A PREHISTORIC
BIBLIOGRAPHY

A PREHISTORIC BIBLIOGRAPHY

By WILFRID BONSER

Librarian to the University of Birmingham, 1929–52

Extended and Edited

by JUNE TROY

formerly Asst. Librarian, City & Guilds Engineering Library,
Imperial College, London, 1956–60

OXFORD · BASIL BLACKWELL · MCMLXXVI

0 631 17090 1

PRINTED IN GREAT BRITAIN
BY R. & R. CLARK LTD, EDINBURGH
BOUND BY KEMP HALL BINDERY LTD., OSNEY MEAD, OXFORD

FOREWORD

This bibliography was conceived by the late Dr Wilfrid Bonser, and the abstracting was nearly completed when illness forced him to stop work.

The present editor took over the work at this stage and it is a source of great regret that it was not finished before Dr Bonser died. The arrangement of the material and the indexing were the work of the editor, who accepts full responsibility for all errors of judgment and of scholarship.

The arrangement was, to a certain extent, dictated by the material itself, which in most cases consisted of a title only. The modern archaeologist will appreciate the difficulty of classifying, for example, something with the title "A Druidic Temple", without consulting the original paper. It would have been impossible to do this in all cases in a work of this size.

The geographical zoning used to divide the various sections was intended originally to be Sir Cyril Fox's Highland Zone and Lowland Zone, but again the nature of the material dictated the final decision. The six zones chosen are given their Council of British Archaeology Group numbers, both in the text and in a list immediately following the contents pages.

Thanks are due to Sir Basil Blackwell for his patience in waiting for the completion of the work philosophically and not without humour. To Mr Leslie Grinsell, F.S.A., must go both the thanks of the editor for his introduction to the work, and apologies for having failed to deliver the goods with reasonable despatch. Miss Phoebe Johnson has given much valuable help in answering queries related to sites in Cumbria, which has saved the editor a great deal of time searching for the answers in the literature. Officers of other local archaeological and natural history societies who have helped to answer queries, where reference to all the original paper was either not possible or of no help, are: The Librarian of the Society of Antiquaries; Miss B. de Cardi of the Council for British Archaeology; the Curator of the Royal Institution of Cornwall; Dumfriesshire and Galloway Natural History and Antiquarian Society; Gloucester City Librarian; Lancashire and Cheshire Antiquarian Society; Surrey Archaeological Society; and the Woolhope Naturalists' Field Club. The editor is grateful for their help.

February 1973

J. D. TROY

PUBLISHER'S NOTE

In the period between the publication of Dr. Bonser's *Romano-British Bibliography* and the preparation of the present volume for the press, the costs of production rose so greatly that there seemed little hope of publishing at a manageable price this volume which completes Dr. Bonser's projected bibliographical trilogy. Publication has now been made practicable through a generous grant in aid by Mr. E. H. L. Sexton.

Dr. Bonser was unable to complete his work on this third volume, and but for the devoted services of Miss June Troy, who had already undertaken to extend, complete and index the work, the book would not have appeared. Miss Troy had also undertaken to see it through the press but, circumstances preventing this, Mr. W. J. Furneaux undertook to read the proofs and to resolve as far as possible the numerous small editorial problems which were inevitable in a work of this magnitude, compiled over a long period. Some errors, omissions and inconsistencies will be found, but the publisher hopes that those who use the book may take into account the chequered history of its preparation, and weighing its merits charitably pardon its deficiencies.

Abbreviation of the titles of journals and the order of details of publication are not always consistent; reference to the list of Journals Searched will be helpful.

The spelling of place-names occasionally may be obsolete, since some of the entries have been taken from early Eighteenth Century sources; some of the place-names cannot be found in current works of reference.

The geographical zoning used to divide the various sections is translated into C.B.A. Group equivalents on page ix, but at the time of going to press some of the county boundaries had been altered, and the list has not been revised to take this into account.

Some entries attributed to anonymous contributors may be in fact extracts from editorial comment.

Miss Troy who unfortunately was unable to read the proofs of this book discovered a number of corrigenda, mainly of proper names, in the finished work. A list of these appears at the end of the book.

CONTENTS

GEOGRAPHICAL ZONES
WITH THEIR CBA GROUP EQUIVALENTS

ZONES	CBA GROUPS	COUNTIES
1	7, 9, 10, 11A, 11B, 14	Bedfordshire, Berkshire, Buckinghamshire, Cambridge, Essex, Greater London, Hertfordshire, Huntingdonshire, Isle of Ely, Kent, Lincolnshire, Norfolk, Northamptonshire, Nottinghamshire, Oxfordshire, Peterborough, Suffolk, Surrey, Sussex
2	12	Dorset, Hampshire and the Isle of Wight, Wiltshire
3	8, 13	Cornwall, Devonshire, Gloucestershire, Herefordshire, Shropshire, Somerset, Staffordshire, Warwickshire, Worcestershire
4	3, 4, 5, 6	Cheshire, Cumberland, Derbyshire, Durham, Leicestershire, Lancashire, Northumberland, Rutland, Westmorland, Yorkshire
5	2	Wales and Monmouthshire
6	1	Scotland: plus Ireland and Isle of Man

JOURNALS SEARCHED

The dates given after the name of a journal show the period during which items were abstracted when this was available. Where journals were renamed, merged or reverted to a former title, the changes are given in chronological order. Cross-reference should be made in the list to ascertain the search period of individual journals in a group.

Further information can be obtained as to the inauguration and other details on journals or publications from *The British Union Catalogue of Periodicals*.

Aberystwyth Studies. 1910–1936
Advancement of Science. 1882–1955
Annals of Archaeology and Anthropology. 1908–1948
Annual Reports. University of London Institute of Archaeology: Bulletin etc. 1938–1966
Annual Report. Woolwich Antiquarian Society. 1895–1954
Annual Report. Yorkshire Philosophical Society. 1824–1955
Anthropological Review : Journal : Transactions of the Anthropological Society of London : Journal of the Ethnological Society of London : Journal of the Royal Anthropological Institute of Great Britain and Ireland. 1863–1965
Antiquarian Magazine : Walford's Antiquarian. 1882–1887
Antiquaries Journal : (Proceedings of the Society of Antiquaries of London). 1921–1965
Antiquary. 1880–1915
Antiquities of Sunderland. 1900–1921
Antiquity. 1927–1965
Archaeologia. 1770–1965
Archaeologia Æliana. 1816–1965
Archaeologia Cambrensis. 1846–1965
Archaeologia Cantiana. 1858–1964
Archaeologia Oxoniensis. 1892–1895
Archaeologia Scotica : (Transactions of the Society of Antiquaries of Scotland). 1792–1890
Archaeological Journal. 1844–1964
Archaeological News Letter. 1948–1965
Archaeological Review : Folk-lore. 1888–1965
Archaeology. 1948–1965
Archaeometry. 1958–1965
Bedfordshire Archaeologist. 1955–1959
Bedfordshire Magazine. 1947–1967
Bericht. Romisch-germanisch Kommission. 1904–1964
Berkshire Archaeological Journal. 1895–1964
Biometrika. 1901–1967
Bradford Antiquary. 1888–1964
Brighton and Hove Archaeologist. 1914–1926
British Museum Quarterly. 1926–1966
British Numismatic Journal : (Proceedings of the British Numismatic Society). 1903–1958
Brycheiniog : (Brecknock Society). 1955–1965
Bulletin. Board of Celtic Studies. 1921–1966
Bulletin. British Museum (Natural History) A: Geology. 1959–1967
Bulletin. University of London Institute of Archaeology. 1959–1966 see Annual Reports, University of London, etc.

Bury Historical Review and Notes and Queries. 1909–1911
Cambridge Historical Journal : Historical Journal. 1923–1967
Ceredigion : (Cardiganshire Antiquarian Society). 1950–1965
Cheshire Historian. 1951–1960
Collectania Antiqua. 1848–1880
Collectania Archaeologica : (Communications to the British Archaeological Association). 1866–1871
Collections (Historical and Archaeological) relating to Montgomeryshire : Montgomeryshire Collections. 1868–1964
Cornish Archaeology. 1962–1966
Y Cymmrodor : (Transactions of the Honorable Society of Cymmrodorion). 1892–1966
Cymru fu : (Notes and Queries relating to the Past History of Wales and the Border Counties). 1887–1891
Devon (and Cornwall) Notes and Queries. 1900–1967
Essex Naturalist. 1880–1887 see Trans. of the Epping Forest and County of Essex Naturalists Field Club.
Essex Review. 1892–1957
Folk-lore. 1891–1965 see Archaeological Review.
Geographical Journal : (Proceedings of the Royal Geographical Society, London). 1893–1965
Geography : Geographical Teacher
Gloucestershire Notes and Queries. 1881–1914
Hampshire Notes and Queries. 1883–1898
Hertfordshire Countryside. 1946–1965
Historical Journal. 1958–1967 see Cambridge Historical.
History of Berwickshire Naturalists' Field Club. 1835–1964
History Teachers' Miscellany. 1923–1929
History To-day. 1951–1967
Home Counties Magazine. 1900–1912 see Middlesex and Hertfordshire Notes and Queries.
Illustrated Archaeologist : The Reliquary (and Illustrated Archaeologist). 1893–1909
Journal (& Memoirs) Anthropological Institute Gt. Britain and Ireland. 1870–1965 see Anthropological Review.
Journal. Antiquarian Association of the British Isles. 1930–1932
Journal. Architectural, Archaeological and Historic Society of Chester. 1849–1962
Journal. British Archaeological Association. 1845–1965
Journal. Chester and North Wales Archaeological and Historical Society. 1849–1957
Journal. Derbyshire Archaeological and Natural History Society. 1879–1966
Journal (Trans.) Ethnological Society of London. 1844–1870 see Anthropological Review.
Journal (Proceedings) of the Geological Society of London : Quarterly Journal Geological Society of London. 1826–1967
Journal. Royal Institution of Cornwall. 1864–1966
Journal. Torquay Natural History Society. 1909–1964
Leicestershire and Rutland Notes and Queries (and Antiquarian Gleaner). 1891–1895
Lincolnshire Historian : Lincolnshire Magazine. 1932–1958
Lincolnshire Notes and Queries. 1888–1936
London Devonian Association Yearbook. 1910–1960
Man. 1901–1965
Memoirs of the Anthropological Society see Anthropological Review.
Middlesex and Hertfordshire Notes and Queries : Home Counties Magazine. 1895–1912

Montgomeryshire Collections see Collections etc., relating to Montgomeryshire. 1868–1964

Natural History Transactions of Northumberland and Durham : Transactions of the Natural History Society of Northumberland, Durham and Newcastle-upon-Tyne : Tyneside Naturalists' Field Club. 1831–1913

Norfolk Archaeology. 1874–1960

Northern Flintshire. 1913

Northern Notes and Queries : Scottish Antiquary : Scottish Historical Review. 1904–1955

Northamptonshire Notes and Queries. 1886–1923

Notes of the Bedfordshire Architectural and Archaeological Society. 1853–1867

Notes and Queries. 1849–1965

Notes and Gleanings. 1888–1892

Notes and Queries for Somerset and Dorset. 1890–1966

Notts and Derbyshire Notes and Queries. 1893–1898

Numismatic Journal : Numismatical Chronicle. 1836–1964

Oxoniensia. 1937–1963 see Proceedings of the Oxfordshire Architectural and Historical Society.

Papers. Eastbourne Natural History Society : Transactions of the Eastbourne etc. 1870–1955

Papers. Purbeck Society. 1855–1868

Papers and Proceedings. Hampshire Field Club (and Archaeological Society). 1885–1963

Papers, Reports etc. Halifax Antiquarian Society : Transactions of the Halifax etc. 1902–1965

Philosophical Transactions. Royal Society of London. 1833–1851

Proceedings. Archaeological Institute. 1846–1858

Proceedings. Bath Natural History and Antiquarian Field Club. 1867–1909

Proceedings. Cambridge Antiquarian : (Antiquarian Communications. 1859–1965)

Proceedings. Cleveland Naturalists' Field Club. 1895–1932

Proceedings. Clifton Antiquarian Club. 1884–1912

Proceedings. Cotteswold Naturalists' Field Club. 1853–1956

Proceedings. Coventry and District Natural History and Scientific Society. 1930–1966

Proceedings and Transactions. Croydon Natural History and Scientific Society. 1871–1956

Proceedings. Devon Archaeological Exploration Society. 1829–1966

Proceedings. Dorset Natural History and Archaeological Society. 1877–1964

Proceedings. Geological Society of London : Quarterly Journal of the Geological etc. see Journal Geological Soc. 1826–1927

Proceedings and Papers. Historic Society of Lancashire and Cheshire : Transactions of the Historic etc. 1848–1965

Proceedings. Isle of Wight Natural History (and Archaeology) Society. 1920–1965

Proceedings. Llandudno (and District) Field Club. 1906–1950

Proceedings. London and Middlesex Archaeological Society : Transactions of the London etc. 1870–1965

Proceedings. Manchester Field Club. 1899–1903

Proceedings. Oxfordshire Architectural (and Historical) Society : Oxoniensia. 1860–1963

Proceedings. Philosophical and Literary Society of Leeds. 1925–1966

Proceedings. Prehistoric Society of East Anglia : Proceedings of the Prehistoric Society. 1911–1935 (1967)

Proceedings. Prehistoric Society see Proceedings of the Prehistoric Society of East Anglia. 1911–1967

Proceedings. Society of Antiquaries. 1843–1920

Proceedings. Society of Antiquaries of Newcastle-upon-Tyne. 1855–1956
Proceedings. Society of Antiquaries of Scotland. 1851–1963
Proceedings. Somerset Archaeological and Natural History Society (Bath Branch).
    1904–1947
Proceedings. Somersetshire Archaeological Society. 1849–1963
Proceedings. Suffolk Institute of Archaeology. 1849–1964
Proceedings. University of Durham Philosophical Society. 1896–1959
Proceedings. West Cornwall Field Club. 1953–1959
Proceedings. Yorkshire Philosophical Society. 1847–1854
Publications. Cambridge Antiquarian Society. Nos. 1–6
Publications. Flintshire Historical Society. 1911–1966
Quarterly Bulletin. Colchester Archaeological Group. 1958–1959
Quarterly Bulletin. Huddersfield Archaeological Society. 1958–?
Quarterly Journal. Geological Society of London. 1901–1967 see Journal of the
    Geological Society of London.
Quarterly Journal. Suffolk Institute of Archaeology. 1869
Reading Naturalist. 1949–1967
Record of Buckinghamshire. 1854–1964
Reliquary (and Illustrated Archaeologist), The. 1896–1909 see Illustrated Archae-
    ologist.
Reports and Papers. Archaeological Society of the County of Lincoln. 1936–1964
Reports and Papers. Associated Architectural Societies. 1850–1935
Reports and Transactions. Devonshire Association for the Advancement of Science.
    1862–1965
Reports and Transactions. East Kent Scientific and Natural History Society, Series
    II. 1901–1913
Reports and Papers. Leicestershire Architectural and Archaeological Society.
Reports. Oxfordshire Archaeological Society. 1887–1951
Research Papers. Surrey Archaeological Society. 1949–1959
Rutland Magazine. 1903–1912
Scottish Antiquary (or Northern Notes and Queries). 1904–1955 see Northern Notes
    and Queries.
Scottish Geographical Magazine. 1885–1959
Scottish Historical Journal. (?)
Scottish Historical Review : Northern Notes and Queries (or the Scottish Anti-
    quary) : Scottish Antiquary (or Northern Notes and Queries). 1904–1955
South Eastern Naturalist and Antiquary. 1890–1930 : 1935–1967
Surrey Archaeological Collections. 1858–1965
Sussex Archaeological Collections. 1848–1965
Sussex County Magazine. 1926–1956
Sussex Notes and Queries. 1926–1963
Transactions. Anglesea Antiquarian Society and Field Club. 1913–1963
Transactions. Archaeological Society of North Oxford. 1853–1858
Transactions Anthropological Society of London see Anthropological Review.
Transactions. Banffshire Field Club and Scientific Society. 1880–1881
Transactions. Berkshire (Archaeological and Architectural Society) Ashmolean
    Society. 1879–1888
Transactions and Proceedings. Birmingham Archaeological Society. 1870–1962
Transactions. Bristol and Gloucestershire Archaeological Society. 1876–1965
Transactions. British Archaeological Association. 1844–1851
Transactions. Buchan (Field) Club. 1887–1940
Transactions. Caernarvonshire Historical Society. 1939–1966
Transactions. Cambridgeshire and Huntingdonshire Archaeological Society. 1900–
    1952
Transactions. Caradoc and Severn Valley Field Club. 1909–1947

Transactions. Cardiff Naturalists' Society. 1867–1964

Transactions. Cardiganshire Antiquarian Society. 1909–1939

Transactions. Carmarthen Antiquarian Society and Field Club : (Carmarthen Antiquary). 1905–1951

Transactions. Cumberland and Westmorland Antiquarian and Archaeological Society. 1874–1964

Transactions. Dartford District Antiquarian Society. 1931–1938

Transactions and Journal of the Proceedings. Dumfriesshire and Galloway Natural History and Antiquarian Society. 1862–1966

Transactions. Durham and Northumberland Architectural and Archaeological Society. 1862–1965

Transactions. East Herts Archaeological Society. 1899–1955

Transactions. East Kent (Scientific and) Natural History Society. 1901–1913

Transactions. East Riding Antiquarian Society. 1893–1949

Transactions. Eastbourne Natural History Society. 1882–1955 see Papers. Eastbourne Natural History Society.

Transactions. Edinburgh Geological Society. 1870–1905

Transactions. Epping Forest and County of Essex Naturalists' Field Club : Essex Naturalist. 1880–1965

Transactions. Essex Archaeological Society. 1858–1964

Transactions. Ethnological Society of London. 1844–1870 see Anthropological Review

Transactions. Glasgow Archaeological Society. 1868–1956

Transactions. Greenwich (and Lewisham) Antiquarian Society. 1905–1961

Transactions. Halifax Antiquarian Society. 1930–1965 see Papers, Reports, etc. Halifax etc.

Transactions. Hampstead Antiquarian and Historical Society. 1898–1907

Transactions. Hawick Archaeological Society. 1863–1958

Transactions. Hertfordshire Natural History Society and Field Club. 1859–1957

Transactions. Historic Society of Lancashire and Cheshire. 1855–1965 see Proceedings and Papers Historical Society Lancs. and Cheshire.

Transactions. Honorable Society of Cymmrodorion : (Y Cymmrodor). 1892–1966

Transactions. Hunter Archaeological Society of Sheffield. 1914–1958

Transactions. Inverness Scientific Society and Field Club. 1875–1899

Transactions. Lancashire and Cheshire Antiquarian Society. 1883–1964

Transactions. Leicester Architectural and Archaeological Society. 1866–1964

Transactions. Leicester Literary and Philosophical Society. 1886–1959

Transactions. London and Middlesex Archaeological Society. 1878–1965 see Proceedings of London and Middlesex Archaeological Society.

Transactions. Natural History Society of Northumberland, Durham and Newcastle-upon-Tyne see Natural History Transactions of Northumberland and Durham

Transactions. Neath Antiquarian Society, 2nd Series. 1930–1939

Transactions. Newbury and District Field Club. 1870–1956

Transactions. Newcomen Society. 1920–1963

Transactions. Norfolk and Norwich Naturalists' Society. 1949–1967

Transactions and Annual Reports. North Staffordshire (Naturalists') Field Club. 1866–1960

Transactions. Northern Naturalists' Union. 1931–1953

Transactions. Radnorshire Society. 1931–1966

Transactions. Royal Historical Society. 1869–1966

Transactions. Royal Society of Literature. 1827–1919

Transactions. Salisbury Field Club. 1891–1894

Transactions. St. Albans and Hertfordshire Architectural and Archaeological Society. 1884–1961

Transactions. Shropshire Archaeological Society. 1878–1964

Transactions. Southend-on-sea Antiquarian and Historical Society. 1921–1951
Transactions. Stirling Natural History and Archaeological Society. 1878–1939
Transactions. Thoroton Society. 1897–1966
Transactions. Tyneside Naturalists' Field Club see Natural History Transactions of
    Northumberland and Durham
Transactions. Watford Natural History Society and Hertfordshire Field Club.
    1859–1957
Transactions. Woolhope Naturalists' Field Club. 1852–1959
Transactions. Worcestershire Archaeological Society. 1923–1963
Ulster Journal of Archaeology. 1853–1965
Vasculum : Vasculum Substitute. 1915–1925 : 1940–1942
Walford's Antiquarian. 1886–1887 see Antiquarian Magazine.
Wiltshire Archaeological Magazine. 1854–1963
Wiltshire Notes and Queries. 1893–1916
Yearbook. East Derbyshire Field Club. 1911–1912
Yorkshire Archaeological Journal. 1870–1965
Yorkshire Notes and Queries. 1904–1909

A. MEN AND METHODS IN ARCHAEOLOGY

1. ARCHAEOLOGISTS AND THEIR WORK

1 Alexander (E. M. M.). Father John MacEnemy: scientist or charlatan? Devonshire Ass. Rpts. & Trans., 96, 1964, 113–46, + 3 plates.

2 [Anon.] Menhios, and Mr. George F. Playne. Glos. N. & Q., 1, pp. 70–72. 1881.

3 Armstrong (Albert Leslie). Obituary. Trans. Hunter archaeol. Soc., 8 ii, 1960, 101–6 + 1 plate.

4 Ashmole, Josten (C. H.), *Editor*. Elias Ashmole, 1617–1692; his autobiographical and historical notes, his correspondence and other contemporary sources relating to his life and work, 5 vols., 26 plates. Oxford. 1966.

5 Bagshawe (Richard W.) *and* **Bagshawe** (Thomas W.). An early antiquary and his friends [Rev. Thomas Leman, F.S.A.]. Beds. Mag., 9, No. 66, 1963, 57–60.

6 Bailey, *Sir* Edward. Charles Lyell. (British Men of Science.) pp. 214, 16 plates, 20 figures, Edinburgh. 1962.

6(b) Bonser (Wilfrid). A bibliography of prehistoric Britain. Oxford, Blackwell, 1975.

7 Brady (*Sir* Antonio). In memoriam. Trans. Essex Fld. Club, 3, 1883, 94–101.

8 Breese (Charles E.). Obituary. Arch. Camb. 87, ii, 1932, 422.

9 Britton (John). Memoir of Aubrey, *etc*. Wiltshire Topographical Society. pp. x, 131 + portrait. 4º. London, 1845.

10 Campbell, J. L. *and* **Thomson**, Derick. Edward Llwyd in the Scottish Highlands, 1699–1700. pp. xxxii, 319 + 23 plates. Oxford, 1963.

11 Childe (V. Gordon). Valediction. Bull. Inst. of Arch. London, 1, 1958, 1–8.

12 —— Gordon Childe Memorial Fund. Archaeology, XI (4), 1958, 287.

13 Clark (John Grahame Douglas), Anglo-French cooperation in archaeology. Proc. prehist. Soc., 4, 1938 340–1.

14 —— Council of British Archaeology: Grants for publications. Proc. prehist. Soc., 18, 1952, 235.

15 —— Osbert Guy Stanhope Crawford, 1886–1957. pp. 16 + 1 plate. Oxford 1959. [Proc. Brit. Acad., 44, 1959 281–96.]

16 Clark (Ronald W.). Sir Mortimer Wheeler. pp. 107 + 11 plates. London (Phoenix House), 1960.

17 Clarke, L. K. Pioneers of prehistory in England. (No. 10, Newman History and Philosophy of Science.) pp. 112. London, Sheed & Ward, 1961.

18 Clark, (W. G.). In memoriam (obituary). Proc. PSEA, 5 i, 1925, 89–90 + 1 plate.

19 Clerk (*Sir* John, of Penicuik). A journie to Galloway in 1721. [Excavated "Roman" cairn with cremation in urn inverted upon stone slab!] Trans. Dumfries, 41, 1962/3, 186–200.

20 Cotton, M. Aylwin. Conference of young archaeologists. [Discussion of various excavations.] Antiquity, 37, 1963, 130–2.

21 Cottrell (Leonard). Digs and Diggers, *illustrated with photographs*. A comprehensive introduction to world archaeology, ranging in time from European prehistory to the great cultures of pre-Columbian America, and describing the ancient civilizations of the Middle East, Egypt, China, India and Europe. Lutterworth Press. 1966.

22 Dawkins (*Sir* William Boyd). William Pengelly, F.R.S., and Kent's Hole. J. Torquay Nat. Hist. Soc., 4, 1924, 118–21.

23 Dobie (Marryat R.). The antiquarian jaunts of Thomas Johnston. [Extracts from note-book of Soc. Antiq. Scot. recording researches in Dumfriesshire and the Stewartry from 1825 to 1827; with notes.] Trans. Dumfries. Ant. Soc., 35, 36 (1957–58), pp. 98–114. 1959.

24 Evans (*Sir* E. Vincent). Obituary. Arch. Camb., 90 i, 1935, 167.

25 Ewbank, James M. Antiquary on horseback. Collections of the Rev. Thos. Machell, Chaplain to King Charles II, towards a History of the Barony of Kendal. 150 pp., 33 figures, 1 map. Titus Wilson 25s. Kendal, 1963.

26 Garrod (D. A. E.). Henri Breuil: 1877–1961. Man, 61, 1961, 205–7 + 1 plate + 1 figure.

27 Gray (Harold St. George). A memoir of General Pitt-Rivers. Proc. Somerset Arch. Soc., 47 (1901), pp. 123–37 +portrait. 1902.

28 —— A memoir of Lieut.-General Pitt-Rivers. Fox *afterwards* Pitt-Rivers (A. H. L.): Excavations in Cranborne Chase, vol. 5, pp. ix–xxxvi + 2 portraits. 1905.

29 —— Lieut.-General Pitt-Rivers. Dryden (A.): Memorials of old Wiltshire, pp. 47–65 +portrait. 1906.

30 Hall (R. de Z.). A West Coker antiquary of 1848, (James Fussell Moore). Proc. Somerset A.&N.H.S., 106, 1962, 88–97.

31 Halls (H. H.). Obituary. Proc. Prehist. Soc., N.S. 1, 1935, 161.

32 Harrison (*Sir* Edward). The riddle of the Old Stones: a personal retrospect. [Figure. Name of Benjamin Harrison's house at Ightham. On eoliths.] Archaeol. Cant., 71 (1957), pp. 47–52. 1958.

33 Hearne (Thomas). A letter to Mr Ralph Thoresby, F.R.S., occasion'd by some antiquities lately discovered near Bramham-Moor, Yorkshire. [BA–socketed axes]. Phil. Trans. Roy. Soc., xxvi, 1708, 395–412.

34 Hughes (H. Harold). Obituary. Arch. Camb., 95 i, 1940, 85–87 + 1 plate.

35 Jewitt (Llewellynn). The late Thomas Bateman, Esq., of Lomberdale house, and Middleton-by-Youlgreave, [Derbs.]. Reliquary, 2, pp. 87–97 + portrait. 1862.

36 Jones (E. D.). Professor Thomas Jones Pierce: Obituary. Arch. Camb., 113, 1964, 170–172.

37 Julian (Mr. H. Forbes). A short sketch of the life of William Pengelly. J. Torquay nat. Hist. Soc., 1, 1913, 225–232 +1 plate and part 2: 1, 1914, 296–306 +1 plate.

37(c) Julian (Mrs. H. Forbes). A short sketch of the life of William

Pengelly, F.R.S., F.G.S. (part 3). J. Torquay nat. Hist. Soc., 2, 1916, 88–95.

38 Julian (Hester Forbes). The Scientific correspondence of Charles Kingsley and William Pengelly [ref. to flint implements etc.]. J. Torquay nat. Hist. Soc., 2, 1920, 361–373.

39 —— William Pengelly and the Museum Jubilee. J. Torquay nat. Hist. Soc., 4, 1924, 101–102 +1 plate.

41 Keith (*Sir* Arthur). Centenary of the birth of Lord Avebury. [Portrait.] Man. 34, pp. 49–51 +portrait. 1934.

42 Kelley (P. Harper). Obituary. Man. 63, 1963, 55.

43 Knowlton (Thomas). Extracts of two letters to Mr. Mark Catesby, F.R.S., concerning the situation of the ancient town Delgovicia. Phil. Trans. Roy. Soc., XLIV, 1746, 100–102.

44 Krämer (Werner). Gerhard Bersu zum Gedächnis (Obituary). Ber. Römgerman. Komm., 45, 1964, 1–2 +1 plate.

45 Lankester, *Sir* Edwin Ray. Obituary. Proc. PSEA, 6 ii, 1929, 142 +1 plate.

46 Layard (Nina Frances). Obituary. Proc. Prehist. Soc., N.S. 1, 1935, 160–161 +1 plate.

47 Leach (Arthur L.). The Rev. G. N. Smith: a Pembrokeshire antiquarian [Gilbert Nicholas Smith]. Arch. Camb., 98 ii, 1945, 248–254 +5 figures.

48 Lloyd (J. D. K.). Wilfrid James Hemp. Obituary. Arch. Camb., 111, 1962, 167–169.

49 Lowe (Harford J.). The Rev. John MacEnery and Kent's Cavern. J. Torquay nat. Hist. Soc., 3, 1921, 3–14.

50 Lukis (Frederick C.). Archaeological notes made by Captain Francis Dubois Lukis . . . during a visit to Buxton, Derbyshire, in 1865. [4 figures +2 plans.] Reliquary, 8, pp. 81–87 + plan. 1868.

51 Markham (*Sir* Clements R.). Pythias, the discoverer of Britain. [3 maps, 3rd *c*. B.C.]. Geog. J., 1, pp. 504–24. 1893.

52 Marr (J. E.). Obituary. Proc. PSEA, 7 ii, 1932–34, 277.

53 Matson (Colin). William Rolfe: a noted Sandwich antiquarian. Arch. Cant., 76, 1961, pp. 180–185 +1 plate.

54 Meyer (Diennt). Bibliographie

Gerhard Bersu. Ber. Röm-german. Komm. 45, 1964, 3–10.

55 Meyrick (Owen). Sir Richard Colt Hoare and William Cunnington. [Barrows, etc.]. Wilts. Archaeol. Mag., 52, pp. 213–18. 1948.

56 Mitchell (Samuel). Letter to Thomas Bakeman, 26 October, 1850, [describing Ramsley Moor. Unpublished. Sheffield City Museum.]

57 Moir (James Reid). Prehistoric archaeology and Sir Ray Lankester. pp. vii, 160 + portrait. 8° Ipswich, 1935.

58 Morgan (P. T. J.). The Abbé Pezron and the Celts. Trans. Hon. Soc. Cymmrodorion, 1965, pt. II 287–295.

59 Nash-Williams (Victor Erle). Obituary. Arch. Camb., 105, 1956, 150–151.

60 Oakley (Kenneth P.). The life and work of Samuel Hazzledine Warren, F.G.S. Essex Naturalist, 30 iii, 1959, 143–147 + 1 plate.

61 —— A List of published papers and records by S. Hazzledine Warren. Essex Naturalist, 30 iii, 1959, 147–161.

62 Ogilvie (Arthur Hebden). Mac-Enery Centenary: Early exploration of Kent's Cavern. Trans. and Proc. Torquay nat. Hist. Soc., 8, 1941, 103–104.

63 —— Arthur Hebden Ogilvie—an appreciation. J. Torquay nat. Hist. Soc., 10, 1951, 157–158.

64 Pengelly (William). Obituary. Trans. Edinburgh Geol. Soc., 7, 1894/98, 74–76.

65 Piggott (Stuart). William Stukeley, an eighteenth-century antiquary. pp. xvi, 228 + 9 plates. 8°. Oxford, 1950. [Pp. 92–135, Avebury, Stonehenge and the Druids.]

66 —— Vere Gordon Childe 1892–1957. Oxford, 1959, pp. 8 + 1 plate.

67 Pool (P. A. S.). William Borlase, the scholar and the man. J.R.I.C. N.S., 5, 1966, 120–172 + 2 plates.

68 —— The Borlase-Stukeley correspondence. Cornish Arch., 5, 1966, 11–13.

69 Prevost (W. A. J.). Sir John Clerk's journey into Galloway in 1735. Trans. Dumfries, 42, 1965, 133–139.

70 Radford (C. A. Ralegh) *and* **Ranlins** (C. W. H.). Harold St. George Gray, 1872–1963. Proc. Somerset A.&N.H.S., 107, 1963, 111–116.

71 Roberts (Thomas). Obituary. Arch. Camb., 87 ii, 1932, 422–23.

72 Sandell (R. E.). Sir Richard Colt Hoare. W.A.M., 58, 1961, No. 209, 1–6.

73 Scott (*Sir* Lindsay). Sir Lindsay Scott, K.B.E., D.S.C., F.S.A. Proc. prehist. Soc., 18, 1952, 234.

74 Sherratt (A. G.). Hayman Rooke, F.S.A.—an eighteenth century Nottinghamshire antiquary. Trans. Thoroton. Soc., 69, 1965, 4–18.

75 Simpson, Gavin. Local archaeological societies, 1850–1865. Antiquity, 36, 1962, pp. 216–219.

76 Simpson (W. Douglas). Sir Daniel Wilson and its Prehistoric Annals of Scotland: a centenary study. Proc. Soc. Ant. Scotland, 96, 1962–63, 1–8 + 1 plate.

77 Smallcombe (W. A.) *and* **Collins** (A. E. P.). The late George W. Smith of Reading. [Figure. His prehistoric collection in Reading Museum.] Berks. Archaeol. J., 49, pp. 62–66 + 4 plates. 1946.

78 Smith (Isobel F.). Bibliography of the publications of Professor V. Gordon Childe. Proc. Prehist. Soc., 21, 1955, 295–304.

79 Sturge (W. Allen). Obituary. Proc. Prehist. Soc. E.A., 3 i, 1918/19, 12–13 + 1 plate.

80(a) Taylor (Margerie Venables). Obituary. Flints. hist. Soc. publns., 21, 1963, 98 + 1 plate.

80(b) Thomas (E. G. Kaines). History of the Newbury District Field Club. Trans. Newbury Dist. Fld. Club, XI i, 1960, 5–11.

81 Thompson (M. W.). The First Inspectors of Ancient Monuments. J. Brit. archaeol. Ass., 23, 1960, 103–124 + 4 plates.

82 Wainwright (Frederick Thresfall), Obituary. W.A.M., 58, 1962, No. 210, 230.

83 Wheeler (*Sir* Robert Eric Mortimer). Archaeology from the earth. pp. xi, 221 + 23 plates. [20 figures + map.] 84. Oxford, 1954. ——. Penguin Books. pp. 252 + 24 plates. [20 figures + 2 maps.] 8°. Harmondsworth, 1956.

84 Wheeler (Mortimer). Alms for Oblivion: an antiquary's scrapbook. 4 pp. illustrations. [This collection of essays ranges over a wide area of subjects]. London. 1966.

85 Wilkins, Judith. Worsaae and British antiquities. Antiquity, 35, 1961, pp. 214–220.

86 Kirwan (L. P.). Sir Leonard Wooley: obituary. Geog. Journ., 126, 1960, 256–57.

87 Woolley, *Sir* Leonard. As I seem to remember. pp. 113, London, 1962.

88 Wright (C. E.). Four Stukeley notebooks. Brit. Mus. Quart, 27, 3/4, 1963/4, 61–65.

89 Young (Robert M.). An early antiquary of Co. Antrim. Ulster J. Arch., 4, 1897, 68.

2. GENERAL THEORIES

90 Acland (H. D.). Bronze and the Bronze People. J. Torquay nat. Hist. Soc., 4, 1923, 13–14 + 1 plate.

91 Airne (C. W.). The story of prehistoric and Roman Britain told in pictures. pp. 64. [*c.* 550 figures.] 8°. Manchester [19–?].

92 Almagro (Martin). Manual de Historia Universal: Tomo I. Prehistoria. Madrid, 1960, pp. 918, figures 944, 13 maps, 8 plates + 19 tables.

93 Arnal (Jean) *and* **Burnez** (Claude). Die Struktur des französischen Neolithikums auf Grund neuester stratigraphischer Beobachtungen. Ber. Röm.-ger. Komm., 37, 1956, 1–90 + 38 figures.

94 Ashe, (Geoffrey). Land to the West. London, 1967. pp. 352, 8 plates, 3 maps.

95 Ault (Norman). Life in ancient Britain. A survey of the social and economic development of the people of England from earliest times to the Roman conquest. pp. xiv, 260. 8°. London, 1920.

96 Barnes (William). A study of the Belgae in south Britain. Proc. Dorset Antiq. F.C., 6, pp. 33–40, 1885.

97 Bayley (Harold). Archaic England. An essay in deciphering prehistory from megalithic instruments, earthworks, customs, coins, place-names and fairie superstitions. pp. viii, 894. 8°. London, 1919.

98 Beddoe (John). A contribution to the anthropology of Wiltshire. [Pp. 15–19, Prehistoric.] Wilts. Archaeol. Mag., 34, pp. 15–41 + diagram. 1905.

99 —— *and* **Rowe** (Joseph Hambley). The ethnology of West Yorkshire. [9 tables.] Yorks. Archaeol. J., 19, pp. 31–60 + map. 1907.

100 Bell (William). Cursory remarks on the pre-historic history of Great Britain. [4 figures.] J. Brit. Archaeol. Ass., 7, pp. 132–40. 1851.

101 Bibby (H. C.). The evolution of man and his culture. London [Gollancz], 1938.

102 Birchall (Ann). The Aylesford-Swarling Culture : the problem of the Belgae reconsidered. Proc. Prehist. Soc., 31, 1965, 241–367 + 44 figures.

103(a) Boas (Franz). The mind of primitive man. Revised edition. pp. v, 285. 8°. New York, 1938.

103(b) Bordes (D. de Sonneville). L'Age de la pierre (No. 948 of "Que sais-je?" Series). pp. 125, 8 line figures. Presse Univ., N.F. 2.50. Paris. 1961.

104 Bordes, François. Typologie au paléolithique ancien et moyen [some reference to Clactonian]. Memoire No. 1, Institut de Préhistoire de l'Université de. pp. 85 + 11 figures + 108 plates. Bordeaux, 1961.

105(a) Bosch-Gimpera (Pedro). El problema indoeuropeo em. 23, pp. 385, 10 maps. México, 1960.

105(b) —— Les indo-européens: problèmes archéologiques. Paris, 1961. pp. 283, 10 maps.

106 Bowles (W. L.). Hermes Britannicus. A dissertation on the Celtic deity Teutates, the Mercurius of Caesar, in further proof and corroboration of the origin and design of the great temple at Abury in Wiltshire. pp. 149. 8°. London, 1828.

107 Bradley (Henry). Some prehistoric river-names. (A bunch of guesses.) English Miscellany presented to Dr. Furnivall, 1901, pp. 110–14: reprinted in collected papers, 1928.

108 Brash (Richard Rolt). Marianan Mac Lir, his mythical connexion with the Isle of Man. Arch. Camb., 3rd S. 12, pp. 137–51. 1866.

109 Briard (Jacques). L'Age du bronze (Que sais-je? No. 835). Paris, 1959. pp. 126, 4 figures.

110 Brodrick (Alan Houghton). Early man; a survey of human origins. pp. 288 + maps. 8º. London, 1948.

111 —— Man and his ancestry. London, 1960. pp. 256, 16 plates.

112 Brothwell (D. R.) Cannibalism in Early Britain. Antiquity, 35 (1961). pp. 304–307.

113 Brothwell (Don). The Palaeopathology of early British man: an essay on the problems of diagnosis and analysis. J. R. anthrop. Inst., 91, 1961, 318–344 + 8 plates.

114 Brown (Jonathan Allen). On the continuity of the Palaeolithic and Neolithic periods. J. Anthrop. Inst., 23, pp. 66–98 + 4 plates (flints). 1892.

115 Brown (P. W. F.). Letter on place name Badda, and association with Iron Age camps. Folklore 73, 1962, 58.

116 Brown (Theo.). The Trojans in Devon. [Map. Legend of Brutus.] Rpt. of Trans. Devon. Assoc., 87, pp. 63–76 + 2 plates. 1955.

117 Bryan (Alan Lyle). Towards the reunification of Anthropology. Man. (62, 1962, 135–136.

118 Bryce (Thomas H.). On certain points in Scottish ethnology. [4 figures.] Scot. Hist. Rev., 2, pp. 275–86 + 3 plates. 1905.

119 Burchell (James Percy Tufnell). The Middle Mousterian culture and its relation to the Coombe Rock of post-Early Monsterian times. [10 figures (flints).] Antiq. J., 14, pp. 33–39. 1934.

120 Burkitt, M. C. The Transition between Palaeolithic and Neolithic times, ie. the Mesolithic period. PPSEA, 5 i, 1925, 16–33, 9 plates.

121 —— Our early ancestors. An introductory study of Mesolithic, Neolithic and Copper Age cultures in Europe and adjacent regions. pp. xii, 243 + 30 plates. 8º. Cambridge, 1926.

122 Burrow (Edward John). From cave man to Roman in Britain. pp. 60. 8º. London [1926].

123 Camden (William). Britannia: a chorographical description of the flourishing kingdoms of England, Scotland and Ireland . . . from the earliest antiquity. Translated and enlarged by R. Gough. 4. vols. fol. London, 1806.

125 Cary (Max *and* **Warmington** (Eric Herbert). The ancient explorers. pp. 270 + 15 maps. [Pp. 33–40, Pytheas.] 8º. London, 1929.

126 Case (H.). The prehistoric period. The Oxford region: ed. A. F. Martin and R. W. Steel. Brit. Ass. pp. 76–84. [4 maps.] 1954.

127 Celebonovic (Stevan) *and* **Grigson** (Geoffrey). Old Stone Age. London, 1957. pp. 92, 72 plates, 20 figures.

128 Chadwick (Nora). Celtic Britain. 238 pp. (incl. 32 plates, 27 line-drawings + 8 maps). London, 1963.

129 Chadwick (Nora K.). The Colonization of Brittany from Celtic Britain. Proc. Brit. Acad., 51, 1965, 235–299.

130(a) Childe (Vere Gordon). The dawn of European civilization. London, 1925, xvi, 328.

130(b) —— 2nd Edition 1927.

130(c) —— 3rd Edition 1939. xviii, 351. Enlarged and rewritten.

130(d) —— 4th Edition 1947. xviii, 362. Enlarged and rewritten.

130(e) —— 5th Edition 1950. xix, 362. Revised.

130(f) —— 6th Edition 1957. xiii, 368. Revised.

130(g) —— The Bronze Age. pp. xii, 258 + plate + map. [31 figures.] 8º. Cambridge, 1930.

131(a) —— Prehistoric communities of the British Isles. pp. 274 + 16 plates. [96 figures.] 8º. London, 1940.

131(b) —— 2nd Edition 1947

131(c) —— 3rd Edition 1949.

132 —— The Final Bronze Age in the Near East and in temperate Europe. Proc. prehist. Soc., 14, 1948, 177–195 + 10 figures + 6 plates.

133 —— Neolithic house-types in temperate Europe. Proc. prehist. Soc., 15, 1949, 77–86 + 7 figures.

135 Chitty (Lily Frances). The Irish Sea in relation to Bronze Age culture. Trans. Caradoc and Severn Valley F.C., 10, pp. 72–74. 1936.

136 Christiansen (R. T.). Studies in Irish and Scandinavian Folktales. Copenhagen (Rosenkilde & Bagger) 1959.

137 Church (Alfred John). Early Britain. *Story of the Nations*. pp. xx, 382 + map. 8º. London, 1889. [17 figures. Pp. 1–10 + plate (with 6 figures), Britain before the Romans.]

138 Clark (John Grahame Douglas).

The dual character of the Beaver invasion. [2 figures + 4 distribution maps.] Antiquity, 5, pp. 415–26 + plate (pottery). 1931.

139 —— The Mesolithic Age in Britain. pp. xxiii, 222 + 2 maps. [60 figures.] 4°. Cambridge, 1932.

140 —— The classification of a microlithic culture: the Tardenoisian of Horsham. [11 figures + map.] Archaeol. J., 90 (1933), pp. 52–77. 1934.

141 —— Eskimo parallels for Mesolithic types. Proc. prehist. Soc. N.S., 2, 1936, 239–240.

142 —— The Mesolithic Settlement of Northern Europe: a study of the food-gathering peoples of northern Europe during the early post-glacial period, (Camb., 1936) pp. xvi, 284 + 8 plates + map. 4.5.70.

143 —— Prehistoric houses. Proc. prehist. Soc., 3, 1937, 468–469.

144 —— Archaeology and society. pp. xv, 220 + 24 plates. 31 figures. London, 1939.

145 —— Europe and the Orient. Proc. prehist. Soc., 5, 1939, 259–60.

146 —— Prehistoric England. pp. viii, 120. Plates 110. Illustrated by drawings, diagrams and photographs. 8°. London, 1 Batsford, 1940. 4th Edition pp. viii, 120, 8°. London, 1948. 1st pb. edition pp. 200 + 50 plates. London, 1962.

147 —— Prehistoric Europe : the Economic Basis. With 16 plates and 180 text illustrations (1952).

148 —— How the earliest peoples lived. [2 figures + map + plan.] The Heritage of early Britain, pp. 33–55. 1952.

149 —— Perspectives in prehistory— presidential address. Proc. prehist. Soc., 25, 1959, 1–14 + 3 figures.

150 —— World prehistory—[with maps]. Cambridge, 1961, pp. xiii, 283, 12 plates, 7 maps. 2nd edition, 16 pp. plates, 13 tables, 10 maps. 1969.

151 —— and **Piggott** (Stuart). Prehistoric Societies. London, 1965, 356 pp. 8 plates. + 95 figures + 4 maps.

152 Clark (*Sir* W. E. Le Gros). The Antecedents of man [pp. 374, 152 text figures]. Edinburgh, The University Press. 1959.

153 Clegg (E. J.). The Study of man—an introduction to human biology. London, 1968. pp. ix + 212 + 51 figures.

154 Clinch (George). The Neolithic dwelling. [10 figures + plan (hut floors, Hay is common).] Reliquary, 3rd 5.11, pp. 25–37. 1905.

155 —— Celtic antiquities. Mundy (P. D.): Memorials of old Sussex, pp. 9–17 + plate. 1909.

156 —— Suggestions for a scheme of classification of the megolithic and analogous prehistoric remains of Great Britain and Ireland. Annals of Archaeology, 2, pp. 46–48 + 2 plates. 1909.

157 Coles (J. M.) C.B.A. Conference on the British Bronze Age, 1960 [Notes & News]. Antiq., 35, 1961, pp. 63–66.

158 —— and **Higgs** (E. S.) The Archaeology of Early Man, 188 line illustrations, maps and diagrams, and 12 illustrations from photographs. cr. 4°. (Spr. 69) (571 08838 4) £7 10s. ($18.00). 2.12.68.

159 —— and **Simpson** (D. D. A.) Editors. Studies in Ancient Europe: essays presented to Stuart Piggott. 14 pp. plates, 75 text figures, 11½″ × 8¼″. 1968.

160 Cole (Sonia). Races of man. London, (?1963). pp. 131, 12 plates, 34 figures.

161 Cooper (William Durrant). On the retention of British and Saxon names in Sussex. Sussex Arch. Collns., 7, pp. 1–21. 1854.

162 Cornwall (Ian W.) *and* **Maitland** (M.). The Making of man [pp. 63, 61 text figures, 2 tables]. London (Phoenix House), 1960.

163 —— The Ground beneath our feet. Bull. Inst. Arch., London, 3, 1962, 47–53 + 3 figures + 1 plate.

164 —— The World of ancient man. London, 1964, 271 pp., 71 maps, diagrams and drawings.

165 Cottrell (Leonard). A Concise encyclopedia of archaeology (pp. 512, 16 colour plates, 160 monochrome plates (incl. 10 line maps)). London, 1960.

166 Council for British Archaeology. British archaeology: a book list. London, 1960, pp. 44.

167 Crawford (Osbert Guy Stanhope). Man and his past. pp. xv, 227 + 10 plates + 2 maps. 8°. London, 1921.

168 —— A prehistoric invasion of

England. [By first wave of Celtic-speaking peoples at close of the Bronze Age (c. 800–700 B.C.).] Antiq. J., 2, pp. 27–35. 1922.

169 Daniel (Glyn Edmund). The dual nature of the Megalithic colonisation of prehistoric Europe. Proc. prehist. Soc., 7, 1941, 1–49 + 16 figures.

170 —— A hundred years of archaeology. pp. 323. 8º. London, 1950.

171 —— The peoples of prehistoric Britain. The Heritage of early Britain, pp. 11–32. 1952.

172 —— The Idea of prehistory. Cleveland, 1963. 220 pp. + 8 plates.

173 —— Man Discovers his Past. With 90 photographs and maps. Cr. 4º. 1966.

174 Davidson (Thomas). Notions concerning the Wieland Saga. Folklore, 69, 1958, 193–195.

175 Davies (Edward). Celtic researches on the origin, traditions and language of the ancient Britons: with some introductory sketches in primitive society. pp. lxxiii, 561. 8º. London, 1804.

176 Dawkins (*Sir* William Boyd). Early man in Britain and his place in the Tertiary period. pp. xxiv, 537. [167 figures + map.] 8º. London, 1880.

177 —— On the present phase of the antiquity of man. Advm. of Science, 52, 1882, 597–604.

178 —— The ancient ethnology of Wales. Cymmrodor, 5, pp. 209–23. 1882.

179 —— On the relation of the Palaeolithic to the Neolithic period. J. Anthrop. Inst., 23, pp. 242–57 + map. 1894.

180 —— The influence of the Mediterranean peoples in prehistoric Britain. Nature, 65, pp. 39–40. 1901.

181 —— The arrival of man in Britain in the Pleistocene age. [2 figures + 3 maps.] J. R. Anthrop. Inst., 40, pp. 233–63. 1910.

182 —— The arrival of man in Britain. Na Fura, 85, pp. 122–24. 1910.

183 —— The settlement of Britain in the prehistoric age. Essays presented to William Ridgeway on his 60th birthday, pp. 427–34. 1913.

184(a) —— The ethnology of Somerset from the Neolithic Age to the close of the Roman dominion. Proc. Somerset Arch. Soc., 68 (1922), pp. 1–7. 1923.

184(b) De Camp (L. Sprague) *and* **De Camp** (Catherine C.). Ancient ruins and archaeology. London, 1964. xviii, 294 pp., 16 figures + 25 plates.

185 Deuel (Leo). The Treasures of time. ?London, 1962. 319 pp., 16 plates, end-paper map.

186 Doblhofer (Ernst). Voices in stone [pp. 327, 16 plates, 94 text figures]. London Souvenir Press, 1961.

187 Dowie (H. G.). The Origin of the British Race. J. Torquay nat. Hist. Soc., 4, 1923, 38–43.

188 —— The Aryans. Trans. & Proc. Torquay nat. Hist. Soc., 5, 1927, 57–62.

189 Dudley (Donald R.). The Rebellion of Boudicca. History Today, 10, 1960, 387–394.

190 —— *and* **Webster**, Graham. The Rebellion of Boudicca. London. pp. xiv, 165, 4 text-figures. 1962.

191 Duncan (Stewart). Evidence as to the scene of man's evolution and the prospects of proving the same by palaeontological discovery. Advm. Sci., 1882, 605–606.

192 Edmonds (Richard). On the name Britain and the Phoenicians. Rpt. & Trans. Devon Assoc., 4 pp., 418–22. 1871.

193 Edwards (O. M.). Celtic Britain. [13 figures.] Traill (H. D.) and Mann (J. S.): Social England, 3rd ed., 1, pp. 1–37. 1901.

194 Ehrich (Robert W.), Editor. Chronologies in Old World archaeology. Chicago, 1965. 557 pp. + 88 figures.

195 Elliot (George Francis Scott). The romance of early British life, from the earliest times to the coming of the Danes. pp. 357. [30 figures.] 8º. London, 1909.

196 —— Prehistoric man and his story. A sketch of the history of mankind from the earliest times. pp. 398. [64 figures.] 8º. London, 1915.

197 Ettlinger (Ellen). The invulnerable hero in Celtic legend. Man, 42, pp. 43–45. 1942.

198 —— Omens and Celtic warfare. Man, 43, pp. 11–17. 1943.

199 Evans (*Sir* Arthur John). Greek and Italian influences in pre-Roman Britain. Archaeol. Oxon., pp. 159–64. 1893.

200 Evans (Emyr Estyn). The sword-bearers. Figure + 3 maps (Winged axes, bronze swords and bugle-shaped objects). [Comparative study of late Bronze Age cultures.] Antiquity, 4, pp. 157–72 + 5 plates. 1930.

201 —— Irish folk ways. pp. xvi + 324, 91 text figures, 16 plates. London, 1961.

202 Evans (*Sir* John). The Bronze period. [3 figures.] Proc. Soc. Antiq., 25·5, pp. 392–419 + 3 plates. 1873.

203 —— Petit album de l'Age du Bronze de la Grande Bretagne. 24 plates + descriptions. 8º. Londres, 1876.

204 —— A Few words on Tertiary man. Trans. Herts. N.H.S. & F.C., 1, 1879/81, 145–150.

205 —— The Bronze Age. Trans. Herts. N.H.S. & F.C., 8, 1894/96, 1–12 + 3 plates.

206 Everett (C. H.). Were Britons cannibals? J. Antiq. Assoc. Brit. Isles, 3, pp. 28–32. 1932.

207 Fell (Clare Isobel). Bronze Age connections between the Lake District and Ireland. [2 maps.] Trans. Cumb. & Westm. Ant. Soc., N.S. 40, pp. 118–30 + 4 plates. 1940.

208(a) Filip (Jan). Die Keltische Zivilisation und ihr Erbe. Prague, 1961. pp. 218 + 52 figures + 40 plates.

208(b) —— Celtic civilisation and its heritage. Prague, 1963. pp. 215 + 40 plates + 52 figures.

209 Fleure (Herbert John) *and* **Whitehouse** (Wallace E.). Early distribution and valley-ward movement of population in south Britain. [4 maps + plan.] Arch. Camb., 6th S. 16, pp. 101–40. 1916.

210 Fleure (Herbert John). The races of England and Wales. pp. 118 + 5 plates. 8º. London, 1923.

211 —— A natural history of man in Britain conceived as a study of changing relations between men and environments. pp. xviii, 349 + 64 plates. 8º. London, 1951. [76 figures. Pp. 100–21, Romans and Britons.]

212 Forrest (M. E.). Palaeolithic man and the Ice-sheet. Trans. Caradoc &

Severn Valley, F.C., 9, pp. 182–88. 1934.

213 —— A revision of the glacial phenomena in Britain in relation to palaeolithic man. [3 maps.] Trans. Caradoc & Severn Valley, F.C., 10, pp. 5–12. 1935.

214 Fox (*Sir* Cyril). The Early Iron Age in England and Wales. Proc. Camb. Antiq. Soc., 30, pp. 52–53. 1928.

215 —— The personality of Britain: its influence on inhabitants and invaders. Man, 32, pp. 202, 204–5. 1932.

216 —— The personality of Britain: its influence on inhabitant and invader in prehistoric and early historic times. *National Museum of Wales*. pp. 99 + 15 maps. 4º. Cardiff, 1932, 1933, 1938, 1943, 1947.

217 Frere (Sheppard Sunderland). The Iron Age in southern Britain. Antiquity, 33, pp. 183–88. 1959.

218 —— Problems of the Iron Age in southern Britain. University of London Institute of Archaeology Occasional Paper No. 11, 1961, pp. xii, 308 + 14 plates + 28 figures.

219 Garrod (Dorothy Annie Elizabeth). The Upper Palaeolithic Age in Britain. pp. 211 + plate + map + plan. 8º. Oxford, 1926. [41 figures + 8 plans.]

220 —— The Upper Palaeolithic in the light of recent discovery. Proc. prehist. Soc., 4, 1938, 1–26 + 7 figures + 4 plates.

221 Geikie (James). The Antiquity of man in Europe; being the Munro Lectures, 1913. Edinburgh, 1914. 8º. pp. xx, 328.

222 Geoffrey of Monmouth. Histories of the kings of Britain. Translated by Sebastian Evans. *Everyman's Library*. pp. xxvi, 262. 8º. London, 1920. [Pp. 251–62, Indices (personal names, place names, folklore), compiled by W. Bonser.]

223 —— The Historia regum Britanniae. pp. xiii, 672 + 16 plates. 8º. New York, 1929.

224 Glob (P. V.). The Bog People: Iron-Age man preserved, 79 *h/t* illustrations and 2 maps. London, 1969.

225 Greatheed (Samuel). Inquiries concerning the origin of the inhabitants of the British Islands. Archaeologia, 16, pp. 95–122. 1812.

226 Grimes (William Francis). Recent books on British archaeology. Antiquity, 9, pp. 424–34. 1935.

227 —— Wales and Ireland in prehistoric times: some meditations. Arch. Camb., 113, 1964. 1–15.

228 Grinsell (Leslie Valentine). Scheme for recording the folklore of prehistoric remains. Folk-lore, 50, pp. 323–32. 1939.

229 Gross (Charles). The sources and literature of English history from the earliest times to about 1485. pp. xx, 618. 8⁰. London, 1900.

230 Guest (Edwin). Origines Celticae . . . and other contributions to the history of Britain. 2 vols. 8⁰. London, 1883.

231 Hansen (Søren). Englands forhistoriske Anthropologi. Kritiske bemærkinger. Aarbøger nordisk Oldkyndighed og Historie, 1915, pp. 222–74. 1915.

232 Hawkes (Charles Francis Christopher) *and* **Dunning** (Gerald Clough). The second Belgic invasion. A reply to Mrs. Cunnington [12, pp. 27–34 + Map.] Antiq. J., 12, pp. 411–30. 1932.

233 —— Die Erforschung der Spätbronzezeit, Hallstalt -und Latène-Zeit in England und Wales von 1914 bis 1931. [60 figures.] 21. Bericht der Römisch-germanischen Kommission, 1931, pp. 86–175 + 27 plates. 1933.

234 —— Prehistoric Britain in 1931 and 1932. (1933–1935). A review of periodical publications. Archaeol. J., 89 (1932), pp. 275–97: 90 (1933), pp. 315–38: 91 (1934), pp. 301–29: 92 (1935), pp. 334–60. 1933–36.

235 —— Current British archaeology. Univ. London, Inst. Archaeol., Ann. Rpt., 1 (1937), pp. 47–69. 1938.

237 —— The prehistoric foundations of Europe to the Mycenean age. pp. xv, 414 + 12 plates + 6 maps and tables. 8⁰. London, 1940. [27 figures. *See* Britain *in index.*]

238 —— British prehistoric archaeology: recent aims, methods and results. Proc. Roy. Instn., 33, pp. 588–95. 1946. *Summarised in* Nature, 157, pp. 717–20. 1946.

239 —— From Bronze Age to Iron Age: Middle Europe, Italy, and the North and West. Proc. prehist. Soc., 14, 1948, 196–218 + 2 figures + 1 plate.

240 —— British prehistory half-way through the century. Proc. prehist. Soc., 17, 1951, 1–15.

241 —— The ABC of the British Iron Age. [3 figures + map.] Antiquity, 33, pp. 170–82. 1959.

242 Hawkes (Jessie Jacquetta). Early Britain. *Britain in pictures.* pp. 48 + plates. 8, + 26 figures. 8⁰. London, 1945.

243(a) —— *and* Charles Francis Christopher. Prehistoric Britain. *Pelican Books.* pp. 134. 8⁰. Harmondsworth, 1943.

243(b) —— *and* ——. *Ditto.* pp. xvi, 280. 8⁰. London, 1947. [30 plates and figures.]

244 Hawkes (Jacquetta). Archaeology and the present. S.E. Naturalist & Antiquary, 53, 1948, 1–14.

245 —— Changing Britain: Stone Age to the Saxon conquest. [4 figures.] History today, 1 (June), pp. 23–30. 1951.

246 —— Archaeology and the concept of progress. History Today, 10, 1960, 73–82 + 8 plates.

247 —— The World of the past. Vol. I pp. xix + 601 + v; maps 6; figures 18; plates xxiv. Vol. II, pp. xv + 709 + iv; maps 8; figures 22; plates xxiv. London, 1963.

248 —— *and* **Woolley** (*Sir* Leonard). Prehistory and the beginning of civilization (History of Mankind. Cultural and Scientific development. Vol. I). xlviii + 873 pp., 56 plates, 92 text-figures, 19 maps, 3 charts. London, 1963.

249 Heizer, R. F. (*Editor*). Man's discovery of his past: literary landmarks in archaeology. Englewood Cliffs, N.J. 1962, pp. 179, 6 figures.

250 Hemmy (A. S.). Racial contributions to civilization. Trans. & Proc. Torquay nat. Hist. Soc., 6, 1930–34, 145–156.

251 Herbert (A.). Cyclops Christianus; or, an argument to disprove the supposed antiquity of the Stonehenge and other megalithic erections in England and Britanny. pp. iv, 247. 8⁰. London, 1849.

252 Heyden (A. A. M.) van der *and* **Scullard** (H. H.), *Editors.* Atlas of the classical world. London, 1963. pp. 222, incl. 73 maps in 6 colours, 475 gravure plates, 29 pp. index. Trade routes etc.

253 Hibben (Frank C.). Prehistoric man in Europe. Man 60, 1960, 188.

254 Hickey (Elizabeth). The legend of Tara. pp. 36. 8°. Dundalk, 1953.

255 Hicks (Henry). On the migrations of preglacial man. Advm. Sci., 1887, 912.

256 —— Prehistoric man in Britain. Trans. Herts. N.H.S. & F.C., 5, 1887/89, 147–154.

257 Hodgkin (Thomas). The history of England from the earliest times to the Norman Conquest. *Political history of England*, 1. pp. xxi, 528 + 2 maps. 8°. London, 1906. [Pp. 1–17, Pre-Roman period.]

258 Hodson, F. R. Reflections on 'The ABC of the British Iron Age' [Notes and News]. Antiq. 34 (1960) pp. 138–140.

259 —— La Tène Chronology, continental and British. Brit. Inst. of Arch., London 4. 1962, 123–141 + 6 figures.

260 —— Cultural grouping within the British pre-Roman Iron Age. Proc. prehist. Soc., 30, 1964, 99–110 + 1 figure.

261 Hogg (Alexander Hubert Arthur). The Votadini. [Map + plan. Tribe between Tyne and Forth.] Aspects of archaeology. Essays presented to O. G. S. Crawford, pp. 200–20. 1951.

262 —— The Survival of Romano-British place-names in Southern Britain. Antiquity, 38, 1964, 296–99.

263 Holmes (Thomas Rice Edward). Ancient Britain and the invasion of Julius Caesar. Second impression, containing corrections by the author. pp. xvi, 764. 8°. London, 1936. [pp. 13–300, Palaeolithic Age: Neolithic Age: Bronze Age and voyage of Pytheas: Early Iron Age: pp. 375–517, Ethnology, Stonehenge (pp. 468–82): Cassiterides.]

264 Holt (R. B.). The reliability of British records and traditions. Cymru Fu, 1, pp. 66–72. 1888.

265 Home (Gordon). The evolution of an English town. Being the story of . . . Pickering, etc. pp. xix, 293 + plates + map. 8°. London, 1905. [Pp. 12–52 + 7 plates, Prehistory.]

266 Horsley (S.). Man's place in nature's scale of life. Proc. & Trans. East Kent Scient. nat. Hist. Soc., Ser. II 1, 1901, 1–6.

267 Howells (William White). The Iron Age population of Great Britain. Amer. J. Phys. Anthr., 23, pp. 19–29. 1937.

268 Hubert (Henri). Les Celtes depuis l'époque de la Tène et la civilisation celtique. pp. xvii, 368. 8°. Paris, 1950.

269 Huebner (Emil). Britanni. Pauly-Wissousa: Real-Encyclopädie, 3, col. 858–79. 1897.

270 Hunt (James). Report on explorations into the archaic anthropology of the islands of Unst, Brassay, and the mainland of Zetland. [9 figures.] Mems. Anthrop. Soc. London, 2, pp. 294–338 + plate. 1866.

271 Hunt (J. W.). The Finger-hair test of prehistoric origins, an experiment in the West Mendip area, 1962. N. & Q. Somerset and Dorset 28, 1964, Part. 279, pp. 170–75.

272 Hunt (Robert). Popular romances of the west of England, or the drolls, traditions, and superstitions of old Cornwall. Third edition, revised and enlarged. pp. 480. 8°. London, 1881. [Pp. 172–87 (rom. lectrs. etc.).]

273 Jabet (George). The ethnology of Warwickshire, traced in the names of places. B'ham & Midland Inst., Arch. Section, Trans., 4 (1873), pp. 1–26. 1874.

274 Jackson (Kenneth Hurlston). Language and history in early Britain. pp. xxvi, 752. 8°. Edinburgh, 1953.

275 —— The International popular tale and early Welsh tradition. Cardiff, 1961, pp. 141.

276 —— The Oldest Irish tradition: a window on the Iron Age. Cambridge, 1964, 55 pp.

277 Jankuhn (Herbert) *and* **Schmitz** (Heinz). Ackerfluren der Eisenzeit und ihne Bedeutung für die frühe Wirtschaftsgeschichte [reference to English sites]. Ber. Röm. german. Komm. 37–38, 1956–57, 148–214 + 3 plates + 14 figures.

278 Jerman (H. Noel). Collections of Drawings of Welsh antiquities. Arch. Camb. 94 i, 1939, 93–95 + 2 figures.

279 Jerrold (Douglas). An introduction to the history of England, from the earliest times to 1204. pp. 614 + maps. 8°. London, 1949.

280 Jessup (Ronald). The Story of archaeology in Britain. London, 1964, 214 pp. + 44 plates.

281 —— Age by Age: landmarks of British archaeology, illustrated by Alan Sorrell, London, 1966.

282 Jewitt (Llewellynn). Passing notes on some stone circles and other remains of past ages in the Isle of Man. Discovery of an oak-tree canoe at Ballakaighen [Isle of Man]. [6 figures.] [Various.] Reliquary, 25, pp. 193–205 + plates. 1885.

283 Jones (D. F.). Rome and her British clients [reference to earlier Iron Age society]. History Today 14, 1964, 350–357 + 5 figures.

284 Keith (*Sir* Arthur). The Bronze Age invaders of Britain. J. R. Anthrop. Inst., 45, pp. 12–22. 1915.

285 —— The antiquity of man. New edition. 2 vols. 8⁰. London, 1925.

286 —— New discoveries relating to the antiquity of man. pp. 512 + plate. [186 figures.] 8⁰. London, 1931.

287 Kendrick (*Sir* Thomas Downing). The axe age: a study in British prehistory. pp. xii, 177. [17 figures + 2 plans.]. 8⁰. London, 1926.

287(a) —— The word 'palstave'. [2 figures.] Antiquity, 5, pp. 322–29 + plate. 1931.

288 —— Die Erforschung der Steinzeit und der älteren und mittleren Bronzezeit in England und Wales von 1914–1931. [50 figures.] 21. Bericht der Römisch-germanischen Kommission, 1931, pp. 11–85 + 11 plates. 1933.

289 Kenyon (Kathleen Mary). A survey of the evidence concerning the chronology and origins of Iron Age A in southern and midland Britain. [22 figures (pottery) + map.] Univ. London, Inst. Archaeol., Ann. Rpt., 8, pp. 29–78. 1952.

290 —— Beginnings in archaeology. London, 1964, 228 pp. + 8 plates + 14 figures.

291 King (Edward). Monumenta antiqua. 4 vol. fol. London, 1799–1805. [Vol. 1 (pp. 345), Prehistory.]

292 Kitchin (E. Hugh). River Drift man and hafted implements. pp. 15. 8⁰. Bournemouth, 1929. [Cauford cliffs district and inland.]

293 Koenigswald (G. H. R. von). Early man: facts and fantasy. Jl. R. anthrop. Inst. 94, 1964, 67–79.

294 Lacaille (A. D.). The northward march of Palaeolithic man in Britain. Proc. Geol. Ass., 57, pp. 57–81 + maps. 1946.

295 Leroi-Gourhan (André.) La Préhistoire. (L'Histoire et ses problèmes No. 1). Paris, 1966. pp. 366 + figures 54.

296 Lethbridge (T. C.). Shell mounds and winkle pens. Arch. Cambrensii 83 i, 175–181 + 2 figures. 1928.

297 Lewis (A. L.). The builders of the megalithic monuments of Britain. [Abstract and discussion.] J. Anth. Inst., 1, pp. 70–73. 1871.

298 Lewis-Abbott (W. J.). Prehistoric races of Hastings. St. Leonards, pp. 12 + 1 plate. 1898.

299 Lincoln (E. F.). Britain's unwritten history. pp. 208 + 16 plates. 8⁰. London, 1959.

300 Lindsay, (Jack). A Short history of culture. London, 1962, pp. 439 + plates lii + many line drawings.

301 —— Our Celtic heritage. pp. 134, 24 text-figures and maps.) 1962. London.

302 Louis (Maurice). Les Origines préhistoriques de la danse. Cahiers de Préhistoire et d'Archéologie, 1955, pp. 3–37.

303 Lukis (John Walter). The lake dwellings and the customs of their inhabitants. Cardiff Nat. Soc. Rpt. of Trans., 7 (1875), pp. 53–58. 1876.

304 Lysons (Samuel) *F.S.A.* Our British ancestors, who and what were they? An inquiry serving to elucidate the traditional history of the early Britons, by means of recent excavations, . . . inscriptions, craniology, *etc.* 8⁰. Oxford & London, 1865.

305 Mackie (Euan W.). The Origin and development of the broch and wheelhouse building cultures of the Scottish Iron Age. Proc. prehist. Soc., 31, 1965, 93–146 + 8 figures + 4 plates.

306 MacLagan (Robert Craig). Our ancestors, Scots, Picts and Cymry, and what their traditions tell us. pp. xi, 447. 8⁰. London, 1913.

307 McNeill (F. Marian). The silver bough. A four volume study of the national and local festivals of Scotland. 8⁰. Glasgow, 1957.

308 MacRitchie (David). Mound-dwellings and mound-dwellers. Trans. Glasgow Archaeol. Soc., N. S. 4, pp. 179–94. 1903.

309 Marien (M. E.). Oud-België van de eerste Landbouwers tot de Komst van Caesar. Antwerp, 1952, pp. 527 + 398 illustrations.

310 —— La Période de la Tène en Belgique: le Groupe de la Haine. Brussels, 1961.

311 Marr (J. E.). Man and the Ice Age. Presidential Address. Proc. prehist. Soc. E.A. 3 ii, 1919/20, 177–191.

312 Massingham (Harold John). Pre-Roman Britain. Benn's sixpenny library, 40. 8⁰. London [192?].

313 Megan (J. V. S.) Penny whistles and prehistory. Antiquity, 34 (1960), pp. 6–13.

314 —— Penny whistles and pre-history: Further notes. Antiq. 35, 1961, 55–57.

315 —— Across the North Sea: A review. Antiq. 35, 1961, pp. 45–52.

316 Milton, John. The history of Britain, that part especially now call'd England; continu'd to the Norman Conquest. Works, Columbia Univ. Press, 10. 8⁰. New York, 1932. pp. 316.

317 Mitchell (Margaret). The Beaker invasion of Britain. Antiquity, 6, pp. 90–93. 1932.

318 Moir (James Reid). The Position of prehistoric research in England. Proc. P.S.E.A., 2 iii, 1916/17, 381–391 + 2 figures.

319 —— Tertiary man in England. pp. 654–55. [20 figures.] Natural History, 24, pp. 36–55. 1924.

320 —— Tertiary man, reprinted from Nature 1 Feb. 1930. Proc. P.S.E.A., 6 i, 1928–9, 11.

321 —— The Culture of Pliocene man. Proc. P.S.E.A., 7 i, 1932–34, 1–17 + 14 figures + 2 plates.

322 Momigliano (Arnaldo). Ricerche preistoriche in Inghilterra. Rivista storica Italiana 61, pp. 275–84. 1949.

323 Montelius (Oscar). The chronology of the British Bronze Age. Archaeologia, 61, pp. 97–162. 1908.

324 —— The chronology of the Bronze Age in Great Britain and Ireland.

[6 figures. Pp. 121–28, Criticisms by Sir Arthur Evans.] Proc. Soc. Antiq., 2S. 22, pp. 120–29 + plate (bronze objects of iron Age). 1908.

326 Mummery (John R.). On the relations which dental caries (as discovered amongst the ancient inhabitants of Britain and amongst existing aboriginal races) may be supposed to hold to their food and social condition. pp. 79 + 2 tables. 8⁰. London, 1870. [Reprinted from Trans. Odontol. Soc., with additional notes. Pp. 3–11, Pre-history.]

327 Munro (Robert). Prehistoric problems. Edinburgh, 1897.

328 —— On the transition between the Palaeolithic and Neolithic civilizations in Europe. Archaeol. J., 65, pp. 205–44 + plate. 1908.

329 —— Prehistoric Britain. *Home University Library.* pp. 256. 8⁰. London, 19—.

330 —— Palaeolithic man and Terramara settlements in Europe. pp. xxiv, 507 + 75 plates. 8⁰. Edinburgh, 1912. [174 figures. Pp. 105–15, Britain.]

331 Nall (J. F.). Ancient man. Trans. & Proc. Torquay nat. Hist. Soc., 5, 1929, 189–197 + 1 plate.

332 Narr (Karl J.). Formengruppen und Kulturkreise im europäischen Paläolithikum. Ber. Römisch-german. Komm. 34, 1951, 1–40 + 11 figures.

333 Navarro (J. M. de). A survey of research on an early phase of Celtic culture. [La Tène.] Proc. Brit. Acad., 22, pp. 297–341. 1936.

334 —— The British Isles and the beginning of the northern Early Bronze Age. Early cultures of N.W. Europe (H. M. Chadwick mem. stud.) ed. Sir C. Fox & Bruce Dickins, pp. 75–105. 1958.

335 North (F. J.). Sunken cities: some legends of the coast and lakes of Wales. Univ. S. Wales Press, 1957, pp. 256 + 13 plates + 17 figures.

336 Oakley (Kenneth Page). Mesolithic men in Britain. Proc. prehist. Soc., 29, 1963, 426–427.

337 —— The Problem of man's antiquity. An historical survey. Bull. BM (Nat. Hist.) Geology 9, 1964, No. 5, 83–155 + 3 plates + 44 figures.

338 Oakeshott (R. Ewart). The

Archaeology of weapons [pp. 359, 22 plates, 179 text figures]. London, 1960.

339 Oman (*Sir* Charles William Chadwick). England before the Norman Conquest, *etc. Methuen's History of England*, 1. Ninth edition. pp. xiv, 679 + 3 maps. 8º. London, 1949.

340 O'Rahilly (Thomas Francis). The Goidels and their predecessors. Proc. Brit. Acad., 21, pp. 323–72. 1935.

341 —— Early Irish history and mythology. pp. x, 568. 8º. Dublin, 1957.

342 Ozanne (Paul.) Indigenes or invaders? Antiquity, 37, 1963, pp. 229–231.

344 Parsons (Frederick Gymer). On the Long Barrow race and its relationship to the modern inhabitants of London. [16 figures.] J. R. Anthrop. Inst., 51, pp. 55–81. 1921.

345 Peake (Harold John Edward). The Bronze Age and the Celtic world. pp. 201 + 14 plates. [22 figures + 4 maps.] 4º. London, 1922.

347 —— The introduction of civilization into Britain. J. R. Anthrop. Inst., 58, pp. 19–31. 1928.

348 Peate (Iorwerth Cyfeiliog). The Kelts in Britain. Antiquity, 6, pp. 156+60. 1932.

349 —— The Kelts: a linguistic contribution. Arch. Camb. 87 ii, 1932, 260–264.

350 Peers (*Sir* Charles Reed). The beginnings of prehistoric studies in Britain. Man, 32, p. 202. 1932.

351 Peet (T . Eric). Roughstone monuments and their builders. *Harper's Library of Living Thought*. pp. xii, 172 + 3 plates. [8 figures + 14 plans. Pp. 15–33, England and Wales: pp. 34–51, Scotland and Ireland.] London, 1912

352 Pegge (Samuel). Observations on the chariots of the ancient Britons. [Temp. Caesar.] Archaeologia, 7, pp. 211–13. 1785.

353 Pengelly (William). Presidential Address to the Anthropological Section of the British Association [antiquity of man]. Advm. Sci., 1883, 549–561.

354 Petrie (Henry). Monumenta historica Britannica, or materials for the history of Britain, from the earliest period. pp. 146, clxxiii 1035, pl. xxvii. 1848.

354 Petrie (*Sir* William Matthew Flinders). The entry of the Bronze users [into Britain]. [Map.] Man, 25, pp. 74–76. 1925.

356 Pettersson (Max). The Stages of social evolution of man and his ancestors. Man, 62, 1962, 103–104.

357 Phené (John Samuel). On the uniformity of design and purpose in the works and customs of the earliest settlers in Britain, evidenced by comparative archaeology. J. Brit. Archaeol. Ass., 29, pp. 27–36. 1873.

358 Piggott (Stuart). The Hercules myth—beginnings and ends. [His cult in Britain: Cerne giant, etc.] Antiquity, 12, pp. 323–31 + 4 plates. 1938.

359 —— Les relations entre l'ouest de la France et les Îles Britanniques dans la préhistoire. Annales du Midi, 65, pp. 5–20. 1953.

360 —— The Neolithic cultures of the British Isles: a study of the stone-using-agricultural communities of Britain in the second millennium, B.C. pp. xix + 420 + 12 plates. 8º. Cambridge, 1954.

361 —— *Home University Library*, 205. British prehistory. pp. 208. 8º. London, 1949.

363 —— Approach to archaeology [pp. 134, 8 plates, 12 figures]. London, 1959.

364 —— The Dawn of civilization. pp. 404, 940 illustrations. London, 1961.

365 —— Archaeology and prehistory —Presidential address. Proc. prehist. Soc., 29, 1963, 1–16.

366 —— Ancient Europe from the beginnings of agriculture to classical antiquity. Edinburgh, 1965, pp. xxiii + 343, plate LI + 143 figures.

369 Powell (T. G. E.). The Celts (Ancient Places and Peoples), 79 photographs, 25 line drawings, 10 maps.

370 Proudfoot (Bruce). The British Association for the Advancement of Science Section H. A Report of the annual meeting 1961. Archaeol. News Letter 7, 1961, 108–116 + 1 figure.

371 Radford (Courtenay Arthur Ralegh). The culture of southwestern Britain in the Early Iron Age. [Figure + 2 plans.] Homenagen a Martins Sarmento (Guimatães, Portugal), pp. 320–331 + map. 1933.

373 —— The Tribes of Southern Britain. Proc. prehist. Soc., 20, 1954, 1–26 + 6 figures.

374 —— Contributions to a study of the Belgae. Proc. prehist. Soc., 21, 1955, 249–256.

375 **Raftery** (Joseph), *Editor*. The Celts. Cork, 1964, 83 pp. Mercier Press.

376 **Raymond** (Percy Edward). Prehistoric life. pp. ix, 324. 8º. Cambridge, Mass., 1939.

377 **Reclus** (Éli). Primitive folk. Studies in comparative ethnology. pp. xiv, 339. 8º. London, 1891.

378 **Rees** (Alwyn) *and* **Rees** (Brinley). Ancient tradition in Ireland and Wales. London, 1961, pp. 427 + 14 figures.

379 —— Celtic heritage: ancient tradition in Ireland and Wales. pp. 427, 14 in-text figures. 50s. London: Thames & Hudson, 1961.

380 **Reid** (Clement). The relation of Palaeolithic man to the glacial Epoch. Rep. Brit. Ass., 1896.

381 **Renard** (G.). Life and Work in Prehistoric Times, 8 pp. plates (The History of Civilization). London. 1st ed. 1929, pp. 228, 25 illustrations.

382 **Rhys** (*Sir* John). The early ethnology of the British Isles. Rhind lectures for 1889. Scottish Rev., 15, pp. 233–52. 1890.

383(a) **Richardson** (Ralph). Kent's Cavern and Sir Henry H. Howorth's "Flood" theory. Trans. Edinburgh Geol. Soc., 7, 1894/98, 21–26.

383(b) **Rivers** (Augustus Henry Lane Fox Pitt). Address to the Antiquarian section at the annual meeting of the [Royal Archaeological] Institute, held at Lewes [1884]. Archaeol. J., 41, pp. 58–78. 1884.

383(c) —— Inaugural address to the annual meeting of the [Royal Archaeological] Institute, held at Salisbury, [1887]. Archaeol. J., 44, pp. 261–77. 1887.

384 **Rivet** (H. L. F.). Cross channel. Archaeol. News Letter, 6, pp. 210–12. 1958.

385 **Roe** (D. A.). The British Lower and Middle Palaeolithic: some problems, methods of study and preliminary results. Proc. prehist. Soc., 30, 1964, 245–267 + 21 figures + 1 plate.

386 **Roger** (E. H.). The Iron Age. Trans. & Proc. Torquay nat. Hist. Soc., 9, 1946, 103–110.

387 **Rouse** (Irving). The Place of 'peoples' in prehistoric research. J. R. anthrop. Inst., 95, 1965, 1–15.

388 **Savory** (H. N.). The "Swordbearers". A reinterpretation. Proc. prehist. Soc., 14, 1948, 155–176 + 5 figures.

389 —— Neolithic Britain: a review. Antiquity, 28, pp. 143–46. 1954.

390 **Sayce** (Archibald Henry). The legend of King Bladud. Cymmrodor, 10, pp. 207–21. 1889.

391 **Sayce** (Roderick Urwick). The Celtic Iron Age. [Iron Age B movements into Britain, Celtic fields, etc.]. Trans. Lancs. & Ches. Ant. Soc., 66 (1956), pp. 1–21. 1957.

392 **Schrader** (Otto). Reallexikon der indogermanischen Altertumskunde. Grundzüge einer Kultur -und Völkergeschichte Alteuropas. pp. xl + 1048. la. 8º. Strassburg, 1906.

393 **Scott** (*Sir* Lindsay). The Problem of the Brochs. Proc. prehist, Soc., 13, 1947, 1–36 + 10 figures.

394 —— Gallo - British Colonies. The Aisted round-house culture in the North. Proc. prehist. Soc., 14, pp. 46–125 + 17 figures + 10 plates. 1948.

395 **Sellman** (R. R.). Prehistoric Britain. Illustrated by the author and Alan Sorrell. 1958, pp. iv +62. f'cap. 4º.

396 **Shotton** (Frederick William). The Problems and contributions of methods of absolute dating within the Pleistocene period. Q. J. Geol. Soc., London. 122, 1966, 357–383 + 3 figures.

397 **Smith** (*Rev.* Frederick). The Stone Ages in north Britain and Ireland with an Introduction by A. H. Keane. pp. xxiv, 377. 8º. London, 1909.

398 **Smith** (Harold Clifford). Jewellery. *Connoisseur's Library*. pp. xlviii, 410 + 54 plates. 8º. London, 1908.

400 **Soudský** (B). *and* **Pleslova** (E). L'Europe à la fin de l'âge de la pierre. Actes du symposium Internat. consacré aux problèmes du néolithique Européen. Prague 1961. pp. 644, 46 plates, 79 figures.

401 **Stackhouse** (Thomas). Two lectures on the remains of ancient

pagan Britain, etc. pp. iv, 74 + 40 plates. 4⁰. London, 1833.

402 Stevenson (Robert B. K.). Pins and the chronology of brochs. Proc. prehist. Soc., 21, 1955, 282–294 + 2 figures.

403 Stone (Gilbert). England from the earliest times to the Great Charter. pp. xx, 618 + 51 plates + 2 maps. 8⁰. London, 1916.

404 Stone (J. F. S.) *and* **Thomas**, L. C. The use and distribution of faience in the ancient East and prehistoric Europe—with notes on the spectro-chemical analysis of faience. Proc. prehist. Soc., 22, 1956, 37–84, 4 figures, 6 tables, 2 plates.

405(a) Stow (John). Annales, or, a general chronicle of England. pp. 1090. fol. Londini, 1631.

405(b) Stratford (Esmé Wingfield). The history of British civilization. pp. xix, 1332. 8⁰. London, 1930.

406 Sturge (W. Allen). The Chronology of stone age. Proc. prehist. Soc., East Anglia li, 1908/10, 43–105 + plates + 2 figures.

407 Summers (Walter C.). The Modernness of the ancients. Trans. & Proc. Torquay nat. Hist. Soc., 6, 1930–1934, 241–250.

408 Swift (Henry). Weapons of the British. [4 figures.] J. Antiq. Assoc. Brit. Isles, 1, pp. 53–59. 1930.

409 Szövérffy (Josef). Irischer Erzählgut im Abendland. Berlin 1957. pp. ix + 193.

410 Taeymans, J. Merveilles de l'Antiquité: Europe. pp. 184, 130 text photographs. Paris and Brussels, 1960.

411 Taylor (Isaac) *and* **Maskell** (J.). Who were the Belgae? [*See also* 7S.1, pp. 441–42, 461–62]. N. & Q., 7S.2, pp. 1–3. 1886.

412 Thomas (David). Animal call-words. A study of human migration. pp. xiv, 170 + 13 plates + map + plan. Cards. Ant. Soc., Trans. 14. 1939.

413 Thompson, M. W. Marxism and culture. Antiquity, 39, 1965, pp. 108–116.

414 Trevelyan (George Macaulay). History of England. pp. xx, 723, London, 1926. 8⁰. pp. xxii, 756, 1937. 8⁰. new and enlarged. pp. xxii, 756, 1945. 3rd reissue London 1952.

415 Tyler (John M.). The New Stone Age in northern Europe. pp. 310 + 22 plates. 8⁰. London, 1921.

416 Ucko (Peter J.), **Tringham** (Ruth) *and* **Dimbleby** (G. W.), *Editors.* Man, Settlement and Urbanism. London, 1972.

417 Underwood (Leon). Le Bâton de commandement. Man, 65, 1965, 140–143 + 5 figures.

418 Vallancey (Charles). An essay on the primitive inhabitants of Great Britain and Ireland, proving that they were Persians or Indo-Scythiae, *etc.* pp. xviii, 219. 8⁰. Dublin, 1807.

419 Vembergue (F. E.). Remarks on the origin of the Celtic nations. Arch. Camb., 1, pp. 173–74. 1846.

420 Vulliamy (Colwyn Edward). Our prehistoric forerunners. pp. 214, 33 illustrations. 8⁰. London, 1925.

421 Waddell (Lawrence Austine). The Phoenician origin of Britons, Scots and Anglo-Saxons, *etc.* 8⁰. London, 1924.

422 Wainwright (F. T.). Archaeology and place-names and history—an essay on problems of co-ordination. London, 1962, pp. xiv-136 + 5 maps.

423 Ward (Gordon). The Iceni—Teutons or Celts? Norfolk Archaeology, XXXII (ii), 1959, 99–103.

424 —— The Belgic Britons: men of Kent in B.C. 55. pp. 150. 4⁰. Sevenoaks [1961]. [27 figures + 5 maps + 2 plans.]

425 Washburn (Sherwood L.). Social life of early man. London, 1962. pp. ix + 299 + 32 figures.

426 Wickham (*Rev.* J.). Records by spade and terror. Historical side-lights from the discovery of Stone-Age, Celtic and Roman remains. 8⁰. Bath. 1912.

427 Wilson (Daniel). Prehistoric man—researches into the origin of civilisation in the old and the new world. London, 2 vols. 8⁰. pp. 488 + 483 illustrations. 1862.

428 Winbolt (Samuel Edward). Britain B.C. *Pelican Books.* pp. 160. 8⁰. Harmondsworth, 1943.

429 Windle (*Sir* Bertram Coghill Alan). Life in early Britain, *etc.* pp. xv, 244 + map. [67 figures and plans.] 8⁰. London, 1897.

431 Woodhead (A. G.). The Greeks in the West. (Ancient Peoples and

Places, Vol. 28). London, 1962, pp. 243, plates 81, 26 text-figures.

432 Worth (Richard Nicholls). The myth of Brutus the Trojan. Snell (F. J.): Memorials of old Devonshire, pp. 20–33. 1904.

433(a) Wright (Thomas). The Celt, the Roman and the Saxon. A history of the early inhabitants of Britain. 1st edition 1852. 2nd revised. 3rd edition, 1861. 4th edition, pp. 562, plates 20, 1885. 6th edition. 8°. London, 1902.

434 Yates (Edward). The Evolution of the dwelling house. S.E. Naturalist & Antiquary, 49, 1945, 12–16.

435 Yeatman (John Pym). An introduction to the study of early English history. pp. xi, 352. 8°. London, 1874.

436 Young (Alison). Brochs and Dune. Proc. Soc Ant. Scotland 95, 1961–62, 171–198 + 4 figures + 4 plates.

437 Young (R.). Prehistoric remains in the Balearic Isles. Ulster J. Arch., 3, 1897, 278–79.

3. SCIENTIFIC METHODS

438 Aitken (Martin Jim). Magnetic dating I. Archaeometry 1, 1958, 16–20 + 1 figure.

439 —— and Harold (M. R.). Magnetic dating II. Archaeology 2, 1959, 17–19 + 1 figure.

440 —— Magnetic prospecting II. Archaeometry 2, 1959, 32–36.

441 —— Magnetic prospecting IV: The Proton Magnetometer. Archaeometry 2, 1959, 40–42.

442 —— Magnetic dating. Archaeometry 3 (1960) 41–44 + 1 figure.

443 —— Magnetic prospecting: the proton gradiometer. Archaeometry 3, 1960, 38–40 + 1 figure.

444 —— Physics and archaeology. New York [Interscience] 1961. pp. x, 181, 28 plates + 50 text figures.

445 —— Magnetic location in Britain. Archaeometry 4, 1961, 83–84.

446 —— and Tite (M. S.). Proton magnetometer surveying on some British hill-forks. Archaeometry 5, 1962, 126–134 + 4 figures.

447 —— and Weaver (G. H.). Magnetic dating: some archaeomagnetic measurements in Britain. Archaeometry 5, 1962, 4–24 + 3 figures.

448 Alexander, (John). The Directing of Archaeological Excavations, plates and drawings. 1969.

449 Allen (G. W. G.). *and* **Nash-Williams** (Victor Evle). Air-photography and archaeology. *National Museum of Wales.* pp. 35. 8°. Cardiff, 1938.

450 Ashbee (Paul) *and* **Cornwall** (Ian W.) An Experiment in field archaeology. Antiquity, 35, 1961, pp. 129–134.

451 Azzaroli (Augusto). The Geological age of the Cromer Forest Bed. Proc. prehist. Soc., 17, 1951, 168–170.

452 Barker (Harold) *and* **Mackey** (C. John). British Museum natural radiocarbon measurements, 1. Brit. Mus. Quart., 22, 1960, 94–101.

453 —— British Museum natural radiocarbon measurements, II. Brit. Mus. Quart., 23, 1960/1, 118–123.

454 —— British Museum natural radiocarbon measurements, III. Brit. Mus. Quart., 27 1/2, 1963, 48–58.

455 Beer (Gavin de). Iktin. Geographical Journal 126, 1960, 160–67 + 2 figures.

456 Belshé (J. C.). Surveys in and around Cambridgeshire. Archaeometry 4, 1961, 73.

457 Biek (Leo.) Archaeology and the microscope. The scientific examination of archaeological evidence. London, 1963, 287 pp., 26 plates (2 in colour).

458 Boswell (P. G. H.). Problems of the borderland of archaeology and geology in Britain. Presidential address for 1936. Proc. prehist. Soc. N.S. 2, 1936, 149–160.

459 Bowen (Emrys George). Introductory background [to historical geography]: prehistoric south Britain. [7 maps.] Derby (H. C.): An historical geography of England before A.D. 1800, pp. 1–29. 1936.

460 Bowen (E. G.). From antiquarianism to archaeology in Cardiganshire, 1909–1959. Ceredigion 3, No. 4, 1959, 257–264.

461 Britton (C. E.). A meteorological chronology to A.D. 1450. Meteorological office, geophysical memoirs, 70. pp. 176. 4°. London, 1937.

462 **Brooks** (Charles Ernest Pelham). The Correlation of the Quaternary Deposits of the British Isles with those of the continent of Europe. Smithsonian Report for 1917, pp. 277–375.

463 —— The evolution of climate in north-west Europe. Man, 21, pp. 104–105. 1921.

464 —— The climate of prehistoric Britain. [2 figures.] Antiquity, 1, pp. 412–18. 1927.

465 **Brothwell** (D.) *and* **Higgs** (E.), *Editor.* Science in archaeology: a Comprehensive survey of progress and research. London: 1963, 595 pp., 32 plates, 92 figures, 66 tables.

466 **Brown** (M. A.) *and* **Stoyle** (A. E. Blin). A sample analysis of British Middle and Late Bronze Age material using optical spectrometry (based on analyses by R. V. Jolowicz, A. E. Blin-Stoyle and C. C. Humphreys). Proc. prehist.Soc ., 25, 1959, 188–208 + 5 figures.

467 **Buckman** (James). On the chemical composition of some ancient British and Roman beads. [3 figures.] Archaeol. J., 8, pp. 351–54. 1851.

468 **Burchell** (James Percy Tufnell). The Northfleet [Kent] 50-foot submergence later than the Coombe rock of post-early Mousterian times. [37 figures, Flake-implements, *etc.*] Archaeologia, 83, pp. 67–92. 1933.

469 —— Land-shells as a critical factor in the dating of post-Pleistocene deposits. Proc. prehist. Soc., 23, 1957, 236–39.

470 —— Land shells and their role in dating deposits of post-glacial times in South-East England. Archaeol. News Letter, 7, ii, 1961, 34–38.

471 **Butzer** (Karl W.). Environment and archaeology. London, 1964, pp. xviii + 524, 19 tables, 84 figures.

472 **Carrier** (E. H.). Historical geography of England and Wales (Southern Britain). 8⁰. London, 1925. [Pp. 11–44, prehistoric.]

473 **Chart** (David Alfred). Air-photography in Northern Ireland. [Plan.] Antiquity, 4, pp. 453–59 + 7 plates. 1930.

474 **Childe** (Vere Gordon). Changing methods and aims in prehistory. Presidential Address for 1935. Proc. prehist. Soc., N.S. 1, 1935, 1–15.

475 **Churchill** (D. M.). A Report on the pollen analyses of the muds from the Medulla tissues of two fossil human skeletons: Tilbury man and Thatcham Man. Proc. prehist. Soc., 29, 1963, 427–8.

476 **Clark** (John Grahame Douglas). The Separation of Britain from the Continent. Proc. prehist. Soc., N.S. 2, 1936, 239.

477 —— Dendrochronology. Proc. prehist. Soc., 3, 1937, 183–185 + 1 plate.

478 —— The Separation of Britain from the Continent. Proc. prehist. Soc., 4, 1938, 230–231.

479 —— *and* **Peake** (H. J. E.). Final insulation of Britain. Proc. prehist. Soc., 4, 1938, 343–44.

480 —— Further note on the Tufa deposit at Prestatyn, Flintshire. Proc. prehist. Soc., 5, 1939, 201–202.

481 —— Radiocarbon dating and the expansion of farming culture from the Near East over Europe. Proc. prehist. Soc., 31, 1965, 58–73 + 4 figures.

482 —— Radio carbon dating and the spread of farming economy. Antiquity, 39, 1965, 45–48.

483 **Clarke** (D. L.). Matrix analysis and archaeology with particular reference to British beaker pottery. Proc. prehist. Soc., 28, 1962, 371–382 + 5 figures.

484 —— *and* **Connah** (G.). Remanent magnetism and Beaker chronology. Antiquity, 36, 1962, pp. 206–209.

485 —— Analytical Archaeology, with 170 line illustrations. Describes and evaluates the sweeping changes that are now overtaking archaeological methodology, and which derive from developments in other disciplines and from the introduction of the computer, whose applications are here reviewed at length. London, 1968.

486 **Clarke** (W. G.). Some aspects of striation. Proc. prehist. Soc., E.A. 1, iv, 1913/14, 434–38 + 2 plates.

487 **Connah**, Graham. An archaeology experiment with the '4c' mine detector. Antiquity, 36, 1962, pp. 305–306.

488 —— *and* **McMillan** (Nora F.) Snails and archaeology. Antiquity, 38, 1964, pp. 62–64.

489 **Cook** (Robert M.) *and* **Belshé** (John C.). Dating by archaeomagnetism. Archaeology 12 (3), 1959, 158–162.

490 Cookson (M. B.). Photography for archaeologists. pp. 123 + 13 plates. 8º. London, 1954.

491 —— The Photographic Department of the Institute. Bull. Inst. of Arch. London, 4, 1964, 25–27 + 1 figure.

492 Cornwall (Ian W.). Soil science and archaeology with illustrations from some British Bronze Age monuments. Proc. prehist. Soc., 19, 1953, 129–147 + 12 figures + 1 plate.

493 —— Soil for the archaeologist [pp. 230, 19 text figures.] London, 1958.

494 Council for British Archaeology. A Guide to air-photographic archaeology in the South-West 1961.

495 Crampton (C. B.) *and* **Webley** (D. P.). Preliminary studies of the historic succession of plants and soils on selected archaeological sites in South Wales. Bull. Board Celtic Studies 20 iv, 1964, 440–449 + 4 figures + 1 table.

496 Crawford (Osbert Guy Stanhope). Prehistoric geography. [Map. Pp. 258–59 + map. Examples of ancient British forts (Bronze Age).] Geog. Rev., 12, pp. 257–63. 1922.

497 —— Notes on air-photograph of Harrow hill [Sussex]. Sussex Arch. Collns., 67, pp. 147–48 + plate. 1926.

498 —— Air survey and archaeology. [2 maps.] Geog. J., 61, pp. 342–66 + 4 plates. 1923.

499 —— Lyonesse. [Figure + map (coast-line of Scilly Isles if raised 60 feet).] Antiquity, 1, pp. 1–14 + 3 plates. 1927.

500 —— Air-photographs near Dorchester, Oxon. [2 plans.] Antiquity, 1, pp. 469–74 + 2 plates. 1927.

501 —— Wessex from the air, pp. xii, 264 + 50 plates. 4º. Oxford, 1928. [61 figures and maps. Camps, villages, ancient fields, barrows (pp. 16–17, Roman).]

502 —— Air survey and archaeology. *Ordnance Survey, Prof. Papers, N.S.*7. pp. 42 + maps. 1928.

503 —— Woodbury, [Wilts.]. Two marvellous air-photographs. Antiquity, 3, pp. 452–35 + plate. 1929.

504 —— Some recent air discoveries. [Figure.] Antiquity, 7, pp. 290–96 + 6 plates. 1933

505 —— Air photography, past and future. Presidential Address for 1938. Proc. prehist. Soc., 4, 1938, 233–238.

506 Curwen (Eliot Cecil). Air-photography and economic history: the evolution of the corn-field. *Economic History Society.* pp. 31 + 2 plates. 8º. London, [1929]. [4 figures + map + 2 plans.]

507 Davies (Margaret). Megalith builders and tidal currents. Arch. Camb., 100, ii, 1949, 275.

508 —— Early man and the soils of Glamorgan. [2 maps.] Cardiff Nat. Soc. Rpt. & Trans., 79 (1945/48), pp. 55–57. 1950.

509 Davison (E. H.). On the geology of Castle-au-Dinas wolfram mine. Geol. Mag. 57, 1920, 347–351 + 2 figures.

510 Dawkins (*Sir* William Boyd). The geography of Britain at the time of the arrival of man. J. Manch. Geog. Soc., 36, pp. 1–5. 1920.

511 Desch (C. H.). Metallurgical aids to archaeology. Trans. Newcomen Soc., 27, 1949/51, 121–129.

512 Dewar (H. S. L.). Geological siting of some Durotrigian and Romano-British farms. Proc. Dorset. N.H. & A.S., 83, 1962, 100.

513 —— Submerged forest at Combwich. N. & Q. Somerset & Dorset, 28, 1962, part 275, p. 59.

514 Dewey (H.). The Relationship of geology to archaeology. Trans. & Proc. Torquay nat. Hist. Soc., 9, 1944, 1–9.

515 Dimbleby (Geoffrey William). Pollen analysis as an aid to the dating of prehistoric monuments. Proc. prehist. Soc., 20, 1954, 231–236 + 1 figure.

516 —— Thatcham—pollen analysis. Berks. Arch. J., 57, 1959, 25–33.

517 —— The Development of British heathlands and their soil (Oxford Forestry Memoirs No. 23). Oxford 1962, pp. 120, 1 + 31 figures, 9 colour plates, 2 + 7 tables.

518 —— Overton Down experimental earthwork. Antiquity, 39, 1965, pp. 134–136.

519 —— Environmental studies and archaeology. Bull. Inst. Arch. London, 6, 1966, 1–14 + 1 figure.

520 —— Plants and Archaeology, 25 *pp. plates,* roy. 8º. London, 1967.

521 Dymond (Charles Williams). A graphic method of finding the point of sunrise on midsummer day. [Figure.] Antiquary, 45, pp. 218–19. 1909.

522 Edmunds (Francis H.). Note on the gravel deposit from which the Piltdown Skull was obtained. Q.J. Geol. Soc., London, 106, 1960, 133–134.

523 Emery (G. T.) Dental pathology and archaeology. Antiquity, 37, 1963, pp. 274–281.

524 Evans (Emyr Estyn). Culture and environment: essays in honour of Sir Cyril Fox. Antiquity, 38, 1964, 152–53.

525 Evens (E. D.). *and others*. 4th Report of the Sub-Committee of the South-Western Group of Museums and Art Galleries on the Petrological identification of stone axes (with *L. V. Grinsell, S. Piggott* and *F. S. Wallis*). Proc. prehist. Soc., 28, 1962, 209–266 + 6 figures.

526 Fagan (Brian M.). Cropmarks in antiquity. Antiquity, 33, pp. 279–81. 1959.

527 —— Cropmarks in antiquity. Antiq., 34, pp. 279–281, 1960.

528 Foster (I. Ll.) *and* **Alcock** (Leslie), *Editors*. Culture and environment. Essays in honour of Sir Cyril Fox. pp. xix + 538 + 28 plates + 111 figures. London, 1963.

529 Fowler (P. J.). Magnetic prospecting III: An archaeological note about Madmarston. Archaeometry, 2, 1959, 37–39.

530 Garrod (D. A. E.). Nova et vetera: a plea for a new method in Palaeolithic archaeology. Presidential address. Proc. PSEA, 5 iii, 1927, 260–272 + 4 figures.

531 Gedye (I.) *and* **Hodges** (Henry W. M.). The Teaching of archaeological conservation. Bull. Inst. of Arch. London, 4, 1962, 83–87.

532 Gerlach (Arch. C.). The Work of the Ordnance Survey. Geog. Journ., 126, 1960, 243–244.

533 Gilbert (Charles Jesse). Earth movements during the closing stages of the Neolithic depression. Q.J. Geol. Soc., 76, 1930, 94–95.

534 Godwin (Henry). The English archaeologist's handbook. pp. xii, 276. 8°. Oxford, 1867.

535 —— The Relationship of bog stratigraphy to climatic change and archaeology. Proc. prehist. Soc., XII, 1946, 1–11.

536 —— The History of the British flora. Cambridge, 1956, pp. viii + 384, 119 figures, plates xxvi.

537 Gomme (*Sir* George Lawrence). The geography of early London. Geog. Teacher, 5, pp. 321–34. 1910.

538 Gresham (C. A.). Earthworms and archaeology [Notes and News]. Antiquity, 35, 1961, pp. 235–237.

539 Griffiths (W. E.). Radiocarbon dates for the Bronze Age in North Wales. Proc. prehist. Soc., 28, 1962, 387.

540 Grimes (William Francis). Early man and the soils of Anglesey. [2 maps]. Antiquity, 19, pp. 169–74. 1945.

541 —— Air photography and archaeology. Trans. London & Middx. Arch. Soc., N.S. 11, pp. 1–9. 1954.

542 Hall (E. T.). Some uses of physics in archaeology. Yearbook of the Physical Society, 1958, 22–34 + 8 figures.

543 —— Chemical investigation of museum objects. Archaeometry, 2, 1959, 43–49 + 3 tables.

544 —— *and* **Aitken** (M. J.). Availability of magnetic surveys: 1959. Archaeometry, 2, 1959, 63.

545 —— X-ray fluorescent analysis applied to archaeology. Archaeometry, 3, 1960, 29–35 + 4 figures.

546 —— Surface enrichment of buried metals. Archaeometry, 4, 1961, 62–66 + 2 figures.

547 Harden (Donald Benjamin). Archaeological air-photography in Britain. [Figure (enclosures at Northfield farm, Long Wittenham, Berks.).] Trans. Newbury F.C., 10 i, pp. 19–26 + 8 plates. 1953.

548 Harris (S.). Distribution maps and early movements into Britain, and their relation to legendary history. Arch. Cambrensis, 83 i, 1928, 182–191 + 1 map.

549 Haward (F. N.). The Chipping of flints by natural agencies. Proc. prehist. Soc. E.A., 1 ii, 1910/12, 185–93 + 12 plates.

550 Hawkes (Charles Francis Christopher). The O.S. Map of the Iron Age. Antiquity, 36, 1962, pp. 293–299.

551 Heizer (Robert F.) *and* **Cook** (Sherburne F.). The application of quantitative methods in archaeology. Chicago, 1960. pp. x + 358, 12 plates, 9 text figures. Quadrangle Books.

552 Hewitt (H. Dixon). Some experiments on patination. Proc. prehist. Soc. E.A., 2 i, 1914/15, 45–51.

553 Holden (E. W.). A Simple method of levelling. Archaeol. News Letter, 7 i, 1961, 8.

554 Homes (Ronald). Commonground—British archaeology and the electrical engineer. Electronics & Power, 13(5), 1967, 162–167 + 8 figures.

555 Hornblower (A. P.). Archaeological applications of the electron probe microanalyser. Archaeometry 5, 1962, 108–112 + 1 figure.

556 Hoskins (William George), *Editor*. The making of the English landscape. pp. 128. [Pp. 25–32, Prehistory.]. 8°. London, 1957.

557 Irving (A.). Some recent work on later quaternary geology and anthropology, with its bearing on the question of Pre-boulder-clay man. [2 figures. Thorley (Herts.) prehistoric site, *etc.*] J. R. Anthrop. Inst., 44, pp. 385–93. 1914.

558 Jamieson (A. W.). The Clay with flints. Proc. prehist. Soc. E.A. 1 iv, 1913/14, 458–460.

559 Jewell (Peter A.), *Editor*. The Experimental earthwork of Overton Down, Wiltshire 1960. London, (B.A. for Advancement of Science), 1963, 108 pp., 8 plates, 38 figures.

560 —— *and* **Dimbleby** (G. W.). The Experimental earthwork on Overton Down, Wiltshire, England: the first four years. Proc. prehist. Soc., 32, 1966, 313–342, 3 figures, 10 plates, 13 tables.

561 Johnson, Jotham, *Editor*. Archaeology. New York, 1963, 367 pp. + 24 plates.

562 Keiller (Alexander) *and others* [Stuart Piggott and F. S. Wallis]. First report of the Sub-Committee of the South-Western Group of Museums and Art Galleries on the petrological identification of stone axes. Proc. prehist. Soc., 7, 1941, 50–72 + 3 figures + 1 plate + 1 map.

563 Kelly (D. B.). Maidstone Museum. Implement petrology survey [Neolithic—EBA]. Arch. Cantiana, 79, 1964, 229–25.

564 Kerrich (J. E.) *and* **Clarke** (D. L.). Notes on the possible misuse and errors of cumulative percentage frequency graphs for the comparison of prehistoric artefact assemblages. Proc. prehist. Soc., 33, 1967, 57–69 + 5 figures.

566 Lewis, (J. M). Aeriel reconnaissance in Wales. Notes & News. Antiquity, 36, 1962, p. 59.

567 Livens (R. G.). Petrology of Scottish Stone implements. Proc. Soc. Antiq. Scotland 92, 1958–59, 56–69 + 7 figures.

568 McBurney (C. M. B.). The Geographical study of the older Palaeolithic stages in Europe. Proc. prehist. Soc., 16, 1950, 163–183 + 2 maps.

569 —— Potassium-argon dating [Notes and News]. Antiq., 34 (1960), pp. 213–215.

570 Maréchal (Jean R.). Application de la thermodynamique à l'explication de la métallurgie ancienne. A report of the Ancient Mining and Metallurgy Committee. Man 63, 1963, 33–38 + 2 figures.

571 Marriott (R. A.). The Last glaciation and the submerged forests. J. Torquay nat. Hist. Soc., 2, 1917, 163–176.

572 Moir (J. Reid). The Geological age of the earliest Palaeolothic flint implements. Geol. Mag., 57, 1920, 221–224.

573 —— Some archaeological problems. PPSEA, 4 ii, 1923/24, 234–240.

574 Morey (June E). Petrographical identification of stone axes. Proc. prehist. Soc., 16, 1950, 191–193.

575 Morris (John H.). Finds of Neolithic and Bronze Age antiquity from under the submerged forest beds at Rhyl. [2 figures.] Arch. Camb., 78, pp. 151–53. 1923.

576 Oakley (Kenneth Page). Geological monuments. Proc. prehist. Soc., 9, 1943, 55–56.

577 —— A Note on the Late Post-Glacial Submergence of the Solent Margins. Proc. prehist. Soc., 9, 1943, 56–59.

578 —— Account of the "fluorine test" for determining the relative antiquity of fossil bones. Q.J. Geol. Soc., London 106, 1950, iii–v.

579 —— Folklore of fossils Part i. Antiquity, 39, 1965, 9–16.

580 —— Folklore of fossils, Part ii. Antiquity, 39, 1965, pp. 117–125.

581 O'Kelly (M. J.). The Experimental earthwork on Overton Down, Wiltshire 1960. Antiquity, 38, 1964, 150–151.

582 Ordnance Survey. Notes on archaeological information incorporated in the Ordnance Survey maps, 1. The long barrows and stone circles in . . . the Cotswolds and Welsh Marches. By O. S. G. Crawford. *Professional Papers, N.S.6.* pp. 11 + plate + map + plan. 8°. London, 1922.

583 —— Air survey and archaeology. By O. S. G. Crawford. *Professional Papers, N.S.7.* pp. 39 + 13 plates + 2 maps. 4°. London, 1924.

584 —— Air-photography for archaeologists. By O. S. G. Crawford. *Professional Papers, N.S.12.* pp. 44 + 19 plates. 4°. London, 1929.

585 —— Ordnance survey map of Southern Britain in the Iron Age. Map scale 1 : 625,000; text pp. 55, 8 distribution maps. Chessington, 1962.

586 Ashmolean Museum (Oxford). Guide to an exhibition of air-photographs of archaeological sites. Nov. 1948 to Feb. 1949. pp. 19 + 16 plates. 4·0 Oxford, 1948.

587 Palmer (L. S.). Elementary graphical archaeometry. Proc. Somerset A & NHS 104, 1959/60, 43–61 + 9 figures.

588 —— Geoelectrical surveying of archaeological sites. Proc. prehist. Soc., 26, 1960, 64–75 + 7 figures + 1 plate.

589 Paterson (T. T.). Studies on the Palaeolithic Succession in England No. 1. The Barnham Sequence. Proc. prehist. Soc., 3, 1937, 87–135 + 27 figures.

590 Peers (*Sir* Charles Reed). A research policy for field work. Antiq. J., 9, pp. 349–53. 1929.

591 Petch (D. F.). Aerial survey of archaeological sites. Lincs. A. & A. S. Rpts. & Papers, 9, 1961, 1–3.

592 Phillips (C. W.). Air-photographs of fields at Barnack, Northants. Proc. prehist. Soc., N.S., 1, 1935, 156–157 + 1 plate.

593 —— The Ordnance Survey and archaeology, 1791–1960. Geog. Journ., 127, 1961, 1–9.

594 Pidgeon (D.). On some recent discoveries in the submerged forest of Torbay [? date BA?]. J. Geol. Soc., London, 41, 1885, 9–22 + 4 figures.

595 Piggott, Stuart. Archaeological draughtsmanship: principles and practice, Part i: principles and retrospect. Antiquity, 39, 1965, pp. 165–176.

596 Platt (Colin). The Punched feature card in archaeological recording. Bull. Inst. of Arch. London, 5, 1965, 61–66 + 2 figures.

597 Poole (G. S.). On the recent geological changes in Somerset, and their date relatively to the existence of man and of certain extinct mammalia [below peat]. J. Geol. Soc., London, 20, 1864, 118–120.

598 Praeger (R. Lloyd). The "Preservation" of ancient monuments. Ulster J. Arch., 4, 1898, 100–101.

599 Preston (F. L.). The Scheme for archaeological research: a second report. Trans. Hunter archaeol. Soc., 9 i , 1964, 51–54.

600 Prestwich (Joseph). On the presence of a raised beach on Portsdown Hill, near Portsmouth, and on the occurrence of a flint implement on a high level at Downton. J. Geol. Soc., London, 28, 1872, 38–41 + 1 figure.

601 —— Considerations on the date, duration, and conditions of the glacial period, with reference to the antiquity of man. J. Geol. Soc., London, 43, 1887, 393–410.

602 —— On the age, formation, and successive drift-stages of the valley of the Darent; with remarks on the Palaeolithic implements of the district, and on the origin of its chalk escarpment. [Kents date]. J. Geol. Soc., London, 47, 1891, 126–163 + 3 plates + 12 figures.

603 Proudfoot (Bruce). Experiments in archaeology. Science Journal 3(11), 1967, 59–64 + 6 figures.

604 Pyddoke (Edward). Stratification for the archaeologist. pp. 124, 8 plates, 18 figures. London, 1961.

605 —— The Scientist and archaeology. London, 1963, 208 pp. + 24 plates + 32 figures.

606 —— What is archaeology? London, 1964, 64 pp. + 8 plates + 5 figures.

607 Raikes (Robert). Water, Weather and Prehistory: preface by Sir Mortimer Wheeler, plates and maps. London, 1967.

608 Richards (E. E.). Spectrographic and magnetic examination of some baked clay slab-moulds. Archaeometry, 2, 1959, 53–54 + 3 tables.

609 Riley (D. N.). Archaeology from the air in the upper Thames valley. [6 maps + plan. Iron Age and Romano-British sites.] Oxoniensia, 8/9, pp. 64–101 + 8 plates. 1944.

610 Rivet (A. L. F.). Ordnance Survey map of Southern Britain in the Iron Age. 1962. 1:625,000. pp. 5 + 3 tables + 8 maps.

611 Roberts (G.). X-ray microanalyser. Archaeometry, 3, 1960, 36–37 + 1 figure.

612 Rogers (Ernest Henry). The raised beach, submerged forest and kitchen midden of Westward Ho and the submerged stone row of Yelland. [8 figures + plan.] Proc. Devon. Archaeol. Expl. Soc., 3, pp. 109–35 + 8 plates + map + 2 plans. 1946.

613 St. Joseph (John Kenneth Sinclair). Air photographs and archaeology. *Kodak exhibition*. pp. 8. 8°. London, 1948.

614 —— Air reconnaissance in Britain: some recent results. [Map (Cropmarks, Maxey, Northants.). Pp. 277–89, Prehistoric.] Recent archaeol. excavations in Britain, pp. 275–96 + 4 plates. 1956.

615 —— Aerial reconnaissance in Wales. Antiquity, 35, 1961, pp. 263–275.

616 —— Air reconnaissance: recent results. Antiquity, 38, 1964, 217–18.

617 —— Air reconnaissance: recent results, 2. Antiquity, 38, 1964, 290–91.

618 —— Air reconnaissance: recent results, 3. Antiquity, 39, 1965, 60–64.

619 —— Air reconnaissance: recent results, 4. Antiquity, 39, 1965, pp. 143–145.

620 —— Air reconnaissance: recent results, 5. Antiquity, 39, 1965, pp. 223–25.

621 Schwarz (G. Theodor). The "Zirkelsonde": a new technique for resistivity surveying. Archaeometry, 4, 1961, 67–70 + 3 figures.

622 —— Stereoscopic views taken with an ordinary single camera—a technique for archaeologists. Archaeometry, 7, 1964, 36–42 + 5 figures.

623 Scollar (Irwin). Electromagnetic prospecting methods in archaeology. Archaeometry, 5, 1962, 146–153 + 1 figure.

624 —— International Colloquium on air archaeology [report of the meeting held in Paris, August, Sept. 1963]. Antiquity, 37, 1963, pp. 296–297.

625 Serra (Joseph Correa de). On a submarine forest, on the east coast of England. Phil. Trans. Roy. Soc., 89, 1799, 145–156.

626 Shotton (F. W.) *and others* [Chitty (L. F.) *and* Seaby (W. A.)]. A new centre of stone axe dispersal on the Welsh border: First report by the West Midlands group of the Council for British Archaeology, for the petrological investigation of stone axes. Proc. prehist. Soc., 17, 1951, 159–167 + 3 figures + 1 plate.

627 —— New petrological groups based on axes from the West Midland (2nd Report of the West Midland Group of the CBA on the Petrological Investigation of Stone Axes). Proc. prehist. Soc., 25, 1959, 135–143 + 1 figure.

628 Simmons, Harold C. Archaeological photography, 23 line illustrations, 16 photographs. London, 1969.

629 Smith (Frederick). Prehistoric man and the Cambridge gravels. pp. viii, 121 + 38 plates. 8°. Cambridge, 1926.

630 Smith (Reginald Allender) *and* **Dewey** (Henry). Stratification at Swanscombe, [Kent]: report on excavations made on behalf of the British Museum and H.M. Geological Survey. [19 figures + 2 maps. Flints, *etc.*] Archaeologia, 64, pp. 177–204 + plate. 1913.

631 —— Plateau deposits and implements. Proc. PSEA, 2 iii, 1916/17, 392–408 + 1 figure.

632(a) Spence (Joseph E.). Report of the Committee for prehistoric sciences, 1933–1935. Trans. Cumb. & Western Ant. Soc., N.S. 35, pp. 170–81 + plate: 37, pp. 98–103 + plate: 40, pp. 99–117. 1935.

632(b) —— Report of the Committee for prehistoric sciences, for 1936.

632(c) —— Report of the Committee for prehistoric sciences, 1937–1939.

633 Spencer (Harold E. P.). The pleistocene period and work for the amateur geologist. S.E. Naturalist & Antiquary, 59, 1954, 26–31.

634 Stone (John F. S.) *and* **Wallis** (F. S.). Second Report of the Sub-Committee of the South-Western group of Museums and Art Galleries on the petrological indentification of Stone axes. Proc. prehist. Soc., 13, 1947, 47–55.

635 Stone (John F. S.). The petrological identification of stone axes. Arch. News Letter, 3, p. 6. 1950.

636 Stone (John F. S.) *and* **Wallis** (F. S.). Third report of the sub-committee of the South-Western group of museums and art galleries on the petrological identification of stone axes. Proc. prehist. Soc., 17, 1951, 99–158 + 9 figures + 3 plates.

637 Stroh (Frederick). Notes on Pleistocene history. Proc. I. of Wight N.H. Arch. Soc., 4, pp. 17–32 + table. 1946.

638 Thompson, M. W. The Origin of 'scheduling'. Antiquity, 37, 1963, pp. 224–5.

639 Thomson (James Oliver). History of ancient geography. pp. xi, 427 + 2 plates. 8⁰. Cambridge, 1948. [66 figures. Caesar, Pytheas, Ptolemy, *etc.*]

640 —— History of ancient geography. Cambridge, 1948. pp. 427 + 66 figures + 2 plates.

641 Tite (M. S.). Alternative instruments for magnetic surveying: comparative tests at the Iron Age hill-fort at Rainsborough. Archaeometry, 4, 1961, 85–90 + 1 figure.

642 —— *and* **Waine** (J.). Thermoluminescent dating: a re-appraisal. Archaeometry, 5, 1962, 53–79 + 12 figures.

643 Tozer (Henry Fanshawe). A history of ancient geography. Second edition, with additional notes by M. Cary. pp. xxiii, 387 + 10 maps. 8⁰. Cambridge, 1935.

644 Treacher (M. S.) *and others* [W. J. Arkell *and* K. P. Oakley]. On the ancient channel between Caversham and Henley, Oxfordshire, and its contained flint implements [Clactonian to Acheulian]. Proc. prehist. Soc., 14, 1948, 126–154 + 50 figures + 1 plate.

645 Ullyott (Philip). A note on the zoogeographical history of North Western Europe [for dating]. Proc. prehist. Soc. N.S. 2, 1936, 169–177 + 4 figures + 1 plate.

646 Underwood (W.). Recent discoveries in palaeontology and the works of early man. Proc. prehist. Soc. E.A., 1 ii, 1910/12, 135–39.

647 Voce (Eric). Scientific evidence concerning metal-working techniques. A report of the Ancient Mining and Metallurgy Committee. Man., 61, 1961, 68–71 + 2 figures.

648 Walker (George P. W.). The lost Wantsum channel: its importance to Richborough castle. [3 maps. Pp. 96–98 + map, Prehistoric period.] Arch. Cant., 39, pp. 91–111. 1927.

649 Wallace (Portia). Tree ring records from Britain. Bull. Inst. of Arch. London, 3, 1962, 69–77 + 2 figures.

650 Wallis (F. S.). Rocks and the archaeologist. Trans. Bristol & Glos. A.S., 79, 1960, pt. II, 155–58.

651 Warren (Samuel Hazzledine). The dating of surface flint implements and the evidences of the submerged peat surface. Proc. prehist. Soc., E.A., 3 i, 1918/19, 94–104 + 2 figures.

652 —— A Natural "Eolith" factory. J. Geol. Soc. London, 76, 1920, 238–253 + 5 figures + 1 plate.

653 —— Archaeology of the submerged land surface of the Essex coast. Proc. prehist. Soc., N.S. 2, 1936, 178–210 + 14 figures + 6 plates.

654 —— Geological and prehistoric traps [in Essex]. [Figure & map. Flaked flints, eoliths, *etc.*] Essex Nat., 27, pp. 2–19. 1940.

655 Warry (Mrs. C. King). Where was Ictis? [?Portland Isle.] Antiquary, 48, pp. 338–41, 440. 1912.

656 Waterbolk (H. T.). The 1959 Carbon-14 Symposium at Groningen. Antiq., 34 (1960), pp. 14–18.

657 Watson (J. Wreford) *and* **Sissons**, (J. B.), *Editors*. The British Isles: a systematic geography. London, 1964, 464 pp., 51 figures.

658 Webster, Graham *and* **Hobley,** Brian. Aerial reconnaissance over the Warwickshire Avon. [10 plates + 11 figures + 2 pull-out maps.] Arch. J. 121, 1964, 1–22.

659 Wheeler (Robert Eric Mortimer). The administration of archaeology in Wales in 1931. Arch. Camb., 86 ii, 1931, 340–352.

660 Widdows (Bernard). The scheduling and listing of monuments and buildings. D.A.J., 79, 1959, 126– 129.

661 Wooldridge (Sydney William) *and* **Linton** (D. L.). The loam-terrains of south east England and their relation to its early history. [Map. Pp. 473–75. Reply by Sir Cyril Fox.] Antiquity, 7, pp. 297–310. 1933.

662 —— Some aspects of the physiography of the Thames Valley in relation to the Ice Age and early man. Proc. prehist. Soc., 23, 1957, 1–19 + 4 figures.

663 —— *and* **Cornwall** (Ian W.). A contribution to a new datum for the prehistory of the Thames valley. Bull.

Inst. Arch., London, 4, 1962, 223–232.

664 West (R. G.) *and* **McBurney** (C. M. B.). The Quaternary deposits at Hoxne, Suffolk and their archaeology. Proc. prehist. Soc., 20, 1954, 131–154 + 11 figures + 1 plate.

665 Wymer (John). The Lower Palaeolithic succession in the Thames Valley and the date of the ancient channel between Caversham and Henley, Oxon. Proc. prehist. Soc., 27, 1961, 1–27 + 23 figures.

666 Zeuner (Friedrich E.). A comparison of the Pleistocene of East Anglia with that of Germany. Proc. prehist. Soc., 3, 1937, 136–157 + 1 figure.

667 —— Archaeology and geology. S.E. Naturalist & Antiquary, 55, 1951, 5–16.

668 —— Loess and Palaeolithic chronology. Proc. prehist. Soc., 21, 1955, 51–64.

669 —— Soils and shorelines as aids to chronology. Bull. Inst. of Arch., London, 4, 1962, 233–250.

B. FIELD ARCHAEOLOGY

1. REGIONAL SURVEYS: GENERAL

670 Alcock (Leslie). Settlement patterns in Celtic Britain. Antiquity, 36, 1962, pp. 51–54.

671 Allen (F. A.). Lake dwellings, at home and abroad. Trans. Caradoc & Severn Valley F.C., 5, pp. 91–100. 1910.

672 Atkinson (Richard John Copland). Field archaeology. Second edition, revised. pp. x, 238 + 12 plates. 1st. 1946. 2nd. 8°. London, 1953.

673 Bacon (Edward). Digging for history (pp. 320, 58 plates). London, 1960.

674 Barnwell (Edward Lowry). Celtic monuments. Arch. Camb., 3rd S. 7, pp. 46–71. 1861.

675 Bibby (Geoffrey). The Testimony of the Spade. London, 1957, pp. 448, 32 plates, figures 63.

676 Blundell (Frederick Ods). Crannogs. Trans. Hist. Soc. Lancs. & Ches., 75 (1923), pp. 203–07 + 5 plates. 1924.

677 Boult (Joseph). Glimpses of pre-Roman civilization in England. Trans. Hist. Soc. Lancs. & Ches., [26] 3 S.2, pp. 113–44. 1874.

678 Bowen (Emrys George). Prehistoric south Britain. [7 maps.] Darby (H. C.) *Editor*, Historical geography of England, pp. 1–29. 1936.

679 Bradford (John). Ancient landscapes: studies in field archaeology. London, 1957, pp. xvii + 297, 25 figures, 75 plates.

680 Brown (Donald F.), *Editor*. COWA Surveys and bibliographies Series I (1958–9); Series II (1960–1). Cambridge, Mass.

681 Buckland (Anne Walbank). Notes on some Cornish and Irish prehistoric monuments. J. Anthrop. Inst., 9, pp. 146–66. 1879.

682 Buckley (Francis). A Microlithic industry of the Pennine chain, related to the Tardenois of Belgium. pp. 7. 8°. U.P. 1924. [2 figures.]

683 Bu'lock (J. D.). The Bronze Age in the North-West. Trans. Lancs.

& Cheshire Antiq. Soc. 71, 1961, 1–42
+ 5 figures.

684 Cantrill (Thomas Crosbee) *and*
Jones (D. T.). Note on the discovery
of prehistoric hearths. Arch. Camb.,
6th S. 6, pp. 17–34. 1906.

685 —— Prehistoric cooking-places
in Britain. Trans. Caradoc & Severn
Valley F.C. 6, pp. 142–45. 1917.

686 Case (Humphrey). Long Barrows, Chronology and Causewayed
Camps. [Report of Prehistoric Society
Spring Conference, 1962]. Antiquity,
36, 1962, pp. 212–216.

687 Chadwick (N.), **Jackson** (K.).
and others. Edited. Celt and Saxon:
Studies in the early British border.
Cambridge, 1963, pp. 365.

689 Clark (E. V.) *and* **Ford** (E. B.).
An above-ground storage pit of the
La Tène period. Proc. prehist. Soc., 19,
1953, 121–126 + 1 figure + 2 plates.

691 Clark (J. G. D.). Notes on
excavations in England during 1935.
Proc. prehist. Soc., N.S. 1, 1935, 130–
138 + 3 plates.

692 —— Notes on excavations in
England, the Irish Free State, Northern
Ireland, Scotland and Wales, during
1936. Proc. prehist. Soc., N.S. 2, 1936,
211–228.

693 —— The "Eastern" facies of the
Maglemose culture. Proc. prehist. Soc.,
N.S. 2, 1936, 240–41.

694 —— Archaeological distributions. Proc. prehist. Soc., N.S. 2, 1936,
247–248.

695 —— Notes on excavations in
England, the Irish Free State, Northern
Ireland, Scotland and Wales during 1937.
Proc. prehist. Soc., 3, 1937, 437–459 +
2 plates.

696 —— Reindeer hunters' summer
camps in Britain? Proc. prehist. Soc.,
4, 1938, 229 + 1 figure.

697 —— Microlithic industries from
Tufa deposits at Prestatyn, Flintshire
and Blashenwell, Dorset. Proc. prehist.
Soc., 4, 1938, 330–334 + 2 figures.

698 Collingwood (Robin George)
and **Myres** (John Nowell Linton).
Roman Britain and the English settlements. Second edition. *Oxford History
of England*, 1. pp. xxvi, 515. [Pp. 1–15,
Pre-Roman.] 8⁰. Oxford, 1937.

699 Congresses—*First International*

*Congress of Prehistoric and Protohistoric
sciences, London, 1932*. A handbook of
the prehistoric archaeology of Britain.
pp. 75 + plan (Stonehenge). 8⁰.
Oxford, 1932. [22 figures and plans.]

700 Copley (Gordon J.). An archaeology of south-east England. pp. 324
+ 16 plates. 4⁰. London, 1958. [20
figures + 12 maps. Pp. 31–129, Prehistoric: pp. 231–311, Gazeteer.]

701(a) Corcoran (J. X. W. P.). The
Young field archaeologist's guide. London, 1966, 216 pp. + 4 plates + 50
figures.

701(b) Cornwall (*Sir* James Marshall).
The military geography of the Welsh
marches. Geog. Mag., 30, pp. 1–12.
1957.

702 Cotton (M. A.). A matter of
time. Archaeol. News Letter, 7 i, 1961,
7–8.

**703 Council for British Archae-
ology.** A survey and policy of field
research in the archaeology of Great
Britain. 1. Prehistoric and early ages to
the seventh century A.D. pp. 120. [Pp.
13–56, 79–99, Prehistory.] 8⁰. London,
1948.

704 COWA Survey. Current work
in Old World archaeology, 1955–57.
Area 1. British Isles, 1, 1958, *in progress.*
2 plates. 4⁰. Cambridge, Mass., 1958–.

705 Cox (T.) *and* **Hall** (A.). Magna
Britannia et Hibernia, or, a new survey
of Great Britain. 6001. 4⁰. London,
1730–31. [Vol. 1, pp. 1–16, Prehistory.]

706 Crawford (Osbert Guy Stanhope). Archaeology in the field. pp.
280 + 24 plates. [40 figures + 3 plans.]
4⁰. London, 1953.

707 Daniel (Glyn Edmund). Some
megalithic follies. Antiq., 34, 1960,
pp. 282–284.

708 Davis (James W.). Report of
the Committee appointed for the purpose of ascertaining and according the
localities of the British Islands in which
evidence of the existence of prehistoric
inhabitants of the country are found.
Advm. of Sci., 1887, 168–172.

709 —— English Lake Dwellings.
Natural Science 1 (1892) 40–43.

710 Dawkins (*Sir* William Boyd).
Cave hunting, researches on the evidence of caves respecting the early
inhabitants of Europe. pp. xxiv, 455 +

plate. [122 figures + 3 maps + 4 plans. Historic caves in Britain, *etc.*] 8°. London, 1874.

711 —— On the evidence afforded by the caves of Great Britain as to the antiquity of man. J. Anthrop. Inst., 7, pp. 151–85. 1878.

712 —— Notes on Durham, York and Manchester in prehistoric times. Archaeol. J., 66, pp. 171–74. 1909.

713 Feachem (Richard). The North Britons: the prehistory of a Border people. London, 1965, 240 pp. + 12 plates + 24 figures.

714 Fergusson (James). Rude stone monuments in all countries: their age and uses. pp. xix, 559 + plate + map. [233 figures and plans. Pp. 61–174, England: pp. 175–238, Ireland; pp. 239–74, Scotland.]

715 Field (N. H.) *and others*. New Neolithic sites in Dorset and Bedfordshire, with a note on the distribution of Neolithic storage pits in Britain (with C. L. Matthews, I. F. Smith and with a Report on animal bones, by Jane M. Ewbank). Proc. prehist. Soc., 30, 1964, 352–381 + 7 figures.

716 Fowler (Margaret J.). The transition from Late Neolithic to Early Bronze Age in the Peak district of Derbyshire and Staffordshire. [5 figures + 2 maps + 3 plans. Pp. 81–97, Debased-megalithic features in barrows, by J. W. X. P. Corcoran.] J. Derbs. Archaeol. Soc., 75, pp. 66–122 + 15 plates. 1955.

717 Fowler (P. J.) *and* **Ashbee** (Paul), *Editors*. The Field Archaeologist: essays in honour of Leslie V. Grindsell's sixtieth birthday. Many plates, diagrams, maps. 1971.

718 Fox (Lady Aileen Mary). Early settlements on Dartmoor and in North Wales. [LBA]. Arch. Camb., 101 ii, 1951, 167–168 + 1 plate.

719 —— South west England. (Ancient Places and People Series, Vol. 41), London, 1964, pp. 254, plates xcviii, figures 36, maps 15.

720 —— South west England. 8°. London, 1964.

721 Fox (*Sir* Cyril). Life and death in the Bronze Age. An archaeologist's field work. pp. xxvii, 193 + 49 plates + 3 maps. 4°. London, 1959.

723 Godwin (H. *and* M. E.). British Maglemose harpoon sites. [2 figures.] Antiquity, 7, pp. 36–48. 1933.

724 Gore (W. Ormsby). Illustrated regional guide to ancient monuments. *Office of Works*. 3 vol. 8°. London, 1936.

725 Grimes (William Francis). Excavations on Defence Sites 1939–1945: I, Mainly Neolithic-Bronze Age. [pp. 259, 102 text figures, 48 plates]. London, H.M.S.O. 1960.

726 Hallam (S. J.). Villages in Roman Britain: some evidence. [1 plate, 2 tables, 2 maps]. Ant. J. 44, 1964, 19–32.

727 Hanbury (J. A. S.). Two days' excursion to Silchester, Avebury & Silbury hill, May 30th and 31st, 1906. [5 figures.] B'ham. Arch. Soc., Trans., 32 (1906), pp. 7–23. 1907.

728 Hawkes (Jessie Jacquetta). A guide to the Prehistoric and Roman monuments in England and Wales. pp. xxiii, 312 + 12 plates + 5 maps. 8°. London, 1951.

729 Hodgson (Katherine S.). Some notes on prehistoric remains of the Border district. [2 plans (cairns).] Trans. Cumb. & Westm. Ant. Soc., N.S. 43, pp. 167–74 + plate. 1943.

730 Hunter Arch. Soc. Research Committee. Field Research. 1 Circle survey; 2 Moorland survey. Trans. Hunter archaeol. Soc., 8 i, 1958, 24.

731 Jackson (John Wilfrid). Cave hunting. Trans. Rochdale Lib. & Sci. Soc., 19, pp. 72–81. 1937.

732 Jessup (Ronald). Curiosities of British archaeology. London, 1961, pp. xii + 215.

733 Jones (Glanville). Settlement patterns in Celtic Britain. Antiquity, 36, 1962, pp. 54–55.

734 —— Settlement patterns in Anglo-Saxon England [From pre-history to —]. Antiquity, 35, 1961, pp. 221.

735 Keller (Ferdinand). The lake dwellings of Switzerland and other parts of Europe. Second edition, . . . translated . . . by John Edward Lee. 2 vol. 8°. London, 1878.

736 Kendall (Henry George Ommanney). Windmill Hill, Avebury, and Grime's Graves. Proc. PSEA 2 ii, 1915/16, 230–239 + 5 figures.

737 —— More about Windmill Hill,

Avebury, and Grime's Graves. Proc. PSEA, 2 iv, 1917/18, 563–575 + 5 figures.

738 —— Windmill Hill, Avebury, and Grime's Graves cores and choppers. PSEA 3 i, 1918/19,104–108 + 2 figures.

739 —— Windmill Hill, Avebury, and Grime's Graves:: cores and choppers PSEA, 3 ii, 1919/20,192–199 + 3 figures.

740 —— On Avebury and Grime's Graves. Proc. Soc. Antiq., 2 S. 31, pp. 78–108. 1919.

741 Kendrick (*Sir* Thomas Downing) *and* **Hawkes** (Charles Francis Christopher). Archaeology in England and Wales, 1914–31. pp. xix, 371 + 30 plates. London, 1932.

742 Leask (H. G.). Notes on excavations in Eire, England, Northern Ireland, Scotland and Wales, during 1938. Proc. prehist. Soc., 4, 1938, 314–325.

743 Lee (Philip G.). Notable Celtic monuments. [Pp. 3–13 + 2 figures, Prehistoric (Ireland).] J. Antiq. Assoc. Brit. Isles, 1, pp. 2–24. 1930.

744 Leeds (Edward Thurlow). Early settlements from the Neolithic to the Saxon period. Nat. Hist. of the Oxford district, editor, J. J. Walker, pp. 27–29. 1926.

745 Lewis (A. L.). Remarks on some archaic structures in Somersetshire and Dorsetshire. [Stanton Drew, Welton-tumulus, Gorwell ring, *etc.*] J. Anthrop. Inst., 11, pp. 117–22. 1881.

746(a) Lewis (J. M.) *and others*. [D. W. Crossley *and* L. A. Butler]. Excavations and discoveries [standing-stones and raths]. Bull. Bd. Celtic Studies, 21 iii, 196–, 250–275 + 6 figures + 4 plates.

746(b) Lhuyd (Edward) (see also under **Lhwyd**). Archaeologia Britannica, giving some account additional to what has hitherto been published, of the languages, histories and customs of the original inhabitants of Great Britain: from collections and observations in travels through Wales, Cornwall, Bois-Bretagne, Ireland and Scotland, Vol. 1: Glossography. fol. Oxford, 1707 [no more published].

746(c) Lhwyd (Edward) (see also under **Lhuyd**). Extract from several letters to Dr Richard Richardson (M.D.) of North Bierly in Yorkshire, containing observations in natural history and antiquities, made in his travels thro' Wales and Scotland. Phil. Trans. Roy. Soc., 28, 1713, 97–101.

747 Lukis (William Collings). Report on the prehistoric monuments of Wilts., Somerset, and South Wales. Proc. Soc. Antiq., 2 S.9, pp. 344–55. 1883.

748 —— Megalithic monuments. Archaeol. Rev., 1, pp. 352–54. 1888.

749 McBurney (C. B. M.). Report on the first season's fieldwork on British Upper Palaeolithic cave deposits. Proc. prehist. Soc., 25, 1959, 260–269 + 1 figure + 7 plates.

751 Martel (E. A.). Irelande et Cavernes Anglaises. Paris lib. Delagrave, 1897, 121 plates, 18 plans, 3 figures.

752 Martin (Edward A.). Dewponds. Antiquity, 4, pp. 347–51 + 2 plates. 1930.

753 Megan (J. V. S.). The Neolithic in the South-West of England: a reply and some further comments. Cornish archaeol., No. 2, 1963, 4–18 + 7 figures.

754 Meldola (Raphael). Presidential address. Trans. Essex Fld. Club 3, 1883, 59–93.

755 —— Local science societies and the minor prehistoric remains of Britain. Advm. of Sci., 1883, 571. Also Nature, Nov. 1, 1883, p. 19.

756 —— Local scientific societies, and the minor pre-historic remains of Britain. Trans. Essex Fld. Club 4, 1885, 116–122.

757 Merewether (John). Diary of the examination of barrows and other earthworks in the neighbourhood of Silbury hill and Avebury, Wilts., in July and August, 1849. Proc. Archaeol. Inst., [5] Salisbury, 1849, pp. 82–112 + 29 plates + 6 plans. 1851.

758 Midgley (J. H.). The National Trust for places of historic interest or natural beauty. J. Torquay nat. Hist. Soc., 4, 1923, 75–78 + 2 plates.

759 Ministry of Works. Ancient monuments in England and Wales. A list . . . corrected to 31st December, 1954. pp. 99. [Pp. 6–11, Prehistoric (introduction).] 8°. London, 1955.

760 Morris (Lewis). Celtic remains. [Edited by D. S. Evans.] *Cambrian Archaeological Association*. pp. 7, lxxxv, 442. 8°. London, 1878.

761 Munro (Robert). Dwellings or crannogs. With a supplementary chapter on remains of lake-dwellings in England. pp. xx, 326. 8⁰. Edinburgh, 1882.

762 —— The Archaeological importance of ancient British lake-dwellings and their relation to analogous remains in Europe. Advm. of Sci., 1885, 1221.

763 —— The archaeological importance of ancient British lake-dwellings and their relation to analogous remains in Europe. J. Anthrop. Inst., 15, pp. 453–70. 1886.

764 —— The lake-dwellings of Europe. *Rhind Lectures for 1888.* pp. xl, 600. 8⁰. London, 1890. [199 figures. Pp. 349–494, Great Britain & Ireland.]

765 Nennius. Ancient British cities. [List from Nennius.] N. & Q., 9 S. 8, pp. 359–60. 1901.

766 O'Neil (Bryan Hugh St. John). War and archaeology in Britain. [With list of sites, prehistoric, *etc.*, excavated.] Antiq. J., 28, pp. 20–44. 1948.

767 Ordnance Survey. Ancient Britain. North sheet. (South sheet.) pp. 36 + map. (pp. 36 + map). 8⁰. Chessington, 1951.

768 Ó'Ríordáin (Seán Pádraig). Archaeology: the prehistoric period. A view of Ireland (British Assoc., Dublin), pp. 149–63 + plate. 1957.

769 Piggott (Stuart). Late Bronze Age enclosures in Sussex and Wessex. Proc. prehist. Soc., 16, 1950, 193–194 + 1 figure.

770 Powell (T. G. E.). Notes on the Bronze Age in the East Midlands. Proc. prehist. Soc., 16, 1950, 65–80 + 8 figures.

771 Radford (C. A. Ralegh). The Neolithic in the Southwest of England. Cornish archaeology No. 1, 1962, 4–17 + 5 figures + 2 plates.

772 Raistrick (Arthur). Mesolithic sites of the North East coast of England. Proc. PSEA, 7 ii, 1932–34, 188–198 + 5 figures.

773 —— The distribution of Mesolithic sites in the north of England. Yorks. Archaeol. J., 31, pp. 141–87, 1934.

774 Rankine (W. F.). Mesolithic research in southern England. Arch. News Letter, 5, pp. 37–40. 1954.

775 —— The Mesolithic of Southern England. Surrey archaeol. Soc. Res. Paps. 4, 1956, 1–63 + 12 figures.

776 Richmond (I. A.). Roman and native in North Britain. (pp. x and 16 + 18 plates + 8 maps + 6 text figures). London, 1958.

777 Rivet (A. L. F.). The Iron Age in Northern Britain. Antiquity, 36, 1962, pp. 24–31.

778 —— The Iron Age in Northern Britain. Edinburgh, 1966, pp. viii + 155, 4 plates, in-text-figures, and maps.

779 Royal Commission on Historical Monuments (England). A matter of time: an archaeological survey of the river gravels of England. [pp. 64, 10 text figures, 13 plates]. London, H.M.S.O., 1960.

780 —— Monuments threatened or destroyed: a select list 1956–1962. London 1963, pp. 89, plates 68, figures 46.

781 "S" (E. P.). On crannogs, and remains discovered in them. [2 figures.] Archaeol. J., 3, pp. 44–49. 1846.

782 Savory (H. N.) *and* **Jones** (G. D. B.). Excavations and discoveries. Bull. Board Celtic Studies, 19 iii, 1961, 250–55 + 3 figures.

783(a) Simpson (Grace). Britons and the Roman army. A study of Wales and the Southern Pennines in the 1st–3rd centuries. London, 1964, 191 pp., 3 plates, 24 figures.

783(b) Smith (Charles Roach). Collectanea Antiqua; etchings and notices of ancient remains, illustrative of the habits, customs, and history of past ages, 6 vol. London, 1848–68. 8⁰.

784 Smith (Worthington George). Man the primeval savage, his haunts and relics from the hill-tops of Bedfordshire to Blackwall. pp. xvi, 349. [242 figures.] 8⁰. London, 1894.

785 Steers (J. A.). Field studies in the British Isles. London, 1964. 552 pp. + 85 figures.

786 Stewart (James). Archaeological guide and glossary. Kendal, 1958, pp. 237 + 28 plates + many figures.

787 —— An archaeological guide and glossary. Second edition, revised. [pp. 237. [28 figures. Pp. 1–84, pre-Roman (8 figures).] 8⁰. London, 1960. [1st edition, 1958].

788 Stukeley (William). Itinerarium curiosum; or, an account of the antiquities and remarkable curiosities in nature or art observed in travels thro' Great Britain. Illustrated with copper plates. 1st edition. fol. London, 1724. 2nd edition 2 pts., 1776. [*See index* to Centuria I.]

789 Thomas (Nicholas Wolfstan de L'Eglise). A Guide to prehistoric England, (pp. 268 incl. 69 figures and photographs). London, Batsford, 1960.

790 Vale (Edmund). Ancient England. A review of monuments, *etc.* pp. 150 + plates. [147 figures.] 8°. London, 1941.

791 Wainwright (G. J.). Three microlithic industries from South-west England and their affinities. Proc. prehist. Soc., 26, 1960, 193–201 + 5 figures + 1 table.

792 Waring (J. B.). Stone monuments, tumuli and ornament of remote ages, *etc.* pp. xi, 96 + 108 plates. fol. London, 1870.

793 Warre (F.). On British cattle stations. Proc. Somerset Arch. Soc., 9 (1859), pp. 142–48. 1860.

794 Webster (Graham). Practical archaeology. London, 1963. 176 pp. + 8 plates + 20 figures.

795 Whatmore (A. W.). Insulae Britannicae. The British Isles, their geography, history and antiquities down to the close of the Roman period. 8°. 1913.

796 Wheeler (*Sir* Robert Eric Mortimer). British field archaeology, past and future. S.E. Naturalist, 37, pp. 1–11. 1932.

798 Williams (John). Druidic stones. Arch. Camb., N.S.1, pp. 1–9, 100–07. 1850.

799 Windle (*Sir* Bertram Coghill Alan). Remains of the prehistoric age in England. Second edition. *Antiquary's Books.* 8°. London, 1904.

800 Wood (Eric S.). Collins field guide to archaeology in Britain. London, 1963, pp. 384, 32 plates, 19 maps, 5 tables, 2 indexes.

801 Wood (P. D.). Strip lynchets reconsidered. Geog. Jl. 127, 1961, 449–459 + 7 figures.

802 Wright (William). The prehistoric and early historic inhabitants of England. Hunterian Lectures, 6 parts. 8°. London, 1907/08. Reprinted from Middlesex Hospital J., 1907/08.

803 Wymer (John). Archaeology of the Lower Palaeolithic in Britain, colour and monochrome plates, figures, maps, med 4°. 1967.

2. REGIONAL SURVEYS BY ZONE

(a) Zone 1 [CBA Groups 7, 9, 10, 11A, 11B, 14]

804 Abbott (W. J. Lewis). The older prehistoric races of Sussex. Trans. Eastbourne N.H. Soc., N.S. 4 iii, pp. 16–23. 1910.

805(a) Abell (Henry Francis). History of Kent. pp. vii, 328. [Pp. 1–151, Prehistoric Kent.] 8°. Ashford, 1898.

805(b) Allen (Edward Heron). Selsey bill: historic and prehistoric. pp. xvi, 404 + 57 plates + 3 maps. [Pp. 69–74 + 7 plates: Prehistoric.] 4°. London, 1911.

806 Allen (Thomas). History of the counties of Surrey and Sussex. 2 vols. 8°. London, 1829.

807 —— The History of the County of Lincoln, from the earliest period to the present time. London. 4°. 2 vols. 1833/34, illustrations.

808 [Anon.] Prehistoric Oxford. Archaeol. Oxford., pp. 1–6 + plate + plan. 1892.

809 [Anon.] Ancient monuments in Sussex. Sussex Arch. Collns., 85, pp. 138–40. 1946.

810 [Anon.] Archaeological sites on the South Downs. Sussex N. & Q., 14, pp. 69–70. 1954.

811 Apling (Harry). Bronze Age settlements in Norfolk. Proc. PSEA, 6 iv, 1931, 365–370 + 3 figures.

812 Armstrong (J. R.). A history of Sussex. pp. 72. 8°. London, 1961.

813 Arundell (Edward Dudbridge). Excavations at Seaford head. Sussex N. & Q., 13, pp. 193–95. 1952.

814 Astbury, A. K. The Blackfens. [pp. 217, 55 plates, 5 text figures, one folding map.] Cambridge, The Golden Head Press, 1958.

815 Astley (Hugh John Dukinfield). Early man in Norfolk. J. Brit. Archaeol. Ass., N.S. 23, pp. 89–114. 1917.

816 Baker (Frederick Thomas). Ancient monuments scheduled in Lincolnshire. Lincs. Historian, 2 iii, pp. 34–36: 2 iv, pp. 1–3. 1956/57.

817 Barker (H. L.). List of ancient monuments in Nottinghamshire. Trans. Thoroton Soc., 70, 1966, 5–8.

818 Barritt (E. E.) *and* **Kettle** (B. M.). Notes on the Romano-British archaeology of Chelmsford and District. Trans. Essex Arch. Soc., 3 Ser. 1, 1962, pt. 2, 165–66.

819 Beamont (George F.) *and* **Gould** (Isaac Chalkley). Early men [in Essex]. [2 figures.] V.C.H., Essex, 1, pp. 261–74 + 8 plates + map. 1903.

820 Beesley (Alfred). The history of Banbury. 2 vol. 8⁰. London, 1848.

821 Besant (*Sir* Walter). Early London. pp. x, 370 + 8 plates. 4⁰. London, 1908.

822 Blomefield (Francis). The History of the ancient city and burgh of Thetford. Fersfield. 4⁰. 1739. pp. 136 + 7 plates.

823 Brent (John). Canterbury in the olden time. Second edition, enlarged. pp. viii, 308 + 31 plates. 8⁰. Canterbury, 1879.

824 Brown (John Allen). The Thames-valley surface-deposits of the Ealing District and their associated palaeolithic floors. J. Geol. Soc., London, 42, 1886, 192–200 + 1 figure.

825 —— Palaeolithic man in Middlesex. pp. 237 + 8 plates. 8⁰. London, 1887.

826 Bunbury (*Sir* Henry) *bart.* Roman and British antiquities discovered at Mildenhall, in Suffolk. Archaeologia, 25, pp. 609–12. 1834.

827 Burchell (James Percy Tufnell) *and* **Moir** (James Reid). The implementiferous deposits of the lower Thames valley and of East Anglia. Man, 33, pp. 31–32. [Figure.] 1933.

828 —— Fresh facts relating to the Boyn hill terrace of the lower Thames valley. [4 figures (flints).] Antiq. J., 14, pp. 163–66 + plate. 1934.

829 —— The Upchurch marshes, Kent. [i. Neolithic occupation "floor", Lower Halstow: ii. Romano-British briquetage site, Lower Halstow: iii. Mesolithic "floor", Lower Halstow: iv. Romano-British briquetage site, Stayhills Saltings.] Arch. News Letter, 6, pp. 89–91. 1957.

830 —— *and* **Frere** (Sheppard Sunderland). The occupation of Sandown park, Esher, during the Stone Age, the Early Iron Age, and the Anglo-Saxon period. (The Iron Age finds from the Warren, Esher, by S. Frere). [12 figures + 2 maps + 3 plans.] Antiq. J., 27, pp. 24–46. 1947.

831 Bury (Henry). The Farnham terraces and their sequence. Proc. prehist. Soc., 1, 1935, 60–69 + 8 figures.

832 Canterbury Excavation Committee. Pre-Roman, Roman and mediaeval Canterbury as so far revealed by the work of the . . . Committee. Third edition. pp. 15. 8⁰. Canterbury, 1954.

833 Carey (Alfred Edward). Prehistoric man on the highlands of east Surrey. pp. 39. 8⁰. London, [1908].

834 Carpenter (L. W.). Some Mesolithic sites in north-east Surrey. [Figure.] Archaeol. News Letter, 6, pp. 155–58. 1958.

835 Case (Humphrey). Archaeological notes: Eynsham, Oxon. [collared urns, two ring-ditches, frag. of stone axe]. Oxonensia 23, 1958, 132 + 1 figure.

836 —— Archaeological notes. Cassington, Oxon. [wrist guard + shale button]. Eynsham, Oxon. [ring ditch with 8 beakers]. Frilford, Berks. [polished flint axe]. Fyfield, Berks. [polished axe]. Harwell, Berks. [barrow]. Hatford, Berks. [EIA sherds]. Oxonensia 24, 1959, 98–102.

837 —— *and* **Sturdy** (David). Archaeological notes. Oxonensia 25, 1960, 131–36.

838 —— Notes on the finds and on ring-ditches in the Oxford Region. [Neolithic, Beaker and ETA]. Oxoniensia 28, 1963, 19–52.

839 Chaplin (Raymond E.) *and* **Coy** (Jennie P.). Researches and discoveries in Kent: Cliffe, 1961. Arch. Camb. 76, 1961, pp. 205–6.

840 Clark (John Grahame Douglas) *and* **Lethbridge** (Thomas Charles). The archaeology of Cambridgeshire. [Pp.

80–90 + 2 maps, Prehistory.] Brit. Ass. Rpt., 1938, pp. 80–95. 1938.

841 Clark (John Grahame Douglas). Early man [in Cambridgeshire]. [28 figures.] V.C.H., Cambs., 1, pp. 247–303 + 8 plates + map. 1938.

842 —— A Microlithic industry from the Cambridgeshire Fenland and other industries of Sauveberrian affinities from Britain. Proc. prehist. Soc., 21, 1955, 3–20 + 7 figures + 1 plate.

843 —— *and* **Godwin**, H. The Neolithic in the Cambridgeshire Fens. Antiquity, 36, 1962, pp. 10–23.

844 Clarke (Roy Rainbird). An Iron Age hut at Postwick and an earthwork on East Wretham heath, Norfolk. Norfolk Arch., 26, pp. 271–80 + 2 plates + 2 plans. 1938.

845 —— The Iron Age in Norfolk and Suffolk. (—2. A revised estimate of the Stutton hut-urn). [10 figures + 2 maps + plan.] Archaeol. J., 96 (1939), pp. 1–113 + 20 plates + 2 maps: pp. 223–25. 1940.

846 —— Prehistoric and Roman Suffolk. Archaeol. J., 108 (1957), pp. 129–31. 1952.

847 —— Notes on recent archaeological discoveries in Norfolk (1943–8). [Snettisham hoard (jewellery and coins of Iron Age, 6 plates), *etc.*] Norfolk Arch., 30, pp. 156–59 + 6 plates. 1952.

848 —— Archaeological discoveries in Norfolk, 1949–54. [Pp. 395–400, Prehistoric.] Norfolk Arch., 31, pp. 395–416. 1957.

849 —— East Anglia (Ancient Peoples and Places series) [58 photographs, 28 line drawings, 13 maps]. London, Thames & Hudson, 1960.

850 Clarke (William George). Two North-West Suffolk floors [Neolithic and EIA]. PSEA 2 i,1914/15, 39–41.

851 —— *and* **Halls** (H. H.). Cone cultures in the Wensnin Valley [Upper Palaeolithic]. Proc. PSEA, 2 ii, 1915/16, 194–209 + 2 plates + 5 figures.

852 —— Norfolk in prehistoric times. Antiquary, 44, pp. 327–32. 1908.

853 Clinch (George). Palaeolithology [at Church Field] near the source of the Ravensbourne [Kent]. Antiquary, 9, pp. 212–15. 1884.

854 —— Some account of ancient excavations in Well wood and chalk-pit field, West Wickham, Kent, pp. 12 + plate. 8°. West Wickham, 1884.

855 —— Prehistoric man in the neighbourhood of the Kent and Surrey border: Neolithic Age. [2 figures + 2 plans (Hut circle, Hayes common).] J. Anthrop. Inst., 29, pp. 124–41 + 2 plates. 1899.

856 —— Early man [in Norfolk]. [11 figures.] V.C.H., Norfolk, 1, pp. 253–78 + 2 plates + map. 1901.

857 —— Early man [in Surrey]. [12 figures. Pp. 249–50, Roads.] V.C.H. Surrey, 1, pp. 227–54 + 4 plates + map. 1902.

858 —— Early man [in Buckinghamshire]. [8 figures.] V.C.H., Bucks., 1, pp. 177–93 + map + 2 plans. 1905.

859 —— Early man [in Sussex]. [4 figures + plan (Cissbury flint mines).] V.C.H., Sussex, 1, pp. 309–31 + 5 plates + map + plans. 1905.

860 —— Early man [in Kent]. V.C.H., Kent, 1, pp. 307–38 + 11 plates + map. 1908.

861 Clutterbuck (Robert). The history and antiquities of the county of Hertford. 3 vol. fol. London, 1813–27.

862 Coles (Rupert). The past history of the forest of Essex. [6 maps. Pp. 115–20 + map, Prehistory.] Essex Nat., 24, pp. 115–33. 1933.

863 Conybeare (John William Edward). A history of Cambridgeshire. *Popular County Histories*. pp. xxviii, 307. 8°. London, 1897. [Pp. 1–15, pre-Roman period.]

864 Covernton (J. G.). Prehistoric sites at Finchingfield. [Map.] Trans. Essex Archaeol. Soc., N.S. 19, pp. 230–41 + 4 plates (Stone implements). 1930.

865 Cox (John Charles). Essex. *The Little guides*. 4th edition. pp. xiii, 312 + 32 plates + map. [Pp. 53–56, Prehistoric antiquities.] Sm. 8°. London, 1926.

866 Crawford (O. G. S.). Field archaeology of the Royston district. Proc. prehist. Soc., N.S. 2, 1936, 97–105 + 9 plates.

867 Curwen (Eliot) *and* (Eliot Cecil). Notes on the archaeology of Burpham and the neighbouring downs. Sussex Arch. Collns., 63, pp. 1–53 + map. 1922.

868 —— Sussex lynchets and their

associated field-ways. Sussex Arch. Collns., 64, pp. 1–65 + 2 plans. 1923.

869 Curwen (Eliot). Bibliographical index to archaeological matter relating to Sussex, appearing elsewhere than in the publications of the Sussex Archaeological Society. [Pp. 495–502, Prehistoric.] Sussex Arch. Collns., General index to 51–75, pp. 493–522. 1936.

870 —— Bibliographical index to archaeological matter relating to Sussex, appearing elsewhere than in the publications of the Sussex Archaeological Society. [pre-Roman.] Sussex Arch. Collns., General index to 51–75, pp. 493–522. 1936.

871 Curwen (Eliot Cecil). Prehistoric Sussex. pp. xiv, 172 + 32 plates. 8º. London, 1929. [8 figures + 2 maps + 2 plans. Pp. 97–129 Roman. Prehistoric roads.]

872 —— The Iron Age in Sussex. Sussex Arch. Collns., 80, 214–16 + map (habitation sites on South Downs). 1939.

873 —— The archaeology of Sussex. *County Archaeologies.* Second edition, revised. pp. xx, 330 + 32 plates. 8º. London, 1954. [94 figures and plans. Pp. 1–282, Prehistory.]

874 —— The Prehistory of Sussex. Arch. J., 116, 1959, 226–27.

875 Dallaway (James). The history of the western division of the county of Sussex. 2 vol. 4º. London, 1815/30. [Vol. 1, pp. 8–24, Roman period.)

876 Dawkins (*Sir* William Boyd). On the traces of the early Britons in the neighbourhood of Oxford. Proc. Oxford. Archit. & Hist. Soc., 1, pp. 108–16. 1862.

877 Dewey (Henry). Surface changes since the Palaeolithic period in Kent and Surrey. Proc. PSEA, 2 i, 1914/15, 107–116 + 2 plates + 1 figure.

878 —— Palaeolithic Thames deposits. Proc. PSEA, 6 iii, 1930, 147–155 + 1 plate.

879 —— The Palaeolithic deposits of the Lower Thames valley. Q.J. Geol. Soc., 88, 1932, 35–56 + 7 figures.

880 Dunkin (E. Hadlow Wise). On the megalithic remains in mid-Kent. Reliquary, 12, pp. 67–80 + plan. 1871.

881 Dutt (William Alfred). Notes on some East Suffolk Neoliths. Proc.

Suffolk Inst. Arch., 11, pp. 326–34 + plate. 1903.

882 —— Norfolk. Revised by E. T. Long. *Little guides.* pp. xii, 188 + 47 plates + maps. Sm. 8º. London, 1949.

883 Dyer (James F.) *and* **Hales** (Anthony J.). Pitstone Hill—a study in field archaeology [3 plates + 5 figures]. Record of Bucks., 17(1), 1961, 49–56.

884 Dyer (James) *and others.* The Story of Luton (by J. Dyer, Frank Stygall and John Dory). Luton, 1964, pp. 224 + plates xlviii and line drawings.

885 Evans (*Sir* John). An archaeological survey of Hertfordshire. [By place, with references.] Archaeologia, 53, pp. 245–62 + map. 1892.

886 —— The Stone Age in Hertfordshire. Trans. Herts. N.H.S. & F.C. 8, 1894/96, 169–187, 7 figures + 6 plates.

887 —— The prehistoric period [in Hertfordshire]. [7 figures.] V.C.H., Herts., 1, pp. 223–50 + 2 plates (coins, verulam) + map. 1902.

889 Falkner (J. Meade). A history of Oxfordshire. *Popular County Historics.* pp. 327. 8º. London, 1899.

890 Fell (Clare Isobel). Prehistoric Northamptonshire. Archaeol. J., 110 (1953), pp. 177–78. 1954.

891 Fox (*Sir* Cyril). The archaeology of the Cambridge region. pp. xxv, 360 + 37 plates + 5 maps. 8º. Cambridge, 1923.

892 —— *and* **Burkitt** (Miles Crawford). Early man [in Huntingdonshire]. [6 figures + 2 maps.] V.C.H., Hunts., 1, pp. 193–218 + 3 plates + map. 1926.

893 Fox (Cyril). The Distribution of man in East Anglia, *c.* 2300 B.C.–50 A.D. Proc. PSEA, 7 ii, 1932/34, 149–164 + 10 figures.

894 —— Reflections on "The archaeology of the Cambridge region". Camb. Hist. J., 9, pp. 1–21. 1947.

895 Fox (Nancy Piercy). Earthworks and hut circles on Hayes common and unpublished Bronze Age flint implements from Millfield, Keston. Arch. Cant., 66 (1953), pp. 162–63. 1954.

896 Frere (Sheppard Sunderland). A survey of archaeology near Lancing. [15 figures + map + plan. Pp. 142–58, Palaeolithic-Iron Age.] Sussex Arch. Collns., 81, pp. 140–72. 1940.

897 Froom (F. R.). The Mesolithic

around Hungerford, Part I. Trans. Newbury Dist. Fld. Club, XI ii, 1963, 62–69 + I figure.

898 —— An Investigation into the Mesolithic around Hungerford, Part II: The Wawcott District. Trans. Newbury Dist. Fld. Club, XI ii, 1963, 70–73.

899 —— The Mesolithic around Hungerford, Part III: Excavations at Wawcott IV. Trans. Newbury Dist. Fld. Club, XI ii, 1963, 74–87 + 4 figures.

900 —— The Mesolithic around Hungerford, Parts IV–V. Trans. Newbury Dist. Fld. Club, XI iii, 1965, 45–51 + 1 figure.

901 Frost (Marian). The early history of Worthing . . . from prehistoric times to a century ago. pp. vii, 99. 8º. Hove, 1929.

902 Furley (Robert). A history of the weald of Kent, with an outline of the early history of the county. 2 vol. [in 3]. 8º. Ashford, 1871–74.

903 George (T. J.). Early man [in Northamptonshire]. V.C.H., Northants., 1, pp. 135–56 + 5 plates + map. 1902.

904 Gordon (E. O.). Prehistoric London: its mounds and circles. 3rd edition, with appendix by J. Griffith. pp. 234. 8º. London, 1932.

905 Granger (Frank). Early man [in Nottinghamshire]. V.C.H., Notts., 1, pp. 183–91 + plate + map. 1906.

906 Grinsell (Leslie Valentine). The Lower and Middle Palaeolithic periods in Sussex. [Figure + map.] Sussex Arch. Collns., 70, pp. 172–82. 1929.

907 —— Sussex in the Bronze Age. [Figure.] Sussex County Mag., 4, pp. 922–26. 1930.

908 —— Sussex in the Bronze Age. [4 figures + 3 maps. *See also* Sussex N. & Q., 4, pp. 85–86, 1932, Addenda and corrigenda: 10, pp. 186–87, 1945.] Sussex Arch. Collns., 72, pp. 30–68. 1931.

909 —— Notes on the White Horse hill region. Berks. Archaeol. J., 43, pp. 135–37. 1939.

910 —— White Horse hill and surrounding country. pp. 66 + map. [7 figures.] 8º. London, 1939.

911 Hancox (Edward R. H.). Neolithic Suffolk. Proc. Suffolk inst. Arch., 11, pp. 200–64 + 2 plates: pp. 335–36 + 2 plates. 1903.

912 Hasted (Edward). The history and topographical survey of the county of Kent. 12 vol. 8º. Canterbury, 1797/1801. [Vol. 1, pp. 1–12, Prehistory.]

913 Hawkes (Charles Francis Christopher). Prehistoric Lincolnshire. [4 figures.] Archaeol. J., 103 (1946), pp. 4–51 + 2 plates. 1947.

914 Hawley (C. D.), *Editor*. List of antiquities in the administrative county of Surrey. 4th edition. Kingston-upon-Thames, 1951, xvi + 211 pp.

915 Haydon (W. T.). A Neolithic find near Dover. S.E. Naturalist, 1, pp. 33–36. 1890.

917 Head (John Frederick). Early man in south Buckinghamshire. An introduction to the archaeology of the region. pp. xix, 175 + 8 maps. 8º. Bristol, 1955. [36 figures and plates. i. Setting: ii. Soils and settlements: iii. Communications].

918 Hewitt (H. Dixon). A Neolithic site near Thetford. Proc. prehist. Soc., E.A. 2 i, 1914/15, 42–45 + 1 plate.

919 Hindi (W.). On the approximate dates of Weyland Smith's cave and the White Horse of Berkshire. [Bronze or Iron Age, *c.* 1500 B.C.–700 A.D.]. Berks., Bucks. & Oxon. Archaeol. J., 25, pp. 63–70. 1919.

920 Hooper (Wilfrid). The pigmy flint industries of Surrey. [4 figures.] Surrey Archaeol. Collns., 41, pp. 50–78. 1933.

921 —— Reigate: its story through the ages. *Surrey Archaeological Society*. pp. 217 + 11 plates + 2 plans. 8º. Guildford, 1945. [Pp. 13–19 + 2 plates, prehistoric Reigate.]

922 Hore (S. Coode). Navestock in olden days: stray notes, prehistoric, Saxon, and Norman. Essex Natr., 8, pp. 223–44. 1894.

923 Horsfield (Thomas Walker). The history and antiquities of Lewes and its vicinity. 2 vol. 4º. Lewes, 1824–27.

924 —— The history . . . of Sussex. 2 vols. 4º. Lewes, 1835.

925 Hughes (Thomas McKenny). The archaeology and geography of the Fenland. J. Brit. Archaeol. Ass., N.S. 5, pp. 277–99. 1899.

926 Hull (Mark Reginald). Iron Age Essex. Colchester Archaeol. Group,

Quart. Bull., 1, p. 46 + map: 2, p. 2. 1958/59.

927 Hunt (Alfred). Prehistoric Lincolnshire. Sympson (E. M.): Memorials of old Lincolnshire, pp. 1–23. 1911.

928 —— Pre-historic man in Lincolnshire. Trans. Lincs. Nat. Union, 1958, pp. 289–303. 1909.

929 —— The pygmy flint age in Lincolnshire. *Lincoln Museum Publications*, 2. pp. 8 + 1 plate. 8°. Lincoln, 1908.

930 Huntingford (George Wynn Brereton). Wayland's smithy and the White Horse. Berks., Bucks. & Oxon. Archaeol. J., 31, pp. 19–24. 1927.

931 Hurd (Howard). Late-Celtic discoveries at Broadstairs. Arch. Cant., 30, pp. 309–12 + 2 plates + plan. 1914.

932 Innocent (R. W.). Evidence of prehistoric occupation in South-West Hertfordshire. Trans. Herts. N.H.S. & F.C. 22, 1943/47, 110.

933 Ireland (William Henry). England's topographer, or a new and complete history of the county of Kent. 4 vols. 8°. London, 1828. [Vol. 1, pp. 1–12, Prehistory.]

934 Jessup (Frank W.). A history of Kent. pp. 191. 8°. London, 1958. [Pp. 1–18, Prehistory.]

935 Jessup (Ronald Frederick). The archaeology of Kent. *County archaeologies*. pp. xiv, 272 + 13 plates + map. 8°. London, 1930. [27 figures + 4 maps + 4 plans. Pp. 1–163, Prehistory.]

936 —— Ancient monuments in Kent. [Alphabetical by place.] Arch. Cant., 61 (1948), pp. 122–25. 1949.

937 Johnson (J. P.). The Palaeolithic period in the Thames basin. [7 figures.] Essex Nat., 13, pp. 97–112 + map. 1913.

938 Johnston (Philip Mainwaring). A schedule of antiquities in the county of Surrey. *Surrey Archaeological Society*. pp. viii, 80 + 33 plates. [37 figures.] 8°. Guildford, 1913.

939 Kelly (David B.). Researches and discoveries in Kent: Bearshed. [R.B. pottery]. Arch. Cant., 76, 1961, pp. 191–2.

940 —— Researches and discoveries in Kent: Langley [Middle-Acheulean Land-axe]. Arch. Cantiane, 77, 1962, 205.

941 —— Researches and discoveries in Kent: Borough Green. [Belgic gold staker and Late Middle Acheulean land-axe]. Arch. Cantiana, 79, 1964, 218.

942 Kendall (H. G. O.). Some Palaeolithic pits and periods in Hertfordshire [Acheulean-Mousterian]. Proc. PSEA, 2 i, 1914/15, 135–139.

943 King (C. Cooper). A history of Berkshire. *Popular County Histories*. pp. 294. 8°. London, 1887.

944 King (W. B. R.) *and* **Oakley** (K. P.). The Pleistocene succession in the lower parts of the Thames Valley. Proc. prehist. Soc., N.S. 2, 1936, 52–76 + 1 figure + 1 plate.

945 Kuhlicke (F. W.). The Beaker folk: prehistoric invaders of Bedfordshire. [4 figures.] Beds. Mag., 2, pp. 103–07. 1950.

946 Lacaille (A. D.). Mesolithic facies in Middlesex and London. Trans. London & Middlesex Arch. Soc., 20 iii, 1961, 101–150 + 9 figures.

947 —— Mesolithic industries beside Colne Waters in Iver and Denham, Buckinghamshire [3 plates + 13 figures]. Record of Bucks., 17(3), 1963, 143–181.

948 —— Mesolithic facies in Middlesex and London, Part I. Archaeol. News Letter, 7 xi, 1965, 243–248 + 1 figure.

949 Lambert (B.). The history of London and its environs from the earliest period to the present time. 4 vol., 8°. London, 1806.

950 Lambert (Joyce M.) *and* **Jennings** (J. N.). The Making of the Broads— a reconsideration of their origin in the light of new evidence (Royal Geographical Research Series No. 3). 8°. London, 1960, pp. 153, plates 11, maps, plans, sections and diagrams, 63.

951 Larksby (J. Russell). Evidences of prehistoric man in West Kent. [5 figures.] Essex Nat., 13, pp. 328–36. 1904.

952 —— Notes on prehistoric man in west Kent. [11 figures, + map.] Antiquary, 41, pp. 95–100, 529–33. 1905.

953 Lasham (Frank). Palaeolithic man in West Surrey. [2 figures.] Surrey Archaeol. Collns., 11, pp. 25–29 + 2 plates. 1893.

954 —— Neolithic and Bronze Age man in west Surrey. [11 figures.] Surrey Archaeol. Collns., 11, pp. 244–51 + 2 plates. 1893.

955 —— Eolithic man in west Surrey. Surrey Archaeol. Collns., 24, pp. 162–68 + plate + plan. 1911.

956 Lawrence (G. F.). The prehistoric antiquities of Wandsworth. J. Brit. Archaeol. Ass., 46, p. 78. 1890.

957 Layard (Nina). Prehistoric cooking places in Norfolk (with a brief account of heating stones, their history and significance). Proc. PSEA, 3 iv, 1921/22, 483–498 + 5 figures + 2 plates.

958 Lowther (Anthony William George). Bronze-Iron Age and Roman finds at Ashtead. Surrey Archaeol. Collns., 41, pp. 93–98. 1933.

959 Malden (Henry Elliot). A history of Surrey. *Popular County Histories*. pp. viii, 321. 8°. London, 1900.

960 Manning (Percy) *and* Leeds (Edward Thurlow). An archaeological survey of Oxfordshire. Archaeologia, 71, pp. 227–65 + map. 1921.

961 Martin (Peter J.). Notice of a British settlement and walled tumulus, near Pulborough. [2 figures.] Sussex Arch. Collns., 9, pp. 109–118. 1857.

962 Matthews (C. L.). Ancient Dunstable. Dunstable: Manshead Archaeol. Soc., 1963.

963 Maynard (Guy). The Britons of Essex and the Roman conquest. Relway (A. C.): Memorials of old Essex, pp. 19–32 + 2 plates. 1908.

964 —— Recent archaeological field work in Suffolk. Proc. Suffolk Inst., Arch., 25, pp. 205–16. 1952.

965 Miller (Samuel Henry) *and* Skertchley (Sydney B. J.). The Fenland, past and present. pp. xxxii, 649 + 27 plates + map. large 8°. Wisbech, 1878, [Pp. 26–34, prehistoric.]

966 Moir (James Reid). Pre-Palaeolithic man [in Suffolk]. Proc. Suffolk Inst. Arch., 15, pp. 9–15 + plate (cross-section of Gipping valley). 1915.

967 —— On a series of ancient "floors" in a small valley near Ipswich. Proc. PSEA, 3 iv, 1921/22, 559–579 + 19 figures.

968 —— The antiquity of man in East Anglia. pp. xiv, 172 + 25 plates. [75 figures.] 8°. Cambridge, 1927.

969 —— Ancient man in the Gipping-Orwell Valley, Suffolk. Proc. PSEA, 6 iii, 1930, 182–221 + 55 figures.

970 Montmorency (James Edward Geoffrey de). Pre-historic and Roman Greenwich. Trans. Greenwich Antiq. Soc., 1, pp. 123–32 + map. 1912.

971 —— Prehistoric Greenwich. Trans. Greenwich Antiq. Soc., 1, pp. 363–72. 1915.

972 Morris (George). Some Neolithic sites in the upper valley of the Essex, Cam. Essex Nat., 20, pp. 49–68 + 2 plates. 1924.

973 Morton (John). The natural history of Northamptonshire. pp. 551 + 14 plates + map. fol. London, 1712.

974 Mothersole (Henry). Notes on some relics of early man in the neighbourhood of Chelmsford. Essex Nat., 10, pp. 305–06. 1898.

975 Nevill (Ralph). Early settlements in south-west Surrey: British, Roman and Saxon. With observations on the march of Aulus Plantius and Vespasian. A.D. 43. pp. 27. 4°. Guildford, 1889.

976 Neville (Richard Cornwallis) *4th Baron Braybrooke*. Ancient Cambridgeshire. A comprehensive survey of vestiges of early occupation in Cambridgeshire and adjacent parts of Essex, *etc.* Archaeol. J., 11, pp. 207–15. 1854.

977 Norwich Castle Museum. Catalogue of antiquities found principally in East Anglia. Edited by Walter Rye, compiled by Frank Leney. pp. x, 152. [Pp. 1–20, Stone Age: pp. 20–33 + plate, Bronze and Early Iron periods.] 8°. Norwich, 1909.

978 O'Reilly (Maureen Margaret). Archaeological notes, 2—Beaker period. Proc. Camb. Antiq. Soc., 29, pp. 105–06 + plate. 1928.

979 Owles (Elizabeth) *and* Smedley (Norman). Archaeology in Suffolk, 1962. Proc. Suffolk Inst. Arch., 29 ii, 1962, 166–74.

980 —— Archaeology in Suffolk, 1963. Proc. Suffolk Inst. Arch., 29 iii, 1963, 348–54.

981 —— Archaeology in Suffolk, 1964. Proc. Suffolk Inst. Arch., 30 i, 1964, 116–23.

982 Parker (John). Prehistoric man with some allusions to his relationship

to Buckinghamshire. Records of Bucks., 5, pp. 289–320 + plate. 1878.

983 Parsons (Frederick Gymer). The earlier inhabitants of London. pp. 240. 8º. London, 1927.

984 Payne (George). An archaeological survey of Kent. Archaeologia, 51, pp. 447–68 + map. 1888.

985 —— Collectanea Cantiana: or, archaeological researches in the neighbourhood of Sittingbourne, and other parts of Kent. pp. xvi, 218. 8º. London, 1893. [Pp. 1–54 + 3 plates, Pre-Roman period.]

986 —— Researches and discoveries in Kent, 1912–1915. Twydall [near Faversham]. Arch. Cant., 31, pp. 275–278 + 8 plates + plan. 1915.

987 Peake (A. E.). The Gravel at No Man's Land Common, Hertfordshire [Aurignacian-Mouberian]. Proc. PSEA, 2 ii, 1915/16, 222–229 + 3 figures.

988 Peake (Harold John Edward). Archaeological finds in the Kennet gravels near Newbury. Antiq. J., 2, pp. 125–30. 1922.

989 —— The archaeology of Berkshire. *County Archaeologies.* pp. xi, 260 + 8 plates + map. 8º. London, 1931. [23 figures + 5 maps. Pp. 1–82, Pre-historic.]

990 —— The Newbury district in the Neolithic Age. Trans. Newbury F.C., 7 (1934/37), pp. 275–85. 1937.

991 —— The origin of Newbury. Trans. Newbury F.C., 8, pp. 204–15. 1940.

992 —— The earliest inhabitants of Newbury. Trans. Newbury F.C., 8, pp. 272–79. 1946.

993 Perkins (John Bryan Ward). Iron Age sites [near Hollesley] in Suffolk. Antiq. J., 17, pp. 195–97. 1937.

994 Petch (D. F.). Archaeological notes for 1955. (— for 1956). Lincs. Archit. & Archaeol. Soc., Rpts. & Papers, 48 (N.S.6), pp. 61–65; 49, pp. 1–9 + plate. 1956/57.

995 —— Archaeological notes for the year 1957. Lincs. Arch. & Archaeol. Soc., Rpts. & Papers, N.S.7, pp. 91–99 + 2 plates. 1958.

996 —— Prehistoric sites at Barrowby. Rpts. & Papers Lincs. Arch. & Archaeol. Soc., 9, 1961.

998 Petrie (*Sir* William Matthew Flinders). Notes on Kentish earthworks. Arch. Cant., 13, pp. 8–16 + 2 plates (14 plans). 1880.

999 Phené (John Samuel). "Old London" in pre-Roman times. Its Italian and Greek colonists, *etc.* J. Brit. Archaeol. Ass., N.S.3, pp. 89–102 + map, pp. 192–205. 1897.

1000 —— The commercial importance of Peterborough in pre-Roman times. J. Brit. Archaeol. Ass., N.S.6, pp. 324–31. 1900.

1001 Phillips (Charles William). The present state of archaeology in Lincolnshire. [5 figures + 2 maps + 2 plans.] Archaeol. J., 90 (1933), pp. 106–49 + 12 plates + 5 maps; 91 (1934), pp. 97–187 + 9 plates + 3 maps + plan. 1934/35.

1002 —— Field archaeology in Lincolnshire. Lincs. Historian, 1, pp. 42–54, 92–99. 1948.

1003 Philp (B. J.). Reports from local secretaries and groups: West Kent Border Excavation Group. Arch. Cantiana, 78, 1963, lvi.

1004 Picton (Harold). Observations on the bone beds at Clacton. Proc. prehist. Soc., E.A. 1 ii, 1910/12, 158–9.

1005 Plot (Robert). The natural history of Oxfordshire. pp. 358 + map. fol. Oxford, 1677. 2nd edition, pp. 366. fol. Oxford, 1705.

1006 Plowright (Charles B.). Neolithic man in West Norfolk. Trans. Norfolk & Norwich Nat. Soc., 5, 1892, 250–264.

1007 Pollitt (William). An introduction to the prehistoric antiquities of Southend-on-sea and district. *Museum handbook*, 1. pp. 14 + 6 plates. 8º. Southend-on-sea.

1008 —— Southend before the Norman Conquest. pp. 82. 8º. Southend-on-Sea, 1953. [21 figures + map. Pp. 10–30, Prehistory (7 figures).]

1009 Pull (J. H.). The Stone Age villages of downland. [11 figures + 3 plans.] Sussex County Mag., 9, pp. 437–39, 498–500, 577–79, 636–38, 725–728, 781–84. 1935.

1010 —— Further discoveries at Church hill, Findon. Sussex County Mag., 27, pp. 15–21. 1953.

1011 Rankine (William Francis). A

Mesolithic Survey of the west Surrey Greensand. *Research Papers of the Surrey Archaeological Society*, 2. pp. 50 + plate. 17 figures.] 4°. Guildford, 19 ?.

1012 —— Mesolithic chipping floors in the wind-blown deposits of west Surrey. Surrey Archaeol. Collns., 50, pp. 1–8 + 2 plates. 1949.

1013 —— Mesolithic research in Surrey. [Figure + map of sites.] Surrey Archaeol. Collns., 52, pp. 1–10. 1952.

1014 Raven (John James). The history of Suffolk. *Popular County Histories.* pp. viii, 287. 8°. London, 1895.

1015 Rice (Robert Garroway). [Report on antiquities from Sussex, 1911]. Proc. Soc. Antiq., 2 S. 23, pp. 371–86. 1911.

1016 Rooke (Peter E.). Cheshunt, prehistoric and Roman. Herts. Countryside, 9, p. 149. 1955.

1017 Rouse (E. Clive). Archaeological work in Buckinghamshire. S.E. Nat'list. & Antiq., 49, 1945, 17–19.

1018 Royal Commission on Historical Monuments (England). An Inventory of the historical monuments in the city of Cambridge. 2 vols. London, 1959, pp. cxxix, + 480 plates, 310.

1020 Rye (Walter). A history of Norfolk. *Popular County Histories.* pp. viii, 316. 8°. London, 1885.

1021 Sainty (J. E.). Norfolk prehistory. Brit. Ass., Rpt., 1935 Appendix, pp. 60–71. 1935.

1022 —— Mesolithic sites in Norfolk. [Kelling, *etc.*] Norfolk Arch., 28, pp. 234–37 + 2 plates. 1945.

1023 —— *and* **Clarke** (Roy Rainbird). A century of Norfolk prehistory. Norfolk Arch., 29, pp. 8–40 + 8 plates. 1946.

1024 Sandford (K. S.), **Leeds** (Edward Thurlow) *and* **Savory** (H. N.). Early man [in Oxfordshire], 1. The Quaternary geology of Oxfordshire with reference to Palaeolithic man. (2. Mesolithic-Neolithic Age: 3. Bronze Age: 4 Early Iron Age). [16 figures.] V.C.H., Oxford, 1, pp. 223–66a + 12 plates + map. 1939.

1025 Seaby (Wilfred Arthur). The distribution of prehistoric and early historic man in the middle Thames basin. S.E. Naturalist, 39, pp. 91–97. 1934.

1026 Sharpe (*Sir* Montagu). Middlesex in British, Roman and Saxon times.

Second edition, pp. xix, 250 + 9 maps. [12 figures.] 8°. London, 1932.

1027 Shrubsole (O. A.) *and* **Clinch** (George). Early man [in Berkshire]. V.C.H., Berks., 1, pp. 173–96 + 11 plates + map. 1906.

1028 Smedley (Norman) *and* **Aberg** (F.A.). Archaeology in Suffolk, 1957. Proc. Suffolk Inst. Archaeol., 27, pp. 178–85; 28, pp. 90–96. 1958–59.

1029 Smedley (Norman) *and* **Owles** (Elizabeth). Archaeology in Suffolk, 1960. Proc. Suffolk Inst. Arch., 28 iii (1960), 290–96.

1030 —— Archaeology in Suffolk, 1961. Proc. Suffolk Inst. Arch., 29 i, 1961, 91–102.

1031 Smith (A. G.). The Context of some Late Bronze Age and Early Iron Age remains from Lincolnshire. Proc. prehist. Soc., 24, 1958, 78–84 + 2 figures + 1 plate.

1032 Smith (Reginald Allender). Excavations on early sites near Leatherhead and Shamley Green. [3 figures.] Proc. Soc. Antiq., 2 S. 18, pp. 251–58. 1901.

1033 —— Antiquities discovered at Desborough, Northants. [3 figures.] Proc. Soc. Antiq., 2 S. 22, pp. 333–37 + 2 plates (pottery). 1908.

1034 —— On Late-Celtic antiquities discovered at Welwyn, Herts. [22 figures + plan. Pottery, *etc.*] Archaeologia, 63, pp. 1–30 + 3 plates. 1912.

1035 —— *and* **Dewey** (Henry). The high terrace of the Thames: report on excavations made on behalf of the British Museum and H.M. Geological Survey in 1913. Archaeologia, 65, pp. 187–212 + plate. 1914.

1036 —— High-level finds in the Upper Thames Valley [St. Acheul and Le Moustier]. Proc. PSEA, 2 i, 1914/15, 99–107.

1037 Smith (Worthington George). Primaeval man in the valley of the Lea. Trans. Essex Fld. Club, 3, 1883, 102–147 + 24 figures.

1038 —— Primaeval man in the valley of the Lea. [35 figures (implements, *etc.*).] Essex Nat., 1, pp. 36–38, 83–91, 125–37. 1887.

1039 —— Early man [in Bedfordshire]. [64 figures]. V. C. H., Beds., 1, pp. 145–74 + map. 1904.

1040 Spurrell (Flaxman Charles John). Dartford antiquities. Notes on British, Roman and Saxon remains there found. Arch. Cant., 18, pp. 304–18 + map. 1889.

1041 Stevens (Joseph). On the earliest known traces of man in the Thames drift, at Reading. Trans. Berks. Arch. Soc., 1881/82, pp. 1–18 + 2 plates. 1882.

1042 Sturdy (David) *and* **Case** (Humphrey). Archaeological notes, 1962–63. Oxoniensis 28, 87–93, 1963.

1043 Sturge (W. Allen), **Dutt** (William Alfred) *and* **Clinch** (George). Early man [in Suffolk]. [9 figures +map.] V.C.H., Suffolk, 1, pp. 235–77 + 6 plates + map. 1911.

1044 Surrey Archaeological Society. A survey of the prehistory of the Farnham district. Prepared by K. P. Oakley, W. F. Rankine, and A. W. G. Lorothar. Including a report on the Badshot long barrow by Alexander Keiller and Stuart Piggott. pp. xv, 270 + 25 plates + 5 maps. 8⁰. Guildford, 1939. [114 figures. Palaeolithic to Roman.]

1045 Swinnerton (H. H.). The prehistoric pottery sites of the Lincolnshire coast. Antiq. J., 12, pp. 239–53. 1932.

1046 —— The story of early man in Nottinghamshire. Trans. Thoroton Soc., 54 (1950), pp. 63–74 + 3 maps 1951.

1047 Sympson (Edward Mansel). Lincoln. *Ancient cities*. pp. xvi, 448 + 11 plates. 8⁰. London, 1906.

1048 Thompson (Frederick Hugh). Archaeological notes for 1952 and 1953. (—for 1954.) Lincs. Archit. & Archaeol. Soc., Rpts. & Papers, 47 (N.S. 5), pp. 75–80 + 4 plates; 48, pp. 1–6 + plate. 1954–55.

1049 Thompson (Percy L.). Prehistoric man in Essex. Essex: an outline scientific survey. *Editor*, G. E. Hutchings. (Congress of S.E. Union of Scientific Societies at Colchester.) pp. 28–33. 1926.

1050 Treacher (Llewellyn). Palaeolithic man in east Berks. Berks., Bucks. & Oxon. Archaeol. J., 2, pp. 16–18, 39–43. 1896.

1051 Turner (Fred). History and antiquities of Brentford. pp. 227. 4⁰. Brentford, 1922.

1052 Underhill (F. M.). Notes on recent antiquarian discoveries in Berkshire. Berks. Archaeol. J., 41, pp. 33–41 + 3 plates: 42, pp. 20–28; 49, pp. 49–61. 1937–38, 1946.

1053 Osborn (Henry Fairfield). The Pliocene man of East Anglia. J. An. Mus. N.H., 21, vi. 1921.

1054 Vincent (William Thomas). Early man in Kent. Woolwich Ant. Soc., Ann. Rpt., 10, pp. 28–38 + plate. 1905.

1055 Vulliamy (Colwyn Edward). The archaeology of Middlesex and London. *County Archaeologies*. pp. xx, 308 + 11 plates + map. 8⁰. London, 1930. [38 figures + 3 maps. Pp. 1–141, Prehistory.]

1056 Waddington (Quintin). Vestiges of pre-Roman London. J. Brit. Archaeol. Ass., N.S. 39, pp. 382–94 + 7 plates. 1933.

1057 Wade (A. G.) *and* **Smith** (Reginald Allender). A Palaeolithic succession at Farnham, Surrey. [Acheulian: middle-late]. Proc. PSEA, 7 iii, 1934, 348–353 + 2 figures.

1058 Wake (Thomas). Some recent archaeological discoveries in Norfolk. Norfolk Arch., 28, pp. 23–28 + 2 plates. 1942.

1059 Warren (Samuel Hazzledine). The classification of the prehistoric remains of eastern Essex. [3 figures.] J. R. Anthrop. Inst., 42, pp. 91–127 + 8 plates (flints, *etc.*). 1912.

1060 —— Palaeolithic remains from Clacton-on-Sea, Essex. Essex Nat., 17, p. 15. 1912.

1061 —— The study of pre-history in Essex, as recorded in the publications of the Essex Field Club. Essex Nat., 18, pp. 145–86. 1916.

1062 —— Pre-history in Essex, as recorded in the journal of the Essex Field Club. *Essex Field Club Special Memoirs, 5.* pp. 44. 8⁰. Stratford, 1918.

1063 —— Prehistoric timber structures associated with a briquetage site [at Ingoldmells] in Lincolnshire. Antiq. J., 12, pp. 254–56 + 2 plates. 1932.

1064 —— The Palaeolithic industries of the Clacton and Dovercourt districts. [5 figures.] Essex Nat., 24, pp. 1–29 + plate. 1932.

1065 —— The Correlation of the Lea

Valley Arctic Beds [Lake Lavallois]. Proc. prehist. Soc., 4, 1938, 328–29 + 1 figure.

1066 —— Some geological and pre-historic records of the north-west border of Essex. Essex Nat., 27, pp. 173–80. 1945.

1067 Westell (William Percival). Historic Hertfordshire. pp. xiii, 198 + 8 plates + map. 8⁰. Hertford, 1931. [Pp. 36–54 + plate (pottery and glass), Roman period.]

1068 Wheeler (*Sir* Robert Eric Mortimer). "Old England", Brentford. Antiquity, 3, pp. 20–32 + 5 plates. 1929.

1069 Whimster (Donald Cameron). The archaeology of Surrey. *County Archaeologies.* pp. xiv, 254 + 12 plates + map. [35 figures + 4 maps + plan. Pp. 1–123, Prehistory.]

1070(a) —— The archaeology of Surrey. *County Archaeologies.* pp. xiv, 254 + 12 plates + map. 8⁰. London, 1931. [32 figures + 9 maps + 4 plans. Pp. 1–123, Prehistory.]

1070(b) White (Charles Harold Evelyn). The Aldreth causeway, its bridge and surroundings. Trans. Cambs. & Hunts. Arch. Soc., 1, pp. 1–28 + 3 plates. 1904.

1070(c) White (G. M.). Prehistoric remains from Selsey Bill, with a commentary on the pottery by Christopher Hawkes. [6 figures (pottery). Early Iron Age.] Antiq. J., 14, p40–52.p. 1934.

1071 Whitley (H. Michell). Recent archaeological discoveries in the Eastbourne district. British remains at Mill Gap, Eastbourne. Sussex Arch. Collns., 37, pp. 111–12. 1890.

1072 Whitwell (J. B.). Iron Age huts and Roman ditches, Ancaster. Rpts. & paps., Lincs., A. & A.S. 10, 1963.

1073 Wickham (Humphrey). Celtic remains found in the hundred of Hoo. [Little Coombe farm.] Arch. Cant., 11, pp. 123–25 + 3 plates (metal implements). 1877.

1074 Wilson (Arthur Ernest). Archaeology in Sussex. Arch. News Letter, 2, pp. 143–44, 161–63. 1950.

1075 —— The Archaeology of the Worthing area. S.E. Naturalist & Antiquary 58, 1953, 10–13.

1076 Winbolt (Samuel Edward). Pre-Roman finds at Folkestone. [5 figures.] Antiq. J., 5, pp. 63–67. 1925.

1077 Wood (Eric S.). Neolithic sites in West Surrey. (With a note on a medieval flint mine at East Horsley.) [4 figures + 2 plans.] Surrey Archaeol. Collns., 52, pp. 11–28 + 2 plates. 1952.

1078 Wyatt (James). Supposed British remains. [5 figures.] Notes Beds. Archit. & Archaeol. Soc., 1, pp. 225–227. 1867.

1079 Wymer, J. Archaeological notes. [12 figures.] Berks. Arch. J., 57, 1959, 119–124.

(b) Zone 2 [CBA Group 12]

1080 Acland (John Edward). Roman and prehistoric sites in and near Dorchester. Fifth edition: pp. 16 + 2 plates + plan. 8⁰. Dorchester, 1928.

1081 Annable (F. K.). Mesolithic sites in north Wiltshire. Wilts. Arch. Mag., 57, pp. 14–15. 1958.

1082 —— Wilsford down and Normanton down, Amesbury. [Neo-lithic and Bronze Age barrows: ? Early Bronze Age earthwork enclosure.] Wilts. Arch. Mag., 57, pp. 228–29. 1959.

1083 [Anon.] A complete list of the ancient monuments in Wiltshire scheduled under the Ancient Monuments Act, 1913 (up to March, 1925). Wilts. Archaeol. Mag., 43, pp. 175–79. 1925.

1084 [Anon.] Antiquities at Savarnake. [Knowle farm. Flint implements.] J. Brit. Archaeol. Ass., N.S. 7, pp. 264–265. 1901.

1085 Applebaum (Shimon). The distribution of the Romano-British population in the Basingstoke area. [4 maps. Pp. 134–8, Early Iron Age and Roman sites in the Basingstoke district.] Papers and Proc. Hants. F.C., 18, pp. 119–38. 1954.

1086 Barker, R. L. Finds from some Settlement-Sites in Cranborne Chase [La Tene III brooch and Romano-British sherds]. Proc. Dorset N.H. & A.S. 82, 1961, 83–85.

1088 Bennett (F. J.). A sketch history of Marlborough in Neolithic times. pp. 12. 8⁰. Marlborough, 1892.

1089 Bowen (H. Collin) *and* **Fowler** (Peter J.). The Archaeology of Fyfield and Overton Downs, Wilts. Interim Report. Barrows; Settlements; Earthworks and Sarsen enclosures; Fields; Ditches; Roads and Tracks; Ponds and Wells; Arrangements of Sarsens. WAM 58, 1962, 210, 98–115, 2 plates, 1 figure.

1090 —— Earthwork circles and mounds on Studland Heath, Dorset. Antiquity, 37, 1963, pp. 220–223.

1091 Brailsford (John). Early Iron Age "C" in Wessex. Proc. prehist. Soc., 24, 1958, 101–119 + 6 figures + 2 plates.

1092 Bury (Henry). Some aspects of the Hampshire plateau Gravels. PPSEA, 4 i, 1922/24, 15–41 + 5 figures.

1093 Calkin (John Bernard). Around Bournemouth in prehistoric and Roman times. pp. 6 + map. 8°. Bournemouth, 1934.

1094 —— The Bournemouth district in the Bronze Age. S.E. Naturalist, 40, pp. 21–31 + 5 plates + map. 1935.

1095 —— A local survey of the Early Bronze Age. [3 figures.] Proc. Bournemouth Nat. Sci. Soc., 28, pp. 46–56 + 2 plates + map. 1936.

1096 —— The Isle of Purbeck in the Iron Age. [12 figures + map.] Proc. Dorset Archaeol. Soc., 70 (1948), pp. 29–59 + 5 plates. 1949.

1097 —— Prehistoric Pokesdown. [2 figures.] Proc. Bournemouth N. Sci. Soc., 40, pp. 79–88 + plate. 1951.

1098 —— Agriculture and population in prehistoric Bournemouth. [Figure.] Proc. Bournemouth N. Sci. Soc., 41, pp. 49–55 + plate. 1952.

1099 —— The Bournemouth area in Neolithic and Early Bronze Age times. [2 figures + 2 maps.] Proc. Dorset Archaeol. Soc., 73 (1951), pp. 32–70 + 3 plates + 3 maps. 1952.

1100 —— Some archaeological discoveries in the Isle of Purbeck. [3 figures.] Proc. Dorset Archaeol. Soc., 74 (1952), pp. 48–54. 1953.

1101 —— Some arch. discoveries in the Isle of Purbeck, Part II: Early Bronze Age remains at Lynchard, Langton Matravers, and a summary of other local EBA discoveries [1 plate + 1 figure]. Proc. Dorset N.H. & A.S., 81, 1960. 116–118.

1102 —— The Bournemouth area in the Middle and Late Bronze Age, with the 'Deverel-Rimbury' problem reconsidered. [6 Appendices; 17 figures + 1 plate.] Arch. J., 119, 1962, 1–65.

1103 —— Some early Iron Age sites in the Bournemouth area [Pottery of IA, A, B & C]. Proc. Dorset N.H. & A.S., 86, 1964, 120–130. [8 figures + 2 tables].

1104 Crawford (Osbert Guy Stanhope). Prehistoric, Roman and Saxon Nursling. Papers & Proc. Hants. F.C., 6 Suppl., pp. 36–38. 1913.

1105 —— **Ellaway** (J. R.) *and* **Willis** (G. W.). The antiquity of man in Hampshire. Papers & Proc. Hants. F.C., 9, pp. 173–88 + plate. 1922.

1106 Cunnington (Maud Edith). Romano-British Wiltshire. Being a list of sites occupied during the Roman period with the addition of some pre-Roman villages. Wilts. Archaeol. Mag., 45, pp. 166–216 + map. 1930.

1107 —— An introduction to the archaeology of Wiltshire from the earliest times to the pagan Saxons. pp. xii, 156. [28 figures + map.] 8°. Devizes, 1933.

1108 Dawkins (*Sir* William Boyd). Early man [in Hampshire]. [2 maps.] V.C.H., Hants., 1, pp. 253–63. 1900.

1109 —— The dwellers in Wiltshire in prehistoric times. Archaeol. J., 78, pp. 251–63. 1921.

1110 Draper (J. C.). Mesolithic sites in south Hampshire. (Further *ditto*). Arch. News Letter, 4, pp. 60–61, 193, 1851–53.

1111 —— Mesolithic and Neolithic distribution in south-east Hampshire. Arch. News Letter, 5, pp. 199–250. 1955.

1112 —— Hampshire. Survey of islands in Langstone harbour. Archaeol. News Letter, 6, p. 204. 1958.

1113 Dunkin (E. Hadlow Wise). Some account of the megalithic remains in south Dorset. Reliquary, 11, pp. 145–57 + 2 plans. 1871.

1114 Dunning (Gerald Clough). Belgic hut and barrows in the Isle of Wight. Antiq. J., pp. 355–58. 1935.

1115 —— The history of Niton, Isle of Wight. Proc. I. of W. N.H. & Arch. Soc., 4, pp. 191–204 + 3 plates + map. 1951.

1116 Farrar (Raymond Anthony Holt). Archaeological notes (Archaeological fieldwork in Dorset). Proc. Dorset Archaeol. Soc., 70 (1948), pp. 60–64; and in each subsequent volume. 1949—.

1117 —— A list of scheduled ancient monuments . . . in Dorset. Proc. Dorset Archaeol. Soc., 74 (1952), pp. 79–84. 1953.

1118 —— Archaeological notes and news for 1959. Miscellaneous discoveries and accessions. Proc. Dorset N.H. & A.S., 81, 1960, 106–109.

1119 —— Miscellaneous discoveries and accessions. Proc. Dorset N.H. & A.S., 82, 1961, 85–86.

1120(a) —— Miscellaneous discoveries and accessions. Proc. Dorset N.H. & A.S., 84, 1963, 111–116.

1120(b) Freeman (John Peere Williams). An introduction to field archaeology as illustrated by Hampshire. pp. xxii, 462 + plates + map + plans. 8°. London, 1915.

1120(c) —— Pre-Roman Winchester. S.E. Naturalist, 36, pp. 82–89. 1951.

1121 Garson (J. G.). Observations on recent explorations made by General Pitt-Rivers at Rushmore. Advm. of Sci., 1887, 912–914.

1122 Goddard (Edward Hungerford). A list of prehistoric, Roman and pagan Saxon antiquities in the county of Wilts. arranged under parishes. Wilts. Archaeol. Mag., 38, pp. 153–378. 1913.

1123 —— The antiquities of Wilts. Arch. Camb., 6th S. 14, pp. 59–86. 1914.

1124 Godwin (H.). "The Ancient forest of Blackamore." Antiquity, 35, 1961, pp. 244–245.

1125 Grinsell (Leslie Valentine). Archaeological gazetteer [of Wiltshire]. V.C.H., Wilts., li, pp. 21–279 + 9 maps. 1957.

1126 —— The archaeology of Wessex. pp. xv, 384 + 15 plates + 6 maps + 18 figures. 8°. London, 1958.

1127 Hawkes (Charles Francis Christopher) and **Piggott** (Stuart). Britons, Romans and Saxons round Salisbury and in Cranborne chase. Reviewing the excavations of General Pitt-Rivers, 1881–1897. Archaeol. J., 104 (1947), pp. 27–81 + 3 plans. 1948.

1128 Hawkes (Charles Francis Chris-topher). Hampshire and the British Iron Age, 1905–1955. Papers & Proc. Hants. F. C., 20, pp. 14–22. 1956.

1130 Hillier (George). The history and antiquities of the Isle of Wight. pp. 104 + 6 plates. 4°. London, [1854?].

1131 Hoare (*Sir* Richard Colt) *bart*. The Ancient history of south Wiltshire. fol. London, 1814–21.

1132 —— The ancient history of north Wiltshire. pp. 128 + 16 plates. fol. London, 1819.

1133 Hutchins (John). The history and antiquities of the county of Dorset. 3rd edition, *etc.* 4 vol. fol. Westminster, 1861–70.

1134 Lewis (A. J.). On the Longstone [at Mottistone] and other prehistoric remains in the Isle of Wight. J. Anthrop. Inst., 14, pp. 45–47. 1884.

1135 Milner (John). The history . . . of Winchester. 2 vol. 4°. Winchester, 1809.

1136 Moule (Henry Joseph). Dorchester antiquities. pp. vi, 96. 8°. Dorchester, 1906.

1137 Oliver (Vere Langford). The pre-Roman and Roman occupation of the Weymouth district. Proc. Dorset Antiq. F.C., 44, pp. 31–55. 1923.

1138 —— A list of ancient monuments in Dorset, scheduled under the Act of 1913, (up to May 1928). Proc. Dorset Archaeol. Soc., 50, pp. 203–06. 1929.

1139 Ordnance Survey. Map of Neolithic Wessex. pp. 35 + map. 8°. Southampton, 1933.

1140 Palmer (L. S.). Some correlations between the prehistory of Hampshire and Africa. S.E. Naturalist, 35, pp. 94–101. 1930.

1141 Passmore (A. D.). Notes on recent discoveries [in Wiltshire]. Wilts. Archaeol. Mag., 34, pp. 308–12 + 3 plates. 1906.

1142 —— Prehistoric and Roman Swindon. Wilts. Archaeol. Mag., 38, pp. 41–47 + plate. 1913.

1143 —— Notes on field-work in N. Wilts., 1921–1922. Wilts. Archaeol. Mag., 42, pp. 49–51. 1922.

1144 —— Early Iron Age antiquities from N. Wilts. Wilts. Archaeol. Mag., 43, pp. 343–44 + 2 plates. 1926.

1145 —— Fieldwork in N. Wilts., 1926–28. [Barrows, *etc.*] Wilts. Archaeol. Mag., 44, pp. 240–45 + 2 plates. 1928.

1146 Piggott (Stuart). Butser hill [Hants.]. Antiquity, 4, pp. 187–200 + 3 plates + 2 plans. 1930.

1147 —— The Early Bronze Age in Wessex. Proc. prehist. Soc., 4, 1938, 52–106 + 24 figures + 5 plates.

1150 Poole (Hubert Frederick). An outline of the Mesolithic flint cultures of the Isle of Wight. [Figure + 3 maps.] Proc. I. of W. N.H. & Arch. Soc., 2, pp. 551–81 + 8 plates. 1936.

1151 —— The Stone Age in the Isle of Wight: a review and some unrecorded phases. [2 figures.] Proc. I. of W. N.H. & Arch. Soc., 3, pp. 33–49 + 3 plates. 1938.

1152 Powell (John Undershell). The early history of the upper Wylye valley. Wilts. Archaeol. Mag., 33, pp. 109–31. 1903.

1153 Price (F.). The Salisbury Guide . . . to which is added an accurate account of Stonehenge, *etc.* 30th edition. 12º. Salisbury, 1825. [1st edition, 1769. 2nd edition, 1771.]

1154 Pugh (R. B.) *and* **Crittall** (Elizabeth), *Editor.* The Victoria County History of Wiltshire, Vol. 1, part 1. Oxford, 1957. pp. xxii + 280, 1 plate, 3 figures + 9 maps.

1155 Rankine (W. F.). Mesolithic sites in Hampshire. Some notes on flints from Beaulieu. [6 figures (flints).] Papers & Proc. Hants. F.C., 14, pp. 230–40. 1939.

1156 —— Mesolithic research in east Hampshire. The Hampshire Greensand. [4 figures + 2 maps (sites).] Papers & Proc. Hants. F.C., 18, pp. 157–72 + plate. 1954.

1157 —— Mesolithic finds in Wiltshire. [4 figures.] Wilts. Archaeol. Mag., 56, pp. 149–61. 1955.

1158 —— The Mesolithic Age in Dorset and adjacent areas [4 figures]. Proc. Dorset N.H. & A.S., 83, 1962, 91–99.

1159(a) Reid (Clement). Note on the Palaeolithic gravel of Savernake forest, Wiltshire. Man, 3, pp. 55–56. 1903.

1159(b) Rivers (Augustus Henry Lane Fox Pitt). Excavations in Granborne Chase near Rushmore, on the borders of Dorset and Wilts. 5 vol. 4º. London, 1887–1905.

1159(c) —— On an ancient British settlement excavated near Rushmore, Salisbury. J. Anthrop. Inst., 17, pp. 190–201. 1888.

1160 Savage (James). The history of Dorchester, *etc.* pp. 220. 8º. Dorchester, 1833.

1161 Shore (Thomas William). The distribution and density of the Old British population of Hampshire. J. Anthrop. Inst., 18, pp. 334–46 + 2 plans. 1889.

1162 —— Characteristic survivals of the Celts in Hampshire. J. Anthrop. Inst., 20, pp. 3–20. 1890.

1163 —— Observations on some of the prehistoric earthworks and tumuli in Hampshire. Hants. N. & Q., 6, pp. 121–24. 1892.

1164 —— A history of Hampshire. *Popular County Histories.* pp. ix, 286. 8º. London, 1892. [Pp. 1–36, Prehistory.]

1165 —— The Candover valley and its prehistoric inhabitants. Papers & Proc. Hants. F.C., 2, pp. 283–94. 1893.

1166 —— Prehistoric races and their remains in the old Clere country of Hampshire. Papers & Proc. Hants. F.C., 3, pp. 171–82. 1895.

1167 Smith (Alfred Charles). Vestiges of the earliest inhabitants of Wiltshire. Wilts. Archaeol. Mag., 9, pp. 97–136 + 4 plates (jewellery, flints, urns). 1866.

1168 —— On British stone and earthworks on the Marlborough downs. [2 figures + 2 plans.] Wilts. Archaeol. Mag., 19, pp. 45–67. 1881.

1169 —— Guide to the British and Roman antiquities of the north Wiltshire downs. pp. xv, 241 + 7 plates + map. [110 figures.] fol. Marlborough, 1884.

1170 —— Guide to the British and Roman antiquities of the north Wiltshire downs in a hundred square miles round Abury. *Wiltshire Archaeological Society.* second edition. pp. xviii, 247 + 7 plates + map. 4º. Devizes and Guildford, 1885.

1171 —— Guide to the British and Roman antiquities of the north Wiltshire downs in a hundred square miles round Abury. Wilts. Archaeol. Mag., 23, pp. 59–62. 1887.

1172 **Smith** (Harry Peace). The occupation of the Hamworthy peninsula in the late Keltic and Romano-British periods. Proc. Dorset Archaeol. Soc., 52, pp. 96–130 + 10 plates + map + plan. 1931.

1173 **Smith** (Isobel F.). Windmill Hill and Avebury. Excavations by Alexander Keiller, 1925–1939. Oxford, 1965, 265 pp. + 41 plates + 7 tables + 83 figures.

1174 **Solly** (H. Sharn). Early man in Dorset. Proc. Dorset Antiq. F.C., 36, pp. 28–40. 1915.

1175 **Stevens** (Joseph). Relics of early races in the upper Test valley, Hampshire. Trans. Berks. Arch. Soc., 1879/80, pp. 49–61. 1880.

1176 **Stone** (B.). Prehistoric and Roman remains in West Dorset and the neighbourhood of Bridport. Bridport, 1893.

1177 **Stone** (John F. S.). Early Iron Age villages or farmsteads on Boscombe down, south Wilts. Arch. News Letter, lxi, pp. 9–10. 1949.

1178(a) —— Wessex before the Celts (Ancient Peoples and Places Series). London, 1958, pp. 207, plates lxxii, figures 22.

1178(b) **Stone** (W. G. Boswell). Prehistoric and Roman remains in west Dorset, and the neighbourhood of Bridport. pp. 20. 8º. Bridport, 1893.

1179 **Sumner** (Heywood). A map of ancient sites in the New Forest, Cranborne Chase and Bournemouth district. 1923.

1180 —— Local papers, archaeological and topographical, Hampshire, Dorset and Wiltshire. pp. 248. 8º. London, Chiswick Press, 1931. [43 plates, figures, maps and plans.]

1181 **Sydenham** (John). Baal Duro Frigensis. pp. 65 + plate. 8º. London 1841.

1182 **Thomas** (Nicholas Wulfstan de l'Eglise). Excavation and field-work in Wiltshire: 1956. Wilts. Archaeol. Mag., 56, pp. 231–52. 1956.

1183 **Toms** (Herbert S.). Bronze Age, or earlier, lynchets. Proc. Dorset Antiq. F.C., 46, pp. 89–100 + 2 plans. 1925.

1184 **Warne** (Charles). Observations on the primeval archaeology of Dorsetshire. Trans. Brit. Archaeol. Ass., 3,

Congress at Gloucester, 1846, pp. 74–85. 1848.

1185 —— Dorsetshire: its vestiges, Celtic, Roman . . . classified, *etc.* pp. vii, 56 + map + plan. 8º. London, 1865.

1186 —— Ancient Dorset. The Celtic, Roman, Saxon, and Danish antiquities. pp. 343 + 18 plates. fol. Bournemouth, 1872.

1188 **Winbolt** (Samuel Edward). Two Bronze Age discoveries in Hants. Papers & Proc. Hants. F.C., 10, pp. 249–51 + 2 plates. 1931.

(c) Zone 3 [CBA Groups 8, 13]

1191 **Andrews** (William). Recent progress in geological and archaeological investigation in Warwickshire and neighbourhood. pp. 13. 8º. Warwick, 1904.

1192 —— Two addresses [to the Warwickshire Naturalists' and archaeologists' Field Club]. 1. The ancient British place names in Warwickshire. 2. The ancient British language in Warwickshire. pp. 35 + map. 8º. Warwick, 1905.

1193 [**Anon.**] The mystical history of Devon. 1. The legend of Brutus the Trojan. Devonian Y.B., 3, pp. 107–11, 1912.

1194 [**Anon.**] Cumulative index of Cornish archaeology: List no. 1 (1932–1952); List no. 2 (1953–1954, with addenda to list 1), *etc.* Proc. West Cornwall F.C., N.S. 1, pp. 7–14, 78–80, and each succeeding part, 1953, *etc.*

1195 **Arthur** (J. P.). Neolithic and other remains found near Harlyn bay. Cornwall. [2 figures]. Antiquary, 40, pp. 104–10, 134–38, 1904.

1196 **Ashbee** (Paul). Fieldwork in the Isles of Scilly, 1950. Proc. West Cornwall F.C., N.S. 1, pp. 76–77. 1954.

1197 —— Flint industries in the Isles of Scilly. Proc. West Cornwall F.C., N.S. 1, pp. 125–26. 1955.

1198 **Auden** (Thomas). Prehistoric man in Shropshire. Trans. Caradoc F.C., 4, pp. 138–46. 1907.

1199 —— Early man [in Shropshire]. V.C.H., Shropshire, 1, pp. 195–203 + 2 plates + map. 1908.

1200 —— Shropshire. *Oxford county histories.* pp. 192 + map. 8⁰. Oxford, 1912.

1201 Baddeley (Welbore St. Clair). A history of Cirencester. pp. 329, xii + 15 plates + 5 plans. 8⁰. Cirencester, 1924. [Pp. 17–30, Pre-Roman evidence.]

1202 Barber, J. 28th Report on archaeology and early history [4 figures + 2 plates]. Rept. & Trans. Devon Assoc., 97, 1965, 88–109.

1204 Bate (Charles Spence). Report on the prehistoric antiquities of Dartmoor. J. Anth. Inst., 1, pp. c–cxxi + 6 plates. 1871.

1205(a) —— On the prehistoric antiquities of Dartmoor. Rpt. of Trans. Devon. Assoc., 4, pp. 491–516 + 6 plates. 1871.

1205(b) Bath (William Harcourt). Palaeolithic man in Devonshire. N. & Q., 186, pp. 64–6. 1944.

1206 Beddoe (John). Remarks on the constructors of Stanton Drew circles, Maes Knoll camp and the Wansdyke. Proc. Clifton Antiq. Club, 1, pp. 12–13. 1888.

1207 Bemrose (G. J. V.). List of scheduled monuments in Staffordshire. Trans. Ann. Rpt. North Staffs. F.C. 91, 1958, 102–04.

1208 Betjeman, John. Cornwall. London, 1964, 144 pp. + 140 plates + 4 maps.

1209 Bird (Henry). The prehistoric races of men, in Somersetshire and the adjoining counties. Proc. Bath N.H. & Ant. F.C., 4, pp. 239–43. 1881.

1210 Blake (J. E. H.). Note on remains of the Bronze Age [from Malvern] in Worcestershire. [2 figures. Palstaves.] B'ham Arch. Soc., Trans., 40 (1914), p. 83. 1915.

1211 Bloxam (Matthew Holbeche). On certain ancient British, Roman and Anglo-Saxon pagandom remains, mostly sepulchral, found in Warwickshire, chiefly in the vicinity of Rugby. pp. 4. [13 figures.] 1884.

1212 Borlase (William Copeland). Antiquities, historical and monumental, of the county of Cornwall. pp. xvi, 464. fol. London, 1769.

1213 —— Naenia Cornubiae, a descriptive essay illustrative of the sepulchres and funereal customs of the early

inhabitants of . . . Cornwall. pp. xvi, 288. 8⁰. London, 1872. [Figures.]

1214 —— Vestiges of early habitation in Cornwall. [Chapel Euny, Chysauster, *etc.*] Archaeol. J., 30, pp. 324–48 + 2 plates + 2 plans. 1873.

1214(b) —— Account of the exploration of tumuli at Trevelgue, or Trevalga, in the parish of St. Columb Minor, Cornwall; with notes on a singular "cliff castle" on the same estate. [Plan (cliff castle).] Archaeologia, 44, pp. 422–27. 1873.

1215 —— Archaeological discoveries in the parishes of St. Just-in-Penwith and Sennen. [2 figures + 4 plans.] J. Roy. Instn. Cornwall, 6, pp. 190–212 + 2 plates + plan (Ballowall cairn). 1879.

1216 Bowen (A. R.). The distribution of prehistoric remains in the Worcester–Malvern area. Trans. Worcs. Archaeol. Soc., N.S. 27 (1950), pp. 24 + map. 1951.

1217 Brailsford (John William). Bronze Age stone monuments of Dartmoor. Antiquity, 12, pp. 444–63 + 4 plates. 1958.

1218 Brassington (William Salt). Historic Worcestershire. pp. xxiii, 328. 4⁰. Birmingham, 1894.

1219 Brent (Francis). On a group of prehistoric remains on Dartmoor. J. Brit. Archaeol. Ass., 39, pp. 217–22. 1883.

1220 Bulleid (Arthur). The lake-villages of Somerset. *Somerset Folk Series, 16.* pp. 78 + 27 plates + map. 8⁰. London, 1924. [6 figures.]

1221 —— Prehistoric man around Bath. *Book of Bath* (B.M.A.), pp. 11–19. 1925.

1222 Bullen (R. Ashington). Harlyn Bay and the discoveries of its prehistoric remains. Third edition. pp. 173 + 24 plates + map. 8⁰. Padstow, 1912. [20 figures + 2 maps.]

1223 Burgess (Joseph Tom). Ancient British remains and earthworks in the forest of Arden. J. Brit. Archaeol. Ass., 29, pp. 37–44. 1873.

1224 Burnard (Robert). The disappearing stone monuments of Dartmoor. Rpt. & Trans. Devon. Assoc., 34, pp. 136–67. 1902.

1225 —— Early man [in Devon]. [11 figures + 15 plans.] V.C.H., Devon, 1, pp. 341–72 + 2 plates + map + plan. 1906.

1226 Burton (R. Jowett). Archaeology of Longtree hundred [Glos.]. [Enclosures, long barrows, round barrows, hut-circles.] Trans. Bristol & Glos. Arch. Soc., 50, pp. 313–18. 1928.

1227 —— Archaeology of Bisley hundred, [Glos.]. Trans. Bristol & Glos. Arch. Soc., 51, pp. 253–60. 1929.

1229 Carter (George Edward Lovelace). The pebbled mounds of Aylesbeare common. Proc. Devon Archaeol. Expl. Soc., 3, pp. 92–97 + 2 plates. 1938.

1230 Chanter (John Roberts). The early history and aborigines of north Devon, and the site of the supposed Cimbric town Artavia. Rpt. & Trans. Devon. Assoc., 2, pp. 57–69. 1867.

1231 Chanter (John Frederick) *and* **Worth** (Richard Hansford). The rude stone monuments of Exmoor and its borders. Rpt. & Trans. Devon. Assoc., 37, pp. 375–97 + 2 plates + 8 plans; 38, pp. 538–52 + plate + 8 plans. 1905–06.

1232 —— The parishes of Lynton and Countisbury. Rpt. & Trans. Devon. Assoc., 38, pp. 114–254 + 6 plates. 1906.

1233 —— Celtic Devon. Rpts. & Trans. Devon. Assoc., 57, pp. 39–66. 1926.

1234 Chatwin (Philip Boughton). Prehistoric finds at Wolston, near Coventry. B'ham Arch. Soc., Trans., 65 (1943–44), p. 143 + plate (urn and quern). 1949.

1235 —— Scheduled ancient monuments in Warwickshire and Staffordshire. B'ham Arch. Soc., Trans., 68 (1949–50), pp. 121–24. 1952.

1236 Chitty (Lily Frances). The Bronze Age in Shropshire. Trans. Caradoc & Severn Valley F.C., 71, pp. 205–06. 1927.

1237 —— An introduction to Shropshire archaeology. Prehistoric. Archaeol J., 113 (1956), pp. 178–81. 1957.

1238 Clark (John Grahame Douglas). Mesolithic sites on the Burtle Beds, near Bridgwater, Somerset. [2 figures.] Man, 33, pp. 63–65. 1933.

1239 Clifford (Elsie Margaret). Notes on the Neolithic period in the Cotteswolds. Proc. Cotteswold N.F.C., 6, pp. 33–49. 1936.

1240 —— The Beaker folk in the Cotswolds. Proc. Prehist. Soc., 3, 1937, 159–63 + 1 plate + 2 figures.

1241 —— The beaker phase in Cotswold. [Map.] Proc. Cotteswold N.F.C., 26, pp. 256–64 + plate. 1938.

1242 Clinch (George). Early man [in Warwickshire]. [4 figures.] V.C.H., Warwick, 1, pp. 213–22 + plate + map. 1904.

1243 —— Early man [in Herefordshire]. V.C.H., Hereford, 1, p. 157. 1908.

1244 —— Early man [in Staffordshire]. [3 figures.] V.C.H., Staffs., 1, pp. 169–81 + 2 plates + map. 1908.

1245 Cornish (J. B.). Early man [in Cornwall]. [Figure (Trethevy).] V.C.H., Cornwall, 1, pp. 353–74 + 3 plates + 4 plans. 1906.

1246 Cotton (William). Illustrations of stone circles, cromlechs, and other remains of the aboriginal Britons in the west of Cornwall, pp. iv, 46 + 21 plates. 4°. London, 1827.

1247 Cowling (John) *and* **Worth** (Richard Hansford). Archaeological notes from the valley of the Lyd. Rpt. & Trans. Devon. Assoc., 68; pp. 303–05 + 4 plates. 1936.

1248(a) Crawford (Osbert Guy Stanhope). The ancient settlements at Harlyn Bay [Cornwall]. Antiq. J., 1, pp. 283–99. 1921.

1248(b) —— The long barrows of the Cotswolds. A description of long barrows, stone circles and other megalithic remains in the area covered by sheet 8 of the quarter-inch Ordnance Survey comprising the Cotswolds and the Welsh marches. pp. xv, 246 + map. [74 figures and plans.] 4°. Gloucester, 1925.

1249 Crossing (William). The old stone crosses of the Dartmoor Borders; with notices of the scenery and traditions of the district, pp. xiv, 152 + 15 plates + 3 figures. 8°. Exeter & London, 1892.

1250 Cummings (Alfred H.). On a few antiquities from the Lizard district, Cornwall. J. Brit. Archaeol. Ass., 29, pp. 341–53 + plate. 1873.

1251 Devonshire Association— Dartmoor Exploration Committee. Second (third, *etc.*) report. Rpt. & Trans. Devon. Assoc., 27, pp. 81–92 + plate + 6 plans, *and in subsequent volumes,* 1895, *etc.*

1252 Davidson (James). The British and Roman remains in the vicinity of Axminster in the county of Devon. pp. v, 90 +4 plans. 8⁰. London, 1933.

1253 Dawkins (*Sir* William Boyd). Early man [in Somerset]. V.C.H., Somerset, 1, pp. 167–204 + 6 plates. 1906.

1254 Dewar (H. S. L.) *and* **Godwin** (H.). Archaeological discoveries in the raised bogs of the Somerset Levels, England. Proc. Prehist. Soc. 29, 1963, 17–49 + 10 figures + 1 plate.

1255 Dobson (Diana Portway). The archaeology of Somerset. *County Archaeologies*, pp. xv, 272 + 8 plates + map. 8⁰. London, 1931. [23 figures + 5 plans. Pp. 1–129, Prehistory.]

1256 —— Finds of the Beaker period [from the Mendips] in Somerset. Antiq. J., 14, pp. 54–55. 1954.

1257 Douch (H. L.). Archaeological discoveries recorded in Cornish newspapers before 1855. Cornish archaeology No. 1, 1962, 92–98.

1258 Dudley (Dorothy) *and* **Patchett** (Florence M.). Excavations on Kerrow farm, Zennor, 1935. Proc. West Cornwall F.C., N.S. 1, pp. 44–47. 1954.

1259 Dudley (Dorothy). Recent work in Cornish archaeology. Proc. West Cornwall F.C., N.S. 1, pp. 147–52. 1956.

1260 —— Late Bronze and Early Iron Age settlements in Sperris Croft and Wicca Round, Zennor, Cornwall. [Map + 2 plans.] J. Roy. Instn. Cornwall, N.S. 3, pp. 66–82 + 3 plates + plan. 1957.

1261 —— The Early Iron Age in Cornwall. Proc. West Cornwall F.C., 2, pp. 47–54. 1958.

1262 Earle (John). A guide to the knowledge of Bath ancient and modern. pp. vi, 350. 8⁰. London, 1864.

1263 Edmonds (Richard). The Celtic and other antiquities of the Land's End district of Cornwall. Arch. Camb., 3rd S., 3, pp. 275–95 +plate +map; pp. 350–368 + 2 plates; 4, pp. 66–76, 173–83, 274–283. 1857–58.

1264 —— The Land's End district: its antiquities, *etc.*, pp. 270 +6 plates + map. 8⁰. London, 1862.

1265(a) Eyton (John). Eyton's "Antiquities": a Shropshire landmark. Notes & Queries, N.S. 7, 205, 1960, 444–46.

1265(b) Eyton (Robert William). Antiquities of Shropshire. 12 vols. 8⁰. London, 1854–60.

1266 Fortey (Charles). Explorations upon the Old Field near Ludlow, December 1884. Arch. Camb., 5th S., 6, pp. 193–97 +plate (plan and pottery). 1889.

1267 Fox (*Lady* Aileen Mary). Celtic fields and farms on Dartmoor, in the light of recent excavations at Kestor. Proc. prehist. Soc., 20, 1954, 87–102 +7 figures + 2 plates.

1268 —— The prehistoric monuments of Dartmoor. [3 plans (Shovel down & Grimspound).] Archaeol. J., 114 (1957), pp. 152–59. 1959.

1269 —— Twenty-fifth Report on the Archaeology and early history of Devon. [3 figures + 2 plates.] Rep. & Trans. Devonshire Association, xci, 1959, 168–177.

1270 —— Twenty-sixth Report on ancient monuments. Rep. & Trans. Devonshire Association, xcii, 1960, 347.

1271 —— Twenty-fifth [*sic*] [27th] Report on the Archaeology and early history of Devon. [8 figures + 3 plates.] Rpt. & Trans. Devons. Ass., 93, 1961, 61–80.

1272 —— 27th Report on ancient monuments. Devonshire Ass. Rpt. & Trans., 95 (1963), 71–73.

1273 —— 27th Report on archaeology and early history. Devonshire Ass. Rpt. & Trans., 95, 1963, 74–86 + 1 plate + 1 figure.

1274 —— 28th Report on Ancient Monuments. Rept. & Trans. Devon. Ass., 97, 1965, 86–87.

1275 Fring (James Hurly). The Briton and the Roman on the site of Taunton. pp. 138 + 3 plates. 8⁰. Taunton, 1880.

1276(a) Gardner (Keith). Mesolithic Survey—North Devon. [2 figures + map.] Rpt. & Trans. Devon. Assoc., 89, pp. 160–74. 1957.

1276(b) Garrett (C. Scott). Romano-British sites at Chestnuts Hill and Popes Hill, Forest of Dean. Trans. Bristol & Gloucester Arch. Soc., 75, 1956, 199–202 + 1 figure.

1277(a) Gilbert (C. S.). An historical survey of the county of Cornwall. 3 vol. 4⁰. Plymouth-dock. 1817–20.

1277(b) Gould (Sabin Baring). Some

Devon monoliths. [At Lew Trenchard.] Rpt. & Trans. Devon. Assoc., 20, pp. 158–62. 1888.

1278 Gracie (H. S.). The Mesolithic Age with special reference to Gloucestershire. Proc. Cotteswold Naturalists' F.C., 33, iii, 1959, 107–09.

1279 Gray (Harold St. George). On some antiquities found at Hamdon or Ham hill, Somerset, and in the neighbourhood. Proc. Soc. Antiq., 2 S. 21, pp. 128–39 + plate. 1906.

1280 —— Experiences in excavating in Somerset. Somerset Arch. Soc., Proc. Bath branch [6], 1929–33, pp. 497–502 + 2 plates. 1933.

1281 Greig (O.) *and* **Rankine** (William Francis). A Stone Age settlement system near East Week, Dartmoor; Mesolithic and post-Mesolithic industries. [6 figures + 2 maps.] Proc. Devon Archaeol. Expl. Soc., 5, pp. 8–26 + 2 plates. 1953.

1282 Grinsell (Leslie Valentine), *Editor*. A Survey and policy concerning the archaeology of the Bristol Region, Part I—to the Norman Conquest. Bristol, 1964.

1285 Harding (G. T.). Parish of Great Witcombe, two Romano-British sites [RB pots and mention of trackway Sarn way]. Trans. BGAS, 81, 1962, 214–15.

1286 Harding (Joan R.). Prehistoric sites on the north Cornish coast between Newquay and Perranporth. [7 figures + 2 maps + 2 plans.] Antiq. J., 30, pp. 156–69. 1950.

1287 Hartshorne (Charles Henry). Salopia antiqua, or an enquiry from personal survey into the druidical, military and other early remains in Shropshire and the north Welsh borders. pp. vii, xxii, 640. 8º. Cambridge, 1841.

1288 Hawkes (Jacquetta). The Archaeology of the Channel Isles, Vol. II: The Bailiwick of Jersey. Jersey, 1939. [pp. 320 + 12 plates + 92 figures.]

1289 Hencken (Hugh O'Neill). The archaeology of Cornwall and Scilly. *County Archaeologies*. pp. xvii, 340 + 12 plates + map. 8º. London, 1932.

1290 —— Notes on the megalithic monuments in the Isles of Scilly. [8 figures + 5 plans.] Antiq. J., 13, pp. 13–29 + plate. 1933.

1291 Hirst (F. C.). Courtyard house sites in West Cornwall. [Figure + map + 2 plans.] J. Brit. Archaeol. Ass., 3rd S. 2, pp. 71–97. 1937.

1292 Hitchins (Fortescue). The history of Cornwall, from the earliest records and traditions, to the present time. Edited by Samuel Drew. 2 vol. 4º. Helston, 1816–24. [Vol. I, pp. 1–309, Prehistory.]

1293 Hoskins (William George). Devon. *A new survey of England*. pp. xx, 600 + 28 plates + 18 maps. 8º. London, 1954. [Pp. 24–35, Prehistoric and Celtic Devon.]

1294 —— Devon and its people. pp. 176 + 12 plates. 8º. Exeter, 1959. [4 figures + 2 maps. Pp. 7–18, Prehistoric Devon.]

1295 Hudd (Alfred Edmund). On some prehistoric remains near Bristol. Proc. Clifton Antiq. Club, 3, pp. 142–48. 1897.

1296(a) Hutchinson (Peter Orlando). On the hill fortresses, tumuli, and some other antiquities of eastern Devon. J. Brit. Archaeol. Ass., 18, pp. 53–66 + 3 plates + map. 1862.

1296(b) Hyslop (C. W. Campbell) *and* **Cobbold** (Edgar Sterling) *eds.* Church Stretton. Vol. 3: Pre-Roman, Roman and Saxon archaeological remains. 8º. Shrewsbury, 1903.

1297(a) Iago (William). On some recent archaeological discoveries in Cornwall. J. Roy. Instn. Cornwall, 10, pp. 185–262 + 11 plates + 2 maps + 2 plans, pp. 449–51. 1890.

1297(b) Jones (A. E.). Roman and other sites near Bredon hill (Worcs.). [Jewellery, flints, pottery, *etc.*] B'ham. Arch. Soc., Trans., 52 (1927), pp. 288–91. 1930.

1298 Kelly (John). Celtic remains on Dartmoor. Rpt. & Trans., Devon. Assoc., 1 v, pp. 45–48. 1866.

1299 Kelly (Thomas). Celtic remains on Dartmoor. J. Roy. Instn. Cornwall, 2, pp. 125–28 + plate. 1866.

1300 Kempe (Alfred John). Account of some monuments conjectured to be British, still existing upon Dartmoor. Archaeologia, 22, pp. 429–35 + plan. 1829.

1301 Kendall (*Rev.* Henry George Ommanna). Flint industries in North

Cornwall. Proc. prehist. Soc. E.A. 1 iv, 1913–14, 438–40.

1302 Kenyon (R. Lloyd). Pre-historic Shropshire. Trans. Shropshire Archaeol. Soc., 2nd S. 4, pp. 264–86. 1892.

1303 Kirwan (Richard). Notes on the pre-historic archaeology of East Devon. Rpt. & Trans., Devon. Assoc., 3, pp. 495–500; 4, pp. 295–304 + 4 plates; pp. 641–53 + 2 plates. 1869–71.

1304 —— Notes on the pre-historic archaeology of east Devon. [2 figures.] Archaeol. J., 29, pp. 34–44 + 4 plates; pp. 151–65 + 2 plates. 1872.

1305 Langdon (Arthur Gregory). Prehistoric and other objects found together near Buttern hill, Cornwall. Proc. Soc. Antiq., 2 S, 21, pp. 456–61. 1907.

1306 Lattimore (M.). Some prehistoric evidence in the Plymouth area. Rpt. & Trans., Devons. Ass., 93, 1961, 286–303.

1307 Lewis (A. L.). A description of some archaic structures in Cornwall and Devon. J. Anth. Inst., 1, pp. i–ix. 1870.

1308 —— Rude stone monuments on Bodmin moor. J. Roy. Instn. Cornwall, 13, pp. 107–13 + plate + plan. 1895.

1309 —— Prehistoric remains in Cornwall. Part 1.—East Cornwall. (Part 2.—West Cornwall.) [Figure. (Figure + map).] J. Anthrop. Inst., 25, pp. 2–16 + plate + plan; 35, pp. 427–34. 1895, 1905.

1310 Lowe (Harford J.). The Dartmoor antiquities and their builders. J. Torquay nat. Hist. Soc., 2, 1917, 131–41 + 1 figure.

1311 Luff (George). Neolithic man and his remains in Shropshire. Trans. Shropshire Archaeol. Soc., 11, pp. 211–222 + 2 plates. 1888.

1312 Lukis (William Collings). On some Megalithic monuments in western Cornwall. J. Brit. Archaeol. Ass., 33, pp. 291–96. 1877.

1313 —— A report on the prehistoric monuments of Devon and Cornwall. Proc. Soc. Antiq., 2 S. 8, pp. 285–93. 1880.

1314 —— Report on the monuments of Dartmoor, its avenues, large circles, burial mounds, hut circles and holed stones. Proc. Soc. Antiq., 2 S. 8, pp. 470–81. 1881.

1315 —— The prehistoric stone monuments of the British Isles—Corn-wall. pp. viii, 31 + 4 plates + map. *Society of Antiquaries.* fol. London, 1885.

1316 McMurtrie (James). Notes on ancient British and Romano-British remains discovered in the Tyning and Kilmersdon road quarries at Radstock. Proc. Somerset Arch. Soc., 45, pp. 108–124 + 3 plates. 1899.

1317 Marsden (John G.). Some unrecorded prehistoric sites in Penwith. J. Roy. Instn. Cornwall, 21, pp. 169–74 + 2 plates. 1923.

1318 Meehan (J. F.). Eight episodes in the history of Bath. pp. 48 + 8 plates. 8°. Bath, 1909.

1319 Megaw (J. Vincent S.). The Neolithic period in Cornwall. The West Cornwall F.C., 2, pp. 13–25. 1958.

1320 —— New light on the most ancient West. Cornish Arch., 4, 1965, 46–50.

1321 Moir (James Reid). Ancient man in Devon. Proc. Devon Archaeol. Expl. Soc., 2, pp. 264–82 + 2 plates. 1936.

1322 Morgan (Thomas). On the Briton, Roman, and Saxon in Staffordshire. J. Brit. Archaeol. Ass., 29, pp. 394–412. 1873.

1323 Neal (S. Cooper). The Stone Age at Linton. Trans. Woolhope N.F.C., 1927–29, pp. 137–41 + plate. 1931.

1324 Ordnance Survey. Map of the Trent basin, showing the distribution of long barrows, megaliths, habitation sites. pp. 31 + map. 8°. Southampton, 1933. [Scale 4 miles to one inch.]

1325 Ormerod (George). An account of some ancient remains existing in the district adjacent to the confluence of the Wye and the Severn, in the counties of Gloucester and Monmouth; namely [pp. 5–13] the probable line of the British Akeman Street, *etc.* [i.e. later material]. Archaeologia, 29, pp. 5–31 + plate + map. 1842.

1326 —— Strigulensia. Archaeological memoirs relating to the district adjacent to the confluence of the Severn and the Wye. pp. viii, 118, + 11 plates. 8°. London, 1861. [Pp. 10–42 + 1 plate, On British and Roman remains; illustrating communications with Venta Silurum, ancient passages of the Bristol Channel, and Antonine's Iter XIV.]

1327 Ormerod (G. Wareing). Notice of prehistoric remains formerly existing near the Drewsteignton cromlech: observed by R. Polwhele prior to 1793, and mapped by William Grey in 1838. Rpt. & Trans. Devon. Assoc., 5, pp. 73–74 + plan. 1872.

1328 Painter (K. S.). The Severn Basin. London, 1964, 72 pp. incl. 44 figures and photographs + frontispiece map.

1329 Patchett (Florence M.). Archaeology in Cornwall. Arch. News Letter, 4, pp. 7–9. 1951.

1330 Pengelly (William). Recent discoveries in the parishes of Chagford and Manaton, Devonshire. Kist ovens and hut circles.] Rpt. & Trans. Devon. Assoc., 12, pp. 365–79. 1880.

1331 Peter (Otho B.). The ancient earth-fenced town and village sites of Cornwall. [Figure.] J. Roy. Instn. Cornwall, 15, pp. 107–19 + 2 plans. 1901.

1332(a) Peter (Thurstan C.). Provisional list of ancient Cornish monuments, as adopted by the County Committee, . . . 1913. J. Roy. Instn. Cornwall, 19, pp. 446–55. 1914.

1332(b) Phillipps (James Orchard Halliwell). Rambles in western Cornwall . . . with notes on the Celtic remains of the Land's End district and the Islands of Scilly. 8⁰. London, 1861.

1333 Phillips (Charles William). The Ordnance Survey and archaeology in Somerset. Proc. Somerset A. & N.H.S., 104, 1959/60, 126–28.

1335 Playne (G. F.). On the early occupation of the Cotteswold hills by man. Proc. Cotteswold Nat. Club, 5, pp. 277–93 + 3 plates + map. 1871.

1336 Polwhele (Richard). The history of Devonshire. 3 vol. fol. London, 1797.

1337 Pring (James Hurly). On some evidences of the occupation of the ancient site of Taunton by the Britons. [Figure.] Archaeol. J., 37, pp. 94–98. 1880.

1338 Prior (C. E.). Archaic stone monuments [on Dartmoor]. Assoc. Archit. Socs.' Rpts., 11, pp. 343–60 + 2 plates + 3 plans. 1872.

1339 Pritchard (John Emanuel). Prehistoric Iron Age [finds in Bristol], 1902.

Proc. Clifton Antiq. Club, 5, pp. 241–43 + 2 plates. 1904.

1340 Prowse (Arthur Bancks). The ancient metropolis of Dartmoor. Rpt. & Trans. Devon. Assoc., 23, pp. 307–14 + map. 1891.

1341 —— The antiquities of Ockery and Roundhill, Dartmoor. Rpt. & Trans. Devon. Assoc., 33, pp. 495–99 + map. 1901.

1342 Pye (W. R.). Report on prehistoric finds in north-west Herefordshire. Trans. Woolhope N.F.C., 36 (1958), pp. 80–83 + 3 plates. 1959.

1343 Radford (Courtenay Arthur Ralegh). Prehistoric settlements on Dartmoor and the Cornish moors. Proc. prehist. Soc., 18, 1952, 55–84 + 13 figures + 4 plates.

1344 —— The county of Devon. Archaeol. J., 114 (1957), pp. 128–35. 1959.

1345 —— The Devon Archaeological Exploration Society, Report for the years 1958–60. Rep. & Trans. Devonshire Association, xcii, 1960, 449.

1346(a) Robinson (R. S. Gavin-). Prehistoric man in Herefordshire. Herefordshire (Woolhope F.C.), pp. 107–19 + 2 maps. 1954.

1346(b) Rogers (Charles William Pilkington). The date of the Dartmoor antiquities. [Map.] Rpt. & Trans. Devon. Assoc., 64, pp. 379–88. 1932.

1347 Rogers (E. H.). Some phases of Devon prehistory. Trans. & Proc. Torquay nat. Hist. Soc., 8, 1942, 171–185.

1348 Royce (David). "Finds" on, or near to, the excursion of the Society at Stow-on-the-Wold. Trans. Bristol & Glos. Arch. Soc., 7, pp. 69–80 + plate + plan. 1883.

1349 Russell (Vivien). Check-list of the antiquities of west Penwith. 1. Parish of St. Just-in-Penwith. Proc. West Cornwall F.C., 2, pp. 95–103. 1959.

1350 —— Parochial check-list of antiquities. Cornish archaeology No. 1, 1962, 107–18.

1351 —— Parochial check-list of antiquities. Cornish archaeol. No. 2, 1963, 64–72.

1352 —— Parochial check-list of antiquities. Cornish archaeol. 3, 1964, 90–99.

1353 —— Parochial check-list of antiquities. Cornish archaeol. 4, 1965, 70–81.

1354 —— Parochial check-list of antiquities. Cornish archaeol. 5, 1966, 63–82.

1355 Seaby (Wilfred Arthur). Archaeology of the Birmingham plateau and its margins. Arch. News Letter, 2, pp. 85–90. 1949.

1356 —— A chert-working floor at Fideoak park, Bishops Hull, Taunton, and other Mesolithic sites in Somerset. [Figure. *See also* p. 173 (note by C. M. Sykes): 4, p. 69 (note by A. D. Lacaille).] Arch. News Letter, 3, pp. 123–28. 1951.

1357 —— Mesolithic cultures in Somerset. Archaeol. J., 107 (1950), pp. 86–87. 1952.

1359 Shorter (Alfred H.). Ancient fields in Manaton parish, Dartmoor. [Plan. Dartmoor hut-circles pre-Roman: ? date of terraces.] Antiquity, 12, pp. 183–89 + 4 plates. 1938.

1360 —— Hut circles and ancient fields near Challacombe, Dartmoor. Proc. Devon Archaeol. Expl. Soc., 4, pp. 104–105. 1951.

1361 Shortt (William T. Peter). Collectanea curiosa antiqua Dumnonia; or, an essay on some druidical remains in Devon, and also on its noble ancient camps and circumvallations, . . . and notices of late discoveries of Roman coins, pottery, and other remains in Exeter and Devon. pp. 100 + 3 plates + 2 plans. 8º. Exeter, [1840?].

1362 Shotton (Frederick William). The distribution of Neolithic, Bronze Age, and Iron Age relics around Coventry. [2 Maps.] Proc. Coventry N.H. Soc., 1, pp. 184–92. 1938.

1363 Simpson (Charlotte). Report of the Archaeological Section 1957/58. Proc. Cotteswold Naturalists F.C. 33 i/ii pp. 17–19. 1957/58

1364 Smith (A. H.). The Place-names of Gloucestershire. 4 pts. Pt. 1. The River and Road Names. The East Cotswolds, xiii, 268, 1964. Pt. 2. The N. & W. Cotswolds, xiii, 262, 1964. Pt. 3. The Lower Severn Valley. The Forest of Dean, xiv, 269. Pt. 4. Introduction, Bibliography, Analyses, Index, Maps, xv, 274. 1965. 8º. Cambridge, 1964/65.

1365 Smith (C. Nancy S.) *revised and ed. by W. F. Grimes.* A catalogue of the prehistoric finds from Worcestershire. [4 figures + 4 maps.] Trans. Worcs. Arch. Soc., N.S. 34 (1957), pp. 1–27 + 2 plates. 1958.

1366 Smith (Reginald Anthony Lendon). Bath. pp. 118 + 84 plates. 8º. London, 1944.

1367 Somervail (Alexander). Prehistoric Torbay. Rpt. & Trans. Devon. Assoc., 28, pp. 533–46. 1896.

1368 Steel (R. Elliot). Early Iron Age finds in Somerset. Antiq. J., 8, pp. 522–23. 1928.

1369 Symonds (P. Biddulph). Some notes on prehistoric discoveries at Linton. Trans. Woolhope N.F.C., 1927–29, pp. 142–43. 1931.

1370 Tebbs (B. N.). A Review of Cornish prehistory. Trans & Proc. Torquay nat. Hist. Soc., 9, 1945, 45–59.

1371 Thomas (Anthony Charles). The Principal antiquities of the Land's End district. West Cornwall Field Club, Field Guide. 8º. pp. 19, 1954; 8º. pp. 24, 1956; 8º. pp. 23, 1957; with **Pool** (Peter Aubrey Seymour) 8º pp. 27, 1959; 8º. pp. 23, 1962.

1372 Thomas (Charles). The Palaeolithic and Mesolithic periods in Cornwall. [Figure.] Proc. West Cornwall F.C., 2, pp. 5–12. 1958.

1373 —— Minor sites in the Gwithian area (Iron Age to recent times). Cornish Archaeol. 3, 1964, 37–62 + 11 figures.

1374 —— The Society's 1962 excavations: interim report. Cornish archaeol., No. 2, 1963, 47–48.

1375 Thomas, (Nicholas) *and* **Gunstone,** (A. J. H.) An Introduction to the prehistory of Staffordshire [Note of Summer meeting at Keele 1963]. Arch. J., 120, 1963, 256–62.

1376 Timmins (Sam). A history of Warwickshire. *Popular County Histories.* pp. 300. 8º. London, 1889.

1377 Tratman (E. K.). The prehistoric archaeology of the Bristol region. [4 maps.] Bristol and its adjoining counties, pp. 147–62. 1955.

1378 Tyler (Francis Cameron). The stone remains in Drewsteignton. Rpt. & Trans. Devon. Assoc., 62, pp. 249–604. 5 plates + plan. 1930.

1379 —— Cyclopean-shaped block of granite [near the foot of Buttern hill, parish of Altarnon] in Cornwall. Devon

& Cornwall N. & Q., 171, pp. 203–06. 1933.

1380 Wailes (Bernard). The Bronze Age in Cornwall. [Map.] Proc. West Cornwall F.C., 2, pp. 26–35. 1958.

1382 Warner (Richard). The history of Bath. pp. 402, 123. 4º. Bath, 1801. [Pp. 1–6, British history.]

1383 Webster (Graham). Amateur archaeology in the West Midlands. Archaeol. News Letter, 7 x, 1964, 219–21.

1384 Whitley (D. Gath). Footprints of vanished races in Cornwall. J. Roy. Instn. Cornwall, 15, pp. 267–302. 1902.

1385 Wilkinson (*Sir* John Gardner). British remains on Dartmoor. J. Brit. Archaeol. Ass., 18, pp. 22–53 + 2 plates; pp. 111–33 + plate + 2 plans. 1862.

1386 Willock (E. H.). Neolithic man on Haldon. Trans. & Proc. Torquay nat. Hist. Soc., 7, 1938, 241–49.

1387 Windle (*Sir* Bertram Coghill Alan) *and* **Bund** (John William Willis). Early man [in Worcestershire]. [4 plans.] V.C.H., Worcs., 1, pp. 179–98 + plate + 5 maps + plan. 1901.

1388 Witts (George Blackhouse). British and Roman antiquities in the neighbourhood of Cheltenham. Trans. Bristol & Glos. Arch. Soc., 4, pp. 199–213. 1880.

1389 —— Archaeological handbook of the county of Gloucester. 8º. Cheltenham, 1883. pp. 121, v + map.

1390 Woods (Roland MacAlpine). List of scheduled monuments: Devonshire. Proc. Devon Archaeol. Expl. Soc., 1, pp. 15–17. 1930.

1391 Worth (Richard Hansford). The Dartmoor hut-circles. [6 figures + map + 4 plans.] Rpt. & Trans. Devon. Assoc., 77, pp. 225–56 + 7 plates + plans. 1945.

1392 —— Prehistoric Tavistock. [Figure + plan.] Rpt. & Trans. Devon. Assoc., 79, pp. 125–28 + 2 plates. 1947.

1393 Worth (Richard Nicholls). Notes upon some Dartmoor antiquities. Notes & Gleanings . . . Devon & Cornwall, 3, pp. 17, 36–37, 59–60, 67–68, 95–96, 108–09, 125–27. 1890.

1394(a) —— The rude stone monuments of Cornwall. J. Roy. Inst. Cornwall, 12, pp. 76–95, 187–203. 1893–95.

(d) Zone 4 [CBA Groups 3, 4, 5, 6]

1394(b) Addy (Samuel Oldall). The "harbour" and barrows at Arbour-lows. [Figure + map.] J. Derbs. Archaeol. Soc., 33, pp. 39–58. 1911.

1395 [Anon.] Bury [Lancs.] in the Bronze Age. Bury Hist. Rev., 1, p. 15 + plate. 1909.

1396 [Anon.] Prehistoric relics from Middleton [-on-the-Wolds]. Yorks. N. & Q. (ed. Forshaw), 5, p. 173. 1909.

1397 [Anon.] Scarborough and Hallstatt. [Figure. Early Iron Age. Bronze armlet.] Antiq. J., 14, pp. 301–02. 1934.

1398 Armstrong (Albert Leslie). Palaeolithic man in the north Midlands. [5 figures.] J. Derbs. Archaeol. Soc., 63 (N.S. 16), pp. 28–60. 1942.

1399 —— Exploration of prehistoric sites in east Derbyshire. J. Derbs. Archaeol. Soc., 69 (N. 3.22), pp. 69–73; 70, pp. 88–91; and each subsequent year. 1949, *etc.*

1400 —— Prehistory: Palaeolithic. Neolithic, and Bronze Ages. [2 figures + 2 maps.] Sheffield and its region, ed. D. L. Linton, *Brit. Ass.*, pp. 90–110 + map. 1956.

1401 Auden (George Augustus). Prehistoric archaeology [of Yorkshire]. Historical . . . survey of York and district, (B.A. meeting, 1906), pp. 1–14 + 1 plate. 1906.

1402 "W. B." Iron Age settlements in Penigent gill. [4 plans.] Yorks. Archaeol. J., 341, pp. 412–19. 1939.

1403 Barber (Henry). The pre-historic remains of Furness and Cartmel. pp. 31. 8º. Ulverston, 1869.

1404 Barker (Mabel Mary). Some excavations in the Carrock area. Trans. Cumb. & Westm. Ant. Soc., N.S. 50, pp. 201–02. 1950.

1405 Barnes (F.) *and* **Hobbs** (J. L.). Newly discovered flint-chipping sites in the Walney Island locality. [Figure.] Trans. Cumb. & Westm. Ant. Soc., N.S. 50, pp. 20–29. 1950.

1406 Bateman (Thomas) *and* **Glover** (Stephen). Vestiges of the antiquities of Derbyshire, and the sepulchred usages of its inhabitants from the most remote ages, *etc.* pp. vii, 247 + plate. 8º. London, 1848.

1407 Bateman (Thomas). Primeval antiquities of Stanton and Hart-hill moor, near Bakewell, Derbyshire. [Figure (urns).] Trans. Brit. Archaeol. Ass. [2] Congress at Winchester, 1845, pp. 192–96. 1846.

1408(a) Bates (Cadwallader John). The history of Northumberland. *Popular County Histories.* pp. vi, 303. 8⁰. London, 1895.

1408(b) Beynon (Vernon Bryan Crowther). Report for Rutland. Proc. Soc. Antiq., 2S. 22, pp. 46–50. 1908.

1408(c) —— Early man [in Rutland]. V.C.H., Rutland, 1, pp. 81–84 + plate + map. 1908.

1409 Birley, Eric. The Archaeology of Cumberland and Westmorland. Arch. J., 115, 1958, 209–14.

1410(a) Bowman (William). Reliquiae antiquae Eboracenses. Leeds, 1855.

1410(b) Brewis (William Parker) *and* **Dixon** (David Dippie). Pre-Roman remains in upper Coquetdale. Proc. Soc. Antiq. Newc., 3rd S. 7, pp. 37–47. 1915.

1411 Browne (Montagu). Evidences of the antiquity of man in Leicestershire. Trans. Leic. Lit. & Phil. Soc., N.S. 1 ix, pp. 7–37 + 3 plates. 1888.

1412 Buckley (Francis). The Microlithic industries of Northumberland. [3 figures.] Arch. Æl., 4th S. 1, pp. 42–47. 1925.

1413 Bu'lock (J. D.). The Celtic, Saxon, and Scandinavian settlement at Meols in Wirral. Trans. Hist. Soc. Lancs. & Ches., 112, 1960, pp. 1–28 + 7 figures.

1414 Burchell (J. P. T.). Upper and Lower Palaeolithic man in East Yorkshire. Flamborough Head. Proc. PSEA, 6 iii, 1930, 226–33 + 2 plates + 7 figures.

1415 Clark (Mary Kitson), *etc.* Iron Age sites in the vale of Pickering. Yorks. Archaeol. J., 30, pp. 157–72 + 4 plates + maps. 1931.

1416 Clarke (David T. D.). The archaeology of Leicestershire. [Pp. 154–155, select bibliography.] Archaeol. J., 112 (1955), pp. 152–55. 1956.

1417 —— Archaeology in Leicestershire High Cross (467593). Trans. Leicester Arch. Soc., 33, 1957, 64.

1418 —— Archaeology in Leicestershire. Thuonby (647038). Trans. Leicester. Arch. Soc., 34, 1958, 84.

1419 —— Archaeology in Leicestershire and Rutland. Breedon-on-the-Hill (406234). Trans. Leic. Arch. Soc., 39, 1963–64, 50.

1420 Clinch (George). Prehistoric Yorkshire. Memorials of old Yorkshire, ed. (T. M. Fallow) pp. 1–10 + 1 plate. 1909.

1421 —— Early man [in Yorkshire]. V.C.H., Yorks., 1, pp. 357–414 + 11 plates + map. 1907.

1422 —— Early man [in Leicestershire]. [Figure.] V.C.H., Leicester, 1, pp. 167–77 + 2 plates + map. 1907.

1423 Cokayne (Andreas Edward). Archaeology in Derbyshire. J. Brit. Archaeol. Ass., 48, pp. 127–38. 1892.

1424 Cole (Edward Maule). On the entrenchments on the Yorkshire wolds. [3 plans.] Antiquary, 22, pp. 109–12, 163–67, 194–98. 1890.

1425 Collingwood (Robin George). An introduction to the prehistory of Cumberland, Westmorland and Lancashire north of the Sands. Trans. Cumb. & Westm. Ant. Soc., N.S. 33, pp. 163–200 + 5 maps. 1933.

1426 Collingwood (William Gershom). An inventory of the ancient monuments of Cumberland. Trans. Cumb. & Westm. Ant. Soc., N.S. 23, pp. 206–76. 1923.

1427 —— An inventory of the ancient monuments of Westmorland and Lancashire-north-of-the-Sands. Trans. Cumb. & Westm. Ant. Soc., N.S. 26, pp. 1–62. 1926.

1428(a) Colls (J. M. N.). Some early remains discovered [on Rombalds moor and Baildon common] in Yorkshire. Archaeologia, 31, pp. 299–307 + plate + map. 1846.

1428(b) Cotsworth (M. B.). Preglacial man in Yorkshire. Yorks. N. & Q. (ed. Forshaw), 3, p. 55. 1906.

1429 Collyer (Robert) *and* **Turner** (Joseph Horsfall). Ilkley: ancient and modern. pp. 283, xcvi. 8⁰. Otley, 1885.

1430 Cowper (Henry Swainson). Some prehistoric remains in North Lonsdale [Lancs.]. Trans. Cumb. & Westm. Ant. Soc., 9, pp. 200–05 + map; pp. 497–504 + plate + 2 plans. 1888.

1431 —— The ancient settlements, cemeteries, and earthworks of Furness. [13 plans.] Archaeologia, 53, pp. 389–426 + map. 1893.

1435 Curwen (Eliot). Ancient cultivations at Grassington, Yorkshire. Antiquity, 2, pp. 168–72. 1928.

1436 Davies (J.). Some recent prehistoric finds of Lake District origin from the Yorkshire Pennines [2 figures]. Trans. C.& W.A. & A.S., N.S. 63, 1963, 53–60.

1437 Davis (James W.). Pre-Roman Yorkshire. Old Yorkshire, ed. William Smith, N.S. 1, pp. 247–57. 1889.

1438 Dawkins (*Sir* William Boyd). Lancashire and Cheshire in pre-historic times. Trans. Lancs. & Ches. Ant. Soc., 2 (1884), pp. 1–7. 1885.

1439 —— Opening address of the Antiquarian section [of the Royal Archaeological Institute] at the Scarborough meeting. Archaeol. J., 52, pp. 336–47. 1895.

1440 Dobson (John). Two reports dealing with finds of prehistoric remains in the Furness district. *North Lonsdale Field Club.* pp. 24 + 2 plates. 8º. Ulverston, 1923.

1441 Dodds (Madeleine Hope). The parishes of Ovingham, Stamfordham and Ponteland. [Pp. 8–15 + 4 plates, Prehistoric period.] Hist. Nhb., 12, pp. xix, 611 + 26 plates. 1926.

1442 —— The parishes of Heddon-on-the-Wall, Newburn, Long Benton and Wallsend, *etc.* Hist. Nhb., 13, pp. xvi, 593 + 26 plates. 1930.

1443 —— The parishes of Alnham, Chalton, *etc.* [Pp. 21–67 + 3 plates + 2 maps, Prehistoric section with schedule.] Hist. Nhb., 14, pp. xviii, 615 + 21 plates + 3 maps. 1935.

1444 —— The parish[es] of Simonburn, Rothbury, Alwinton. [Pp. 17–62 + 5 plates + 2 maps, Prehistoric section with schedule.] Hist. Nhb., 15, pp. xxiii, 526 + 58 plates and maps. 1940.

1445 Dudley (Harold Edgar). The history and antiquities of the Scunthorpe & Frodingham district. pp. xvi, 247 + plates. 8º. Scunthorpe, 1931. [64 figures.]

1446 Eccleston (J.). Ancient remains at Lacra and Kirksanton. Trans. Cumb. & Westm. Ant. Soc., 1, pp. 278–81 + plate + map. 1874.

1447 Eden (*Sir* Timothy). Durham. *County Books series.* 2 vol. 8º. London, 1952.

1448 Edwards (William). The early history of the North Riding. pp. xvi, 267 + 37 plates + map. 4º. London, 1924.

1449 Elgee (Frank). Early man in north-east Yorkshire. pp. xvi, 259 + 29 plates. 4º. Gloucester, 1930. [67 figures and maps. Pp. 1–193, Prehistory; pp. 237–45, bibliography.]

1450 —— Prehistoric archaeology in Yorkshire, 1906–1931. Brit. Ass. Rpt., 1932, Appendix, pp. 40–51. 1932.

1451 —— *and* **Elgee** (Harriet Wragg). The archaeology of Yorkshire. *County Archaeologies.* Pp. xv, 272 + 12 plates + 2 maps. 8º. London, 1933. [Pp. 1–120, Prehistory.]

1452 Ellis (Colin Dare Bernard). History in Leicester, 55 B.C.–A.D. 1500. pp. 138. 8º. Leicester, 1948.

1453 Fair (Mary Cicely). The Neolithic occupation of the west and south Cumberland corn belt. Trans. Cumb. & Westm. Ant. Soc., N.S. 32, p. 183. 1932.

1454 —— The Prehistory of West Cumberland from Solway Firth to Duddon Estuary. Proc. Prehist. Soc., N.S. 1, 1935, 149–50 + 1 plate.

1455 —— The Gosforth area in prehistory. A co-ordination of recorded finds to 1942. Trans. Cumb. & Westm. Ant. Soc., N.S. 43, pp. 50–54 + plate. 1943.

1456 Fell (Clare Isobel) *and* **Hildyard** (Edward John Westgarth). Prehistoric Weardale—a new Survey. (More flints from Weardale—a postscript.) [7 figures (flints).] Arch. Æl., 4th S. 31, pp. 98–115 + map; 34, pp. 131–37. 1953–56.

1457 —— The Beaker period in Cumberland, Westmorland, and Lancashire north-of-the-sands. [Map.] Early cultures of N.W. Europe (H. M. Chadwick mem. stud.) ed. *Sir* C. Fox and Bruce Dickins, pp. 41–50 + 2 plates. 1958.

1458 Ferguson (Richard Saul). Report on the archaeology of [Cumberland], and especially on the prehistoric remains. Proc. Soc. Antiq., 2 S. 8, pp. 490–94. 1881.

1459 —— Report on ancient monuments in Cumberland and Westmorland. Trans. Cumb. & Westm. Ant. Soc., 10, pp. 271–74. 1889.

1460 —— A history of Cumberland. *Popular County Histories.* pp. 312. 8⁰. London, 1890.

1461 —— An archaeological survey of Cumberland and Westmorland. And of Lancashire north-of-the-sands, by H. Swainson Cowper. [By place, with references.] Archaeologia, 53, pp. 485–531, 531–38 + map. 1893.

1462 —— A history of Westmorland. *Popular County Histories.* pp. viii, 312. 8⁰. London, 1894. [Pp. 8–20, The early inhabitants.]

1463 —— Early man [in Cumberland]. [3 plates + 2 maps + 4 plans.] V.C.H., Cumb., 1, pp. 225–52. 1901.

1464 Fishwick (Henry). A history of Lancashire. *Popular County Histories.* pp. vii, 305. 8⁰. London, 1894.

1465 Garstang (John). Early man [in Lancashire]. V.C.H., Lancs., 1, pp. 211–256 + 5 plates + map. 1906.

1466 Gibbs (G. Bennett). Neolithic man in county Durham. [Pp. 23–28, sites.] Ant. Sunderland, 19 (1929/32), pp. 13–28. 1939.

1467 Gill (Thomas). Vallis Eboracensis: comprising the history and antiquities of Easingwold and its neighbourhood. pp. 456 + 14 plates. 8⁰. London, 1852.

1468 Glossop (William). Ancient British remains on Baildon moor. Bradford Antiquary, 1, pp. 88–89 + plate. 1888.

1469 Greenwell (William). Early man [in County Durham]. [4 figures.] V.C.H., Durham, 1, pp. 199–209 + plate + map. 1905.

1470 Hadfield (C. N.). Charnwood Forest—a survey. Leicester, 1952, xvii + 104 pp.

1471 Hall (George Rome). An ancient British remains near Birtley and Barrasford, North Tyne. Arch. Æl., N. [2nd] S. 7, pp. 3–17 + 3 plates (12 camp plans) + map. 1876.

1472 —— On ancient remains, chiefly prehistoric, in Geltsdale, Cumberland. Trans. Cumb. & Westm. Ant. Soc., 6, pp. 456–80 + map. 1883.

1473 Hallam (J. S.). Distribution of Mesolithic sites in Lancashire and Yorkshire. Huddersfield Archaeol. Soc., Quart. Bull., 2, pp. 2–4. 1958.

1474 Hardwick (Charles). Ancient British remains at Over Darwen. Trans.

Hist. Soc. Lancs. & Ches. [18] N.S. 6, pp. 273–78 + plate (pottery). 1866.

1475 Hargrove (William). History and description of the ancient city of York. 2 vol. 8⁰. York, 1818.

1476 Harker (Bailey J.). Discovery of prehistoric remains at Grassington, in Craven, Yorkshire. Antiquary, 26, pp. 147–49. 1892.

1477 Harker (John). On further discoveries of British remains at Lancaster moor. J. Brit. Archaeol. Ass., 28, pp. 80–82. 1872.

1478 Hay (Thomas). Early settlements near the head of Ullswater. Trans. Cumb. & Westm. Ant. Soc., N.S. 36, pp. 71–75 + table. 1936.

1479 —— Our early settlements and their physiographic setting. [Lake District.] Trans. Cumb. & Westm. Ant. Soc., N.S. 40, pp. 136–40. 1940.

1480 —— Threlkerd settlement. Trans. Cumb. & Westm. Ant. Soc., N.S. 43, pp. 20–24. 1943.

1481 —— Buttermere settlements. Trans. Cumb. & Westm. Ant. Soc., N.S. 45, pp. 116–21. 1945.

1482 Heathcote (John Percy). Birchover. Its prehistoric and druidical remains. pp. 25, 8⁰. Winster [1927].

1483 —— Excavations on Stanton moor [1931–33]. [3 figures + 2 plans.] J. Derbs. Archaeol. Soc., 60 (N.S. 13), pp. 105–15 + plate. 1939.

1484 —— Excavations in Derbyshire during 1938. J. Derbs. Archaeol. Soc., 59 (N.S. 12, 1938), pp. 81–83. 1939.

1485 —— Scheduled ancient monuments. DAJ, 81, 1961, 136–37.

1486 —— Stanton Moor. Arch. J., 118, 1961, 216.

1487 —— Scheduled ancient monuments. DAJ, 83, 1963, 94–96.

1488 Hedley (Robert Cecil). Notes on a prehistoric camp and avenue of stones on Thockrington Quarry House farm. Arch. Æl., N. [2nd] S. 12, pp. 155–58 + plan. 1887.

1489 Hedley (William Percy). The three northern counties—prehistory. Headlam (*Sir* Cuthbert) *bart., ed.,* The three northern counties of England, pp. 62–66 + 2 plates. 1939.

1490 —— Prehistoric man in Northumberland. Vasculum, 12, pp. 42–46. 1926.

1491 Hodgson (Katherine S.). Some excavations in the Bewcastle district. Trans. Cumb. & Westm. Ant. Soc., N.S. 40, pp. 154–66 + 4 plates. 1940.

1492 Hogg (Alexander Hubert Arthur). Native settlements of Northumberland. Antiquity, 17, pp. 136–47. 1943.

1493 —— A new list of the native sites of Northumberland. Proc. Soc. Antiq. Newc., 4th S. 11, pp. 140–53. 1947.

1494 —— Doddington and Horton moors. Arch. Æl., 4th S. 34, pp. 142–49. 1956.

1495 Honeyman (Herbert Lewis). Northumberland. *County Books series.* pp. xii, 288 + map. 8⁰. London, 1949.

1496 Horwood (A. R.). Prehistoric Leicestershire. Dryden (A.): Memorials of old Leicestershire, pp. 46–68 + plate. 1911.

1497 Hughes (R. G.). Archaeological sites in the Trent Valley, South Derbyshire. DAJ, 81, 1961, 149–50 + 1 plate.

1498 Hutchinson (William). The history and antiquities of the county palatine of Durham. 3 vol. 4⁰. Newcastle, 1785–94.

1499 —— The history of Cumberland. 2 vol. 4⁰. Carlisle, 1794.

1500 Jackson (John Wilfrid). The prehistory of the Manchester region. Anc. Monuments Y.B. & Proc., 1934–5, pp. 48–53. 1935.

1501 —— Contributions to the archaeology of the Manchester region. [2 figures.] North Western Naturalist, pp. 110–19 + 2 plates. 1936.

1502 —— Contributions to the archaeology of the Buxton region. [3 figures.] North Western Naturalist, pp. 1–7. 1936.

1503 —— Some early references to prehistoric and Roman antiquities in Lancashire and Cheshire. Trans. Lancs. & Ches. Ant. Soc., 50 (1934–35), pp. 162–76. 1936.

1504 —— The prehistoric archaeology of Lancashire and Cheshire. Trans. Lancs. & Ches. Ant. Soc., 50 (1934–35), pp. 65–106. 1936.

1505 —— A review of the Neolithic and Bronze Ages of the Buxton district.

pp. 9. 8⁰. Buxton, 1941. [Reprinted from the Buxton Advertiser.]

1506 —— Stone Age relics from the Hartington district. J. Derbs. Archaeol. Soc., 72 (N.S. 25), pp. 120–24. 1952.

1507 Jobey (George). A Note on scooped enclosures in Northumberland. Arch. Æliana, 40, 1962, 47–58 + 7 figures.

1508 —— Additional rectilinear settlements in Northumberland. Arch. Æliana, 41, 1963, 211–15 + 3 figures.

1509 —— Enclosed stone built settlements in North Northumberland. Arch. Æliana, 42, 1964, 41–64 + 10 figures.

1510 —— Hill Forts and settlements in Northumberland. Arch. Æliana, 43, 1965, 21–64 + 18 figures.

1511 Jones (Glanville R.). Basic patterns of settlement distribution in northern England. [4 maps.] Adv. of Sci., 18, pp. 192–200. 1961.

1512 Jopling (Charles M.). Remains ascribed to the era of the Druids in Furness, north of Lancashire. [3 figures + map + plan.] Archaeologia, 31, pp. 448–453 + 3 plates (with plans). 1846.

1513 Kirke (Henry). On some ancient British and Anglo-Saxon names of places, *etc.*, existing at the present day in the Peak of Derbyshire. Reliquary, 6, pp. 59–63. 1866.

1514 Lawrence (C. F.). A prehistoric Cheshire town. Cheshire N. & Q., 3 S. 9, pp. 25–28. 1912.

1515 Leigh (Charles). The natural history of Lancashire, Cheshire, and the Peak in Derbyshire; with an account of the British, Phoenician, Armenian, Greek and Roman antiquities in those parts. 3 pts. fol. Oxford, 1700.

1516 Lewis (A. L.). On the past and present condition of certain rude stone monuments in Westmorland. J. Anthrop. Inst., 15, pp. 165–70. 1885.

1517(a) Longbotham (A. T.). Prehistoric remains in Barkisland. Trans. Halifax Antiq. Soc., 1932, pp. 153–82 + 7 plates.

1517(b) Lowndes (R. A. C.). "Celtic" fields, farmsteads, and burial-mounds in the Lune Valley [3 figures (which are pull-out maps)]. Trans. C. & W.A. & A.S., N.S. 63, 1963, 77–95.

1518 Lukis (William Collings). On the flint implements and tumuli of the neighbourhood of Wath, near Ripon, Yorks. pp. 11 + 3 plates. 8⁰. n.p., 1865.

1519 —— On the flint implements and tumuli of the neighbourhood of Wath. Yorks. Arch. J., 1, pp. 116–26 + 5 plates + map. 1870.

1520 Mackenzie (E.). An historical, topographical and descriptive view of Northumberland, *etc.* Second edition, enlarged. 2 vol. 4⁰. Newcastle upon Tyne, 1825.

1521 Manby (T. G.). Some Mesolithic sites in the Peak District and Trent Basin. DAJ, 83, 1963, 10–23 + 3 figures.

1522 March (Henry Colley). The Neolithic men of Lancashire and those of Brittany considered and compared. Trans. Lancs. & Ches. Ant. Soc., 2 (1884), pp. 8–20 + 2 plates. 1885.

1523 Mitchelson (N.). The Bronze Age in Cleveland. Arch. News Letter, 4, pp. 127–28. 1952.

1524 Monkman (C.). On discoveries in recent deposits in Yorkshire. J. Ethnolog. Soc., N.S. 2, pp. 157–69 + 2 plates. 1870.

1525 Moore (John W.). Mesolithic sites in the neighbourhood of Flixton, North-east Yorkshire. Proc. prehist. Soc., 16, 1950, 101–08 + 4 figures + 1 plate.

1526 Mortimer (John Robert). An ancient British settlement, consisting of a double row of pits on Danby North moor, Yorkshire. [Map + plan.] Archaeol. J., 55, pp. 155–65. 1898.

1527 Newton (Charles). Map of British and Roman Yorkshire. Drawn and engraved by W. Hughes. 23½″ × 29″, London, 1847. [Scale, 5 inches = 20 miles.]

1528 Oliver (George). The history and antiquities of . . . Beverley, *etc.* pp. xxiii, 575. 4⁰. Beverley, 1829.

1529 Pennington (Rooke). Notes on some tumuli and stone circles near Castleton, Derbyshire. J. Anthrop. Inst., 4, pp. 377–86 + plan. 1875.

1530 —— Notes on the barrows and bone-caves of Derbyshire. With an account of a descent into Elden hole. 8⁰. London, 1877.

1531 Petch (James Alexander). Early man in the district of Huddersfield: with an appendix on the nature of graving

tools, by Francis Buckley. *Tolson Memorial Museum Publications, Handbook 3.* pp. 95. 8⁰. Huddersfield, 1924. [45 figures.]

1532 Phené (John Samuel). The early occupants in the vicinity of the Mersey, Morcambe bay, and Manchester. J. Brit. Archaeol. Ass., N.S. 1, pp. 1–10. 1895.

1533 Picton (*Sir* James Allanson). Prehistoric remains in Lancashire. Arch. Camb., 3rd S., 14, pp. 206–08. 1868.

1534 Posnansky (Merrick). Note on the presence of prehistoric field systems in Derbyshire. J. Derbs. Archaeol. Soc., 76, p. 71. 1956.

1535 Powell (T. G. E.). Notes on two Bronze Age discoveries in Leicestershire. Trans. Leic. Arch. Soc., 25, pp. 51–55. 1949.

1536 Preston (Henry). Prehistoric relics at Stamford. [1000–500 B.C.] Rutland Mag. 12, pp. 191–92. 1906.

1537 —— Flint work-sites in northeast Durham. [2 figures.] Vasculum, 15, pp. 137–41. 1929.

1538 —— Microlithic and other industries of the Wear valley. [Figure.] Proc. Soc. Antiq. Newc., 4th S. 6, pp. 109–16. 1933.

1539 Radley (Jeffrey). Recent prehistoric finds in the Peak District. DAJ, 83, 1963, 96–100 + 1 figure.

1540 —— *and* **Marshall** (Geoffrey). Mesolithic sites in South-west Yorkshire. Yorkshire Arch. Journ. 41 (i), 1963, 81–97 + 7 figures.

1541 —— *and* ——. Maglemosian sites in the Pennines. Yorks. Arch. Journ. 41 (iii), 1965, 394–402 + 3 figures.

1542 Raistrick (Arthur). The Bronze Age in West Yorkshire. Yorks. Archaeol. J., 29, pp. 554–65 + 9 plates + 2 maps. 1929.

1543 —— *and* **Chapman** (S. E.). The Lynchet groups of upper Wharfedale, Yorkshire. [Figure + 3 maps + 2 plans.] Antiquity, 3, pp. 165–81 + 5 plates. 1929.

1544 —— Bronze Age settlement of the north of England. Arch. Æl., 4th S. 8, pp. 149–65 + 3 maps. 1931.

1545 —— *and* **Westoll** (T. S.). A prehistoric site [near the mouth of Crimden Beach] on the south Durham coast.

[Figure.] Vasculum, 19, pp. 139–44. 1933.

1546 —— Prehistoric invasions of Northumberland and Durham. Trans. Northern Naturalists' Union 1 iii, 1934, 187–99 + 4 figures.

1547 —— Iron-Age settlements in West Yorkshire. [7 figures + map.] Yorks. Archaeol. J., 34, pp. 115–50. 1939.

1548 Rawnsley (Hardwick Drummond). Prehistoric man at Bristowe hill, Crosthwaite. [Neolithic.] Trans. Cumb. & Westm. Ant. Soc., N.S. 4, pp. 254–56 + plate. 1904.

1549 Roeder (Charles). Prehistoric glimpses of Eddisbury hundred (Cheshire). [Figure + 3 plans.] Trans. Lancs. & Ches. Ant. Soc., 24 (1906). pp. 113–25 + 2 plates. 1907.

1550 —— Kersal moor [Lancs.] and Kersal cell: a sketch from Neolithic days to present times. Trans. Lancs. & Ches. Ant. Soc., 25 (1907), pp. 81–94 + 2 plates. 1908.

1551 Rooke (Hayman). A further account of some druidical remains in Derbyshire. Archaeologia, 7, pp. 175–78 + 2 plates. 1785.

1552 —— Druidical and other British remains in Cumberland. Archaeologia, 10, pp. 105–13 + plate + 2 plans. 1792.

1553 —— An account of some druidical remains in Derbyshire. Archaeologia, 12, pp. 41–49 + 4 plates. 1799.

1554 Rowe (Joseph Hambley). Vestiges of the Celts in the West Riding. Bradford Antiquary, [4] N.S. 2, pp. 324–51. 1905.

1555(a) —— Prehistoric vestiges. British Medical Association, 92nd meeting, Bradford, July 1924. pp. 1–8. 1924.

1555(b) Rowntree (Arthur), *Editor.* The History of Scarborough. pp. xx, 456. London and Toronto. 8°. 1931.

1556 S. (J.). The founder of the city of Leicester, king Leir (Anno mundi) 3105. Leic. & Rutland N. & Q., 1, pp. 5–9. 1889.

1557 Sainter (J. D.). A few words upon Comb's Moss, and some of the prehistoric remains thereon, and in its neighbourhood. Reliquary, 23, pp, 241–44. 1883.

1558(a) Saull (William Devonshire). On the earlier British villages or loca-

tions, particularly in reference to one on the moor near Sealing & Yorkshire. [Plan.] Trans. Brit. Archaeol. Ass., 3, Congress at Gloucester, 1846, pp. 152–59. 1848.

1558(b) Sheaham (James Joseph). History and topography of the city of York and the North Riding of Yorkshire. Beverley, 1857–71. 3 vols. 8°.

1559 Sheppard (Thomas). Pre-historic man in Holderness. [Figure.] Assoc. Archit. Socs'. Rpts., 25, pp. 231–249 + plate + plan (Skipsea earthworks). 1899.

1560 —— Prehistoric man in Holderness. [2 figures.] Antiquary, 36, pp. 38–44, 80–87. 1900.

1561 —— Notes on the antiquities of Brough, East Yorkshire. [5 figures.] Antiquary, 38, pp. 80–83, 103–07. 1902.

1562 —— Pre-historic man in East Yorkshire. Yorks. N. & Q. (ed. Forshaw), 2, p. 343. 1906.

1563 —— Yorkshire lake dwellings. Yorks. N. & Q. (ed. Forshaw), 3, pp. 99–102. 1906.

1564 —— Notes on the more important archaeological discoveries in East Yorkshire. Trans. E. Riding Antiq. Soc., 14, pp. 45–66. 1907.

1565 —— Prehistoric remains in East Yorkshire. [8 figures.] Sheppard (T.): Handbook to Hull (Brit. Ass. 1922), pp. 185–200. 1922.

1566 —— Prehistoric Bridlington. [5 figures.] Hist. Teachers' Miscellany, 1, pp. 136–44. 1923.

1567 —— Iron-Age relics from East Yorkshire. Yorks. Archaeol. J., 31, pp. 132–36 + 2 plates. 1934.

1568 —— The natural history of Goathland dale & Archaeology. North Western Naturalist, 1, pp. 308–19. 1941.

1569 Shrubsole (George W.). On a settlement of prehistoric people in Delamere forest. J. Chester Arch. Soc., N.S. 4, pp. 96–112. 1892.

1570 —— List of [8] prehistoric remains found in Cheshire. J. Chester Arch. Soc., N.S. 4, p. 190. 1892.

1571 Simpson (Henry Trail). Archaeologia Adelensis, or a history of the parish of Adel, *etc.* pp. xii, 297. 8°. London, 1879.

1572 Simpson (Robert). The history

and antiquities of the town of Lancaster. pp. xv, 376. 8º. Lancaster, 1852.

1573 Smith, A. H. The Place names of the West Riding of Yorkshire. Cambridge, 1963. pp. 207.

1574 Smith (Reginald Allender). Pre-Roman remains at Scarborough. [58 figures.] Archaeologia, 77, pp. 179–200 + 2 plates. 1928.

1575 Speight (Ernest E.). Prehistoric remains in upper Wharfedale. Antiquary 27, pp. 121–23. 1893.

1576 —— Recent exploration in upper Wharfedale. Antiquary, 28, pp. 98–100. 1893.

1577 —— Prehistoric Craven. The work of excavation in upper Wharfedale. Bradford Antiquary, N.S. 1, pp. 134–36. 1900.

1578 Spence (Joseph E.). Ancient enclosures on Town Bank, Kinniside. Trans. Cumb. & Westm. Ant. Soc., N.S. 38, pp. 63–70 + 3 plans. 1938.

1579 Spencer (Allan). Preliminary report on archaeological investigations near Radcliffe, Lancashire. Trans. Lancs. & Ches. Ant. Soc., 62 (1950–51), pp. 196–203 + 2 plates (implements). 1953.

1580 Stead (C. M.). The La Tène Cultures of Eastern Yorkshire. York, 1965, 135 pp. + 38 figures.

1581 Strange (Patrick). Scheduled ancient monuments in Derbyshire. DAJ 86, 1966, 92–93.

1582 Sylvester (Dorothy). Whence came Cheshire folk? Cheshire Historian 10, 1960, 15–20.

1583 Tate (George). The antiquities of Yevering Bell and Three Stone burn, among the Cheviots in Northumberland, with an account of excavations made into Celtic forts, hut dwellings, barrows and stone circle. [Plan (stone circle).] Hist. Berwick. Nat. Club, 4, pp. 431–53 + plate + plan. 1862.

1584 —— On Celtic remains found in the neighbourhood of Wooler. Hist. Berwick. N.C., 3, pp. 154–55. 1853.

1585 Taylor (M. Waistell). The prehistoric remains at Moordivock, near Ullswater. Trans. Cumb. & Westm. Ant. Soc., 8, pp. 323–47 + plate + 5 plans. 1886.

1586 Thomas (F.). "Celtic Fields" at Blackwell, Taddington. DAJ 81, 1961, 147–48 + 1 figure + 1 plate.

1587 —— Ancient field boundaries at Blackwell, near Taddington. DAJ 83, 1963, 106–108 + 2 figures.

1588 Thornber (William). Traces on the British, Saxons, and Danes in the Foreland of the Fylde. Hist. Soc. Lancs. & Ches., Proc., 4, pp. 100–18. 1852.

1589 Timperley (W. A.). Discoveries at Oakes Park, Norton, Derbyshire. J. Derbs. Archaeol. Soc., 71 (N.S. 24), pp. 70–71: 72 (N.S. 25), pp. 48–64 + plate. 1951–52.

1590 Tomlinson (John). The level of Hatfield Chase and parts adjacent. pp. 322 + map. 4º. Doncaster, 1882.

1591 Trechmann (C. T.). Notes on Neolithic chipping-sites in Northumberland and Durham. Trans. nat. Hist. Soc., N. & D. New Series 6, 1909–13, 67–85 + 4 plates.

1592 Tucker (W. Trueman). On some supposed British remains from Rothley, Leicestershire. pp. 15 + 4 plates. 8º. Loughborough, 1896.

1593 Tudor (Thomas Linthwaite). List of ancient monuments in Derbyshire scheduled by H. M. Commissioners of Works. (Monuments scheduled in 1933, *and subsequent years.*) J. Derbs. Archaeol. Soc., 53 (N.S. 6, 1932), pp. 100–02, 54, pp. 19–21, *etc.* 1933, *etc.*

1594 Varley (William James). Early man in the Cheshire plain. J. Chester & N. Wales Arch. Soc., N.S. 29, pp. 50–65. 1932.

1595 —— Prehistoric Cheshire. pp. 116 + 8 plates + 6 maps + table. 8º. Chester, 1940.

1596 Veitch (W. Y.). Prehistoric Middlesbrough. Cleveland N.F.C., Record of Proc., lii, pp. 5–12. 1899.

1597 Walker (John William). Wakefield, its history and people. pp. xvi, 728. 2nd edition, revised and enlarged. 8º. Wakefield, 1939.

1598 Wallis (Alfred). On some prehistoric remains near Sheffield, beyond the Derbyshire border. J. Brit. Archaeol. Ass., 30, pp. 61–66. 1874.

1599 Wallis (John). The natural history and antiquities of Northumberland, *etc.* 2 vol. 4º. London, 1769.

1600 Ward (J. Clifton). On some archaeological remains in Keswick district. [Palaeolithic—Iron Age.] Trans. Cumb. & Westm. Ant. Soc., 1, pp. 215–221. 1874.

1601 —— Notes on archaeological remains in the Lake District. [5 plans.] Trans. Cumb. & Westm. Antiq. Soc., 3, pp. 241–65. 1878.

1602 Ward (John). Recent diggings at Harborough docks, Derbyshire. [17 figures.] Reliquary, N.S. 3, pp. 216–30 + 4 plates (skulls). 1889.

1603 —— Notes on the archaeology of Derbyshire. 8°. 1895. [Pp. 1–9, Prehistory. Reprinted from Bulmer's History and directory of Derbyshire.]

1604 —— A sketch of the archaeology of Derbyshire. [Pp. 4–15, Prehistory.] J. Brit. Archaeol. Ass., N.S. 6, pp. 1–25. 1900.

1605 —— Early man [in Derbyshire]. V.C.H., Derbs., 1, pp. 159–90 + map. 1905.

1606 —— Notes on some Derbyshire antiquities from Samuel Mitchell's memoranda. J. Derbs. Archaeol. Soc., 30, pp. 155–72. 1908.

1607 Wardell (James). British remains on Baildon common, Yorkshire. [Figures of urns, *etc.*] Bowman (William). Reliquiae Antiquae Eboracenses (Leeds), pp. 87–94. 1855.

1608 Watson (John). Druidical remains in or near the parish of Halifax in Yorkshire. Archaeologia, 2, pp. 353–63 + plate. 1773.

1609 —— The history and antiquities of the parish of Halifax in Yorkshire. pp. 394. 4°. London, 1775.

1610 Webster (Graham) *and* **Leach** (G. B.). The archaeologist in the field. Cheshire Historian, 1, pp. 19–30 + 3 plates. 1951.

1611 Wheeler (*Sir* Robert Eric Mortimer). Prehistoric Scarborough. (Appendix: The "linear earthworks" of the Scarborough district). Rowntree (Arthur) *ed.*: The history of Scarborough, pp. 9–39 + 8 plates. 1931.

1612 Whellan (T.). History and topography of the city of York; and the North Riding of Yorkshire. Compiled by James Joseph Sheahan. 3 vol. 8°. Beverley, 1857–71.

1613 Whitaker (Thomas Dunham). An history of the original parish of Whalley, and honor of Clitheroe, in the

counties of Lancaster and York. pp. v, 483, 14. 4°. Blackburn, 1801.

1614 Whiting (Charles Edwin). Excavations on Sutton common, [near Askern], 1933, 1934, 1935. Yorks. Archaeol. J., 33, pp. 57–80 + 6 plates. 1938.

1615 Widdrington (*Sir* Thomas). Analecta Eboracensia: or some remaynes of the ancient city of York. London, 1897. 4°. pp. xxxvi + 327 + 26 plates.

1616 Wildridge (Thomas Tindall), *Editor*. Northumbria: a repository of antiquities, Book I. London, 1888. pp. 140 + vii, illus.

1617 —— Lake-dwellings of Yorkshire. Bygone Yorkshire, *ed.* William Andrews, pp. 1–38. 1892.

1618 Wilkinson (*Sir* John Gardner). On some vestiges of the Britons near Hathersage. [7 figures.] Reliquary, 1, pp. 159–66 + 2 plates. 1861.

1619 Wilkinson (Thomas Turner). On the Druidical rock basins in the neighbourhood of Burnley. Trans. Hist. Soc. Lancs. & Ches., [17] N.S. 5, pp. 1–12 + 2 plates. 1865.

1620 Willmot, G. F. *and others* (*editors*). York: a survey 1959 [Pp. 198, 16 maps and figures]. York, British Association, 1959.

1621 —— The prehistory of the vale of York. [2 figures + 2 maps.] York, a survey, 1959. (Brit. Ass.), pp. 85–94. 1959.

1622 Wilson (G. H.). Cave hunting holidays in Peakland. pp. 93. 8°. Chesterfield, 195–? [30 figures.]

1623 Wood (Butler). Prehistoric antiquities of the Bradford district. pp. 11 + 4 plates + 3 maps. 8°. Bradford, 1902.

1624 —— Prehistoric antiquities of the Bradford district. Bradford Antiquary, [4] N.S. 2, pp. 113–123 + 4 plates + 2 maps. 1905.

1625 Wood (Eric S.). Some current problems of Yorkshire archaeology. Arch. News Letter, I iv, pp. 12–14. 1948.

1626 —— Notes on archaeology in Yorkshire, 1948–1950. Arch. News Letter, 3, pp. 96–99. 1950.

1627 Wright (Thomas). On the remains of a primitive people in the south-east corner of Yorkshire; with some remarks on the early ethnology of Britain. pp. 16 + 2 plates. 8°. [Leeds, 1884.]

1628 —— On the early history of
Leeds, in Yorkshire, and on some questions of prehistoric archaeology agitated
at the present time. A lecture read before
the philosophical and Literary Society of
Leeds, April 19th, 1864. pp. 30. [Pp. 4–
20, Prehistory.] 8°. Leeds, 1864.

(e) Zone 5 [CBA Group 2]

1629 Allen (John Romilly). The preservation of ancient monuments in
Wales. Cymmrodor, 11, pp. 1–14. 1890.

1630 [Anon.] Prehistoric remains,
Llanbedr, Merionethshire. [Figure + 2
plans.] Arch. Camb., 6th S. 12, pp. 227–
304 + plate. 1912.

1631 Anwyl (*Sir* Edward). The early
settlers of Brecon. [Neolithic.] Arch.
Camb., 6th S., 3, pp. 16–38. 1903.

1632 —— The early settlers of Carnarvonshire. Arch. Camb., 6th S. 4, pp.
197–212. 1904.

1633 —— The early settlers of Cardigan. Arch. Camb., 6th S. 6, pp. 93–120.
1906.

1634 —— The early settlers of Carmarthen. [Pp. 381–83, List of 63 prehistoric hearths.] Arch. Camb., 6th S. 7,
pp. 361–88. 1907.

1635 —— The early settlers of Anglesey. Arch. Camb., 6th S. 8, pp. 1–28,
121–48. 1908.

1636 —— The early settlers of Monmouthshire. [Figure.] Arch. Camb., 6th
S. 9, pp. 261–82. 1909.

1637 —— Early man in Wales. Proc.
Llandudno F.C., 3 (1908–09), pp. 61–66.
1910.

1638 —— Cardiganshire antiquities.
Antiquary, 47, pp. 60–64. 1911.

1640 Banks (Richard William). On
the prehistoric remains in the Edwy
valley, Radnorshire. Arch. Camb., 4th
S. 6, pp. 246–55 + plate + plan, pp. 291–
292, 383. 1875.

1641 Barnwell (Edward Lowry).
Primaeval Merioneth. Arch. Camb., 4th
S. 4, pp. 84–95 + 6 plates. 1873.

1642 —— Early remains in Carmarthenshire. Arch. Camb., 4th S. 8, pp. 81–
96 + 5 plates. 1877.

1643 Baynes (Edward Neil). The
megalithic remains of Anglesey. Trans.

Hon. Soc. Cymmr., 1910–11, pp. 3–91 +
37 plates + map + 2 plans. 1912.

1644 —— Prehistoric cooking-places
in Anglesey. pp. 14. [2 figures + 3
plans.] Anglesey Ant. Soc. Trans., [1],
Suppl. 1913.

1645 —— Prehistoric cooking-places
[at Penrhos Lligwy] in Anglesey. [2
figures + 3 plans.] Arch. Camb., 6th S.
13, pp. 201–14. 1913.

1646 —— Prehistoric man in Anglesey. Anglesey Ant. Soc. Trans., [2], pp.
1–18. 1914.

1647 —— The Bronze Age in Anglesey. Anglesey Ant. Soc. Trans., 1923,
pp. 21–31. 1923.

1648 —— Neolithic Anglesey. Anglesey Ant. Soc. Trans., 1926, pp. 20–23.
1926.

1649 Bowen (Emrys George). Cardiganshire in prehistoric times. Trans.
Cards. Ant. Soc., 11, pp. 12–20. 1936.

1650 —— *and* **Gresham** (C. A.). The
History of Merioneth, vol. 1 (Merioneth
Historical and Record Society). Dol-
gellau, 1967, pp. xiv, 298 + 110 figures
+ 12 plates.

1651(a) Bromwich, Rachel, *Editor*.
Trioedd yuys Prydein. The Welsh
triads. Cardiff. 1961. pp. cxliv, 555 + 2
plates. (Univ. of Wales Press.)

1651(b) Bund (John William Willis).
The true objects of Welsh archaeology.
Cymmrodor, 11, pp. 103–32. 1891.

1652(a) —— Early Cardiganshire.
Arch. Camb., 6th S. 5, pp. 1–37. 1905.

1652(b) Burgess (C. B.). The Bronze
Age in Radnorshire: a re-appraisal.
Trans. Radnors. Soc. 32, 1962, 7–24 + 6
figures.

1653 Buxton (Leonard Halford Dudley) *and* **Higham** (T. F.). Cave exploration in the Gower peninsula. Man, 29,
pp. 206–07. 1929.

1654 Cantrill (Thomas Crosbee) *and*
Jones (O. T.). Prehistoric cooking-
places in South Wales. Arch. Camb.,
6 S. 11, pp. 253–86. 1911.

1655 —— Flint chipping-floors in
south-west Pembrokeshire. [11 figures
+ map + 2 plans.] Arch. Camb., 6th S.
15, pp. 157–210, 337–38. 1915.

1656 Clinch (George). A preliminary
report on the antiquities of the Cader
Idris district. Liverpool Committee for
excavation and research in Wales and the

Marches, Ann. Rpt., 1 (1908), pp. 49–52. 1909.

1657 Crampton (C. B.) *and* **Webley** (D.). The Correlation of prehistoric settlement and soils in the Vale of Glamorgan. Bull. Board Celtic Studies 18 iv, 1960, 387–96 + 2 figures.

1658 —— *and* —— The Correlation of prehistoric settlement and soils: Gower and South Wales Coalfield. Bull. Board Celtic Studies 20 iii, 1963, 326–37 + 3 figures.

1659 Craster (O. E.). Ancient monuments of Anglesey. *Ministry of Works*. pp. 30 + 8 plates + map + plan (Holyhead mountain hut circles). 8°. London, 1953.

1660 Davies (A. Stanley). Bronze Age sites on the Plynlymon moorland. Bull. Board Celtic Studies, 7 1, pp. 29–30. 1934.

1661 —— Bronze Age finds from central Wales. Bull. Board Celtic Studies, 7, pp. 333–34. 1934.

1662 Davies (Ellis). Denbighshire antiquities. [Figure. Late Bronze Age horse trappings, from St. George, Abergele.] Arch. Camb., 80, p. 210. 1925.

1663 —— The prehistoric and Roman remains of Denbighshire. pp. xxiii, 426 + map. 8°. Cardiff, 1929.

1664 —— Prehistoric and Roman remains of Flintshire. Cardiff, 1929, pp. 426 + 146 figures. 2nd, 1949, pp. 464 + 183 figures + 3 maps.

1665 —— The prehistoric and Roman remains of Flintshire. With a short appendix. pp. xxvi, 464 + 3 maps. 8°. Cardiff, 1949.

1666 Dawkins (*Sir* William Boyd). The place of the Welsh in the history of Britain. Collns. rel. to Montgom., 23, pp. 241–60. 1889.

1667 —— Certain fixed points in the prehistory of Wales. Arch. Camb., 6th S. 12, pp. 61–108. 1912.

1668 Dunn (C. J.). Further archaeological discoveries in the Radnor Basin. Trans. Radnors. Soc. 35, 1965, 10–20 + 5 figures.

1669 Edwards (Griffith). History of the parish of Llangadfan. Collns. rel. to Montgom., 3, pp. 317–44. 1869.

1670 Evans (T. Zodwig). The people of Pembrokeshire. pp. 39. 8°. Tenby, 1920.

1671 Farrington (Richard). Snowdonia Druidica. 1769. (Unpublished ms. in National Library of Wales.)

1672 Fleure (Herbert John). Welsh archaeology and anthropology. Arch. Camb., 6th S. 13, pp. 153–58. 1913.

1673 —— Ancient Wales—Anthropological evidences. Trans. Hon. Soc. Cymmr., 1915–16, pp. 75–164 + 3 maps. 1917.

1674 —— An outline story of our neighbourhood. [Pp. 111–20, Pre-historic.] Aberystwyth Stud., 4, pp. 111–23. 1922.

1675 —— Problems of Welsh archaeology. Arch. Camb., 78, pp. 225–42. 1923.

1677 Foster (I. Ll.) *and* **Daniel** (Glyn), *Editors*. Prehistoric and Early Wales. 9¼ + 6¼, pp. 240, illustrated. 1965.

1678 Fox (*Lady* Aileen Mary). The Dual Colonisation of East Glamorgan in the Neolithic and Bronze Ages. Arch. Camb. 91 i, 1936, 100–117 + 3 figures.

1679 Fox (*Sir* Cyril). North Wales in prehistoric times: problems presented by some recent discoveries. Anglesey Ant. Soc. Trans., 1930, pp. 23–25. 1930.

1680 —— Excavations at pre-Roman and Roman sites in South Wales in 1930. Welsh housing and development year book, 1931, pp. 85–88. 1932.

1681 —— The Megalithic monuments of Gower—their relation to topography. Arch. Camb. 92 i, 1937, 159–61 + 1 figure.

1682 —— Life in Anglesey 2000 years ago. An Early Iron Age discovery. Antiquity, 18, pp. 95–97 + 2 plates. 1944.

1683 —— Field archaeology in South Wales, 1939–45: personal reflections and record. Bull. Bd. Celtic Stud., 12, pp. 52–56. 1946.

1684 Freeman (T. W.). The early settlement of Glamorgan. [3 maps.] Scot. Geog. Mag., 52, pp. 12–33 + 2 plates. 1936.

1685 Giraldus de Barri. The itinerary of Archbishop Baldwin through Wales . . . translated . . . with annotations . . . by Sir Richard Colt Hoare, *bart.* 2 vol. 4°. London, 1806.

1686 Griffiths (William Eric). The hut circles of North Wales. Proc. Llandudno F.C., 23, pp. 43–45. 1950.

1687 —— Early settlements in Caernarvonshire. Arch. Camb. 101 i, 1950, 38–71 + 2 plates + 9 figures.

1688 Grimes (William Francis). South Wales megaliths—survey. [List.] Bull. Bd. Celtic Stud., 6, pp. 88–89. 1931.

1689 —— The rude stone monuments of South Wales. Neath Ant. Soc., Trans., 2 S. 2, pp. 90–93. 1932.

1690 —— Prehistoric archaeology in Wales since 1925. Proc. PSEA, 7 i, 1932–1934, 82–106 + 7 figures + 5 plates.

1691 —— Contributions to a field archaeology of Pembrokeshire: I. The archaeology of Skomer Island [IA settlement, field-system, *etc.*]. Arch. Camb. 101 i, 1950, 1–20 + 5 figures + 5 plates.

1692 —— The prehistory of Wales, Second edition. *National Museum of Wales*. pp. xvii, 288 + 19 plates. 8⁰. Cardiff, 1951. [78 figures.]

1693 —— Prehistoric and Roman Pembrokeshire. Arch. J., 119, 1962, 310–11.

1694 H (E.). Ancient Arwystli, [Montgomeryshire]. Arch. Camb., 3rd S. 14, pp. 1–23 + 3 plans. 1868.

1695 Hancock (Thomas W.). Llanrhaiadr-yn-Mochnant; its . . . antiquities. Collns. rel. to Montgom., 4, pp. 201–48 + plate + 2 plans. 1871.

1696 Hemp (Wilfrid James). A list of mounds, cairns, and circles on the northern Flintshire plateau. Bull. Bd. Celtic Studies, 1, pp. 353–70. 1923.

1697 —— *and* **Gresham** (Colin A.). Hut-circles in north-west Wales. [Map + 5 plans.] Antiquity, 18, pp. 183–96. 1944.

1698 —— *and* **Gresham** (C.). Hut-circles in north-west Wales. Antiquity, 27, pp. 29–32. 1953.

1699 Hicks (Henry). Evidence of preglacial man in North Wales. Advm. Sci. 1886, 839.

1700 Higgins (Leonard S.). An Investigation into the problem of the sand dune areas on the South Coast of Wales. Arch. Camb., 88 i, 1933, 26–67 + 6 figures.

1701 Hogg (Alexander Hubert Arthur). Gwynedd and the Votadini. Antiquity, 19, pp. 80–84. 1945.

1702 Howse (William Henry). Radnorshire. pp. 347 + 18 plates + map.

[Pp. 23–27, Prehistoric.] 8⁰. Hereford, 1949.

1703 —— Scheduled ancient monuments in Radnorshire. Radnorshire Soc., Trans., 24, pp. 20–25. 1954.

1704 Hughes (Henry Harold) *and* **Lowe** (W. Bezant). Dinas Llanfairfechan. Excavations by the Colwyn Bay and district field club. [12 figures + map + 2 plans.] Arch. Camb., 80, pp. 342–64. 1925.

1705 —— Caer-y-Twr and the hut-circles at Ty Mawr on Holyhead mountain. Proc. Llandudno F.C., 12 (1925–1926), pp. 10–13. 1926.

1706 Hughes (Ieuan T.). The background of Llandysul. Ceredigion, 3, pp. 101–13. 1957.

1707 Jarrett, Michael G. Early Roman campaigns in Wales [Mention of Bronze Hoard including native objects]. Arch. J., 121, 1964, 23–39.

1708 Jerman (H. Noel). Recent finds on the Kerry hills, Montgomeryshire. Bull. Bd. Celtic Stud., 6, pp. 381–82. 1933.

1709 —— The Bronze Age in Montgomeryshire. A suggested interpretation of the data. Collns. rel. to Montgom., 44, pp. 57–76 + map. 1935.

1710 —— The Bronze Age in Radnorshire. [Figure + map.] Radnorshire Soc., Trans., 6, pp. 33–48; 8, pp. 38–46. 1936–38.

1711 Jones (Basil Evan). The ancient monuments of Radnorshire. The Royal Commission's inventory. Collns. rel. to Montgom., 37, pp. 157–80. 1915.

1712 Jones (Harry Longueville). List of the prehistoric (early British) remains in Wales, arranged according to counties. [*See also* 3rd S. 1, pp. 214–16 (notes).] Arch. Camb., N.S. 5, pp. 81–87, 203–07; 3rd S. 1, pp. 18–27, 110–14, 175–81, 262–270; 3rd S. 2, pp. 81–90, 193–98. 1854–55.

1713 —— On the study of Welsh antiquities. Arch. Camb., 3rd S. 14, pp. 78–86, 187–93. 1869.

1714 Jones (Morgan Hugh). Carmarthenshire in the Bronze and Iron Age. Trans. Carmarthenshire Ant. Soc., 16, pp. 20–23 + 2 plates. 1922.

1715 Jones (O. T.). The blue stones of the Cardigan district. Antiquity, 30, pp. 34–36. 1956.

1716 Jones (T. Simpson) *and* **Owen**

(Robert). A history of the parish of Guilsfield (Cegidva). [2 plans.] Collns. rel. to Montgom., 31, pp. 129–200. 1900.

1717 Jones (Theophilus). A history of the county of Brecknock. 2 vols. 4°. Brecknock, 1805–09.

1718 Lacaille (A. D.) *and* **Grimes** (William Francis). The Prehistory of Caldey. Arch. Camb., 104, 1955, 85–165 + 15 figures + 16 plates.

1719 —— *and* —— The Prehistory of Caldey. Arch. Camb., 110, 1961, 30–70 + 12 figures.

1720 Leach (Arthur). Prehistoric cooking-places on the Pembrokeshire and Carmarthenshire coasts. [Figure.] Arch. Camb., 6 S. 11, pp. 433–36. 1911.

1721 Lewis (A. L.). On some rude stone monuments in North Wales. [Figure.] J. Anthrop. Inst., 7, pp. 118–123. 1878.

1722 Lines (H. H.). Ancient remains around Conway: Dwygyfylchi, Meini Hition, Maen y Campian, *etc*. Antiquary, 24, pp. 150–55. 1891.

1723 Llangattock Local History Society, Llangattock Parish Scrap-book. Brycheiniog, 7, 1961, 118–57 + 1 map.

1724 Lloyd (*Sir* John Edward). A history of Wales. Second edition. 2 vols. 8°. London, 1912.

1725 —— A history of Carmarthenshire. 2 vol. fol. Cardiff, 1935–39.

1726 Llwyd (Angharad). A History of the Island of Mona, or Anglesey. Ruthin 1833, pp. 413.

1727 Lowe (W. Bezant). Prehistoric remains on the uplands of north Carnarvonshire. [15 figures + 3 maps + 4 plans.] Arch. Camb., 6th S. 12, pp. 39–60, 199–210. 1912.

1728 —— The prehistoric remains of the Penmaenmawr uplands. [9 figures + map + 2 plans.] Anglesey Ant. Soc. Trans., [1], pp. 7–21. 1913.

1729 —— Prehistoric remains in north Carnarvonshire. [9 figures + 4 maps + 3 plans.] Arch. Camb., 79, pp. 80–112. 1924.

1730 —— Some recent discoveries of prehistoric remains in the uplands of north Carnarvonshire. [11 figures + 4 maps + 3 plans.] Proc. Llandudno F.C., 10 (1923–24), pp. 19–47. 1925.

1731 —— Notes on the position and distribution of hut-circles, *etc*., in north

Carnarvonshire. [4 figures.] Proc. Llandudno F.C., 10 (1923–24), pp. 52–58. 1925.

1732 —— Hut circles and various enclosures on the south-eastern slopes of Moel Faban, near Bethesda. [Plan.] Proc. Llandudno F.C., 10 (1923–24), pp. 48–51. 1925.

1733 —— Hut circles and various enclosures on the south-eastern slopes of Moel Faban, near Bethesda. Proc. Llandudno F.C., 12 (1925–26), pp. 6–10. 1926.

1734 Lowe (Walter Bezant). The heart of northern Wales as it was and as it is, being an account of the prehistorical and historical remains of Aberconway and the neighbourhood. 2 vol. 8°. Llanfairfechan, 1912, 1927. [Vol. 1, pp. 12–122 + 99 figures; vol. 2, pp. 4–131 + 82 figures, Prehistory.]

1736 Mathias (A. G. O.). South Pembrokeshire early settlements. Arch. Cambrensis, 82 i, 1927, 188–95 + 4 figures.

1737(a) Meyrick (Samuel Rush). The history and antiquities of the county of Cardigan. pp. xix, cclxxviii, 538 + 20 plates. 4°. London, 1810.

1737(b) Oakeley (Mary Ellen Bagnall) *and* **Oakeley** (William Bagnall). An account of some of the rude stone monuments and burial mounds in Monmouthshire. *Monmouthshire and Caerleon Antiquarian Association*. pp. 22 + 9 plates. 4°. Newport, 1889.

1738 Owen (D. E.). Notes on antiquities in the parish of Llanelwedd. Radnorshire Soc. Trans., 18, pp. 3–20. 1948.

1739 Owen (Edward). Ancient British camps, *etc*., in Lleyn, co. Carnarvon. Transcribed from the British Museum Additional MSS. no. 28,860. [Written by J. G. Williams of Pwllheli in 1871.] Arch. Camb., 6th S. 3, pp. 251–62. 1903.

1740 Owen (Elias). Arvona antiqua —Ancient remains, Hufottai, *etc*. Arch. Camb., 3rd S. 13, pp. 102–08– + map. 1867.

1741 —— On the circular huts, sometimes called Cyttiau'r Gwyddelod, and their inhabitants. Cymmrodor, 9, pp. 120–40, 334–48 + 2 plans. 1888.

1742 —— The abodes of Neolithic man in North Wales. Trans. Hist. Soc.

Lancs. & Ches., 45, pp. 81–98 + plate + 4 plans. 1894.

1743 Peake (Harold John Edward). The Bronze Age in Wales. Aberystwyth Stud., 4, pp. 13–18. 1922.

1744 Prichard (Hugh). Mona antiqua. Arch. Camb., 4th S. 2, pp. 300–12 + 2 plans. 1871.

1745 Pughe (William Owen). Antiquities of northern Pembrokeshire. Arch. Camb., 3rd S. 1, pp. 271–74 + plate. 1855.

1746 Randall, H. J. The Vale of Glamorgan, Newport (Mon.), 1961, pp. 109, 12 plates + 8 maps + text figures.

1747 Roberts (C. F.). Presidential Address to the Cambrian Archaeological Association. Arch. Camb., 90 ii, 1935, 175–188.

1748 Roberts (J.). Druidical remains and antiquities of the ancient Britons, principally in Glamorgan, *etc*. 8°. Swansea, 1842.

1749 Robinson (George E.). Hutdwellings [at Craig Rhiwarth] in Montgomeryshire. Arch. Camb., 4th S. 11, pp. 25–30 + 2 plates. 1880.

1750 Roderick, A. J., *Editor*. Wales through the ages: Vol. 1, from the earliest times to 1485. [Pp. 200 + 12 plates + 3 maps.] Llandybie, Carmarthenshire: Christopher Davies 1959.

1751 Rowlands (Henry). Mona antiqua restaurata. An archaeological discourse on the antiquities of . . . Anglesey, the ancient seat of the British druids. pp. viii, 383. 4°. Dublin, 1723.

1752 Royal Commission on Ancient & Historical Monuments in Wales and Monmouthshire. An inventory of the historical monuments in Anglesey. pp. clxxxix, 189 + 184 plates. 4°. London, 1937.

1753 —— An Inventory of the Ancient monuments in Caernarvonshire. Vol. 1: East. [Pp. lxxviii + 215, 188 text figures + 100 plates.] London, H.M.S.O., 1956.

1754 —— An Inventory of the ancient monuments in Caernarvonshire. Vol. 11: Central. [Pp. 287, 194 text figures + 82 plates.] London, H.M.S.O., 1960.

1755 —— An Inventory of the ancient monuments in Caernarvonshire. Vol. 111: West, the Cantref of Lleyn. London, 1964. pp. 367 + 68 plates.

1756 Rutter (J. G.). Prehistoric Gower: the early archaeology of West Glamorgan. pp. 90 + 14 plates. 8°. Swansea, 1948.

1757 Sansbury (Arthur R.) *and* **Davies** (D. Ernest). Recent [prehistoric] finds in Cardiganshire. [3 figures.] Cards. Antiq. Soc. Trans., 7, pp. 72–74; 9, pp. 32–35 + plate. 1930, 1933.

1758 Savory (Hubert Newman). Archaeology in Wales, 1946–1948. Arch. News Letter, 1 ix, pp. 5–6; 1 x, pp. 8–9. 1949.

1759 —— Discoveries on Merthyr Mawr warren (Glam.). Bull. Bd. Celtic Stud., 14, pp. 170–71 + plate. 1951.

1760 —— Early Iron Age discoveries on Merthyr Mawr warren (Glam.). Bull. Bd. Celtic Stud., 16, pp. 53–54. 1954.

1761 —— Prehistoric Brecknock. [Figure + 3 maps + 3 plans.] Brycheining, 1, pp. 79–125 + 8 plates. 1955.

1762 —— The Late Bronze Age in Wales: some new discoveries and new interpretations. Arch. Camb., 107, pp. 3–63 + 6 plates. 1958.

1763 —— The Late Bronze Age in Wales. Some new discoveries and new interpretations. Arch. Camb., 107, 1958, 3–63 + 17 figures + 5 plates.

1764 —— *and others* [T. W. Burke and G. C. Bacon]. Current work in Welsh archaeology. Bull. Board Celtic Studies, 19 ii, 1961, 163–92 + 5 figures + 4 plates.

1765 —— Current work in Welsh archaeology: excavations and discoveries [Barrows, spearhead, palstave]. Bull. Bd. Celtic Studies, 21 iv, 1966, 368–76 + 4 figures.

1766 Seward (Edwin). The formation of a record of prehistoric remains in Glamorganshire. Cardiff Nat. Soc. Rpt. & Trans., 23, pp. 21–25. 1891.

1767 Skinner (John). Ten days' tour through the Isle of Anglesey. pp. 89. Arch. Camb., 6th S. 8, supplement. 1908.

1768 Smith (F. Gilbert). Prehistoric remains at Bryn Newyold, Prestatyn. [2 figures.] Proc. Llandudno F.C., 13 (1926–27), pp. 62–72. 1927.

1769 Stanley (Hon. William Owen). Memoirs on remains of ancient dwellings in Holyhead island . . . Cyttiau'r Gwyddelod, explored in 1862 and 1863. 4 pts. 8°. London, 1871. 8°. London, 1876.

1770 —— [and **A. Way**]. Memoirs of remains of ancient dwellings in Holyhead Island, chiefly of circular form, called Cyttiau'r Gwyddelod, explored in 1862 and 1868. With notices of relics found in the recent excavations there, and also in various parts of Anglesey. 4 pts. 8°. London, 1876.

1771 Thomas (David Richard). Prehistoric and other remains in Cynwil Gaio [Glamorgan]. Arch. Camb., 4th S. 10, pp. 55–62 + 3 plates. 1879.

1772 Wareman (Thomas). Prehistoric remains in Monmouthshire. [Plan (Castell Penrose).] Arch. Camb., 3rd S. 1, pp. 14–17, 120–23. 1855.

1773 Watson (Katherine). Regional archaeologies—North Wales. Cory Adams Mack, 1965. pp. 92 + 49 figures.

1774 Wheeler (*Sir* Robert Eric Mortimer). Archaeology in Wales, Jan. 1914–Sept. 1921. (Current work in Welsh archaeology.) Bull. Bd. Celtic Studies, 1, pp. 64–90, 168–91, 276–87, 339–70: *continued in each subsequent part.* 1921, *etc.*

1775 —— Some problems of prehistoric Chronology in Wales. [2 figures.] Arch. Camb. 76, pp. 1–18. 1921.

1776 —— Prehistoric and Roman Wales. pp. 299 + 4 maps. 8°. Oxford, 1925. [i. Cave-man; ii. New Stone Age; iii. Megaliths & map; iv. Beaker-folk; v. Bronze Age + 2 maps; vi. Early Iron Age; vii. Roman occupation + map; viii. Summary. 109 figures.] pp. 217–274; figures 93–109.]

1777 —— Wales and archaeology. 1929. Sir John Rhys Memorial Lecture, B.A. Proc. British Academy, vol. xv.

1778 Willans (J. B.). A history of the parish of Hyssington. Collns. rel. to Montgom., 35, pp. 177–237 + plate (Mitchell's Ford) + map. 1910.

1779 Williams (Albert Hughes). An introduction to the history of Wales. 1. Prehistoric times to A.D. 1063. 8°. Cardiff, 1941.

1780 Williams (Jonathan). History of Radnorshire. Arch. Camb., 3rd S. 1, pp. 191–207. 1855.

1781 Williams (Richard). A history of the parish of Llanbrynmair. Chapter 9, Archaeological. Collns. rel. to Montgom., 22, pp. 307–14 + plate + plan. 1888.

1782 Williams (W. Wynn). Early remains at Penrhos Lligwy, Anglesey. [4 figures + 2 plans.] Arch. Camb., 3rd S. 13, pp. 50–56. 1867.

1783 —— Mona antiqua. Arch. Camb., 4th S. 2, pp. 34–40 + 3 plates + plan. 1871.

1784 —— Dinas Cynfor and Morwydd Ymrawyr. Arch. Camb., 4th S. 7, pp. 103–12 + 2 plans. 1876.

1787 Woodward (Bolingbroke Bernard). The history of Wales, from the earliest times. pp. vi, 608. 4°. London, 1852.

(f) Zone 6 [CBA Group 1, plus Ireland and Isle of Man]

1788 Allen (John Romilly). Notice of prehistoric remains near Tealing in Forfarshire. J. Brit. Archaeol. Ass., 37, pp. 254–61 + 3 plates (cup-marks, etc.). 1881.

1789 Anderson (George). On some of the stone circles and cairns in the neighbourhood of Inverness. [5 plans.] Archaeol. Scot., 3, pp. 211–22. 1831.

1790 Anderson (James). An account of [various] ancient monuments and fortifications in the Highlands of Scotland. (A further description, *etc.*). [Figure.] Archaeologia, 5, pp. 241–66 + 3 plans; 6, pp. 87–99 + 2 plates. 1779–1782.

1791 Anderson (Joseph). Report on the ancient remains of Caithness, and results of explorations. Mems. Anthrop. Soc. London, 2, pp. 226–50 + 2 plates. 1866.

1792 —— Scotland in pagan times; the Bronze and Stone Ages. pp. xxiii, 397. 8°. Edinburgh, 1886; The Iron Age. *Rhind Lectures*, 1881. pp. xx, 314. 8° Edinburgh, 1883.

1793 [Anon.] Lanarkshire antiquities. J. Brit. Archaeol. Ass., 17, pp. 18–21 + 3 plates, pp. 110–12 + 3 plates, pp. 208–11 + 3 plates. 1861.

1794 [Anon.] Ancient lake-dwellings in Scotland. [3 figures.] Antiquary, 7, pp. 66–69. 1883.

1795 [Anon.] Discoveries at Timpendean Muir, near Jedburgh. Reliquary, 12, p. 123. 1871.

1796 [Anon.] Prehistoric discoveries

at Glenborrodale: relics dating back 20,000 to 30,000 years. J. Brit. Archaeol. Ass., N.S. 26, p. 206. 1920.

1797 Armitage (Harold). Early man in Hallamshire. pp. xii, 307 + 16 plates. 8°. London, 1939.

1798 Armstrong (Edmund Clarence Richard). Note on the Hallstatt period in Ireland. Antiq. J., 2, pp. 204–07. 1922.

1799 Barnwell (Edward Lowry). Notes on the stone monuments in the Isle of Man. [Plan.] Arch. Camb., 3rd S. 12, pp. 46–60 + 6 plates + plan. 1866.

1800 Barry (*Sir* Francis Tress) *bart.* Prehistoric brochs of Caithness. pp. 16. 8°. n.p. 1899.

1801 Bord Failte Eireann. The National monuments of Ireland in the charge of the Commissioners of Public Works in Ireland. Dublin, 1964, 116 pp. + 12 plates + 56 drawings + 7 sketch maps.

1802 Boyd (William). The stone age in Buchan. Trans. Buchan F.C., 1, 1890.

1803 Bremer (Walther). Ireland's place in prehistoric and early historic Europe. Dublin, 1928. 38 pp. + 19 figures.

1804 Bryden (J.). Antiquities of one pre-historic period of the Hawick district. Trans. Hawick Archaeol. Soc., 1873.

1805 Burchell (James Percy Tufnell), Some littoral sites of early post-glacial times located in North Ireland. Proc. PSEA 7 iii, 1934, 366–72. 12 figures + 1 table.

1806 Cadell (Henry M.). A Map of the ancient lakes of Edinburgh. Trans. Edinburgh Geol. Soc., 6, 1890/93, 287–296 + 1 map.

1807 Calder (Charles S. T.). Cairns, neolithic houses and burnt mounds in Shetland. Proc. Soc. Ant. Scotland, 96, 1962–63, 37–86, 6 plates + 18 figures.

1808 Callander (John Graham). The Early Iron Age in Scotland. Trans. Banff. F.C., 28. 1908.

1809 —— Dumfriesshire in the Stone, Bronze and Early Iron Ages. Trans. Dumfries. Ant. Soc., 3 S. 11 (1923–24). pp. 97–119 + 4 plates. 1925.

1810 —— Recent archaeological research in Scotland. [9 figures + 3 plans.]

Archaeologia, 77, pp. 87–110 + 3 plates. 1928.

1811 Campbell (Marion) *and* **Sandeman** (Mary L. S.). Mid Argyll: a field survey of the historic and prehistoric monuments. Proc. Soc. Ant. Scotland, 95, 1961–62, 1–125 + 6 figures.

1812 Cardi (Beatrice) de. The fourth Scottish summer school in archaeology. A report of the meeting held in Edinburgh in July, 1955. Arch. News Letter, 6, pp. 12–19. 1955.

1813 Chambers (Rosa). Episode on an Irish farm [mention of Rath and Souterraine]. Folklore, 71, 1961, 345–47.

1814 Charlesworth (J. Kaye). Ireland in Pleistocene times. Man, 28, pp. 120–22. 1928.

1815 Childe (Vere Gordon). The early colonization of north-eastern Scotland. [3 figures + 6 maps + 4 plans.] Proc. Roy. Soc. Edinb., 50, pp. 51–78 + 2 plates. 1930.

1816 —— Neolithic settlement in the west of Scotland. [Map.] Scot. Geog. Mag., 50, pp. 18–25 + 2 plates. 1934.

1817 —— The prehistory of Scotland. pp. xv, 285 + 16 plates + 4 maps. 8°. London, 1935. [82 figures and plans.]

1818 —— Some results of archaeological research in Scotland, 1932–7. [3 figures + 5 plans.] Univ. London, Inst. Archaeol., Ann. Rpt., 2 (1938), pp. 29–45 + 2 plates. 1939.

1819 —— Scotland before the Scots, being the Rhind lectures for 1944. pp. vii, 144 + 16 plates. 8°. London, 1946.

1820 Clark (Grahame). The Prehistory of the Isle of Man. Proc. Prehist. Soc., 1, 1935, 70–92 + 13 figures.

1821 Coffey (George). The Bronze Age in Ireland. pp. xi, 107 + 11 plates. 8°. Dublin, 1913. [85 figures.]

1822 Coles (John M.). New aspects of the Mesolithic settlement of South-West Scotland. Trans. Dumfries, 41, 1962/3, 67–98 + 3 figures.

1823 Conwell (Eugene Alfred). Handbook to the Lougherew hills, county Meath, Ireland. pp. 25 + map. 8°. Dublin, 1868.

1824 Cooke, John. Handbook for travellers in Ireland. London, 1896.

1825 Corkill (W. H.). Manx mines and megaliths. Mems. & Proc. Manch. Lit. & Phil. Soc., 65. 1921.

1826 Corrie (J. M.). Kirkcudbright-shire in the Stone, Bronze, and Early Iron Ages. [5 figures + plan.] Trans. Dumfries. Ant. Soc., 3 S. 14 (1926–28), pp. 272–99 + 11 plates + 3 tables. 1930.

1827 Craw (James Hewat). Fort and hut-circles on the Upper Whitadder [Berwickshire]. Hist. Berwick. Nat. Club, 21, pp. 206–10. 1910.

1828 Cree (James E.). Palaeolithic man in Scotland. Antiquity, 1, pp. 218–221. 1927.

1829 Curle (James). Roman and native remains in Caledonia. [7 figures + 2 plans.] J.R.S., 3, pp. 98–115 + 3 plates. 1913.

1830 Curwen (Eliot Cecil). The Hebrides: a cultural backwater. [2 figures + 9 plans.] Antiquity, 12, pp. 261–89 + 5 plates. 1938.

1831 Cuming (Henry Syer). On Irish antiquities. [Figure.] J. Brit. Archaeol. Ass., 10, pp. 165–76 + plate. 1854.

1832 Davies (Margaret). Types of megalithic monuments of the Irish Sea and North Channel coastlands: a study in distributions. [6 maps + 3 plans.] Antiq. J., 25, pp. 125–44. 1945.

1833 —— The diffusion and distribution pattern of the megalithic monuments of the Irish Sea and North Channel coastlands. [10 maps.] Antiq. J., 26, pp. 38–60. 1946.

1834 Eogan (George). The Later Bronze Age in Ireland in the light of recent research. Proc. prehist. Soc., 30, 1964, 268–351 + 20 figures + 4 plates.

1835 Evans (Emyr Estyn) *and* **Gaffikin** (M.). Belfast Naturalists' Field Club Survey of antiquities: Megaliths and raths. Irish Naturalists' J., 5, pp. 1–11 + map. 1935.

1836 —— Archaeological investigations in northern Ireland. A summary of recent work. Antiq. J., 15, pp. 165–73 + 2 plates. 1935.

1837 —— Irish heritage. pp. 190 + 6 plates. 8º. Dundalk, 1942. [114 figures.]

1838 —— Archaeological research in Ireland, 1939–1948. [4 figures.] Archaeology, 2, pp. 69–72. 1949.

1839 —— Ulster's place in British archaeology. Trans. Lancs. & Ches. Ant. Soc., 64 (1954), pp. 19–23 + map. 1955.

1840 Fairhurst (Harold). The Clyde in prehistory. The Glasgow region. (Brit. Ass., Glasgow, 1958), pp. 119–28. 1958.

1841 Fairhurst (Horace). The geography of Scotland in prehistoric times. [Figure + map.] Trans. Glasgow Archaeol. Soc., N.S. 13, pp. 1–16. 1954.

1842 Feacham (Richard William de Fécamp). Iron Age and early mediaeval monuments in Galloway and Dumfriesshire. Trans. Dumfriess. Ant. Soc., 3rd S. 33 (1954–55), pp. 58–65. 1956.

1843 —— Unenclosed platform settlements. Proc. Soc. Ant. Scotland, 94, 1960/61, 79–85 + 4 figures.

1844 —— A Guide to prehistoric Scotland. London, 1963, 223 pp. + 50 figures + 2 maps.

1845 Fleure (Herbert John) *and* **Neely** (G. J. H.). Cashtal yn Ard, Isle of Man. [Figure + 2 plans.] Antiq. J., 16, pp. 373–95 + 3 plates. 1936.

1846 Gibson (W. G.). Note on the antiquities of the Stone, Bronze, and Iron periods, found in Dumfriesshire and Galloway. Trans. Dumfries. Ant. Soc., 1, pp. 47–51. 1863.

1847 Goudie (Gilbert). The Celtic and Scandinavian antiquities of Shetland. pp. xvi, 305. 8º. Edinburgh, 1904.

1848(a) Hardy (James). On some British remains near Oldcambus. Hist. Berwick. Nat. Club, 11, pp. 159–62. 1885.

1848(b) Harttung (Julius), *afterwards* **Pflugk-Harttung** (Julius von). The druids of Ireland. Trans. Roy. Hist. Soc., N.S. 7, pp. 55–75. 1893.

1849 Holleyman (G. A.). Tiree [Inner Hebrides] craggans. [4 figures.] Antiquity, 21, pp. 205–11. 1947.

1850 Horsburgh (James). Notes of cromlechs, duns, hut-circles, chambered cairns, and other remains, in the county of Sutherland. [Figure.] Proc. Soc. Antiq. Scot., 7, pp. 277–79. 1870.

1851 Hunter (James). Description of pit dwellings at Dilly-Moenan and the Miaave crag, Tarfair, near Macduff, Banffshire. Proc. Soc. Antiq. Scot., 7, pp. 465–71. 1870.

1852 Jamieson (Thomas F.). On some remains of the Stone period in the Buchan districts of Aberdeenshire. Proc. Soc. Antiq. Scot., 6, pp. 240–45. 1868.

1853 Keiller (Alexander). Megalithic monuments of north-east Scotland, pp. 25. 8⁰. London, 1934.

1854 Kermode (P. M. C.). The ancient monuments of the Isle of Man. Presidential Address. Arch. Camb., 84 ii, 1929, 167–78.

1855 Kinvig (Robert Henry). The Isle of Man and Atlantic Britain: a study in historical geography. [11 maps.] Institute of Brit. Geographers Publication No. 25. Trans. & Papers, pp. 1–27. 1958.

1856 Kirk (William). Prehistoric sites at the sands of Forvie, Aberdeenshire. [4 figures + 3 plans.] Aberdeen Univ. Rev., 35, pp. 150–71 + 4 plates. 1953.

1857 Knight (G. A. Frank). Antiquities in the neighbourhood of Otter Ferry, Loch Fyne [Argyllshire]. Trans. Glasgow Archaeol. Soc., N.S. 9, pp. 7–25. 1937.

1858 Lacaille (Armand Donald). The Stone Age background of Scotland (with particular reference to the south-west and south). [9 figures + 3 maps.] Trans. Dumfriess. Ant. Soc., 3rd S. 26 (1947–1948), pp. 9–40 + 2 plates + map. 1949.

1859 —— The Stone Age in Scotland. *Publns. Wellcome Hist. Med. Museum*, N.S. 6. pp. xxii, 345 + 9 plates + map. 8⁰. London, 1954. [140 figures.]

1860 Laing (Samuel). Prehistoric remains of Caithness, with notes on the human remains, by Thomas H. Huxley, pp. 160. 8⁰. London, 1866. [68 figures.]

1861 Lewis (A. L.). Notes on some Irish antiquities. J. Anthrop. Inst., 9, pp. 137–45 + plate. 1879.

1862 Lhwyd (Edward). Several observations relating to the antiquities and natural history of Ireland made in his travels thro' that Kingdom. Phil. Trans. Roy. Soc., xxvii, 1712, 503–06.

1863 Macalister (Robert Alexander Stewart). Ireland in pre-Celtic times. pp. xvi, 374. 8⁰. Dublin, 1921. [115 figures + 7 plans.]

1864 —— The antiquities of Ireland. [12 figures.] Art & Archaeology, 15, pp. 125–37. 1923.

1865 —— The Archaeology of Ireland. Methuen 1927? 1928?

1866 —— The archaeology of Ireland. pp. xvi, 373 + 15 plates. 8⁰. London, 1928. [2 figures.]

1867 —— Archaeological research in the Irish Free State. Antiq. J., 15, pp. 205–08. 1935.

1868 —— The chronology of megalithic monuments in Ireland. Man, 46, pp. 97–98. 1946.

1869 Macdonald (*Sir* George). The archaeology of Scotland. Brit. Ass. Rpt., 1928, pp. 142–49. 1929.

1870 —— Prehistoric Scotland. pp. 161. 4⁰. n.d. [Typescript. Initial chapters of an unfinished work in Library of the Society of Antiquaries.]

1871 McDonald (R. H.). The hill of Tara. [Figure + 2 plans.] J. Brit. Archaeol. Ass., N.S. 1, pp. 271–79. 1895.

1872 Macfarlane (Walter). Geographical collections relating to Scotland [mainly between 1721 and 1730.]. Edited from Macfarlane's transcript in the Advocates' Library by Sir Arthur Mitchell. *Publications of the Scottish Historical Society*, 51–53. 3 vol. 8⁰. Edinburgh, 1906–08.

1873 McKenzie (Colin). An account of some remains of antiquity in the island of Lewis, one of the Hebrides. Archaeol. Scot., 1, pp. 282–92 + plate. 1792.

1874(a) Mackinlay (John). Notice of two crannoges, or palisaded islands, in Bute. Proc. Soc. Antiq. Scot., 3, pp. 43–46 + plan. 1862.

1874(b) Maclagan (Christian). The hill forts, stone circles and other structural remains of ancient Scotland. pp. x, 148 + 19 plates + 20 plans. fol. Edinburgh, 1875.

1875 MacLean (Hector). The ancient peoples of Ireland and Scotland considered. J. Anthrop. Inst., 20, pp. 154–179. 1890.

1876 MacRitchie (David). Some Hebridean antiquities. [13 figures + plan.] Reliquary, N. [3rd] S. 1, pp. 200–215. 1895.

1877 —— Hut-circles at Auchingaich glen, Dumbartonshire. Antiquary, 36, pp. 377–78. 1900.

1878 Mahr (Adolf). New aspects and problems in Irish prehistory. Presidential Address for 1937. Proc. prehist. Soc., 3, 1937, 262–436, 29 figures + 7 plates.

1879 Mapleton (R. J.). Report on prehistoric remains in the neighbourhood of the Crinan canal, Argyllshire.

J. Ethnolog. Soc., N.S. 2, pp. 146–55. 1870.

1880(a) Martin (Cecil P.). Prehistoric man in Ireland. pp. xi, 184 + 11 plates. 4°. London, 1935. [6 figures.]

1880(b) Martin (William Gregory N.). The lake dwellings of Ireland: or ancient lacustrine habitations of Erin, commonly called crannogs. pp. xxii, 268 + 49 plates. 8°. Dublin, 1886. [189 figures.]

1881 Marwick (Hugh). Ancient monuments in Orkney. Ministry of Works. pp. 38 + 12 plates + map. 8°. Edinburgh, 1952.

1882 Maxwell (*Sir* Herbert Eustace). A history of Dumfries and Galloway. *County histories of Scotland*. pp. xv, 411. 8°. Edinburgh, 1896.

1883 Michie (A.). Prehistoric remains in the Allan Water district. Trans. Hawick Archaeol. Soc., 1879.

1884 Michie (*Rev.* J. G.). Traces of early human habitations on Deeside and vicinity [BA—Pictish]. Advm. Sci., 1885, 1232.

1885 Milne (John). Traces of early man in Buchan. Trans. Buchan F.C., 2. 1892.

1886 Movius (Hallam C.), *jr.* The Irish stone age, its chronology, development & relationships. pp. xxiv, 329 + 7 plates. 4°. Cambridge, 1942. [55 figures + 4 maps.]

1887 Munro (Robert). Ancient Scottish lake-dwellings or crannogs: with a supplementary chapter on remains of lake-dwellings in England. pp. xx, 326 + 3 plates + 2 plans. 8°. Edinburgh, 1882. [264 figures.]

1888 —— Prehistoric Scotland and its place in European civilisation. *County Histories of Scotland*. pp. xix, 502. 8°. Edinburgh, 1899.

1889 —— On a Bronze Age cemetery and other antiquities at Largs, Ayrshire. [4 figures.] Archaeologia, 62, pp. 239–50. 1910.

1890 Neilson (George). The monuments of Caithness. Scot. Hist. Rev., 9, pp. 241–52 + 6 plates. 1912.

1891 Norman (Edward Robert *and* St Joseph (J. K. S.). The Early Development of Irish Society: the evidence of aerial photography (Cambridge Air Survey, 3). 70 plates, 2 diagrams, 11 in. by 7⅝ in. Camb. 1969.

1892 Ó Ríordáin (Seán Pádraig). Palaeolithic man in Ireland. Antiquity, 5, pp. 360–62. 1931.

1893 —— Early Irish homesteads. Trans. Lancs. & Ches. Ant. Soc., 63 (1952–53), pp. 178–82 + plate + plan. 1954.

1894 —— Tara. [Figure.] Myth or legend? Pp. 59–68 + 2 plates. 1956.

1895 Orr (James). Standing stones and other relics in Mull. [3 figures + map + 3 plans.] Trans. Glasgow Archaeol. Soc., N.S. 9, pp. 128–34. 1938.

1896 Petrie (George). Description of antiquities in Orkney recently examined. Proc. Soc. Antiq. Scot., 2, pp. 56–62 + plan. 1859.

1897 Piggott (Stuart). Scotland before history. pp. viii, 112. 8°. London, 1958. [32 figures.]

1898 —— The Prehistoric people of Scotland. London, 1962. ix + 165 pp., 8 plates, 16 text-figures.

1899 Pococke (Richard), *bp. of Meath*. An account of some antiquities found in Ireland. Archaeologia, 2, pp. 32–41 + 3 plates. 1773.

1900 Powell (T. G. E.). The Celtic settlement of Ireland. [Map.] Early cultures of N.W. Europe (H. M. Chadwick mem. stud.) *ed.* Sir C. Fox *and* Bruce Dickins, pp. 171–95. 1958.

1901 Power (P.). Prehistoric Ireland. A manual of Irish pre-Christian archaeology. pp. 96. 8°. Dublin, 1923.

1902 Pownall (Thomas). Further Observations on the early Irish antiquities. Archaeologia, 7, pp. 164–69 + 2 plates. 1785.

1903 Raftery (Joseph). Prehistoric Ireland. pp. xvi, 228 + 16 plates. 8°. London, 1951. [267 figures.]

1904 Reid (R. W.). Prehistoric archaeology in Aberdeen district. Brit. Ass., Rpt., 1934, Appendix, pp. 68–76. 1934.

1905 Royal Commission on the Ancient and Historical Monuments of Scotland. Stirlingshire. An inventory of the ancient monuments, vol. I. 1963, Edinburgh, H.M.S.O., xxxix, 272 pp. + 110 figures + 115 plates. Vol. II, xiv, 216 pp. + 70 figures + 115 plates.

1906 Scott (Archibald Black). The historical sequence of peoples, culture and characteristics in Scotland, from 400

B.C. to 950 A.D. [pp. 1–6, Prehistoric.] Trans. Buchan F.C., 15, pp. 1–18. 1934.

1907 Scott (*Sir* W. Lindsay). Neolithic culture of the Hebrides. Antiquity, 16, pp. 301–06. 1942.

1908 —— The Colonisation of Scotland in the second millennium B.C. Proc. prehist. Soc., 17, 1951, 16–82 + 3 figures.

1909 Simpson (William Douglas). The province of Mar: being the Rhind Lectures in Archaeology, 1941. *Aberdeen University Studies*, 121. pp. xi, 167 + 89 plates. 4⁰. Aberdeen, 1943. [43 figures.]

1910 Skene (William Forbes). Celtic Scotland. 3 vol. 8⁰. Edinburgh, 1876–90.

1911 Smith (John). Prehistoric man in Ayrshire. 8⁰. London, 1895.

1912 Snadden (James). The prehistoric remains on the Nine Stane Rig. Trans. Hawick Archaeol. Soc., 1923, pp. 20–24. 1923.

1913 Somerville (Boyle). Prehistoric monuments in the Outer Hebrides, and their astronomical significance. [Figure + map + 6 plans.] J. R. Anthrop. Inst., 42, pp. 23–52 + 3 plates + plan (Callanish). 1912.

1914 Steer (Kenneth Arthur). Scientific survey of south-eastern Scotland. *British Association, Edinburgh, 1951*. 8⁰. Edinburgh, 1951.

1915 —— Roman and native in Southern Scotland. [Note for Summer Meeting 1964.] Arch. J., 121, 1964, 164–67.

1916 Stuart (John). On the earlier antiquities of the district of Cromar, in Aberdeenshire. Proc. Soc. Antiq. Scot., 1, pp. 258–63. 1865.

1917 —— Notice of a group of artificial islands in the Loch of Dowalton, Wigtonshire, and of other artificial islands or crannogs throughout Scotland. [2 figures. Pp. 174–77, List of sites.] Proc. Soc. Antiq. Scot., 6, pp. 114–78 + 2 plates + plan. 1868.

1918 —— Account of excavations in groups of cairns, stone circles and hut-circles on Balnabroch, parish of Kirkmichael, Perthshire, and at West Persie, in that neighbourhood. Proc. Soc. Antiq. Scot., 6, pp. 402–10. 1868.

1919 Stewart (Margaret E. C.). Strath Tay in the second Millennium

B.C. A field survey. [Clyde-Carlingford tombs; cup-and-ring marks; beakers.] Proc. Soc. Antiq. Scotland, 92, 1958–59, 71–84, p figures + 3 plates.

1920 Stirling, *County Council*. Ancient monuments in Stirlingshire: list. Trans. Stirling H.N. & Arch. Soc., 1912–13, pp. 85–89. 1913.

1921 Tait (Lawson). Notes on the shell-mounds, hut-circles, and kist-vaens of Sutherland. Proc. Soc. Antiq. Scot., 7, pp. 525–32. 1870.

1922 Tate (Ralph). Report of Zetland archaeological expedition. Mems. Anthrop. Soc., London, 2, pp. 239–47. 1866.

1923 Taylor (R. Mascie). Discovery of ancient lake-dwellings at Boho, Fermanagh, Ireland. J. Brit. Archaeol. Ass., 36, pp. 371–72. 1880.

1924 Thomas (F. W. L.). Account of some of the Celtic antiquities of Orkney including the stones of Stenness, tumuli, Picts-houses, &c., with plans. [11 figures + 3 plans.] Archaeologia, 33, pp. 88–136 + 6 plans. 1852.

1925 —— Notice of beehive houses in Harris and Lewis; with traditions of the Each-uisge, or water-horse, connected therewith. Proc. Soc. Antiq. Scot., 3, pp. 127–34 + plate. 1862.

1926 —— Description of beehive houses in Uig, Lewis, and of a Pict's house and cromlech, &c., Harris. Proc. Soc. Antiq. Scot., 3, pp. 134–44 + 4 plates + 3 plans. 1862.

1927 Traill (William). General remarks on the dwellings of prehistoric races in Orkney; with a special notice of the Pict's house of Skerrabrae, in the parish of Sandwick, showing the present state of the excavations lately made there. [Figure.] Proc. Soc. Antiq. Scot., 7, pp. 426–39. 1870.

1928 Truckell (A. E.). The mesolithic in Dumfries and Galloway: recent developments. Trans. Dumfries & Galloway nat. Hist & Antiq. Soc., 40, 1961/1962, 43–47.

1929 Wainwright (Frederick Threlfall). Souterrains in Scotland. [6 plans. Earth-houses, *etc*.] Antiquity, 27, pp. 219–32. 1953.

1930 —— *editor*. The Northern Isles. London, 1962, pp. 224, 23 plates + 37 text-figures.

1931 —— The Souterrains of southern Pictland. London, 1963, pp. 234, 61 figures + 32 plates.

1932 Watts, W. A. C-14 Dating and the Neolithic in Ireland. Antiq. 34 (1960), pp. 111–16.

1933 Whelan (C. Blake). Ireland in Pleistocene times. Man, 28, pp. 74–76. 1928.

1934 Wilson (Daniel). The archaeology and prehistoric annals of Scotland. 2nd edition. 2 vols. 8°. Edinburgh, 1863.

1936 Wyatt (M. Digby). A few observations on the early habitations of the Irish, and especially the crannoges or lake castles. pp. 5. 4°. 1858.

1937 Young (James). Recent archaeological discoveries in the parish of Lesmahagow. Trans. Glasgow Archaeol. Soc., N.S. 3, pp. 498–503 + 2 plates. 1899.

1938 Young (Robert S.). Archaeological rambles in the Inisowen Mountains. Ulster J. Arch., 3, 1897, 196–99.

1939 Young (Robert). Ireland and the East. Ulster J. Arch., 3, 1897, 201.

1940 Young (Robert S.). Archaeological rambles in the Inisowen Mountains. Ulster J. Arch., 4, 1897, 17–22 + 1 figure.

1941 Young (Robert M.). Vestiges of primitive man in the County Down. Ulster J. Arch., 4, 1897, 44–47 + 2 figures.

C. SPECIFIC SITES

1. BURIALS IN GENERAL

1942 Ashbee (Paul). Stake and post circles in British round barrows. [Diagram + map + plan. P. 9, Provisional list.] Archaeol. J., 114 (1957), pp. 1–9 + plate. 1959.

1943 —— The Bronze Age round barrow in Britain. [Pp. 222, 23 textfigures + 32 plates.] London, 1960.

1944 —— The Earthen Long Barrow in Britain, 36 plates, 18 line drawings. London, 1972.

1945 Bateman (Thomas) *and* **Isaacson** (Stephen). General account of the barrows opened in Derbyshire and Staffordshire, during the season of 1845. [2 figures.] Trans. Brit. Archaeol. Ass., [2] Congress at Winchester, 1848, pp. 205–17. 1846.

1946 —— On the sepulchral antiquities of various nations, illustrative of the custom of tumular interment, as practised by the primeval inhabitants of Britain. Bowman (William): Reliquiae Antiquae Eboracenses (Leeds), pp. 1–9 + 2 plates. 1855.

1947 —— Ten years' diggings in Celtic and Saxon grave hills, in the counties of Derby, Stafford, and York, from 1848 to 1858, *etc.* pp. xi, 302. 8°. London, 1861. [59 figures and plans.]

1948 Clark (John Grahame Douglas). Megaliths and collective burial. Proc. prehist. Soc., 3, 1937, 470–72.

1949 —— Earthen long barrows. Proc. prehist. Soc. 3, 1937, 173–75 + 1 figure.

1950 —— Mortality in prehistoric times. Proc. prehist. Soc., 4, 1938, 226–228.

1951 Clinch (George). Neolithic burial. [5 figures + 10 plans.] Reliquary, 3rd S. 11, pp. 145–61. 1905.

1952 Copsey (H. W.). A List of barrows around the Berkshire–Surrey–Hampshire boundary. Berks. Arch. J., 61, 1963/4, 20–27.

1953 Crawford (Osbert Guy Stanhope). Barrows. [9 figures.] Antiquity, 1, pp. 419–34 + 2 plates. 1927.

1954 —— Stone cists. Antiquity, 2, pp. 418–22 + 6 plates. 1928.

1955 Daniel (Glyn Edmund). The "dolmens" of southern Britain. Antiquity, 11, pp. 183–200. 1937.

1956 —— The Transepted gallery graves of Western France. Proc. prehist. Soc., 5, 1939, 143–65 + 9 figures.

1957 —— *and* **Powell** (T. G. E.). The Distribution and date of the passage-graves of the British Isles. Proc. prehist. Soc., 15, 1949, 169–87 + 2 figures.

1958 —— The prehistoric chamber tombs of England and Wales. pp. xiv, 256 + 16 plates. 8°. London, 1950. [33 figures.] pp. 177–250, Inventory.]

1959 —— The long barrow in western Europe. [2 maps + plan.] Early cultures of N.W. Europe (H. M. Chadwick mem. stud.) ed. Sir C. Fox and Bruce Dickins, pp. 1–20. 1950.

1960 —— Prehistoric chamber tombs of England and Wales. [Letter.] Arch. News Letter, 3, p. 143; 4, pp. 3–4. 1951.

1961 —— *and* **Arnal** (J.). Les monuments mégalithiques et la forme des tumuli en France et en Angleterre. Bull. Soc. pré. franç., 1952, p. 34. 1952.

1962 —— The Chronology of the French collective tombs. Proc. prehist. Soc., 24, 1958, 1–23 + 3 figures. [Analogies with British.]

1963 Davis (Joseph Barnard). On the interments of primitive man. [6 figures.] North Staffs. N.F. Club, Rpts., [1], pp. 52–67 + 3 plates. 1875.

1964 Evans (John H.). Notes on the folklore and legends associated with the Kentish megaliths. Folk-lore, 57, pp. 36–43. 1946.

1965 Fox (*Sir* Cyril) *and others*. Cairn cemeteries (with Fox, *Lady* Aileen Mary and Hemp, Wilfrid James). Bull. Bd. Celtic Stud., 7, pp. 419–20; 8, pp. 92–94; 8, pp. 274–75. 1935–36.

1966 Greenwell (William). Ancient British tumuli. Q. J. Suffolk Inst. Arch., 1, pp. 8–12. 1869.

1967 —— British barrows . . . with a description of figures of skulls, general remarks on prehistoric crania and an appendix by George Rolleston. pp. xi, 763. 8⁰. Oxford, 1877. [177 figures.]

1968 —— Recent researches in barrows in Yorkshire, Wiltshire, Berkshire, *etc.* [33 figures. Pottery, *etc.*] Archaeologia, 52, pp. 1–72 + 2 plates. 1890.

1969 Grinsell (Leslie Valentine). Bell-barrows. Proc. PSEA, 7 ii, 1932–34, 203–30 + 13 figures.

1970 —— The ancient burial-mounds of England. 2nd edition. pp. xviii, 278 + 24 plates. 8⁰. London, 1953. [12 figures.]

1971 Hawkes (Jessie Jacquetta). The prehistoric chamber tombs of England and Wales. [Letter.] Arch. News Letter, 3, pp. 159–60. 1951.

1972 Hemp (Wilfrid James). A possible pedigree of Long Barrows and chambered cairns. Proc. prehist. Soc., N.S. 1, 1935, 108–14 + 6 figures.

1973 Jewitt (Llewellynn). Grave-mounds and their contents . . . as exemplified in the burials of the Celtic, the Romano-British and the Anglo-Saxon periods. pp. xxiv, 306. 8⁰. London, 1870. [489 figures and plans. pp. 1–108, prehistoric.]

1974 Jones (Jack Davies). The technique of barrow excavation. [Map of Bronze Age burials in Cheshire.] Cheshire Historian, 2, pp. 28–33 + 2 plates. 1952.

1975 Jones (John). The cromlech. Arch. Camb., 4, pp. 82–93. 1849.

1976 Lukis (William Collings). On cromlechs. J. Brit. Archaeol. Ass., 20, pp. 228–37. 1864.

1977 —— On some peculiarities in the construction of chambered barrows. J. Brit. Archaeol. Ass., 22, pp. 249–63 + 3 plates + 17 plans. 1866.

1978 Piggott (Stuart). A Note on the relative chronology of the English long barrows. Proc. prehist. Soc., N.S. 1, 1935, 115–26 + 7 figures.

1979 —— Grooved stone cists, Scotland and the Scillies. Antiquity, 15, pp. 81–83 + plate. 1941.

1980 —— Heads and hoofs. Antiquity, 36, 1962, pp. 110–18.

1981 Rolleston (George). On the people of the long barrow period. J. Anth. Inst., 5, pp. 120–73 + 3 plans. 1875.

1982 Sprockhoff (Ernst). Central European Urnfield Culture and Celtic La Tène: an outline. Proc. prehist. Soc., 21, 1955, 257–81 + 14 figures. [BA–IA].

1983 Stackhouse (Thomas). Illustration of the tumuli or ancient barrows; exhibiting the principles which determined the magnitude and position of each, *etc.* pp. x, 33 + 7 plates. 8⁰. London, 1806.

1984 Valéra (Ruiadhri de). The "Carlingford Culture", the Long Barrow and the Neolithic of Great Britain and Ireland. Proc. prehist. Soc., 27, 1961, 234–52 + 1 map.

1985 Ward (John). Barrow notitia. Antiquary, 50, pp. 294–98. 1914.

1986 Wells, (Calvin). A Study of cremation. Antiq., 34 (1960), pp. 29–37.

1987 Whiting (Charles Edwin). Ancient log coffins in Britain. Trans.

Archit. Soc. Durham & Nhb., 8, pp. 80–
105 + 3 plates. 1937.

1988 Young (George Malcolm). Pond
barrows. Antiquity, 8, pp. 459–61.
1934.

2. BURIALS BY ZONES

(a) Zone 1 [CBA Groups 7, 9, 10, 11A, 11B, 14]

1989 Abbott (W. J. Lewis). Notes on
a remarkable barrow at Sevenoaks. (Pp.
137–45 + 2 plates, Notes on some
specialised and diminutive forms of flint
implements from [it].) J. Anthrop. Inst.,
25, pp. 130–36 + 2 plates. 1895.

1990 Adams (John). An account of
the opening of a barrow in Berkshire. J.
Brit. Archaeol. Ass., 22, pp. 448–50.
1866.

1991 —— An account of the opening
of a barrow at Great Shefford, Berks.
Trans. Newbury F.C., 1, pp. 130–31 +
plate (thuribulum). 1871.

1992 Akerman (John Yonge). Account of the opening by Matthew Bell
of an ancient British barrow, in Iffins
Wood, near Canterbury, in the month of
January, 1842. Archaeologia, 30, pp.
57–61. 1844.

1993 —— Observations on the cele-
brated monument at Ashbury, in the
county of Berks., called "Wayland
Smith's cave". Archaeologia, 32, pp.
312–14 + plate (with plan). 1947.

1994 —— Notes on antiquarian researches in . . . 1854. Teddington,
Middlesex. Archaeologia, 36, pp. 175–
76. 1855.

1995 —— *and* **Stone** (Stephen). An
account of the investigation of some
remarkable circular trenches, and the
discovery of an ancient British cemetery,
at Stanlake, Oxon. Archaeologia, 37,
pp. 363–70 + 2 plans. 1857.

1996 Alexander (John). Addington:
the Chestnuts megalithic tomb. Archaeol. Cant., 72 (1958), pp. 191–92. 1959.

1997 —— The Excavation of the
Chestnuts Megalithic tomb at Addington,
Kent. Arch. Camb. 76, 1961, pp. 1–57 +
15 figures.

1999 [Anon.] The Kentish cromlech,
Kit's Coty house. [Trans.] Brit. Arch-

aeol. Ass., 5, Congress at Worcester,
1848, pp. 192–98. 1851.

1998 Anderson (A. Whitford). Late
Celtic burial, Abbots Langley, Herts.
[Figure (cinerary urn and bowl).] Antiq.
J., 2, pp. 259–60. 1922.

2000 [Anon.] Cromlechs at Addington
& Trottescliffe, [Kent]. [Trans.] Brit.
Archaeol. Ass., 5, Congress at Worcester,
1848, pp. 198–99. 1851.

2001 [Anon.] Ancient British barrow
at Teddington. Surrey, Archaeol. Collns.
1, pp. 74–76 + plate of weapon. 1858.

2002 [Anon.] Barrow openings in
Berkshire. Reliquary, 21, p. 127. 1880.

2003 [Anon.] Excavation of a barrow
at Eye. J. Brit. Archaeol. Ass., N.S. 17,
pp. 88–89. 1911.

2004 [Anon.] Bronze Age. Discovery
of burials at Dunstable. J. Brit. Archaeol. Ass., N.S. 32, pp. 136–37. 1926.

2005 [Anon.] Bronze Age burial site
at Dedham, Essex. [Plan.] Colchester
Archaeol. Group, Quart. Bull., 1, pp. 36–
38. 1958.

2006 Ashbee (Paul) *and* **Dunning**
(Gerald Clough). The Round barrows of
East Kent. Arch. Camb. 74, 1960, pp.
48–57 + 4 figures.

2007 Atkinson (Richard John Copland). A Middle Bronze Age barrow at
Cassington, Oxon. Oxoniensia, 11/12,
pp. 5–26 + 3 plates. 1947.

2008 —— The excavations at Dor-
chester, Oxfordshire, 1946–1951. [Plan.
Neolithic and Bronze Age.] Arch. News
Letter, 4, pp. 56–59. 1951.

2009 ——, **Piggott** (Cecily Margaret)
and **Sandars** (N. K.). Excavations at
Dorchester, Oxon. First report. Sites I,
II, IV, V and VI, with a chapter on henge
monuments, by R. J. C. Atkinson. pp.
xii, 151 + 10 plates. 4°. Oxford,
1951. [32 figures, maps and plans + 9
tables.]

2010 —— Excavations in Barrow Hills
field, Radley, Berks., 1944–45. Barrows
2, 3 and 7 and a Romano-British cemetery. [5 figures + 4 plans.] Oxoniensia,
17/18 (1952/53), pp. 14–35 + plate.
1954.

2011 —— Wayland's Smithy. Antiquity, 39, 1965, pp. 126–00.

2012 Barkley (C. W.). Celtic remains
at [Coldvane farm,] Addington, co. Kent.
[Cromlech.] N. & Q., 4 S. 6, p. 120. 1870.

2013 Bateman (Thomas). On early burial-places discovered in the county of Nottingham. J. Brit. Archaeol. Ass., 8, pp. 183–92 + 3 plates. 1852.

2014 Bennett (F.). Coldrum monument [Kent] and exploration 1910. [Figure + map + 3 plans.] J. R. Anthrop. Inst., 43, pp. 76–85. 1913.

2015 De La Bere (R.). Excavation of barrow at Silk Willoughby. [Early Iron Age.] Lincs. N. & Q., 22, pp. 106–08, 125–28. 1933.

2016 Blake (Bryan P.). Excavation of a Bronze Age barrow at Dedham Essex. Trans. Essex Archaeolog. Soc., XXVIII, 1960, 344–57 + 8 figures + 1 plate.

2017 Booker (R. P. L.). Urn burial at Stoke Poges. [Late Bronze Age.] Records of Bucks., 10, p. 105. 1816.

2018 Boyle (Richard G.). Reports from local secretaries and groups: Malling [Chestnuts megalithic burial chamber]. Arch. Cantiana, 78, 1963, liii.

2019 Boys (William). Observations on Kits Coity house, in Kent. Archaeologia, 11, pp. 38–44. 1792.

2020 Bradford (John Spencer Purvis). Excavations at Cassington, Oxon., 1947. [2 figures. Romano-British interment superimposed on one of Beaker period.] Oxoniensia, 16 (1951), pp. 1–4 + 3 plates. 1953.

2021 Bradshaw (J.). Reports from local secretaries and groups: Ashford [Boughton Aluph barrow]. Arch. Cantiana, 79, 1964, li–lii.

2022 Bramwell (F. G. S.). Barrow formerly existing in Preston Drove, Brighton. [Plan. ?Neolithic long barrow.] Sussex N. & Q., 7, pp. 73–76. 1938.

2023 Brinson (J. G. S.). Two burial groups of Belgic age, Hothfield common, near Ashford. [Figure (urn) and plan.] Arch. Cant., 56 (1943), pp. 41–47 + 2 plates. 1944.

2024 Briscoe (Grace) *Lady*. Bronze Age burials at How hill, Icklingham [Suffolk]. [Figure.] Proc. Camb. Antiq. Soc., 48 (1954), pp. 6–9. 1955.

2025 —— Swale's tumulus: a combined Neolithic Age and Bronze Age barrow at Worlington, Suffolk. [4 figures + plan.] Proc. Camb. Antiq. Soc., 50 (1956), pp. 101–12. 1957.

2026 —— Bronze Age cremation urn at Rabbit Hill, Lakenheath [Suffolk.] [1 figure]. Proc. Camb. Ant. Soc., LIV (1961), 19–21.

2027 Brothwell, D. R.). Cremated remains from Rabbit Hill, Lakenheath. Proc. Camb. Ant. Soc., LIV (1961), 21.

2028 Brown (B. J. W.), *etc.* Excavations at Grimstone End, Pakenham. [9 figures + map + plan. Ring barrow containing un-urned. Early Bronze Age cremation.] Proc. Suffolk Inst. Arch., 26, pp. 189–207 + 6 plates. 1955.

2029 Budgen (William). A La Tène III inhumation. [Figure (urn).] Antiq. J., 11, pp. 71–73. 1931.

2030 Burstow (George Philip). A Late Bronze Age urnfield. Steyning Round Hill discoveries. [2 figures.] Sussex County Mag., 24, pp. 85–88. 1950.

2031 —— A Late Bronze Age urnfield on Steyning round hill. [*See also* 3, p. 7 (note by Harold E. P. Spencer)]. Arch. News Letter, 2, p. 184. 1950.

2032 —— A Late Bronze Age urnfield on Steyning Round hill, Sussex. Proc. prehist. Soc., 24, 1958, 158–64 + 4 figures.

2032(a) Campbell (John Duncan Vaughan), *5th earl Cawdor and* **Fox** (Sir Cyril). The Beacon Hill barrow, Barton Mills, Suffolk; with a report on the osteology by W. L. H. Duckworth; and a note on the flint objects by Miles Burkitt. Proc. Camb. Antiq. Soc., 26, pp. 19–65 + plate + plan. 1923.

2033 Case (Humphrey J.). The Lambourn seven barrows. Oxoniensia, 15 (1950), pp. 110–14 + map. 1952.

2034 —— The Lambourn seven barrows. [6 figures. Bronze Age.] Berks. Archaeol. J., 55, pp. 15–31 + 3 plates + plan. 1957.

2035 —— A Late Belgic burial at Watlington, Oxon. Oxoniensia, 23, 1958, 139–41 + 1 figure.

2036 Catling (H. W.). A Beaker-culture barrow at North Stoke, Oxon. Oxoniensia, 24, 1959, 1–12 + 5 figures + 1 plate.

2037 Caton (Louisa L. F.). Spade work in North-West Suffolk. Proc. prehist. Soc., E.A., 2 i, 1914/15, 35–38.

2039 Chester (Greville J.). Account of the discovery of ancient British remains, near Cromer. Norfolk Arch., 5, pp. 263–67. 1859.

2040 Clarke (Edward Daniel). Observations upon some Celtic remains, lately discovered by the public road leading from London to Cambridge, near to the village of Sawston. Archaeologia, 18, pp. 340–43 + 2 plates. 1817.

2041 Clarke (Roy Rainbird) *and* **Apling** (H.). An Iron Age tumulus on Warborough hill, Stiffkey, Norfolk. Norfolk Arch., 25, pp. 408–28 + plan. 1935.

2042 —— and Wells (Calvin P. B.). Early Bronze Age burials at Barton Bendish, Norfolk. Norfolk Arch., 31, pp. 324–30 + plate. 1955.

2043 Clarke (William George). Norfolk barrows. Antiquary, 49, pp. 416–23. 1913.

2044 Clinch (George). Coldrum, Kent, and its relation to Stonehenge. [Figure + 2 plans.] Man, 4, pp. 20–33. 1904.

2045 Coghlan (Herbert Henry). An Unusual prehistoric burial at Lambourn. Trans. Newbury Dist. Fld. Club, 10 iii, 1956, 53.

2047 Collyer (H. C.). Notes on the opening of some tumuli on the South Downs. Proc. Croydon N.H. & Sci. Soc., 4, pp. 179–84. 1895.

2048 Cooper (T. S.). Notes on a barrow discovered on Blackheath, Surrey. Surrey Archaeol. Collns., 14, p. 156. 1899.

2049 Corcoran (J. X. W. P.). Excavation of two mounds on Thursley Common. Surrey Arch. Collections, 58, 1961, 87–91 + 1 plate.

2050 —— Excavation of the bell-barrows in Deerleap Wood, Wotton. Surrey Arch. Collections, 60, 1963, 1–18 + 9 figures + 4 plates.

2051 Cotton (M. A.) *and* **Richardson** (K. M.). A Belgic cremation site at Stone, Kent. Proc. prehist. Soc., 7, 1941, 134–41 + 5 figures + 2 plates.

2052 Crawford (Osbert Guy Stanhope). Lowland long barrows. Antiquity, 4, pp. 357–58. 1930.

2053 Curwen (Eliot). The Hove tumulus. pp. 6 + plate + map. 8°. Brighton, 1918.

2054 —— and Curwen (Eliot Cecil). Notes on inhumation and cremations on the London Road, Brighton. Sussex Arch. Collns., 64, pp. 191–93. 1923.

2055 —— and —— The Hove tumulus. [Map.] Brighton & Hove Archaeologist, 2, pp. 20–28 + 3 plates. 1924.

2056 —— and —— Two unrecorded long barrows [on Stoughton down]. [Plan and sections.] Sussex Arch. Collns., 66, pp. 172–75. 1925.

2057 —— and —— Lynchet burials [i.e. at edge of ploughed fields at Asheham, Rodmell] near Lewes. [4 figures.] Sussex Arch. Collns., 71, pp. 254–57. 1930.

2058 Curwen (Eliot). On three barrows, in the parishes of Iford and Rodmell. Sussex N. & Q., 4, pp. 70–72. 1932.

2059 Curwen (Eliot Cecil). The Tegdown barrow. Sussex N. & Q., 6, pp. 225–27. 1937.

2060 D. (H.). The dolmens at Rollright and Enstone. Oxfordshire Archaeol. Soc., Rpts., 1897/1898, pp. 40–51 + 2 plates (with plans). 1899.

2061 Dauncey (Kenneth Douglas Masson) *and* **Hurrell** (D. J.). The excavation of a round barrow at Cromwell, Nottinghamshire. [Bronze Age.] Trans. Thoroton Soc., 55 (1951), pp. 1–2 + plate. 1952.

2062 Davidson (H. R. Ellis). Weland the Smith. Folklore, 69, 1958, 145–59.

2063 Donaldson (T. L.). Wayland Smith's cave or cromlech, near Lambourn, Berks. Wilts. Archaeol. Mag., 7, pp. 315–20 + plan. 1862.

2064 Dunkin (E. Hadlow Wise) *and others*. Kit's Coty House. N. & Q., 4 S. 5, pp. 32, 162, 260. 1870.

2065 Dunning (Gerald Clough). Second interim report on the excavation of a Bronze Age tumulus at Dunstable, Bedfordshire. [2 figures + plan.] Man, 28, pp. 146–51. 1928.

2066 —— and Wheeler (*Sir* Robert Eric Mortimer). A barrow at Dunstable, Bedfordshire. Part 1, The archaeological evidence. (Part 2, The skeletal material, by Doris Dingwall). Archaeol. J., 88 (1931), pp. 193–217 + 10 plates. 1932.

2067 Dyer (James F). Barrows of the Chilterns. [1 figure + 11 tables + pull-out map]. Arch. J., 116, 1959, 1–24.

2068 —— The Five Knolls [Neolithic

and BA cemetery]. Beds. Mag., 8, No. 57, 1961, 15–20 + 5 figures.

2069 —— Correction: Photograph of burial from Five Knolls barrows. [2nd Neol.] Beds. Mag., 8, No. 58, 1961, 64.

2070 Edwardson (A. R.). A Bronze Age burial at Barnham, [Suffolk]. Proc. Suffolk Inst. Archaeol., 27, pp. 186–90. 1958.

2071 —— A Beaker burial at West Stow. Proc. Suffolk Inst. Arch., 29, pt. i, 1961, 73–77 + 3 figures.

2072 Erith (F. H.). A Bronze Age urn-field at Vinces farm, Ardleigh, near Colchester. Colchester Archaeol. Group, Quart. Bull., 1, pp. 11–12 + plate. 1958.

2073 —— *and* **Longworth** (Ian H.). A Bronze Age urnfield on Vinces Farm, Ardleigh, Essex. Proc. prehist. Soc., 26, 1960, 178–92. + 8 figures

2074 Erwood (Frank Charles Elliston). The megaliths of the old road. Woolwich Ant. Soc., Ann. Rpt., 13, pp. 74–84. 1908.

2075 —— The examination of a tumulus at Abbey Wood, [Kent]. [Figure.] Woolwich Ant. Soc., Ann. Rpt., 18 (1912), pp. 82–83. 1913.

2076 Evans (*Sir* John). Opening of a barrow in Easneye wood [near Ware, Herts.]. Proc. Soc. Antiq., 2 S. 18, pp. 8–9. 1899.

2077 —— Opening of a barrow in Easneye wood. East Herts. Archaeol. Soc., Trans., 1, pp. 137–8. 4°. 1900.

2078 Evans (John Henry). Smythe's megalith. Arch. Cant., 61 (1948), pp. 135–40. 1949.

2079 —— Kentish megalith types. Arch. Cant., 63 (1950), pp. 63–81 + plan (Coldrum). 1951.

2080 Fawssett (Bryan). Inventorium sepulchrale: an account of some antiquities dug up at Gilton, Kingston, Sibertswold, etc. in Kent. Edited by Charles Roach Smith. 4°. London, 1856.

2080(b) Fell (Clare Isobel). A Late Bronze Age urnfield and grooved-ware occupation at Honington, Suffolk. Proc. Camb. Antiq. Soc., 45 (1951), pp. 30–43. 1952.

2081 Fereday (Joy). Long barrow near Pitsford, Northants. Antiquity, 23, pp. 218–20. 1949.

2082 Figg (William). On the opening of a barrow at Growlink, in Friston.

[Figure.] Sussex Arch. Collns., 5, pp. 207–12. 1852.

2083 Forde (Cyril Daryll). Report on the excavation of a Bronze Age tumulus at Dunstable, Bedfordshire. [3 figures + 2 plans. Pp. 25–27 (+ plate + 2 figures), Report on the human remains found in no. 5 barrow, 67 G. Elliot Smith.] Man, 27, pp. 21–27 + plate. 1927.

2084 Fox (*Sir* Cyril) *and* **Lethbridge** (Thomas Charles). The La Tène and Romano-British cemetery, Guilden Morden, Cambs. Proc. Camb. Antiq. Soc., 27, pp. 49–63. 1926.

2085 Fox (E. V. Piercy). Reports from local secretaries and groups: Bromley. Arch. Cantiana, 78, 1963, l.

2086 Franks (*Sir* Augustus). British barrows near Chichester. Proc. Archaeol. Inst., [9] Chichester, 1853, pp. 51–54. 1856.

2087 Frere (Sheppard Sunderland). An early Bronze Age burial at Epsom College. Surrey Archaeol. Collns., 47, pp. 92–95 + plate. 1941.

2088 Gedge (J. D.). Examination of Suffolk tumuli: the Seven hills, Ampton: Barton hill. G. J. Suffolk Inst. Arch., 1, pp. 19–20. 1869.

2089 —— *and* **Hunt** (Alfred Leigh). examination of Suffolk tumuli. [Risby, Long Heath field.] Q. J. Suffolk Inst. Arch., 1, pp. 37–42. 1869.

2090 Greenfield (Ernest). The Bronze Age round barrow on Codicote Heath, Hertfordshire. Trans. St. Albans & Herts. archit. & archaeol. Soc., 1961, 5–20 + 5 figures + 2 plates.

2099 Grinsell (Leslie Valentine). Long-barrows and bell-barrows in Sussex. Sussex N. & Q., 3, pp. 69–71 + plate. 1930.

2094 —— A classification of Downland tumuli. Sussex N. & Q., 3, pp. 140–43. 1931.

2095 —— The barrows of the South Downs. Sussex County Mag., 5, pp. 396–401. 1931.

2096 —— A grave-mound cluster on Mill hill, near Rodmell. [Figure.] Sussex N. & Q., 3, pp. 231–33. 1931.

2097 —— Ancient burial-mounds. Sussex County Mag., 8, pp. 94–97. 1934.

2098 —— Sussex barrows. Sussex Arch. Collns., 75, pp. 216–75. 1934.

2099 —— An analysis and list of

Surrey barrows. Surrey Archaeol. Collns., 42, pp. 26–60 + 5 plates. 1934.

2100 —— A Chambered long barrow near Lambourn. Proc. Prehist. Soc., N.S. 1, 1935, 149.

2101 —— An analysis and list of Berkshire barrows. Berks. Archaeol. J., 39, pp. 171–91 + 6 plates; 40, pp. 20–58 + 2 plates + 2 plans; 42, pp. 102–16; 43, pp. 9–21 + 3 maps + figure. 1935–39.

2102 —— The Lamborne chambered long barrow. Berks. Archaeol. J., 40, pp. 59–62 + 2 plates + plan. 1936.

2103 —— Sussex barrows: supplementary paper (Supplement no. II). Sussex Arch. Collns., 81, pp. 210–14 + 2 maps; 82 (1941), pp. 115–23. 1940–42.

2104 —— Puttenham—barrow on the Hog's Back. Surrey Arch. Collections, 60, 1963, 84.

2105 Gurney (Frederick G.) *and* **Hawkes** (Charles Francis Christopher). An Early Iron Age inhumation burial at Egginton, Bedfordshire. Antiq. J., 20, pp. 230–44 + 2 plates. 1940.

2106 Hales (John Wesley). The Highgate barrow: a theory for its origin. Middsx. & Herts. N. & Q., 1, pp. 6–11. 1895.

2107 Hannah (Ian Campbell). Bronze Age burial at Chichester. Antiq. J., 12, pp. 170–71. 1932.

2108 Harden (Donald Benjamin) *and* **Treweeks** (R. C.). Excavations at Stanton Harcourt, Oxon., 1940, II. [3 figures + map + plan. Ring-ditches and barrow.] Oxoniensia, 10, pp. 16–41 + 7 plates. 1945.

2109 Hassall (M. W. C.). Archaeology of Holton. Oxoniensia, 23, 1958, 145–46.

2110 Head (John Frederick). The excavation of the Cop round barrow, Bledlow. Records of Bucks., 13, pp. 313–46 + 2 plates + plan. 1938.

2111 Hogg (A. H. A.). Preliminary report on the excavation of a long barrow at West Rudham, Norfolk. Proc. prehist. Soc., 4, 1938, 334–36 + 1 figure.

2112 —— A long barrow at West Rudham, Norfolk. Norfolk Archaeol., 27, pp. 315–31 + 5 plates + map + 2 plans. 1940.

2113 Holden (E. W.). Sussex barrows. Sussex N. & Q., 15, pp. 126–27. 1959.

2114 Holleyman (G. A.) *and* **Yeates** (C. W.). Excavations in the Ditchling Road area north of Brighton, 1950–1957. Sussex Arch. Collections, 98, 1960, 133–149 + 8 figures + 1 plate.

2116 Hughes (Thomas McKenny). On a tumulus in Buckenham Fields, Norfolk, explored August 1900, by Lord Amherst of Hackney. J. Brit. Archaeol. Ass., N.S. 7, pp. 183–88. 1901.

2117 Jessup (Ronald Frederick). Excavations at Julliberrie's grave, Chilham, Kent. Antiq. J., 17, pp. 122–37 + 5 plates + plan. 1937.

2118 —— Further excavations at Julliberrie's grave, Chilham. Antiq. J., 19, pp. 260–81 + 4 plates + 2 plans. 1939.

2119 Kelly (David B.). Researches and discoveries in Kent: Maidstone. Arch. Cantiana, 78, 1963, 194–6 + 1 figure.

2120 King (Samuel William). Examination of an ancient cemetery at Hempnall, Norfolk. Norfolk Arch., 5, pp. 49–52 + plan. 1859.

2121 Knox (W. Crawford). Excavation of a mound in Weston Wood, Albury. Surrey Arch. Collections, 60, 1963, 71–81.

2122 Leaf (C. S.). Crouched skeleton from Chippenham, Cambridgeshire. Antiq. J., 15, pp. 61–63 + plate (axe-hammer), pp. 213–14. 1935.

2123 —— Two Bronze Age barrows at Chippenham, Cambridgeshire. Proc. Camb. Antiq. Soc., 36, pp. 134–55 + 7 plates + 2 plans; 39, pp. 29–68 + 2 plates + 3 plans. 1936–40.

2124 Leeds (Edward Thurlow). On the excavation (Further excavations) of a round barrow at Eyebury, near Peterborough. Proc. Soc. Antiq., 2 S. 24, pp. 80–94; 26, pp. 116–27 + plan. 1912–15.

2125 —— Round barrows and ring-ditches in Berkshire and Oxfordshire. Oxoniensia, 1, pp. 7–23 + 2 plates. 1936.

2126 —— Further excavations in Barrow Hills field, Radley, Berks. Oxoniensia, 3, pp. 31–40 + 2 plates. 1938.

2127 Lethbridge (Thomas Charles). Bronze Age burials at Little Downham, Cambs. [Figure.] Antiq. J., 10, pp. 162–164 + plate. 1930.

2128 —— Further excavations in the

Early Iron Age and Romano-British cemetery at Guilder Morden. [4 figures.] Proc. Camb. Antiq. Soc., 36, pp. 109–20 + 10 plates + plan. 1936.

2129 —— Excavation of the Snailwell group of Bronze Age barrows. [2 figures + 10 plans.] Proc. Camb. Antiq. Soc., 43 (1949), pp. 30–49 + 4 plates. 1950.

2130 —— Burial of an Iron Age warrior at Snailwell. [3 figures + plan.] Proc. Camb. Antiq. Soc., 47 (1953), pp. 25–37 + 8 plates. 1954.

2131 Lewis (A. L.). On a rude stone monument [at Colderham or Coldrum Lodge, near Addington] in Kent. J. Anthrop. Inst., 7, pp. 140–42. 1878.

2132 —— The Coldrum monument. Man, 4, p. 39. 1904.

2133 Lewis (Geoffrey D.). Inhumation burial from Tolmare Farm, Findon. Sussex Arch. Collections, 98, 1960, 13.

2134 —— Middle Bronze Age cremation from Heyshott. Sussex Arch. Collections, 98, 1960, 15 + 1 figure.

2135 —— Beaker burial at Burpham. Sussex Arch. Collections, 98, 1960, 15 + 1 figure.

2136 —— Middle Bronze Age cremation from Stonington. Sussex Arch. Collections, 98, 1960, 15–16 + 1 figure.

2137 Lowerison (Bellerby). Mounds on Manor Farm, Heacham. Proc. prehist. Soc. E.A., LIII, 1912/13, 345–46.

2138 McCrerie (Alan). Kits Coty house: Smythe's megalith: The General's tombstone. Archaeol. Cant., 70 (1956), pp. 250–52. 1957.

2139 Manning (Charles Robertson). Notice of the examination of some British barrows in the parish of Bergh Apton. Norfolk Arch., 5, pp. 180–84. 1859.

2140 Margrett (Edward). Prehistoric remains in the Thames valley. Berks., Bucks. & Oxon. Archaeol. J., 11, pp. 27–29 + plate. 1905.

2141 Maynard (Guy) *and* **Benton** (Gerald Montagu). A burial of the Early Bronze Age discovered at Berden. Trans. Essex Archaeol. Soc., N.S. 15, pp. 278–294; 16, p. 144. 1921–23.

2142 —— *and* **Spencer** (H. E. P.). Report on the removal of a tumulus on Martlesham heath, Suffolk. [12 figures + plan. Bronze Age remains.] Proc. Suffolk Inst. Arch., 24, pp. 36–57. 1949.

2143 Neville (Richard Cornwallis), *4th Baron Braybrooke*. Examination of a group of barrows, five in number, in Cambridgeshire. ["Five Hill field": 1½ miles from Royston.] Archaeologia, 32, pp. 357–61. 1847.

2144 —— Sepulchra exposita: or an account of the opening of some barrows . . . discovered in the neighbourhood of Audley End, Essex. pp. vi, 98 + 15 plates + 2 plans. 8º. Saffron Walden, 1848.

2145 Norris (Norman Edward Stanley). A Bronze Age burial at Lower Tongdean, Hove. [Figure (urn).] Sussex N. & Q., 6, pp. 186–88. 1937.

2146 Parker (James). Garford barrow, near Abingdon. Proc. Oxford Archit. & Hist. Soc., 3, pp. 6–13. 1872.

2147 Parsons (Frederick Gymer). A round barrow at St. Margaret's Bay, [Kent.] Man, 29, pp. 53–54. 1929.

2148 Payne (George). A Celtic interment at Sittingbourne, Kent. Proc. Soc. Antiq., 2 S. 10, pp. 29–30. 1884.

2149 —— Celtic interments discovered at Shorne, [Kent]. Proc. Soc. Antiq., 2 S. 18, pp. 73–77. 1900.

2150 —— Celtic interments discovered at Shorne. Arch. Cant., 24, pp. 86–90 + plan. 1900.

2151 Peacock (Edward). An account of the opening of a Celtic grave-mound, at Cleatham, Lincolnshire. Reliquary, 8, pp. 224–26 + plate. 1868.

2152 Peake (Harold John Edward). Excavations on the Berkshire downs. Trans. Newbury F.C., 7 (1934–37), pp. 90–108. 1934.

2153 —— *and* **Padel** (John). Exploration of three round barrows on Woolley down, Berks. Trans. Newbury F.C., 7 (1934–37), pp. 30–48 + 2 plates + 2 plans. 1937.

2154 ——, *etc.* Excavations on Churn plain, Blewbury, Berks. Trans. Newbury F.C., 7 (1934–37), pp. 160–74. 1937.

2155 Peers (*Sir* Charles Reed) *and* **Smith** (Reginald Allender). Wayland's smithy, Berkshire. Antiq. J., 1, pp. 183–198. 1921.

2156 —— *and* —— Wayland's smithy, Berkshire. Berks, Bucks. & Oxon. Archaeol. J., 32, pp. 74–82; 33, pp. 17–23. 1928–29.

2157 Pegge (Samuel). Observations on Kit's Cotty house, in Kent. Archaeologia, 4, pp. 110–16. 1777.

2158 Petch (D. F.). The excavation of a barrow, Kirmond le Mire, 1859. Rpts. & Papers, Lincs. A. & A.S. 8 (1959), 3–4.

2159 —— Bronze Age barrows at Stroxton and Great Ponton. Rpts. & Papers, Lincs. A. & A.S., 9, 1961, 11.

2160 —— Round barrows at Brocklesby. Rpts. & Papers, Lincs. A. & A.S., 9, 1961, 11.

2161 —— A Barrow at South Willingham. Rpts. & Papers, Lincs. A. & A.S., 9, 1961, 11–12.

2162 Phillips (Barclay). Discovery of a tumulus at Hove, near Brighton, containing an amber cup, *etc*. [Figure.] Sussex Arch. Collns., 9, pp. 119–24. 1857.

2163 Phillips (Charles William). The long barrows of Lincolnshire. [10 plans.] Archaeol. J., 89 (1932), pp. 174–202 + plate + 2 maps. 1933.

2164 —— Some new Lincolnshire long barrows. Proc. PSEA, 7 iii, 1934, 423.

2165 —— A Re-examination of the Therfield Heath long barrow, Royston, Hertfordshire. Proc. prehist. Soc., N.S. 1, 1935, 101–07 + 5 figures.

2166 —— The excavation of the Giants' Hills long barrow, Skendleby, Lincolnshire. Archaeologia, 85, pp. 37–106 = 11 plates + 2 plans. 1936.

2167 Piggott (Stuart). Excavation of a round barrow near Pewit farm, Charlton down, Berks. Trans. Newbury F.C., 8, pp. 109–16. 1939.

2169 Prigg (Henry). The tumuli of Warren Hill, Mildenhall. Proc. Suffolk Inst. Arch., 4, pp. 287–99 + 2 plates. 1874.

2170 Pryor (Marlborough R.). Prehistoric interment at Weston, Stevenage. East Herts. Archaeol. Soc., Trans., 1, p. 195. 1900.

2171 Radcliffe (Fabian). Excavation at Logic Lane, Oxford. The prehistoric and early medieval finds. Oxoniensia, 26/27, 1961/62, 38–69 + 16 figures + 3 tables.

2172 Rahtz (P. A.). Two mounds on Row Down, Lambourn, Berks. Berks. Arch. J., 58, 1960, 20–32.

2173 —— Farncombe Down Barrow, Berkshire. Berks. Arch. J., 60, 1962, 1–24.

2174 Ransom (William). An Account of British and Roman remains found in the neighbourhood of Hitchin. Trans. Herts. N.H.S. & F.C., 4, 1886/88, 39–48 + 4 plates.

2175 Read (*Sir* Charles Hercules). The opening of the tumulus on Parliament Hill, Hampstead, known as Boadicea's grave. Proc. Soc. Antiq., 2 S. 15, pp. 240–45. 1894.

2176 —— The Highgate barrow: an account of the excavations. Midsx. & Herts. N. &. Q, 1, pp. 4–6. 1895.

2177(a) Repton (John Adey). An account of the opening of the great barrow at Stow-heath, near Aylsham, in Norfolk, in July 1808. Archaeologia, 16, pp. 354–55 + plate. 1812.

2177(b) Rivers (August Henry Lane Fox Pitt). Opening of the Dyke road, or Black Burgh tumulus, near Brighton, in 1872. J. Anth. Inst., 6, pp. 280–87. 1877.

2178 Roberts (Edward). On an ancient British cemetery on Sunbury common at Ashford, Middlesex. J. Brit. Archaeol. Ass., 27, pp. 449–52. 1871.

2179 Sainty (J. E.). Long barrow at West Rudham, Norfolk. Antiq. J., 18, p. 172, 410 (correction). 1938.

2180 ——, **Watson** (A. Q.) *and* **Clarke** (Roy Rainbird). The first Norfolk long barrow. Interim report on excavations at West Rudham, 1937. Norfolk Arch., 26, pp. 315–29 + plate. 1938.

2181 Scott (*Sir* W. Lindsay). Whiteleaf barrow, Monks Risborough. [Neolithic A2 pottery.] Records of Bucks., 14, p. 298. 1945.

2182 —— Excavation of a Neolithic barrow on Whiteleaf Hill, Bucks. Proc. prehist. Soc., 20, 1954, 212–30 + 7 figures + 3 plates.

2183 Sheppard (Thomas). Bronze Age burials at Cleethorpes. Lincs. N. & Q., 23, pp. 129–32 + plate (urns). 1935.

2184 Shrubsole (O. A.). On a tumulus containing urns of the Bronze Age, near Sunningdale, Berks., and on a burial place of the Bronze Age at Sulham, Berks. Proc. Soc. Antiq., 2 S. 21, pp. 303–14. 1907.

2185 Simpson, W. G. *and* **Case**, Humphrey. A Beaker-culture burial at

Dorchester, Oxford. Oxoniensia, 28, 1963, 93–95 + 1 figure.

2186 Smith (Henry). Notes on prehistoric burial in Sussex. Sussex Arch. Collns., 22, pp. 57–76. 1870.

2187(a) Smith (Reginald Allender). The seven barrows at Lambourn [Berks.]. Archaeol. J., 78, pp. 47–54. 1921.

2187(b) —— A remarkable long barrow. B.M.Q., 10, p. 56. 1935.

2188 Spokes (Sidney). A Bronze Age barrow. [2 figures + plan.] Sussex County Mag., 6, pp. 651–56. 1932.

2189 Stebbing (William Pinckard Delane). Cherry Gardens Hill tumulus, Folkestone. With a report on the human remains by A. J. E. Cave. Arch. Cant., 56 (1943), pp. 28–33. 1944.

2190(a) Swanton (E. W.). Note on a late Keltic burial ground recently discovered at Haslemere. Surrey Archaeol. Collns., 19, pp. 33–38 + 3 plates. 1906.

2190(b) Taylor (Brian Hope). A newly discovered round barrow on Croham Hurst, near Croydon. Surrey Archaeol. Collns., 49, pp. 98–100. 1946.

2191(a) Thompson (M. W.). Excavation of a supposed Roman barrow at South Ockendon, Essex. Trans. Essex Archaeol. Soc., XXVII (1958), 271–72.

2191(b) Tildesley (Miriam Louise). Report on human skeleton from a depth of 13 ft. near Grosvenor road, Westminster. Man, 31, pp. 179–84. 1931.

2192 Toms (Herbert S.). Long barrows in Sussex. [Figure + 5 plans.] Sussex Arch. Collns., 63, pp. 157–65. 1922.

2193 Trollope (Arthur). Account of the examination of tumuli at Broughton, Lincolnshire. Archaeol. J., 8, pp. 341–351 + plate (urns) + plan. 1851.

2194 Trump (D. H.). The Bronze Age barrow and Iron Age settlement at Thriplow. [3 figures + plan.] Proc. Camb. Antiq. Soc., 49 (1955), pp. 1–12. 1956.

2196 Vine (Francis Thomas). On three tumuli in Gorsley Wood, near Bridge, and Canterbury. Arch. Cant., 15, pp. 311–17 + plan. 1883.

2197 W (I.). Berkshire antiquities. Archaeol. J., 5, pp. 279–91 +plate. 1848.

2198 Warhurst (Alan). A Belgic burial from Borough Green. Arch. Cant., 66 (1953), pp. 157–60. 1954.

2199 Warren (S. Hazzledine). On a prehistoric interment near Walton-on-Naze. Essex Nat., 16, pp. 198–208 + plate. 1911.

2200 Watson (A. Q.). Tumulus on Massingham Heath excavated August 27th, 1931. Proc. PSEA, 6 iv, 1931, 375–376 + 1 figure.

2201 Whitwell (J. B.). Two barrows destroyed, Haugham. Rpts. + papers, Lincs. A. & A.S., 10, 1964, 58.

2202 —— Urn and cremation from Bronze Age barrow, Stroxton. Rpts. + papers, Lincs. A. & A.S., 10, 1964, 59–60 + 1 plate.

2203 Wilkerson, J. C. Bronze Age barrows at Melbourn. Cambridge Antiq. Soc. Proc., 5 LIII, 1960, 55.

2204 Williams (*Mrs.* Audrey). Excavations in Barrow Hills field, Radley, Berkshire, 1944. Oxoniensia, 13, pp. 1–17 + 2 plates. 1948.

2205 Williams (John Foster). Excavation of a barrow at Cley-next-the-Sea. Norfolk Arch., 22, pp. 206–08 + plate. 1925.

2206 Wilson (J.). The seven barrows. Trans. Newbury F.C., 1, pp. 178–82. 1871.

2207 Winbolt (Samuel Edward). Cremation trenches near Peaslake. Surrey Archaeol. Collns., 40, p. 117. 1932.

2208 —— A Bronze-Age burial on Duncton down. Sussex N. & Q., 4, p. 218. 1933.

2209 Woodruff (Cumberland Henry). On Celtic tumuli in east Kent. Arch. Cant., 9, pp. 16–30 + 2 coloured plates. 1874.

2210 —— An account of discoveries made in Celtic tumuli [at Ringwould] near Dover, Kent. [Figure.] Archaeologia, 45, pp. 53–56 + plate (urns). 1877.

2211 Yeates (Charles W.). The Ditchling Field discoveries. Sussex County Mag., 24, p. 408. 1950.

2212 —— Prehistoric man in the Cold Dean area. Sussex County Mag., 25, pp. 377–80. 1951.

(b) Zone 2 [CBA Group 12]

2213 Acland (John Edward). List of [54] Dorset barrows opened by E. Cunnington: or described by him. Proc. Dorset Antiq. F.C., 37, pp. 40–47. 1916.

2214 Adorian (Paul) *and* **Keil** (Fred). An excavation in a mound at Encombe, Corfe Castle. Proc. Dorset N.H. & A.S., 83, 1962, 85.

2215 Akerman (John Yonge). Note on the opening of four ancient British barrows in south Wilts. Archaeologia, 35, pp. 480–83. 1853.

2216 Alexander (John). Report on the investigation of a round barrow on Arreton Down, Isle of Wight. Part I: The barrow. Proc. I.O.W. nat. Hist. & archaeol. Soc., 5 v, 1960, 189–204, 6 figures + 2 plates.

2217 —— *and others.* Report on the investigation of a round barrow on Arreton Down, Isle of Wight. Part I: The barrow; Part II: The pre-barrow occupation, by P. C. Ozanne and A. Ozanne; Part III: The Early Bronze Age in the Isle of Wight. Proc. prehist. Soc., 26, 1960, 263–302, 10 figures + 2 plates.

2218 —— Report on the investigation of a round barrow on Arreton Down, Isle of Wight. Part III: The Early Bronze Age in the Isle of Wight. Proc. I.O.W. nat. Hist. & archaeol. Soc., 5 vii, 1962, 301–09.

2219 Andrews (Samuel). A short list of some tumuli in north Hampshire. Papers & Proc. Hants. F.C., 4, pp. 47–50. 1898.

2220 Andrew (Walter Jonathan). Report of the first (second) excavations at Oliver's Battery in 1930 (1931). Papers & Proc. Hants. F.C., 12, pp. 5–10, 163–168. 1932–33.

2221 Annable (F. K.). Earlswood long barrow. [Plan.] Wilts. Arch. Mag., 57, pp. 3–5. 1958.

2222 —— The Snail Down barrow cemetery: Bronze Age. Wilts. Arch. Mag., 57, pp. 5–8. 1958.

2223 —— Codford Down barrow group. Wilts. Arch. Mag., 57, pp. 8–9. 1958.

2224 —— Lamb down, Codford and Down farm, Pewsey: Bronze Age barrow group. Wilts. Arch. Mag., 57, pp. 231–232. 1959.

2225 —— The Milton Hill farm [near Pewsey] barrow group: Bronze Age. Wilts. Arch. Mag., 57, pp. 230–31. 1959.

2226 [Anon.] Bronze Age finds. J.

Brit. Archaeol. Ass., N.S. 27, p. 233. 1921.

2227 [Anon.] Barrow at Winterslow hut opened 1844. Wilts. Archaeol. Mag., 43, pp. 336–37. 1926.

2228 [Anon.] Moncton long barrow. Wilts. Archaeol. Mag., 55, pp. 82–83. 1953.

2229 [Anon.] The Earlswood long barrow. Arch. News Letter, 6, p. 92. 1957.

2232 apSimon (A. M.). Dagger graves in the "Wessex" Bronze Age. [2 figures.] Univ. London, Inst. Archaeol., Ann. Rpt., 10, pp. 37–62. 1954.

2233 Ashbee (Paul). Excavation of the great barrow at Bishop's Waltham, Hampshire. Possible burial of a chief. Arch. News Letter, 5, pp. 109–10. 1954.

2234 —— The great barrow at Bishop's Waltham, Hampshire. Papers & Proc. Hants. F.C., 19, pp. 184–86. 1956.

2235 —— The excavation of a round barrow on Canford heath, Dorset, 1951. [2 figures + map + plan.] Proc. Dorset Archaeol. Soc., 76 (1954), pp. 39–50, + 3 plates. 1956.

2236 —— The Great Barrow at Bishop's Waltham, Hampshire. Proc. prehist. Soc., 23, 1957, 137–66, 12 figures + 4 plates.

2237 —— *and* **Smith** (Isobel). The Windmill Hill long barrow [Notes & News.] Antiq., 34 (1960), pp. 297–98.

2238 —— Normanton Down, Grimsell's barrow No. 33a (SO/10864148). Note of excavation. WAM, 58 (1962), No. 210, 241.

2239 —— Normanton Down barrow: Grimsell's No. 33a. WAM, 58, 1963, No. 211, 468.

2240 —— The Radiocarbon dating of the Fussell's Lodge long barrow. Antiquity, 38, 1964, 139–40.

2241 Ashburnham (C.). Opening of the round barrow at Melcombe Bingham. Proc. Dorset Antiq. F.C., 38, pp. 74–80. 1918.

2242 Atkinson (Richard John Copland), **Brailsford** (John William), *and* **Wakefield** (Hugh George). A pond barrow at Winterbourne Steepleton, Dorset. Archaeol. J., 108 (1951), pp. 1–24 + plate. 1952.

2243 —— The Neolithic long mound at Maiden Castle. [2 figures.] Proc.

Dorset Archaeol. Soc., 74 (1952), pp. 36–38. 1953.

2244 Austen (John H.). On the tumuli of the St. Aldhelm's head district. Papers of the Purbeck Society, 1, pp. 33–46 + 3 plates. 1855.

2245 —— On the tumuli, etc., of the chalk range. Papers of the Purbeck Society, 1, pp. 110–15 + plate; 231–38 + plate; 157–63 + plate; 231–38 + plan; 2, pp. 55–58. 1857–58.

2246 Babington (Charles Cardale). An account of the excavation of tumuli, made by J. J. Smith, near Bincombe, in Dorsetshire, in 1842. Antiq. Comm. (Camb. Antiq. Soc.), 1, pp. 141–44 + 2 plates (pottery). 1854.

2247 Barrow (Benjamin). Notes on the opening of the tumuli on Ashey Down. J. Brit. Archaeol. Ass., 10, pp. 162–65 + plate + plan. 1864.

2248 Best (M. E.). Excavation of three barrows on the Ridgeway, Bincombe. Proc. Dorset N.H. & A.S., 86, 1964, 102–03.

2249 Bond (N.). Flower's barrow. Papers of the Purbeck Society, 1, pp. 98–109 + plan. 1857.

2250 Salkin (John Bernard). A late Bronze Age urn-field at Kinson, Dorset. [2 figures + map + plan.] Proc. Dorset Archaeol. Soc., 54, pp. 78–86. 1933.

2251 —— Romano–British graves at Putlake Farm, Langton Matravers [1 figure.] Proc. Dorset N.H. & A.S., 81, 1960, 122–23.

2252 Case (Humphrey). The Excavation of two round barrows at Poole, Dorset. Proc. prehist. Soc., 18, 1952, 148–59 + 5 figures.

2253 Chaffers (William). Barrows in Wiltshire, excavated in 1842. Collectanea Antiqua, 1, pp. 95–96. 1848.

2254 Chapman (Gillian). A Beaker burial at Weeke, Winchester. With a report on the skeleton by I. W. Cornwall. [Figure]. Papers & Proc. Hants. F.C., 19 (1956), pp. 276–80. 1957.

2255 Christie (Patricia M.). Excavation and fieldwork in Wiltshire 1961: Amesbury, Earl's Down Farm, Bronze Age barrows. Grimsell's Nos. 70 and 71. WAM, 58, 1962, No. 210. 240,

2256 —— A Barrow-cemetery of the Second Millennium B.C. in Wiltshire, England—excavation of a round barrow, Amesbury, G.71 on Earl's Farm Down, Wilts. Proc. prehist. Soc., 33, 1967, 336–366, 8 figures, 8 plates + 2 tables.

2257 Clay (Richard Challoner Cobbe). The Woodminton group of barrows, Bowerchalke. Wilts. Archaeol. Mag., 43, pp. 313–24 + 5 plates + map + plan. 1826.

2258 —— An unrecorded disc barrow on Gallow's hill, Alvediston. Wilts. Archaeol. Mag., 43, p. 324. 1926.

2259 —— Round barrow by the side of Dobson's Drove, Long down, Ebbesbourne Wake, opened 22nd July, 1924. Wilts. Archaeol. Mag., 43, pp. 324–25. 1926.

2260 —— The excavation of the barrow on Barrow hill, Ebbesbourne Wake, April 1924. Wilts. Archaeol. Mag., 43, pp. 325–26. 1926.

2261 —— The barrows on Middle down, Alvediston. [2 figures + plan.] Wilts. Archaeol. Mag., 43, pp. 432–39. 1926.

2262 —— A Late Bronze Age urn-field at Pokesdown, Hants. [13 figures + plan.] Antiq. J., 7, pp. 465–84 + 2 plates. 1927.

2263 —— The barrows in Marleycombe hill, Bowerchalke (1926). Wilts. Archaeol. Mag., 43, pp. 548–56. 1927.

2264 —— Pre-Roman coffin burials with particular reference to one from a barrow at Fovant. Wilts. Archaeol. Mag., 44, pp. 101–05. 1928.

2265 —— A crouched burial at Winterslow. Wilts. Archaeol. Mag., 44, pp. 260–61. 1928.

2266 —— The excavation of an oval barrow in Hadden's Hill plantation, Bournemouth. Antiq. J., 8, pp. 87–89. 1928.

2267 Clinch (George). Discovery of a Bronze Age cemetery in the Isle of Portland. Reliquary, 3rd S. 10, p. 144. 1904.

2268 Crawford (Osbert Guy Stanhope). Discovery of a cist-burial at Sheepwash, near Freshwater, in the Isle of Wight. Proc. Soc. Antiq., 2 S. 25, pp. 189–93. 1913.

2269 —— Excavations at Rancombe, near Shorwell, Isle of Wight, August, 1920. Papers & Proc. Hants. F.C., 9, pp. 210–13 + 2 plates. 1922.

2270 —— Excavations at Roundwood

during 1920. [3 figures + plan. i. The round barrow; ii. The twin barrows; iii. The disc barrow (with plan).] Papers & Proc. Hants. F.C., 9, pp. 189–209 + 2 plates. 1922.

2271 Cunnington (Benjamin Howard). "Blue hard stone, ye same as at Stonehenge", found in Boles (Bowles) barrow (Heytesbury, I). [Copy of a letter from William Cunnington, 1801.] Wilts. Archaeol. Mag., 41, pp. 172–74. 1920.

2272 —— The "blue stone" from Boles barrow. Wilts. Archaeol. Mag., 42, pp. 431–37 + 2 plates. 1924.

2273 Cunnington (Edward). The Helstone on Ridge hill, Portesham. Proc. Dorset Antiq. F.C., 15, pp. 52–54. 1894.

2274 Cunnington (Henry). A description of three barrows [one at Rockley and two on Ogbourn down] opened on the occasion of the visit of the Wiltshire Archaeological Society to Marlborough, August, 1879. Wilts. Archaeol. Mag., 19, pp. 67–74 + 2 plates. 1881.

2275 Cunnington (Maud Edith). Notes on the opening of a Bronze Age barrow at Manton, near Marlborough. [16 figures.] Reliquary, 3rd S. 13, pp. 28–46. 1907.

2276 —— Notes on a barrow of the Bronze Age at Oliver's camp, near Devizes. [2 figures.] Reliquary, 3rd S. 14, pp. 199–202. 1908.

2277 —— Notes on the opening of a Bronze Age barrow at Manton, near Marlborough. [2 figures.] Wilts. Archaeol. Mag., 35, pp. 1–20 + 7 plates. 1907.

2278 —— The discovery of a chamber in the long barrow at Lanhill, near Chippenham. Wilts. Archaeol. Mag., 36, pp. 300–10 + 3 plates. 1909.

2279 —— Notes on barrows on King's Play down, Heddington. Wilts. Archaeol. Mag., 36, pp. 311–17. 1909.

2280 —— Bronze Age barrows on Arn hill, Warminster. Wilts. Archaeol. Mag., 37, pp. 539–41 + plate (urns). 1912.

2281 —— List of the long barrows of Wiltshire. Wilts. Archaeol. Mag., 38, pp. 379–414. 1914.

2282 —— Opening of a barrow at Market Lavington. [Figure.] Wilts. Archaeol. Mag., 43, pp. 396–97 + 2 plates. 1926.

2283 —— Barrow near Shepherds' Shore. Wilts. Archaeol. Mag., 43, pp. 397–98. 1926.

2284 —— Two Bronze Age beaker burials at Netheravon. Wilts. Archaeol. Mag., 43, pp. 490–91. 1926.

2285 —— Unrecorded long barrow at Imber. Wilts. Archaeol. Mag., 45, p. 83. 1930.

2286 Cunnington (William). Account of a barrow on Roundway hill, near Devizes. Wilts. Archaeol. Mag., 3, pp. 185–88. 1857.

2287 —— Account of a barrow on Oldbury hill, Wilts., opened February, 1858. Wilts. Archaeol. Mag., 6, pp. 73–74. 1860.

2288 —— An account of ancient British and Anglo-Saxon barrows on Roundway hill, in the parish of Bishop's Cannings. [Plan.] Wilts. Archaeol. Mag., 6, pp. 159–67. 1860.

2289 —— Notes on a long barrow on Oldbury hill. Wilts. Archaeol. Mag., 13, pp. 103–04. 1872.

2290 —— Barrows on Roundway hill. Wilts. Archaeol. Mag., 22, pp. 340–41. 1885.

2291 —— On the recent exploration of Bowls's barrow. Advm. Sci., 1886, 841.

2292 —— Notes on Bowl's barrow [or Bowlsbury]. Wilts. Archaeol. Mag., 24, pp. 104–25 + plate. 1889.

2293 —— Notes on a group of barrows on Beckhampton downs. Wilts. Archaeol. Mag., 24, pp. 346–47. 1889.

2294 —— Account (Further account) of tumuli opened in Wiltshire in three letters to Aylmer Bourke Lambert, F.R.S. F.S.A. Archaeologia, 15, pp. 122–29 + 7 plates; pp. 338–46 + 4 plates. 1806.

2295 Drew (Charles Douglas) *and* **Piggott** (Stuart). The Excavation of long barrow 163a on Thickthorn Down, Dorset. Proc. prehist. Soc., N.S. 2, 1936, 77–96 + 5 figures + 7 plates.

2296 —— *and* —— Two Bronze Age barrows excavated by Edward Cunnington. [Figure. Clandon barrow and Ridgeway barrow no. 7.] Proc. Dorset Archaeol. Soc., 58 (1936), pp. 17–25 + 5 plates + plan. 1937.

2297 Dunning (Gerald Clough). A Late Bronze Age urnfield at Barnes, Isle of Wight, and notes on the Late Bronze

Age in the Isle of Wight. Proc. I. of W. N.H. & Arch. Soc., 2, pp. 108–17 + 6 plates + map. 1931.

2298 —— Notes on the excavation of two round barrows at Niton, and a Bronze Age hut on Gore down, Chale. [6 figures.] Proc. I. of W. N.H. & Arch. Soc., 2, pp. 196–210 + 6 plates + plan. 1932.

2299 —— A new long barrow [at South Wouston] in Hampshire. [Figure (flint scraper) + map.] Antiq. J., 26, pp. 185–86 + plate. 1946.

2300 Farrar (Raymond Anthony Holt). A collection of antiquities, and a note on the excavation of a Late Bronze Age barrow at East Down House, Winterborne, Whitchurch. Proc. Dorset Archaeol. Soc., 74 (1952), pp. 104–06. 1953.

2301 —— Three cist burials near Kimmeridge. Proc. Dorset N.H. & A.S. 81, 1960, 94–97.

2302 —— A Cist burial at Putton Lane Brickyards, Chickerell. Proc. Dorset N.H. & A.S. 85, 1963, 100–01.

2303 —— The Badbury-Hamworthy Roman Road, and a possible Bronze Age Barrow. Proc. Dorset N.H. & A.S., 85, 1963, 106.

2304 Farrer (Percy). Bronze Age interment at Ratfyn, Amesbury. Wilts. Archaeol. Mag., 41, pp. 190–91. 1920.

2305 Fowler (Peter J.). A Romano-British barrow, Knob's Crook, Woodlands, Dorset. Proc. Dorset N.H. & A.S., 81, 1960, 99–100.

2306 —— The Excavation of a supposed barrow on Corfe Hills, Corfe Mullen. Proc. Dorset N.H. & A.S., 86, 1964, 109–10.

2307 Fox (C. Frederick). Tumuli on Netley Hill, Bursledon. Papers & Proc. Hants. F.C., 12, pp. 72–74. 1932.

2308 Frend (William Hugh Clifford). A Bronze Age barrow on Knowle hill near Corfe Castle. Proc. Dorset Archaeol. Soc., 76 (1954), pp. 51–55. 1955.

2309 Goddard (Edward Hungerford). Notes on barrows at Lake, from MS. note book by E. Duke. Wilts. Archaeol. Mag., 35, pp. 582–86. 1908.

2310 —— Bronze implements found in barrows at Amesbury, 1770. Wilts. Archaeol. Mag., 38, p. 115. 1913.

2311 —— Early Bronze Age interment at the Central Flying School, Upavon. Wilts. Archaeol. Mag., 40, pp. 6–7. 1917.

2312 —— Objects from barrows in Scratchbury camp. Wilts. Archaeol. Mag., 41, pp. 193–94. 1920.

2313 Goddard (C. V.). Bronze Age interment at Wilton. Wilts. Archaeol. Mag., 36, p. 489. 1910.

2314 Gray (Harold St. George) and Prideaux (Charles S.). Barrow-digging at Martinstown, near Dorchester, 1903. Proc. Dorset Antiq. F.C., 26, pp. 6–39 + 7 plates + 2 plans. 1905.

2315 Green (Charles). Giant ditch in barrow near Stonehenge. Archaeol. News Letter, 7 ii, 1961, 44.

2316 Grimes (W. F.). Excavations in the Lake Group of barrows, Wilsford, Wiltshire, in 1959. Bull. Inst. of Arch., London, 4, 1962, 89–121 + 12 figures.

2317 Grinsell (Leslie Valentine). Hampshire barrows. [6 figures + 4 plans.] Papers & Proc. Hants. F.C., 14, pp. 9–40 + 7 plates + 4 maps; pp. 195–229 + 5 plates; pp. 346–65 + 3 plates. 1938–40.

2318 —— and Sherwin (Gerald Ambrose). Isle of Wight barrows. [Pp. 193–213, List.] Proc. I. of W. N.H. & Arch. Soc., 3, pp. 179–222 + 4 plates + map. 1940.

2319 —— The Bronze Age round barrows, Wessex. Proc. prehist. Soc., 7, 1941, 73–113 + 2 figures + 2 plates + 4 maps.

2320 —— Dorset barrows. Dorset N.H. & Arch. Society. pp. 192 + 11 plates + 6 maps. 4°. Dorchester, 1959.

2321 Hawkes (Jacquetta). The Longstone, Mottistone. Antiquity, 31, pp. 147–52 + plate. 1957.

2322 Hawley (William). Notes on barrows in south Wilts. Wilts. Archaeol. Mag., 36, pp. 615–28 + plates + plan. 1910.

2323 Hillier (William). Discovery of an ancient tumulus, at Winterbourne-Monkton, [Wilts.]. Wilts. Archaeol. Mag., 1, pp. 303–04. 1854.

2324 Johnston (David E.). A Group of barrows near Shalbourne, Wilts. WAM, 58 (1963), No. 211, 362–69 + 6 figures + 1 plate.

2325 Keiller (Alexander) and Piggott (Stuart), Excavation of an untouched chamber in the Lanhill long barrow. Proc. prehist. Soc., 4, 1938, 122–50 + 2 figures + 18 plates.

2326 Kell (Edmund). On the discovery of two cemeteries in the Isle of Wight. [i. British, at Swanmore, near Ryde. Urns, etc.] J. Brit. Archaeol. Ass., 23, pp. 215–16. 1867.

2327 Kidner (H.). New Forest round barrows which do not conform to either of the three standard types. Papers & Proc. Hants. F.C., 9, pp. 126–31. 1920.

2328 King (D. Grant). The Lanhill Long Barrow, Wiltshire, England: an essay in reconstruction (with appendices by W. E. V. Young, A. J. Clarke, A. J. Cain and G. W. Dimbleby). Proc. prehist. Soc., 32, 1966, 73–85 + 5 figures + 1 plate.

2329 Kitchin (V. P.). The Opening of a round barrow at West Lulworth in 1916 [1 figure]. Proc. Dorset N.H. & A.S., 81 (1960), 92–93.

2330 Knocker (G. M.), *Group Capt.* Excavation of a round barrow in Rag Copse, near Hurstbourne Tarrant, Hants. Papers & Proc. Hants. F.C., 22, pt. iii, 1963, pp. 125–50 + 9 figures + 5 plates.

2331 Leeds (Edward Thurlow). Barrow at Knowle farm, Little Bedwyn. Wilts. Archaeol. Mag., 38, pp. 640–41. 1914.

2332 Lukis (William Collings). Tumuli in north Wiltshire. Proc. Soc. Antiq., 2 S. 3, pp. 213–16. 1866.

2333 —— Notes on barrow-diggings in the parish of Collingbourne Dacis. [2 figures + 3 plans.] Wilts. Archaeol. Mag., 10, pp. 85–103 + 2 plates + plan. 1867.

2334 McGregor (R.). A Late Bronze Age barrow at Berry Wood, near Burley, New Forest, Hampshire. Papers & Proc. Hants. F.C., 22, pt. ii, 1962, pp. 45–50 + 3 figures.

2338 March (Henry Colley). The ritual of barrows and circles. Proc. Dorset Antiq. F.C., 29, pp. 225–50. 1908.

2339 Mellor (A. Shaw). Excavation of a circular mound on Totney hill, Kingsdown, Box. August, 1934. Wilts. Archaeol. Mag., 47, pp. 169–76. 1935.

2340 Miles (William Augustus). A description of the Deverel barrow [Dorset] opened A.D. 1825. Also, a minute account of the Kimmeridge coal money,

a most mysterious and nondescript article, pp. 1–29 + 6 plates, 31–53. 8⁰. London, 1826.

2341 Money (Walter). An ancient interment at Kingsclere. Papers & Proc. Hants. F.C., 71, pp. 110–11. 1914.

2342 Musty (J. W. G.) *and* **Stone** (John F. S.). An Early Bronze Age barrow and Late Bronze Age urnfield on Heale hill, Middle Woodford. [3 figures + plan.] Wilts. Archaeol. Mag., 56, pp. 253–61. 1956.

2343 Newall (Robert Stirling). Barrow 85 Amesbury [Goddard's list]. Wilts. Archaeol. Mag., 45, pp. 432–58 + map + plan + table. 1931.

2344 Oliver (Vere Langford). The Helstone. Proc. Dorset Antiq. F.C., 42, pp. 36–41. 1922.

2345 —— Disc barrows of Dorset. Proc. Dorset Archaeol. Soc., 50, pp. 117–124. 1929.

2346 Ozanne (Paul C.) *and* **Ozanne** (Audrey). Report on the investigation of a round barrow on Arreton Down, Isle of Wight. Part II: The pre-barrow occupation. Proc. I. of W. nat. Hist. & archaeol. Soc., 5 vi, 1961, 251–58 + 1 figure.

2347 —— *and* —— Report of the investigation of a round barrow on Arreton Down, Isle of Wight. Part II: The pre-barrow occupation. Proc. I. of W. nat. Hist. & archaeol. Soc., 5 vii, 1962, 288–302 + 1 figure.

2348 Parke (Aubrey L.). The excavation of a bell-barrow, Oakley down, Wimborne St. Giles. Proc. Dorset Archaeol. Soc., 75 (1953), pp. 36–44 + 2 plates + plan. 1955.

2349 Passmore (A. D.). The Devil's Den dolmen, Clatford bottom. An account of the monument and of work undertaken in 1921 to strengthen the north-east upright. [5 figures + plan.] Wilts. Archaeol. Mag., 41, pp. 523–30. 1922.

2350 —— Earthwork on Sugar hill, Wanborough. [Plan.] Wilts. Archaeol. Mag., 42, pp. 248–49. 1923.

2351 —— Chambered long barrow in West Woods. Wilts. Archaeol. Mag., 42, pp. 366–67. 1923.

2352 —— An unrecorded long barrow at West Kington. Wilts. Archaeol. Mag., 48, p. 466 + plate. 1939.

2353 —— Barrow no. 2, Wylye, Wilts. Wilts. Archaeol. Mag., 49, pp. 117–18 + 2 plates. 1940.

2354 —— A disc barrow containing curious flints near Stonehenge. Wilts. Archaeol. Mag., 49, p. 238. 1940.

2355 —— Barrow 19 Aldbourne (Goddard). Wilts. Archaeol. Mag., 49, pp. 239–40. 1940.

2356 —— Bronze Age burial from Swindon. Wilts. Archaeol. Mag., 50, p. 100. 1942.

2357 —— Chute, barrow 1. Wilts. Archaeol. Mag., 50, pp. 100–01. 1942.

2358 Payne (Eric H.). The Bincombe barrow, Ridgeway hill, Dorset. Excavated September, 1922, by Charles S. Prideaux. Proc. Dorset Archaeol. Soc., (6571943), pp. 38–52 + 11 plates. 1944.

2359 Piggott (Cecily Margaret). A Middle Bronze Age barrow and Deverel–Rimbury urnfield, at Latch Farm, Christchurch, Hampshire. Proc. prehist. Soc., 4, 1938, 169–87 + 11 figures + 2 plates.

2360 —— Excavation of fifteen barrows in the New Forest 1941–2. Proc. prehist. Soc., 9, 1943, 1–27 + 18 figures + 8 plates.

2361 —— Three turf barrows at Hurn, near Christchurch. Papers & Proc. Hants. F.C., 15, pp. 248–62 + 6 plates. 1943.

2362 —— An Iron Age barrow in the New Forest. [4 figures + map + 2 plans.] Antiq. J., 33, pp. 14–21 + plate. 1953.

2363 Piggott (Stuart). Bronze Age and Late Celtic burials from Yateley, Hants. [Figure (pottery).] Berks., Bucks. & Oxon. Archaeol. J., 32, pp. 69–73. 1928.

2364 —— The Excavation of a long barrow in Holdenhurst Parish, near Christchurch, Hants. Proc. PSEA, 3 (1937), 1–14 + 7 figures + 7 plates.

2365 —— The Badbury barrow, Dorset, and its carved stone. Antiq. J., 19, pp. 291–99 + plate. 1939.

2366 —— *and* **Piggott** (Cecily Margaret). Excavation of barrows on Crichel and Launceston downs, Dorset. Archaeologia, 90, pp. 47–80 + 9 plates + plan (Crichel down). 1944.

2367 —— *and* —— The excavation of a barrow on Rockbourne down. Papers & Proc. Hants. F.C., 15, pp. 156–62 + 2 plates + plan. 1945.

2368 —— Probable long barrow and stones near Eggardon. Proc. Dorset Archaeol. Soc., 67 (1945), p. 39. 1946.

2369 —— The chambered cairn of the Grey mare and colts [at Gorwell, above Portesham, Dorset]. [Plan.] Proc. Dorset Archaeol. Soc., 67 (1940), pp. 30–33. 1946.

2370 —— Notes on some north Wiltshire chambered tombs. [2 plans.] Wilts. Archaeol. Mag., 52, pp. 57–64 + plate + plan (West Kennet long barrow). 1947.

2371 —— Destroyed megaliths in north Wiltshire. Wilts. Archaeol. Mag., 52, pp. 390–92. 1948.

2372 —— *and* **Dimbleby** (Geoffrey). A Bronze Age barrow on Turners Puddle heath. Proc. Dorset Archaeol. Soc., 75 (1953), pp. 34–35 + plate. 1955.

2373 —— The West Kennet Long Barrow: excavations 1955–56. Ministry of Works Archaeological Reports, No. 4, pp. xii, 103 + 27 plates + 20 figures.

2374 —— The excavation of the West Kennet [Wilts.] long barrow: 1955–6. Antiquity, 32, pp. 235–42 + 2 plates. 1958.

2375 —— From Salisbury Plain to South Siberia [a re-evaluation of Upton Lovell BA barrow]. WAM, 58, 1961, No. 210, 93–97 + 1 figure + 1 plate.

2376 —— The West Kennet long barrow. Excavations 1955–56. pp. 140. 4°. London. 1962.

2377(a) Pleydell (John Clavell Mansell). The barrows of Dorset. Proc. Dorset Antiq. F.C., 5, pp. 20–23 + 4 plates. 1881.

2377(b) —— An ancient interment on the Verne, Portland. [Plan.] Proc. Dorset Antiq. F.C., 13, pp. 232–38. 1892.

2377(c) —— On a . . . British barrow at Bagber, Milton Abbas, *etc.* Proc. Dorset Antiq. F.C., 17, pp. 131–34 + 2 plates. 1896.

2377(d) Ponting (Charles Edwin). Description of a barrow recently opened on Overton hill. (Opening of barrow on Overton hill. By William Cunnington.) Wilts. Archaeol. Mag., 20, pp. 342–45 (345–47). 1882.

2378 Poole (H. F.) *and* **Sherwin** (Gerald Ambrose). A Belgic incineration in the Isle of Wight. Antiq. J., 12, pp. 296–98. 1932.

2379 Preston (J. P.) *and* **Hawkes** (Charles Francis Christopher). Three Late Bronze Age barrows on the Cloven Way [Hants.]. Antiq. J., 13, pp. 414–54. 1933.

2380 Price (John Edward) *and* **Price** (Frederick George Hilton). Excavations of tumuli on the Brading downs, Isle of Wight. J. Anthrop. Inst., 12, pp. 192–96 + plan. 1882.

2381 Prideaux (C. S.). The barrows of Dorset. Perkins (T.) & Pentin (H.): Memorials of old Dorset, pp. 19–27 + plate. 1907.

2382 Proudfoot (Edwina V. W.). Report on the excavation of a bell barrow in the parish of Edmondsham, Dorset, England, 1959. Proc. prehist. Soc., 29, 1963, 395–425 + 10 figures + 3 plates.

2383 Rawlence (E. A.). Prehistoric interments near Porton, Wilts. Wilts. Archaeol. Mag., 33, pp. 410–14 + plate (urn). 1904.

2384 Rickman (Charles). Recent discoveries at Okeford Fitzpaine. [Burials.] Proc. Dorset Antiq. F.C., 4, pp. 91–94. 1880.

2385 Russell (Percy). White's schedule of the Dorset Beacons. Proc. Dorset N.H. & A.S., 81, 1960, 103–06.

2386 Seaby (W. A.). A barrow on Wooton common, Hants. Papers & Proc. Hants. F.C., 17, pp. 116–21 + plate. 1952.

2387 Simpson (D. D. A.) *and* **Smith** (Isabel F.). West Overton, Overton Hill: barrows. Grinsell's Nos. 6, 6a, 6b, 7. WAM, 58, 1963, No. 211, 467–498.

2388 Smart (T. William Wake). An analysis of "The Celtic tumuli of Dorset", by Charles Warne. Proc. Dorset Antiq. F.C., 9, pp. 55–77. 1888.

2389 Smith, I. F. *and* **Simpson**, D. D. A. A heatherworker's grave from North Wiltshire. Antiquity, 38, 1964, pp. 57–61.

2390 —— *and* —— Excavation of a round barrow on Overton Hill, North Wiltshire. Proc. prehist. Soc., 32, 1966, 122–55 + 8 figures + 6 plates.

2391 Stevens (Frank) *and* **Stone** (John F. S.). The barrows of Winterslow.

Wilts. Archaeol. Mag., 48, pp. 174–82 + 5 plates + plan. 1938.

2392 Stevens (Joseph). Early British cemetery found at Dummer, Hants. J. Brit. Archaeol. Ass., 45, pp. 112–22 + plate. 1889.

2393 Stone (John F. S.). A Middle Bronze Age urnfield on Easton down, Winterslow. Wilts. Archaeol. Mag., 46, pp. 218–24 + 2 plates + plan. 1933.

2394 —— Excavations at Easton down, Winterslow, 1931–1932. Wilts. Archaeol. Mag., 46, pp. 225–42 + 7 plates + 2 plans. 1933.

2395 —— Skeleton found in a barrow at Idmiston. Wilts. Archaeol. Mag., 46, pp. 387–88. 1933.

2396 —— Excavations at Easton down, Winterslow, 1933–1934. Wilts. Archaeol. Mag., 47, pp. 68–80 + plate (dog's skeleton). 1935.

2397 —— An Early Bronze Age grave in Fargo plantation near Stonehenge. [2 figures (pottery) + plan.] Wilts. Archaeol. Mag., 48, pp. 357–70 + plan. 1938.

2398 —— *and* **Hill** (N. Gray). A round barrow on Stockbridge down, Hampshire. Antiq. J., 20, pp. 39–51 + 4 plates + plan. 1940.

2399 —— A Beaker interment on Stockbridge down, Hampshire, and its cultural connexions. [Plan.] Antiq. J., 28, pp. 149–56 + plate. 1948.

2400 Stoves (J. L.). Report on hair from the barrows of Winterslow. Wilts. Archaeol. Mag., 52, pp. 126–27. 1947.

2401 Sydenham (John). An account of the opening of some [25] barrows in south Dorsetshire. Archaeologia, 30, pp. 327–38 + plate. 1844.

2402 Thomas (Nicholas) *and* **Thomas** (Charles). Excavations at Snail down, Everleigh: 1953, 1955. An interim report. Wilts. Archaeol. Mag., 56, pp. 127–48. 1955.

2403 Thompson (M. W.) *and* **Ashbee** (P.). Excavation of a barrow near the Hardy Monument, Black Down, Portesham, Dorset (with a report on pollen analysis by G. W. Dimbleby). Proc. prehist. Soc., 23, 1957, 124–36 + 7 figures + 1 plate.

2404 Thorp (John). Description of an ancient British barrow in the Isle of Wight. J. Brit. Archaeol. Ass., 38, pp. 109–10 + plate. 1882.

2405 —— Ancient barrow in the Isle of Wight. Antiquary, 5, p. 119. 1882.

2406 Thurnam (John). On the [long] barrow at Lanhill near Chippenham, *etc.* [2 plans.] Wilts. Archaeol. Mag., 3, pp. 67–86 + map. 1857.

2407 —— On a cromlech-tumulus called Lugbury, near Littleton Drew [Wilts.]. Wilts. Archaeol. Mag., 3, pp. 164–77 + plate + plan. 1857.

2408 —— On the examination of a chambered Long-barrow at West Kennet, Wiltshire. [14 figures + 3 plans.] Archaeologia, 38, pp. 405–21. 1860.

2409 —— Examination of barrows on the downs of north Wiltshire. Wilts. Archaeol. Mag., 6, pp. 317–36 + plate. 1860.

2410 —— On Wayland's smithy, and on the traditions connected with it. Wilts. Archaeol. Mag., 7, pp. 321–33 + plan. 1862.

2411 —— Four flint implements . . . found in a barrow near Stonehenge. Proc. Soc. Antiq., 2 S. 2, pp. 427–31. 1864.

2412 —— Examination of a chambered long barrow, at West Kennet, Wiltshire. [3 figures.] Wilts. Archaeol. Mag., 10, pp. 130–35 + 2 plates + plan. 1867.

2413 —— On ancient British barrows [and their contents], especially those of Wiltshire and the adjoining counties. Part 1, Long barrows. (Part 2, Round barrows). [238 figures + 4 plans.] Archaeologia, 42, pp. 161–244 + 3 plates + plan; 43, pp. 285–552 + 11 plates. 1869–71.

2414 —— On long barrows and round barrows. Wilts. Archaeol. Mag., 13, pp. 339–43. 1872.

2415 Underwood (Guy). Farleigh Wick. Wilts. Archaeol. Mag., 52, pp. 270–71 + 2 plates. 1948.

2416 Vatcher (Faith de Mallet Morgan) *and* **Ashbee** (Paul). The excavation of two long barrows in Wessex. Antiquity, 32, pp. 104–11 + 2 plates. 1958.

2417 —— The Excavation of a Long Barrow at Nutbane, Hants. Proc. prehist. Soc., 25, 1959, 15–51 + 11 figures + 10 plates.

2418 —— The Radio-carbon dating of the Nutbane Long Barrow. Antiq., 34 (1960), p. 289.

2419 —— The Excavation of the Long Mortuary Enclosure on Normanton Down, Wilts. Proc. prehist. Soc., 27, 1961, 160–73 + 7 figures + 4 plates.

2420 —— Winterbourne Stoke, Greenlands Farm: Bronze Age barrows (SU/098442). WAM, 58, 1962, No. 210, 241.

2421 —— The Excavation of the barrows on Lamb Down, Codford St. Mary. WAM, 58, 1963, No. 211, 417–41 + 9 figures + 1 plate.

2422 Vatcher (H. F. W. L.). Bronze Age barrows: Grinsell's Nos. 12, 13, 31 and 5. WAM, 58, 1962, No. 210, p. 242.

2423 Warefield (Hugh George). The excavation of a "pond-barrow" at Winterborne Steepleton, Dorset, 1947–8. Arch. News Letter, 1 xii, pp. 11–12. 1949.

2424 Warne (Charles). On the Celtic tumuli of Dorsetshire. Trans. Brit. Archaeol. Ass. [2] Congress at Winchester, 1845, pp. 171–78. 1846.

2425 —— The Celtic tumuli of Dorset. An account of personal and other researches in the sepulchral mounds of the Durotriges. pp. 76 + 13 plates. fol. London, 1866.

2426 Willis (G. W.). Bronze Age burials round Basingstoke. Papers & Proc. Hants. F.C., 18, pp. 60–61 + 5 plates. 1954.

2427 Young (George Malcolm). Pond barrows. Wilts. Archaeol. Mag., 47, pp. 496–98. 1936.

2428 Young (W. E. V.). Beckhampton, Wilts. Arch. News Letter, lv, p. 6. 1948.

2429 —— A beaker interment at Beckhampton. Wilts. Archaeol. Mag., 53, pp. 311–31 + 2 plates. 1950.

(c) Zone 3 [CBA Groups 8 and 13]

2430 Antiquarius. The tumulus at Uley. Glos. N. & Q., 2, pp. 10–11. 1884.

2431 Ashbee (Paul). Stone cists in the Isles of Scilly. Arch. News Letter, 3, p. 135. 1951.

2432 —— Two stone cists in St. Mary's, Isles of Scilly. [Figure + map + plan.] Proc. West Cornwall F.C., N.S. 1, pp. 28–31. 1953.

2433 —— Recent work on the Cornish Bronze Age. Proc. West Cornwall F.C., N.S. 1, pp. 129–35. 1956.

2434 —— The excavation of Tregulland Barrow, Treneglos parish, Cornwall. Antiq. J., 38, pp. 174–96 + 3 plates. 1958.

2435(a) Barber (S.). The prehistoric cemetery at Harlyn Bay [Cornwall]. Reliquary, 3rd S. 7, pp. 189–94. 1901.

2435(b) Barnwell (Edward Lowry). The Bredwardine cromlech [Herefordshire]. Arch. Camb., 4th S. 4, pp. 275–276 + plate. 1873.

2436 Bate (Charles Spence). Researches into some ancient tumuli on Dartmoor. Rpt. & Trans. Devon. Assoc., 5, pp. 549–57 + plate + plan. 1872.

2437 —— Researches into some ancient tumuli on Dartmoor. Rpt. & Trans. Devon. Assoc., 6, pp. 272–75 + plate. 1873.

2438 —— Prehistoric interment recently found at Trethil in Sheviock. J. Roy. Instn. Cornwall, 7, pp. 136–38. 1882.

2439 Beesley (George J.). Mên-antol revisited. Antiquary, 48, pp. 134–39; 51, pp. 386–89. 1912, 1915.

2440 Belleville (Guy). A Crouched burial found in King Street, Brixham. Proc. Devon arch. expl. Soc., v iv, 1956, 124.

2441 Bellows (William). Opening of a round barrow near Haresfield, Glos. Proc. Cotteswold Nat. Club, 15, p. 258. 1906.

2442 Berry (*Sir* James). Belas Knap Long barrow, Gloucestershire, report of the excavations of 1929. (Second report, ... 1930.) Trans. Bristol & Glos. Arch. Soc., 51, pp. 273–303 + 21 plates + plan; 52, pp. 123–50 + 15 plates + plan. 1929–30.

2443 Bird (H.). Notes on the tumuli of the Cotteswold hills, and the human remains found therein. Proc. Cotteswold Nat. Club, 6, pp. 332–40. 1876.

2444 Blight (John Thomas). An account of a barrow with kist-vaen, in the parish of Sancreed, Cornwall. Arch. Camb., 3rd S. 10, pp. 243–45 + 2 plates. 1864. *Reprinted in* J. Roy. Instn. Cornwall, 1 iii, pp. 19–20 + 2 plates. 1865.

2445 —— Notice of a barrow with kistvaen on Trewavas head in the parish of St. Breage, Cornwall. Arch. Camb., 3rd S. 13, pp. 334–42 + 2 plates. 1867.

2446 —— Notice of a barrow with kist-vaen on Trewavas head in the parish of S. Breage. J. Roy. Instn. Cornwall, 2, pp. 306–13 + 2 plates. 1867.

2447 Borlase (William Copeland). Excavations ... in subterranean chambers at Chapel Euny, Sancreed, Cornwall. Proc. Soc. Antiq., 2 S. 4, pp. 161–70. 1868.

2448 —— Barrows in Cornwall. Arch. Camb., 3rd S. 15, pp. 32–38 + plate. 1869.

2450 —— Typical specimens of Cornish barrows. Archaeologia, 49, pp. 181–198 + 4 plates with plans. 1885.

2451 Bousfield (Paul) *and* **Bousfield** (Sigrid). Late Bronze Age burial at St. Just in Roseland, with an archaeological survey of the Roseland peninsula. [4 figures + map.] J. Roy. Instn. Cornwall, N.S. 1, pp. 130–48 + map. 1952.

2452 Brothwell (D. R.). A Romano-British burial at South Cerney, Gloucestershire. Trans. Bristol & Glos. A.S., 76, 1957, 157–60 + 2 plates + 1 figure.

2453 Brown (Jonothan Allen). Uley barrow or Hetty Pegler's rump. Glos. N. & Q., 5, pp. 219–28 + plate. 1894.

2454 Buckman (James). Notes on an ancient British tumulus at Nympsfield, opened by the Cotteswold Club. Proc. Cotteswold Nat. Club, 3, pp. 184–90. 1865.

2455 Bulleid (Arthur). The Murtry hill stones. Proc. Somerset Arch. Soc., 57 (1911), pp. 35–40. 1912.

2456 —— Notes on some chambered long barrows of north Somerset. Proc. Somerset Arch. Soc., 87 (1941), pp. 56–71 + 2 plates + plan. 1942.

2457 Burnard (Robert). Notes on Dartmoor kistvaens. Rpt. & Trans. Devon. Assoc., 22, pp. 200–07. 1890.

2458 —— Dartmoor kistvaens. Reliquary, N. [3rd] S. li, pp. 161–65. 1895.

2459 Burton (R. Jowett). Avenis barrow. Trans. Bristol & Glos. Arch. Soc., 47, pp. 348–50. 1925.

2460 Bush (Thomas S.). Excavation of twin-barrows April–May, 1909. Somerset Arch. Soc., Proc. Bath branch [2] 1909–13, pp. 28–32 + 6 plates. 1909.

2461 —— Tumulus, Lansdown, September–October, 1909. Somerset Arch.

Soc., Proc. Bath branch [2] 1909–13, pp. 34–39 + 3 plates + plan. 1909.

2462 —— Barrows on Charmy down. Somerset Arch. Soc., Proc. Bath branch [2] 1909–13, pp. 66–68 + plate + plan. 1910.

2463(a) —— Lansdown explorations, 1911. Two barrows in the Race field, Lansdown, excavated May–June, 1911. Mound near the Grenville monument. Tumulus in British camp, September, 1911. Somerset Arch. Soc., Proc. Bath branch [2] 1909–13, pp. 122–26 + 4 plates. 1911.

2463(b) —— Summary of the Lansdown explorations, 1905–1912. Somerset Arch. Soc., Proc. Bath branch [2] 1909–13, pp. 246–52 + 4 plates + 2 plans. 1913.

2464 Cantrill (Thomas Crosbee). Clent heath . . . prehistoric remains. Trans. Worcs. Archaeol. Soc., N.S. 6 (1929), pp. 145–46. 1930.

2465(a) Carrington (Samuel). Some account of a Celtic tumulus at Throwley, Staffordshire. Reliquary, 5, pp. 171–73. 1865.

2465(b) —— Some account of Long-Low, near Wetton, Staffordshire. [4 figures.] Reliquary, 5, pp. 26–30. 1865.

2466 Carter (George Edward Lovelace). Unreported mounds on Woodbury common. Proc. Devon Archaeol. Expl. Soc. 2, pp. 283–94 + 4 plates + 2 plans. 1936.

2467 Chitty (Lily Frances). Bronze Age cist burial found at Eyton, near Alberbury, Shropshire. Preliminary notes. [Figure.] Trans. Shropshire Archaeol. Soc., 51, pp. 139–41 + plate. 1943.

2468 Christie (Patricia M.). Crig-a-Mennis, a Bronze Age barrow at Liskey, Perranporth: interim note. [Plan.] Proc. West Cornwall F.C., 2, pp. 104–10. 1959.

2469 —— Crig-a-mennis: a Bronze Age barrow at Liskey, Perrangabuloe, Cornwall. Proc. prehist. Soc., 26, 1960, 76–97 + 6 figures + 5 plates.

2470 Clifford (Elsie Margaret). Notgrove barrow. Trans. Bristol & Glos. Arch. Soc., 56, pp. 1–2 + plan. 1934.

2471 —— Jackbarrow, Duntisbourne Abbots [Glos.]. Trans. Bristol & Glos. Arch. Soc., 59, pp. 334–37 + plate. 1937.

2472 —— Notgrove Long barrow, Gloucestershire. Archaeologia, 86, pp. 119–61 + 13 plates + plan. 1937.

2473 —— The Excavation of Nympsfield long barrow. Gloucestershire. Proc. prehist. Soc., 4, 1938, 188–213 + 6 figures + 9 plates.

2474 —— Beaker [interment] found at Prestbury, Glos. Trans. Bristol & Glos. Arch. Soc., 60, pp. 348–49. 1938.

2475 —— The Soldier Grave, Frocester, Gloucestershire. Proc. prehist. Soc., 4, 1938, 214–18 + 3 figures + 1 plate.

2476 —— and **Daniel** (Glyn E.). The Rodmarton and Avening portholes [Gloucestershire]. Proc. prehist. Soc., 6, 1940, 133–65 + 7 figures + 6 plates.

2477 —— The Cotswold megalithic culture. The grave goods and their background. Early cultures of N.W. Europe (H. M. Chadwick mem. Stud.) *ed.* Sir C. Fox & Bruce Dickins, pp. 21–40. 1950.

2478 —— The Ivy Lodge round barrow [near Stroud, Glos.]. Trans. Bristol & Glos. Arch. Soc., 69 (1950), pp. 59–77 + plate. 1952.

2479 —— Burial at Kingscote, Gloucestershire. Trans. BGAS, 82, 1963, 205–207 + 1 figure.

2481 Crook (B. A.), *Dr. and* **Crook** (K. M.). A beaker burial near Corston, Bath. [Figure.] Antiq. J., 21, pp. 151–52. 1941.

2482 Daniel (Glyn Edmund). The Long Barrows of the Cotswolds. Trans. BGAS, 82, 1963, 5–17 + 2 figures.

2483 Devonshire Association. First (second, *etc.*) report of the Barrow Committee. Rpt. & Trans. Devon. Assoc., 11, pp. 146–60, *and in subsequent volumes.* 1879, *etc.*

2484 Dewey (Henry). Note on an unrecorded cromlech in north Cornwall. J. Roy. Instn. Cornwall, 18, pp. 362–64 + plate + map + plan. 1911.

2485 Dimbleby (G. W.). Pollen analysis from two Cornish barrows. JRIC, N.S. 4, 1963, 364–75.

2486 Doe (George). The examination of two barrows near Torrington. Rpt. & Trans. Devon. Assoc., 7, pp. 102–05 + plate. 1875.

2487 Donovan (Helen Evangeline). Adlestrop hill barrow, Gloucestershire.

Trans. Bristol & Glos. Arch. Soc., 60, pp. 152–64 + 2 plates + plan. 1938.

2488 Dorington (J. E.). Remains on a round barrow, in Hungerfield, in the parish of Cranham. Trans. Bristol & Glos. Arch. Soc., 5, pp. 133–36. 1881.

2489 Dowie (H. G.). A Prehistoric burial site at Slapton. Trans. & Proc. Torquay nat. Hist. Soc., 5, 1927, 3–5 + 1 plate.

2490 Dudley (Dorothy). The Excavation of the Otterham Barrow, Cornwall. JRIC, N.S. 4, 1961, 62–80 + 5 figures + 10 plates.

2491 —— The Excavation of the Carvinack barrow, Tregavethan, near Truro, Cornwall. JRIC, N.S. 4, 1964, 414–51 + 6 figures + 10 plates.

2492 —— *and* **Thomas** (Charles). An Early Bronze Age burial at Rosecliston, Newquay. Cornish arch., 4, 1965, 10–17 + 2 figures + 1 plate.

2493 —— *and* **Jope** (E. M.). An Iron Age cist-burial with two brooches from Trevone, North Cornwall. Cornish arch., 4, 1965, 18–23 + 3 figures.

2494 Dunkin (E. Hadlow Wise). Notes on the discovery of a kistvaen on Tredinney hill, near Land's End. Reliquary, 10, pp. 241–43 + plan. 1870.

2495 —— On the original use of the Mên-an-tol, . . . Madron. J. Roy. Instn. Cornwall, 4, pp. 152–54. 1872.

2496 Dymond (Charles William). Notes on the Men-an-tol and Chywoon quoit, Cornwall. J. Brit. Archaeol. Ass., 33, pp. 176–78 + 2 plates (with plans). 1877.

2497 —— Trethevy stone. J. Brit. Archaeol. Ass., 37, pp. 112–22 + 2 plates + plan. 1881.

2498 —— The Mên-an-tol: a recent theory examined. Antiquary, 50, pp. 47–49. 1914.

2499 Elworthy (Frederick Thomas). An ancient British interment. [2 figures.] Proc. Somerset Arch. Soc., 42, pp. 56–66 + 2 plates. 1896.

2500 Falcon (T. A.). Dartmoor: a note on graves. Rpt. & Trans. Devon. Assoc., 37, pp. 457–61. 1905.

2501 Falconer (J. P. E.). Bronze Age round barrow, Woodchester, [Glos.]. Trans. Bristol & Glos. Arch. Soc., 52, pp. 309–12 + plate (beaker). 1930.

2502 Forrest (H. E.). Prehistoric burial at Alberbury: some unusual features. Trans. Shropshire Archaeol. Soc., 51, pp. 142–45. 1943.

2503 Fowler (Hugh). On the opening of an ancient British barrow at Huntshaw. Rpt. & Trans. Devon. Assoc., 2, pp. 187–89. 1867.

2504 Fox (*Lady* Aileen Mary). The Broad Down (Farway) necropolis and the Wessex culture in Devon. Proc. Devon. Archaeol. Expl. Soc., 4, pp. 1–19 + 5 plates + plan. 1948.

2505 Gardiner (Charles Irving). Jackbarrow. A recently discovered Cotswold long barrow. [Pp. 72–75, Human remains, by M. L. Tildesley.] Proc. Cotteswold N.F.C., 25, pp. 69–75 + plate. 1933.

2506 —— Adlestrop hill barrow. (second report). Proc. Cotteswold N.F.C., 25, pp. 301–02; 26, p. 104: 1935–36. 1936.

2507 Garrett (C. Scott). Tidenham chase barrow. [7 figures + 2 plans.] Trans. Bristol & Glos. Arch. Soc., 74 (1955), pp. 15–35 + 3 plates. 1956.

2508 Gettins (G. L.), **Taylor** (Herbert) *and* **Grinsell** (Leslie Valentine). The Marshfield barrows. Trans. Bristol & Glos. Arch. Soc., 72 (1953), pp. 23–44 + 3 plates + 2 plans. 1954.

2509 Gray (Harold St. George). Huish Champflower barrow, near Raleigh's Cross, on the Brendon hills. N. & Q., Som. & Dorset, 8, pp. 303–05. 1903.

2510 —— Report on the excavations at Wick barrow, Stogursey, Somersetshire. pp. iv, 78 + 10 plates + map + plan. 8°. Taunton, 1908. [20 figures + map + plan.]

2511 —— Report on the Wick barrow excavations. Proc. Somerset Arch. Soc., 54 (1908), pp. 1–78 + 10 plates + plan. 1909.

2512 —— Human remains from Dinder. N. & Q., Som. & Dorset, 11, pp. 355–56. 1909.

2513 —— Excavations at Murtry hill, Orchardleigh park, 1920. Proc. Somerset Arch. Soc., 67 (1921), pp. 39–55 + plate + plan. 1922.

2514 —— Battlegore, Williton. Proc. Somerset Arch. Soc., 77 (1931), pp. 7–36 + 3 plates + 2 plans. 1932.

2515 —— Rude stone monuments of

Exmoor. Part 5. Proc. Somerset Arch. Soc., 83 (1937), pp. 166–70. 1938.

2516 —— Stone cist found at Walton park, Clevedon, in 1898. Proc. Somerset Arch. Soc., 89 (1943), pp. 86–87. 1944.

2517 Green (Charles). An Iron Age cremation burial in the Cotswolds. [Figure.] Antiq. J., 22, pp. 216–18. 1942.

2518 —— The Birdlip Early Iron Age burials: a review. Proc. prehist. Soc., 15, 1949, 188–90 + 1 figure + 1 plate.

2519 —— A round barrow near Haresfield, Gloucestershire. Antiq. J., 29, pp. 80–81. 1949.

2520 —— A Round barrow at Astley, Worcestershire. Trans. Worcs. A.S., N.S. vol. 38, 1961, 1–8 + 3 figures + 4 plates.

2521 Grey (Gerald J.). Exploration of tumulus, Hampton down. Somerset Arch. Soc., Proc. Bath branch [1] 1904–1908, pp. 51–54 + plan. 1905.

2522 Grinsell (Leslie Valentine). Some rare types of round barrow on Mendip. Proc. Somerset Arch. Soc., 85 (1939), pp. 151–66 + 2 plates. 1940.

2523(a) —— A Decorated cist-slab from Mendip. Proc. prehist. Soc., 23, 1957, 231–32 + 1 plate.

2523(b) —— A round barrow on Mendip. N. & Q., Som. & Dorset, 27, pp. 202–03. 1958.

2524 —— The Marshfield Barrows: Supplementary note. Trans. Bristol & Glos. A.S., 77, 1958, 151–55 + 1 figure.

2525 —— Work at the Pool Farm stone cist, Mendip. N. & Q., Somerset & Dorset, 27, pt. 259, 1959, 243–4.

2526 Gunstone (A. J. H.). The Dale of the three Shire Stones, near Batheaston [sham megalith]. Trans. BGAS, 82, 1963, 210–11.

2527 Hamilton (W. G.). A Bronze Age burial site at Southend, Mathon. [Herefordshire]. Trans. Woolhope N.F.C., 1936–38, pp. 120–27 + 3 plates + plan. 1940.

2528 Hancock (F.). Two barrows on the Brendon hills. Proc. Somerset Arch. Soc., 42, pp. 22–25. 1896.

2529 Hemp (Wilfrid James). Belas Knap Long barrow, Gloucestershire. [Figure.] Trans. Bristol & Glos. Arch. Soc., 51, pp. 261–72 + 9 plates + 2 plans. 1929.

2530 —— Arthur's Stone, Dorstone,

Herefordshire. Arch. Camb., 90 ii, 1935, 288–92 + 3 figures.

2531 Hill (Herbert C.). Northfield tumulus, Cheltenham. Trans. Bristol & Glos. Arch. Soc., 52, pp. 305–08. 1930.

2532 Hirst (F. C.). Supposed Iron Age burial at Mawganporth. J. Roy. Instn. Cornwall, 24, pp. 319–27. 1935.

2533 Hitchins (Malachi). Account of . . . a cromlech discovered in the parish of Madron. Archaeologia, 14, pp. 224–30. 1803.

2534 Hoare (Sir Richard Colt), bart. An account of a stone barrow, in the parish of Wellow, at Stoney Littleton in the county of Somerset, which was opened and investigated in the month of May 1816. Archaeologia, 19, pp. 43–48 + 2 plates + plan. 1821.

2535 Horne (Ethelbert). Excavation of Pool farm barrow, West Harptree, Somerset. Proc. Somerset Arch. Soc., 76 (1930), pp. 85–90 + plate + plan. 1931.

2536 King (H.) and Polkinghorne (B. C.). Excavation of a barrow on Chapel Carn Brea, Cornwall. Man, 9, pp. 147–48. 1909.

2537 Kirwan (R.). Memoir of the examination of three barrows at Broad Down, Farway, near Honiton. Rpt. of Trans. Devon Assoc., 2, pp. 619–49 + 9 plates (pottery, etc.). 1868.

2538 —— Sepulchral barrows at Broad Down, near Honiton [Devon], and an unique cup of bituminous shale found there. Archaeol. J., 25, pp. 290–311 + 3 plates. 1868.

2539 Lawrence (W. L.). Examination of a chambered long barrow in Gloucestershire. Proc. Soc. Antiq., 2 S. 3, pp. 275–80. 1866.

2540 Lewis (A. L.). Cornish quoits and French dolmens—a comparison. J. Roy. Instn. Cornwall, 18, pp. 409–12 + 2 plates. 1911.

2541 Lewis (H. A.). Cist at St. Martin's, Scilly. Antiq. J., 29, pp. 84–85 + plate. 1949.

2542 Lukis (Frederick Collings). Observations on the Celtic megaliths, and the contents of Celtic tombs, chiefly as they remain in the Channel Islands. Archaeologia, 35, pp. 232–58. 1853.

2543 Lysons (Samuel). Opening of a

tumulus at Rodmarton in Gloucester-shire. Proc. Soc. Antiq., 2 S. 2, pp. 275-79. 1863.

2544 MacLean (*Sir* John). Description of the chambered tumuli of Uley and Nympsfield. Trans. Bristol & Glos. Arch. Soc., 5, pp. 86–118 + 2 plates + 2 plans. 1881.

2545 Marshall (George). Two Early Bronze Age burials in the Olchon valley, Herefordshire. Bull. Bd. Celtic Stud., 6, pp. 378–86. 1933.

2546 —— Report on the discovery of two Bronze Age cists in the Olchon valley, Herefordshire. Trans. Wool-hope N.F.C., 1930-32, pp. 147–53 + 6 plates. 1935.

2547 Moore (Henry Cecil). Arthur's stone, Dorestone. Trans. Woolhope N.F.C., 1900-02, pp. 194–99 + 2 plates. 1903.

2548 Morgan (C. Lloyd). The Water-stone dolmen, Somersetshire. Proc. Clifton Antiq. Club, 3, pp. 192–94 + plate. 1897.

2549 O'Neil (Bryan Hugh St. John). The excavation of Knackyboy cairn, St. Martin's, Isles of Scilly, 1948. Antiq. J., 32, pp. 21–34 + 6 plates + plan. 1952.

2550 —— A triangular cist in the Isles of Scilly. Antiq. J., 54, pp. 235–37 + plate. 1954.

2551 O'Neil (Helen) *and* **Grinsell** (Leslie V.). Gloucestershire barrows [No. 8 of Regional Surveys of English barrows]. Trans. Bristol. & Glos A.S., 79, 1960, pt. 1, 5–149 + 5 figures + 1 map.

2552 O'Neil (Helen E.). Fifield Long Barrows I and II; on Oxfordshire and Gloucestershire county boundary. Trans. Bristol & Glos. A.S., 79, 1960, pt. ii, 298–301 + 1 figure.

2553 Ormerod (G. Wareing) *and* **Rowlands** (J. Bowen). Drewsteignton cromlech. N. & Q., 3 S. 2, pp. 20, 119, 395. 1862.

2554 —— The fall and restoration of the cromlech at Drewsteignton, 1862. Rpt. & Trans. Devon Assoc., 4, pp. 409–11. 1871.

2555 —— Drewsteington cromlech. Antiquary, 3, pp. 91–92. 1881.

2556 Paine (Alfred E. W.). Note on a long barrow, near Bisley. Proc.

Cotteswold Nat. Club, 17, pp. 341–43 + plate (skull). 1912.

2557(a) Pape (T.). Excavation of a round barrow at Swinscoe. North Staffs. F.C., Trans., 64, pp. 89–96 + plan. 1930.

2557(b) Passmore (A. D.). A bee-hive chamber at Ablington, Gloucester-shire. [Figure + plan.] Trans. Bristol & Glos. Arch. Soc., 56, pp. 95–98 + 2 plates. 1934.

2558 Piper (George H.). Arthur's stone, Dorstone. Trans. Woolhope N.F.C., 1881–82, pp. 175–80 + 2 plates. 1888.

2559 Pool (Peter A. S.). Lanyon quoit: the fall of 1815. Proc. West Cornwall F.C., N.S. 1, pp. 167–69. 1956.

2560 —— Tolcreeg Barrow, Gulval. Cornish arch., 3, 1964, 105–07 + 1 figure.

2561 —— To a fallen Cromlech. Cornish Arch., 5, 1966, 16.

2562 Radford (Courtenay Arthur Ralegh). Belas Knap barrow, Glouces-tershire. Report on work carried out during the winter 1930–31. Trans. Bristol & Glos. Arch. Soc., 52, pp. 295–99. 1930.

2563 —— *and* **Rogers** (Ernest Henry). The excavation of two barrows at East Putford. [3 plans.] Proc. Devon Archaeol. Expl. Soc., 3, pp. 156–63 + 3 plates. 1947.

2564 —— The Chambered tomb at Broadsands, Paignton. Proc. Devon Arch. Expl. Soc., v v + vi, 1957/58, 147–67 + 6 figures + 2 plates.

2565 Rahtz (P. A.). The excavation of a twin-barrow near Marshfield, Glos. Arch. News Letter, I xii, p. 8. 1949.

2566 Reece (Richard). The Oakley Cottage Romano-British cemetery, Cir-encester. Trans. BGAS, 81, 1962, 51–72 + 3 figures.

2567 Rogers (John) *Canon of Exeter*. Some account of the opening of a barrow near Newquay with a few remarks on urn burial. Ann. Rpt. Roy. Instn. Cornwall, 22 (1840), pp. 60–63. 1841.

2568 Rogers (Ernest Henry). The excavation of a barrow on Brownstone farm, Kingswear. Proc. Devon Ar-chaeol. Expl. Soc., 3, pp. 164–66 + 2 plates. 1947.

2569 Rolleston (George). The pre-historic interments of the Cotteswold district. Trans. Bristol & Glos. Arch. Soc., 1, pp. 55–58. 1876.

2570 —— *and* **Rivers** (Augustus Henry Lane Fox Pitt). Report of excavation of a twin-barrow, and a single round barrow at Sigwell (Six wells), parish of Compton, Somerset. (Observations on the topography of Sigwell). J. Anthrop. Inst., 8, pp. 185–94 + 3 plans. 1878.

2571 —— *and* —— Report of exvacation of a twin barrow and a single round barrow, at Sigwell, parish of Charlton Horethorne, Somerset. Proc. Somerset Arch. Soc., 24 (1878), pp. 75–88. 1879.

2572 Russell (Vivien). A possible long barrow at Brane in Sancreed. Proc. West Cornwall F.C., N.S. 1, p. 26 + plan. 1953.

2573 Sanford (W. A.). Notice of a burial by cremation, of the Bronze period, in the parish of West Burkland. Proc. Somerset Arch. Soc., 13 (1865–1866), pp. 261–62. 1867.

2574 Scantlebury (T. J.). A barrow group [at Trenderway, Bodmin moor], in east Cornwall. Proc. West Cornwall F.C., 2, pp. 31–33. 1957.

2575 Scarth (Harry Mengden). Remarks on ancient chambered tumuli, as illustrative of the tumulus still existing at Stoney Littleton, near Wellow, in the county of Somerset. Proc. Somerset Arch. Soc., 8 (1858), pp. 35–62 + 3 plates (with plan). 1859.

2576 —— Tumulus at Nempnett, now destroyed. Proc. Bath N.H. & Ant. F.C., 3, pp. 20–25. 1877.

2577 Scott (M. H.). Note on a dolmen at Stoke Bishop. Proc. Bath N.H. & Ant. F.C., 10, pp. 318–19 + plate. 1905.

2578 Smith (Reginald Allender). On a Jersey megalithic monument at Henley-on-Thames. [4 plans.] Proc. Soc. Antiq., 2 S. 31, pp. 133–45. 1919.

2579 Stanes (R. G. F.). Chapman barrows. Devon & Cornwall Notes & Queries, 29 vii, 1963, 206.

2580 Stone (J. Harris). On the Ballowal cairn at St. Just, and on inverted urns. Antiquary, 47, pp. 86–89, 145–50. 1911.

2581 Tebbs (B. N.). The Long barrows of the Cotswolds. Trans. & Proc. Torquay nat. Hist. Soc., 7, 1937, 187–95 + 1 plate.

2582 Tebbutt (Charles Frederick). A cist in the Isles of Scilly. Antiq. J., 14, pp. 302–04 + plate. 1934.

2583 Thomas (Charles). Megalithic tombs on the island of Teän, Scilly. [2 plans.] Proc. West Cornwall F.C., 2, pp. 33–36. 1957.

2584 Thurnam (John). Description of a chambered tumulus, near Uley, Gloucestershire. [2 plans.] Archaeol. J., 11, pp. 315–27 + 2 plates. 1854.

2585 Wainwright (G. J.). The Excavation of a cairn at St Neot, Bodmin Moor. Cornish arch. 4, 1965, 4–9 + 3 figures.

2586 Warner (R. B.). Burrow Belles: a new chambered tomb near Truro. Cornish Arch., 5, 1966, 14–15.

2587 Watkins (Alfred). Arthur's stone. Trans. Woolhope N.F.C., 1927–1929, pp. 149–51 + plate + plan. 1931.

2588 Were (Francis). Report on the excavation at Druid Stike. Trans. Bristol & Glos. Arch. Soc., 36, pp. 217–19 + plate. 1913.

2589 Whitley (D. Gath). The builders and antiquity of our Cornish dolmens. J. Roy. Instn. Cornwall, 16, pp. 84–99. 1903.

2590 Williams (Audrey). Excavation of barrows at Ston Easton, Somerset. Proc. Somerset Arch. Soc., 88 (1942), pp. 77–79. 1943.

2591 —— Bronze Age barrows near Chewton Mendip, Somerset. Proc. Somerset Arch. Soc., 93 (1947), pp. 39–67 + 8 plates. 1949.

2592 —— Bronze Age barrows on Charmy down and Lansdown, Somerset. [4 figures + 3 plans.] Antiq. J., 30, pp. 34–46 + 2 plates. 1950.

2593 Witts (George Blackhouse). Randwick long barrow. Proc. Cotteswold Nat. Club, 8, pp. 156–60 + plate. 1884.

2594 —— Notgrove long barrow. [Plan.] Proc. Cotteswold Nat. Club, 18, pp. 43–46. 1912.

2595 Wood (James George). The Arthur stone. Trans. Woolhope N.F.C., 1918–20, pp. 200–03. 1921.

2596(a) Worth (Richard Hansford)

and **Tyler** (F. C.). Kistvaens at Thornworthy (and stone rows). Devon & Cornwall N. & Q., 16, pp. 49–50 + plate, pp. 115–19. 1930.

2596(b) Wright (Thomas). Treago, and the large tumulus at St. Weonards. [Plan.] Arch. Camb., 3rd S. 1, pp. 161–74 + plate. 1855.

(d) Zone 4 [CBA Groups 3, 4, 5, 6]

2598(a) Alcock (Leslie) *and* **Alcock** (Elizabeth). Ringham Low: the rediscovery of a Derbyshire chambered tomb. [2 plans.] Antiquity, 26, pp. 41–43; 27, pp. 41–42. 1952–53.

2598(b) Allen (John Romilly). On the circle of stones at Calderstones, near Liverpool. J. Brit. Archaeol. Ass., 39, pp. 304–16 + 2 plates (cup-marks, *etc.*). 1883.

2598(c) —— The Calderstones, near Liverpool. J. Brit. Archaeol. Ass., 44, pp. 71–82. 1888.

2599 Allies (Jabez). Sepulchral vase, and other antiquities, discovered near Scarborough, and preserved in the Scarborough Museum. [Figure.] Archaeologia, 30, pp. 458–62. 1844.

2600 Anderson (W. D.). The tumulus on Great Meg fell. [Plan.] Trans. Cumb. & Westm. Ant. Soc., N.S. 23, pp. 112–14. 1923.

2601 Andrew (Walter Jonathan). Excavation of the tumulus on Sponds hill, east Cheshire. Trans. Lancs. & Ches. Ant. Soc., 30 (1912), pp. 184–94 + plate + plan. 1913.

2602 [Anon.] The opening of a barrow on Grin Low [Derbs.]. Illus. Arch., 2, pp. 52–53. 1894.

2603 [Anon.] Discovery of interments of the Early Iron Age at Danes' Graves, near Driffield, Yorkshire. [Figure.] Reliquary, N. [3rd] S. 3, pp. 224–30. 1897.

2604 [Anon.] Cinerary urn of the Bronze Age found in barrow near Thorpe hall, near Bridlington, Yorks. [Figure.] Reliquary, 3rd S. 12, p. 270. 1906.

2605 [Anon.] Excavation of the Quernhow tumulus, Yorkshire. Arch. News Letter, 2, pp. 169–71. 1950.

2606 apSimon (A.) *etc.* Excavation of the Barnby Howes barrows, Yorkshire. Arch. News Letter, 4, pp. 126–27. 1952.

2607 Armstrong (Albert Leslie) A sepulchral cave at Tray Cliffe Castleton, Derbyshire. J. R. Anthrop Inst., 53, pp. 123–31. 1923.

2608 Ashbee (Paul) *and* **Ashbee** (R. C. L.). Excavation of a barrow at Hindlow, Derbyshire. Arch. News Letter, 5, pp. 134–35. 1954.

2609 —— *and* **apSimon** (A. M.). Barnby howes, Barnby, East Cleveland, Yorkshire. Yorks. Archaeol. J., 39, pp. 9–31 + 2 plates + plan. 1956.

2610 —— Excavations on Kildale moor, North Riding of Yorkshire. Yorks. Archaeol. J., 39, pp. 179–92 + 3 plates + plan. 1957.

2611 Askew (Gilbert). Report on the excavation of two Bronze Age burials at Benthall, Northumberland. [Map.] Arch. Æl., 4th S. 15, pp. 149–55 + plate. 1938.

2613 Bagshawe (Benjamin). Notice of a barrow near Grindlow, Derbyshire. [Figure.] Reliquary, 3, pp. 205–06. 1863.

2614 Baggaley (J. W.). The Crookes urn burial. Trans. Hunter Arch. Soc., 3, pp. 334–36 + 1 plate. 1929.

2615 Ball (Thomas). Opening of barrows in Swinburne park. [Plan.] Proc. Soc. Antiq. Newc., 4th S. 4, pp. 75–81 + plate. 1929.

2616 Barker (Mabel Mary). Tumuli near Carrock Fell. [2 plans.] Trans. Cumb. & Westm. Ant. Soc., N.S. 34, pp. 107–12. 1934.

2617 Bartlett (J. E.). The excavation of a barrow at Lodge Moor, Sheffield, 1954–55. Trans. Hunter Arch. Soc., 7, pp. 321–30 + 3 plates + plan. 1957.

2618 Bateman (Thomas). Account of some Celtic barrows lately opened [at] Bakewell, Derbyshire. Trans. Brit. Archaeol. Ass. [1] Congress at Canterbury, 1844, pp. 77–88. 1845.

2619 —— Remarks upon a few of the barrows opened at various times in the more hilly districts near Bakewell, [Derbs.]. J. Brit. Archaeol. Ass., 7, pp. 210–20 + plate. 1851.

2620 —— On excavations at Gib Hill tumulus [Derbs.]. J. Brit. Archaeol. Ass., 15, pp. 151–53. 1859.

2621 Bateman (William). An account of the opening of tumuli, principally at Middleton, by Youlgrave, Derbyshire, from 1821 to 1832. Collectanea Antiqua (edited by C. R. Smith), 1, pp. 49–60 + 2 plates. 1848.

2622 Bennett (W.). Giants' graves, Penygent. Yorks. Archaeol. J., 33, pp. 318–19 + plan. 1938.

2623 —— Report on excavations near Burnley. Trans. Lancs. & Ches. Ant. Soc., 62 (1950–51), pp. 204–06 + plate (urns) + plan. 1953.

2624 Bosanquet (Robert Carr). The Ellsnook tumulus near Rock. Proc. Soc. Antiq. Newc., 4th S. 6, pp. 146–49 + plate (beaker). 1933.

2625 Brewis (Parker). A Bronze Age burial at Kyloe, Northumberland. Arch. Æl., 4th S. 5, pp. 26–29 + 2 plates. 1928.

2626 Bryan (Benjamin). On a cromlech formerly standing on Riber hill, Matlock, in the county of Derby. [Figure.] J. Derbs. Archaeol. Soc., 91, pp. 39–44. 1887.

2627 Bulmer (William). Note on a cist at Summerhill, Blaydon. Arch. Æl., 4th S. 15, pp. 218–21. 1938.

2628 —— A note on two more cists at Summerhill, Blaydon. Arch. Æl., 4th S. 16, pp. 260–63. 1939.

2629 Bu'lock (J. D.) *and* **Rosser** (C. E. P.). Winter Hill, a composite cairn of the Bronze Age. Trans. Lancs. & Cheshire antiq. Soc., 70, 1960, 66–73 + 2 figures.

2630 Burman (C. Clark). Report on the examination and description of human remains from an ancient British grave discovered at High Buston, Northumberland, on 18th October, 1912. Arch. Æl., 3rd S. 9, pp. 44–53. 1913.

2631 Butterfield (Allan). Structural details of a long barrow on Black Hill, Bradley Moor, West Yorkshire. Yorks. Archaeol. J., 34, pp. 222–27. 1939.

2632 Cherry (J.). Cairns in the Birker Fell and Ulpha Fell area. Trans. C. & W.A. & A.S., N.S. 61, 1961, 7–15.

2633 —— *and* **Fletcher** (W.). Cairn on Birker Moor, rescue dig. Trans. C. & W.A. & A.S., N.S. 64, 1964, 371.

2635 Clark (E. Kitson). Excavation at Pule hill, near Marsden, on the Huddersfield and Manchester road. Yorks.

Archaeol. J., 16, pp. 38–42 + 2 plates. 1902.

2636 Clark (Mary Kitson). Bronze Age burial, Inglebank gravel pit, Boston Spa. (Report on human remains, by A. J. E. Cave.) Yorks. Archaeol. J., 31, pp. 36–43 + plate. 1934.

2637 Cole (Edward Maule). On the recent opening of a tumulus in Yorkshire. Antiquary, 33, pp. 71–72. 1897.

2638 —— Duggleby howe. Trans. E. Riding Antiq. Soc., 9 (1901), pp. 57–61. 1902.

2639 —— Notes on tumuli in the wolds, East Riding of Yorkshire. Antiquary, 39, pp. 261–64. 1903.

2640 Collier (Carus V.). Notes on a barrow at Bradwell. J. Brit. Archaeol. Ass., 48, p. 80. 1892.

2641 Collingwood (Edward F.), **Cowen** (John David) *and* **Shaw** (A. F. Bernard). A prehistoric grave at West Lilburn. Arch. Æl., 4th S. 24, pp. 217–229 + plate. 1946.

2642 —— *and* —— A prehistoric grave at Haugh Head, Wooler. Arch. Æl., 4th S. 26, pp. 47–54. 1948.

2643 —— *and* **Jobey** (George). A Food vessel burial at West Lilburn. Arch. Æliana, 39, 1961, 373–78 + 3 figures.

2644 Collingwood (William Gershorn). Tumulus at Grayson-lands, Glassonby, Cumberland. Trans. Cumb. & Westm. Ant. Soc., N.S. 1, pp. 295–302 + plate (urn). 1901.

2646 Conyngham (*Lord* Albert Denison) *afterwards* **Denison** (Albert) *1st Baron Londesborough*. Account of discoveries made in barrows near Scarborough. [6 figures.] J. Brit. Archaeol. Ass., 4, pp. 101–07. 1849.

2647 —— An account of the opening of some tumuli in the East Riding of Yorkshire. [Figures + 2 plans.] Archaeologia, 34, pp. 251–58 + plate. 1852.

2648 Cordeaux (John). Ancient British interment. Lincs. N. & Q., 2, pp. 17–18. 1890.

2649 Cowen (John David). A cist-burial at West Horton, near Doddington. [Map.] Proc. Soc. Antiq. Newc., 4th S. 8, pp. 195–96. 1938.

2650(a) Craw (James Hewat). A Neolithic cairn at Byrness, Northumberland. Hist. Berwick. Nat. Club, 27, p. 239. 1931.

2650(b) —— The excavation of two Bronze Age cairns on Coldsmouth hill, near Yetholm [Northumberland]. [Figure + 2 plans.] Hist. Berwick Nat. Club, 27, pp. 379–84 + plate. 1931.

2651 Cross (*Hon.* Marjorie). The excavation of two cairns in the Duddon valley. Trans. Cumb. & Westm. Ant. Soc., N.S. 50, p. 200. 1950.

2652 Crossley (Ely Wilkinson). Removal of a tumulus at Scarborough. Yorks. Archaeol. J., 21, pp. 111–12 + plate. 1911.

2653 Cust (*Sir* Edward). The prehistoric man of Cheshire: or, some account of a human skeleton found under the Leasowe shore in Wirral. Trans. Hist. Soc. Lancs. & Ches. [16] N.S. 3, pp. 193–200. 1863.

2654 Davis (Joseph Barnard). Notice of the opening of a barrow at Scale house, in the West Riding of Yorkshire; and the comparison of that barrow with certain others in Jutland. [9 figures.] Reliquary, 6, pp. 1–11 + plate. 1866.

2655 Dawes (Matthew). British burial places near Bolton, Co. Lancashire. Hist. Soc. Lancs. & Ches., Proc., 4, pp. 130–32 + plate + plan. 1852.

2656 Dawkins (*Sir* William Boyd). On the exploration of prehistoric sepulchral remains of the Bronze Age at Bleasdale by S. Jackson, Esq. Trans. Lancs. & Ches. Ant. Soc., 18 (1900), pp. 114–24 + 2 plates + plan. 1901.

2657 Dixon (David Dippie). Notes on the discovery of British burials on the Simonside hills, parish of Rothbury, in Upper Coquetdale, Northumberland. Arch. Æl., N.[2nd] S. 15, pp. 23–32 + 2 plates (urns). 1892.

2658 —— [Pre-historic coffin formed out of a tree trunk exhumed at Cartington farm, Rothbury, Northumberland.] [Figure + plan.] Proc. Soc. Antiq. Newc., 3rd S. 6, pp. 79–84 + plate. 1913.

2659 Dixon (James A.) *and* **Fell** (Clare Isobel). Some Bronze Age burial circles at Lacra, near Kirksanton [Cumb.]. [3 figures + 4 plans.] Trans. Cumb. & Westm. Ant. Soc., N.S. 48, pp. 1–22 + 6 plates. 1948.

2660 Dobson (John). Report on the exploration of the Sunbrick disc barrow.

Trans. Cumb. & Westm. Ant. Soc., N.S. 27, pp. 100–09. 1927.

2661 Elgee (Harriet Wragg *and* Elgee** (Frank). An Early Bronze Age burial in a boat-shaped wooden coffin from North-East Yorkshire. Proc. prehist. Soc., 15, 1949, 87–106 + 12 figures.

2662 Erskine (J. S.). A Birkrigg burial. Trans. Cumb. & Westm. Ant. Soc., N.S. 36, pp. 150–57 + plate. 1936.

2663 Evans (*Sir* Arthur John). Megalithic monuments in their sepulchral relations. [2 figures.] Trans. Lancs. & Ches. Ant. Soc., 3 (1885), pp. 1–31 + plate. 1886.

2664 Fawcett (Edward). Report on a Bronze Age burial at Sutton Bank, near Thirsk, Yorkshire. Yorks. Archaeol. J., 33, pp. 418–25 + 2 plates. 1938.

2665 Fawcett (James William). Two hitherto unrecorded burial cists in Satley parish, Co. Durham. Proc. Soc. Antiq. Newc., 4th S. 9, pp. 225–26. 1941.

2666 Fell (Clare Isobel). A Beaker burial on Sizergh fell, near Kendal. [Figure.] Trans. Cumb. & Westm. Ant. Soc., N.S. 53, pp. 1–5. 1954.

2667 —— Some cairns in High Furness. Trans. Cumberland & Westm. Ant. Soc., N.S. 64, 1964. 1–5.

2668 Ferguson (Richard Saul). On a tumulus at Old Parks, Kirkoswald: with some remarks on one at Aspatria, and also on cup, ring and other rock markings in Cumberland and Westmorland. [Figure.] Trans. Cumb. & Westm. Ant. Soc., 13, pp. 389–99 + 7 plates. 1895.

2669 Filby (E. A.). Pre-historic burials near Bamburgh. [2 plans.] Proc. Soc. Antiq. Newc., 3rd S. 2, pp. 121–24 + plate, pp. 194–95. 1905.

2670 Fishwick (Henry). Discovery of ancient British barrow in Todmorden, in the county of Lancaster. Reliquary, 3rd S. 9, pp. 276–79. 1903.

2673 Garson (J. G.). A description of the skeletons found in Howe hill barrow. J. Anthrop. Inst., 22, pp. 8–20 + table. 1892.

2674 Gatty (Reginald A.). How Tallon. [2 figures + plan.] Reliquary, N.-[3rd] S. 4, pp. 105–08. 1898.

2675 Gelderd (Charles), **Randall** (James) *and* **Dobson** (John). Some Birkrigg barrows. Trans. Cumb. & Westm.

Ant. Soc., N.S. 14, pp. 466–79 + plate. 1914.

2676 Gibson (John Pattison). Some notes on prehistoric burials on Tyneside and the discovery of two cists on the bronze period in Dilston park. [7 figures.] Arch. Æl., 3 S. 2, pp. 126–49. 1906.

2677 Greenfield (Ernest). The second Bronze Age round barrow at Swarkeston, Derbyshire. Interim report. J. Derbs. Archaeol. Soc., 76, pp. 34–39. 1956.

2678 —— *and* **apSimon** (A. M.). The Excavation of barrow 4 at Swarkeston, Derbyshire. DAJ, 80, 1960, 1–48 + 11 figures + 8 plates.

2679 Greenwell (William). An account of the opening of two barrows situated in the parish of Ford, and county of Northumberland. Hist. Berwick Nat. Club, 4, pp. 390–94 + plate. 1862.

2680 —— Notes on the opening of ancient British tumuli in north Northumberland in 1863 and 1865. Hist. Berwick Nat. Club, 5, pp. 195–205 + plate. 1865.

2681 —— Notices of the examination of ancient grave-hills in the North Riding of Yorkshire. [7 figures.] Archaeol. J., 22, pp. 97–117, 241–63 + 4 plates. 1865.

2682 —— *and* **Embleton** (D.). On the ancient burial at Ilderton, Northumberland, with notes on the skull. Natural History Transactions of Northumberland and Durham 1, 1866, 143–48 + 2 plates.

2683 —— On two ancient interments at Wooler and Ilderton. Hist. Berwick. Nat. Club, 6, pp. 415–20. 1872.

2684 —— Tumuli of Cumberland and Westmorland. Trans. Cumb. & Westm. Ant. Soc., 1, pp. 19–26. 1874.

2685 —— Early Iron Age burials in Yorkshire. Archaeologia, 60, pp. 251–324 + plate. 1906.

2686 Hall (George Rowe). On the opening and examination of a barrow of the British period at Warkshaugh, North Tynedale. Nat. Hist. Trans. Northumberland & Durham, 1, 1866, 151–167 + 1 figure + 1 plate.

2687(a) —— Recent explorations in ancient British barrows, containing cup-marked stones, near Birtley, North Tynedale. Arch. Æl., N.[2nd.]S. 12, pp. 241–67 + plate. 1887.

2687(b) Hand (Charles Robert). The story of the Calderstones. Fifth edition. pp. 32. [4 figures.] 8°. Liverpool, 1970.

2687(c) —— Captain William Latham and [his picture of] the Calderstones [in the Manchester Reference Library]. Trans. Hist. Soc. Lancs. & Ches., 67 (1915), pp. 1–6 + 3 plates. 1916.

2688 Hardy (James). Further discoveries of pre-historic graves, urns, and other antiquities: on Lilburn Hill farm, on the Lilburn Tower estate. Arch. Æl., N.[2nd.]S. 13, pp. 350–56 + plate (urns). 1889.

2689 —— On three British cists, one of them containing an urn, found near Callaly Castle, Northumberland, in 1891. Hist. Berwick. Nat. Club, 14, pp. 390–391. 1893.

2690 Harker (John). British interments at Lancaster moor. J. Brit. Archaeol. Ass., 21, pp. 159–61 + plate. 1865.

2691 —— British interments at Lancaster. J. Brit. Archaeol. Ass., 33, pp. 125–27 + plate. 1877.

2692 Harkness (Robert) *and* **Stalker** (Vallance). Notice of the discovery of a cist and its contents at Moorhouse farm, Brougham, Westmoreland. Archaeologia, 45, pp. 411–16. 1877.

2693 Harris (J. A.). Secondary Neolithic burials at Church Dale, near Monyash, Derbyshire, 1937–39. Proc. prehist. Soc., 19, 1953, 228–230 + 2 figures.

2694 Hayes, Raymond H. Note on the Burton Howes. Antiquity, 35, 1961, p. 128.

2695 Heathcote (John Percy). Excavations (Further excavations) at barrows on Stanton moor. J. Derbs. Archaeol. Soc., 51 (N.S. 4, 1930), pp. 1–44 + 12 plates + plan; 57 (N.S. 10, 1936, pp. 21–42 + 6 plates + 2 plans. 1931–37.)

2696 —— Bronze Age cist from Gib hill. J. Derbs. Archaeol. Soc., 61 (N.S. 14) pp. 66–68 + plate. 1940.

2697 —— Excavations on Stanton moor, [1953]. J. Derbs. Archaeol. Soc., 74, pp. 128–33. 1954.

2698 Hedley (Robert Cecil). A prehistoric burial at the Sneep, North Tynedale. Arch. Æl., N.[2nd.]S. 15, pp. 49–51 + plate (urns). 1892.

2699 —— Ancient British burials, Northumberland. Antiquity, 2, p. 470 + plate. 1928.

2700 —— Bronze Age burial at West Wharmley. Proc. Soc. Antiq. Newc., 4th S. 3, pp. 176, 187–89 + 2 plates. 1928.

2701 Hedley (William Percy). Pre-historic burial at Corbridge. Proc. Soc. Antiq. Newc., 3rd S. 10, pp. 281–82. 1922.

2702 Henderson (A. N.). The excavation of a barrow remnant at Lodge moor, Sheffield, 1956–1957. Trans. Hunter Arch. Soc., 7, pp. 331–37. 1957.

2703 —— Barrow No. 9 Ramsley Moor, North East Derbyshire. Trans. Hunter Arch. Soc., 8 ii, 1960, 71–7 + 3 figures.

2704 Herbert (H. B.). Bronze Age cists at Beadnell, [Northumberland]. Hist. Berwick. Nat. Club, 29, p. 218. 1936.

2705 Hodgson (John Crawford). A pre-historic barrow near South Charlton, Northumberland. Arch. Æl., 3rd S. 14, pp. 124–32. 1917.

2706 Hodgson (Katherine S.) *and* **Harper** (Kenneth). The prehistoric site at Broomrigg near Ainstable: the excavations of 1948–49. Trans. Cumb. & Westm. Ant. Soc., N.S. 50, pp. 30–42 + 4 plates. 1950.

2707 Hogg (Alexander Hubert Arthur). Cist at Clifton farm near Morpeth. Proc. Soc. Antiq. Newc., 4th S. 10, pp. 156–61. 1944.

2708 Hogg, Robert. Beckfoot fort, cemetery site [1 plate]. 1. Stone cist. 2. Bronze disc brooch. Trans. C. & W.A. & A.S., N.S. LXII, 1962, 323–24.

2709 Hornsby (William) *and* **Stanton** (Richard). British barrows near Brotton [-in-Cleveland]. Yorks. Archaeol. J., 24, pp. 263–68 + 2 plates. 1917.

2710 —— *and* **Laverick** (John D.). The British remains at Hinderwell beacon. Yorks. Archaeol. J., 25, pp. 495–447 + 3 plates. 1920.

2711 —— *and* —— British barrows round Boulby [Cleveland]. Yorks. Archaeol. J., 25, pp. 48–52 + 3 plates + map. 1920.

2712 —— The mound-breakers of Cleveland. Proc. Cleveland N.F.C., 3, pp. 209–15. 1926.

2713 Hudleston (Christopher Roy). A Bronze Age burial on Little Mell fell. [Figure.] Trans. Cumb. & Westm. Ant. Soc., N.S. 52, pp. 178–80. 1952.

2714 Hughes (T. Cann). Discoveries at Bleasdale, Lancs. J. Brit. Archaeol. Ass., N.S. 7, pp. 171–73 + plate (3 cinerary urns). 1901.

2715 Hughes (Thomas McKenny). Some notes on mound opening, with a description of one recently explored on Sizergh fell, Westmorland. ((On another tumulus on Sizergh fell). Trans. Cumb. & Westm. Ant. Soc., N.S. 4, pp. 71–79 + plan, pp. 201–04 + plate. 1904.

2716 Hunter Arch. Soc. Excavation 1955. Lodge Moor, Sheffield. Trans. Hunter archeol. Soc., 8 i, 1958, 29–5.

2717 Jeffreys (R. H.). Discovery of pre-historic burials at Fatfield, Co. Durham. [Plan.] Proc. Soc. Antiq. Newc., 3rd S. 3, pp. 150–55 + 2 plates. 1907.

2718 Jewitt (Llewellynn). A word on "barrow digging" [in Yorkshire]. Reliquary, 8, pp. 79–80. 1868.

2719 Jobey (George). A Beaker burial at Shipley, Alnwick, Northumberland. Arch. Æliana, 38, 1960, 244–47 + 1 figure.

2720 —— *and others*. An Early Bronze Age burial on Reaverhill Farm, Barrasford, Northumberland. Arch. Æliana, 43, 1965, 65–75 + 3 figures + 1 plate.

2721(a) —— Stott's House "tumulus" and the Military Way. Walker. Arch. Æliana, 43, 1965, 77–86 + 3 figures.

2721(b) Johnston (J. L. **Forde-**). Megalithic art in the North-west of Britain the Calderstones, Liverpool. Proc. prehist. Soc., 23, 1957, 20–39 + 8 plates + 7 figures.

2721(c) —— The Excavation of a round barrow at Gallowsclough Hill, Delamere Forest, Cheshire. Trans. Lancs. & Cheshire antiq. Soc., 70, 1960, 74–83 + 4 figures.

2721(d) —— The Excavation of two barrows on Chelmorton Low, Derbyshire. DAJ, 82, 1962, 82–90 + 3 figures + 2 plates.

2722 Kirk (John Lamplugh). The opening of a tumulus near Pickering. Ann. Rpts. Yorks. Phil. Soc., 1911, pp. 57–62 + 3 plates. 1912.

2723 Lamplough (W. H.) *and* **Lidster** (J. R.). Neolithic burial cave at Ebberstan, Yorkshire. Arch. News Letter, 4, pp. 141–42. 1952.

2724 Livens, R. G. East Hesterton long barrow, Yorkshire: the Eastern half. Antiquity, 39, 1965, 49–53.

2724(b) Lubbock (John) *1st baron Avebury*. On Mr. Bateman's researches in ancient British tumuli [in Derbyshire]. Trans. Ethnology. Soc., N.S. 3, pp. 307–21 + 4 tables. 1865.

2725 Lucas (John F.) *and* **Jewitt** (Llewellynn). Notice of the opening of some Celtic gravemounds in the High Peak. Reliquary, 3, pp. 159–64 + plate. 1863.

2726 —— Notice of the opening of a Celtic and Anglo-Saxon grave-mound at Tissington, Derbyshire. Reliquary, 5, pp. 165–69. 1865.

2727 Lukis (J. F.). Notice of the opening of a barrow on Grey Cap hill, Cressbrook, October 15, 1867. Reliquary, 8, pp. 177–78. 1868.

2728 McCall (Hardy Bertram). An account of the opening of a barrow at Kirklington, with some observations on prehistoric burials. Yorks. N. & Q. (ed. Forshaw), 1, pp. 146–47. 1904.

2729 Manby (T. G.). Chambered tombs of Derbyshire. J. Derbys. A. & N.H. Soc., 78, 1958, 25–39 + 8 figures + 2 plates.

2730 —— The Excavation of the Willerby Wold Long Barrow, East Riding of Yorkshire. Proc. Prehist. Soc., 29, 1963, 173–205 + 8 figures + 2 tables + 4 plates.

2731 —— The Excavation of Green Low chambered tomb. DAJ, 85, 1965, 1–24 + 8 figures + 7 plates.

2731(b) Manners (John Henry Montagu) *9th duke of Rutland*. Bronze Age burial in Leicestershire. Antiq. J., 15, pp. 59–61. 1935.

2733 Marsden (Barry M.). The Re-excavation of Green-Low—a Bronze Age round barrow on Alsop Moor, Derbyshire. DAJ, 83, 1963, 82–89 + 3 figures + 1 plate.

2734 —— The Excavation of a Bronze Age barrow on Haddow Grove Farm, Lathkill Dale, Derbyshire. DAJ, 84, 1964, 102–12 + 5 figures.

2735 Maryon (Herbert). Excavation

of two Bronze Age barrows at Kirkhaugh, Northumberland. Arch. Æl., 4th. S. 13, pp. 207–17. 1936.

2736 Mawson (James). An account of the opening and subsequent removal of an ancient British barrow upon the Hackthorpe hall estate, in the parish of Lowther. Trans. Cumb. & Westm. Ant. Soc., 2, pp. 11–14 + plate (urn) + plan. 1876.

2737 May (Thomas). Notes on a Bronze Age barrow [near Kenya Hall farm, Winwick, Lancs.]. Trans. Lancs. & Ches. Ant. Soc., 21 (1903), pp. 120–126 + 2 plates + map. 1904.

2738 Moffatt (James G.). Pre-historic grave from the Lilburn Hill farm, on the Lilburn Tower estate. [2 figures.] Arch. Æl., N.[2nd.]S. 10, pp. 220–22 + plate. 1885.

2739 Mortimer (John Robert). A notice of the opening of Calais Wold barrow, on Bishop Wilton wold, in the East Riding of Yorkshire: with some notes upon its contents by J. Barnard Davis. [Figure.] Reliquary, 6, pp. 185–90 + 2 plates. 1866.

2740 —— Notice of a barrow at Helperthorpe, Yorkshire. Reliquary, 8, pp. 77–79, 185–87. 1868.

2741 —— An account of the opening of a Celtic tumulus near Fimber, Yorkshire. [3 figures (urns).] Reliquary, 9, pp. 65–69 + plate + plan. 1868.

2742 —— Kemp How, Cowlam [near Driffield]. J. Anthrop. Inst., 9, pp. 394–97 + plan. 1880.

2743 —— Account of the discovery of six ancient dwellings, found under and near to British barrows on the Yorkshire wolds. J. Anthrop. Inst., 11, pp. 472–78 + plan. 1882.

2744 —— An account of the exploration of Howe hill barrow, Duggleby, Yorkshire. J. Anthrop. Inst., 22, pp. 3–8. 1892.

2745 —— The opening of a barrow near Sledmere. Trans. E. Riding Antiq. Soc., 2, pp. 18–23. 1894.

2746 —— The opening of six mounds at Scarborough, near Beverley. Trans. E. Riding Antiq. Soc., 3, pp. 21–23. 1895.

2747 —— The grouping of barrows, and its bearing on the religious beliefs of the ancient Britons. Trans. E.

Riding Antiq. Soc., 3, pp. 53–62 + plan. 1895.

2748 —— The Danes' graves. Ann. Rpt. Yorks. Phil. Soc., 1897, pp. 1–10 + table + 2 plates + plan. 1898.

2749 —— Report on the opening of a number of so-called Danes' Graves at Kilham, E.R. Yorks., and the discovery of a chariot-burial of the Early Iron Age. [Figure + plan.] Proc. Soc. Antiq., 2 S. 17, pp. 119–28. 1898.

2751 —— Forty years' researches in British and Saxon burial mounds of East Yorkshire, including Romano- British discoveries, and a description of the ancient entrenchments on a section of the Yorkshire wolds. pp. lxxxvi, 452 + 125 plates. 4°. London, 1905.

2752 —— Opening of a barrow near "Borrow Nook". Yorks. Archaeol. J., 20, pp. 491–92. 1909.

2753 —— Opening of two barrows in the East Riding. Yorks. Archaeol. J., 21, pp. 214–17 + 2 plates (pottery). 1911.

2754 —— Danes' graves. Trans. E. Riding Antiq. Soc., 18 (1911), pp. 30–52. 1912.

2755 Newbigin (Nancy). The Devil's lapful long cairn, near Kielder [in the Cheviots]. [2 figures.] Proc. Soc. Antiq. Newc., 4th S. 7, pp. 166–67. 1936.

2756 —— Excavations of a long and a round cairn on Bellshiel Law, Redesdale. [Figure + 2 plans.] Arch. Æl., 4th. S. 13, pp. 293–309 + plate + plan. 1936.

2757 Pegge (Samuel). A disquisition on the lows or barrows in the Peak of Derbyshire. Archaeologia, 7, pp. 131–48 + plate. 1785.

2758 —— Discoveries in opening a tumulus in Derbyshire. Archaeologia, 9, pp. 189–92 + plate. 1789.

2759 Pennington (Rooke). Notes on barrow opening near Castleton. Reliquary, 14, pp. 85–88. 1873.

2760 —— On the relative ages of cremation and contracted burial in Derbyshire in the Neolithic and Bronze periods. J. Anth. Inst., 4, pp. 265–76. 1874.

2761 Posnansky (Merrick). The excavation of a Bronze-Age round barrow at Lockington. Trans. Leic. Arch. Soc., 31, pp. 17–29 + plate + plan. 1955.

2762 —— The Bronze Age round barrow at Swarkeston. J. Derbs. Archaeol.

Soc., 75, pp. 123–39 + 2 plates + plan: 76, pp. 10–26. 1955–56.

2763 Preston (F. L.). A barrow group at Burbage, Sheffield. Trans. Hunter Arch. Soc., 7, p. 200 + plan. 1955.

2764 Preston (William). Account of opening one of the largest barrows on Sandford moor, Westmoreland. Archaeologia, 3, p. 273. 1775.

2765 Proctor (William). Report of the proceedings of the Yorkshire Antiquarian Club in the excavation of barrows from the year 1849. pp. 15. 8°. York, 1854.

2766 —— British barrow at Hutton-Cranswick. [Urns.] Bowman (William): Reliquiae Antiquae Eboracenses: (Leeds), pp. 38–38. 1855.

2767 —— Report of the proceedings of the Yorkshire Antiquarian Club, in the excavation of barrows from the year 1849. [Acklam, Huggate, Thixendale, Aldrow, Arras, Danes Dale, Hutton-Cranswick, Ampleforth, Skipwith.] Proc. Yorks. Phil. Soc., 1849–54, pp. 176–89. 1855.

2768 Purvis (J. B.). A group of prehistoric graves at Bedlington. Proc. Soc. Antiq. Newc., 4th S. 10, pp. 322–24 + 2 plates. 1946.

2769 Radley (Jeffrey). Glebe Low, Great Longstone. DAJ, 86, 1966, 54–69, + 3 figures + 2 plates.

2770 Raistrick (Arthur). Prehistoric burials at Waddlington and at Bradley, West Yorkshire. Yorks. Archaeol. J., 30, pp. 248–55 + 2 plates. 1931.

2771 Reaney (D.). A Beaker burial at Aston-on-Trent. DAJ, 86, 1966, 103.

2772 Riley (D. N.). A Early Bronze Age cairn on Harland Edge, Beeley Moor, Derbyshire. DAJ, 86, 1966, 31–53 + 11 figures.

2773 Robinson (John). Ancient remains discovered at Grindon hill, near Sunderland. [Plan.] Proc. Soc. Antiq. Newc., 3rd S. 2, pp. 197–99. 1905.

2774 Rooke (Hayman). Discoveries in a barrow [Fin Cop, near Ashford] in Derbyshire. [Urns and skeletons.] Archaeologia, 12, pp. 327–33 + plate + plan. 1799.

2775 Ross (W. H.) and Hayes (R. H.). Prehistoric enclosure (Chambered cairn) on Great Ayton moor, [Yorks.]. Arch. News Letter, 5, pp. 207–08. 1955.

2777 Selby (P. J.). Notice of two ancient tombs or graves discovered and opened in spring 1851, upon Adderstone Low mill farm, in the parish of Bamburgh. [2 plans.] Hist. Berwick. N.C., 3, pp. 123–24. 1853.

2778 Sheppard (Thomas). Burial customs in East Yorkshire over 2,000 years ago. Yorks. N. & Q. (ed. Forshaw), 1, p. 348. 1905.

2779 —— A burial in east Yorkshire over two thousand years ago. Reliquary, 3rd S. 11, pp. 61–62. 1905.

2780 —— Note on a British chariot-burial at Hunmanby, in East Yorkshire. Yorks. Archaeol. J., 19, pp. 482–88 + 1 plate. 1907.

2781 —— British chariot-burial. Yorks. N. & Q. (ed. Forshaw), 4, pp. 75–77. 1907.

2782 —— Catalogue of the Mortimer collection of prehistoric remains from East Yorkshire barrows. *Hull Museum publication*, 162. pp. viii, 146. 8°. Hull, 1929. [Pp. 113–46, figures.]

2783 Short (David Call). A Bronze Age cist at Humbleton, Wooler. [2 figures.] Hist. Berwick. Nat. Club, 27, pp. 385–90. 1931.

2784 Simpson (F. R.). An account of an ancient British grave discovered at North Sunderland; with a description of the caluarium of a skeleton found therein, by J. Barnard Davis. Hist. Berwick. Nat. Club, 4, pp. 428–30 + plate. 1862.

2785 Smith (Henry Ecroyd). An ancient British cemetery at Wavertree. Trans. Hist. Soc. Lancs. & Ches., [20] N.S. 8, pp. 131–46 + plate + plan. 1868.

2787 Spence (Joseph E.). A tumulus in Mecklin park, Santon Bridge. Trans. Cumb. & Westm. Ant. Soc., N.S. 37, pp. 104–05 + plate. 1937.

2788 Stead (Ian M.). A chariot burial on Pexton moor, North Riding. Antiquity, 33, pp. 214–16 + plate. 1959.

2789 —— The Excavation of beaker burials at Staxton, East Riding, 1957. Yorks. Arch. Journ. 40 (i), 1959, 129–144 + 8 figures + 2 plates.

2790 —— A Distinctive form of La Tène barrow in eastern Yorkshire and on the Continent. Ant. J., 41, 1961, 44–62.

2791 Stickland (H. J.). The excavation of five Bronze Age barrows on Broxa and Hackness moors, Yorkshire. Arch. News Letter, 3, p. 87. 1950.

2792 Tate (George). On cist-vaens and sepulchral urns in a tumulus or barrow near Lesbury, Northumberland. [Plan.] Hist. Berwick. N.C., 3, pp. 63–67. 1851.

2793 Taylor (Michael Waistell). On the discovery of prehistoric remains at Clifton, Westmorland. Trans. Cumb. & Westm. Ant. Soc., 5, pp. 79–97 + 2 plates + plan. 1881.

2794 Thomas (G. W.). Barrows at North Newbold, Yorkshire. [Figure (incense cup).] Proc. Soc. Antiq., 2 S. 7, pp. 321–25. 1878.

2795 Thompson (Frederick Hugh). Notes on excavations and finds in Cheshire during 1960: Bronze Age burial, Beech Hall School, Macclesfield. Trans. Lancs. & Cheshire antiq. Soc., 70, 1960, 65.

2796 —— Miscellanea: Bronze Age burial from Beech Hall, Macclesfield. Chester Arch. Soc. Jl., 48, 1961, 43–45.

2797 —— Miscellanea: Supposed barrow in Dunham New Park. Chester Arch. Soc. Jl., 48, 1961, 45.

2798 Thompson (George H.). Notes on urns and cists found at Amble, Northumberland, in 1883 and 1884. Hist. Berwick. Nat. Club, 10, pp. 523–530 + 2 plates. 1884.

2799 Tissiman (John). Report on excavations in barrows, in Yorkshire. J. Brit. Archaeol. Ass., 6, pp. 1–5 + 2 plates. 1850.

2800 —— Celtic remains from a tumulus near Scarborough. Archaeologia, 33, pp. 446–49 + plate. 1852.

2801 Trechmann (C. T.). Recent finds of prehistoric remains at Hasting hill, near Otterton. Ant. Sunderland, 14, pp. 1–5. 1913.

2802 —— Prehistoric burials in the county of Durham. Arch. Æl., 3rd S. 11, pp. 119–76. 1914.

2803 Varley (William James). A plan of the Blaesdale [Lancs.] sepulchral circle. Annals of Archaeology, 19, p. 28 + plan. 1932.

2804 —— Bleasdale and the idea of timber circles. Annals of Archaeology, 20, pp. 187–94. 1933.

2805 —— A note on Bleasdale circle. Trans. Lancs. & Ches. Ant. Soc., 49 (1933), pp. 159–62. 1935.

2806 —— The Bleasdale circle. Antiq. J. 18, pp. 154–71 + 6 plates. 1938.

2807 Vasey (Richard). British remains near Whitby. Yorks. N. & Q. (ed. Forshaw), 1, pp. 129–31. 1904.

2808 Ware (Thomas) *and* **Wright** (Richard Pearson). An Early Bronze Age cist at Kelloe Law, Co. Durham. [Figure. Pp. 217–26, Report on the skeletons, by C. Howard Tonge.]. Arch. Æl., 4th S. 29, pp. 213–20, 1951 + plate.

2809 Wake (Thomas). A Bronze Age burial cist found near Denton burn. [Northumb.] [2 figures.] Proc. Soc. Antiq. Newc., 4th S. 7, pp. 226–27. 1936.

2810 Walker (John William). The tumuli at Twemlow hall, Cheshire. Trans. Hist. Soc. Lancs. & Ches., 91 (1939), pp. 205–07. 1940.

2811 Ward (John). Barrows at Haddon Fields, Derbyshire. J. Derbs. Archaeol. Soc., 10, pp. 47–55 + 2 plates. 1888.

2812 —— On some diggings near Brassington, Derbyshire. J. Derbs. Archaeol. Soc., 12, pp. 108–38 + 4 plates. 1890.

2813 —— The Grinlow barrow, Buxton. Reliquary, N. [3rd] S. 5, pp. 179–188. 1899.

2814 —— Five-wells tumulus, Derbyshire. Reliquary, 3rd S. 7, pp. 229–42. 1901.

2815 —— Notes on a pre-historic burial-place at Megdale, near Matlock Bridge. J. Derbs. Archaeol. Soc., 23, pp. 40–47. 1901.

2816 —— Prehistoric burials in Derbyshire. Cox (J. C.): Memorials of old Derbyshire, pp. 39–69 + 6 plates + 2 plans. 1907.

2817 Wardell (James). British barrow, at Winteringham, [East Riding]. Bowman (William): Reliquiae Antiquae Eboracenses: (Leeds), pp. 57–59, 75–76. 1855.

2818 Waterman (Dudley U.). Quernhow: a food-vessel barrow in Yorkshire. [4 figures + map + 2 plans.] Antiq. J., 31, pp. 1–24 + 5 plates + plan. 1951.

2819 Wildridge (Thomas Tindall). The British barrow at Marton. Trans. E. Riding Ant. Soc., 1, pp. 46–52. 1893.

2820 Williamson (William Crawford). Description of the tumulus, lately opened at Gristhorpe, near Scarborough, illustrated with engravings of the coffin, weapons, etc. pp. 18 + plate. 4°. Scarborough, 1834.

2821 —— Description of the tumulus, lately opened at Gristhorpe, near Scarborough, illustrated with engravings of the coffin, weapons, etc. Second edition. pp. 18 + plate. 4°. Scarborough, 1836.

2822 —— Description of the tumulus opened at Gristhorpe, near Scarborough, with engravings of the coffin, weapons, etc. pp. 23. 8°. Scarborough, 1872.

2823 Wright (William). Skulls from the Danes' graves, Driffield. J. Anthrop. Inst., 33, pp. 66–73 + 2 plates. 1903.

2824 —— Notes on the human remains found in the Danes Graves. Archaeologia, 60, pp. 313–24 + plate. 1906.

2825 Yates (George Charles) *and* **Jackson** (S.). Bronze Age burials on Fairsnape farm, Bleasdale, Lancashire. Reliquary, 3rd S. 6, pp. 258–63. 1900.

(e) Zone 5 [CBA Group 2]

2826 Abaris. Cromlech at Gaerllwyd, Newchurch, near Caerwent, Monmouthshire. [Figure.] Arch. Camb., 1, pp. 277–79. 1846.

2827 Allen (H. Mortimer). The Dolwilym cromlech, [Carmarthenshire]. Reliquary, 3rd S. 12, p. 48 + plate. 1906.

2828 [Anon.] Cromlech at Bryn Celli Dam, Anglesey. [Figure.] Arch. Camb., 2, pp. 3–6. 1847.

2829 [Anon.] The exploration of a tumulus [on top of Mwdwl Eithin], in west Denbighshire. J. Brit. Archaeol. Ass., N.S. 18, p. 102. 1912.

2830 [Anon.] The Grave of Sawyl Benisel, king of the Britons. Arch. Camb., N.S. 2, pp. 159–62. 1851.

2831 [Anon.] Cromlech[s] in the Isle of Anglesea. [Trans.] Brit. Archaeol. Ass., 5, Congress at Worcester, 1848, pp. 188–91. 1851.

2832 [Anon.] Bryn Celli Ddu cromlech. Arch. Camb., 6th S. 8, pp. 67–71 + 2 plates. 1908.

2833 **Appleton** (Sylvia E.). The Longhouse cromlech. Arch. Camb., 80, pp. 422–23. 1925.

2834 **Lubbock** (John) *1st baron Avebury.* Description of the Park Cwm tumulus. J. Ethnolog. Soc., N.S. 2, pp. 416–419 + plan. 1870. *Reprinted in* Arch. Camb., 4th S. 2, pp. 168–70 + plan. 1871.

2835 —— *and* **Vivian** (*Sir* H. Hussey) *bart.* Description of the Park Cwm tumulus. Arch. Camb., 5th S. 4, pp. 192–201 + plate + plan. 1887.

2837 **Banks** (Richard William). The four-stones, Old Radnor. Arch. Camb., 4th S. 5, pp. 215–17 + plate. 1874.

2838 —— The four stones, Old Radnor. Trans. Woolhope N.F.C., 1886–89, pp. 211–12 + plate.

2839 **Barnwell** (Edward Lowry). Cromlechs in North Wales. [3 figures + plan.] Arch. Camb., 3rd S. 15, pp. 118–47 + 6 plates + plan. 1869.

2840 —— Notes on some South Wales cromlechs. [6 figures.] Arch. Camb., 4th S. 3, pp. 81–143 + 7 plates. 1872.

2842 —— South Wales Cromlechs. Arch. Camb., 4th S. 5, pp. 59–73 + 4 plates. 1874.

2843 —— The chambered mound at Plas Newydd. Arch. Camb., 4th S. 11, pp. 81–96 + 3 plates + 2 plans. 1880.

2844 —— On some South Wales cromlechs. Arch. Camb., 5th S. 1, pp. 129–44 + 7 plates. 1884.

2845 —— Sepulchral chamber at Tyn-y-Coed, near Capel Garmon, Denbighshire. Arch. Camb., 5th S. 5, pp. 60–61 + 3 plates + plan. 1888.

2846 **Baynes** (Edward Neil). The excavation of Lligwy cromlech, in the county of Anglesey. [7 figures + 2 plans.] Arch. Camb., 6th S. 9, pp. 217–231. 1909.

2847 —— The excavation of two barrows at Ty'n-y-Pwll, Llanddyfnan, Anglesey. Arch. Camb., 6th S. 9, pp. 312–32. 1909.

2848 —— Notes on the excavation of two barrows at Llanddyfnan, Anglesey. Proc. Soc. Antiq., 2nd S. 22, pp. 368–73. 1909.

2849 —— *and* **Evans** (S. J.). Bedd Branwen. Anglesey Ant. Soc. Trans., [1], pp. 22–27. 1913.

2850 —— Some dolmens in North Wales. Proc. Llandudno F.C., 8 (1913–1915), pp. 48–60. 1917.

2851 —— Lligwy cromlech. Anglesey Ant. Soc. Trans., 1932, pp. 37–38 + plate. 1932.

2852 —— The cromlech at Cromlech farm, Llanfechell. Anglesey Ant. Soc. Trans., 1936, p. 124 + plate. 1936.

2854 **Blight** (John Thomas). Cromlech at Llansantffraid, near Conway, [Denbighshire]. [Figure + plan.] Arch. Camb., 3rd S. 11, pp. 278–80 + 2 plates. 1865.

2855 **Cantrill** (Thomas Crosbee). The contents of a carn at Ystradfellte, Co. Brecon. [2 figures + plan.] Arch. Camb., 5th S. 15, pp. 248–64. 1898.

2856 —— Notes on a collection of objects obtained during the recent exploration of a cairn in Breconshire. J. Anthrop. Inst., 28, pp. 3–4. 1899.

2857 **Cobb** (W. W.). Note on the cromlechs of Tan-y-Murian, Rhiw, [Carn.]. [2 figures.] Arch. Camb., 6th S. 17, pp. 135–38. 1917.

2858 **Cocks** (Alfred Heneage). Antiquities on the Voelas estate, Denbighshire. Arch. Camb., 6th S. 18, pp. 123–132. 1918.

2859 **Daniel** (Glyn E.). The Four Crosses burial chamber, Caernarvonshire. Arch. Camb., 92 i, 1937, 165–67 + 5 figures.

2860 —— The Chambered barrow in Parc Le Breos, Cwm, S. Wales. Proc. prehist. Soc., 3, 1937, 71–86 + 4 figures.

2861 —— Excavations at Trehill, Glamorgan, June, 1936. Arch. Camb., 92 ii, 1937, 287–93 + 4 figures.

2862 **Daniel** (John E.), **Evans** (Emyr Estyn) *and* **Lewis** (Trevor). Excavations on the Kerry Hills, Montgomeryshire. Arch. Cambrensis, 82 i, 1927, 147–60 + 7 figures.

2863 **Davies** (A. Stanley). A Cromlech on the Breiddens, Montgomeryshire. Arch. Camb., 89 i, 1934, 179–82 + 3 figures.

2864 **Davies** (David). Celtic sepulture on the mountains of Carno, Montgomeryshire. Arch. Camb., 3rd S. 3, pp. 301–05. 1857.

2865 **Davies** (Ellis). Tumulus destroyed. [Map.] Arch. Camb., 6th S. 15, pp. 436–38. 1915.

2866 —— Some Lleyn antiquities. Arch. Camb., 78, pp. 306–10. 1923.

2867 —— Partial excavation of a tumulus on Crown Farm, Whitford, Flintshire. Arch. Camb., 84 i, 1929, 151–54 + 1 figure.

2868 —— Plas Heaton cave, tumulus and beaker. Proc. Llandudno F.C., 17, pp. 65–68. 1933.

2869 —— An interesting Bronze Age discovery made near Nefyn, Caernarvonshire. Arch. Camb., 106, 1957, 117–18.

2870 Davies (V. E.). Cairn on the Black Mountains, Breconshire. Arch. Camb., 79, pp. 410–11. 1924.

2871 Dawkins (*Sir* William Boyd). On the recent exploration of Gop Cairn and cave. Report of the 56th meeting of the BA for the Advm. Sci. 1886 (1887) 839–41.

2872 —— On the cairn and sepulchral cave at Gop, near Prestatyn. Archaeol. J., 58, pp. 322–41. 1901. *Reprinted in* Arch. Camb., 6th S. 2, pp. 161–81. 1902.

2873 Dearden (James). Some remarks on the opening of certain tumuli near Tenby. [On Ridgeway.] Arch. Camb., N.S. 2, pp. 291–94 + 2 plates + map. 1851.

2874 Dunn (C. J.). Surface finds from a barrow and its immediate vicinity, near Walton, Radnorshire. Trans. Radnors. Soc., 36, 1966, 9–14 + 1 figure.

2875 Evans (Evan). Pentraeth [Anglesey]: barrow excavated. Arch. Camb., 6th S. 8, p. 119. 1908.

2876 Evans (Franklen George). The St. Nicholas cromlechs. Cardiff Nat. Soc. Rpt. & Trans., 13 (1881), pp. 41–48. 1882.

2877 Evans (George Eyre). Traces of early man in the neighbourhood of Llandyssul [Cards.]. Arch. Camb., 79, pp. 214–15. 1924.

2878 —— Llanboidy: Gwal y Filiast dolmen. Trans. Carmarthenshire Ant. Soc., 28, p. 87 + plate. 1938.

2879(a) Evans (*Sir* John). Carnedd and cromlech at Capel Garmon, near Llanrwst. [Figure.] Arch. Camb., 3rd S. 2, pp. 91–95 + plan. 1856.

2879(b) Evans (M. Bevan) *and* Hayes (Peter). Excavation of a cairn on Cefn-Golen near Moel Famman. (—Second report). Flintshire Hist. Soc. Publns., 13, pp. 91–97 + 2 plates + 2 maps ; 15,

pp. 112–40 + 5 plates + plan. 1953–55.

2880 Evans (W. F.). Prehistoric remains in the Ogmore sandhills. Arch. Camb., 6 S. 11, pp. 441–43. 1911.

2882 Fenton (John). Cromlech at Llanwnda, Pembrokeshire. Arch. Camb., 3, pp. 283–85. 1848.

2883 —— On the ancient modes of burial of the Cymri, or Celtic Britons. [3 figures.] Arch. Camb., 3rd S. 6, pp. 25–33. 1860.

2884 Ffoulkes (W. Wynne). Tumuli, Denbighshire. Arch. Camb., N.S. 2, pp. 219–25, 274–81. 1851.

2885 —— Tumuli, Merionethshire. Arch. Camb., N.S. 3, pp. 65–68, 96–104, 214–20. 1852.

2886 —— Tumuli, Merioneth.—Tomen Pentref. Arch. Camb., 4th S. 5, pp. 313–19 + plate. 1874.

2887 Forde (Cyril Daryll). A Middle Bronze Age burial in Cardiganshire. Bull. Bd. Celtic Stud., 8, p. 271. 1936.

2888 —— A Middle Bronze Age burial in Cardiganshire. [2 figures.] Antiq. J., 17, p. 79. 1937.

2889 —— Dysgwylfa Fawr barrow, Cardiganshire—a food vessel and dug-out trunk cremation burial. Bull. Bd. Celtic Stud., 9, pp. 188–89. 1938.

2890 —— Dysgwylfa Fawr barrow, Cardiganshire. A food vessel and dug-out trunk cremation burial. Cards. Ant. Soc. Trans., 13, pp. 72–73. 1938.

2891 —— Dysgwylfa Fawr barrow, Cardiganshire: a food-vessel and dug-out trunk cremation burial. Antiq. J., 19, pp. 90–92 + plate. 1939.

2892 —— Two Bronze Age cairns near Bridgend, Glamorgan. Trans. Cards. Ant. Soc., 13, pp. 72–73. 1938.

2893 Fox (*Lady* Aileen Mary) *and* Threipland (Leslie Murray). The Excavation of two cairn cemeteries near Hirwaun, Glamorgan. Arch. Camb., 97 i, 1942, 77–92 + 9 figures + 2 plates.

2895 Fox (*Sir* Cyril). On a burial place of dwellers in the upper Taf valley, near Whitland, Carmarthenshire, in the Bronze Age. [10 figures + map + 2 plans.] Arch. Camb. 8°. pp. 275–88. 1925.

2896 —— A Bronze Age barrow on Kilpaison burrows, Rhoscrowther, Pembrokeshire. Arch. Camb., 81, pp 1–35. 1926.

2897 —— The Food-vessel from the barrow on Linney Burrows, Castle-martin, Pembroke. Arch. Cambrensis, 81 ii, 1926, 401–04 + 2 figures.

2898 —— *and* **Grimes** (W. F.). Corston Beacon: an early Bronze Age cairn in South Pembrokeshire. Arch. Cambrensis, 83 i, 1928, 137–74 + 10 figures.

2899 —— *and* **Fox** (*Lady* Aileen Mary). An Early Bronze Age cairn, near Bridgend, Glamorgan. Bull. Bd. Celtic Stud., 9, pp. 84–85. 1937.

2900 —— Two Bronze Age cairns in South Wales: Simondston and Pond cairns, Coity Higher parish, Bridgend. [6 figures + map + plan.] Archaeologia, 87, pp. 129–80 + 25 plates + 2 plans. 1938

2901 —— Two Bronze Age cairns near Bridgend, Glamorgan. Man, 38, pp. 90–91. 1938.

2902 —— Stake-circles in turf barrows: a record of excavation in Glamorganshire, 1939–40. Antiq. J., 21, pp. 97–127 + 8 plates + 3 plans. 1941.

2903 —— A datable ritual barrow in Glamorganshire. Antiquity, 15, pp. 142–61 + 5 plates + plan. 1941.

2904 —— *and* **Fox** (*Lady* Aileen Mary). The Golden Mile barrow in Colwinston Parish, Glamorgan. Arch. Camb., 96 ii, 1941, 185–92 + 1 figure.

2905 —— A Beaker barrow, enlarged in the Middle Bronze Age, at South hill, Talbenny, Pembrokeshire. [8 figures + 2 maps.] Archaeol. J., 99 (1942), pp. 1–32 + 8 plates + 2 plans. 1943.

2906 —— A Bronze Age barrow (Sutton 268') in Llandow parish, Glamorganshire. Archaeologia, 89, pp. 89–126 + 12 plates + plan. 1943.

2907 —— Burial ritual and custom in the Bronze Age (illustrated by recent excavations in South Wales). [Map and plan.] Early cultures of N.W. Europe (H. M. Chadwick mem. stud.) ed. Sir C. Fox and Bruce Dickins, pp. 51–73 + 2 plate + 4 plans. 1958.

2908 Gardner (Willoughby). The cromlech on the Great Orme. Proc. Llandudno F.C., 1 (1906–07), pp. 7–15. 1912.

2909 —— Excavations of tumuli in Eglwys Bach, Denbighshire. Arch. Camb., 6th S. 13, pp. 817–38. 1913.

2910 —— A Newly discovered Car-

marthenshire megalith. Arch. Camb., 95 i, 1940, 80–83 + 2 figures + 2 plates.

2912 Griffith (John E.). Portfolio of photographs of the cromlechs of Anglesey and Carnarvonshire. 41 plates. Oblong fol. London, 1900.

2913 —— Some Rhondda cairns. Cardiff Nat. Soc. Rpt. & Trans., 36 (1903), pp. 118–25 + 2 plates. 1904.

2914 Griffiths (William Eric). The megalithic tombs of Wales. Proc. Llandudno F.C., 22, pp. 16–18. 1949.

2915 Grimes (William Francis). An Early Bronze Age burial from Stormy down, Pyle, Glam. Bull. Bd. Celtic Stud., 4, pp. 173–74. 1928.

2916 —— An Early Bronze Age burial from Stormy Down, Pyle, Glamorgan. Arch. Camb., 83 ii, 1928, 330–37 + 4 figures.

2917 —— A Beaker-burial from Ludchurch, Pembrokeshire. Arch. Camb., 83 ii, 1928, 338–43 + 3 figures.

2918 —— Barrows in Llanboidy parish, Carmarthenshire. Bull. Bd. Celtic Stud., 5, p. 81. 1924.

2919 —— Beaker-burial at Llanharry, Glamorgan. Bull. Bd. Celtic Stud., 5, pp. 80–81. 1929.

2920 —— Burial mounds in the Parish of Llanboidy, Carmarthenshire. Arch. Camb., 84 ii, 1929, 325–32 + 4 figures.

2921 —— A Bronze Age burial at Knighton, Radnorshire. Bull. Bd. Celtic Stud., 8, p. 94. 1935.

2922 —— Bronze Age burial from Llandegla, Denbighshire. Bull. Bd. Celtic Stud., 8, p. 95. 1935.

2923(a) —— Preliminary note on a Bronze Age burial mound near Knighton, Radnorshire. Radnorshire Soc. Trans., 5, p. 78. 1935.

2923(b) Grimes (William Francis). Map of South Wales showing the distribution of long barrows and megaliths. *Ordnance Survey.* Southampton, 1936.

2923(c) —— The Megalithic monuments of Wales. Proc. prehist. Soc., N.S. 2, 1936, 106–39 + 31 figures + 2 plates.

2924 —— The Long cairns of the Brecknockshire Black Mountains. Arch. Camb., 91 ii, 1936, 259–82 + 20 figures.

2925 —— Two Bronze Age burials from Wales. Arch. Camb., 91 ii, 1936, 293–304 + 6 figures.

2926 —— Pentre Ifan burial chamber, Nevern, Pembrokeshire. Bull. Bd. Celtic Stud., 8, pp. 270–71; 9, pp. 82–84. 1936–37.

2927 —— Bronze Age burials near Crug-coy, Llanarth, Cardiganshire. Bull. Bd. Celtic Stud., 8, pp. 271–72. 1936.

2928 —— A round barrow of the Bronze Age near Jackets well, Knighton. Radnorshire Soc., Trans., 7, pp. 23–29. 1937.

2929 —— A barrow on Breach farm, Llanbleddian, Glamorgan. Cardiff Nat. Soc. Rpt. & Trans., 69 (1936), pp. 49–70 + 5 plates + plan. 1938.

2930 —— A Barrow on Breach Farm, Llanbleddian, Glamorgan. Proc. prehist. Soc., 4, 1938, 107–21 + 8 figures + 3 plates.

2931 —— Ty-isaf long cairn, Breconshire. Bull. Bd. Celtic Stud., 9, 283–85. 1938.

2932 —— The Excavation of Ty-isaf long cairn, Brecknockshire. Proc. prehist. Soc., 5, 1939, 119–42 + 8 figures + 5 plates.

2933 —— Pentre-Ifan burial chamber, Pembrokeshire. Arch. Camb., 100 i, 1948, 3–23 + 6 figures + 7 plates.

2934 —— Pentre-Ifan burial chamber, Nevern, Pembrokeshire. *Ministry of Works*, p. 11. 8º. London, 1953. [Map + plan.]

2935 —— Caper Garmon chambered long cairn. pp. 10. 8º. London, 1958. [Plan.]

2936 —— Devil's Quoit burial chamber, Angle. Arch. J., 119 (1962), 347.

2938 —— Dry Burrows barrow group. Arch. J., 119, 1962, 348.

2939(a) **Halhed** (William B.). The Maen Pebyll, Mynydd Hiraethog, Denbighshire. [Figure + 2 plans.] Arch. Camb., 6th S. 9, pp. 246–48. 1909.

2939(b) **Hemp** (Wilfrid James). Maen Pebyll long cairn [at Nebo, Denbighshire]. [2 figures + plan.] Arch. Camb., 78, pp. 143–47. 1923.

2940 —— The Capel Garmon chambered long cairn. Arch. Cambrensis, 82 i, 1927, 1–43 + 21 figures.

2941 —— The chambered cairn of Bryn Celli Ddu. [2 figures + plan.] Archaeologia, 80, pp. 179–214 + 15 plates + plan. 1930.

2942 —— The Chambered cairn of Bryn Celli Ddu. Arch. Camb., 86 ii, 1931, 216–58 + 20 figures.

2943 —— The Chynnog collar and the Carnguwch Cairn. Arch. Camb., 86 ii, 1931, 354–55 + 1 plate.

2944 —— Maen Hir in Glynllivon Park [Carnarvon]. Arch. Camb., 87 i, 1932, 199–201 + 1 figure.

2945 —— Carneddau Hengwm, Merionethshire. Arch. Camb., 91 i, 1936, 25–29 + 3 figures.

2946 —— The chambered cairn known as Bryn yr Hen Bobl near Plas Newydd, Anglesey. Archaeologia, 85, pp. 253–292 + 12 plates + plan. 1936.

2947 —— Remains of barrows at Llanddyfnan, Anglesey. Arch. Camb., 96 i, 1941, 97–98 + 1 figure.

2948 —— Bryn Celli Ddu, Anglesey, *Ministry of Works*. pp. 4. 8º. London, 1946. [Plan, Chambered cairn.]

2949 —— Merioneth cairns and barrows in Llandrillo and neighbouring parishes. Bull. Bd. Celtic Stud., 14, pp. 155–65 + plate + map. 1951.

2950 —— Bryn yr Hen Bobl chambered cairn, Plas Newydd, Anglesey. Anglesey Ant. Soc. Trans., 1953, pp. 2–20 + 8 plates + plan. 1953.

2951 **Houlder** (C. H.). The excavation of a barrow in Cardiganshire. Ceredigion, 3, pp. 11–23, 118–23. 1956–57.

2952 **Hughes** (Harold). Merddyn Gwyn barrow, Pentraeth. Arch. Camb., 6th S. 8, pp. 211–20, 297. 1908.

2953 —— Parc le Breos, Gower. Arch. Camb., 92 i, 1937, 175–76 + 1 figure.

2954 —— A Beaker burial at Llithfaen, Caernarvonshire. Arch. Camb., 94 i, 1939, 95–97 + 1 figure.

2955 **Jackson** (R. H.). The Gopior y Gopa, tumulus—Flintshire. [Figure + plan.] Arch. Camb., 3rd S. 4, pp. 152–56. 1858.

2956 **Jerman** (H. Noel). The excavation of a barrow on Caebetin hill, Kerry, Montgomeryshire. Collns. rel. to Montgom., 42, pp. 176–81 + map + plan. 1932.

2957 —— Excavation of a barrow near Kerry, Montgomeryshire. Arch. Camb., 88 i, 1933, 102–05 + 2 figures.

2958 —— Cromlechs in Anglesey and Caernarvon. Arch. Camb., 91 i, 1936, 147–48.

2959 —— A barrow in Llangurig parish, Mont. Bull. Bd. Celtic Stud., 8, pp. 377–78. 1937.

2960 Jones (Harry Longueville). On the cromlechs extant in the isle of Anglesey. Archaeol. J., 3, pp. 39–44. 1846.

2961 —— Cromlech at Llanvaelog, Anglesey. [Figure.] Arch. Camb., 3rd S. 10, pp. 44–46. 1864.

2962 —— Pembrokeshire antiquities. Cromlechs, Newton, Manorbeer, St. David's head, Pentre Ifan. Arch. Camb., 3rd S. 11, pp. 281–85 + 4 plates. 1865.

2963 —— *and* **Prichard** (Hugh). Cromlech, Henblas. [Plan.] Arch. Camb., 3rd S. 12, pp. 466–71 + plate. 1866.

2964 Jones (Herbert C.). A prehistoric burial in Clun valley. [Plan.] Trans. Caradoc & Severn Valley F.C., 10, pp. 74–80. 1936.

2965 Jones (**J. F.**). Orchard Park, [Laugharne]. Beaker burial. Carmarthen Antiquary, 2 (1947/8), pp. 57–59. 1951.

2966 Jones (S. J.) *and* **Davies** (D. Ernest). Excavations at Pen-y-Glogau, south Cardiganshire. [3 figures + 2 plans.] Cards. Antiq. Soc. Trans., 7, pp. 118–24. 1930.

2967 Keith (*Sir* Arthur). Skeletons found in the barrow at Pentraeth, Anglesey. Arch. Camb., 6th S. 9, pp. 254–55. 1909.

2968 —— The human remains (St. Nicholas chambered tumulus). [3 figures.] Arch. Camb., 6th S. 16, pp. 268–294. 1916.

2969 Kempe (Alfred John). "Arthur's stone", a cromlech in the district of Gower. Archaeologia, 23, pp. 420–425 + plate. 1831.

2970 Laws (Edward). An old picture of the dolmen at Pentre Evan. Arch. Camb., 5th S. 2, pp. 72–73 + plate. 1885.

2971 Leach (G. B.). Excavation of an earth mound on Mynydd Axton. Flint. hist. Soc. publns., 21, 1963, 101–04 + 2 figures.

2972 Lewis (A. L.). Notes on some rude stone monuments in Glamorganshire. Man, 7, pp. 37–39. 1907.

2973 Lewis (D. Phillips). Tumulus at Berriew, Montgomeryshire. Arch. Camb., 3rd S. 3, pp. 296–99. 1857.

2974(a) Lewis (Henry). Find of barrows near Llanfihangel Nant Melan. Arch. Camb., 6th S. 12, p. 336. 1912.

2974(b) Lewis, J. M. Harold's Stone [short note]. Arch. J., 119 (1962), 348.

2975 Lines (H. H.). Gwern Einion, near Harlech. [2 cromlechs, *etc.*] Antiquary, 28, pp. 236–54. 1893.

2976 —— The carnedd or tomb of Bronwen, Anglesea. Antiquary, 30, pp. 9–12. 1894.

2977 —— Mona, Anglesea. [Bonafon cromlech.] Antiquary, 30, pp. 71–74; 31, pp. 87–89, 249–53, 302–03. 1894–95.

2978 Lloyd (*Sir* John Edward). The cromlechs of North Wales. Jones (E. A.): Memorials of old North Wales, pp. 188–92. 1913.

2979 Luck (Richard). Cromlechs at Llanfairfechan, Carnarvonshire. Arch. Camb., 5th S. 5, pp. 168–70. 1888.

2980 Lukis (John Walter). Chambered tumuli. Cardiff Nat. Soc. Rpt. & Trans., 4 (1872), pp. 27–35. 1873.

2981 —— On the St. Lythan's and St. Nicholas' cromlechs and other remains, near Cardiff. Arch. Camb., 4th S. 6, pp. 171–85 + 3 plates + 2 plans. 1875.

2982 —— St. Nicholas cromlechs. Cardiff Nat. Soc. Rpt. & Trans., 6 (1874), pp. 73–82. 1875.

2983 Matthews (Arthur Weight). Marros: chambered cairn. Trans. Carmarthenshire Ant. Soc., 20, p. 82 + plate. 1927.

2984 Morgan (W. E. T.) *and* **Marshall** (George). Excavation of a long barrow at Llanigon, Co. Brecon. Arch. Camb., 76, pp. 296, 299. 1921.

2985 —— *and* —— Report on the excavation of a long barrow at Llanigon, Co. Brecon. Trans. Woolhope N.F.C., 1921–23, pp. 30–40 + 2 plates + plan. 1925.

2986 Morgan (W. L.). Discovery of a megalithic sepulchral chamber on the Penmaen burrows, Gower, Glamorganshire. Arch. Camb., 5 S. 11, pp. 1–6 + plate + plan. 1894.

2987 Morris (Robert Prys). Cistfaen at Aberganolwyn. Arch. Camb., 4th S. 9, pp. 64–66. 1878.

2988 Nash-Williams (Victor Eme). A Beaker-burial from Llanharry, Glamorgan. Arch. Camb., 85 ii, 1930, 402–05 + 2 figures.

2989 Newall (Robert Stirling). The Smaller cairn at Bryn Celli Ddu. Arch. Camb., 86 ii, 1931, 259–62 + 1 figure.

2990(a) Newstead (Robert). Grave mounds at Penmaenmawr. J. Arch. & Hist. Soc. Chester, N.S. 6, pp. 145–51 + plate (stone implements). 1899.

2990(b) Oakeley (William Bagnall). The chambered tumulus at Heston Brake, Monmouthshire. Proc. Clifton Antiq. Club, 2, pp. 64–66 + plan. 1893.

2991 Ordnance Survey. Map of South Wales, showing the distribution of long barrows and megaliths. [Introduction by W. F. Grimes.] pp. 56 + map. 8°. Southampton, 1936. [Scale: 4 miles to one inch.]

2992 Owen (Elias). Cromlech, Llandegai. Arch. Camb., 3rd S. 13, pp. 62–63 + plate. 1867.

2993 Owen (Elijah). Notice of the discovery of ancient British sepulchral remains at Penmon, Anglesey. Arch. Camb., 5th S. 6, pp. 59–62. 1889.

2994 Owen (M. N.). A prehistoric tomb at Garthbeibio [Montgom.]. Trans. Caradoc & Severn Valley F.C. 7, pp. 108–10. 1923.

2995 Parry (T. Lowe D. Jones). Cromlech on Gynydd Cefn Anrmlch, Caernarvonshire. [Figure.] Arch. Camb., pp. 97–99. 1847.

2996 Peate (Iorwerthe C.). A Beaker burial from Llannon, Carmarthenshire. Arch. Camb., 85 ii, 1930, 309–14 + 3 figures.

2997 Phillips (Charles William). An Examination of the Ty Newydd chambered tomb, Llanfaelog, Anglesey. Arch. Camb., 91 i, 1936, 93–99 + 3 figures.

2998 Powell (Thomas George Eyre). Excavation of the megalithic tomb of Barclodiad y Gawres. Summary of first season's work, June, 1951. (—Second season's work, June, 1953). Anglesey Ant. Soc. Trans., 1952, pp. 69–70; 1953, pp. 47–48. 1952–53.

2999 —— Excavations at Gwaenysgor (Flints.) 1951. Arch. Camb., 103, 1954, 109–111 + 1 figure.

3000 —— *and* **Daniel** (Glyn Edmund). Barclodiad y Gawres. The excavation of a megalithic chamber tomb in Anglesey, 1952–1953. pp. xiv, 80 + 40 plates. 4°. Liverpool, 1956. [9 figures + 4 maps + 5 plans.]

3001 —— The Chambered cairn at Dyffryn Ardudwy. Antiquity, 37, 1963, pp. 19–24.

3002 Price (Frederick George Hilton). The opening of a barrow in the parish of Colwinston, Glamorganshire. Proc. Soc. Antiq., 2 S. 11, pp. 430–38. 1887. *Reprinted in* Arch. Camb., 5th S. 5, pp. 83–93. 1888.

3003 Prichard (Hugh). Crûg Lâs, Malldraeth, Anglesey. [Plan. *See also* p. 394.] Arch. Camb., 3rd S. 11, pp. 196–200. 1865.

3004 —— Cromlech at Pantry–Saer, Anglesey. [Figure.] Arch. Camb., 3rd S. 14, pp. 89–90. 1868.

3005 —— Barclodiad y Gawres [cromlech], and camp at Trecastell [Anglesey]. Arch. Camb., 3rd S. 15, pp. 403–07 + plate + 2 plans. 1869.

3006 —— Cromlech at Ty Mawr [Anglesey]. Arch. Camb., 4th S. 4, pp. 22–31 + plate. 1873.

3007(a) Richards (Melville). Carn Ymenyn [Mynachlog-Ddu, Pemb.]. Arch. Camb., 113, 1964, 176–77.

3007(b) Rivers (Augustus Henry Lane Fox Pitt). On the opening of two cairns near Bangor, North Wales. J. Ethnolog. Soc., N.S. 2, pp. 306–24 + plate. 1870.

3008 Rix (Mathew). Parc le Breos, Gower. Arch. Camb., 91 ii, 1936, 321–323 + 2 figures.

3009 Savory (Hubert Newman). A Middle Bronze Age barrow at Crick, Monmouthshire. Arch. Camb., 95 ii, 1940, 169–91 + 9 figures.

3010 —— Two Middle Bronze Age palisade barrows at Letterston, Pembrokshire. Arch. Camb., 100 i, 1948, 67–87 + 7 figures.

3011 —— Palisade barrows at Letterston, Pembrokeshire. Bull. Bd. Celtic Stud., 12, pp. 123–25. 1948.

3012 —— A cist-burial on Merthyr Mawr warren, Glamorgan. Bull. Bd. Celtic Stud., 13, pp. 111–12. 1949.

3013 —— A supposed barrow at Newton Nottage, Glamorgan. Bull. Bd. Celtic Stud., 13, pp. 112–13. 1949.

3014 —— A cist burial on Merthyr Mawr warren, Glamorgan. Cardiff Nat. Soc. Rpt. & Trans., 79 (1945/48), p. 59 + plate. 1950.

3015 —— The Tinkinswood and St.

Lythans long cairns, Glamorgan. *Ministry of Works*. pp. 7. 8⁰. London, 1950. [2 plans.]

3016 —— Examination of a long cairn at Pipton (Breckn.). Bull. Bd. Celtic Stud., 14, pp. 166–68. 1951.

3017 —— Burial cave at Llanferres (Denb.). Bull. Bd. Celtic Stud., 14, pp. 174–75 + plate. 1951.

3018 —— Excavation of a group of round barrows on Stormy down near Pyle (Glam.). Bull. Bd. Celtic Stud., 15, pp. 70–72. 1952.

3019 —— The excavation of Twlc-y-filiast cromlech, Llangynog (Carm.). Bull. Bd. Celtic Stud., 15, pp. 225–28. 1953.

3020 —— The Excavation of the Pipton long cairn, Brecknockshire. Arch. Camb., 105, 1956, 7–46 + 4 figures + 7 plates.

3021 —— The excavation of the Twlc-y-Filiast cromlech, Llangynog (Carm.). [2 figures + plan.] Bull. Bd. Celtic Stud., 16, pp. 300–08 + 3 plates. 1956.

3022 —— Some unrecorded round barrows in east Glamorgan. Trans. Cardiff Nat. Soc., 86 (1956–57), pp. 25–27. 1959.

3023 —— Beaker cist near Brymbo (Denb.). Bull. Bd. Celtic Stud., 18, pp. 192–93 + plate. 1959.

3024 —— Excavation at a third round barrow at Pen-Dre, Letterston (Pemb.) 1961. Bull. Board Celtic Studies, 20 iii, 1963, 309–25 + 4 figures + 6 plates.

3025 **Scott** (W. Lindsay). The Chambered tomb of Pant-y-Saer, Anglesey. Appendix I: Report on human bones, by John Cameron. Appendix II: Report on animal bones from chamber, by J. Wilfrid Jackson. Arch. Camb., 88 ii, 1933, 185–228 + 20 figures.

3026 **Solly** (Nathaniel Neal). Account of Ystumcegid cromlech, in the parish of Llanfihangel-y-Pennant, county of Carnarvon. Archaeologia, 33, pp. 66–67 + plate. 1852.

3027 **Stanley** (*Hon.* William Owen). Cromlech at Trefigneth [near Holyhead, Anglesey]. Arch. Camb., 3rd S. 13, p. 234 + plate. 1867.

3028 —— Ancient interments and sepulchral urns found in Anglesey and North Wales, with notes on examples in some other localities. [5 figures.] Arch-

aeol. J., 24, pp. 13–34 + 7 plates. 1867.

3029 —— Ancient interments and sepulchral urns found in Anglesey and North Wales, with some account of examples in other localities. With additional observations by Albert Way. Arch. Camb., 3rd S. 14, pp. 217–93 + 6 plates. 1868.

3030 —— On the tumulus in Plas Newydd park, Anglesey. Arch. Camb., 4th S. 1, pp. 51–58 + 7 plates + 2 plans. 1870.

3031 —— The chambered tumulus in Plas Newydd park, Anglesey. [Figure + 6 plans.] Archaeol. J., 28, pp. 85–96 + 8 plates. 1871.

3032 —— Cromlech at Trefigneth, [Anglesey]. Archaeol. J., 31, pp. 1–2 + plate. 1874.

3033 —— Notices of sepulchral deposits with cinerary urns found at Porth Dafarch, in Holyhead Island, in 1848; and of recent excavations in the sandmounds adjacent in 1875–6. [2 figures.] Archaeol. J., 33, pp. 129–43 + 8 plates + 2 plans. 1876. *Reprinted in* Arch. Camb., 4th S. 9, pp. 22–38 + 8 plates + plan. 1878.

3034 **Stapleton** (Philip). Exploration of tumuli near Caewys, Flintshire. [Figure.] Arch. Camb., 6th S. 8, pp. 295–96. 1908.

3035 —— The Bryngwyn tumuli [Flintshire]. [6 figures + 2 plans (2 figures).] Arch. Camb., 6th S. 8, pp. 359–76; 9, pp. 361–66. 1908–09.

3036 **Stephens** (T.). On the names of cromlechan. Arch. Camb., 3rd S. 2, pp. 99–109. 1856.

3037 **T** (T. H.). Pembrokeshire cromlechan. [Figure (Tre-llys) + plan (Longhouse).] Cymru Fu, 2, pp. 227–28. 1890.

3038 **Tegid.** Cromlechs, &c. in Pembrokeshire. Arch. Camb., 2, pp. 373–374. 1847.

3039 **Thomas** (David Richard). Early interments at Cefn, near St. Asaph. Arch. Camb., 3rd S. 15, pp. 197–98. 1869.

3040 **Thomas** (Eva). Cromlech at Capel Garmon. [Figure + plan.] Proc. Llandudno F.C., 3 (1908–09), pp. 13–15. 1910.

3041 **Thomas** (E. Lorimer). Discovery of prehistoric burial-ground in Cardiganshire. [2 figures. Bronze Age.

Arch. Camb., 6th S. 10, pp. 373–79; 12, pp. 345–56. 1910–12.

3042 Thomas (J. E.). An account of the opening of a tumulus known as Twyn y Beddall, near Hay. Arch. Camb., 4th S. 3, pp. 1–4 + plan. 1872.

3043 Thorne (Charles). Construction of cromlechs. Arch. Camb., 3rd S. 15, pp. 198–99. 1869.

3044 Treherne (George Gilbert). Note of digging in a tumulus in Tafarn Diflas field [Llandawke]. Trans. Carmarthenshire Ant. Soc., 9, pp. 54–55 + plate (axe-head). 1913.

3045 Vulliamy (Colwyn Edward). The excavation of a megalithic tomb in Breconshire. (Further excavations in the long barrows at Ffostill). [Figure + 3 plans (2 plans).] Arch. Camb., 76, pp. 300–05; 78, pp. 320–24. 1921–23.

3046 —— Note on a long barrow in Wales. [Plan.] Man, 22, pp. 11–13. 1922.

3047 —— Excavation of a long barrow in Breconshire. [Figure + 2 plans.] Man, 22, pp. 150–52. 1922.

3048 —— Excavation of an unrecorded long barrow [at Little Lodge farm, near Glasbury, Breconshire] in Wales. [Plan.] Man, 29, pp. 34–36. 1929.

3049 Ward (John). Prehistoric interments near Cardiff. Arch. Camb., 6th S. 2, pp. 25–32 + 2 plates. 1902.

3050 —— Cadno tumulus, Pendine. Trans. Carmarthenshire Ant. Soc., 5, pp. 30–31. 1909.

3051 —— Notes on digging in a tumulus on Bigning mountain, Castle Lloyd. Trans. Carmarthenshire Ant. Soc., 6, pp. 18–20 + plan. 1910.

3052 —— The St. Nicholas chambered tumulus, Glamorgan. [11 figures + 5 plans (4 figures + plan).] Arch. Camb., 6th S. 15, pp. 253–320; 16, pp. 239–67. 1915–16.

3053 —— Some prehistoric sepulchral remains near Pendine, Carmarthenshire. Arch. Camb., 6th S. 18, pp. 35–79. 1918.

3054 —— Prehistoric burials, Merthyr Mawr warren, Glamorgan. Arch. Camb., 6th S. 19, pp. 323–52. 1919.

3055 Way (Albert). The cromlechs of Anglesey. [29.] Archaeol. J., 28, pp. 97–108. 1871.

3056 Webley (D. P.). Unrecorded round barrows in Glamorgan and Monmouthshire. Bull. Bd. Celtic Stud., 16, pp. 211–12. 1955.

3057 —— Valley bottom cairns in south Brecknockshire. Bull. Bd. Celtic Stud., 17, p. 54. 1956.

3058 —— An unrecorded chambered long cairn in Brecknockshire. Bull. Bd. Celtic Stud., 17, pp. 54–55. 1956.

3059 —— Cairn cemeteries [at Vaynor] in south Breconshire. Bull. Bd. Celtic Stud., 17, pp. 117–18. 1957.

3060 —— Unrecorded round barrows in Glamorgan and Monmouthshire. [Monknash, Glam. and Barbados Green, Tintern, Mon.] Bull. Bd. Celtic Stud., 18, p. 76. 1958.

3061 —— A cairn cemetery and secondary Neolithic dwelling on Cefn Cilsanws, Vaynor (Breckn.). [Figure + 2 plans.] Bull. Bd. Celtic Stud., 18, pp. 79–88 + 2 plates. 1958.

3062 —— Twyn Bryn Glas: the excavation of a round cairn at Cwm Cadlan, Breconshire. Bull. Board Celtic Studies, 19 i, 1960, 56–71 + 5 figures + 2 plates.

3063 —— Y Garn Llwyd, Newchurch West, Monmouthshire: a reassessment. Bull. Board Celtic Studies, 19 iii, 1961, 255–58 + 1 figure.

3064 Wheeler (*Sir* Robert Eric Mortimer). A tumulus at Garthbeibio, Montgomeryshire. Arch. Camb., 78, pp. 279–90. 1923.

3065 —— Crouched burial at Merthyr Mawr, Glamorgan. Bull. Bd. Celtic Studies, 2, pp. 161–63. 1924.

3066 —— A Bronze Age barrow at Kilpaison Burrows, Rhoscrowther, Pembrokeshire. Bull. Bd. Celtic Stud., 3, pp. 74–75. 1926.

3067 —— A burial place of dwellers in the upper Taf valley near Whitland, Carmarthenshire, in the Bronze Age. Bull. Bd. Celtic Stud., 3, p. 75. 1926.

3068 —— A tumulus at Garthbeibio, Montgomeryshire. Collns. rel. to Montgom., 40, pp. 109–19. 1928.

3069 Wilkinson (*Sir* John Gardner). Avenue and carns about Arthur's Stone in Gower. [2 figures. (plan).] Arch. Camb., 4th S. 1, pp. 23–45 + 2 plates + 2 plans; 117–21 + plate + plan. 1870.

3070 **Wilkinson** (*Sir* John Gardner). Cromlechs and other remains in Pembrokeshire. Collectanea Archaeol., 2, pp. 219–40 + 6 plates and plans. 1871.

3071 **Williams** (Audrey). A Megalithic tomb at Nicholaston, Gower, Glamorgan. Proc. prehist. Soc., 6, 1940, 178–81 + 4 figures + 2 plates.

3072 —— Chambered cairn, Nicholaston, Glamorgan. Bull. Bd. Celtic Stud., 10, pp. 187–88. 1940.

3073 —— Two Bronze Age barrows on Fairwood Common, Gower, Glamorgan. Arch. Camb., 98 i, 1944, 52–63 + 7 figures + 5 plates.

3074 **Williams** (Howel). Excavation of Bronze Age tumulus, near Gorsedd, Holywell, Flintshire. [13 figures + plan.] Arch. Camb., 76, pp. 265–89. 1921.

3075 **Williams** (Jacob Picton Gordon). Kipaison (Kilpatrick's ton) Bronze Age cemetery. Trans. Carmarthenshire Ant. Soc., 19, pp. 54–56 + plan (barrow). 1925.

3076 —— Linney burrows—a Bronze Age Stone mound. Arch. Camb., 81, pp. 186–90. 1926.

3077 **Williams** (W. Wynn). Cromlech, Lligwy [Anglesey]. [Plan.] Arch. Camb., 3rd S. 13, pp. 135–37 + 2 plates. 1867.

3078 —— Cromlech, Bonafon mountain [Anglesey]. [Figure.] Arch. Camb., 3rd S. 13, pp. 344–46 + plate. 1867.

3079 —— Cromlech, Bodowyr, Llanidan. (Ruined cromlech, Perthi Duon, Llanidan): [Anglesey]. Arch. Camb., 3rd S. 15, pp. 263–64 + 2 plates. 1869.

3080 —— Excavations at Pant y Saer cromlech, Anglesey. Arch. Camb., 4th S. 6, pp. 341–48 + plate + plan. 1875.

(f) Zone 6 [CBA Group 1 plus Ireland and Isle of Man]

3081 **Aitken** (W. G.). Two Bronze Age cist burials. (i) Lochlands Farm, Pattray, (ii) Ballimenach, near Campbeltown, Argyll. Proc. Soc. Ant. Scotland, 95, 1961–62, 126–133 + 4 figures + 1 plate.

3082 **Alexander** (*Sir* J. E.). Opening of the Fairy Knowe of Pendreith, Bridge of Allan [Stirlingshire]. Proc. Soc. Antiq. Scot., 7, pp. 519–23 + plate. 1870.

3083 **Allen** (John Romilly). Notes on a cist with axe-head sculptures, near Kilmartin, Argyleshire. J. Brit. Archaeol. Ass., 36, pp. 146–50 + plate. 1880.

3084 **Anderson** (Joseph). On the chambered cairns of Caithness, with results of recent explorations. Proc. Soc. Antiq. Scot., 6, pp. 442–51 + plate. 1868.

3085 —— Report on excavations in Caithness cairns. Mems. Anthrop. Soc. London, 3 (1867–69), pp. 216–42. 1870.

3086 —— On the horned cairns of Caithness. Mems. Anthrop. Soc. London, 3 (1867–69), pp. 266–73. 1870.

3087 —— On the horned cairns of Caithness: their structural ararngement, contents of chambers, &c. [7 figures + 6 plans.] Proc. Soc. Antiq. Scot., 7, pp. 480–512. 1870.

3088 [**Anon.**] Notes on the rude stone monuments of Sligo and their contents. Archaeol. Rev., 4, pp. 375–79. 1889.

3089 [**Anon.**] Irish megaliths. Antiquity, 1, pp. 97–98 + plate. 1927.

3090 **Bersu** (Gerhard). A Cemetery of the Ronaldsway Culture at Ballateare, Quaby, Isle of Man. Proc. prehist. Soc., 13, 1947, 161–169 + 4 figures + 2 plates.

3091 **Bishop** (A. Henderson). Note on a burial after cremation. Trans. Dumfries. Ant. Soc., 3 S. 6 (1918–19), pp. 44–48 + 4 plates. 1919.

3092 **Buckland** (Anne Walbank). The Monument known as "King Orry's Grave" compared with tumuli in Gloucestershire. Advm. Sci. 1888, 854.

3093 —— The monument known as "King Orry's grave", compared with tumuli in Gloucestershire. J. Anthrop. Inst., 18, pp. 346–53 + plate. 1889.

3094 **Bryce** (Thomas H.). Cairns and tumuli of Bute. Scot. Hist. Rev., 1, p. 109. 1903.

3095 **Calder** (Charles S. T.). Note on a Bronze Age cist at Redden farm, Sproriston, Roxburghshire. Hist. Berwick. Nat. Club, 31, p. 241 + plate. 1949.

3096 —— Report on a Bronze Age grave discovered on Cumledge estate, near Duns. Hist. Berwick. Nat. Club, 32, pp. 46–48 + 3 plates + plan. 1950.

3097 Callander (J. Graham). Prehistoric burial at Alva. Trans. Stirling N.H. & Arch. Soc., 1914–19, pp. 83–85. 1919.

3098 —— Horned cairn, Cairnhoby (Kirkcudbright). Trans. Dumfries. Ant. Soc., 3 S. 13 (1925–26), pp. 246–47. 1927.

3099 —— Prehistoric graves in the Roman fort at Old Kilpatrick, Dunbartonshire. Trans. Glasgow Arch. Soc., N.S. 8, pp. 53–61 + 2 plates. 1930.

3100 —— Mausoleums in the island of Rousay, Orkney. Antiq. J., 14, pp. 423–24. 1934.

3101 Campbell of Kilberry (Marion) *and others* [Scott (J. G.) and Piggott (Stuart)]. The Badden cist slab. Proc. Soc. Ant. Scotland, 94, 1960/61, 46–61 + 4 figures + 2 plates.

3102 Chalmers (James Hay) *and* **Davidson** (C. B.). Notice of the discovery of a stone cist at Broomend, near Inverurie, Aberdeenshire. [Figure.] Proc. Soc. Antiq. Scot., 7, pp. 110–18, 561–62. 1870.

3103 Chardenal (C. A.). On the probable origin and age of the stone tumuli along the firth of Clyde. Trans. Glasgow Archaeol. Soc., 2, pp. 173–78. 1883.

3104 Childe (Vere Gordon). Scottish megalithic tombs and their affinities. [4 figures + 3 plans.] Trans. Glasgow Arch. Soc., N.S. 7, pp. 120–37. 1933.

3105 —— The chambered cairns of Ronsay. [Map.] Antiq. J., 22, pp. 139–142. 1942.

3106 —— Megalithic tombs in Scotland and Ireland. Trans. Glasgow Archaeol. Soc., N.S. 11, pp. 7–21. 1947.

3107 Clark (John Grahame Douglas). Megalithic research in the North of Ireland. Proc. prehist. Soc., 3, 1937, 166–172 + 3 figures.

3108 Coffey (George). New Grange, and other incised tumuli in Ireland. Dublin, pp. 118 + 95 figures. 1912.

3109 Coles (Frederick R.). The tumulus and stone-circles at Cauldside. [Kirkcudbright.] Trans. Dumfriess. Ant. Soc., 6 (1887–90), pp. 83–84. 1890.

3110 Coles (Frederick R.). The cairns of Kirkcudbrightshire. Trans. Dumfries. Ant. soc., 10 (1893–94), pp. 59–66. 1894.

3111 —— A record of the [16] kistvaens found in the Stewartry of Kirkcudbright. Reliquary, N.[3rd]S. 3, pp. 1–19. 1897.

3112 Coles (John M.) *and* **Simpson** (D. D. A.). The Excavation of a Neolithic round barrow at Pitnacree, Perthshire, Scotland (with an appendix, by C. B. Denston). Proc. prehist. Soc., 31, 1965, 34–57 + 5 figures + 7 plates.

3113 Collins, A. E. P. *and* **Waterman**, D. M. Millin Bay: a late Neolithic cairn in County Down. Belfast, 1955. pp. 84, plates xix, figures 17. Archaeological Research Publications of Northern Ireland, No. 4.

3114 Conwell (Eugene Alfred). On some remarkable archaeological discoveries in Ireland. Trans. Ethnolog. Soc., N.S. 5, pp. 217–20. 1867.

3115 Corcoran (John X. W. P.). The Cadlingford Culture. Proc. prehist. Soc., 26, 1960, 98–148 + 10 figures + 2 plates.

3116 —— The Excavations of three chambered tombs in Caithness during 1961. Archaeol. News Letter, 7 iii, 1962, 155–159 + 3 figures.

3117 —— Excavation of a chambered cairn at Mid Gleniron Farm, Wigtownshire. Interim Report. Trans. Dumfries, 41, 1962/3, 99–110 + 3 figures.

3118 Cormack (W. F.). Prehistoric site at Kirkburn, Lockerbie. Trans. Dumfries & Galloway, 40, 1961/62, 53–59 + 2 figures + 3 plates.

3119 —— Burial site at Kirkburn, Lockerbie. Proc. Soc. Ant. Scotland, 96, 1962–63, 107–35 + 9 figures + 2 plates.

3120 Cramond (William). Tumuli in the Cullen district. Trans. Banff. F.C., 15, 1895.

3121 Craw (James Hewat). Cist and urn found on Harelaw hill, Chirnside [Berwickshire]. Hist. Berwick. Nat. Club, 19, p. 340 + plate. 1905.

3122 Cregreen (Eric). Beaker burial at Kilmory Knap, Argyllshire. [Figure.] Proc. Soc. Antiq. Scot., 90 (1956–57), pp. 227–39. 1959.

3123 Dalrymple (Charles E.). Notes on the excavation of a tumulus, at Auchleven, in the parish of Premnay, and district of Garioch, Aberdeenshire. Proc. Soc. Antiq. Scot., 2, pp. 431–32. 1859.

3124 Davidson (James Milne). Bronze Age burials at Blantyre and Milngavie. [3 figures.] Trans. Glasgow Archaeol. Soc., N.S. 9, pp. 305–12. 1940.

3125 Davies (Oliver) *and* **Evans** (Emyr Estyn). Goward hill cairn, Co. Down. Antiquity, 7, p. 222. 1933.

3126 —— *and* —— Excavation of a horned cairn at Goward, Co. Down. [Figure + plan.] Man, 33, pp. 114–17. 1933.

3127 Dickie (William). Craigdarroch (Sanquhar) tumuli and others. Trans. Dumfries. Ant. Soc., 3 S. 1 (1912–13), pp. 354–59. 1913.

3128(a) Don (John). A prehistoric interment (near Peterhead) in Buchan. Trans. Buchan F. C., 8, pp. 103–05. 1905.

3128(b) Elliot (J. Scott) *Maj.-gen. and* **Rae** (Ian). Whitestanes Moor—Sites 1 and 80. An enclosed cremation cemetery. Trans. Dumfries, 42, 1965, 51–60 + 2 figures.

3129 Eogan, George. A New passage grave in Co. Meath. Antiquity, 37, 1963, pp. 226–28.

3130 Estridge (H.). On an ancient tumulus at New Grange in Ireland. [4 figures + plan.] Proc. Oxford Archit. & Hist. Soc., 1, pp. 303–10. 1864.

3131 Evans (Emyr Estyn) *and* **Davies** (Oliver). Excavation of a horned cairn at Ballyalton, Co. Down. [Figure + plan.] Man, 34, pp. 88–90. 1934.

3132 —— Doey's cairn, Dunloy [Co. Antrim]. Antiq., J., 16, pp. 208–13 + plate. 1936.

3133 —— The Multiple-cist cairn at Mount Stewart, Co. Down, Northern Ireland. Proc. prehist. Soc., 3, 1937, 29–42 + 5 figures + 3 plates.

3134 Fairhurst (Horace) *and* **Scott** (J. G.). The mound at West Carlestoun, Torrance of Campsie, Stirlingshire. Trans. Glasgow Archaeol. Soc., N.S. 14, pp. 20–294 + 2 plates. 1956.

3135 Falconer (Allan A.). Two early graves at Cockburn, Duns. Hist. Berwick. Nat. Club, 27, p. 355. 1931.

3135(b) —— Bronze Age burial at Rig Foot, Longformacus parish. Hist. Berwick. Nat. Club, 28, p. 247. 1934.

3136 Ferguson (W.). Notes on a cist found at Parkhill, Dyce, in October 1881. Advm. of Sci., 1885, 1225.

3137 Finegan (Joseph Thomas). Description of a crom-leach in the county of Kilkenny. Archaeologia, 16, pp. 264–271 + plate. 1812.

3138 Forrest (Archibald). A stone cist found at Middlefield farm, in the parish of Gavinton, near Duns, Berwickshire. Trans. Glasgow Archaeol. Soc., N.S. 12, pp. 15–18. 1953.

3139 Galloway (Alexander). Memorandum as to objects found in a small tumulus on the lands of Slochairn, Baldernock parish, opened August 4, 1859. Trans. Glasgow Archaeol. Soc., 1, pp. 227–35. 1868.

3140 Gourlay (W. R.). The cairns of Stroanfreggan and Cairn Avel. Trans. Dumfries. Ant. Soc., 3 S., 14 (1926–28), pp. 184–94. 1930.

3141 Graham (Angus). Cairnfields in Scotland. Proc. Soc. Antiq. Scot., 90 (1956–57), pp. 7–23. 1959.

3142 —— A Small cairn near Ospisdale [Sutherland]. Proc. Soc. Antiq. Scotland, 91, 1960, 177.

3143(a) Greenwell (William). An account of excavations in cairns near Crinan [Argyleshire]. Proc. Soc. Antiq. Scot., 6, pp. 336–51 + plate. 1868.

3143(b) Gunn (A. Rugg). Megalithic remains, South Uist. [Figure and plan. Dolmen.] Antiquity, 11, pp. 96–99. 1937.

3144 Gunn (Peter B.). Notes on excavations at Falla cairn, Oxnam [near Jedburgh]. Hist. Berwick. Nat. Club, 27, pp. 104–06. 1929.

3145 Hamilton (J. R. C.). Food vessel cist at Doune, Perthshire. Proc. Soc. Antiq. Scot., 90 (1956–57), pp. 231–34. 1959.

3146 Hardy (James). An account of an assemblage of ancient sepulchral monuments in the east of Berwickshire. Hist. Berwick. N.C., 3, pp. 103–11. 1853.

3147 —— On ancient stone cists and human remains discovered at Aycliffe house, near Ayton. Hist. Berwick. Nat. Club, 7, pp. 274–75. 1874.

3148 —— On ancient interments in a tumulus, called the Fairy Knowe, near Stenton, East Lothian. Hist. Berwick. Nat. Club, 9, pp. 101–04. 1879.

3149 —— British cist on Ayton Law farm (parish of Ayton). Hist. Berwick. Nat. Club., 14, p. 392. 1893.

3150 Hardy (James). British cist on Redheugh farm, near Oldcamporbus [Berwick.] Hist. Berwick. Nat. Club, 14, pp. 393–95. 1893.

3151 Hemp (Wilfrid James). Leac Con Mic Ruis, Co. Sligo. Antiquity, 5, pp. 98–101 + 2 plates. 1931.

3152 Henshall (A. S.). A Bronze Age burial at Embo, Sutherland. Proc. Soc. Antiq. Scot., 90 (1956–57), pp. 225–27. 1959.

3153 —— A Dagger grave from the Law of Mauldslie, Carluke, Lanarkshire. Proc. Soc. Ant. Scotland, 95, 1961–62, 307 + 1 figure.

3154 —— and **Wallace** (J. C.). The Excavation of a chambered cairn at Embo, Sutherland. Proc. Soc. Ant. Scotland, 96, 1962–63, 9–36 + 6 figures + 4 plates.

3155 —— and —— A Bronze Age cist burial at Masterton, Pitreavie, Fife. Proc. Soc. Ant. Scotland, 96, 1962–63, 145–54 + 4 figures + 1 plate.

3156 —— The chambered tombs of Scotland, Vol. 1. Edinburgh, 1963, pp. xvi + 456 + 27 plates + 145 figures + 10 maps.

3157 —— Chambered Tombs of Scotland, Vol. 1 1963, Vol. 11 1972 (Edinburgh U.P.).

3158 Herring (I. J.). Knockoneill excavation, Co. Derry. Arch. News Letter, 1 ix, pp. 7–8. 1949.

3159 Holden (J. Sinclair). On some forms of ancient interment in [the Glens] Co. Antrim. J. Anth. Inst., 1, pp. 219–21. 1971.

3160 Innes (Cosmo). Notice of a tomb on the hill of Roseisle, Morayshire, recently opened; also of the chambered cairns and stone circles at Clara, on Nairnside. [Figure.] Proc. Soc. Antiq. Scot., 3, pp. 46–50 + 2 plates. 1862.

3161 Jackson (John Wilfrid). An account of a human burial on the shore near Ballintry harbour. Irish Naturalists' J., 6, pp. 190–91. 1937.

3162 Jervise (Andrew). Account of the discovery of a circular group of cinerary urns and human bones at Westwood, near Newport, on the Tay. Proc. Soc. Antiq. Scot., 6, pp. 388–94 + plate. 1868.

3163 Joass (James M.). Notice of the discovery of cists containing urns and burned bones at Torran Dubh, near Tain [Ross.]. Proc. Soc. Antiq. Scot., 6, pp. 418–19 + plate. 1868.

3164 —— Note of five kists found under a tumulus on the glebe of the parish of Eddertoun, Ross, and of a kist within a circle of standing stones in the same neighbourhood. [2 figures + plan.] Proc. Soc. Antiq. Scot., 7, pp. 268–69. 1870.

3165 Keith (*Sir* Arthur). Report on human remains from cist graves, Rathlin Island [Co. Antrim?]. Man, 29, pp. 98–100. 1929.

3166 Kermode (Philip Moore Callow). Notice of the opening of a Celtic tumulus on Snaefell, in the Isle of Man. Reliquary, 25, pp. 117–18. 1884.

3167 —— Long barrow in the Isle of Man. Antiq. J., 7, pp. 191–92. 1927.

3168 Lawson (Alexander). Notes of urns and sepulchral monuments discovered at various times in the parish of Creich, Fifeshire. [Figure.] Proc. Soc. Antiq. Scot., 7, pp. 401–09. 1870.

3169 Lett (H. W.). Sepulchral cairn on Knock Iveagh. Ulster J. Arch., 4, 1897, p. 67.

3170 Letts (Ernest F.). Burial tumuli in County Louth, Ireland. Trans. Lancs. & Ches. Ant. Soc., 11 (1893), pp. 52–56. 1894.

3171 Lisowski (F. P.) *and* **Spence** (T. F.). The Cremation from Manderstone, Berwickshire. Hist. Berwick. Nat. Hist. Club, 36 ii, 1963, 172–74 + 2 plates.

3172 MacGown (John). Ancient sepulture in Crambrae. Trans. Glasgow Archaeol. Soc., 2, pp. 114–20. 1883.

3173 MacKie (Evan W.). The Lang Cairn, Dumbarton Muir. Proc. Soc. Ant. Scotland, 94, 1960–61, 315–17, 1 figure.

3174 —— Two radio carbon dates from a Clyde–Solway chambered cairn. Antiquity, 38, 1964, pp. 52–54.

3175 Mapleton (R. J.). Notice of a cairn at Kilchoan, Argyleshire, and its contents. Proc. Soc. Antiq. Scot., 6, pp. 351–55. 1868.

3176 —— Note on a cist with engraved stones on the Poltalloch estate, County of Argyll. [Figure.] J. Ethnolog. Soc., N.S. 2, pp. 340–42. 1870.

3177 Maxwell (J. Harrison). A Bronze Age cemetery at Springhill farm, Baillieston, near Glasgow. Trans. Glasgow Archaeol. Soc., N.S. 9, pp. 287–302. 1940.

3178 Megan (J. V. S.) *and* **Simpson** (D. D. A.). A short cist burial of North Uist and some notes on the prehistory of the Outer Isles in the Second Millenium B.C. Proc. Soc. Ant. Scotland, 94, 1960/61, 62–78, 3 figures + 1 plate.

3179 Miller (Alfred G.). Bronze Age graves at Ferniegair, Hamilton. [3 figures.] Trans. Glasgow Archaeol. Soc., N.S. 11, pp. 17–21. 1947.

3180 Mongey (L.). The Portal dolmens of south-eastern Ireland. [Figure + map + plan.] J. Waterford Spelaeological Soc., 1, pp. 1–32 + 3 plates. 1941.

3181 Nevill (Francis). Part of a letter to the Rt. Rev. Lord Bishop of Clogher, containing a relation of several urns and sepulchral monuments lately found in Ireland. Phil. Trans. Roy. Soc., xxviii, 1713, 252–56.

3182 Norman (George). Burial mounds of Ireland. Somerset Arch. Soc., Proc. Bath branch, [3] 1914–18, pp. 238–47. 1917.

3183 O'Kelly, (M. J.) Newgrange, Co. Meath. Antiquity, 38, 1964, 288–90.

3184 O'Neil (Bryan Hugh St. John). The Dwarfie stane, Orkney, and St. Kevin's bed, Glendalough [Co. Wicklow]. Antiq. J., 27, pp. 182–83. 1947.

3185 O'Riordáin (Seán P.). A Burial with faience beads at Tara. Proc. prehist. Soc., 21, 1955, 163–73 + 2 figures + 2 plates.

3186 —— *and* **Daniel**, Glynn. New Grange and the Bend of the Boyne. London, 1964, 168 pp., 48 plates, 31 figures.

3187 Petrie (George). Notice of a barrow containing cists, on the farm of Newbigging, near Kirkwall; and at Isbister, in the parish of Rendall, Orkney. Proc. Soc. Antiq. Scot., 6, pp. 411–18 + plate. 1868.

3188 Piggott (Stuart). An Early Bronze Age sanctuary site in Scottish lowlands. Antiquity, 22, pp. 35–36. 1948.

3189 —— Excavations in three chambered tombs in Galloway, 1949. Arch. News Letter, 2, pp. 108–09. 1949.

3190 —— The excavations at Cairnpapple hill, West Lothian 1947–48. An-

tiquity, 23, pp. 32–39 + 2 plates + plan. 1949.

3191 —— Cairnpapple (N.S. 987717) [Note for Summer Meeting, 1964]. Arch. J., 121, 1964, 181.

3192 Pownall (Thomas). A description of the sepulchral monument at New Grange, near Drogheda, in the county of Meath, in Ireland. Archaeologia, 2, pp. 236–75 + 4 plates + plan. 1773.

3192(b) Ritchie (P. R.) A Chambered cairn at Isbister, South Ronaldsay, Orkney [Orkney–Cromarty Type (ii)]. Proc. Soc. Antiq. Scotland, 92, 1958–59, 25–32, 4 figures + 1 plate.

3193 Roberts (George E.). On the discovery of large kist-vaens on the Muckle Heog in the island of Unst (Shetland), containing urns of chloritic schist. Mems. Anthrop. Soc. London, 1 (1863–64), pp. 296–98 + plate. 1865.

3194 Robertson (Alexander). Notes of the discovery of stone cists at Lesmurdie, Banffshire, containing primitive urns, &c., along with human remains. [3 figures.] Proc. Soc. Antiq. Scot., 1, pp. 205–11. 1855.

3195 Robertson (A. D.). Ancient cromlech at Ardenadam, near Dunoon. [2 figures + plan.] Trans. Glasgow Archaeol. Soc., 1, pp. 486–92. 1868.

3198 Russell (Rev. John). Notes on the opening of a cist, in the parish of Leslie, Aberdeenshire. Advm. of Sci., 1885, 1224–25.

3199 Scott (J. G.). The Excavation of the chambered cairn at Crarae, Loch Fyneside, Mid Argyll. Proc. Soc. Ant. Scotland, 94, 1960/61, 1–27 + 12 figures + 4 plates.

3200 —— Clyde, Carlinford and Connaught Cairns—a review. Antiquity, 36, 1962, pp. 97–101.

3201 —— The chambered cairn at Beacharra, Kintyre, Argyll. Proc. prehist. Soc., 30, 1964, 134–58 + 11 figures + 6 plates.

3202 Scott (W. Lindsay). Discovery of beakers in a cairn at Kraiknish, Loch Eynort, Isle of Skye. [Plan.] Man, 29, pp. 165–66 + plate. 1929.

3204 Seton (A.). Account of a large tumulus or barrow, near the west coast of the peninsula of Cantyre. Archaeol. Scot., 3, p. 43. 1831.

3205 Simpson (*Sir* James Young) *bart*. An account of two barrows at Spottiswood, Berwickshire, opened by the Lady John Scott. Proc. Soc. Antiq. Scot., 5, pp. 222–24 + plate. 1865.

3206 Simpson (William Douglas). A chambered cairn at Allt-nam-Ban, Strathbrora, Sutherland. [Plan.] Antiq. J., 8, pp. 485–88 + plate. 1928.

3207 Stevenson (Robert Barron Kerr). A cist with holed coverstone at Redbrae, Wigtown. (Further note). [Figure.] Trans. Dumfries. Ant. Soc., 3rd S. 25 (1947–48), pp. 129–32 + plate; 27, pp. 208–09. 1949–50.

3208 —— A bone ring from a Breaker burial at Mainsriddle, Kirkcudbrightshire. [Figure.] Proc. Soc. Antiq. Scot., 90 (1956–57), pp. 229–31. 1959.

3209 Stuart (Charles). On British cists at Frenchlaw and Edington hill, Berwickshire. Hist. Berwick Nat. Club, 6, pp. 349–52. 1872.

3210 Stuart (John). Notice of cists and other remains discovered in Cairn Curr, on the farm of Warrackstone, in Aberdeenshire. Proc. Soc. Antiq. Scot., 7, pp. 24–25. 1870.

3211 Tait (Lawson). Note of a cist, with a cup-marked cover, found in a mound on the links of Dornoch. Proc. Soc. Antiq. Scot., 7, p. 270. 1870.

3212 —— Account of cists opened at Kintradiogll, Sutherland. Proc. Soc. Antiq. Scot., 7, pp. 512–15. 1870.

3213 Taylor (George). Notes on the discovery of some ancient graves at Hoprig [farm, Cockburnspath]. Hist. Berwick. Nat. Club, 25, p. 317. 1924.

3214 Tempest (H. G.). Bone objects from an Irish burial cairn. Man, 49, pp. 13–16 + plate. 1949.

3215 Truckell (Alfred Edgar). A Bronze Age cist at Mainsriddle. Trans. Dumfriess. Ant. Soc., 3rd S. 35 (1956–1957), pp. 112–16 + plate. 1958.

3216 Valera (Ruaidhri de). The Court cairns of Ireland. Proc. Roy. Irish Acad., 60, Sect. C, No. 2, pp. 9 + 140 + 37 plates.

3217 —— *and* **Ó'Nualláin** (Seán). Survey of the Megalithic tombs of Ireland, Vol. 1: County Clare. pp. xvii + 116, 59 figures, 22 plates. Dublin, 1961.

3218 —— *and* —— Survey of Mega-lithic tombs of Ireland, Vol. 11: County Mayo. Dublin, 1964, 122 pp., 41 plates, 74 figures + folding map.

3219 Walker (Iain C.). The Clave cairns. Proc. Soc. Ant. Scotland, 96, 1962–63, 87–106 + 2 figures.

3220 Wallace (James Cumming). Bronze Age cairn and cist, with food vessel, at Mollance, near Castle-Douglas, Kirkcudbrightshire. [Figure + 3 plans.] Trans. Dumfriess. Ant. Soc., 3rd S. 30 (1951–52), pp. 159–65. 1953.

3221 —— Burial mound, near Gatelawbridge. Trans. Dumfriess. Ant. Soc., 3rd S. 32 (1953–54), pp. 138–41. 1955.

3222 —— *and* **Walker** (Iain C.). A Cinerary urn cemetery at Easter Culbeuchly, near Banff. Proc. Soc. Ant. Scotland, 94, 1960–61, 317–20 + 1 plate + 1 figure.

3223 Wallace (J. C.). Excavation of a short cist with cremation at Manderstone, near Duns. Hist. Berwick. Nat. hist. Club, 36 ii, 1963, 168–71, plates.

3224 Wells (Lawrence H.). A survey of human remains from long cist burials in the Lothians. Proc. Soc. Antiq. Scot., 90 (1956–57), pp. 180–91. 1959.

3225 —— Remains from a short cist discovered at Leith in 1884. Proc. Soc. Antiq. Scot., 90 (1956–57), p. 222. 1959.

3226 Winckley (S. Thorold). A skull found in [the Hillhead broch] North Caithness. Assoc. Archit. Soc.'s Rpts., 26, p. 464 + plate. 1902.

3227 Wood (James). On cists filled with tough clay, found in Coldingham churchyard. Hist. Berwick. Nat. Club, 11, pp. 192–93. 1885.

3228 Woodham (A. A.) *and* **Woodham** (M. F.). The excavation of a chambered cairn at Kilcoy, Ross-shire. [4 figures + 3 plans.] Proc. Soc. Antiq. Scot., 90 (1956–57), pp. 102–15 + 4 plates. 1959.

3229 —— Two cists at Golspie, Sutherland. Proc. Soc. Antiq. Scot., 90 (1956–57), pp. 234–38. 1959.

3230 Young (Hugh W.). Discovery of an ancient burial place and a symbol-bearing slab at Easterton of Roseisle [Morayshire]. [4 figures + 2 plans. (5 figures).] Reliquary, N.[3rd]S. 1, pp. 142–50: 2, pp. 39–44, 120–21, 1895–96. pp. 237–41 (2 figures + plan), 4, pp. 49–51 (plan).

3231 Yovng (Hugh W.). The graves of Ardkeiling, Strypes, Elginshire [SIC]. Reliquary, N.[3rd]S. 3, pp. 41–47. 1897.

3232 —— Notes on a cairn at Kinsteary, Nairn. Reliquary, 3rd. S. 10, pp. 130–31. 1904.

3233 Young (R. T.). Account of the recent excavations and discoveries at Pendreich, near Bridge of Allan. Trans. Stirling N.H. & Arch. Soc., 1926–27, pp. 91–93. 1927.

3. CIRCLES, HENGES etc. IN GENERAL

3234 Allcroft (Arthur Hadrian). The Celtic circle-moot: some new facts and the inferences. Trans. Hon. Soc. Cymmr. 1918–19, pp. 1–29. 1920.

3237 Dixon (S. E.). Some earthworks and standing stones in East Anglia in relation to a prehistoric solar culture. Proc. PSEA, 2 ii, 1915/16, 171–73.

3239 Engleheart (George). Concerning orientation [of megaliths]. Antiquity, 4, pp. 340–46. 1930.

3241 Gray (John). Who built the British stone circles? Nature, 79, pp. 236–38. 1908.

3242(a) Gurnell (James). Megalithic circles. Trans. Banff. F.C., 6. 1886.

3242(b) Hamper (William). Observations on certain ancient pillars of memorial called hoar-stones; to which is added a conjecture on the Croyland inscriptions. 4°. Birmingham, 1820. p. 27.

3243 Hudson (Herbert). Ancient sun alignments. The meaning of artificial mounds and mark stones. With a commentary by F. A. Bennett. Proc. Suffolk Inst. Arch., 21, pp. 120–38 + diagram. 1933.

3244 James (*Sir* Henry). Plans and photographs of Stonehenge and of the Turnsachan in the island of Lewis; with notes relating to the Druids, and sketches of cromlechs in Ireland. pp. 27 + 15 plates + 4 plans. 4°. Southampton, 1867.

3245 Kerr (James). Druid circles as burial-places. N. & Q., 4 S. 12, p. 206. 1873.

3246 Lewis (A. L.). On the relation of stone circles to outlying stones, or tumuli, or neighbouring hills, with some inferences therefrom. J. Anthrop. Inst., 12, pp. 176–91. 1882.

3247 —— Stone circles of Britain. Archaeol. J., 49, pp. 136–54. 1892.

3248 —— Notes on the relative positions of certain hills and stone circles in England and Wales. Proc. Soc. Antiq., 2 S. 14, pp. 150–54. 1892.

3249 —— Ancient measures in prehistoric monuments. J. Anthrop. Inst., 27, pp. 194–203 + plan. 1897.

3250 —— The stone circles of Cornwall and of Scotland. A comparison. J. Roy. Instn. Cornwall, 14, pp. 378–83. 1900.

3251 —— "King Arthur's hall" on Bodmin moor and some Irish circles. [Plan.] J. Roy. Instn. Cornwall, 18, pp. 117–22. 1910.

3252 Lewis (*Sir* George Cornewall). *bart.* Historical survey of the astronomy of the ancients. pp. viii, 527. 8°. London, 1862. [Pp. 450–57, 481–82, Tin trade of Cornwall.]

3253 Lockyer (*Sir* Joseph Norman). On the observations of stars made in some British stone circles. Preliminary (—Second, Third) note. [The Hurlers, near Liskeard, Stauton Drew: Clock stars, *etc.*: The Aberdeen circles.] Proc. Roy. Soc., 76 A, pp. 177–80: 77 A, pp. 465–72: 80A, pp. 285–89. 1905–8.

3254 —— Stonehenge and other British stone monuments astronomically considered. pp. xii, 340. [61 figures + 4 plans.] 8°. London, 1906.

3255 —— The age and use of British stone-circles. J. Brit. Archaeol. Ass., N.S. 12, pp. 211–12. 1906.

3256 —— The use and age of ancient stone monuments. Trans. Hon. Soc. Cymm., 1908–09, pp. 1–20. 1910.

3257 Lukis (William Collings). Survey of certain megalithic monuments in Scotland, Cumberland, and Westmoreland. Proc. Soc. Antiq., 2 S. 10, pp. 302–20. 1885.

3258 McAldowie (Alexander M.). Prehistoric time measurement in Britain: an astronomical study of some ancient monuments. [Figure.] North Staffs. N.C., Ann. Rpt. & Trans., 46, pp. 155–170 + 11 plates. 1912.

3259 Macbain (Alexander). Druid circles. Trans. Gaelic Soc. Inverness, 10, pp. oo–oo. 1883.

3261 March (Henry Colley). A new theory of stone circles. Trans. Lancs. & Ches. Ant. Soc., 6 (1888), pp. 98–111. 1889.

3262 Milles (Edward). British stone circles. No reference given and not in BM catalogue of published books. London? 1907.

3263 Perry (William J.). Relationship between the geographical distribution of megalithic monuments and ancient mines. Mems. & Proc. Manch. Lit. & Phil. Soc., 60, 1915.

3264 Piggott (Stuart). Timber circles: a re-examination. [3 figures + 11 plans.] Archaeol. J., 96 (1939), pp. 193–222 + plate. 1940.

3265 Pradenne (A. Vayson de). The use of wood in megalithic structures. Antiquity, 11, pp. 87–92 +4 plates. 1937.

3266 Rees (Alwyn D.). Notes on the significance of white stones in Celtic archaeology and folk-lore with reference to recent excavations at Ffynnon Degla, Denbighshire. Bull. Bd. Celtic Stud., 8, pp. 87–90. 1935.

3267 Ross (James). Stone circles. Trans. Inverness Sci. Soc., 1, pp. 2. 1880.

3268 Somerville (Boyle) *Rear-Admiral*. Instances of orientation in prehistoric monuments of the British Isles. [16 figures and plans.] Archaeologia, 73, pp. 193–224. 1923.

3269 Spence (James). Megalithic circles. Trans. Banff. F.C., 6. 1886.

3271 Thom (Alexander). The Solar observations of Megalithic man. [3 figures.] Journ. British Astronomical Assoc., 64 (8), 1954, 396–404.

3272 —— A Statistical examination of the megalithic sites in Britain. [8 figures.] Journ. Roy. Stat. Soc. A *118* (III) 1955, 275–95.

3273 —— The Geometry of Megalithic man. [8 figures.] Mathematical Gazette, XLV (352) May 1961, pp. 83–93.

3274 —— The larger units of length of Megalithic man. [3 figures.] Journ. Roy. Stat. Soc., A, *127* (4) 1964, 527–33.

3275 —— Observatories in ancient Britain. [3 figures.] New Scientist (No. 398) 2 July 1964.

3276 —— Megalithic astronomy: indications in standing stones. [39 figures.] Vistas in Astronomy (ed. A. Beer), Vol. 7, 1–57, 1965. Pergamon.

3277 —— Megalithic Sites in Britain, 77 figures + 1 colour plate. 8º. Oxford. 1966.

3279 Wise (Thomas Alexander). Remarks on Celtic monuments. J. Brit. Archaeol. Ass., 33, pp. 158–69 + plate + plan. 1877.

3280 Worth (Richard Hansford). The prehistoric monuments of Scorhill, Buttern hill, and Shuggledown (Shoveldown), [Dartmoor]. Rpt. & Trans. Devon. Assoc., 64, pp. 279–87 + 3 plates + 3 plans. 1932.

4. CIRCLES, HENGES etc. BY ZONE

(a) Zone 2 [G.B.A. Group 12]

3281 Aitch (Jay). Stonehenge. [Orientation.] N. & Q., 5 S. 4, pp. 83–84. 1875.

3282 Allen (G. W. G.) *and* **Passmore** (A. D.). Earthen circles near Highworth. Wilts. Archaeol. Mag., 47, pp. 114–22 + 4 plates + map. 1935.

3283 Annabus (F. Kenneth). The West Kennet avenue. Wilts. Arch. Mag., 57, pp. 229–30. 1959.

3284 [Anon.] A description of Stonehenge, Abiry, &c. pp. 100. [Pp. 1–39 + 5 plates, Stonehenge.] 12º. Salisbury, 1776.

3285 [Anon.] Guide to the stones of Stonehenge. pp. 2 + plan. 8º. Devizes, 1884.

3286 [Anon.] Sale of Stonehenge. [To C. H. E. Chubb, for £6,600.] J. Brit. Archaeol. Ass., N.S., 21, pp. 272–273. 1915.

3287 [Anon.] Sale of Stonehenge and the Amesbury abbey estate. Wilts. Archaeol. Mag., 39, pp. 392–94. 1916.

3288 [Anon.] The plan for Avebury. An appeal to the nation [for preservation of village and its surroundings]. Antiquity, 11, pp. 490–93 + plate. 1937.

3289 [Anon.] Stonehenge given to the nation [by C. H. E. Chubb of Bemerton Lodge]. Wilts. Archaeol. Mag., 40, pp. 366–68. 1919.

3290 [Anon.] Stonehenge, on Salisbury plain, by the most eminent writers, *etc.* A new edition. pp. 82 + plate + plan. Sm. 8⁰. Salisbury, 1921.

3291 [Anon.] Avebury. [Acquisition by the National Trust.] Antiquity, 17, pp. 94–95. 1943.

3292 [Anon.] Stonehenge: re-erection of trilithon. [Figure + plan.] Archaeol. News Letter, 6, pp. 143, 167. 1958.

3293 [Anon.] Stonehenge restored. Antiquity, 33, pp. 50–51 + plate. 1959.

3294 Antrobus (*Lady* F. C. M.). The recent work at Stonehenge. [Figure.] Nature, 64, pp. 602–03. 1901.

3295 Atkinson (Richard John Copland) *etc.* Excavations at Stonehenge, 1950. Arch. News Letter, 3, pp 3–4. 1950.

3296 —— The Date of Stonehenge. Proc. prehist. Soc., 18, 1952, 236–37 + 1 plate.

3297 ——, **Piggott** (Stuart) *and* **Stone** (J. F. S.). The excavation of two additional holes at Stonehenge, 1950, and new evidence for the date of the monument. Antiq. J., 32, pp. 14–20 + plate. 1952.

3297(b) —— The Dorset cursus. Antiquity, 29, pp. 4–9 + 4 plates + map. 1955.

3298 —— Stonehenge. pp. xv, 210 + 25 plates + plan. [7 figures, maps and plans.] 8⁰. London, 1956.

3299 —— Stonehenge and Avebury. [pp. 63, maps and plans.] London, H.M.S.O. 1959.

3300 Aubrey (John). Monumenta Britannica, or a miscellany of British antiquities. Vol. 1, Section 1, Templa Druidum; Stonehenge. No reference given and not in BM catalogue of published, but quoted in Wiltshire Arch. Mag. by William Long N/D.

3301 —— Fac-similes of Aubrey's plans of Abury. Wilts. Archaeol. Mag., 7, pp. 224–27 + 2 folding plans. 1862.

3302 Awdry (Robert William). Three great Wiltshire stone monuments. [Old Sarum, Stonehenge, Avebury.] Wilts. Archaeol. Mag., 49, pp. 24–27. 1940.

3303 Barclay (Edgar). The ruined temple of Stonehenge, its history and a short account of questions associated

with it. pp. xxv, 75 + plate. [7 figures + 5 plans.] 8⁰. London.

3304 —— Stonehenge. J. Brit. Archaeol. Ass., 49, pp. 179–205 + plan. 1893.

3305 —— Stonehenge. [5 figures.] Ill. Arch., 1, pp. 83–89. 1893.

3306 —— Stonehenge and its earthworks. pp. vii, 152. [44 figures.] 4⁰. London, 1895.

3307 —— Note on Stonehenge. Reliquary, 3rd S. 8, pp. 138–42. 1902.

3308 Barnes (William Miles). Poxwell circle. Proc. Dorset Antiq. F.C., 21, pp. 150–57. 1900.

3309 Bazeley (William). Abury and its literature. Proc. Cotteswold Nat. Club, 10, pp. 192–201 + 2 plates + plan. 1892.

3310 Bensly (Edward). Stonehenge restored by Inigo Jones. N. & Q., 165, p. 175. 1933.

3311 Brentnall (Harold Cresswall). Avebury for the nation. Wilts. Archaeol. Mag., 50, pp. 196–97. 1943.

3312 Brock (Edgar Philip Loftus). Sunrise at Stonehenge on the longest day. J. Brit. Archaeol. Ass., 47, pp. 330–31 + plate. 1891.

3313 Broome (J. H.). Astronomical date of Stonehenge. [977 B.C. (Sirius exactly over heel-stone).] Astron. Register, 7, pp. 202–04 + plate; 8, pp. 36, 39. 1869–70.

3314 Browne (Henry). Illustration of Stonehenge, Abury, *etc.* 8th edition. pp. x, 60. 8⁰. Salisbury, 1867.

3315 Buckingham (W. A.). Avebury. [3 plans.] J. Brit. Archaeol. Ass., N.S. 41, pp. 32–60. 1936.

3316 Calkin (John Bernard). Some archaeological discoveries in the Isle of Purbeck, Part II: A possible avenue to Rempstone Circle. Proc. Dorset N.H. & A.S., 81, 1960, 114–116.

3317 Cambridge (Octavius Pickard). Megalithic remains at Poxwell, Dorset. The Druid's temple, or druidical circle. Proc. Dorset Antiq. F.C., 6, pp. 55–57 + plate. 1885.

3318 Capper (J. E.). Photographs of Stonehenge, as seen from a war balloon. Archaeologia, 60, p. 571 + 2 plates. 1907.

3319 Charleton (Walter). Chorea gigantum; or, the most famous antiquity of Great-Britain, vulgarly called Stone-

heng, *etc.* pp. 64 + plate. 8⁰. London,
1663.

3320 Charleton (Walter). Chorea
gigantum, *etc.* Second edition. pp. 98 +
plate + portrait. fol. London, 1725.

3321 Christie (Patricia M.). The
Stonehenge Cursus. W.A.M., 58, 1963,
No. 211, 370–82 + 5 figures + 1 plate.

3322 Clark (J. G. D.). The Preservation of Avebury. Proc. prehist. Soc.,
3, 1937, 467–68.

3323 Clay (Richard Challoner Cobbe).
Stonehenge avenue. [Figure.] Antiquity, 1, pp. 342–44. 1927.

3324 Cox (R. Hipbisley). A guide to
Avebury and neighbourhood. pp. 68
+ 4 plates. [12 figures.] 8⁰. London,
1909.

3325 Crampton (Patrick). Stonehenge of the Kings, a people appear.
pp. 171. London. 8⁰. 1967.

3326 Crawford (Osbert Guy Stanhope). The Stonhenge avenue: missing
branch found. J. Brit. Archaeol. Ass.,
N.S. 28, pp. 233–37. 1922.

3327 —— Notes on field-work round
Avebury, December, 1921. Wilts. Archaeol. Mag., 42, pp. 52–63 + plan. 1922.

3328 —— The Stonehenge avenue.
[Plan.] Antiq. J., 4, pp. 57–59 + plate.
1924.

3329 —— Durrington Walls [Wilts.].
Antiquity, 3, pp. 49–59 + 3 plates. 1929.

3330 —— The symbols carved on
Stonehenge. [Plan.] Antiquity, 28, pp.
25–31 + 8 plates. 1954.

3331(a) Cunnington (*Mrs.* Maud
Edith). The discovery of a skeleton and
"drinking cup" at Avebury. [2 figures.]
Man, 12, pp. 200–03. 1912.

3331(b) —— The re-erection of two
fallen stones, and the discovery of an
interment with drinking cup, at Avebury. [2 figures.] Wilts. Archaeol. Mag.,
38, pp. 1–11 + plate. 1913.

3332 —— A buried stone in the
Kennet avenue. Wilts. Archaeol. Mag.,
38, pp. 12–14. 1913.

3333 —— Stonehenge. Antiquity, 3,
pp. 223–26. 1924.

3334 —— Prehistoric timber circles.
Antiquity, 1, pp. 92–95 + 2 plates
(Woodhenge). 1927.

3335 —— Woodhenge. A description of the site as revealed by excavations
. . . 1926–7–8. Also of four circles and

an earthwork enclosure south of Woodhenge. pp. viii, 187 + 54 plates + map
+ 2 plans. 4⁰. Devizes, 1929.

3336 —— Stonehenge and the two-
date theory. Antiq. J., 10, pp. 103–13.
1930.

3337 —— The "sanctuary" on Overton hill, near Avebury. Wilts. Archaeol.
Mag., 45, pp. 300–35 + 7 plates + 3
plans. 1931.

3338 —— Niedermendig [Eifel] lava
rock near Avebury. Antiquity, 5, pp.
233–35. 1931.

3338(b) —— Avebury. A guide to
the circles, *etc.*, Silbury hill. pp. 20.
8⁰. Devizes, 1931.

3339 —— Evidence of climate derived from snail shells and its bearing
on the date of Stonehenge. [Damp conditions.] Wilts. Archaeol. Mag., 46,
pp. 350–55. 1933.

3340 Cunnington (Robert Henry).
The recent excavations at Stonehenge.
Wilts. Archaeol. Mag., 44, pp. 332–47
+ plan. 1929.

3341 —— Stonehenge and the two-
date theory. J. Brit. Archaeol. Ass.,
N.S. 36, pp. 229–32. 1930.

3342 —— The "sanctuary" on Overton hill: was it roofed? [Figure.] Wilts.
Archaeol. Mag., 45, pp. 486–88. 1931.

3343 —— The date and orientation
of Stonehenge. [Plan.] J. Brit. Archaeol.
Ass., N.S. 37, pp. 161–71. 1931.

3344 —— Stonehenge and its date.
pp. vii, 135. [11 figures + 3 plans.] 8⁰.
London, 1935.

3345 Cunnington (William). Stonehenge notes. Wilts. Archaeol. Mag., 11,
pp. 347–49. 1869.

3346 —— A guide to the stones of
Stonehenge. Devizes, 1884.

3347 —— Stonhenge notes: the fragments. Wilts. Archaeol. Mag., 21, pp.
141–49 + plan. 1884.

3348 —— Stonehenge: short notes.
Wilts. Archaeol. Mag., 29, pp. 178–81.
1897.

3349 Davis (W. H.). Avebury. Second edition. pp. 26. [6 figures.] 8⁰.
Devizes, 1901.

3350 Dewar (Stephen). Neolithic engineering and Stonehenge. Antiquity,
36, 1962, pp. 137–38.

3351 Douglas (James). Letter . . . on
the original design of Stonehenge and

the neighbouring barrows. Wilts. Arch-aeol. Mag., 20, pp. 237–40. 1882.

3352 Duke (Edward). The druidical temples of the county of Wilts. pp. viii, 203 + 2 plans. 8°. London, 1846.

3353 —— Letter relative to Stone-henge. Proc. Archaeol. Inst., [5] Salis-bury, 1849, pp. 111–20. 1851.

3354 —— The age of Stonehenge. pp. 7. 8°. Salisbury, 1887. [*From* Salisbury & Winchester Journal, Sept. 17, 1887.]

3355 Dunkin (Edwin). Old points of Stonehenge. N. & Q., 4 S. 7, pp. 36, 179, 197. 1871.

3356 Engleheart (George Herbert) *and* **Newall** (Robert Sterling). A second blue-stone lintel at Stonehenge. [2 figures.] Antiq. J., 10, pp. 152–53. 1930.

3357 —— The age of Stonehenge: a criterion. Antiq. J., 12, pp. 17–23. 1932.

3358 —— A second Stonehenge "altar" stone? Wilts. Archaeol. Mag., 46, pp. 395–97 + 2 plates. 1933.

3359 Evans (*Sir* Arthur John). On Stonehenge. Proc. Oxford Archit. & Hist. Soc., 5, pp. 149–57. 1888.

3360 —— Stonehenge. Archaeol. Rev., 2, pp. 312–30. 1889.

3361 Evans (Sebastian). From Stone-henge to Avebury and beyond. pp. 23. 4°. *n.p.*, 1905.

3361(b) Farrer (Percy). Durrington Walls, or Long Walls. Wilts. Archaeol. Mag., 40, pp. 95–103 + plate + plan. 1918.

3362 Field (N. H.). Discoveries at the Knowlton Circles, Woodlands, Dor-set. [3 figures.] Proc. Dorset N.H. & A.S., 84, 1963, 117–29.

3363 Fisher (P. H.). Stonehenge. [Materials.] N. & Q., 2 S. 11, pp. 228–229, 369. 1855.

3364 Gidley (Lewis). Stonehenge viewed by the light of ancient history and modern observation. 8°. Salisbury, 1873.

3365 Goddard (Edward Hunger-ford). Stonehenge—concerning the sar-sens. Man, 27, pp. 12–13. 1927.

3366 Gowland (William). Recent ex-cavations at Stonehenge; with a note on the nature and origin of the rock-fragments found in the excavations, by J. W. Judd. [28 figures +plan.] Archaeo-logia, 58, pp. 37–118 + 3 plates + plan. 1902.

3367 —— The recent excavations at Stonehenge, with inferences as to the origin, construction, and purpose of that monument. [Figure + plan.] Man, 2, pp. 7–11, 22–26 (discussion). 1902.

3368 —— Recent excavations at Stone-henge. With a note [pp. 47–62] on the nature and origin of the rock-fragments found in the excavations, by J. W. Judd. [10 figures.] Wilts. Archaeol. Mag., 33, pp. 1–62 + 3 plates + 2 plans. 1903.

3369 Gray (Harold St. George). The Avebury excavations, 1908–22. [8 fig-ures + plan.] Archaeologia, 84, pp. 99–162 + 19 plates + 2 plans. 1935.

3370 Grigson (Geoffrey). Stonehenge and the imagination. [3 figures.] His-tory today, 1, (Mch.), pp. 22–29. 1951.

3371 Guest (Edwin). On the "Bel-gic ditches", and the probable date of Stonehenge. Archaeol. J., 8, pp. 143–157 + map. 1851.

3372 —— On the "Belgic ditches", and the probable date of Stonehenge. Proc. Archaeol. Inst., [6] Oxford, 1850, pp. 45–59 + map. 1854.

3373 Harrison (W. Jerome). A bib-liography of the great stone monuments of Wiltshire—Stonehenge and Avebury. Wilts. Archaeol. Mag., 32, pp. 1–169 + 4 plates. 1891.

3374 Hatto (A. T.). Stonehenge and midsummer: a new interpretation. [Fig-ure + plan.] Man, 53, pp. 101–06. 1953.

3375 Hawkins (Gerald S.) *and* **White** (John B.). Stonehenge Decoded, pp. viii, 202. London, 1966.

3376 Hawley (William). Stonehenge: interim report on the exploration. (Se-cond *ditto*). [13 (5) figures.] Antiq. J., 1, pp. 19–41 + 3 plates; 2, pp. 36–52 + 2 plates. 1921–22.

3377 —— Recent excavations at Stone-henge. Nature, 109, pp. 781–83. 1922.

3378 —— Third (Fourth) report on the excavations at Stonehenge. [Plan.] Antiq. J., 3, pp. 13–20 + 2 plates; 4, pp. 30–39 + plate. 1923–24.

3379 —— [5th] Report on the ex-cavation at Stonehenge during the season of 1923. [6th] Report . . . (of 1924). Antiq. J., 5, pp. 21–50 + plate + plan; 6, pp. 1–25 + 3 plates + 2 plans. 1925–1926.

3380 —— Report on the excavations at Stonehenge during 1925 and 1926.

[4 figures.] Antiq. J., 8, pp. 149–76 + 2 plates + plan. 1928.

3381 Herbert (*Hon.* Aubrey). New views respecting Stonehenge. Proc. Somerset Arch. Soc., 69 (1923), pp. 1–5. 1924.

3382 Hill (Patrick Arthur). The Sarsens of Stonehenge: the problem of their transportation. Geog. Jl., 127, 1961, 488–92 + 1 figure + 2 plates.

3383 —— The Avebury sarsens: some surface markings. W.A.M., 58, 1961, 39 + 1 plate.

3384 Hill (William Burrough). Stonehenge, an appreciation. pp. 9 + 4 plates. 8°. Southampton, 1914.

3385 Hinks (Arthur R.). Stonehenge and Karnac. Nineteenth Century, July, pp. 119–27. 1925.

3386 Holmes (Mabelle). Stonehenge: old theories and new discoveries. Trans. Hampstead Ant. Soc., [5] 1902–03, pp. 134–41. 1905.

3387 Holmes (Thomas Rice). The age of Stonehenge. Antiq. J., 2, pp. 344–49. 1922.

3388 Hughes (Thomas McKenny). Arbury. (Second Report). Proc. Camb. Antiq. Soc., 10, pp. 277–84; 16, pp. 211–19. 1902–04.

3389 Jones (Inigo). The most notable antiquity of Great Britain, vulgarly called Stone-henge, *etc.* pp. 72 + 8 plates + portrait + 3 plans. fol. London, 1725.

3390 Keiller (Alexander). The West Kennet avenue, Avebury. Antiquity, 8, pp. 344–47. 1934.

3391 —— *and* **Piggott** (Stuart). The recent excavations at Avebury. [3 figures.] Antiquity, 10, pp. 417–27 + 7 plates + plan. 1936.

3392 —— Avebury. Summary of excavations, 1937 and 1938. Antiquity, 13, pp. 223–33 + 4 plates + plan. 1939.

3393 Kemble (John Mitchell). A note about the word Stonehenge. N. & Q., 2 S. 3, pp. 2–3. 1857.

3394 Kendall (Henry George Ommanney). A fragment of blue stone near Avebury, and its accompanyments. Man, 18, pp. 54–55. 1918.

3395 Kennard (A. S.) *and* **Jackson** (John Wilfrid). Reports on 1. The nonmarine mollusca, and 2. The animal remains from the Stonehenge excavations

of 1920–26. Antiq. J., 15, pp. 432–40. 1935.

3396 Kidner (H.). An unrecorded type of circular earthwork in the New Forest. Papers & Proc. Hants. F.C., 8, pp. 310–14. 1919.

3397 King (Bryan). Avebury—The Beckhampton avenue. Wilts. Archaeol. Mag., 18, pp. 377–83. 1879.

3398 King (D. Grant). The Avebury Sarsens. W.A.M., 58, 1962, No. 210, 217–18.

3399 Kibwan (R.). On the origin and appropriation of Stonehenge. Rpt. & Trans. Devon. Assoc., 3, pp. 517–23. 1869.

3400 Learmont (D. A.). Stonehenge and Woodhenge. Empire Survey Rev., 3, pp. 339–43 + 2 plans. 1936.

3401 Lewis (A. L.). On the Wiltshire circles. J. Anthrop. Inst., 20, pp. 277–88 + plan. 1891.

3402 —— On the damage recently sustained by Stonehenge. Man, 1, pp. 24–26. 1901.

3403 —— Stonehenge: an enquiry respecting the fall of trilithons. [Figure (MS. Sloane 2596).] Man, 2, pp. 133–135. 1902.

3404 Lockyer (*Sir* John Norman) *and* **Penrose** (F. C.). An attempt to ascertain the date of the original construction of Stonehenge from its orientation. [2 figures. 1680 B.C.] Proc. Roy. Soc., 69, pp. 137–47. 1901.

3405 —— *and* —— An attempt to ascertain the date of the original construction of Stonehenge from its orientation. [2 figures. 1680 B.C.] Nature, 65, pp. 55–57. 1901.

3406 Long (William). Abury illustrated. pp. 72 + 3 plates + 4 plans. [With additions.] 4°. Devizes, 1858.

3407 —— Abury. [Figure + 3 plans. Vol. 7, p. 227, corrigenda.] Wilts. Archaeol. Mag., 4, pp. 309–63 + 3 plates + 5 plans. 1858.

3408 —— Stonehenge and its barrows. pp. 244 + plan. 4°. Devizes, 1876.

3409 —— Stonehenge and its barrows. [2 figures.] Wilts. Archaeol. Mag., 16, pp. 1–244 + 10 plates + map + 6 plans. 1876.

3410 —— Abury notes. Wilts. Archaeol. Mag., 17, pp. 327–35. 1878.

3411 Lukis (William Collings). Report on the prehistoric monuments of Stonehenge and Avebury. Proc. Soc. Antiq., 2 S. 9, pp. 141–50, 150–57. 1882.

3412 Lynn (William Thynne). The earliest mention of Stonehenge. N. & Q., 8 S. 5, p. 224. 1894.

3413 MacKenzie (Alexander Muir). Prehistoric circles. [Avebury and Stonehenge.] Dryden (A.): Memorials of old Wiltshire, pp. 29–37 + 4 plates. 1906.

3414 McLachlan (D. B.). The meaning of Stonehenge. pp. 30 + plan. 4°. [Wimbledon, 1930]. [Typescript, in library of Society of Antiquaries.]

3415 Maskelyne (Edmund Story). Stonehenge. pp. 39 + plan. 8°. Bath, 1898.

3416 —— On the purpose, the age, and the builders of Stonehenge. Proc. Bath N. H. & Ant. F.C., 91, pp. 1–39 + plan. 1901.

3417 Maskelyne (Nevil Story). Stonehenge: the petrology of its stones. Wilts. Archaeol. Mag., 17, pp. 147–60 + plate. 1878.

3418 Matcham (George). Remarks on two communications respecting Stonehenge, addressed by Edward Duke to the Archaeological Institute, and to the editor of the Gentleman's Magazine. Proc. Archaeol. Inst., [5] Salisbury, 1849, pp. 121–34. 1851.

3419 Maton (William George). Account of the fall of some of the stones of Stonehenge [Jan. 1797]. Archaeologia, 13, pp. 103–06 + 2 plates. 1797.

3420 Newall (Robert Sterling). Stonehenge. (The recent excavations). [Page of plans.] Antiquity, 3, pp. 75–88 + 2 plates + folding plan. *Reprinted in* Wilts. Archaeol. Mag., 44, pp. 348–59 + folding plan. 1929.

3421 —— Stonehenge stone wall. [2 plans.] Antiq. J., 32, pp. 64–67 + plate. 1952.

3422 —— Stonehenge. *Ministry of Works.* pp. 21 + 4 plates + plan. 8°. London, 1955.

3423 —— Stonehenge: a review. Antiquity, 30, pp. 137–41 + plan. 1956.

3424 Nicholson (Brinsley). Stonehenge. Antiquary, 2, pp. 150–51. 1880.

3425 Passmore (A. D.). Notes on an undescribed stone circle at Coate, near Swindon. [Plan.] Wilts. Archaeol. Mag., 27, pp. 171–74. 1893.

3426 —— The Avebury ditch. Antiq. J., 2, pp. 109–11. 1922.

3427 —— Langdean stone circle. [East Kennett.] [Figure + plan.] Wilts. Archaeol. Mag., 42, pp. 364–66. 1923.

3428 —— Avebury: a new stone in the Kennett avenue. [Figure.] Wilts. Archaeol. Mag., 43, pp. 341–43. 1926.

3429 —— The [Sir Henry] Meux excavation at Avebury. Wilts. Archaeol. Mag., 47, pp. 288–89 + plate. 1935.

3430 Payne (Eric H.). The Overton hill retaining-circle. Wilts. Archaeol. Mag., 50, pp. 83–91. 1942.

3431 Peake (Harold John Edward). The earliest structure at Stonehenge. Man, 45, pp. 74–78. 1945.

3432 Petrie (*Sir* William Matthew Flinders). Stonehenge: plans, descriptions and theories. pp. 34 + 2 plans. 4°. London, 1880.

3433 —— Stonehenge—the heel stone. Man, 24, p. 107. 1924.

3434 Phené (John Samuel). Existing analogues of Stonehenge and Avebury, found in the Talayots and Taulas of Minorca. J. Brit. Archaeol. Ass., 48, pp. 265–79. 1892.

3435 Piggott (Stuart). Stukeley, Avebury and the druids. Antiquity, 9, pp. 22–32 + 5 plates. 1935.

3436 —— A potsherd from Stonehenge ditch. Antiquity, 10, pp. 221–222 + plate. 1936.

3437 —— *and* **Piggott** (Cecily Margaret). Stone and earth circles in Dorset. [Figure and 10 plans.] Antiquity, 13, pp. 138–58 + 2 plates. 1939.

3438 —— Stonehenge: a summary note. [Plan.] Archaeol. J., 104 (1947), pp. 4–6. 1948.

3439 —— Stonehenge reviewed. Aspects of archaeology. . . . Essays presented to O. G. S. Crawford, pp. 274–92. 1951.

3440 —— Recent work at Stonehenge. [2 plans.] Antiquity, 28, pp. 221–24 + plate. 1954.

3441 —— The Druids and Stonehenge. Myth or legend, pp. 97–104 + plate. 1956.

3442 —— The Radio-carbon date from Durrington Walls. Antiquity, 33 (1959), pp. 289–90.

3443 Read (*Sir* Charles Hercules). On the recent history of Stonehenge. Proc. Soc. Antiq., 2 S. 31, pp. 1–5. 1918.

3444 Rickman (John). On the antiquity of Abury and Stonehenge. Archaeologia, 28, pp. 399–419 + plate (Stonehenge) + plan (Avebury). 1840.

3445 Rivers (Augustus Henry Lane Fox Pitt). On the proposed exploration of Stonehenge by a committee of the British Association. J. Ethnol. Soc., N.S. 2, pp. 1–5. 1870.

3446 Sayce (Archibald Henry). The Date of Stonehenge. J. Egyptian Archaeology, 1, p. 18, 1 plate. 1914.

3447 Schuchhardt (C.). Stonehenge. Prähist. Z., 2, 292–340 + 42 figures. 1910.

3448 Skeat (Walter William). Stonehenge. N. & Q., 10 S., 10, p. 386. 1908.

3449 Smith (Alfred Charles). Excavations at Avebury, under the direction of the Wiltshire Archaeological Society. Wilts. Archaeol. Mag., 10, pp. 209–16. 1867.

3450 —— Supposed stone-circle near Abury. Wilts. Archaeol. Mag., 17, pp. 253–54. 1878.

3451 Somerville (Boyle T.). Remarks on Mr. Stone's paper on the date of Stonehenge and on the dating of megalithic structures by astronomical means generally. Man, 22, pp. 133–37. 1922.

3452 Spencer (Joseph Houghton). Stonehenge: its relative position with regard to other ancient works. Antiquary, 41, pp. 144–45. 1905.

3453 Stark (C. A.). Stonehenge. pp. 30. 8º. Gainsburgh, 1823.

3454 Stevens (Edward Thomas). Jottings on some of the objects of interest in the Stonehenge excursion, . . . 1876. *Wiltshire Archaeological Society.* pp. xii, 236 + map. [91 figures.] 8º. Salisbury, 1876.

3455 Stevens (Frank). Stonehenge today and yesterday. Revised edition. pp. ii, 90 + plan. 8º. London, H.M.S.O., 1929.

3456 Stone (Edward Herbert). Stonehenge: concerning the four stations. [2 figures + plan.] Nature, 109, pp. 410–12. 1922.

3457 —— Stonehenge. Notes on the midsummer sunrise. [3 figures.] Man, 22, pp. 114–18. 1922.

3458 —— The age of Stonehenge, deduced from the orientation of its axis. Nineteenth Century, Jan., pp. 105–15. 1922.

3459 —— Stonehenge: concerning the four stations. [Figure.] Nature, Feb., pp. 220–22. 1923.

3460 —— The age of Stonehenge, deduced from the orientation of its axis. [1840 B.C.] Antiq. J., 3, pp. 130–134. 1923.

3461 —— The method of erecting the stones of Stonehenge. [8 figures.] Wilts. Archaeol. Mag., 42, pp. 446–56. 1924.

3462 —— Stonehenge—the heel stone. Man, 24, pp. 68–69. 1924.

3463 —— The stones of Stonehenge. pp. xv, 150 + 31 plates + 5 plans. 4º. London, 1924.

3464 —— The story of Stonehenge, based mostly on the results obtained by the excavations undertaken by Colonel Hawley . . . 1921–1925. pp. 7 + plate + plan. 4º. 1925.

3465 —— The orientation of Stonehenge. Nineteenth Century, Sept., pp. 415–21. 1925.

3466 —— The purpose of Stonehenge. Man, 25, pp. 69–72. 1925.

3467 —— Some notes on Stonehenge. Reprint of articles published in the Wiltshire Gazette from 17th December, 1925, to 4th February, 1926. pp. 8. 4º. 1926.

3468 —— Stonehenge—the supposed blue stone trilithon. [Figure + plan.] Man, 26, pp. 42–45. 1926.

3469 —— Stonehenge — concerning the sarsens. Man, 26, pp. 202–04. 1926.

3470(a) Stone (John F. S.). Some discoveries at Ratfyn, Amesbury, and their bearing on the date of Woodhenge. Wilts. Archaeol. Mag., 47, pp. 55–67. 1935.

3470(b) —— The Stonehenge cursus and its affinities. [2 plans.] Archaeol. J., 104 (1947), pp. 7–19 + 4 plates + 2 plans. 1948.

3471 ——, **Piggott** (Stuart) *and* **Booth** (A. St. J.). Durrington Walls, Wiltshire: recent excavations at a ceremonial site of the early second millenium, B.C. Antiq. J., 34, pp. 155–77 + 2 plates. 1954.

3472 Stukeley (William). Stonehenge. a temple restor'd to the British druids. pp. 66 + 35 plates. fol. London, 1740.

3473 —— Abury . . . described. pp. vi, 102, vi + 40 plates. fol. London, 1743.

3474 Teall (J. J. H.). Notes on sections of Stonehenge rocks belonging to W. Cunnington. Wilts. Archaeol. Mag., 27, pp. 66–68. 1893.

3475 Teasdale (Washington). Age and origin of Stonehenge: astronomical theories. Trans. Leeds Astronomical Soc., 7, pp. 1–8 + plate. 1899.

3476 Thomas (Herbert H.). The source of the foreign stones of Stonehenge. Wilts. Archaeol. Mag., 42, pp. 325–40 + 4 plates. 1923.

3477 —— The source of the stones of Stonehenge. Antiq. J., 3, pp. 239–60 + 3 plates. 1923.

3478 Thurnam (John). On an incised marking on the impost of the great trilithon, at Stonehenge. [4 figures.] Wilts. Archaeol. Mag., 9, pp. 268–78. 1866.

3479 Trotter (A. P.). Stonehenge as an astronomical instrument. [Plan.] Antiquity, 1, pp. 42–53 + plate. 1927.

3480 Twining (Thomas). Avebury in Wiltshire. pp. 36 + plan. 4⁰. London, 1723.

3481 W. (W. W.). Stonehenge and Carnac. N. & Q., 4 S. 4, pp. 58–60, 160–64. 1869.

3482 Wallis (S.). Concise account of Stonehenge. pp. 28. [5 figures.] 12⁰. London, 1750.

3483 Webb (John). A vindication of Stone-heng restored, *etc.* Second edition, pp. 228. fol. London, 1725.

3484 Wegeman (Georg). Stonehenge. pp. 9 + 2 plates + map + plans. *Typescript.* 4⁰. Detmold, 1957.

3485 Whitmell (C. T.). Astronomic date of Stonehenge. [1700 B.C.] Nature, 65, pp. 128–29. 1901.

(b) Zones 1, 3–6
[All G.B.A. Groups except 2]

3486 Alcock (Leslie). The Henge Monument of the Bull Ring, Dove Holes, Derbyshire. Proc. prehist. Soc., 16, 1950, 81–86 + 3 figures.

3487 Allcroft (Arthur Hadrian.) Napps circle in Pendine. Trans. Carmarthenshire Ant. Soc., 15, pp. 11–13. 1921.

3488 —— The circle on Pwll mountain in Marros. Trans. Carmarthenshire Ant. Soc., 15, pp. 18–19. 1921.

3491 Anderson (W. D.). Some recent observations at the Keswick stone circle. Trans. Cumb. & Westm. Ant. Soc., N.S. 15, pp. 99–112 + 2 plans. 1915.

3492 —— Elva stone circle. [North of Bassenthwaite lake.] Trans. Cumb. & Westm. Ant. Soc., N.S. 23, pp. 29–32 + plan. 1923.

3493 Andrew (C. K. Croft). Goodaver stone circle. [Altarnum parish, Cornwall.] Devon & Cornwall N. & Q., 19, pp. 350–51. 1937.

3494 —— Another [i.e. unrecorded] Cornish stone circle. [On Craddock moor in parish of St. Cleer.] Devon & Cornwall N. & Q., 19, pp. 354–56. 1937.

3495 Andrew (Walter Jonathan). Excavations at Arbor Low. J. Derbs. Archaeol. Soc., 24, pp. 173–74. 1902.

3496 —— The Bull Ring. A stone circle at Dove Holes. J. Derbs. Archaeol. Soc., 27, p. 86. 1905.

3497 —— The prehistoric stone circles of Derbyshire. Cox (J. C.): Memorials of old Derbyshire, pp. 70–88 + 2 plates. 1907.

3498 [Anon.] The arrows, near Boroughbridge, Yorkshire. Yorks. N. & Q. (ed. Forshaw), 5, p. 257. 1909.

3499 [Anon.] Menhir at Brwyno, Glandyfi, Cardiganshire. Antiq. J., 15, p. 345. 1935.

3501 Armstrong (Albert Leslie). Notes on Arbor Low. Trans. Hunter Arch. Soc., 3, pp. 76–79. 1929.

3502 Atkinson (Richard John Copland). A henge monument at Westwell, near Burford, Oxon. [Plan.] Oxoniensia, 14 (1949), pp. 84–87. 1951.

3503 Barham (Basil). Arbor Low and the holed stone. J. Derbs. Archaeol. Soc., N.S. 3, pp. 79–84 + plate. 1930.

3504 Barnwell (Edward Lowry). Alignments in Wales. [Figure.] Arch. Camb., 3rd S. 14, pp. 169–79 + plate. 1868.

3505 —— Eglwys y gwyddel [stone

circle, Towyn], Merioneth. Arch. Camb., 4th S. 5, pp. 234–42 + plate. 1874.

3506 Barnwell (Edward Lowry). On pillar-stones in Wales. Arch. Camb., 4th S. 6, pp. 299–306 + 5 plates. 1875.

3507 Barry (E. M.). The monolith in Rudston churchyard, Yorkshire. N. & Q., 4 S. 8, pp. 368, 462; 9, pp. 20, 102. 1871–72.

3508 Beesley (Thomas). Rollright-stones. [4 figures.] Trans. N. Oxford Archaeol. Soc., 1, pp. 61–73. 1854.

3509(a) —— The Rollright stones. Trans. Archaeol. Soc. North Oxon., 1853–55, pp. 61–73 + plate + plan. 1855.

3509(b) Bemrose (H. H. Arnold). Geological notes on Arbor Low. J. Derbs. Archaeol. Soc., 26, pp. 78–79. 1904.

3510 Blight (John Thomas). The holed stones of Cornwall. [4 figures.] Arch. Camb., 3rd S. 10, pp. 292–99 + 3 plates. 1864.

3511 —— Castallack Round, in the parish of S. Paul. [2 figures + plan.] J. Roy Instn. Cornwall, liv, pp. 66–70. 1865.

3512 —— Notes on antiquities in North Wales. Circles at Aber, Caernarvonshire. Arch. Camb., 3rd S. 11, pp. 137–38 + 2 plates. 1865.

3513 Bousfield (Paul) *and* **Bousfield** (Sigrid). A notable Cornish henge monument. [Plan. On Lower Woon farm on Bodmin–Truro road.] Proc. West Cornwall F.C., N.S. 1, pp. 35–40. 1954.

3514 Breese (Charles E.). Meini Hirion on Tir Gwyn farm in the parish of Llannor, Carnarvonshire. Arch. Camb., 80, pp. 385–87. 1925.

3515 Brigg (John J.). Catstones Ring. (Castle Stead Ring). Yorks. N. & Q. (ed. Forshaw), 3, pp. 363–64. 1907.

3516 Brown (John). The druidical circle in Troqueer. Trans. Dumfries. Ant. Soc., 6, pp. 33–34. 1890.

3517 Brushfield (Thomas Nadauld). Arbor Low. J. Brit. Archaeol. Ass., N.S. 6, pp. 127–39. 1900.

3518 Bryce (James). An account of excavations within the stone circles of Arran. Proc. Soc. Antiq. Scot., 4, pp. 499–524 + plate. 1863.

3519 Burnard (Robert). Re-erection

of Dartmoor mênhirs. Reliquary, N. [3rd] S. 1, pp. 35–37. 1895.

3520 —— Scorhill circle [Gidleigh common, Dartmoor]. Reliquary, 3rd S. 8, p. 72. 1902.

3521 Bushell (William Done). The stone-circles of Pembrokeshire. Arch. Camb., 6th S. 9, pp. 241–42. 1909.

3522 —— Amongst the Prescelly circles. Arch. Camb., 6 S. 11, pp. 287–33. 1911.

3523 Callender (Henry). Notice of the stone circle at Callernish, in the island of Lewis. Proc. Soc. Antiq. Scot., 2, pp. 380–84 + plate. 1859.

3524 Callander (John Graham). Stone circles in Aberdeenshire. Trans. Bulhard F.C., 14, pp. 204–09. 1934.

3525 Chitty (Lily Frances). The Hoar stone or Marsh pool circle. [Plan.] Trans. Shropshire Archaeol. Soc., 43 (4th S. 10), pp. 247–53. 1926.

3526 Clark (John Grahame Douglas). The Norwich "woodhenge". Antiquity, 9, pp. 465–69 + 4 plates. 1935.

3527 Clark (Grahame). The Timber monument at Arminghall and its affinities. Proc. prehist. Soc., N.S. 2 (1936), 1–51 + 27 figures + 14 plates.

3528 Clarke (David). A stone circle at Wessenden. Huddersfield Archaeol. Soc., Quart. Bull., 3, p. 3 + plate (with plan). 1958.

3529 Coles (Frederick R.). The standing stones of the Stewartry. Trans. Dumfries. Ant. Soc., 11 (1894–95), pp. 78–83 + 3 plates. 1896.

3530 —— The stone-circles of the north-east of Scotland. [6 figures + 3 maps + 17 plans.] Trans. Buchan F.C., 7, pp. 705–38 + plate. 1904.

3531 Collingwood (Robin George) *and* **Bersu** (Gerhard). King Arthur's Round Table [Westmorland]. Interim report on the excavations of 1937. (Final report, including the excavations of 1939, with an appendix on the Little Round Table). [2 figures + map. (Map).] Trans. Cumb. & Westm. Ant. Soc., N.S. 38, pp. 1–31 + 6 plates + 3 plans; 40, pp. 169–206 + 6 plates + plan. 1938–40.

3532(a) Collingwood (William Gershom). An exploration of the circle on Banniside moor, Coniston. [2 figures.] Trans. Cumb. & Westm. Ant. Soc.,

N.S. 10, pp. 342–53 + 4 plates + plan. 1910.

3532(b) Collinson (S. E.). The Bleasdale find: prehistoric rath or stockaded camp of the Bronze Age. Trans. Lancs. & Ches. Ant. Soc., 29 (1911), pp. 19–28 + 2 plates + plan. 1912.

3533 Cowling (E. T.). The Bull stone [on the southern slope of the Chevin above Guiseley]. Yorks. Archaeol. J., 34, pp. 1–2. 1938.

3534 Cox (John Charles). Some notes on Arbor Low. J. Derbs. Archaeol. Soc., 6, pp. 97–108. 1884.

3535 Craw (James Hewat). Duddo stone circle. Hist. Berwick. Nat. Club, 28, pp. 84–86 + plate. 1932.

3536 Crawford (Osbert Guy Stanhope). The Thornborough circles. *British Association, Leeds, 1927, Handbook, 11, pp. 5–11.* 8°. Leeds, 1927.

3537 —— Long Meg [Little Salkeld, Cumberland]. Antiquity, 8, pp. 328–29 + 2 plates. 1934.

3539 Curwen (Eliot). Stone circle on Swarth fell, Ullswater. Trans. Cumb. & Westm. Ant. Soc., N.S. 21, p. 273. 1921.

3540 D. (E. H. W.). Destruction of the Tolmên [or holed-rock in the parish of Constantine, Cornwall]. [Cured rheumatism if one crawled 3, 5, or 9 times through the hole.] N. & Q., 4 S. 3, p. 332. 1869.

3541 Davies (Ellis). Stone circle, Llandrillo in Edeirnion. Arch. Cambrensis, 82 ii, 1927, 397–98.

3542 Davies (Ivor E.). The Druids' circle and ancient cooking mounds, Penmaenmawr. Proc. Llandudno F.C., 18, pp. 122–23. 1935.

3543 Dawkins (*Sir* William Boyd). Arbor Low. Trans. Lancs. & Ches. Ant. Soc., 32 (1914), pp. 273–77. 1915.

3544 Dickson (J.) *Dr.* On certain markings on the Druid circle in Holywood. [*See also* 4 (1883–86), pp. 44–45, notes by Dr. Gilchrist.] Trans. Dumfries. Ant. Soc., 3 (1864–65), pp. 29–32. 1867.

3545 Dodds (George). Observations on the Rudstone monolith. Reliquary, 14, pp. 1–7. 1873.

3546 Drummond (James). Notice of the Clach-a-Charra, a stone of memorial, at Onich, in Lochaber [Inverness]. Proc. Soc. Antiq. Scot., 6, pp. 328–32 + plate. 1868.

3547 Dunkin (E. Hadlow Wise). Remarks on the stone-circles at Boscawen-Un and Boskednan in west Cornwall. [Figure + 2 plans.] Reliquary, 10, pp. 97–102. 1869.

3548 —— On the megalithic circle at Duloe, Cornwall. Arch. Camb., 4th S. 4, pp. 45–50 + plan. 1873.

3549 Dunning (Gerald Clough). A stone circle and cairn on Mynydd Epynt, Brecknockshire. Arch. Camb., 97 ii, 1943, 169–94 + 8 figures + 16 plates.

3550 Dymond (Charles William). The megalithic antiquities at Stanton Drew. J. Brit. Archaeol. Ass., 33, pp. 297–307 + 2 plates + plan. 1877.

3551 —— A group of Cumbrian megaliths. J. Brit. Archaeol. Ass., 34, pp. 31–36 + 4 plans. 1878.

3552 —— Notes on the megalithic antiquities at Stanton Drew. Proc. Somerset Arch. Soc., 23 (1877), pp. 30–37 + plate + plan. 1878.

3553 —— Gunnerkeld stone circle [near Shap, Westmorland]. J. Brit. Archaeol. Ass., 35, pp. 368–71 + plan. 1879.

3554 —— The Hurlers [Cornwall]. J. Brit. Archaeol. Ass., 35, pp. 297–307 + plan. 1879.

3555 —— A group of Cumberland megaliths. J. Brit. Arch. Ass., 34, pp. 31–36. *Reprinted (with additions) in* Trans. Cumb. & Westm. Ant. Soc., 5, pp. 39–57 + 2 plates. 1880.

3556 —— Gunnerkeld stone circle. Trans. Cumb. & Westm. Ant. Soc., 4, pp. 537–40 + plan. 1880.

3557 —— Duloe stone circle [Cornwall]. J. Brit. Archaeol. Ass., 38, pp. 149–55 + plate (with plan). 1882.

3558 —— Mayburgh and King Arthur's Round Table [Eamont Bridge, Westmorland]. Trans. Cumb. & Westm. Ant. Soc., 11, pp. 187–219 + 3 plans. 1891.

3559 —— The ancient remains at Stanton Drew in the county of Somerset. pp. iv, 40 + 2 plans. 4°. Bristol, 1896.

3560 —— An exploration of Sunken Kirk, Swinside, Cumberland, with incidental researches in its neighbourhood. Trans. Cumb. & Westm. Ant. Soc., N.S. 2, pp. 53–76 + 2 plans; N.S. 4, pp. 354–55 (correction). 1902.

3561 Dymond (D. P.). The "Henge"

monument at Nunwick, near Ripon. 1961 excavation. Yorks. Arch. Journ. 41 (i), 1963, 98–107 + 4 figures + 1 plate.

3562 Dymond (D. P.). Ritual monuments at Rudston, E. Yorkshire, England. Proc. prehist. Soc., 32, 1966, 86–95 + 4 figures + 3 plates.

3563 Eogan (George). The Excavation of a stone alignment and circle at Cholwichtown, Lee Moor, Devonshire, England (with an appendix on soil pollen analysis, by I. G. Simmons). Proc. prehist. Soc., 30, 1964, 25–38 + 4 figures + 8 plates.

3564 Evans (*Sir* Arthur John). The Rollright stones and their folk-lore. Folk-lore, 6, pp. 6–51 + 3 plates + plan. 1895.

3565 —— The Rollright stones and their folklore. [2 figures.] Ditchfield (P. H.): Memorials of old Oxfordshire, pp. 22–38 + plate. 1903.

3566 Ferguson (Richard Saul). Stone circle at Gamelands, Bland House brow, township of Raisbeck, parish of Outon, Westmorland. Trans. Cumb. & Westm. Ant. Soc., 6, pp. 183–85 + plan. 1883.

3567 —— Shap stones. [Former existence, from a drawing, of avenue and stone circle south of Shap.] Trans. Cumb. & Westm. Ant. Soc., 15, pp. 27–34 + 3 plates + map. 1899.

3568 Fletcher (W.). Grey Croft stone circle, Seascale, Cumberland. Trans. Cumb. & Westm. Ant. Soc. N.S. 57, pp. 1–8 + 3 plates + plan. 1958.

3569 Fleure (Herbert John) *and* **Dunlop** (Margaret). Glendarragh circle and alignments, The Braid, I.O.M. Antiq. J., 22, pp. 39–53 + 4 plates + plan. 1942.

3571 Fox (*Sir* Cyril). The Ysceifiog circle and barrow, Flintshire. [13 figures + plan.] Arch. Camb., 81, pp. 48–85 + plate + plan. 1926.

3572 Fraser (James). Stone circles of Strathnairn. Trans. Banffshire F.C., 3, 1883.

3573 French (Gilbert J.). The stone circles on Chetham's Close [Turton, Lancs.]. Trans. Lancs. & Ches. Ant. Soc., 12 (1894), pp. 42–51 + 2 plates + plan. 1895.

3574 Gabriel (Jacob Rees) *and* **Evans** (George Eyre). Kilmaenllwyd stones:

Maenhir farm. Trans. Carmarthenshire Ant. Soc., 4, pp. 25–26. 1908.

3575 Gelderd (Charles) *and* **Dobson** (John). Report on the excavations carried out at the "Druids' circle" on Birkrigg in the parish of Urswick [Furness]. Trans. Cumb. & Westm. Ant. Soc., N.S. 12, pp. 262–74 + 3 plates + plan. 1912.

3576 Gilchrist (James). Notes on the Druid circles in the neighbourhood of Inverness. Trans. Dumfries. Ant. Soc., 3 (1864–65), pp. 33–37. 1867.

3577 Goss (William Henry). On Arbor Low. Reliquary, 17, pp. 113–18, 147–54, 193–201; 18, pp. 49–56, 103–108, 156–60, 235–39; 20, pp. 1–8. 1876–1879.

3578 Graham (T. M. B.). The Grey Yauds, a vanished stone circle. [On King Harry fell, 10 miles from Carlisle.] Trans. Cumb. & Westm. Antiq. Soc., N.S. 7, pp. 67–71. 1907.

3580 Gray (Harold St. George). On the excavations at Arbor Low, 1901–1902. [6 figures.] Archaeologia, 58, pp. 461–98 + 6 plates + plan. 1903.

3581 —— Relief model of Arbor Low stone circle, Derbyshire. [2 figures.] Man, 3, pp. 145–46 + plate. 1903.

3582 —— Arbor Low stone circle. Excavations in 1901 and 1902. [13 figures.] J. Derbs. Archaeol. Soc., 26, pp. 41–77 + 8 plates + plan. 1904.

3583 —— The stone circle on Withypool hill, Exmoor. Proc. Somerset Arch. Soc., 52 (1906), pp. 42–50 + plan. 1907.

3584 —— The stone circles of east Cornwall. Proc. Soc. Antiq., 2 S. 22, pp. 29–32. 1907.

3585 —— On the stone circles of east Cornwall. Archaeologia, 61, pp. 1–60 + 5 plates + 3 plans. 1908.

3586 —— The Porlock stone circle, Exmoor. Proc. Somerset Arch. Soc., 74 (1928), pp. 71–77 + plan. 1929.

3587 —— Rude stone monuments of Exmoor (Somerset portion), part 3— [Almsworthy stones]. Proc. Somerset Arch. Soc., 77 (1931), pp. 78–82 + plan. 1932.

3588 —— Rude stone monuments of Exmoor, part 4. [Dunkery beacon, Kit barrows, *etc.*] Proc. Somerset Arch. Soc., 78 (1932), pp. 121–25. 1933.

3589(a) Gray (Harold St. George). Porlock stone circle. Archaeol. J., 107 (1950), p. 87. 1952.

3589(b) Griffith (John). The orientations at Boscawen-un. Antiquary, 45, p. 79. 1909.

3590 Griffiths (William Eyre). Excavation of concentric circles at Penygroes, Caern. Bull. Bd. Celtic Stud., 13, pp. 113–15. 1949.

3591 —— The excavation of stone circles near Penmaenmawr, North Wales. Proc. prehist. Soc., 26, 1960, 303–39 + 8 figures + 2 plates.

3592 Grimes (William Francis). The Cottrell Park standing stone, St. Nicholas, Glamorgan. Cardiff Nat. Soc. Rpt. & Trans., 67 (1934), pp. 104–08 + 2 plates. 1936.

3593 —— Meini Gwyr, Carmarthenshire. Bull. Bd. Celtic Stud., 9, pp. 373–74. 1939.

3594 —— Excavations at Stanton Harcourt, Oxon., 1940. [17 figures + map. Devil's Quoits (standing stones), ring-ditches, etc. Appendix A, Pits within the Quoit circle, by K. S. Sandford: Appendix B, Human remains (& skeletons), by L. F. Cowley.] Oxoniensia, 8/9, pp. 19–63 + 5 plates. 1944.

3595 —— Meini-gwyr. Arch. J., *119* (1962) 342.

3596 —— Ffynnon-Brodyr [short note]. Arch. J., *119* (1962) 342.

3597 Grinsell (Leslie Valentine). Stanton Drew stone circles. *Ministry of Works.* pp. 7. 8°. London, 1956.

3598 Hamper (William). Observations on certain ancient pillars of memorial, called hoar-stones. [Pp. 52–60, list of hoar-stones, and places named from them.] Archaeologia, 25, pp. 24–60. 1834.

3601 Harvey, John H. A Note on Long Meg, Salkeld. Arch. J., *116*, 1959, 262.

3602 Hay (Thomas). An interesting layer at King Arthur's Round Table. Trans. Cumb. & Westm. Ant Soc., N.S. 49, pp. 215–16 + plate. 1949.

3603 Heathcote (J. Clee). Arbor Low . . . a short guide. pp. 28. [3 figures + plan.] 8°. Chesterfield, 1935.

3604 Heathcote (John Percy). Excavations at Doll Tor stone circle, Stanton moor. [2 figures.] J. Derbs. Ar-

chaeol. Soc., 60 (N.S. 13), pp. 116–25 + plate + plan. 1939.

3605 —— The Nine stones, Harthill moor. J. Derbs. Archaeol. Soc., 60 (N.S. 13), pp. 126–28 + plate. 1939.

3606 —— Arbor Low: today, the days of old, and the years of ancient times. A short history, *etc.* Revised edition. pp. 27. [3 figures + map + plan.] 8°. Chesterfield, 1956.

3607 —— Arbor Low. Arch. J. 118, 1961, 216.

3608 Heelis (Arthur John). Maybrough and King Arthur's Round Table. Trans. Cumb. & Westm. Ant. Soc., N.S. 12, pp. 146–54. 1912.

3609 Hodgson (Katharine S.). Notes on stone circles at Broomrigg, Grey Yauds, *etc.* Trans. Cumb. & Westm. Ant. Soc., N.S. 35, pp. 77–79 + 2 plates + 4 plans. 1935.

3610 —— Further excavations at Broomrigg, near Ainstable. Trans. Cumb. & Westm. Ant. Soc., N.S. 52, pp. 1–8 + 11 plates. 1952.

3611 —— Long Meg and her daughter. Arch. J. 115, 1958, 236.

3612 Honeyman (Herbert Lewis). The standing stones of Hethpool. Proc. Soc. Antiq. Newc., 4th S. 6, pp. 116–17. 1933.

3613 Hubbersty (H. A.). Arbor Low. The quarrying and transport of its stones. J. Derbs. Archaeol. Soc., 26, pp. 80–81. 1904.

3613(b) Iago (William). Notes on Duloe circular enclosure. J. Roy. Instn. Cornwall, 12, pp. 96–106 + map. 1893.

3614 Innes (Cosmo). Notice of the stone circle of Calbernish in the Lewis, and of a chamber under the circle recently excavated. [Figure + plan.] Proc. Soc. Antiq. Scot., 3, pp. 110–12. 1862.

3615 Isaacson (Stephen). On the ancient circular temple at Arbor-Low, Derbyshire; with some general remarks on similar structures. [2 figures.] Trans. Brit. Archaeol. Ass. [2], Congress at Winchester, 1845, pp. 197–204. 1846.

3616 Jackson (Magnus). Stone circle near Aberfeldy, Perthshire. Reliquary, 3rd S. 13, p. 47 + plate. 1907.

3617 Jeffcott (John M.). Circle on the Mule [or Mull, parish of Rushen], Isle of Man. Arch. Camb., 3rd S. 12, pp. 306–12 + plan. 1866.

3618 Jewitt (Llewellynn). Passing notes on some stone circles and other remains of past ages in the Isle of Man. [2 figures + plan.] Reliquary, 25, pp. 161–72 + plan. 1885.

3619 Jones (Donald H.). Henllan stone-circle. Neath Ant. Soc. Trans., 2 S. 3, pp. 51–54. 1933.

3620 Jones (Herbert C.). A stone circle. Trans. Caradoc & Severn Valley F.C., 11, pp. 127–29. 1941.

3621 Keiller (Alexander). Interim report upon such of the stone circles of Aberdeenshire and Kincardineshire as have been scheduled as ancient monuments. 8°. *Privately printed.* 1927.

3622 Keith (Edward). Monolith on South Middleton moor [Northumb.]. Proc. Soc. Antiq. Newc., 4th S. 5, pp. 82–83 + plate. 1931.

3623 Kermode (Philip Moore Callow). The Meayll stone circle, Isle of Man. [4 figures + plan.] Ill. Arch., 2, pp. 1–8. 1894.

3624 Kinahan (George Henry). Legends about stone circles, &c. Folk-lore Record, 5, pp. 169–72. 1882.

3625 —— On a circular structure at Cummer, Co. Wexford. J. Anthrop. Inst., 12, pp. 318–22 + plan. 1883.

3626 Leadman (Alexander Dionysius Hobson). The Devil's arrows, near Boroughbridge, Yorkshire. Reliquary, N.S. 4, pp. 1–4 + plate. 1890.

3627 —— The Devil's arrows, near Boroughbridge, Yorkshire. [3 figures.] Antiquary, 39, pp. 8–11. 1903.

3628 Lees (Edwin). An account of some presumed Celtic monuments, called the King and the Queen, and the Bambury stone, on Bredon hill, Worcestershire. Assoc. Archit. Socs'. Rpts., 6, pp. 95–99. 1861.

3629 Lewis (A. L.). The Devil's arrows, Yorkshire. J. Anthrop. Inst., 8, pp. 180–83. 1878.

3630 —— Notes on two stone circles in Shropshire. J. Anthrop. Inst., 11, pp. 3–7 + plan. 1881.

3631 —— On three stone circles in Cumberland with some further observations on the relation of stone circles to adjacent hills and outlying stones. J. Anthrop. Inst., 15, pp. 471–81 + 2 plans. 1886.

3632 —— Stone circles near Aberdeen. J. Anthrop. Inst., 17, pp. 44–57 + plate. 1887.

3633 —— On the connection between stone circles and adjacent hills. Trans. Shropshire Archaeol. Soc., 2nd S. 5, pp. 78–86 + map. 1893.

3634 —— The stone circles of Scotland. [Figure + 3 plans.] J. Anthrop. Inst., 30, pp. 56–73. 1900.

3635 —— Some stone circles in Ireland. [Figure + 2 plans.] J. R. Anthrop. Inst., 39, pp. 517–29. 1909.

3636 —— Stone circles in Derbyshire. [2 figures (Arborlow).] Man, 3, pp. 133–36. 1903.

3637 —— Megalithic monuments in Gloucestershire. [Longstone, Minchinhampton, *etc.*] Man, 12, pp. 40–41. 1912.

3638 —— Standing stones and stone circles in Yorkshire. Man, 14, pp. 163–166. 1914.

3639 Lewis (J. M.). Gors Fawr stone circle. Arch. J., 119, 1962, 342.

3640 Llewellynir, (W.). [Menhirs at] Caer-Hên-Eglwys or Caewye-Hên-Eglwys. Arch. Camb., 5th S. 12, pp. 323–25. 1895.

3641 Logan (James). Observations on several circles of stone in Scotland, presumed to be druidical. Archaeologia, 22, pp. 198–203 + 2 plates; pp. 409–11 + 2 plates. 1829.

3642 Long (William). The druidical temple at Stanton Drew, [Somerset] commonly called the Weddings. Archaeol. J., 15, pp. 199–215 + plan. 1858.

3643 Lowe (Walter Bezant). Some arrow stones and other incised stones in north Carnarvonshire and north Denbighshire. [18 figures + 2 maps.] Arch. Camb., 79, pp. 340–62. 1924.

3644 Lubbock (John) *1st Baron Avebury.* Arbor Low. [3 figures.] Reliquary, 20, pp. 81–85. 1879.

3645 Lukis (William Collings). The Devil's arrows, Boroughbridge, Yorkshire. Proc. Soc. Antiq., 2 S. 7, pp. 134–38. 1877.

3646 Lynch (Frances). The Pikestones, Anglezarke, Lancashire. Proc. prehist. Soc., 32, 1966, 347–48 + 2 figures.

3647 McAldowie (Alexander M.). Notes on the Bawd stone, near Rockhall, on the Roaches. North Staffs. N.C.,

Ann. Rpt. & Trans., 48, pp. 162–68 + 2 plates. 1914.

3648 MacArthur (William). The stone circles on Meayll hill, Isle of Man. N. & Q., 11 S. 7, pp. 383–84. 1913.

3649 McInnes (Isla J.). A Class II Henge in the East Riding of Yorkshire. Antiquity, 38, 1964, 218–19.

3650 McLauchlan (Thomas). Notice of monoliths in the island of Mull. [Figure + map.] Proc. Soc. Antiq. Scot., 5, pp. 46–52. 1865.

3651 MacMichael (J. Holden). Nine Maidens. N. & Q., 10 S. 2, pp. 128, 396–97, 453. 1904.

3652 Marshall (George). The Fedw stone circle, in the parish of Glascwm, Radnorshire. Trans. Woolhope N.F.C., 1927–29, pp. 119–22. 1931.

3653 Martin (Edward A[lfred]). Megaliths on the South Downs. (Reprinted from Knowledge & Scientific News, Feb. 1910.) pp. 4. 8º. London, 1910.

3654 Mason (Joseph Robert). Antiquities at Dean. [Remains of stone circle.] Trans. Cumb. & Westm. Ant. Soc., N.S. 23, pp. 34–35 + 2 plates. 1923.

3655 —— *and* **Valentine** (Herbert). Studfold Gate circle and the parallel trenches at Dean. [2 plans.] Trans. Cumb. & Westm. Ant. Soc., N.S. 25, pp. 268–71 + plate. 1925.

3656 Matthews (T. Arthur). Some notes (Some further notes) on Arbor Low and other lows in the High Peak. [4 figures. (Figure.)] J. Derbs. Archaeol. Soc., 29, pp. 103–12: 33, 87–94. 1907–11.

3657 —— Some menhirs. [Two stones near Wirksworth.] J. Derbs. Archaeol. Soc., 37, pp. 55–58 + 2 plates. 1915.

3658 Mayne (W. Boxer). Meane-an-Tol or Maen rock, *etc.*, Constantine. J. Roy. Instn. Cornwall, 21, pp. 441–450 + plate. 1925.

3659(a) Milne (John). Stone circles in Aberdeenshire. Advm. of Sci., 1885, 1223.

3659(b) Mitchell (H. B.). The Parkhouse circle. Trans. Buchan F.C., 4, 1898.

3660 Moggridge (Matthew). Druidic circle, Rhosmaen, Radnorshire. Arch. Camb., 3rd S. 6, pp. 21–22 + plan. 1860.

3661 Morgan (C. Lloyd). The stones of Stanton Drew: their source and origin. Proc. Somerset Arch. Soc., 33 (1887), pp. 37–50 + plan. 1888.

3662 Mountford (George). Standing stones on Stapley hill. Trans. Shropshire Archaeol. Soc., 46, pp. 200–03. 1932.

3663 Noble (Mary Elizabeth) *Miss.* The stone circle on Knipe Scar [Westmorland]. Trans. Cumb. & Westm. Ant. Soc., N.S. 7, pp. 211–14 + plan. 1907.

3664 Nicholls (R.). The Devil's Ring and Finger. Antiquity, 1, pp. 229–30 + 2 plates. 1927.

3665 North (Oliver Henry) *and* **Spence** (Joseph E.). Stone circle, Summerhouse hill, Yealand Conyers. Trans. Cumb. & Westm. Ant. Soc., N.S. 36, pp. 69–70 + plan. 1936.

3666 North Lonsdale Field Club. Report on the further excavations carried out at the "Druid's circles", on Birkrigg in the parish of Urswick, September–October, 1921. Trans. Cumb. & Westm. Ant. Soc., N.S. 22, pp. 346–352 + plan. 1922.

3667(a) O'Neil (Helen E.). Condicote earthwork, a henge monument, Gloucestershire. Trans. Bristol & Glos. A.S., 76, 1957, 141–46 + 1 figure.

3667(b) Owen (Edward). A boundary stone with a good record. [Hirfaen Gwyddog, Llanycrwys, Carm.] [Figure.] Ill. Arch., 1, pp. 55–58. 1893.

3668 Palmer (Mervyn G.). Standing stones of the Ilfracombe district. Rpt. & Trans. Devon. Assoc., 69, pp. 883–895 + 5 plates + map. 1937.

3669 Parsons (Hamlyn). Investigations into the Burford down stone row, Dartmoor. Rpt. & Trans. Devon. Assoc., 85, pp. 145–47. 1953.

3670 Pegge (Samuel). On the Rudston pyramidal stone. Archaeologia, 5, pp. 95–97 + plate. 1779.

3671 Perfect (H. T.). The megalithic remains at Stanton Drew. Proc. Clifton Antiq. Club, 1, pp. 14–17. 1888.

3672 Peter (Rev. James). The stone circles in Aberdeenshire, with special reference to those in the more lowland parts of the county, their extent and arrangement, singly or in groups, with general observations. Advm. of Sci., 1885, 1221–1223.

3673(a) Piggott (Stuart). The Mull hill circle, Isle of Man, and its pottery. [6 figures + plan.] Antiq. J., 12, pp. 146–57. 1932.

3673(b) Playne (George F.). On the recent destruction of a Gloucestershire menhir. Trans. Bristol & Glos. Arch. Soc., 1, pp. 105–06. 1876.

3674(a) Plint (R. G.). Stone circle on Potter Fell, Nr. Kendal. Tran. C. & W.A. & A.S. N.S.L. x, 1960, 201.

3674(b) Pool (Peter H. S.). *and* **Russell** (Vivien). Preliminary note on two menhir excavations in Gulval, Cornwall. Proc. West Cornwall F.C., 2, pp. 128–29. 1959.

3675 Powell (Thomas George Eyre). Excavation of a circular enclosure at Broadbank, Briercliffe, Lancashire. Trans. Hist. Soc. Lancs. & Ches., 104 (1952), pp. 145–52 + plan. 1953.

3676 Pownall (Thomas). Account of a singular stone among the rocks at West Hoadley, Sussex. ["Great upon little".] Archaeologia, 6, pp. 54–60 + plate. 1782.

3679 Price (Frederick George Hilton). Treblech [Monmouthshire]. J. Anthrop. Inst., 9, pp. 51–53 + plate. 1879.

3680 Prowse (Arthur Bancks). The Rundlestone [near Princetown]. Rpt. & Trans. Devon. Assoc., 40, pp. 219–21. 1908.

3681 Ravenhill (J. W.) *and* **Chatwin** (Philip Boughton). The Rollright stones. [Kingstone.] B'ham. Arch. Soc. Trans., 52 (1927), p. 305. 1930.

3682 Ravenhill (T. H.). The Rollright stones, some facts and some problems. Oxfordshire Archaeol. Soc., Rpts., 71, pp. 121–43. 1926.

3683 —— The Rollright stones, some facts and some problems. pp. 23. 8°. Long Compton, 1927.

3684 —— The Rollright stones and the men who erected them. Second edition. pp. 62 + 2 plates + plan. 8°. Birmingham, 1932.

3685 Rees (William). An account of two druidical circles and a Roman camp on a mountain near Trecastle, Brecknockshire. [Figure.] Arch. Camb., N.S. 5, pp. 125–34 + plan. 1854.

3686 Reid (R. C.). Note on a stone circle near Loch Stroan. Trans. Dumfries Ant. Soc., 3 S. 22 (1938–39), pp. 164–165 + plan. 1942.

3687 Riley (D. N.). Circles and barrows on Ramsley Moor. Trans. Hunter archaeol. Soc. 8 ii, 1960, 68–70 + 1 figure.

3688(a) Robinson (Joseph). Letter on Leaset (sic) Wood stone circle. Proc. Soc. Antiq., 2 S. 8, pp. 389–92. 1880.

3688(b) Robinson (Joseph) *and* **Ferguson** (Richard Saul). Notes on excavations at Leacot hill stone circle, Westmorland. Trans. Cumb. & Westm. Ant. Soc., 5, pp. 76–78 + plan. 1881.

3689 Rogers (Ernest Henry). The Yelland stone row. [On tidal flat on the Taw near Fremington.] Proc. Devon. Archaeol. Expl. Soc., 1, pp. 201–02 + plate. 1932.

3690 Rooke (Hayman). An account of some druidical remains on Stanton and Hartle moor in the Peak, Derbyshire. Archaeologia, 6, pp. 110–15 + 7 plates. 1782.

3691 —— Some account of the Brimham rocks in Yorkshire. Archaeologia, 8, pp. 209–17 + 2 plates. 1787.

3692 —— Description of some druidical remains on Harborough rocks, &c. in Derbyshire. Archaeologia, 9, pp. 206–10 + 2 plates. 1789.

3693 Rudge (Ernest A.). The statistical evidence for a conglomerate alignment in Essex. Essex Nat., 29, pp. 178–86 + plate, pp. 256–58. 1954.

3694 Russell (Vivien) *and* **Pool** (Peter Aubrey Seymour). Excavation of a Menhir at Try, Gulval. Cornish Arch., 3, 1964, 15–26 + 3 figures.

3695 Sainter (J. D.). Notes on a stone circle, called the Bridestones, near Congleton [Cheshire]. Reliquary, 21, pp. 197–200. 1880.

3696 Saunders (A. D.). St. Breock beacon longstone. Proc. West Cornwall F.C., 2, pp. 111–12. 1959.

3697 Savory (Hubert Newman). Examination of a menhir at Knelston, Glamorgan. Bull. Bd. Celtic Stud., 13, pp. 110–11. 1949.

3698 Sayce (Roderick Urwick). The stone-rings on Craig Rhiwarth. Collns. rel. to Montgom., 45, pp. 104–21 + 7 plates. 1937.

3699 Scarth (Harry Mengden). On the megalithic remains at Stanton Drew.

Proc. Somerset Arch. Soc., 14 (1867), pp. 161–72 + plan. 1869.

3700 Senogles (H.). The standing stones of Anglesey. Anglesey Ant. Soc. Trans., 1938, pp. 24–29 + 2 plates. 1938.

3701 Sharp (W. H.). The Goatstones stone circle. Proc. Soc. Antiq. Newc., 4th S. 11, p. 435. 1950.

3702 Sherlock (Helen Travers). The Wyrley [Staffs.] stones. *Caravan essays, 10.* pp. 47 + plate. [15 figures.] 8º. Cambridge, 1929.

3703 Shirley (G. W.). The standing stones of Torhouse, and others. Trans. Dumfries. Ant. Soc., 3 S. 19 (1933–35), pp. 153–61. 1936.

3704 Sibree (Ernest). The Stanton Drew stones. pp. 20. 8º. Bristol, 1919.

3705 Simpson (James). Stone circles near Shap, Westmoreland. Proc. Soc. Antiq. Scot., 4, pp. 443–49 + plate. 1863.

3706 —— Stone circles near Shap, Westmoreland. Trans. Cumb. & Westm. Ant. Soc., 6, pp. 176–82. 1883.

3707 Simpson (John). Megalithic remains on Bilberry knoll, Matlock. J. Derbs. Archaeol. Soc., 37, pp. 59–76 + 2 plates + map. 1915.

3708 Smith (Robert Henry Soden). Notice of circles of stones in the parish of Crosby Ravenswirth, Westmoreland. Archaeol. J., 27, pp. 200–03. 1870.

3709 Somerville (Boyle). The Devil's arrows [Boroughbridge, Yorks.]. Prehistoric stone monuments and their orientation. *British Association, Leeds, 1927, Handbook 18,* pp. 13–20. [Plan.] 8º. Leeds, 1927.

3710 Spain (George Redesdale Brooker). The "Three Kings of Denmark", Redesdale. [Figure + map + plan.] Proc. Soc. Antiq. Newc., 3rd. S. 5, pp. 234–37. 1912.

3711 Spence (James). The stone circles of Old Deer [Aberdeensh.]. Trans. Buchan F.C., 1. 1890.

3712 Spence (Joseph E.). A stone circle in Shap rural parish. Trans. Cumb. & Westm. Ant. Soc., N.S. 35, p. 69 + plan. 1935.

3713 Spooner (B. C.). The stone circles of Cornwall. Folklore, 64, pp. 484–87. 1953.

3714 Stevens (David). Stanton Drew and its tradition. N. & Q., 1st S. 4, pp. 3–4. 1851.

3715 Stout (H. B.). Gretigate stone circles, Sides, Gosforth. [1 figure.] Trans. C. & W.A. & A.S., N.S. 61, 1961, 1–6.

3716 Stuart (John). Notices on various stone circles in the parishes of Cairney, Monymusk, and Tough, Aberdeenshire; and of Inverkeithny, Banffshire. Proc. Soc. Antiq. Scot., 1, pp. 141–42. 1855.

3717 Tait (Lawson). Notes of the opening of a stone circle at Craigmore, in Strathfleet, Sutherlandshire. Proc. Soc. Antiq. Scot., 7, pp. 473–75 + plate. 1870.

3718 Tate (George). The Duddo stones and the urns found in their vicinity. [Figure.] Hist. Berwick. Nat. Club, 10, pp. 542–44 + plate. 1884.

3719 Taylor (Michael Waistell). On the vestiges of Celtic occupation near Ullswater, and on the discovery of buried stone circles by Eamont side. Trans. Cumb. & Westm. Ant. Soc., 1, pp. 154–68 + 2 plates + map. 1874.

3720 Thomas (Charles). Folklore from a northern henge monument. Folk-lore, 64, pp. 427–29. 1953.

3721 —— The Society's 1962 excavations: The Henge at Castilly, Lanivet [no evidence of prehistoric origin]. Cornish archaeol., 3, 1964, 3–14 + 4 figures.

3722 Thomas (Nicholas). The Thornborough circles, near Ripon, North Riding. Yorks. Archaeol. J., 38, pp. 425–45 + 3 plates. 1955.

3723 —— The Devil's ring and finger [Note for Summer Meeting, Keele, 1963]. Arch. J., 120, 1963, 289.

3724 Thompson (D.). The name Arbor Low. J. Derbs. Archaeol. Soc., 76, pp. 67–70. 1956.

3725 Thompson (W. H.). An ancient monolith. [Rudston.] Bygone Yorkshire, ed. William Andrews, pp. 39–45 + plate. 1892.

3726 Thomson (Alexander). Notice of a group of four circles of standing stones in the south corner of the parish of Banchory-Devenick, county of Kincardine. [Plan.] Proc. Soc. Antiq. Scot., 5, pp. 130–35. 1865.

3727 Tregelles (G. F.). Stone circles [in Cornwall]. [4 figures + plan.] V.C.H., Cornwall, 1, pp. 379–406 + 2 plates + 8 plans. 1906.

3728 Tristram (Edward). The stone circle, known as the Bull Ring, at Dove Holes, and the mound adjoining. J. Derbs. Archaeol. Soc., 37, pp. 77–86 + plan. 1915.

3729 Tucker (J. Allon). Stanton Drew. Proc. Bath N.H. & Ant. F.C., 5, pp. 257–64. 1885.

3730 Tudor (Thomas Linthwaite). Further note on a holed stone near Arbor Low. J. Derbs. Archaeol. Soc., 51 (N.S. 4, 1930), pp. 154–56. 1931.

3731 Turner (T. S.). History of Aldborough [Yorks.] and Borough-bridge, containing an account of the Roman antiquities, Devil's arrows, etc. . . . and other curiosities. pp. vi, 190 + plates + plan (of Isurium). 8°. London, 1853.

3732 Tyler (Francis Cameron). Ellipse of stones at Manaton, Devon. Devon & Cornwall N. & Q., 17, pp. 210–12. 1933.

3733 —— Scorhill circle, Dartmoor. Devon & Cornwall N. & Q., 17, pp. 258–61. 1933.

3734 —— Menhir on Bodmin east moor [in Altarnum]. Devon & Cornwall N. & Q., 17, pp. 372–73 + plate. 1933.

3734(b) Vatcher (Faith de Mallet). Thornborough Cursus, Yorks. Yorks. Arch. Journ., 40 (ii), 1960, 169–82 + 3 plates + 4 figures.

3735 Warner (Richard). A Possible Henge at Hargaoras, near Truro. Cornish archaeol. No. 2, 1963, 79–80.

3736 Watkins (Alfred). Alignment of giant's cave and sacrificial stone, Malvern hills. Trans. Woolhope N.F.C., 1924–26, pp. 8–9 + plate.

3737 —— The Devil's Arrows. [Vertical grooves.] N. & Q., 161, pp. 176–177. 1931.

3738 Watson (George). The stone circles of Roxburghshire. Trans. Hawick Archaeol. Soc., [40], pp. 20–28. 1908.

3739 Webley (G. D.). Four standing stones in South Brecknock. Bull. Bd. Celtic Stud., 16, p. 299. 1956.

3740 Wilson (J. S.) *and* **Garfitt** (G. A.). Stone circle, Eyam moor [Derbys.]. [Plan.] Man, 20, pp. 34–37. 1920.

3741 Worth (Richard Hansford). The stone rows of Dartmoor. Parts 6–8. Rpt. & Trans. Devon. Assoc., 35, pp. 426–27 + plan; 38, pp. 535–37 + map; 40, pp. 281–82 + 2 plans; 43, pp. 348–349 + plan; 50, pp. 402–04 + plan. 1903–11.

3742 —— Long Stone Row on Erme [Dartmoor]. Devon N. & Q., 4, pp. 11–12. 1906.

3743 —— Two stone circles on Dartmoor, Swincombe valley, and West Dart valley, with a note on the Grey Wethers. Rpt. & Trans. Devon. Assoc., 71, pp. 321–38 + 2 plates. 1939.

3744 —— The Dartmoor menhirs. Rpt. & Trans. Devon. Assoc., 72, pp. 191–99 + 10 plates. 1940.

3745 —— Retaining-circles associated with stone rows, Dartmoor. [7 plans.] Rpt. & Trans. Devon. Assoc., 73, pp. 227–38 + 2 plates. 1941.

3746 —— A stone circle [on Willings Walls warren] in the Plym valley. [2 plans.] Rpt. & Trans. Devon. Assoc., 74, pp. 207–10 + 2 plates. 1942.

3747 —— The stone rows of Dartmoor. [Plan.] Rpt. & Trans. Devon. Assoc., 78, pp. 285–315 + 4 plates + map + 5 plans; 79, pp. 175–86 + plate. 1946–47.

3748 Worth (Richard Nicholls). The stone rows of Dartmoor. Parts 1–5. [Figure.] Rpt. & Trans. Devon. Assoc., 24, pp. 387–417; 25, pp. 541–46; 26, pp. 296–307; 27, pp. 437–42; 28, pp. 712–13. 1892–96.

3749 Wood (Eric S.). The earth circles on St. Martha's hill, near Guildford. Surrey Archaeol. Collns., 54, pp. 10–46 + 3 plates. 1955.

3750 Young (R. T.). Notes on the stone circles in the Wharrie glen. Trans. Stirling N.H. & Arch. Soc., 1924–25, pp. 158–65. 1925.

5. FORTS, CAMPS AND EARTHWORKS IN GENERAL

3751 Allcroft (Arthur Hadrian). Earthwork of England. Prehistoric, Roman, etc. pp. xix, 711 + map (of South Downs). [224 figures.] 8°. London, 1908.

3752 Chater (A. G.). Earthworks of the hill-spur type. [8 figures.] J. Brit. Archaeol. Ass., N.S. 15, pp. 21–46. 1909.

3753 **Clark** (George Thomas). Some remarks upon earthworks of the British period. Archaeol. J., 37, pp. 217–26. 1880.

3754 **Cotton** (Molly Aylwin). British camps with timber-laced ramparts. Archaeol. J., 111 (1954), pp. 26–105 + plate (Burghead), 1955.

3755 —— Relationships between Iron Age earthworks in France and Britain. Archaeol. News Letter, 7 vii, 1962, 147–52.

3756 **Crawford** (Osbert Guy Stanhope). The "interrupted ditch" [which surrounds the interior of British Neolithic camps]: a possible explanation. Antiquity, 7, pp. 344–45. 1933.

3757 **Curwen** (Eliot Cecil). Neolithic camps. [2 figures (pottery) + 10 plans.] Antiquity, 4, pp. 22–54 + 9 plates. 1930.

3758 **Duckett** (*Sir* George) *bart.* Observations on the water-supply of some of our ancient British encampments, more especially in Wiltshire and Sussex. [Dew-ponds.] Wilts. Archaeol. Mag., 18, pp. 177–80. 1879.

3760 **Johnston** (James Leo Forde). Hillforts of the Iron Age in England and Wales, 150 text figures, 20 plates, cr. 4°. Liverpool Univ. Pr., 1973.

3761 **Fox** (Aileen Mary). Hill-slope forts and related earthworks in southwest England and South Wales. [Map + 10 plans. Early Iron Age B.] Archaeol. J., 109 (1952), pp. 1–22 + plate. 1953.

3761(b) **Freeman** (John Peere Williams). Cross-dykes. [4 maps.] Antiquity, 6, pp. 24–34. 1932.

3763 **Gould** (Isaac Chalkley). Early defensive earthworks. [4 figures + 12 plans. Pp. 17–25, Prehistoric.] J. Brit. Archaeol. Ass., N.S. 7, pp. 15–38 + plate + 5 plans. 1901.

3764 **Gresham** (Colin A.). Multiple ramparts. [E.g. at Maiden Castle.] Antiquity, 17, pp. 67–70. 1943.

3765 **Griffith** (John). English earthworks and their orientation. Nature, 80, pp. 69–72. 1909.

3766 **Hawkes** (Charles John Christopher). Hill-forts. [5 figures + 3 distribution maps + 3 plans. Iron Age, A, B and C.] Antiquity, 5, pp. 60–97 + 2 plates + 3 plans. 1931.

3767(a) **Hemp** (Wilfrid James). Hill

fort problem [analogies in France]. Arch. Camb., 97 i, 1942, 93–95.

3767(b) **Johnston** (J. L. Forde). Earl's Hill, Pontesbury and related hillforts in England and Wales. Arch. J., 119, 1962, 66–91.

3768 **King** (C. Cooper). Ancient earthworks in Britain. [Pp. 34–44, Prehistoric.] Trans. Berks. Arch. Soc., 1879/80, pp. 34–48 + 2 plates. 1880.

3769 **Krämer** (Werner). The *Oppidum* of Manching [mentions British analogies]. Antiq., 34 (1960), pp. 191–200.

3770 **Morgan** (William Llewelyn). The classification of camps and earthworks. Arch. Camb., 6th S. 20, pp. 201–23. 1920.

3771 **Piggott** (Stuart). Castle Law hill-fort and Souterrain. Arch. J., 121, 1964, 186.

3772 **Sayce** (Roderick Urwick). Some suggestions concerning the purpose of hill-top camps. Collns. rel. to Montgom., 42, pp. 132–41. 1932.

3773 **Spurell** (Flaxman Charles John). Deneholes and their relation to other earthworks. J. of Proc. Essex Fld. Club, 4, 1885, lviii–lx.

3774 **Warre** (F.). On the types of ancient British earthworks. Proc. Somerset Arch. Soc., 8 (1858), pp. 63–75 + plate (4 plans). 1859.

3775 **Wheeler** (*Sir* Robert Eric Mortimer). Iron Age camps in northwestern France and southwestern Britain. Antiquity, 13, pp. 58–79 + 6 plates + 3 plans (all French). *See also* pp. 244–45. 1939.

3776 —— Multiple ramparts: a note in reply. Antiquity, 18, pp. 50–52. 1944.

3777 —— Earthwork since Hadrian Allcroft. Archaeol. J., 106 (1949, Clapham Suppl.), pp. 62–82. 1952.

3778 **Wilkinson** (*Sir* John Gardner). On ancient British walls. J. Brit. Archaeol. Ass., 17, pp. 1–8 + 3 plates. 1861.

6. FORTS, CAMPS AND EARTHWORKS BY ZONES

(a) Zone 1
[CBA Groups 7, 9, 10, 11A, 11B, 14]

3779 **Allcroft** (Arthur Hadrian). Some earthworks of west Sussex. [4 plans.]

Sussex Arch. Collns., 58, pp. 65–90. 1916.

3780 Allcroft (Arther Hadrian). Tentative explorations on Rewell hill [near Arundel]. [Figure. Early Iron Age pottery.] Sussex Arch. Collns., 61, pp. 31–39. 1920.

3781(a) The Sussex war dyke: a pre-Roman thoroughfare. Sussex Arch. Collns., 63, pp. 54–85 + map. 1922.

3781(b) Allen (Edward Heron). Archaeological discoveries in Selsey in 1912. Sussex Arch. Collns., 55, pp. 315–18; 57, pp. 224–25. 1912–15.

3782 Applebaum (Erik S.). Excavations at Wilbury hill [Herts.] in 1933. J. Brit. Archaeol. Ass., N.S. 39, pp. 352–61. 1933.

3783 —— Excavations at Wilbury hill, an Iron-Age hill-fort near Letchworth, Hertfordshire, 1933. Archaeol. J., 106 (1949), pp. 12–45. 1951.

3784 Arkell (William Joscelyn). The site of Cherbury camp [Charney Bassett, Berks.]. Oxoniensia, 4, pp. 196–97. 1939.

3785 Avery (Michael) *and others*. Rainsborough, Northants, England: excavations 1961–5 (with J. E. G. Sutton and J. W. Banks and with appendices by M. S. Tite, J. G. Evans, M. J. Aitken, H. N. Hawley and A. J. Cain). Proc. prehist. Soc., 33, 1967, 207–306 + 36 figures + 11 plates + 4 tables.

3786 Bayne (Nicholas). Excavations at Lyneham camp, Lyneham, Oxon. [2 figures + plan. Iron Age.] Oxoniensia, 22 (1957), pp. 1–10 + plate. 1958.

3787 Beldam (Joseph). Excavations . . . made at the Arbury Banks, near Ashwell, Hertfordshire. pp. 7. [Plan, British camp.] Royston 1856.

3788 Berridge (Jesse). Earthworks at Little Baddow. [c. 400 B.C.] Trans. Essex Archaeol. Soc., N.S. 19, pp. 199–200. 1930.

3789 Berry (James) *and* **Bradbrook** (William). Excavations at Norbury camp, Whaddon Chase. [6 figures + map.] Records of Bucks., 10, pp. 106–20 + 4 plates + plan. 1916.

3790 Birch, *Mrs*. A Carshalton camp. Surrey Archaeol. Collns., 36, pp. 102–06. 1925.

3791 Boyden (J. R.). Excavations at Goosehill camp, 1953–5. [3 figures + map + 3 plans. Iron Age.] Sussex Arch. Collns., 94, pp. 70–99 + plate + plan. 1956.

3792 Bradford (John Spencer Purvis). The excavation of Cherbury camp, 1939, an interim report. [Plan.] Oxoniensia, 5, pp. 13–20 + 2 plates. 1940.

3793 —— An Early Iron Age site on Blewburton hill, Berks. [5 figures (Iron Age A pottery).] Berks. Archaeol. J., 46, pp. 97–104 + 2 plates. 1942.

3793(b) Burry (H. T. Pullen). The circus on Park Brow, Sompting. Sussex Arch. Collns., 65, pp. 242–50. 1924.

3793(c) Burstow (George Philip). The prehistory of Highdown hill. [5 figures.] Sussex County Mag., 15, pp. 76–81. 1941.

3794 —— The prehistory of the Caburn. [7 figures.] Sussex County Mag., 15, pp. 214–20. 1941.

3795 —— Finds on Combe hill, Jevington. Sussex N. & Q., 11, pp. 54–56. 1946.

3796 —— *and* **Holleyman** (G. A.) Excavations at Ranscombe Camp, 1959–1960. Sussex Arch. Collections, 102, 1964, 55–67, 4 plates + 12 figures.

3798 Case (Humphrey). The Neolithic causewayed camp at Abingdon, Berks. [4 figures + plan. Pottery, *etc*.] Antiq. J., 36, pp. 11–30. 1956.

3799 Clarke (Rainbird). Holkham Camp, Norfolk. Proc. prehist. Soc., N.S. 2, 1936, 231–33 + 1 plate.

3800 Clinch (George). Ancient earthworks [in Sussex]. V.C.H., Sussex, 1, pp. 453–80 + map. 1905.

3801 —— *and* **Montgomerie** (Duncan N.). Ancient earthworks [in Surrey]. [41 plans.] V.C.H., Surrey, 4, pp. 379–405 + map. 1912.

3802 Coffin (Stephen). Bow hill camp and its south-west corner. [Plan.] Sussex N. & Q., 13, pp. 135–37. 1951.

3803 Cole (William). Report of the Committee appointed to investigate the ancient earthwork in Epping Forest. Known as the "Loughton" or "Cowper's" Camp. Trans. Essex Fld. Club, 3, 1883, 212–30 + 2 plates + 3 figures.

3804 Collins (A. E. P.). Excavations on Blewburton hill, 1947. (——, 1948 and 1949). [6 figures + 3 plans. (10 figures + 6 plans).] Berks. Archaeol. J., 50, pp. 4–29 + 6 plates. 1947; 53, pp. 21–64 + 6 plates. 1953.

3805 Collins (A. E. P.) *and* **Collins** (F. J.). Excavations on Blewburton Hill, 1953. [4 plates + 8 figures + 1 pull-out plan.] Berks. Arch. J., 57, 1959, 52–73.

3806 Colvin (H. M.). An Iron-Age hill-fort at Dover? [Plan.] Antiquity, 33, pp. 125–27. 1959.

3807 Cook (Norman) *and* **Jessup** (Ronald Frederick). Excavations in Rose wood, Ightham, 1933. Arch. Cant., 45, pp. 16–67. 1933.

3808 Cotton (Molly Aylwin). Excavations at Ambresbury Banks, 1956. [Early Iron Age A.] Essex Nat., 30, pp. 43–44. 1957.

3809 —— Alfred's Castle. [plates 1 + figures 1.] Berks. Arch. J., 58, 1960, 44–48.

3810 —— Robin Hood's Arbour: and rectilinear enclosures in Berkshire. [3 plates + 5 figures.] Berks. Arch. J., 59, 1961, 1–35.

3811 —— Berkshire hill forts. [Figure 1.] Berks. Arch. J., 60, 1962, 30–52.

3812 Crouch (Walter). Ancient entrenchments at Uphall, near Barking, Essex. [2 figures + plan.] Essex Nat., 7, pp. 131–38. 1893.

3813 —— Ancient entrenchments at Uphall, near Ilford, Essex. [Plan.] J. Brit. Archaeol. Ass., N.S. 4, pp. 291–93. 1898.

3814 Curwen (Eliot) *and* **Curwen** (Eliot Cecil). Earthworks and Celtic road, Binderton. [Plan.] Sussex Arch. Collns., 66, pp. 163–71. 1925.

3815 —— *and* —— Two wealden promontory forts. Sussex Arch. Collns., 66, pp. 176–80. 1925.

3816 —— *and* —— Excavations in the Caburn, near Lewes. Sussex Arch. Collns., 68, pp. 1–56 + plan. 1927.

3817 —— *and* —— Thundersbarrow hill. Sussex Arch. Collns., 71, pp. 258–59. 1930.

3818 Curwen (Eliot). Rackham bank and earthwork. Sussex Arch. Collns., 73, pp. 168–86. 1932.

3819 —— *and* **Curwen** (Eliot Cecil). Late Bronze Age ditches at Selmeston. Sussex Arch. Collns., 79, pp. 195–98. 1938.

3820 —— *and* —— The earthworks on Rewell hill, near Arundel. Sussex Arch. Collns., 61, pp. 20–30 + plate + plan. 1920.

3821 Curwen (Eliot Cecil). The old people of Mount Caburn. [5 figures.] Sussex County Mag., 1, pp. 10–15. 1927.

3822 —— Excavations in the Trundle, Goodwood, 1928. (—Second session, 1930.) Sussex Arch. Collns., 70, pp. 32–85 + plate + plan; 72, pp. 100–49 + 3 plans. 1929–31.

3823 —— Neolithic camp, Combe hill, Jevington. [Plan.] Sussex Arch. Collns., 70, pp. 209–11. 1929.

3824 —— Wolstonbury. [3 figures + plan. Iron Age camp.] Sussex Arch. Collns., 71, pp. 237–45. 1930.

3825 —— Excavations at Hollingbury [camp]. Sussex N. & Q., 3, p. 187. 1931.

3826 —— Whitehawk Neolithic camp. Sussex N. & Q., 3, pp. 188–89. 1931.

3827 —— *and* **Williamson** (R. J. Ross). The date of Cissbury camp. Being a report on excavations undertaken for the Worthing Archaeological Society. [5 figures + map.] Antiq. J., 11, pp. 14–36 + 4 plates + plan. 1931.

3828 —— Timber palisades at Hollingbury. Antiquity, 5, pp. 491–92 + 2 plates. 1931.

3829 —— The Caburn: its date, and a fresh find. [Figure + plan.] Sussex Arch. Collns., 72, pp. 150–55. 1931.

3830 —— Excavations at Hollingbury camp, Sussex. [Map + 2 plans.] Antiq. J., 12, pp. 1–16 + 4 plates + plan. 1932.

3831 —— The Hollingbury rampart palisades. Antiq. J., 13, pp. 162–63. 1933.

3832 —— Excavations in Whitehawk Neolithic camp, Brighton, 1932–3. Antiq. J., 14, pp. 99–133 + 4 plates + 3 plans. 1934.

3833 —— Cross-ridge dykes [on Downs] in Sussex. Aspects of Archaeology. . . . Essays presented to O. G. S. Crawford, pp. 93–107. 1951.

3834 —— Hollingbury Camp. Arch. J., 116, 1959, 234.

3835(a) Dawkins (*Sir* William Boyd). On Bigbury camp and the Pilgrims' Way. Archaeol. J., 59, pp. 211–18 + 3 plates. 1902.

3835(b) Densham (H. B. A. Ratcliffe) *and* **Densham** (M. M. Ratcliffe). An Anomalous earthwork of the Late Bronze Age on Cock Hill, Sussex.

Sussex Arch. Collections, 99, 1961, 78–101 + 12 plates + 6 figures.

3836 Downman (Edward A.). Ancient earthworks [in Northamptonshire]. V.C.H., Northants., 2, pp. 397–419 + map. 1906.

3837 Dyer (James F.). Ravensburgh castle. [Early Iron Age.] Herts. Countryside, 8, p. 70. 1953.

3838 —— A secondary Neolithic camp at Waulud's Bank, Leagrave, Bedfordshire. Beds. Archaeologist, 1, pp. 9–16 + plan. 1955.

3839 —— Bedfordshire earthworks, 1—Maiden Bower, Dunstable. Beds. Mag. 7, No. 56, 1961, 320–24 + 3 figures.

3840 —— Waulud's Bank, Leagrave. Beds. Mag., 8, N. 58, 1961, 57–64 + 6 figures.

3841 —— The hill-forts of Bedfordshire. Beds. Mag. 8, No. 59, 1961, 112–18 + 7 figures.

3842 —— Dray's Ditches, Bedfordshire, and early Iron Age territorial boundaries in the eastern Chilterns. Ant. J. 41, 1961, pp. 32–43.

3843 —— Earthworks of the Icknield Way: Part One. Beds. Mag., 8, 60, 1962, 161–66 + 5 figures.

3844 —— Earthworks of the Icknield Way: Part two. Beds. Mag. 8, No. 61, 1962, 200–05 + 5 figures.

3845 —— The Chiltern Grim's Ditch. Antiquity, 37, 1963, pp. 46–49.

3846 Fell (Clare Isobel). The Hunsbury hill-fort, Northants. A new survey of the material. Archaeol. J., 93 (1936), pp. 57–100 + 14 plates. 1937.

3847 —— Hunsbury hill. Archaeol. J., 110 (1955), pp. 212–13. 1954.

3848 Fennell (K. R.). Excavations at O.S. 38, Tallington. Rpts. & Papers Lincs., A. & A.S., 9, 1961, 26–34 + 2 figures.

3849 Fowler (P. J.). Excavations at Madmarston Camp, Swalcliffe, 1957–8. Oxoniensia, 25, 1960, 3–48 + 19 figures + 3 plates.

3850 Fox (*Sir* Cyril) *and* **Clarke** (Louis Colville Gray). Excavations in Bulstrode camp. Records of Bucks., 11, pp. 283–88 + 4 plates + plan. 1924.

3851 Francis (Alfred G.). On a causeway at the prehistoric settlement of Southchurch, Essex. [Bronze Age.]

Trans. Southend Ant. Soc., 2, pp. 49–75.

3852 Frere (S. S.). Ivinghoe. Record of Bucks., 17 (4), 1964, 315.

3853 Gould (Isaac Chalkley). Notes upon an earthwork near Harlow railway station. Trans. Essex. Archaeol. Soc., N.S. 5, pp. 95–98 + plan. 1895.

3854 —— Ancient earthworks [in Kent]. [51 plans.] V.C.H., Kent, 1, pp. 389–455 + maps. 1908.

3855 Griffith (J.). Redbourne camp. S. Albans Archit. & Archaeol. Soc., Trans., 1887, pp. 66–69 + plan. 1888.

3856 Hamlin (Ann). Excavations of ring-ditches and other sites at Stanton Harcourt. Oxoniensia, 28, 1963, 1–19 + 10 figures.

3857 Hanworth (Viscountess) *and* **Hastings** (F. A.). Excavation of a mound in Weston Wood, Albury. Surrey Arch. Collections, 58, 1961, 92–103 + 3 figures.

3858 Harden (Donald Benjamin). A ring-ditch at Long Hanborough, Oxon. [Bronze Age.] Oxoniensia, 11/12, p. 175 + plate. 1947.

3859 Hardy (William Kyle). The riddle of Sidown warren. Trans. Newbury F.C., 7 (1934–37), pp. 52–57. 1937.

3860 Harrison (*Sir* Edward). Oldbury hill, Ightham. Arch. Cant., 45, pp. 142–61 + 2 plates. 1933.

3861 Hartley (Brian Rodgerson). The Wandlebury Iron Age hill-fort, excavations of 1955–6. Proc. Camb. Antiq. Soc., 50 (1956), pp. 1–27 + 3 plates. 1957.

3863 Hogg (Alexander Hubert Arthur) *and* **O'Neil** (Bryan Hugh St. John). A causewayed earthwork in Kent. Antiquity, 11, pp. 223–25. 1937.

3864 —— —— *and* **Stevens** (Courtnay Edward). Earthworks on Hayes and West Wickham commons. Arch. Cant., 54 (1941), pp. 28–34 + plan. 1942.

3865 —— An Earthwork at Sutton Hoo. Antiq., 35, 1961, pp. 53–55.

3866 Holden (E. M.). Earthworks on Court hill. Sussex N. & Q., 13, pp. 183–85. 1951.

3867 Holleyman (G. A.). Harrowhill excavation, 1936. Sussex Arch. Collns., 78, pp. 230–51. 1937.

3868 Hollingdale (J. A.). Ranscombe camp [facing Mount Caburn]. Sussex N. & Q., 5, pp. 124–25. 1934.

3869 Hulme (Edward Wyndham). The War dyke. N. H. & Archaeol. Soc., Littlehampton, Rpts. & Proc., 1928–30, pp. 24–34 + plate. 1931.

3870 Huntingford (George Wynn Brereton). The ancient earthworks of north Berkshire. Berks. Archaeol. J., 40, pp. 157–75 + 3 plans. 1936.

3871 Hussey (Richard C.). The British settlement in Bigbury wood, Harbledown. Arch. Cant., 9, pp. 13–15 + plan. 1874.

3872 Jenkins (Frank). Interim report on excavations at Bigberry Camp, Hambledown, near Canterbury, 1962–1963. Arch. Cantiana, 78, 1963, xlvii–xlviii.

3873 Jessup (Ronald Frederick). Trial excavations at Bigberry camp, Harbledown, Kent. Antiq. J., 14, pp. 294–97. 1934.

3874 —— *and* **Cook** (Norman C.). Excavations at Bigberry camp, Harbledown. Arch. Cant., 48, pp. 151–68 + 8 plates + plan. 1936.

3875 —— Objects from Bigberry camp, Harbledown, Kent. Antiq. J., 18, pp. 174–76 + plate. 1938.

3876 Jowitt (Robert Lionel Palgrave). A guide to St. Albans and Verulamium. pp. 216 + 14 plates. 8º. London, 1935.

3877(a) Karslake (J. B. P.). Pre-Roman Silchester. [Plan.] Trans. Newbury F.C., [6] 1930–33, pp. 204–09. 1933.

3877(b) Keef (P. A. M.). Harting hill hut shelters. [5 figures + plan. Pp. 187–91, The Iron Age pottery from huts I and II, by Sheppard Frere.] Sussex Arch. Collns., 89, pp. 179–91. 1950.

3878 Kempe (Alfred John). On an intrenched camp at Wimbledon, in Surrey, and on the termination don or dune in that name. Archaeologia, 31, pp. 518–21. 1846.

3879 Kimball (Day). Cholesbury camp [Bucks.]. J. Brit. Archaeol. Ass., N.S. 39, pp. 187–208 + 7 plates + 2 plans. 1933.

3880 Laver (Henry). A survey of Grymes dyke and the other earthworks on Lexden heath [Colchester]. Trans. Essex Archaeol. Soc., N.S. 11, pp. 19–20 + plan. 1911.

3881 Laver (Philip G.). On an earthwork to the north-east of Essex. Trans. Essex Archaeol. Soc., N.S. 16, pp. 214–15 + 2 plates. 1923.

3882 Leach (Arthur L.). Earthworks in north-west Kent. Woolwich Ant. Soc., Ann. Rpt., 17 (1911), pp. 28–35. 1912.

3883 Leeds (Edward Thurlow). Chastleton camp, Oxfordshire, a hillfort of the Early Iron Age. Antiq. J., 11, pp. 382–98 + 2 plates + plan. 1931.

3884 —— Rectangular enclosures of the Bronze Age in the upper Thames valley. Antiq. J., 14, pp. 414–16 + 2 plates. 1934.

3885 Lowther (Anthony William George). "Caesar's camp", Wimbledon, Surrey. The excavations of 1931. Archaeol. J., 102 (1945), pp. 15–20 + 3 plates. 1946.

3886 —— Report on excavations at the site of the Early Iron Age camp in the grounds of Queen Mary's hospital, Carshalton, Surrey. [14 figures + map.] Surrey Archaeol. Collns., 49, pp. 56–74 + 2 plates + map. 1946.

3887(a) Mackay (R. Robertson). The Excavation of the causewayed camp at Staines, Middlesex. Archaeol. News Letter 7 vi, 1962, 131–38 + 4 plates.

3887(b) Manning (W. H.). The Excavation of a mound near Caesar's camp, Easthampstead. [Figures 2.] Berks. Arch. J., 6, 1963/64, 92–95.

3888 Margary (Ivan Donald). A Celtic enclosure in Ashdown forest. Sussex N. & Q., 3, pp. 71–73. 1930.

3889 —— King's Standing, Ashdown forest. Sussex N. & Q., 3, pp. 72, 74–76. 1930.

3890 —— Dry Hill Camp, Lingfield, Surrey. Surrey Arch. Collections, 61, 1964, 100.

3891 Martin (William). A Sussex hill-fort. Antiquary, 43, pp. 11–13. 1907.

3892 Meldola (Raphael), **Rivers** (A. H. L. F. P.) *and* **Cole** (W.). Preliminary report of the Committee appointed to investigate the ancient earthwork in Epping Forest, known as the "Loughton" or "Cowper's" Camp [1A]. Advm. Sci., 1882, 274–75; 1882, 243–52 + 2 plates.

3893 Money (James H.). A promontory camp above the High Rocks near Tunbridge Wells. Sussex N. & Q., 8, pp. 33–34. 1940.

3894 —— An interim report on excavations at High Rocks, Tunbridge Wells, 1940. Sussex Arch. Collns., 82 (1941), pp. 104–09 + plate + plan. 1942.

3895 Musson (Reginald Coulson). Excavation of Combe hill camp, Jevington, Sussex. Arch. News Letter, 2, pp. 141–42. 1950.

3896 —— An excavation at Combe hill camp near Eastbourne, August 1949. Sussex Arch. Collns., 89, pp. 105–16. 1950.

3897 O'Neil (Bryan Hugh St. John). The promontory fort on Keston common. [Plan. Early Iron Age. Defended on two long sides by bog.] Arch. Cant., 45, pp. 124–28 + plate. 1933.

3898 Oswald (Adrian). Some unrecorded earthworks in Nottinghamshire. Trans. Thoroton Soc., 43 (1939), pp. 1–15 + 4 plates. 1940.

3899 Parker (James). History of Letcombe castle. Trans. Newbury F.C., 2 (1872–75), pp. 181–83. 1878.

3900 Peake (Harold John Edward). Ancient earthworks [in Berkshire]. [26 plans.] V.C.H., Berks., 1, pp. 251–84 + map. 1906.

3901 —— Trial excavation at Lambourne place. [Figure. Iron Age earthwork. Pottery.] Trans. Newbury F.C., 7 (1934–37), pp. 109–12. 1937.

3902 Perkins (John Bryan Ward). Excavations on Oldbury hill, Ightham, 1938. Arch. Cant., 51 (1939), pp. 137–81 + 9 plates + map + 2 plans. 1940.

3903 —— Excavations on the Iron Age hill-fort of Oldbury, near Ightham, Kent. Archaeologia, 90, pp. 127–76 + 8 plates + map + plan. 1944.

3904 Petch (D. F.). Excavation of a site at Tallington. R. & P. Lincs. A. & A.S., 8, 1959, 8–9.

3905 —— Excavations at Tallington. Rpts. & Papers Lincs. A. & A.S., 9, 1961, 12–13.

3906 Phene (John Samuel). The Celtic relics at Letcombe castle. Trans. Newbury F.C., 2 (1872–75), pp. 177–81. 1878.

3907 Phillips (Charles William). Ancient earthworks [in Cambridgeshire]. V.C.H., Cambs., 2, pp. 1–47 + 2 maps. 1948.

3908 Phillipson, David. Bathend Clump: an "Iron Age Hill Fort" of the 18th Century A.D.? Antiquity, 37, 1963, pp. 225–26.

3909 Philp (Brian). Enclosures, Hayes common. Archaeol. Cant., 71 (1957), pp. 233–36. 1958.

3910 —— Reculver: excavations on the Roman Fort in 1957. [Prehistoric layer: Iron Age A sherds.] Arch. Cantiana 73, 1959, pp. 96–115 + 4 figures.

3911 Piggott (Stuart). Trial excavation at Ram's Hill [camp]. Trans. Newbury F.C., 8, pp. 116–17. 1939.

3912 —— and **Piggott** (Cecily Margaret). Excavations at Ram's Hill, Uffington, Berks. Antiq. J., 20, pp. 465–80 + 6 plates + plan. 1940.

3913 —— and —— The excavations at Ram's Hill, 1939. Trans. Newbury F.C., 8, pp. 171–77. 1940.

3914 Potts (William). Ancient earthworks [in Oxfordshire]. [2 maps + 29 plans.] V.C.H., Oxon., 2, pp. 303–349 + map. 1907.

3915 Pydduke (Edward). Water supply for downland camps. Sussex N. & Q., 13, p. 89. 1950.

3916 Rhodes (P. P.). A prehistoric and Roman site at Wiltenham Clumps, Berks. Oxoniensia, 13, pp. 18–31 + plate. 1948.

3917(a) Rivers (Augustus Henry Lane Fox Pitt). An examination into the character and probable origin of the hill forts of Sussex. Archaeologia, 42, pp. 27–76 + 3 plans. 1869.

3917(b) —— Excavations at Mount Caburn camp, near Lewis, September and October 1887, and July 1872. No reference given and not in BM catalogue of published books.

3918 —— On the threatened destruction of the British earthworks near Dorchester, Oxfordshire. J. Ethnolog. Soc., N.S. 2, pp. 412–15 + plate. 1870.

3919 —— Excavations in Cissbury camp, Sussex. J. Anth. Inst., 5, pp. 357–90 + 3 plates + 3 plans. 1876.

3920 —— Report on the excavation of the earthwork known as Ambresbury Banks, Epping Forest. Trans. Epping

Forest & Cty. Essex Fld. Club, 2, 1882, 55–68 + 3 plates.

3921 Rivers (Augustus Henry Lane Fox Pitt). Excavations at Caesar's camp near Folkstone, conducted in June and July, 1878. Archaeologia, 47, pp. 429–65 + 4 plates + plan. 1883.

3925 Robarts (N. F.). Notes on a recently discovered British camp near Wallington [Surrey]. [8 figures.] J. Anthrop. Inst., 35, pp. 387–97. 1905.

3926 —— *and* **Collyer** (Henry C.). Additional notes upon the British camp near Wallington [Surrey]. Man, 11, pp. 38–41, 103–06. 1911.

3928 Simmons (B. B.). Iron Age hill forts in Nottinghamshire. Trans. Thoroton Soc., 67, 1963, 9–20 + 6 figures.

3929 Smith (Charles Roach). The British oppidum at Cobham. Arch. Cant., 11, pp. 121–22. 1877.

3930 —— Holwood and Keston. Arch. Cant., 13, pp. 1–7. 1880.

3931 —— British moated oppidum near Staplehurst. Arch. Cant., 13, pp. 492–93. 1880.

3932 Smith (Reginald Allender). The Hunsbury hill finds. Archaeol. J., 69, pp. 421–32. 1912.

3933 Smith (Worthington George). Maiden Bower [earthwork, Dunstable], Bedfordshire. Proc. Soc. Antiq., 2 S. 27, pp. 143–61. 1915.

3934 Stephenson (R.). The Devil's ditch. Trans. Cambs. & Hunts. Arch. Soc., 3, pp. 287–90. 1914.

3935 Stevens (Joseph). Walbury camp. Trans. Newbury F.C., 2 (1872–1875), pp. 96–101. 1878.

3936 Stevenson (William). Ancient earthworks [in Nottinghamshire]. [24 figures.] V.C.H., Notts., 1, pp. 289–316 + map. 1906.

3937 Taylor (Horace D.). A prehistoric camp in Hadley Wood. [Plan.] Trans. London & Middx. Arch. Soc., N.S. 4, pp. 97–99. 1922.

3938 Thomas (Nicholas). Excavations, Big Rings, Dorchester [Oxon.]. Arch. News Letter, 4, p. 92. 1952.

3939 Toms (Herbert S.). Prehistoric valley entrenchments. Interesting discovery near Falmer. 1 page. [Plan. Extracted from Brighton Herald, Sept. 7, 1907.] 1907.

3940 —— Valley entrenchments near Falmer, Sussex. Antiquary, 43, pp. 427–29. 1907.

3941 —— Excavations at the Beltout valley entrenchments. [2 figures + plan. Bronze Age.] Sussex Arch. Collns., 55, pp. 41–55. 1912.

3942 —— Neolithic entrenchments. Lecture on the Beltout works. Trans. Eastbourne N.H. Soc., N.S. 5, pp. 50–51. 1913.

3943 —— A record of the valley-side entrenchment in Bramble bottom, Eastdean. [Plan.] Trans. Eastbourne N.H., Soc., N.S. 5, pp. 58–62. 1913.

3944 —— Notes on a survey of Hollingbury camp. Brighton & Hove Archaeologist, 1, pp. 12–21 + 2 plates + plan. 1914.

3945 —— The Cissbury earthworks. [Plan.] Antiq. J., 2, pp. 377–78. 1922.

3946 —— Valley entrenchments west of the Ditching road. (*Ditto* east of ditto). [6 plans. (3 figures + 6 plans).] Brighton & Hove Archaeologist, 2, pp. 57–72; 3, pp. 42–61. 1924–26.

3947 —— Miscellaneous earthworks near Brighton. [Figure + 8 plans. Plumpton, Westmeston, Falmer, *etc.*] Sussex Arch. Collns., 68, pp. 178–97. 1927.

3948 —— Earthworks on Middle Brow [Westmeston]. [Plan. ? Late Bronze Age.] Sussex Arch. Collns., 70, pp. 206–09. 1929.

3949 Turner (Edward). On the military earthworks on the Southdowns, with a more enlarged account of Cissbury. Sussex Arch. Collns., 3, pp. 173–84. 1850.

3950 Wall (John Charles). Ancient earthworks. [Map + 20 plans.] V.C.H., Suffolk, 1, pp. 583–631 + map. 1911.

3951 —— Ancient earthworks. [6 plans. Pp. 2–3, Enfield camp.] V.C.H., Middlesex, 2, pp. 1–14 + map. 1911.

3952 Ward (Ogier). The hill-forts of Sussex. Papers of the Eastbourne N.H. Soc., 8 (1875–76), pp. 3. 1876.

3953 Warren (S. Hazzledine). Excavations in pillow mounds at High Beach. [2 figures + map. Iron Age pottery found.] Essex Nat., 21, pp. 214–26 + plate. 1926.

3954 —— Report on excavations in Loughton camp in Epping forest, carried out by the Essex Field Club during 1926 and 1927. [4 figures. Early La Tène.] Essex Nat., 22, pp. 117–38 + 4 plates + plan. 1927.

3955 Wheeler (*Sir* Robert Eric Mortimer). A prehistoric metropolis: the first Verulamium. [6 figures + 2 plans.] Antiquity, 6, pp. 133–47 + 8 plates. 1932.

3956 —— *and* **Verney** (Tessa). Verulamium, a Belgic and two Roman cities. *Reports of the Research Committee of the Society of Antiquaries of London*, 11, pp. xii, 244 + 120 plates. 8º. Oxford, 1936.

3957 —— The Devil's dyke, Wheathampstead. [Pre-Roman (Belgic).] St. Albans Archit. & Archaeol. Soc., N.S. 5, pp. 95–98 + 2 plates. 1939.

3958 White (D. A.). Excavations at the War Ditches, Cherry Hinton, 1961–1962. Proc. Camb. Ant. Soc. LVI/LVII, 1962/63, 9–29.

3959 —— Excavations at the War Ditches, Cherry Hinton, 1949–51. [6 figures.] Proc. Camb. Ant. Soc., LVI/LVII, 1962–63, 30–41.

3960 Whitwell (J. B.). A Rectangular crop mark, Saxilby. Rpts. & paps. Lincs. A. & A.S. 10, 1963, 4.

3961 Williams (*Mrs.* Audrey). Excavations at Langford downs, Oxon. (near Lechlade) in 1943. Oxoniensia, 11/12, pp. 44–64 + 3 plates. 1947.

3962 Williamson (R. P. Ross). Excavations in Whitehawk Neolithic camp, near Brighton. (—Third session, 1935.) Sussex Arch. Collns., 71, pp. 56–96; 77, pp. 60–92 + section + 2 plans. 1930–36.

3963 Wilson (Arthur Ernest). Excavations in the ramparts and gateway of the Caburn, August–October 1937. Interim report. Sussex Arch. Collns., 79, pp. 168–94 + plate + plan. 1938.

3964 —— Excavations at the Caburn, 1930. Sussex Arch. Collns., 80, pp. 193–213. 1939.

3965 —— Report on the excavations on Highdown hill, Sussex, August 1939. Sussex Arch. Collns., 81, pp. 173–203 + plan. 1940.

3966 —— Excavations on Highdown hill, 1947. Sussex Arch. Collns., 89, pp. 163–78. 1950.

3967 —— The Devil's Dyke. Arch. J., 116, 1959, 233.

3968 Winbolt (Samuel Edward). Castle hill camp, Tonbridge. Arch. Cant., 41, pp. 193–95. 1929.

3969 —— Excavations at Holmbury camp, Surrey, April 1930. Surrey Archaeol. Collns., 38, pp. 156–70 + 4 plates. 1930.

3970 —— Excavation at Saxonbury camp [Eridge park]. Sussex Arch. Collns., 71, pp. 222–36. 1930.

3971 —— Excavations at Hascombe camp, Godalming, June–July 1931. [Iron Age. 6 figures + plan.] Surrey Archaeol. Collns., 40, pp. 78–96 + 3 plates. 1932.

3972 —— *and* **Margary** (Ivan Donald). Dry Hill camp, Lingfield. [Early Iron Age. Figure.] Surrey Archaeol. Collns., 41, pp. 79–92 + 3 plates + plan. 1933.

3973 —— Ancient earthworks at [i] Nutbourne common and [ii] Hurston warren, Pulborough. A revision. Sussex N. & Q., 5, pp. 53–54. 1934.

3974 —— An Early Iron Age camp in Piper's copse, Kirdford. [Figure + plan.] Sussex Arch. Collns., 77, pp. 244–49. 1936.

3975 Wolseley (Garnet R.), **Smith** (Reginald Allender) *and* **Hawley** (William). Prehistoric and Roman settlements on Park Brow [Sussex]. [62 figures + 12 plans.] Archaeologia, 76, pp. 1–40. 1927.

3976 Wood (Peter). The Early Iron Age camp called Grimsbury Castle, near Hermitage, Berks. [2 plates + 3 figures.] Berks. Arch. J. 57, 1959, 74–82.

3977 —— *and* **Hardy** (J. R.). Perborough Castle and its field system. [Figures 2.] Berks. Arch. J. 60, 1962, 53–61.

3978 —— Excavations in 1960 at Grimsbury Castle, near Hermitage, Berks. Trans. Newbury Dist. Fld. Club, XI ii, 1963, 53–61 + 4 figures.

3979 Woodard (Peter). Excavations on Wolstonbury hill (1950). Sussex N. & Q., 13, pp. 131–34. 1951.

(b) Zone 2—[CBA Group 12]

3980 Annable (F. Kenneth). Excavation, Windmill hill, Avebury. Neolithic causewayed camp. Wilts. Arch. Mag., 57, p. 3. 1958.

3981 Annable (F. Kenneth). Cow Down, Longbridge Deverell: Early Iron Age enclosures. Wilts. Arch. Mag., 57, pp. 9–10. 1958.

3982 —— Down Barn West, Winterbourne Gunner: a trapezoidal enclosure of probable Early Iron Age AB date. Wilts. Arch. Mag., 57, pp. 10–11. 1958.

3983 —— Nash Hill promontory camp; Early Iron Age. Wilts. Arch. Mag., 57, pp. 16–17 + plate. 1958.

3984 —— Down Barn West, Winterbourne Gunner [Wilts.]: a ditched enclosure of Early Iron Age date. Wilts. Arch. Mag., 57, p. 233. 1959.

3985 [Anon.] Maidun Castle purchased for the Prince of Wales. J. Brit. Archaeol. Ass., N.S. 19, pp. 293–94. 1913.

3986 [Anon.] Hambledon hill. Proc. Dorset Antiq. F.C., 46, pp. 73–74. 1925.

3987 [Anon.] Windmill hill, Wiltshire. Antiquity, 1, pp. 104–05. 1927.

3989 Barnes (William). Cranborne—the so-called castle. Proc. Dorset Antiq. F.C., 4, pp. 134–36. 1880.

3990 —— A study on the Buckley or Bockerley dyke and others in Dorset. Proc. Dorset Antiq. F.C., 5, pp. 49–56. 1881.

3991 —— Some slight notes on Badbury Rings. Proc. Dorset Antiq. F.C., 5, pp. 38–39. 1881.

3992 —— Eggerdon and British tribeship. Proc. Dorset Antiq. F.C., 5, pp. 40–46. 1881.

3993 —— Maiden Castle. Proc. Dorset Antiq. F.C., 14, pp. 55–61. 1893.

3994 Benfield (Eric). The town of Maiden Castle. pp. 70 + 11 plates + map (of Iron Age hill forts of western England). 8º. London, 1947.

3995 Boon (George C.). Excavation at Silchester, 1954–7: an interim report. Papers & proc. Hants. F.C., 21, pt. 1, 1958, pp. 9–21 + 2 plates + 5 figures.

3996 Brailsford (John William) *and* **Richmond** (Ian Archibald). British Museum excavation at Hod hill, Dorset. (Prehistoric hill-fort + Roman fort.] Brit. Mus. Q., 17, pp. 49–50. 1952.

3997 —— Hod Hill: Vol 1, Antiquities from Hod Hill in the Durden Collection, London, 1962. pp. viii + 24, 14 plates, plan, 15 figures.

3998 Bunting (G. H.). Bury Wood Camp, Colerne, Wilts. Appendix IV: Animal bones (seasons 1959, 1960). Wilts. Arch Mag., 58, No. 210, pp. 204–5. 1962.

3999 Chadwick (S. E.) *and* **Thompson** (M. W.). Note on an Iron Age habitation site near Battlesbury camp, Warminster. [Figure (pottery) + plan.] Wilts. Arch. Mag., 56, pp. 262–64. 1956.

4000 Chancellor (Ernest Clive). Badbury Rings reviewed. Proc. Dorset Archaeol. Soc., 66 (1944), pp. 19–30. 1945.

4001 Clay (Richard Challoner Cobbe). Chiselbury camp [Fovant]. Wilts. Archaeol. Mag., 47, pp. 20–24 + plate. 1935.

4002 Clift (J. G. Neilson). Maiden Castle, Dorchester. J. Brit. Archaeol. Ass., N.S. 13, pp. 157–68 + 2 folding plans. 1907.

4003 Cowie (J. W.). Bury Wood Camp, Colerne, Wilts. Appendix II: heated limestone experiments. Wilts. Arch. Mag., 58, No. 210, pp. 200–01. 1962.

4004 Cunnington (Benjamin Howard) *and* **Cunnington** (Maud Edith). Casterley camp [Salisbury plain]. Wilts. Archaeol. Mag., 38, pp. 53–105 + 13 plates + 3 plans. 1913.

4005 Cunnington (Edward). Hambledon hill, Dorset. Proc. Dorset Antiq. F.C., 16, pp. 156–58. 1895.

4006 Cunnington (*Mrs.* Maud Edith). Notes on excavations at Oliver's Camp, near Devizes, Wilts. Man, 8, pp. 7–13. 1908.

4007 —— On a remarkable feature in the entrenchments of Knap Hill camp, Wiltshire. [Plan.] Man, 9, pp. 49–52. 1909.

4008 —— Knap Hill camp. Wilts. Archaeol. Mag., 37, pp. 42–65 + plate. 1911.

4009 —— Lidbury camp [Wilts.]. [Plan. Early Iron Age.] Wilts. Archaeol. Mag., 40, pp. 12–36 + 8 plates + 2 plans. 1917.

4010 —— Pits in Battlesbury camp. Wilts. Archaeol. Mag., 42, pp. 368–73. 1923.

4011 —— Figsbury Rings. An account of excavations in 1924. Wilts. Archaeol. Mag., 43, pp. 48–58. 1925.

4012 —— Yarnbury castle [on Salisbury plain]. Antiquity, 6, pp. 471–74 + plate. 1932.

4013 Cunnington (*Mrs*. Maud Edith). The demolition of Chisenbury trendle [by R.A.F., as danger to landing]. Wilts. Archaeol. Mag., 46, pp. 1–3 + plate. 1932.

4014 —— Excavations in Yarnbury castle camp, 1932. [Iron Age.] Wilts. Archaeol. Mag., 46, pp. 198–213 + 15 plates + 3 plans. 1933.

4015 Davies (W. J.). Bury Wood Camp, Colerne, Wilts. Appendix 1: Topographical Note. Wilts. Arch. Mag., 58, No. 210, pp. 199–200. 1962.

4016 Dunning (Gerard Clough). Chillerton down camp, Gatcombe, Isle of Wight. Proc. I. of W. N.H. & Arch. Soc., 4, pp. 51–53 + 3 plates + plan. 1947.

4017 Farrar (Raymond Anthony Holt). An Early Iron Age fort on Shipton hill, Shipton gorge. Proc. Dorset Archaeol. Soc., 77 (1955), pp. 135–36 + plate. 1956.

4018 Field (N. H.). An Excavation at the earthwork in Bowley's Plantation, Owermoigne. Proc. Dorset N.H. & A.S., 81, 1960, 102–03.

4020 Forster (Robert Henry). Notes on Maiden Castle. J. Brit. Archaeol. Ass., N.S. 13, pp. 169–71 + 2 folding plans. 1907.

4021 Fowler (Peter J.). A rectangular earthwork enclosure at Tisbury, Wilts. Antiquity, 37, 1963, pp. 290–93.

4022(a) —— Interim report on an excavation in Combs Ditch, Dorset, 1964. Proc. Dorset, N.H. & A.S., 86, 1964, 112.

4022(b) Freeman (John Peere Williams). Danebury. [Figure.] Papers & Proc. Hants. F.C., 6, pp. 293–308 + 3 plans. 1909.

4022(c) —— Short cross-valley dykes [in Hants.]. [Plan.] Papers & Proc. Hants. F.C., 13, pp. 55–60 + plate + plan. 1935.

4023 Gelling (P. S.). Excavation at Pilsdon Pen. Proc. Dorset N.H. & A.S., 86, 1964, 102.

4024 Gresham (Colin A.). Spettisbury rings, Dorset. [8 figures + plan. Early Iron Age.] Archaeol. J., 96 (1939), pp. 114–31 + 7 plates. 1940.

4025 Grimes (William Francis). Maiden Castle. Antiquity, 19, pp. 6–10. 1945.

4026 Harding (D. W.). Excavation

of multiple banks, Thickthorn Down. Proc. Dorset N.H. & A.S., 81, 1959, 110–13.

4027 Hawkes (Charles Francis Christopher), **Myres** (John Nowell Linton) *and* **Stevens** (C. G.). Saint Catharine's hill, Winchester. Papers & Proc. Hants. F.C., 11, pp. xvi, 310 + 16 plates. 1929.

4028 —— —— *and* —— St. Catherine's hill, Winchester. pp. 310. 8°. Winchester, 1930. [Iron Age camp (6th–2nd c. B.C.).]

4029 —— The excavation of Buckland rings, Lymington, 1935. [6 figures.] Papers & Proc. Hants. F.C., 13, pp. 124–64 + 10 plates + 6 plans. 1936.

4030 —— The excavations at Quarley hill, 1938. Papers & Proc. Hants. F.C., 14, pp. 136–94 + 14 plates + map + 4 plans. 1939.

4031 —— The excavations at Bury hill, 1939. Papers & Proc. Hants. F.C., 14, pp. 291–337 + 7 plates. 1940.

4032 —— Pilsdon Pen camp. Archaeol. J., 107 (1950), pp. 91–92. 1952.

4033 Hawkes (Jacquetta). The place of origin of the Windmill Hill culture. Proc. prehist. Soc., N.S. 1, 1935, 127–29 + 1 plate.

4034 —— The excavations at Balksbury, 1939. Papers & Proc. Hants. F.C., 14, pp. 338–45 + plate. 1940.

4035(a) Johnston (J. L. Forde). Note on excavations at Bugbury Rings. Proc. Dorset N.H. & A.S., 80, 1958, 107–08.

4035(b) Kerslake (Thomas). Caer Pensauel coit, a long lost unromanised British metropolis, a reassertion occasioned by two reports of an Exploration Committee of the Somersetshire Arch. & Nat. Hist. Soc. [between Wilts. and Somerset, above Kilmington]. pp. 45. 8°. London, 1882.

4036 King (D. Grant). Bury Wood Camp, report on excavations, 1959. WAM, 58, 1961, 40–47 + 2 figures.

4037 —— Bury Wood Camp, report on excavations, 1960. WAM, 58, 1962, No. 210, 185–208 + 6 figures + 1 plate.

4038 Liddell (Dorothy M.). Notes on two excavations in Hampshire. [1.] Chilworth ring, 1928. Papers & Proc. Hants. F.C., 10, p. 224. 1931.

4039 McKnight (W. H. E.). On Ringsbury and other camps in north

Wiltshire. Wilts. Archaeol. Mag., 23, pp. 195–200. 1887.

4040 Major (Albany Featherstone-haugh). The filling-in of the eastern ditch at Oliver's camp, near Devizes. Antiquary, 47, pp. 219–21, 320. 1911.

4041 March (Henry Colley) *and* **Solly** (H. Sharn). A critical and material examination of the hill-fortress called Eggardun. [Figure.] Proc. Dorset Antiq. F.C., 22, pp. 28–42. 1901.

4042 —— Report on excavations on Eggardnn [Dorset], 1900. [Figure.] Proc. Soc. Antiq., 2 S. 18, pp. 258–62. 1901.

4043 Mellor (A. Shaw). Notes on Bury Wood camp, Colerne, Wilts. [Plan. Iron Age.] Wilts. Archaeol. Mag., 47, pp. 504–12. 1936.

4044 Merewether (John). The examination of Silbury hill. Proc. Archaeol. Inst., [5] Salisbury, 1849, pp. 73–81. 1851.

4045 Milner (A. B.). Some earthworks in mid-Hampshire. [3 figures. Tidbury ring: 2 barrows at Hinton Ampner.] Papers & Proc. Hants. F.C., 16, pp. 38–47. 1944.

4046 Montgomerie (Duncan H.). Old Sarum. [5 figures + 3 plans. Pp. 131–136, Early Iron Age, Roman and Saxon periods.] Archaeol. J., 104 (1947), pp. 129–43. 1948.

4047 Morgan (Octavius). Silbury hill. [Opening in 1723. *See also* p. 90.] N. & Q., 4 S. 1, p. 14. 1868.

4048 Moule (Henry Joseph). Chalbury Rings and Rindbury. Proc. Dorset Antiq. F.C., 21, pp. 188–92. 1900.

4049 Musty (J. W. G.). Upton Scudamore earthworks. [EIA "A".] WAM, 58, 1963, No. 211, 469.

4050 Ordnance Survey. Celtic earthworks of Salisbury plain: based on airphotographs. Old Sarum [sheet]. pp. 2 + map. 8°. Southampton, 1934. [Scale—1:25,000.]

4051 Pass (Alfred C.). Recent explorations at Silbury hill. Wilts. Archaeol. Mag., 23, pp. 245–54 + plate + plan. 1887.

4052 —— Recent excavations at Silbury hill. Proc. Clifton Antiq. Club, 1, pp. 130–35 + plate + plan. 1888.

4053 Passmore (A. D.). Liddington castle (camp). Wilts. Archaeol. Mag., 38, pp. 576–84 + 4 plates. 1914.

4054 —— Silbury hill. Wilts. Archaeol. Mag., 41, pp. 185–86. 1920.

4055 —— The earthen hill top camps of Wessex. pp. 7. 8°. Swindon, 1934.

4056 —— Earthwork at Ogbourne St. George. Wilts. Archaeol. Mag., 49, p. 239. 1940.

4057 Petrie (*Sir* William Matthew Flinders). Report on diggings in Silbury hill, August, 1922. Wilts. Archaeol. Mag., 42, pp. 215–18 + plate + plan. 1923.

4058 Piggott (Cecily Margaret). An Iron Age A site on Harnham hill. [6 figures (sections and pottery).] Wilts. Archaeol. Mag., 48, pp. 513–22. 1939.

4059 —— Five Late Bronze Age enclosures in North Wiltshire. Proc. prehist. Soc., 8, 1942, 48–61 + 11 figures + 3 plates.

4060 —— The Grim's Ditch complex in Cranborne chase. Antiquity, 18, pp. 65–71 + map. 1944.

4061 Piggott (Stuart). Ladle hill [Hants.]—an unfinished hillfort. [Figure.] Antiquity, 5, pp. 474–85 + 5 plates + 2 plans. 1931.

4062 —— An unrecorded Iron Age [A] enclosure on Rockbourne down, Hants. [Plan.] Papers & Proc. Hants. F.C., 15, pp. 53–55. 1941.

4063 —— The Neolithic camp on Whitesheet hill, Kilmington parish. [2 figures + plan.] Wilts. Archaeol. Mag., 54, pp. 404–10. 1952.

4064 —— Windmill Hill—East or West? Proc. prehist. Soc., 21, 1955, 96–101 + 1 plate + 1 figure.

4066 Preston (J. P.). Excavations of Early Iron Age site at Landford [Wilts.]. pp. 19. 8°. Cambridge, 1929. [11 figures + plan.]

4067 Radley (Jeffrey). Occupation remains at Bugbury Rings, Tarrant Keynston [IA to Roman]. Proc. Dorset N.H. & A.S., 86, 1964, 113–14.

4068 Rahtz (P. A.). Interim report on excavations at Hog Cliff Hill, Maiden Newton. Proc. Dorset N.H. & A.S., 81, 1960, 94.

4069 —— Interim report on excavations at Bokerly Dyke. [1 figure.] Proc. Dorset N.H. & A.S., 81, 1960, 100–102.

4070 —— Second interim report on excavations at Hog Cliff Hill, Maiden

Newton. Proc. Dorset N.H. & A.S., 82, 1961, 83.

4072 Richardson (Katharine Margaret). Excavations at Poundbury, Dorchester, Dorset, 1939. Antiq. J., 20, pp. 429–48 + 10 plates + map + plan. 1940.

4073(a) Rickman (Charles). Buzbury encampment. Proc. Dorset Antiq. F.C., 4, pp. 95–97. 1880.

4073(b) Rivers (Augustus Henry Lane Fox Pitt). Excavation of the South Lodge camp, Rushmore park: an entrenchment of the Bronze Age. Wilts. Archaeol. Mag., 27, pp. 206–22 + 2 plates + plan. 1894.

4074 Scarth (Henry Mengden). Scratchbury camp [Wilts.]. Archaeol. J., 45, pp. 90–91. 1888.

4075 Shore (Thomas William). A list of ancient camps and other ancient earthworks in Hampshire, and remarks on their present condition. Papers & Proc. Hants. F.C., 1 i, pp. 22–26. 1887.

4076 —— Celtic earthworks in Hampshire, in reference to the density of the Celtic population. Advm. Sci., 1888, 852–53.

4077 —— Celtic earthworks in Hampshire. Shore Memorial Vol. (Hants. F.C.), pp. 36–41. 1911.

4078 Smart (T. William Wake). Badbury Rings. Proc. Dorset Antiq. F.C., 11, pp. 16–26. 1890.

4079 Smith (Alfred Charles). Silbury. Wilts. Archaeol. Mag., 7, pp. 145–91 + plate + 4 plans. 1862.

4080 —— On the ancient earthwork enclosures on the downs of North Wilts., supposed to be British cattle pens. Wilts. Archaeol. Mag., 11, pp. 245–51. 1869.

4081 Smith (Isobel F.). The 1957–8 excavations at Windmill Hill. Antiquity, 32, pp. 268–69. 1958.

4082 —— Excavations at Windmill Hill, Avebury, Wilts., 1957–8. [4 figures + plan. Neolithic.] Wilts. Arch. Mag., 57, pp. 149–62 + plate. 1959.

4083 —— Radio-carbon dates from Windmill Hill [Notes and News]. Antiq., 34 (1960), pp. 212–13.

4084 Solly (H. Sharn). Eggardun hill. Proc. Dorset Antiq. F.C., 42, pp. 31–35. 1922.

4085 Spurgeon (C. J.). Two Pembrokeshire earthworks [Annexed and concentric] univall. [Scollock Rath, Walton West.] Arch. Camb., 112, 1963, 154–58 + 3 figures.

4086 Stallybrass (B.). Outer Ashley down camp. Wilts. Archaeol. Mag., 34, pp. 418–22. 1906.

4087 Stone (John F. S.). An enclosure on Boscombe down east. Wilts. Archaeol. Mag., 47, pp. 466–89 + 2 plates. 1936.

4088 Sumner (Heywood). The ancient earthworks of Cranborne Chase. pp. xiv, 82 + 2 plates + 37 maps and plans. 4°. London, *Chiswick Press*, 1913.

4089 —— The ancient earthworks of Cranborne Chase. Proc. Dorset Antiq. F.C., 34, pp. 31–41 + 4 plans. 1913.

4090 —— The ancient earthworks of the New Forest. pp. x, 142. 4°. London, *Chiswick Press*, 1917. [25 figures, plates and plans.]

4091 —— Geography and prehistoric earthworks in the New Forest district. Geog. J., 67, pp. 244–48. 1926.

4092 —— Combs ditch and Bokerly dyke, reviewed. Proc. Dorset Archaeol. Soc., 52, pp. 59–74 + plate + map. 1931.

4093 —— Ancient earthworks in the New Forest district. pp. 20 + map. 8°. *n.p.*, 1917 [6 plans.]

4094 Symonds (Henry). Dorset prehistoric earthworks as defences against the Spaniards in 1588. N. & Q. Som. & Dorset, 13, p. 125. 1913.

4095 Thompson (M. W.). Recent building at Balkesbury Camp, Andover. Papers & Proc. Hants. F.C., 21, pt. 1, 1958, p. 53.

4096 Toms (Herbert S.). Notes on some surveys of valley entrenchments in the Piddletrenthide district, central Dorset. [Bronze Age.] Proc. Dorset Antiq. F.C., 33, pp. 34–44 + plate + 3 plans. 1912.

4097 —— Chettle down earthwork: an ancient pond. Proc. Dorset Archaeol. Soc., 51, pp. 194–203 + plate + plan. 1930.

4098 Tucker (Charles). Report on the examination of Silbury hill. Proc. Archaeol. Inst., [5] Salisbury, 1849, pp. 297–303 + plan. 1851.

4099 Vatcher (Faith de Mallet Morgan). The Excavation of the Roman earthwork at Winterslow, Wilts. Ant.

J., 43, 1963, 197–213 + 1 map + 2 plates.

4100 Warne (Charles). Vindogladia Celtica. [British Wimborne.] Arch. Camb., 3rd S. 15, pp. 294–95. 1869.

4101 Webster (Graham). Further investigations of the site of the Roman Fort at Waddon Hill, Stoke Abbot, 1960–62. [Native pottery and possible IA biv.] Proc. Dorset N.H. & A.S., 86, 1964, 135–49 + 9 figures.

4102 Western (A. C.). Bury Wood Camp, Colerne, Wilts. Appendix III: Identification of charcoals. Wilts. Arch. Mag., 58, No. 210, pp. 201–04. 1962.

4103 Wheeler (*Sir* Robert Eric Mortimer). The excavation of Maiden Castle, Dorset. First (second, third) interim report. [3 figures + 8 plans.] Antiq. J., 15, pp. 265–75 + 8 plates + map + 3 plans; 16, pp. 265–83 + 8 plates + 2 plans; 17, pp. 361–82 + 13 plates + 5 plans. 1935–37.

4104 —— The excavation of Maiden Castle, Dorset. First (second, third) interim report. [3 figures + 6 plans. Neolithic–Roman.] Proc. Dorset Archaeol. Soc., 56 (1934), pp. 1–10 + 8 plates + map + 3 plans; 57 (1935), pp. 1–17 + 7 plates + map + 2 plans; 58 (1936), pp. 1–17 + 13 plates + 6 plans. 1935–37.

4105 —— Maiden Castle, Dorset. *Reports of the Research Committee of the Society of Antiquaries of London, 12.* pp. xx, 399 + 118 plates + 2 plans. 4°. Oxford, 1943. [pp. 61–78, Roman period; pp. 241–51, Roman pottery; pp. 334–37, Roman coins.]

4106 —— Maiden Castle, Dorset. *Ministry of Works.* pp. 11. 8°. London, 1951. [Plan.]

4107 Whitley (Margaret). Excavations at Chalbury camp, Dorset, 1939. [6 figures (pottery) + 2 plans. Late Bronze–Early Iron Age.] Antiq. J., 23, pp. 98–121 + 7 plates. 1943.

4108 Wilkinson (John). A report on diggings made in Silbury hill, and in the ground adjoining. [2 figures.] Wilts. Archaeol. Mag., 11, pp. 113–18. 1869.

4111 Woolley (*Sir* Charles Leonard). Excavations on Beacon hill, Hampshire, in August, 1912. [Figure + plan.] Fort. Fragment of Bronze Age pottery. Man, 13, pp. 8–10. 1913.

4112 Wrey (*Commander* E. C.). A note on the New Forest from the archaeological angle [Iron Age earthworks]. Paper & Proc. Hants. F.C., 21, pt. III, 1960, pp. 156–59.

(c) Zone 3 [CBA Groups 8, 13]

4113 Amery (Peter Fabyan Spark). Some hitherto unrecorded hill fortresses near Ashburton. Rpt. & Trans. Devon. Assoc., 6, pp. 261–65 + plate (map and plan of Chase castle). 1873.

4114 [Anon.] Maiden Castle, Dorset. [Sale by Lord Alington to Dudley of Cornwall.] N. & Q. Som. & Dorset, 13, p. 262. 1913.

4115 [Anon.] Somerset in the Bronze Age: excavations at Ham hill. J. Brit. Archaeol. Ass., N.S. 28, pp. 237–40. 1922.

4116 Anthony (I. E.). The Iron Age camp at Puston, Herefordshire. *Woolhope Club.* pp. 40 + 3 plates. 8°. Hereford, 1958. [3 figures + 2 maps + 2 plans.]

4117 Atkinson (G. M.). Clifton camps. [3 camps, one at Clifton and two (Bower Walls and Stokeleigh) in Somerset.] Proc. Somerset Arch. Soc., 15 (1868–69), pp. 27–29 + plate. 1870.

4118 Babington (Charles Cardale). Description of the ancient hill fortress of Uleybury. Archaeol. J., 11, pp. 328–29. 1852.

4119 Baddeley (Welbore St. Claire). Uleybury camp. [3 plans. Early Iron Age.] Somerset Arch. Soc., Proc. Bath branch, [7] 1934–38, pp. 67–73. 1935.

4120 Baker (Thomas John Lloyd). An account of a chain of ancient fortresses, extending through the south western part of Gloucestershire. Archaeologia, 19, pp. 161–75 + map + plan (Uleybury). 1821.

4122 Barnwell (Edward Lowry). Chun castle. [2 figures + 2 plans.] Arch. Camb., 3rd S. 11, pp. 187–95. 1865.

4123 Bate (Charles Spence). Grimspound and its associated relics. [5 figures + plan.] J. Plymouth Instn., pp. 120. 1873.

4124 Bladen (William Wells). Terraces and earthworks at Stone. (The Stone terraces and their possible origin.) North Staffs. N.C., Ann. Rpt. & Trans., 32, pp. 134–39, 150–55 + 4 plates + plan. 1898.

4125 Blight (John Thomas). The cliff-castle at Maen, near the Land's End, in the parish of S. Sennen. [2 figures.] J. Roy. Instn. Cornwall, 1 ii, pp. 8–11 + plate + plan. 1864.

4126 —— The cliff-castle at Maen, near the Land's End, in the parish of S. Sennen, Cornwall. [2 figures.] Arch. Camb., 3rd S. 11, pp. 77–81 + plate + plan. 1865.

4127 —— Notice of enclosures at Smallacombe, near the Cheeseloving, Cornwall. [3 figures.] J. Roy. Instn. Cornwall, 3, pp. 10–16 + plate. 1868.

4128 —— The cliff-castle of Kenidjack, in the parish of St. Just in Penwith, Cornwall. J. Roy. Instn. Cornwall, 3, pp. 108–09 + plan. 1868.

4129 Bothamley (C. H.). Ancient earthworks [in Somerset]. [82 plans.] V.C.H., Somerset, 2, pp. 467–532 + map. 1911.

4130 Bowen (A. R.). The hill-forts of Worcestershire and its borders. Trans. Worcs. Archaeol. Soc., N.S. 29 (1952), pp. 33–37. 1953.

4132 Brailsford (John William). Excavations at the promontory fort near Okehampton station. [2 figures + map + 2 plans.] Proc. Devon Archaeol. Expl. Soc., 3, pp. 86–91 + 2 plates. 1938.

4133 Brooks (R. T.). The Rumps, St. Minver: Interim Report on the 1963 excavations. Cornish Arch., 3, 1964, 26–34 + 2 figures.

4134 —— The Rumps, St. Minver: Second Interim Report on the 1965 season. Cornish Arch., 5, 1966, 4–10 + 1 figure.

4135 Burrow (Edward John). The ancient entrenchments and camps of Gloucestershire. pp. 176 + map. 4°. Cheltenham, 1919. New and abridged edition. pp. viii, 132. obl. 8°. Cheltenham [1924].

4137 Burrow (Edward J.). Excavations on Leckhampton hill, Cheltenham, during the summer of 1925. [6 figures + 3 plans. Tumulus and Early Iron Age camp.] Proc. Cotteswold N.F.C.,

22, pp. 95–122 + 6 plates + plan. 1925.

4138 Cantrill (Thomas Crossbee). Earthworks on Haughmond hill, near Shrewsbury. [Plan.] Trans. Caradoc & Severn Valley F.C., 6, pp. 136–42. 1917.

4139 Chanter (John Frederick). Grimspound. J. Brit. Archaeol. Ass., N.S. 33, pp. 87–89. 1927.

4140 Chatwin (Philip Boughton). Excavations on Corley camp, near Coventry. [Iron Age.] B'ham. Arch. Soc., Trans., 52 [1927], pp. 282–87 + 3 plates + plan. 1930.

4141 Clifford (Elsie Margaret). The earthworks at Rodborough, Amberley, and Minchinhampton, Gloucestershire. [2 figures + 2 plans. Pottery, etc.] Trans. Bristol & Glos. Arch. Soc., 59, pp. 287–307 + 10 plates. 1937.

4142 —— Bagendon: a Belgic oppidum; a record of the excavations of 1954–56. pp. xix + 278, 31 plates + 71 figures. 8°. Cambridge, 1961. [Pp. 22–42, The pre-Belgic Iron Age cultures of Gloucestershire, by M. Aylwin Cotton.]

4143 Cobbold (Edgar Sterling). Shropshire earthworks. Trans. Shropshire Archaeol. Soc., 3rd S. 7, pp. 166–176 + 5 plans, etc. 1907.

4144 Collins (W. G.) and **Cantrill** (Thomas Crosbee). Salisbury hill camp, near Bath. Antiquary, 45, pp. 326–31, 419–25, 451–56. 1909.

4145 Cornish (J. B.). Ancient earthworks and defensive enclosures [in Cornwall]. [7 full pages of plans.] V.C.H., Cornwall, 1, pp. 451–73. 1906.

4146 Cotton (M. Aylwin). Cornish cliff castles. [Early Iron Age.] Proc. West Cornwall F.C., 2, pp. 113–21. 1959.

4147 Cotton (William). Account of certain hill castles, situated near Land's End, in Cornwall. Archaeologia, 22, pp. 300–06 + 2 plans (Chun castle and Castle-an-Dinas). 1829.

4148 Cox (J. Stevens). Neolithic evidence, Ham Hill. N. & Q., Somerset and Dorset, 28, 1962, pt. 276, p. 83.

4149 Crofts (C. B.). Maen castle, Sennen: the excavation of an Early Iron Age promontory fort. Proc. West Cornwall F.C., N.S. 1, pp. 98–115 + plate (section). 1955.

4150 Davies (James). The British

and Roman encampments of Herefordshire. Arch. Camb., N.S. 2, pp. 45–51.
1851.

4151(a) Dawkins (*Sir* William Boyd).
Hamden hill camp: the earthworks.
Proc. Somerset Arch. Soc., 32 (1886),
pp. 43–51, 81–83 + 3 plates. 1887.

**4151(b) Devonshire Association—
Dartmoor Exploration Committee.**
First report: The exploration of Grimspound. Rpt. & Trans. Devon. Assoc.,
26, pp. 101–21 + plate + 6 plans. 1894.

4152 Dewey (Henry). In some prehistoric earthworks of unknown origin
near Boscastle. J. Roy. Instn. Cornwall,
19, pp. 137–39 + plate + plan. 1912.

4153 Dudley (Dorothy). Sub-rect-
angular earthworks with rounded cor-
ners. Proc. West Cornwall F.C., N.S. 1,
pp. 54–58. 1954.

4154 Dunning (Gerald Clough). Salmonsbury camp, Gloucestershire. Antiquity, 5, pp. 489–91 + 2 plates. 1931.

4155 —— Salmonsbury camp [Glos.].
Trans. Bristol & Glos. Arch. Soc., 56,
pp. 3–5. 1934.

4156 Dymond (Charles William).
Dolbury and Cadbury: two Somersetshire camps. J. Brit. Archaeol. Ass., 38,
pp. 398–919 + 2 plans. 1882.

4157 —— Dolbury and Cadbury
camps. Proc. Somerset Arch. Soc., 29
(1883), pp. 104–16 + 2 plans. 1884.

4158 —— Worlebury: an ancient
stronghold in the County of Somerset.
pp. i–viii, 1–104 + 11 plates + frontispiece. fol. Bristol, 1886. [Privately
printed.]

4159 —— Worlebury, an ancient
stronghold in the county of Somerset.
A new edition. pp. 124 + 8 plates +
map + 2 plans. 4⁰. Bristol, 1902.

4161 Fell (Clare Isobel). Shenbarrow
Hill Camp, Stanton, Gloucestershire.
Trans. Bristol & Glos. A.S., 80, 1961,
16–41 + 3 plates + 8 figures.

4166 Fox (*Lady* Aileen Mary). The
Castlewitch ringwork: a new henge
monument in S.E. Cornwall. Antiq. J.,
32, pp. 67–70. 1932.

4167 —— Hembury hill-fort. Archaeol. J., 114 (1957), pp. 144–47. 1959.

4168 Fryer (Alfred Cooper). Sub-
sidence of land on Clifton hill camp. J.
Brit. Archaeol. Ass., 49, pp. 159–61.
1893.

4169 Gardner (Willoughby). Ancient
defensive earthworks [in Warwickshire].
V.C.H., Warwick, 1, pp. 345–406 +
map. 1904.

4170 Gelling (Peter S.). Excavations
at Caynham Camp, near Ludlow. First
Interim Report. Trans. Shropshire A.S.,
56 ii, 1959, 145–48 + 2 figures.

4171 —— Excavations at Caynham
Camp, near Ludlow. Second Interim
Report. Trans. Shropshire A.S., 56 iii,
1960, 218–27 + 2 plates + 5 figures.

4172 —— Excavations at Caynham
Camp, near Ludlow. Final Report
[EIA]. Trans. Shropshire A.S., 57 ii,
1962/63, 91–100 + 6 figures + 1
plate.

4173 Gordon (A. S. R.). The excavation of Gurnard's head, an Iron
Age cliff castle in western Cornwall.
[Trereen Dinas.] Archaeol. J., 97 (1940),
pp. 96–111 + 4 plates. 1941.

4174 Gould (Isaac Chalkley). Ancient
earthworks [in Herefordshire]. [101
plans.] V.C.H., Hereford, 1, pp. 199–
262 + map. 1908.

4175(a) Gould (J. T.). Loaches
Banks, Bourne Pool, Aldridge. Trans.
Birmingham Arch. Soc., 77, 1959, 40–42
+ 1 plate + 2 figures.

4175(b) Gould (Sabin Baring). An
exploration of Tregear Rounds [parish of
St. Kew]. J. Roy. Instn. Cornwall, 16,
pp. 73–83 + 3 plates + plan. 1903.

4176 Gracie (H. S.). Bagendon, the
Iron Age camp. [Negative evidence
from area of new estate.] Trans. Bristol
& Glos. A.S., 80, 1961, 179.

4177 Gray (Harold St. George). Ru-
borough camp, in the parish of Broomfield, Somerset. Proc. Somerset Arch.
Soc., 49 (1903), pp. 173–82. 1904.

4178 —— Worlebury camp. Proc.
Somerset Arch. Soc., 51 i (1905), pp.
17–28. 1906.

4179 —— Maesbury camp, or Maesbury castle. Proc. Somerset Arch. Soc.,
53 (1907), pp. 73–81. 1908.

4180 —— Notes on archaeological
remains found on Ham hill, Somerset.
Proc. Somerset Arch. Soc., 56 (1910),
pp. 50–61 + 2 plates. 1911.

4181 —— Trial-excavations at Cadbury castle, S. Somerset, 1913. Proc.
Somerset Arch. Soc., 59 (1913), pp.
1–24 + 4 plates + plan. 1914.

4182 Gray (Harold St. George). Trial-excavations at Cadbury camp, Tickenham, Somerset, 1922. Proc. Somerset Arch. Soc., 68 (1922), pp. 8–20 + plate + plan. 1923.

4183 Hencken (Thalassa Cruso). The excavation of the Iron Age camp on Bredon hill, Gloucestershire, 1935–1937. [21 figures + map.] Archaeol. J., 95 (1938), pp. 1–111 + 31 plates + 6 plans. 1939.

4184(a) Hoare (*Sir* Richard Colt) *bart.* Account of antiquities found at Hamden hill [Somerset], with fragments of British chariots. [British camp.] Archaeologia, 21, pp. 39–42 + 2 plates + plan. 1827.

4184(b) Hodges (T. R.). Meon hill and its treasures. B'ham. Arch. Soc., Trans., 32 (1906), pp. 101–15 + plate. 1907.

4185 Hughes (Ieuan T.). Report on the excavations conducted on Midsummer hill camp. [Middle of 1st c. B.C.]. Trans. Woolhope N.F.C., 1924–1926, pp. 18–27 + 4 plates + 3 plans. 1928.

4186(a) Hume (C. R.) *and* **Jones** (G. W.). Excavations on Nesscliff Hill [Iron Age camp]. Trans. Shropshire A.S., 56 II, 1959, 129–32 + 4 figures.

4186(b) Hunt (J. W.). Banwell Camp [Somerset] univall. Report on excavation by the Banwell Society of Archaeology [some IA "A" finds]. N. & Q. for Somerset & Dorset, 27, pt. 270, 1959, 238–39.

4187 Hutchinson (Peter Orlando). On hill fortresses, sling-stones, and other antiquities in south-eastern Devon. Rpt. & Trans. Devon. Assoc., 2, pp. 372–82 + 3 plans. 1868.

4189 Irving (George Vere). Ancient camps, earthworks, and fortifications in Devon. [List.] Collectanea Archaeol., 2, pp. 18–29. 1871.

4190 —— Ancient camps, earthworks, and fortifications in Cornwall. [List.] Collectanea Archaeol., 2, pp. 160–71 + plate (plans). 1871.

4191(a) Jenkins (H. L.). Ancient camp [at Bantham] at the mouth of the [Devonshire] Avon. Devon N. & Q., 2, pp. 20–23. 1902.

4191(b) Johnston (J. L. Forde-). The Hillfork of Staffordshire. Arch. J., 120, 1963, 262–63.

4191(c) —— Berry Ring. Arch. J., 120, 1963, 288.

4191(d) —— Bury Bank. Arch. J., 120, 1963, 289.

4191(e) —— Castle Ring. Arch. J., 120, 1963, 299–300.

4192 Kenyon (Kathleen Mary). Explorations at Sutton Walls, Herefordshire. Archaeol. J., 110 (1953), pp. 1–87 + 17 plates + map + plan. 1954.

4193 Leeds (Edward Thurlow). Excavations (Further excavations) at Chun castle, in Penwith, Cornwall. Archaeologia, 76, pp. 205–40 + plate; 81, pp. 33–42 + plate. 1927–31.

4194 Liddell (Dorothy Mary). Report on the excavations at Hembury fort, Devon, 1930 (—Second season, 1931). (—Third season, 1932). (4th and 5th seasons, 1934 and 1935). (Honiton). [13 figures.] Proc. Devon Archaeol. Expl. Soc., 2, pp. 39–63 + 21 plates + plan; pp. 90–120 + 20 plates + plan; pp. 162–90 + 17 plates + 5 plans; 3, pp. 135–75 + 16 plates + 4 plans. 1930–35.

4195 —— The palisade at Hembury fort [Devon]. [Plan. Iron Age]. Antiquity, 6, pp. 475–77 + plate. 1932.

4196 Lindley (E. S.). Brackenbury Ditches [Iron Age, but Bronze Age tanged dagger found there]. Trans. Bristol & Glos. A.S., 76, 1957, 150–56 + 1 figure.

4197 Lines (H. H.). The Ladies' glen, or glen of "the stone", on the Malvern hills. [And its connection with the Herefordshire beacon camp.] Antiquary, 21, pp. 205–10. 1890.

4198 —— Titterstone camp and others. Introduction and notes by William Phillips. [Abdon Burrf, Coxam Knoll camp, Gaer ditches, *etc*.] Trans. Shropshire Archaeol. Soc., 2nd S. 3, pp. 1–35 + 5 plans. 1891.

4199 Lewis (J. M.). A section of Offa's Dyke at Buttington Tump, Tidenham [not prehistoric but given as "Standing Stone" on O.S. sheet] [spurious Barrow]. Trans. Bristol & Glos. A.S., 82, 202–04 + 1 figure. 1963.

4200 Lynam (Charles). A few jottings on some Staffordshire camps. North Staffs. N.F. Club, Rpts., 26, pp. 134–40. 1892.

4201 —— Ancient earthworks [in

Staffordshire]. [31 plans.] V.C.H., Staffs., 1, pp. 331–79 + map. 1908.

4202 Mayor (Albany Featherstone-haugh) *and* **Burrow** (Edward John). The mystery of Wansdyke: being the record of research and investigation in one field. pp. viii, 200. 4⁰. Cheltenham, 1926. [112 figures + 100 plans.]

4203 Mallet (Charles de) *baron.* Caynham camp. Trans. Woolhope N.F.C., 1883–85, pp. 74–79 + plan. 1890.

4204 Marshall (George). Interim report on the excavation of an Iron Age camp at Poston, Vowchurch, Herefordshire. Trans. Woolhope N.F.C., 1933–1935, pp. 89–99 + 5 plates + plan. 1938.

4205 —— Lower Pack Wood camp, Poston, in the parish of Vowchurch, and some remarks on the Iron Age in Herefordshire. Trans. Woolhope N.F.C., 1933–35, pp. 21–29 + plate. 1938.

4206 Martin (John May). Broadbury and its ancient earthworks. Rpt. & Trans. Devon. Assoc., 25, pp. 547–51. 1893.

4207 Montgomerie (Duncan H.). Ancient earthworks [in Worcestershire]. [2 plans.] V.C.H., Worcs., 4, pp. 421–434 + map. 1924.

4208 Morgan (Conwy Lloyd). Notes on the Clifton, Burwalls and Stokeleigh camps. Proc. Clifton Antiq. Club, 5, pp. 8–24 + 2 plates + 2 plans. 1904.

4209 —— Burwalls and Stokeleigh camps. Proc. Somerset Arch. Soc., 47 (1901), pp. 217–29 + 2 plates + plan. 1902.

4210 Norris (Hugh). The camp on Hamdon hill. Proc. Somerset Arch. Soc., 30 (1884), pp. 138–48. 1885.

4211 O'Neil (Bryan Hugh St. John). Excavation at Titterstone Clee Hill Camp, Shropshire, 1932. Arch. Camb., 89 i, 1934, 83–111 + 11 figures.

4212 —— Excavations at Titterstone Clee hill camp, Shropshire, 1932. Antiq. J., 14, pp. 13–32 + 5 plates + 3 plans. 1934.

4213 Ormerod (G. Wareing). What is Grimspound? Rpt. & Trans. Devon. Assoc., 5, pp. 41–46. 1872.

4214 Parry (John Augustus). On the remains of ancient fortifications in the neighbourhood of Bideford. [Map + 3 plans.] Rpt. + Trans. Devon. Assoc., 2, pp. 98–105. 1867.

4215 Peter (Thurstan C.). The exploration of Carn Brea. J. Roy. Instn. Cornwall, 13, pp. 92–102 + 7 plates + map + plan. 1895.

4216 Phillips (William). Garmsley camp. Trans. Woolhope N.F.C., 1893–1894, pp. 42–45 + plan. 1896.

4217 Piper (George H.). The camp and ancient British town on the Midsummer and Holly-bush hills, of the Malvern range. Trans. Woolhope N.F.C. 1898/99, pp. 69–71 + plan. 1900.

4217 Piper (George H.). The camp and ancient British town on the Midsummer and Holly-bush hills, of the Malvern range. Trans. Woolhope N.F.C., 1898–99, pp. 69–71 + plan. 1900.

4218 Playne (George F.). On the ancient camps of Gloucestershire. Proc. Cotteswold Nat. Club, 6, pp. 202–46 + 2 plates of plans, etc. + map. 1875.

4219 Powell (T. G. E.). Oxenton hill camp [Glos.]. [Figure (Iron Age pottery).] Trans. Bristol & Glos. Arch. Soc., 55, pp. 383–84. 1933.

4220 Price (Frederick George Hilton). Camps on the Malvern hills. J. Anthrop. Inst., 10, pp. 319–31. 1881.

4221 —— Camps on the Malvern hills. Trans. Woolhope N.F.C., 1877–1880, pp. 217–28. 1887.

4222 Radford (Courtenay Arthur Ralegh). Our prehistoric camps. Proc. Devon Archaeol. Expl. Soc., 1, pp. 5–7. 1929.

4223 —— Castle Dore, 1936. Devon & Cornwall N. & Q., 19, pp. 130–32. 1936.

4224 —— Castle Dore. Interim report on the first season (1936) of excavations. *Cornwall Excavations Committee.* pp. 10 + plate. 8⁰. Truro, 1937.

4225 —— Stoke hill camp. Proc. Devon Archaeol. Expl. Soc., 3, pp. 24–32 + map + plan. 1937.

4226 —— *and* **Cox** (James Stevens). Cadbury castle, South Cadbury. Proc. Somerset Arch. Soc., 99/100, pp. 106–13. 1956.

4227 Ramsden (Josslyn Vere). The hill fort and castle hill at Widworthy. [Plan.] Rpt. & Trans. Devon. Assoc., 79, pp. 193–96. 1947.

4228 Rennie (D. M.). The excavation of an earthwork on Rodborough

Common in 1954–55. Trans. Bristol & Glos. A. S., 78, 1959, 24–43 + 7 figures.

4229 Richardson (Katharine Margaret). Blackbury castle [Devon]. [Plan. Early Iron Age.] Archaeol. J., 114 (1957), pp. 165–66. 1959.

4230 Saunders (A. D.). Excavations at Castle Gotha, St. Austell: second interim report. [IA.] Cornish archaeol., No. 2, 1963, 49–51.

4231 Scarth (Harry Mengden). On ancient earthworks in the neighbourhood of Bath, on the south side of the river Avon. [Plan. Hampton down camp, Stantonberry camp, Maes knoll, Stanton Drew, Wellow tumulus.] J. Brit. Archaeol. Ass., 13, pp. 98–113. 1857.

4232 —— Worlebury, or camp on the Worle hill, immediately over the town of Weston-super-mare. J. Brit. Archaeol. Ass., 31, pp. 266–75 + plan. 1875.

4233 —— Dolebury camp on Mendip. Proc. Bath N.H. & Ant. F.C., 5, pp. 1–8. 1885.

4234 Seaby (W. A.). The Iron Age hill-fort on Ham hill, Somerset. Archaeol. J., 107 (1950), pp. 90–91. 1952.

4235 Sheldon (Gilbert). Hembury fort and the primitive road system of east Devon. Proc. Devon Archaeol. Expl. Soc., 1, pp. 64–69 + 2 maps. 1930.

4236 Simms (B. B.). Recent investigations of the hill fort and camp at Maer. [Berth Hill SJ/788391.] North Staffs. F.C., Trans., 66, pp. 91–100 + plan. 1932.

4237 Stanley (Muriel) *and* **Stanley** (Brian). The Defences of the Iron Age camp at Wappenbury, Warwickshire (1st–3rd centuries). Trans. Birmingham Arch. Soc., 76, 1958, 1–9 + 4 figures.

4238 Stone (John F. S.) *and* **Wicks** (A. T.). Trial excavations at Hayes Wood enclosure, Freshford, Somerset. Proc. Somerset Arch. Soc., 81 (1935), pp. 133–48 + 3 plates + plan. 1936.

4239 Tomkins (Henry George). The ancient stronghold of Worlebury. Proc. Bath N.H. & Ant. F.C., 3, pp. 379–97. 1877.

4240 —— Some account of the ancient (pre-Roman) stronghold of Worlebury, near Weston-super-Mare. Advm. Sci., 1888, 851–52.

4241 Wailes (Bernard). Excavations at Castle-au-Dinas, St. Columb Major: Interim Report. Cornish Archaeol., No. 2, 1963, 51–55 + 1 figure.

4242 —— Castle-au Dinas, St. Columb Major. Cornish Arch., 3, 1964, 85.

4243 —— Castle-au-Dinas, St. Columb Major. Cornish Arch., 4, 1965, 65.

4244 Wall (John Charles). Ancient earthworks [of Devon]. [99 plans.] V.C.H., Devon, 1, pp. 573–630 + map. 1906.

4245 —— Ancient earthworks [in Shropshire]. [128 plans.] V.C.H., Shropshire, 1, pp. 351–413 + map. 1908.

4246 Walter (Richard). Hamdon hill [camp]. Proc. Somerset Arch. Soc., 4 (1853), pp. 78–90 + plan. 1854.

4247 Walter (Richard Hensleigh). Some recent finds on Ham hill, south Somerset. [2 figures.] Antiq. J., 3, pp. 149–50; 4, pp. 51–53. 1923–24.

4248 Warner (S. E.). Wall Hills near Ledbury. Trans. Woolhope N.F.C., 1942–45, pp. 66–69. 1947.

4249 Warre (F.). Ancient earth-work at Norton Fitz-warren. Proc. Somerset Arch. Soc., 1 (1849–50), pp. 38–47 + plan. 1851.

4250 —— Worle camp. Proc. Somerset Arch. Soc., 2 (1851), pp. 64–85, 125–127 + 3 plates + plan; 4 (1853), pp. 124–27. 1852–54.

4251 —— Castle Neroche. Proc. Somerset Arch. Soc., 5 (1854), pp. 29–48 + plan. 1855.

4252 —— Earthworks in the neighbourhood of Bruton. [Pen pits and Cadbury, Milbourne Wick, Temple Combe.] Proc. Somerset Arch. Soc., 7 (1856–57), pp. 42–63. 1858.

4253 Webster (G. R. Harding). The riddle of Abdon Burf. Trans. Shropshire Archaeol. Soc., 45 (4th S. 12), pp. 85–96. 1929.

4254 Wedlake (William James). Excavations at Camerton, Somerset. A record of thirty years' excavation covering the period from Neolithic to Saxon times, 1926–56. *Camerton Excavation Club.* pp. xvii, 284 + 19 plates + 2 maps + 2 plans. 4°. Bath, 1958.

4255 —— The Herefordshire beacon hill fort. [2 plans. Iron Age.] Archaeol. J., 109 (1952), pp. 146–48 + plate.

4256(a) Wilkinson (*Sir* Gardner).

Carn Brea (or Carn Brê), near Redruth, Cornwall. Ann. Rpt. Roy. Instn. Cornwall, 41 (1859), pp. 17–43 + plan. 1860.

4256(b) Willis (L.) *and* **Rogers** (Ernest Henry). Dainton earthworks. [7 figures + map + plan. Iron Age.] Proc. Devon Archaeol. Expl. Soc., 4, pp. 29–101 + 2 plates + plan. 1951.

4257 Windle (*Sir* Bertram Coghill Alan). An excavation in Kemerton Camp [Worcs.]. Man, 5, pp. 133–35. 1905.

4258 Witchell (E. Northam). The camps at Minchinhampton. Proc. Cotteswold Nat. Club, 13, pp. 53–56. 1899.

4259 Wood (Peter). The Early Iron Age camp on Bozedown, Whitchurch, Oxon. [3 figures + plan.]. Oxoniensia, 19 (1954), pp. 8–14. 1955.

4260 Woods (Gertrude MacAlpine). A note on Hembury fort. Proc. Devon Archaeol. Expl. Soc., 1, p. 4 + plan. 1928.

4261 Worth (Richard Hansford). The prehistoric pounds on Dartmoor. [2 figures + 15 plans.] Rpt. & Trans. Devon. Assoc., 75, pp. 273–302 + 3 plates. 1943.

4262 Wright (J.). An enquiry concerning fortified hills near Bath. Proc. Bath N.H. & Ant. F.C., 4, pp. 129–38. 1881.

4263 Young (Alison) *and* **Richardson** (Katharine Margaret). Report on the excavations at Blackbury castle. Proc. Devon Archaeol. Expl. Soc., 5, pp. 43–67 + 7 plates + plan. 1955.

(d) Zone 4 [CBA Groups 3, 4, 5, 6]

4264 Ahier (Philip). The story of Castle hill, Huddersfield, . . . 200 B.C.–A.D. 1945. pp. 96. 8⁰. Huddersfield, 1946. [Figures.]

4265 Armitage (Ella). The non-sepulchral earthworks of Yorkshire. pp. 23. 8⁰. Bradford, 1901.

4266 Armitage (*Mrs*. Ella Sophia) *and* **Montgomerie** (Duncan H.). Ancient earthworks [in Yorkshire]. [74 plans.] V.C.H., Yorks., 2, pp. 1–71 + map. 1912.

4267 Atkinson (William). On some earthworks near Eamont Bridge [Camb.].

Trans. Cumb. & Westm. Ant. Soc., 6, pp. 444–55 + plate + plan. 1883.

4268 Ball (Thomas). Warden hill camp and "the castles" in Weardale. [Plan.] Proc. Soc. Antiq. Newc., 3rd S. 10, pp. 142–48. 1921.

4269 —— A cluster of earthworks near Bolam, Northumberland. [9 plans.] Proc. Soc. Antiq. Newc., 3rd S. 10, pp. 237–50. 1922.

4270 —— Some rectilinear earthworks in Northumberland. (—, Class G). [7 plans. (6 plans).] Proc. Soc. Antiq. Newc., 4th S. 1, pp. 173–78, 223–237. 1923–24.

4271 —— Hill and plateau forts near Otterburn. [Map + 3 plans.] Proc. Soc. Antiq. Newc., 4th S. 1, pp. 21–30. 1923.

4272 —— Blue Crag promontory fort, Colwell, North Tyne, Northumberland. Proc. Soc. Antiq. Newc., 4th S. 2, pp. 23–34 + plate ; pp. 138–43 + 2 plates. 1925–26.

4273 Benson (George). Notes on an intrenchment on Holgate hill, York. Ann. Rpt. Yorks. Phil. Soc., 1904, pp. 49–50 + map + plan + 2 plates (flint implements). 1905.

4274 Boyne (William). Earthworks at Killingbeck, near Leeds. Bowman (William), *Reliquae Antiquiae Eboracenses*, pp. 10–11. 4⁰. Leeds. 1855.

4275 Bu'lock (John D.). The hill-fort of Helsby, Cheshire. Trans. Lancs. & Ches. Ant. Soc., 66 (1956), pp. 107–10 + 3 plates + plan. 1957.

4276 Clarke (David T.-D.). Archaeology in Leicestershire [Leicester]. 2. The Castle [Eaton 796296]. Trans. Leicester. Arch. Soc., 28 (1952), 17–47 + 25 figures + 8 plates.

4277 —— Archaeology in Leicestershire. Breedon-on-the-Hill (406235). Trans. Leicester. Arch. Soc., 34, 1958, 79–80.

4278 Cole (Edward Maule). Danes' dike. Trans. E. Riding Antiq. Soc., 1, pp. 53–58 + plan. 1893.

4279 —— Huggate dikes. Antiquary, 30, pp. 7–9. 1894.

4280 —— Huggate dikes. Trans. E. Riding Antiq. Soc., 2, pp. 12–17. 1894.

4281 Cole (W. M.). The Longshaw earthworks. [Derbysh.] [Probably Iron Age.] Trans. Hunter Arch. Soc., 4, pp. 362–63 + plan. 1937.

4282 Collingwood (Robin George). The hill-fort on Carrock Fell. Trans. Cumb. & Westm. Ant. Soc., N.S. 38, pp. 32–41. 1938.

4283 Collingwood (William Gersham). Three more ancient castles of Kendal. Trans. Cumb. & Westm. Ant. Soc., N.S. 8, pp. 97–112. 1908.

4284 Copley (Harold). The earthworks in Cantslow wood, Rotherham. Preliminary report. [Iron Age.] Trans. Hunter Arch. Soc., 6, pp. 190–91. 1950.

4285 Cox (John Charles). Ancient earthworks [of Derbyshire]. [Figure + 26 plans.] V.C.H., Derbs., 1, pp.(357–96 + map. 1905.

4286 Decker, K. V. *and* **Scollar**, I. Iron Age square enclosures in Rhineland [analogies in Yorkshire]. Antiquities, 36, 1962, pp. 175–78.

4287 Dibbin (H. A.). Castle hill, near Hallaton, Leicestershire. Proc. Soc. Antiq., 2 S. 7, pp. 316–21. 1878.

4288 —— The castle hill and the ancient earthwork near Hallaton, co. Leicester. Leic. & Rutland N. & Q., 1, pp. 170–76. 1890.

4289 Dobson (John). Urswick Stone Walls [Furness]. Trans. Cumb. & Westm. Ant. Soc., N.S. 7, pp. 72–94 + 5 plates + 3 plans. 1907.

4290 Dymond (D. P.) *and* **Stead** (Ian M.). Grimthorpe: a hillfort on the Yorkshire wolds. [2 figures + map + 2 plans. Iron Age B.] Antiquity, 33, pp. 208–13 + plate. 1959.

4291 Elgee (Frank). Report on excavations at Eston camp during 1929. Proc. Cleveland N.F.C., 4, p. 95. 1932.

4293 Gardner (Willoughby) *and* **Cowper** (Henry Swainson). Ancient earthworks [in Lancashire]. [25 plans.] V.C.H., Lancs., 2, pp. 507–60 + map. 1908.

4294 Goodchild (J. G.). The earthworks near Kirkland, known as the Hanging walls of Mark Antony. Trans. Cumb. & Westm. Ant. Soc., 8, pp. 40–47 + plate + plan. 1886.

4295 Gould (Isaac Chalkley). The early defensive earthworks on Comb Moss. J. Derbs. Archaeol. Soc., 23, pp. 108–14. 1901.

4296 —— Carl's wark [on Hathersage moor]. [Figure + plan.] J. Derbs. Archaeol. Soc., 25, pp. 80 + plate. 1903.

4297 —— Ancient earthworks [in County Durham]. [30 plans.] V.C.H., Durham, 1, pp. 343–63 + map. 1905.

4298 Greene (Dorothy). "The Roman ridge", hill top, Kimberworth, near Rotherham. Trans. Hunter Arch. Soc., 6, pp. 95–97 + 2 plates. 1950.

4299 Haigh (Daniel Henry). Caer Ebranc, the first city of Britain. Yorks. Arch. J., 5, pp. 350–61 + 2 tables. 1897.

4300 Harrison (William). The defensive earthworks and fortified enclosures of Cheshire. Trans. Lancs. & Ches. Ant. Soc., 25 (1907), pp. 146–55. 1908.

4301 Hedley (Robert Cecil). Early earthworks in Northumberland. [List, by parishes.] Proc. Soc. Antiq. Newc., 4th S. 1, pp. 81–113 + map. 1923.

4302 —— The prehistoric camps of Northumberland. Arch. Æl., N. [2nd] S. 13, pp. 225–33 + 2 plans; 15, pp. 33–36 + plan (Burgh Hill). 1889–92.

4303 Hills (Gordon Macdonald). Examples of ancient earthworks [in the neighbourhood of Sheffield]. J. Brit. Archaeol. Ass., 30, pp. 406–13 + plan [of Maiden Castle, Dorset]. 1874.

4304(a) Jobey (George). An earthwork at Smalesmouth, Northumberland. Arch. Æliana, 39, 1961, 371–73 + 1 figure.

4304(b) Johnston (J. L. Forde-). The Iron Age hillforts of Lancashire and Cheshire. Trans. Lancs. & Cheshire antiq. Soc., 72, 1962, 9–46 + 29 figures.

4305 Jones (Jack Davies). The hill forts of Cheshire. [Map.] Cheshire Historian, 3, pp. 19–23. 1953.

4306 Kenyon (Kathleen Mary). Excavations at Breedon-on-the-hill, 1946. Trans. Leic. Arch. Soc., 26, pp. 17–82 + 12 plates + map + plan. 1950.

4307 —— Breedon on the Hill camp, [Leics.]. [Iron Age]. Archaeol. J., 112 (1955), p. 172. 1956.

4308 Lomas (John). A Bronze Age site at Parwich, Derbyshire [ring-ditches]. DAJ, 82, 1962, 91–99, 3 figures + 2 plates.

4309 Lowndes (R. A. C.). Allen Knott earthwork, Far Orrest, Windermere, Westmorland. Trans. C. & W.A. & A.S., N.S. 64, 1964, 94–97.

4310 Lynn (Francis). Yeavering Bell, Harehope fort, and Humbleton hill.

Hist. Berwick. Nat. Club, 19, pp. 155–62 + 2 plans. 1904.

4311 Maclauchlan (Henry). Notes on camps in the parishes of Branxton, Carham, Ford, Kirknewton, and Wooler, in Northumberland. Hist. Berwick. Nat. Club, 24, pp. 451–72. 1922.

4312 Maclean (Hector). Caerthannoc or Maidencastle, Southby fell, [Cumb.]. [Prehistoric ring fort.] Trans. Cumb. & Westm. Ant. Soc., N.S. 12, pp. 143–45. 1912.

4313 Mason (Joseph Robert) *and* **Valentine** (Herbert). The British village site at Lanthwaite Green and other earthworks in west Cumberland. [Plan.] Trans. Cumb. & Westm. Ant. Soc., N.S. 24, pp. 117–22 + 4 plates. 1924.

4314 Mitchell (T. Carter). Maiden's Bower, near Topcliffe. Yorks. Archaeol. J., 9, pp. 241–50. 1886.

4345 Musson (Reginald Coulson). Hesketh Roughs ridge, [Gisburn, West Riding]. [Prehistoric earthwork. Plan.] Proc. Leeds. Phil. and Lit. Soc., 5, pp. 249–50. 1943.

4317 Preston (F. L.). Hill-forts in south-west Yorkshire. Trans. Hunter Arch. Soc., 6, pp. 85–94 + map. 1950.

4318 —— Burr Tor camp [near Great Hucklow], Derbyshire. Arch. News Letter, 2, p. 204. 1950.

4319 —— A field survey of the "Roman rig" dyke in south-west Yorkshire. Trans. Hunter Arch. Soc., 6, pp. 197–200, 285–309. 1950.

4320 —— The hill-forts of the Peak. J. Derbs. Archaeol. Soc., 74, pp. 1–31. 1954.

4321 Radley (Jeffrey). A Ring-bank on Beeley Moor. DAJ, 85, 1965, 126–31 + 2 figures + 1 plate.

4322 Raistrick (Arthur). Preliminary excavations of an earthwork at Easington, West Yorks. Yorks. Archaeol. J., 31, pp. 44–48. 1934.

4323(a) Riley (D. N.), **Greene** (Dorothy) *and* **Preston** (F. L.), *etc.* "Roman Ridge" excavation reports. [i. Investigation of entrance through the "Roman Ridge" in Shepherd's plantation, Greasbrough, nr. Rotherham; ii–iii. Two excavations in the "Roman Ridge" dyke; iv. Grimesthorpe road, Sheffield.] Trans. Hunter Arch. Soc., 7, pp. 18–25, 96–97 + 5 folding plates. 1951–52.

4323(b) Rivers (Augustus Henry Lane Fox Pitt). On excavations in the earthwork called Dane's Dyke at Flamborough in October, 1879; and on the earthworks of the Yorkshire wolds. J. Anthrop. Inst., 11, pp. 455–70 + 2 plates + map + 2 tables. 1882.

4324 Sheppard (Thomas). Danes' dyke [Holderness]. Trans. E. Riding Antiq. Soc., 22, pp. 33–42. 1919.

4325 Stanley (John). An Iron Age fort at Ball Cross farm, Bakewell. [2 figures + plan.] J. Derbs. Archaeol. Soc., 74, pp. 85–99 + plate. 1954.

4326 Surtees (Scott Frederick). British pit dwellings in the neighbourhood of Doncaster. pp. 15. 8°. Leeds, 1870.

4327 Thomas (F.). A fresh survey of earthwork on Toothill [variously listed as Bronze Age, or Roman, but evidence inconclusive prob. not prehistoric). Trans. Lancs. & Cheshire antiq. Soc., 70, 1960, 84–87 + 2 figures.

4328 —— Earthworks on Chee Tor, Blackwell, near Taddington [? IA settlement ?BA]. DAJ, 82, 1962, 102–04 + 1 figure.

4329 Thomas (Stanley). Archaeology in Leicestershire and Rutland. Burrough-on-the-Hill (760119). Trans. Leic. Arch. Soc., 36 (1960), 51–2.

4330 Tristram (Edward). The promontory forts of Derbyshire. [2 plans.] J. Derbs. Archaeol. Soc., 33, pp. 1–18 + 4 plates. 1911.

4331 —— Fin Cop prehistoric fort. J. Derbs. Archaeol. Soc., 34, pp. 133–38. 1912.

4332 —— Combs Moss [promontory] fort, Chapel-en-le-Frith, Derbyshire. [2 figures + plan.] Antiquary, 49, pp. 205–211. 1913.

4333 —— Mam Tor earthwork. J. Derbs. Archaeol. Soc., 37, pp. 87–90. 1915.

4334 Tyson (N.) *and* **Bu'lock** (J. D.). The Iron Age fortifications at Planes Wood, Whalley [Lancs.]. Trans. Lancs. & Ches. Ant. Soc., 67 (1957), pp. 115–17 + plate. 1958.

4335 Varley (William James). Maiden Castle, Bickerton [Cheshire]: a summary of the results of the excavations of 1934 and 1935. J. Chester & N. Wales Arch. Soc., N.S. 31, pp. 113–21 + plate + plan. 1935.

4336 Varley (William James). Maiden Castle, Bickerton [Cheshire]. Preliminary excavations, 1934. (Further excavations, 1935). Annals of Archaeology, 22, pp. 97–110 + 8 plates; 23, pp. 101–12 + 6 plates + map + plan. 1935–36.

4337 —— Recent investigations into the origins of [7] Cheshire hill-forts. Trans. Lancs. & Ches. Ant. Soc., 57 (1936), pp. 51–59 + map. 1937.

4338 —— Excavations of the castle ditch, Eddisbury, 1935–1938. Trans. Hist. Soc. Lancs. & Ches., 102 (1950), pp. 1–68. 1951.

4340 Wacher (J. S.). Excavations at Breedon - on - the - Hill, Leicestershire, 1957. Ant. J., 44, 1964, 122–42.

4341 Wall (John Charles). Ancient earthworks [in Leicestershire]. [22 plans. Pp. 274–75, Tumuli.] V.C.H., Leicester, 1, pp. 243–76 + map. 1907.

4342 —— Ancient earthworks [in Rutland]. [8 plans.] V.C.H., Rutland, 1, pp. 107–19 + map. 1908.

4343 Walton (*Capt.* R. H.). Lordenshaws Camp, Rothbury. Hist. Berwicks. Naturalist Club, 35 i, 1959, 17–20 + 1 figure.

4344 Ware (Henry), *Rt. Rev, DD*. A British rath near Kirkby Lonsdale. Trans. Cumb. & Westm. Ant. Soc., 7, pp. 111–13 + plan. 1884.

4345 Wilson (T.). Remains at Hugill, near Windermere, [Westm.]. Trans. Cumb. & Westm. Ant. Soc., 6, pp. 86–90 + plan. 1883.

4346 Wooler (Edward). Shackleton [hill] camp, [co. Durham]. Proc. Soc. Antiq. Newc., 3rd S. 3, pp. 70–71 + plan. 1907.

4347 —— [Stanwick camp, co. Durham]. Proc. Soc. Antiq. Newc., 3rd S. 4, pp. 70–71 + plate + plan. 1909.

(e) Zone 5 [CBA Group 2]

4348 Alcock (Leslie). The hill-fort in Cwrt-yr-Ala park, near Dinas Powis (Glam.). [3 figures + plan. (Section).] Bull. Bd. Celtic Stud., 16, pp. 242–50 + 3 plates; 17, pp. 131–36. 1955–57.

4349 —— Castell Odo: a fortified settlement of the Early Iron Age on Mynydd Ystum, near Aberdaron. Caer-

narvon. Hist. Soc., Trans., 19, pp. 1–7 + 2 plates. 1958.

4350 —— Castell Odo: an embanked settlement on Mynydd Ystum, near Aberdaron, Caernarvonshire [Iron Age village]. Arch. Camb., 109, 1960, 78–135 + 13 figures + 2 plates.

4351 —— Dinas Powys. An Iron Age, Dark Age, and Early Medieval Settlement in Glamorgan. Cardiff, 1963. xxviii + 230, 12 plates + 42 figures.

4352 —— Dinas Powys: an Iron Age, Dark Age and early medieval settlement in Glamorgan. Cardiff, 1963, 230 pp., 12 plates + 41 figures. Univ. of Wales Press.

4353 —— Hillforts in Wales and the Marches. Antiquity, 39, 1965, pp. 184–195.

4354 [Anon.] Earthworks on Bryn Golen. [Plan.] Northern Flintshire, 1, pp. 1–5 + plate. 1913.

4355 [Anon.] Caer Lleion, or the fort on Conway mountain. Proc. Llandudno F.C., 13 (1926–27), pp. 34–36. 1927.

4356 Babington (Charles Cardale) *and* **Jones** (Harry Longueville). On Caercarreg-y-fran [Llanberis] Caernarvonshire. Arch. Camb., 3rd S. 2, pp. 56–59, 96–98 + plan. 1856.

4357 Babington (Charles Cardale). Cyclopean wall near Llanberis. Arch. Camb., 3rd S. 11, p. 277 + plate. 1865.

4358 Ball (Thomas). Discovery of an unrecorded camp near Swinburn, Northumberland. [Plan.] Proc. Soc. Antiq. Newc., 4th S. 2, pp. 101–04. 1925.

4359 Banks (Richard William). Pen Caer Helen [camp], Llanbedr, Carnarvonshire. (Pen-y-Gaer?). Arch. Camb., 4th S. 5, pp. 81–82. 1874.

4360 —— Tomen castle, Radnor forest. [Promontory fort.] Arch. Camb., 4th S. 6, pp. 339–41. 1875.

4361 Barnwell (Edward Lowry). Tre'r Ceiri [fort, Caernarvonshire]. [3 figures + 3 plans.] Arch. Camb., 4th S. 1, pp. 66–88 + 2 plates + plan. 1871.

4362 —— Pembrokeshire cliff-castles. Arch. Camb., 4th S. 6, pp. 74–86 + 3 plans. 1875.

4363 —— Craig-y-Dinas [stone fortress near Clynnog Vawr, Carnarvonshire]. Arch. Camb., 4th S. 9, pp. 217–21 + plate + plan. 1878.

4364 —— Pen Caer Helen [Llanbedr,

Carnarvonshire]. [Hill-fort.] Arch. Camb., 4th S. 14, pp. 192–95 + plate + plan. 1883.

4365 Bersu (Gerhard) *and* **Griffiths** (W. E.). Concentric circles at Llwyn-du Bach, Penygroes, Caernarvonshire. Arch. Camb., 100 ii, 1949, 173–206 + 14 figures + 2 plates.

4367 Blight (John Thomas). Pen Caer Helen, [parish of Llanbedr, near Conway. Arch. Camb., 3rd S. 13, pp. 276–80 + plate + plan. 1867.

4368 Bonney (Thomas George). Pen Caer Helen, Carnarvonshire. [Fort.] Archaeol. J., 25, pp. 228–32 + plan. 1868.

4369 Breese (Charles E.). The Fort of Dinas Emrys. Arch. Camb., 85 ii, 1930, 342–54 + 6 figures.

4370 —— "Castell Odo" Arch. Camb., 87 ii 1932, 372–85 + 11 figures.

4371 Chitty (Lily F.). How did the hill-fort builders reach the Breiddins? Arch. Camb., 92 i, 1937, 129–50 + 1 map.

4372 Christison (D.). The prehistoric fortresses of Treceiri and Eildon. [8 figures + 2 plans.] Arch. Camb., 5th S. 14, pp. 17–40. 1897.

4373 Crossley (D. W.). List of hill-forts and other earthworks in Pembrokeshire. Bull. Board Celtic Studies, 20 ii, 1963, 171–205.

4374 Davies (A. G.). The Excavations at the Bulwarks Llanmadoc (Glam.). September, 1957. Bull. Board Celtic Studies, 21 i, 1964, 100–04 + 4 figures + 1 plate.

4375 Davies (Ellis). An unnoticed British camp in Flintshire. Arch. Camb., 6th S. 17, pp. 433–35. 1917.

4376 —— Mynydd Gaer camp. Proc. Llandudno F.C., 19, pp. 28–29. 1938.

4377 Davies (Francis Robert). Ancient British cities. [Shan Dinas, near Llandudno.] N. &. Q, 9 S. 8, p. 467. 1901.

4378 Dawkins (*Sir* William Boyd). Tre'r Ceiri: introductory note. [Early Iron Age fort.] Arch. Camb., 6th S. 7, pp. 35–37. 1907.

4379 "O.T.E" On the British forts on the coast of Caernarvonshire. Arch. Camb., 1, pp. 169–73 + frontispiece. 1846.

4380 Evans (D. Cledlyn). Y Garn Goch [camps]. Trans. Carmarthenshire

Ant. Soc., 5, pp. 84–85 + plan; 89–91 + plate; pp. 100–02 + plate. 1910.

4381(a) —— Cribyn Clottas, [Cards.]. Some hill-top camps. Cards. Antiq. Soc. Trans., 9, pp. 19–25. 1933.

4381(b) Evans (M. Bevan). Y Gaer, Llai—report on rescue excavations, 1961. Flints. hist. Soc. publns., 21, 1963, 21–31 + 4 figures + 2 plates.

4382 Fenton (John). Breselu [or Presele] hill, [Pembrokeshire]. Arch. Camb., N.S. 4, pp. 81–89 + plate ("British urn"). 1853.

4383 Ffoulkes (W. Wynne). Castra Clwydiana. [i. Moel Multi Menlli; ii. Moel Multi Gaer, part of Moel Famma; iii. Moel Multi Arthur.] Arch. Camb., N.S. 1, pp. 81–89 + plate + plan; pp. 174–87 + 2 plans. 1850.

4384 Forde (Cyril Daryll). Excavations on Pen Dinas hill fort, Aberystwyth, Cards. Bull. Bd. Celtic Stud., 7, pp. 77–80. 1933.

4385 —— Excavations on Pen Dinas hill fort, Cardiganshire, second season, 1934. Bull. Bd. Celtic Stud., 7, pp. 324–327. 1934.

4386 —— *and* **O'Neil** (Bryan Hugh St. John). Breiddin Hill camp. (Excavations, 1934.) Antiq. J., 14, pp. 56–57; 15, pp. 71–73. 1934–35.

4387 —— First (second) season's work on Pen Dinas hill fort, Aberystwyth, Cardiganshire. [2 figures + plan.] Antiq. J., 14, pp. 57–59; 15, pp. 63–66. 1934–35.

4388 —— Excavations on Pen Dinas hill fort, Cardiganshire. Third season, 1936. 8, pp. 378–80; 9, pp. 83–88. 1937.

4389 —— Excavations on Pen Dinas, Cardiganshire, 1937. Antiq. J., 18, pp. 77–81 + plate. 1938.

4390 —— Pen Dinas, Cardiganshire. Antiquity, 12, pp. 99–100. 1938.

4391 Forde (Cyril Daryll) *and others*. Excavations at Pen Dinas, Aberystwyth, (with W. E. Griffiths, A. H. A. Hogg and C. H. Houlder) [dated by duck-stamp pot in Phase IV] [IA "B"] [Multivall. Hillfort.] Arch. Camb., 112, 1963, 125–153 + 11 figures.

4393 Fox (Cyril) *and* **Hemp** (Wilfrid James). Two unrecorded hillforts on Llanymynech Hill, Montgomeryshire, and Blodwell Rock, Shropshire, and their relation to Offa's Dyke. Arch. Cambrensis, 7th S., 81 ii, 1926, 395–400 + 2 figures.

4394 Fox (Cyril). Caer Dynnaf, Llanblethian. A hill-fort of Early Iron Age type in the Vale of Glamorgan. Arch. Camb., 91 i, 1936, 20–24 + 1 figure.

4395 —— Field survey of Glamorgan: the defensive earthworks of Gower. Bull. Bd. Celtic Stud., 8, pp. 364–70. 1937.

4396 Gardner (Willoughby). Note on the defences of Penygaer. [4 figures.] Arch. Camb., 6th S. 6, pp. 257–67. 1906.

4397 —— Ancient hill fort on Penygaer, near Llanbedr-y-Cenin. [4 figures.] Proc. Llandudno F.C., 6 (1911–12), pp. 50–57. 1914.

4398 —— The hill-fort of Dinorben, near Abergele, Denbighshire. Bull. Bd. Celtic Studies, 1, pp. 276–79. 1922.

4399 —— The native hill-forts in North Wales and their defences. Arch. Cambrensis, 81 ii, 1926, 221–82 + 30 figures.

4400 —— Craig Gwrtheyrn Hill Fort, Llanfinangel ar Arth, Caermarthenshire. Arch. Camb., 87 i, 1932, 144–50 + 3 figures.

4401 —— Ffridd Faldwyn Hill-Fort, near Montgomery. Arch. Camb., 87 ii, 1932, 364–71 + 7 figures.

4402 —— Caer y Twr, a hill-fort on Holy Island, Anglesey. Arch. Camb., 89 i, 1934, 156–73 + 14 figures.

4403 —— A promontory fort at Porthkerry, Glamorganshire. Arch. Camb., 90 i, 1935, 135–40 + 3 figures.

4404 —— Y Gardden hill-fort, Ruabon, Denbighshire. Arch. Camb., 92 i, 1937, 151–58 + 4 figures.

4405 —— Dinorwig hill-fort Llanddeiniolen, Caernarvonshire [pre-Roman]. Arch. Camb., 99 ii, 1947, 231–48 + 13 figures.

4406 —— *and* **Savory** (H. N.). Dinorben, a hill-fort occupied in Early Iron Age and Roman times. Cardiff, 1964. 250 pp., 36 plates + 36 figures.

4407 Gould (Sabin Baring), Exploration of the stone camp on St. David's head. [14 figures.] Arch. Camb., 5th S. 16, pp. 105–31 + 3 plans. 1899.

4408 —— Exploration of Moel Trigarn [fort on Prescelly range]. [11 figures. Pp. 200–11, Exploration of the hut-sites.] Arch. Camb., 5th S. 17, pp. 189–211 + plan. 1900.

4409 —— The exploration of Clegyr Voya [camp, near St. David's]. [Figure + plan.] Arch. Camb., 6th S. 3, pp. 1–11. 1903.

4410 —— *and* **Burnard** (Robert). An exploration of some of the cytian in Tre'r Ceiri. [7 figures + 2 plans.] Arch. Camb., 6th S. 4, pp. 1–16 + plate (glass beads). 1904.

4411 Griffith (John). Hen Dre'r Gelli: a buried prehistoric town in the Rhondda valley. Arch. Camb., 6th S. 6, pp. 281–307. 1906.

4412 Griffith (William Eric) *and* **Hogg** (Alexander Hubert Arthur). The hill-fort on Conway mountain, Caernarvonshire. Arch. Camb., 105, 1956, 49–80 + 9 figures + 3 plates.

4413 Grimes (William Francis). Fishponds camp. Bosherston [short note] [Pembs.] Arch. J., 119, 1962, 348.

4414 —— St. David's Head promontory fort and Carn Llidi [short note]. Arch. J., 119, 1962, 336–38.

4415 —— Castlemartin Rath [short note] [Pembs.?] Arch. J., 119, 1962, 347–48.

4416 Hamer (Edward). Ancient Arwystli: its earthworks and other ancient remains. Collns. rel. to Montgom., 1, pp. 209–32 + 3 plans; 2, pp. 42–70 + plate. 1868–69.

4417 Hayes (Peter) *and* **Evans** (J. Sandford). Hope: hill fort of Caer Estyn. Flints. Inst. Soc. publns., 18, 1960, 170–175 + 4 figures + 2 plates.

4418 Hemp (Wilfred James). A "Neolithic" camp in Wales [Llanidloes Dinas]. Arch. Camb., 84 i, 1929, 145.

4419 Higgins (H.). The ancient forts of Wales. Proc. Llandudno F.C., 15, pp. 65–75. 1930.

4420 —— The stone forts of Wales: who erected them? Proc. Llandudno F.C., 15, pp. 75–79. 1930.

4421 —— The single ramparted defensive enclosures of Wales. Proc. Llandudno F.C., 17, pp. 107–17. 1933.

4422 —— Dinas Dinorwic. Proc. Llandudno F.C., 17, pp. 75–76. 1933.

4423 Hogg (Alexander Hubert Arthur). Garn Bodnan and Tre'r Ceiri, excavations at two Caernarvonshire hillforts. [15 figures + 2 plates + 2 tables + 2 pull-out maps.] Arch. J., 117, 1960, 1–39.

4424 Hogg (Alexander Hubert Arthur). List of hill-forts in Cardiganshire. Bull. Board Celtic Studies, 19 iv, 1962, 354–57.

4425 Houlder (Christopher). Rescue excavations at Moel Hiraddng I—excavations in 1954–55. Flints. hist. Soc. publins., 19, 1961, 1–20 + 7 figures +7 plates.

4426 Hughes (Harold). The exploration of Pen-y-Gaer, hill-fort above Llanbedr-y-Cenin. [4 figures + 2 plans. Late-Celtic hill fort.] Arch. Camb., 6th S. 6, pp. 241–56. 1906.

4427 —— Pen-y-Gorddyn or y Gorddyn Fawr [camp]. [2 plans.] Arch. Camb., 6th S. 6, pp. 268–72. 1906.

4428 —— Report on the excavations carried out at Tre'r Ceiri in 1906. [17 figures.] Arch. Camb., 6th S. 7, pp. 38–62 + plan. 1907.

4429 Hughes (Henry Harold). Prehistoric remains on Penmaenmawr (known as Braich y Ddinas). Report on the Survey and excavations. (Report . . . 1912.) (Third report.) [5 figures + 2 plans. (5 figures + plan.) (10 figures + 2 plans).] Arch. Camb., 6th S. 12, pp. 169–82; 13, pp. 353–66; 15, pp. 17–39. 1912–15.

4430 —— Tre'r Ceiri [Llanaelhaiarn]. [9 figures. On summit of Yr Eifl.] Proc. Llandudno F.C., 7 (1912–13), pp. 42–56 + plan. 1935.

4431 Hughes (Henry Harold). Prehistoric remains on Penmaenmawr (known as Braich y Dinas). Fourth (Fifth) report on the survey and excavations. [6 figures. (13 figures).] Arch. Camb., 57, 77, ii, pp. 346–359, 1922. 78, pp. 243–268, 1923.

4432 Hughes (Ieuan T.). A regional survey of north Cardiganshire prehistoric earthworks. [Figure + 6 maps + 28 plans.] Cards. Antiq. Soc., Trans. 4, pp. 22–56. 1926.

4433 —— Some south Cardiganshire earthworks. [6 plans.] Cards. Antiq. Soc. Trans., 7, pp. 112–17. 1930.

4434 —— Some observations on hilltop camps. Cards. Antiq. Soc. Trans., 9, pp. 12–18. 1933.

4435(a) Jabet (George). The British town and fort Caer Seion, near Conway. [Figure.] B'ham & Midland Inst., Arch. Section, Trans., 2 (1871), pp. 15–21 + plan. 1872.

4435(b) Johnston (J. L. Forde-). Fieldwork on the hillforts of North Wales. Flints. hist. Soc. publins., 21, 1963, 1–20 + 6 figures + 2 plates.

4435(c) —— The Hill-forts of the Clwyds. Arch. Camb., 114, 1965, 146–178 + 7 figures + 4 plates.

4436 Jones (Glanville R. J.). Early settlement in Arfon: the setting of Tre'r Ceiri. Trans. Caernarvon hist. Soc., 24, 1963, 1–20 + 3 figures.

4437 Jones (Morgan Hugh). Y Grongaer. Trans. Carmarthenshire Ant. Soc., 2, pp. 158–59. 1906.

4438 Kay (Richard E.). Castell Dinas, Parish of Targarth, Brecknockshire. Brycheiniog 10, 1964, 15–27 + 4 figures.

4439 Kenyon (Kathleen Mary). Ffridd Faldwyn [hill-fort]. Archaeol. J., 113 (1956), pp. 215–17. 1957.

4440 Kingsford (M. S.). A preliminary report on some of the forts on the coast of North Wales, between Llandulas and the Rivals, and in Anglesey, [Figure.] Liverpool Committee for excavation and research in Wales and the Marches, Ann. Rpt., 1 (1908), pp. 40–48. 1909.

4441 Laws (Edward). Pembrokeshire earthworks. Arch. Camb., 4th S. 11, pp. 241–48. 1880.

4442 Lines (H. H.). Breidden hill camp, and other camps in the vicinity. Collns. rel. to Montgom., 23, pp. 321–44 + plate + 4 plans, pp. 413–16 (Crowther camp). 1889.

4443 —— A British caer on Cefn Namor, Tal y fan mountain [Caernarvonshire]. Antiquary, 24, pp. 64–67. 1891.

4444 —— Braich y Ddinas on Penmaenmawr. Antiquary, 29, pp. 11–15. 1894.

4445 —— Bron y Voel, on the western slope of Moelfre, Merionethshire. [Celtic caer.] Antiquary, 29, pp. 248–52. 1894.

4446 —— Dyganwy, Caer Llion, and Caer Seion. Antiquary, 30, pp. 263–70. 1894.

4447 Llewelyn (John Talbot D.). Mynydd Carn Goch, Llangafelach, Glamorganshire. Arch. Camb., 3rd S. 2, pp. 63–67 + plate + plan. 1856.

4448 Moggridge (Matthew) *and* **Jones** (Harry Longueville). Carn Goch, Caermarthenshire. Arch. Camb., 3rd S. 6, pp. 97–104 + plan. 1860.

4449 Morris (A. H.). Maindu camp,

[Monmouthshire]. [Figure (stone celt).] Arch. Camb., 6th S. 9, p. 372. 1909.

4450 Morris (Bernard). "Hen Castell", a re-discovered hill-slope earthwork in Gower. Trans. Cardiff Nat. Soc., 87, 1957/58, 23 + 1 figure.

4462 O'Neil (Bryan Hugh St. John). Breiddin hill camp excavations, 1934. Bull. Bd. Celtic Stud., 7, pp. 327–29; 8, pp. 90–92. 1934–35.

4463 —— Breiddin Hill Camp excavations, 1934 [?EIA]. Arch. Camb., 90 i, 1935, 161–62.

4464 —— Excavations at Breiddin Hill Camp, Montgomeryshire, 1933–35. Arch. Camb., 92 i, 1937, 86–128 + 9 figures.

4465 —— Excavations at Ffridd Faldwyn Camp, Montgomery, 1937. Arch. Camb., 92 ii, 1937, 322–24.

4466 —— Excavations at Ffridd Faldwyn camp, [near] Montgomery, 1937. (—1938). (—1939). Bull. Bd. Celtic Stud., 9, pp. 88–91, 287–90; 10, pp. 190–191. 1937–40.

4467 —— Excavations at Ffridd Faldwyn camp, Montgomery, 1937 and 1938. [Early Iron Age.] Collns. rel. to Montgom., 45, pp. 201–04. 1938.

4468 —— Excavations at Ffridd Faldwyn camp, Montgomery, 1937. [Early Iron Age.] Antiq. J., 18, pp. 81–82. 1938.

4469 —— Excavations at Ffridd Faldwyn Camp, Montgomery, 1938. Arch. Camb., 93 ii, 1938, 249–50.

4470 —— Excavations at Ffridd Faldwyn camp, Montgomery, 1938. (—1939.) [Iron Age B ware. Neolithic and later.] Antiq. J., 19, pp. 92–94; 20, pp. 122–23. 1939–40.

4471 —— Excavations at Ffridd Faldwyn Camp, Montgomery, 1939 [Neolithic—IA]. Arch. Camb., 95 i, 1940, 79–80.

4472 —— Excavations at Ffridd Faldwyn Camp, Montgomery, 1937–39 [occupation from Neolithic to LIA]. Arch. Camb., 97 i, 1942, 1–57 + 15 figures + 12 plates.

4473 —— Ffridd Faldwyn Camp, Montgomery [note on dating]. Arch. Camb., 98 i (1944), 147.

4474 Owen (Elias). Camp on the Llanllechid hill [Carnarvonshire]. [For protection of flocks?] Arch. Camb., 4th S. 6, pp. 220–23 + plan. 1875.

4475 Owen (Hugh). Notes on the study of early camps and forts in Wales. Anglesey Ant. Soc. Trans., 1938, pp. 30–41. 1938.

4476 P. (Clara). Dinas Penmaen or Penmaenmawr, a druidical temple before being a British fortress. Cymmrodor, 5, pp. 154–58. 1882.

4477 Paget (—). Notes on some ancient stone forts in Carnarvonshire. [2 figures + 2 plans.] J. Brit. Archaeol. Ass., N.S. 2, pp. 97–111. 1896.

4478 —— Caves and passages under the British fortress of Pen-y-Gaer, Conway valley. J. Brit. Archaeol. Ass., N.S. 3, pp. 291–93. 1897.

4479 Parry (*Sir* T. Love) and **Jones** (D. Parry). Tre' r Ceiri, Caernarvonshire. Arch. Camb., 3rd S. 1, pp. 254–257 + plan. 1855.

4480 Prichard (Hugh). Early remains of Llanengrad, Anglesey. Arch. Camb., 3rd S. 13, pp. 108–15 + plate. 1867.

4481 —— Twyn y Parc [Anglesey]. Arch. Camb., 4th S. 6, pp. 349–58 + plan. 1875.

4482 —— Braich y Dainas. Arch. Camb., 4th S. 8, pp. 202–35 + 2 plates + plan. 1877.

4483 —— Compound walls in North Wales: Caer Drewyn, Pen y Gaer, Craig y Ddinas, and Tre'r Ceiri. [Figure.] Arch. Camb., 5th S. 4, pp. 241–59 + plan (Caer Drewyn). 1887.

4484 Savory (Hubert Newman). Excavation of an Early Iron Age fortified settlement on Mynydd Bychan, Llysworney, Glam., 1949. Bull. Bd. Celtic Stud., 13, pp. 247–50. 1950.

4485 —— Further excavations at the Early Iron Age settlement on Mynydd Bychan, Llysworney (Glam.), 1950. Bull. Bd. Celtic Stud., 14, pp. 171–74. 1951.

4486 —— Excavation at the Gaer, Aberllynfi (Breck.), Bull. Bd. Celtic Stud., 14, pp. 251–52. 1951.

4487 —— List of hill-forts and other earthworks in Wales. [i. Glamorgan; ii. Monmouthshire; iii. Brecknockshire; iv. Radnorshire; v. Carmarthenshire.] Bull. Bd. Celtic Stud., 13, pp. 152–61, 231–38; 14, pp. 69–75; 15, pp. 73–80, 228–31 (additions to i–iii); 16, pp. 54–69. 1949–1954.

4488 Savory (Hubert Newman). Excavation of an early Iron Age fortified settlement on Mynydd Bychan, Llysworney (Glam.), 1949–50. Arch. Camb., 103, 1954, 85–108 + 3 figures + 4 plates.

4489 —— Excavation of an early Iron Age fortified settlement on Mynydd Bychan, Llysworney (Glam.) 1949–50. Part II. Arch. Camb., 104, 1955, 14–51 + 5 figures + 4 plates.

4490 —— The 1955 excavations at Dinas Emrys hill-fort, Beddgelert (Caern.). [Late Bronze or Early Iron Age.] Bull. Bd. Celtic Stud., 16, pp. 213–214; 17, pp. 55–57 + plate. 1955–56.

4491 —— Dinas Emrys. [Iron Age hill-fort.] Caernarvonshire Hist. Soc. Trans., 17, pp. 1–8 + 4 plates + plan. 1956.

4492 —— Excavations at Dinorben hill-fort, Abergele (Denb.), 1956–57. [Figure + 2 plans.] Bull. Bd. Celtic Stud., 17, pp. 296–309 + 3 plates. 1958.

4493 —— Newly recorded earthworks in east Glamorgan. Trans. Cardiff Nat. Soc., 86 (1956–57), pp. 29–30. 1959.

4494 Stapleton (Philip). Exploration of Moel-y-Gaer [camp], Bodfari, [Flintshire]. [Figure + 2 plans.] Arch. Camb., 6th S. 9, pp. 232–38. 1909.

4495 Tierney (H. Carlton). British camp at Cwmrheiddol. Trans. Carmarthenshire Ant. Soc., 5, pp. 92–95. 1910.

4496 Wainwright (G. J.). Excavations at Castell Bryn Gwyn, Anglesey 1959. Trans. Anglesey Antiq. Soc. Fld. Club, 1960, 50–52.

4497 —— The Excavation of an earthwork at Castell Bryn-Gwyn, Llanidan Parish, Anglesey. Arch. Camb., 111, 1962, 25–58 + 17 figures.

4498 Wight (M.). An Iron Age stronghold. [Tre'r Ceiri.] Country Life, 89, pp. 248–49. 1941.

4499 Williams (Aneurin). Camp circles at Penygroes, Carnarvonshire. [Plan.] Arch. Camb., 6th S. 19, pp. 534–35. 1919.

4500 Williams (Audrey). The Knave promontory fort, Rhossili, Gower. Bull. Bd. Celtic Stud., 9, pp. 286–87. 1938.

4501 —— Excavations at the Knave Promontory fort, Rhossili, Glamorgan. Arch. Camb., 94 ii, 1939, 210–19 + 5 figures.

4502 —— The Excavation of Bishopston Valley promontory fort, Glamorgan. Arch. Camb., 95 i, 1940, 9–19 + 5 figures.

4503 —— Bishopston Valley promontory fort, Gower, Glamorgan. Bull. Bd. Celtic Stud., 10, pp. 188–89. 1940.

4504 —— High Penard promontory fort, Gower, Glamorgan. Bull. Bd. Celtic Stud., 10, pp. 189–90. 1940.

4505 —— A Promontory fort at LLenllan, Cardiganshire. Arch. Camb., 98 ii, 1945, 226–40 + 5 figures + 6 plates.

4506 Williams (H. W.). The exploration of a prehistoric [stone-walled] camp [in the Rhondda valley] Glamorganshire. [4 figures + plan.] Arch. Camb., 6th S. 2, pp. 252–60. 1902.

4507 Williams (J. Graham). Ancient encampments near Aberystwith. Arch. Camb., 3rd S. 13, pp. 284–91 + map. 1867.

4508(a) —— Ancient British camps, etc. in Lleyn, Co. Carnarvon. Pwllheli, 1871. (British Museum Additional MSS. No. 28,860.)

4508(b) Williams (Victor Erle Nash). The fortified hill-settlements at Llanmelin, Monmouthshire. Bull. Bd. Celtic Stud., 5, pp. 274–77. 1930.

4508(c) —— The fortified hill-settlement at Llanmelin, Monmouthshire. [Early Iron Age.] Antiq. J., 11, pp. 70–71. 1931.

4508(d) —— The Early Iron Age Hill Settlement at Llanmelin, Monmouthshire. Arch. Camb., 86 ii, 1931, 365–66.

4508(e) —— The Early Iron Age hill-settlement at Llanmelin, Monmouthshire. Bull. Bd. Celtic Stud., 6, pp. 92–93, 288–89. 1931–32.

4509(a) —— The Fortified hill-settlement at Llanmelin, Monmouthshire. Arch. Camb., 87 ii, 1932, 393.

4509(b) —— An Early Iron Age hill-fort at Llanmelin, near Caerwent, Monmouthshire. With a note on the distribution of hill-forts and other earthworks in Wales and the Marches. The Pottery, by C. F. C. Hawkes. Report on the Osseous remains, Llanmelin Hillfort by Lionel F. Cowley. Arch. Camb., 88 ii, 1933, 237–346 + 57 figures.

4509(c) —— An Early Iron Age coastal camp at Sudbrook, Portskewett,

Monmouthshire. Arch. Camb., 90 i, 1935, 159–61 + 2 figures.

4509(d) Williams (Victor Erle Nash). The Early Iron Age coastal camp at Sudbrook, Portskewett, Monmouthshire. Arch. Camb., 91 i, 1936, 129–31 + 2 figures.

4510(a) —— Sudbrook excavations, 1936. Arch. Camb., 91 ii, 1936, 314–16 + 2 figures.

4510(b) —— Sudbrook excavations, 1936. Bull. Bd. Celtic Stud., 8, p. 275. 1936.

4510(c) —— An Early Iron Age coastal camp at Sudbrook, near the Severn Tunnel, Monmouthshire. Arch. Camb., 94 i, 1939, 42–79 + 9 figures and 9 plates.

4511(a) —— *and* **Savory** (Hubert Newman). Map of Wales showing hillforts and other earthworks. Bull. Bd. Celtic Stud., 13, p. 152 + folding map. 1949.

4511(b) Williams (W. Wynn), *junior.* Fortified British village, Porthamel [Anglesey]. Arch. Camb., 3rd S. 13, pp. 281–84 + plate + plan. 1867.

4512(a) —— Din Sylwy [camp], Anglesey. [5 plans.] Arch. Camb., 3rd S. 15, pp. 56–61 + 8 plates + plan. 1869.

4512(b) —— Pentyrch, Carnarvonshire. [Hill-fort.] Arch. Camb., 4th S. 4, pp. 154–57 + plate + plan. 1873.

4513(a) —— Caer-Creini. Arch. Camb., 4th S. 12, pp. 307–15 + plate + plan. 1881.

4513(b) Wright (Frank S.). Some ancient defensive earthworks near Aberystwyth, with notes on early communications. Aberystwyth Stud., 2, pp. 45–68 + 6 plans. 1914.

(f) Zone 6 [CBA Group 1 plus Ireland and Isle of Man]

4514 Anderson (George). Vitrified forts, with description of Craig Phadrich, near Inverness. Trans. Edinburgh Geol. Soc., 1, 1870, 302–04.

4515 Babington (Charles Cardale). On the Firbolgic forts in the south isles of Aran, [co. Galway], Ireland. [Plan (Dun Aengus).] Arch. Camb., 3rd S. 4, pp. 96–103 + plate (Dun Aengus). 1858.

4516 Barrington (*Hon.* Daines). Observations on the vitrified walls in Scotland. Archaeologia, 6, pp. 100–03. 1782.

4517 Bell (Richard). Forts and their connecting trenches in Eskdalemuir. Trans. Dumfries. Ant. Soc., 17 (1900–1901), pp. 76–85. 1906.

4518 Berry (R. G.). The Royal residence of Rathmore of Moy-linne with notes on other early earthworks in Ulster. Ulster J. Arch., 4, 1898, 123–25.

4519 —— The Royal residence of Rathmore of Moy-linne with notes on other early earthworks in Ulster. [?date]. Ulster J. Arch., 4, 1898, 160–70.

4520 —— The Royal residence of Rathmore of Moy-linne with notes on other early earthworks in Ulster. Ulster J. Arch., 4, 1898, 241–55 + 3 figures.

4521 Childe (Vere Gordon). A promontory fort on the Antrim coast. [3 figures + 4 plans.] Larriban head. Antiq. J., 16, pp. 179–98 + 4 plates. 1936.

4522 —— Kaimes hill fort, Midlothian. Antiq. J., 20, pp. 495–97 + plate. 1940.

4523 Christison (David). Early fortifications in Scotland: notes, camps, and forts. *Rhind Lectures,* 1894. pp. xxvi, 407 + 3 maps. 8°. Edinburgh, 1898. [137 figures in text.]

4524 Coffey (George) *and* **Jamison** (H. L.). Fort and souterrain at Shancoduff, Co. Monaghan. Ulster J. Arch., 3, 1897, 275–76 + 1 figure.

4525 Cormack (W. F.). Prehistoric site at Beckton, Lockerbie. Trans. Dumfries & Galloway N.H. & Ant. Soc. 41, 1962/63, 111–15 + 3 figures.

4526 —— Palisaded enclosure at Harthill, Lockerbie. Trans. Dumfries & Galloway N.H. & Ant. Soc., 41, pp. 116–17 + 2 figures. 1962º63.

4527 Cruden (S. H.). The Chesters. Arch. J., 121, 1964, 175–76.

4528 Curle (Alexander Ormiston). Notice of some excavation on the fort occupying the summit of Bonchester hill, parish of Hobkirk, Roxburghshire. [Early Iron Age?] Trans. Hawick Archaeol. Soc., 1910, pp. 77–80 + plan. 1910.

4529 —— The prehistoric forts of Scotland. Trans. Hawick Archaeol. Soc., 1932, pp. 1–6. 1932.

4530(a) Dickson (John M.). The "Dane's Cast" [Cos. Armagh and Down]. Ulster J. Arch., 3, 1897, 200.

4530(b) Du Noyer (George Victor). On the remains of ancient stone-built fortresses and habitations occurring to the west of Dingle, county Kerry. [Figure + 18 plans.] Archaeol. J., 15, pp. 1–24 + 3 plates + map. 1858.

4531 Drummond, *Mrs*. The prehistory and prehistoric remains of the Hillfoots and neighbouring district. Trans. Stirling N.H. & Arch. Soc., 59 (1936–37), pp. 112–28. 1937.

4532(a) Elliot (J.). The vitrified forts of Scotland. Trans. Hawick Archaeol. Soc., 1871.

4532(b) Elliot (J. Scott), *Maj.-Gen. and* **Coles** (J. M.). Excavations at McNaughton's Fort, Kirkcudbright [Iron Age]. Trans. Dumfries 43, 1966, 73–79 + 3 figures + 3 plates.

4533 Fairhurst (Horace). The Meikle Reive, a hill fort on the Campsies, Stirlingshire. [Iron Age.] Trans. Glasgow Archaeol. Soc., N.S. 14, pp. 64–89 + plate + 2 plans. 1956.

4534 —— An Caisreal: an Iron Age fortification in Mull. Proc. Soc. Ant. Scotland, 95, 1961–62, 199–207 + 3 figures + 2 plates.

4535 Feachem (Richard William de Fécamp). Castlehill wood dun, Stirlingshire. Proc. Soc. Antiq. Scot., 90 (1956–57), pp. 24–51 + plate. 1959.

4536 Fraser (George Milne). Dunnideer and its triple fortresses. pp. 68. 8º. Aberdeen, 1927. [Bibliography.]

4537 Geikie (James). List of hill forts, intrenched camps, etc. in Roxburghshire on the Scotch side of the Cheviots. Hist. Berwickshire Nat. Club, 10, pp. 139–48. 1882.

4538 Gelling (Peter S.). Close ny chollagh: an Iron Age fort at Scarlett, Isle of Man (with a report on animal remains, by W. Potts). Proc. Prehist. Soc., 24, 1958, 85–100 + 6 figures + 7 plates.

4539 Hamilton (Edward). Vitrified forts on the west coast of Scotland. Archaeol. J., 37, pp. 227–43 + 2 plans. 1880.

4540 Hamilton (John R. C.). Excavations at Jarlshof, Shetland. *Ministry of Works, Archaeological reports*, 1. pp.

xiii, 228 + 40 plates + plan. 4º. Edinburgh, 1956.

4541 Hibbert (Samuel). Observations on the theories which have been proposed to explain the vitrified forts of Scotland. [3 figures. Pp. 180–81, List of 44 forts.] Archaeol. Scot., 4, pp. 160–82. 1857.

4542 —— Collections relative to vitrified sites. [3 figures + 8 plans.] Archaeol. Scot., 4, pp. 183–201, 280–98 + plate. 1857.

4543 Home (David Milne). Notices of the remains of ancient camps on both banks of the river Tweed, near Milne-Graden. [Plan.] Hist. Berwick. Nat. Club, 4, pp. 454–58 + plan. 1862.

4544 Honeyman (John). Remarks on the construction of vitrified forts. Trans. Glasgow Archaeol. Soc., 2, pp. 29–34. 1883.

4545 —— Note on a vitrified fort at Rhufresean, Ardmarnock, Argyllshire. Trans. Glasgow Archaeol. Soc., N.S. 1, pp. 340–42 + plan. 1890.

4546 Hughes (Thomas McKenny). On the camp at Ardoch, in Perthshire. [3 plans.] Archaeologia, 54, pp. 267–72. 1895.

4547 Jamieson (John). On the vitrified forts of Scotland. Trans. Roy. Soc. Lit., 2, pp. 227–51. 1832.

4548 Keddie (William). On the remains of a vitrified fort, or site, in the island of Cumbrae, with notes on the vitrified forts of Berigonium, Glen Nevis, Craig Phadrick, Portencross, and Bute. Trans. Glasgow Archaeol. Soc., 1, pp. 236–55. 1868.

4549 Lennox (James). Wood-Castle, Lochmaben. [Circular camp of British origin.] Trans. Dumfries. Ant. Soc., 6 (1887–90), pp. 38–40. 1890.

4550 Lett (H. W.) *and* **Berry** (R. G.). The Great wall of Midia, commonly known as "The Dane's Cast", or "Gleanna-na-muice-duibhe". Ulster J. Arch., 3, 1896, 23–29 + 3 figures + 2 plates and 1897, 65–82 + 1 map.

4551 Lynn (Francis). Bunkle Edge forts. [2 figures + 5 plans.] Hist. Berwick. Nat. Club, 14, pp. 364–76. 1895.

4552 Mackay (Mackintosh). Description of the hill fort of Dùn-da-Làimh, in the parish of Laggan, district

of Badenoch, Inverness-shire. [Plan.]
Archaeol. Scot., 4, pp. 305–12. 1857.

4554 Maclaren (A.). Stanhope Dun,
Peeblesshire. Proc. Soc. Ant. Scotland,
93, 1959–60, 192–201 + 5 figures.

4555 Mapleton (R. J.). Description
of stockaded remains recently discovered
at Arisaig, Inverness-shire. Proc. Soc.
Antiq. Scot., 7, pp. 516–19. 1870.

4556 Maxwell (Herbert Eustace).
Vitrified fortifications [in Galloway].
N. & Q., 9 S. 11, pp. 110–11. 1885.

4557 Maxwell (J. Harrison). The
vitrified fort on Eilean Buidhe, Kyles of
Bute. [4 figures + 2 plans.] Trans.
Glasgow Archaeol. Soc., N.S. 10, pp. 60–
70. 1941.

4558 Michie (A.). The British camp
on Rinkhill. Trans. Hawick Arch. Soc.,
1870.

4559 Neish (James) *and* **Stuart** (John).
Reference notes to plan and views of
ancient remains on the summit of the
Laws, Forfarshire. [Vitrified fort.] Proc.
Soc. Antiq. Scot., 3, pp. 440–54 + plate
+ plan. 1862.

4561 O'Kelly (Michael J.). Excavation of a ring-fort at Garryduff, co. Cork
[late Iron Age]. [4 figures (pottery,
bronze brooch and gold bird).] Antiquity, 20, pp. 122–26. 1946.

4562 Piggott (Cecily Margaret).
South Scottish hill-fort excavations.
[Hownam Rings, Hayhope Knowe, Bonchester.] Arch. News Letter, 4, pp. 45–
47. 1951.

4563 Piggott (Stuart). Excavations at
Braidwood Fort, Midlothian and Craig's
Quarry, Dirleton, East Lothian [EIA
fort and house site]. Proc. Soc. Antiq.
Scotland, 91, 1960, 61–77 + 8 figures + 1
plate.

4564 Riddell (Robert). Observations
on vitrified fortifications in Galloway.
Archaeologia, 10, pp. 147–50. 1792.

4565 Rivet, A. L. F. Eildon Hill-
Fort (NT 555328). [Note for Summer
Meeting with whole page plan.] Arch. J.,
121, 1964, 202–03.

4566 Russell, *Miss*. The vitrified
forts of the north of Scotland, and
the theories as to their history. J. Brit.
Archaeol. Ass., 50, pp. 205–22. 1894.

4568 Simpson (D. D. A.) *and* **Elliot**
(J. Scott), *Maj.-Gen.* Excavations at
Camp Hill, Trohoughton, Dumfries

[LBA–IA palisaded enclosure & later
stone-faced ramparts]. Trans. Dumfries
& Galloway, N.H. & Ant. Soc., 41,
1962/63, 125–34 + 5 figures + 11 plates.

4569 Simpson (Richard). A con-
trast in prehistoric forts near Dunscore.
Trans. Dumfries. Ant. Soc., 17 (1901–
1902), pp. 136–40. 1906.

4570 Skene (James). An account of
the hill fort at the Barmekyne in Aberdeenshire. Archaeol. Scot., 2, pp. 324–27
+ plate + plan. 1822.

4571 Smail (Henry Richardson). Prehistoric camp at Earnsheugh. Hist.
Berwick. Nat. Club, 30, pp. 213–14.
1947.

4572 Stewart (M. E. C.). The Excavation of two circular enclosures at
Dalnaglar, Perthshire [dating uncertain
but 1st cent. B.C. prob.]. Proc. Soc. Ant.
Scotland, 95, 1961–62, 134–58 + 12
figures + 3 plates.

4573 Thomas (Charles). Excavations
at Trusty's Hill, Anwoth, Kirkcudbrightshire, 1960 [Late IA fort]. Trans.
Dumfries & Galloway N.H. & Ant.
Soc., 37, 1959, 58–70 + 6 figures.

4574 Thomas (F. W. L.). On the
duns of the outer Hebrides. [Prehistoric
fortifications.] Archaeol. Scot., 5, pp.
365–415 + 7 plates (with plans), 1890.

4575 Thomson (James). The hill
forts of Angus. pp. 39. Sm. 8⁰. Ar-
broath, [18– ?].

4576 Truckell (Alfred Edgar). Tynron Doon, 1964–65. Trans. Dumfries &
Galloway N.H. & Ant. Soc., 43, pp.
147–49 + 1 figure. 1966.

4577 Walton (*Captain* R. H.). Note
on Castle Hill, Callaby [IA hill-fort].
Hist. Berwicks. Naturalists Club, 34 iii,
1958, 205–10 + 1 figure.

4578 Walton (*Capt.* R. H.). The
Catrail—another theory. N'umberland
—Galashiels. [Linear earthwork—un-
known date.] Yarrow—Melrose—hidden
date. Deil's Dyke. The Picts' Work
Ditch, Selkirk. Hist. Berwicks. Nat'list
Club, 36 i, 1962, 60–63.

4579 Winning (John G.). Ancient
British forts on Chapelhill [near Hawick].
Trans. Hawick Archaeol. Soc., 1929, pp.
22–23. 1929.

4580 Young (Hugh W.). Henderland
hill fort, Peebles-shire. [Figure.] Reliquary, N. [3rd] S. 1, pp. 99–100. 1895.

7. ALL OTHER SITES BY ZONES

(a) Zone 1 [CBA Groups 7, 9, 10, 11A, 11B, 14]

4581 Abbott (G. Wyman). The discovery of prehistoric pits at Peterborough [pp. 333–40 + 6 figures]; and the development of Neolithic pottery, by Reginald A. Smith. [14 figures.] Archaeologia, 62, pp. 333–52 + 3 plates. 1910.

4582 Abbott (W. J. Lewis). The Hastings kitchen middens. Pp. 137–45 + 2 plates, (Notes on some specialised and diminutive forms of flint implements from [the midden]). J. Anthrop. Inst., 25, pp. 122–30 + 2 plates (flints). 1895.

4583 Alexander (John). Early Cambridge: An interim report on the excavations at Castle Hill, Cambridge 1956–1962. Archaeol. News Letter, 7, 1964, 222–26 + 5 figures.

4584 —— The History of Cambridge. Excavations on Castle Hill, 1956–1964. History Today, 15, 1965, 800–02 + 2 figures.

4585 [Anon.] Bronze Age settlement [at Itford hill] in Sussex. Num. Circular, 58, w. 530. 1950.

4586 Apling (Harry). A Hallstatt settlement at West Harling, Norfolk. Proc. PSEA, 7 i, 1932–34, 111–22 + 5 figures.

4587 Applebaum (E. S.). An Early Iron Age site at Holwell, Hertfordshire. [4 figures + map. Pottery, etc.] Antiq. J., 14, pp. 383–88. 1934.

4588 Armstrong (Albert Leslie). A Late Upper Antignacian Station in North Lincolnshire. Proc. PSEA, 6 iv, 1931, 335–39 + 2 figures.

4589 —— A living site of La Tène age [at Willoughton], in north Lincolnshire. [Beads, etc.] Antiq. J., 13, pp. 55–57. 1933.

4590 Arnold (Edward Dudbridge). The Selmeston Mesolithic site. Sussex N. & Q., 13, pp. 312–13 + plate. 1953.

4591 Atkinson (Richard John Copland). Archaeological sites on Port Meadow, Oxford. [Late Bronze and Early Iron Ages. 2 figures, map and plan.] Oxoniensia, 7, pp. 24–35 + 3 plates. 1942.

4592 Barrington (*Hon.* Daines). An account of certain remarkable pits or caverns in the earth, [near Little Coxwell] in the county of Berks. Archaeologia, 7, pp. 236–43. 1785.

4593 Barton (K. J.). Settlements of the Iron Age and Pagan Saxon periods at Linford, Essex [Iron Age A and RB pottery]. Trans. Essex Arch. Soc., 3 Ser. 1 (1962), pt. 2, 59–104 + 2 plates + 18 figures.

4594 Bawtree (M.). Iver: Larbourne Farm, Thorney [Notes]. Record of Bucks., 17 (1) 1961, 88.

4595 Bell (A. M.). The later age of stone, especially in connection with remains found near Limpsfield. pp. 54. 8°. [n.p.], 1888.

4596 —— Palaeolithic remains at Wolvercote, Oxfordshire. [2 figures. (5 figures).] Antiquary, 30, pp. 148–52; 192–98. 1894.

4597 Benton (Gerald Montagu). Early Iron Age site at Braintree, Essex. Antiq. J., 3, p. 148. 1923.

4598 Birchall (Ann). The Belgic problem: Aylesford revisited. Brit. Mus. Quart., 28 1/2 1964, 21–29 + 3 figures + 3 plates.

4599 Blake (Brian). Excavations at Bulmer, Suffolk. Colchester Archaeol. Group, Quart. Bull., 1, p. 22. 1928.

4600 Bowen (A. R.). Observations on the Mesolithic site at Sudbrook, near Grantham. Lincs. Archit. & Archaeol. Soc., Rpts. & Papers, 45, (N.S. 3), pp. 103–08 + plate. 1948.

4601 Boyle (J.). Canterbury: excavations at 10 and 11 Castle Street, 1950. (—1951). Arch. News Letter, 3, pp. 145–47; 4, pp. 157–59. 1951–52.

4602 Boyden (J. R.). Excavations at Hammer wood, Iping: 1957. [Map + plan. Iron Age.] Sussex Arch. Collns., 96, pp. 149–63 + 3 plates. 1958.

4603 Bradford (John Spencer Purvis) *and* **Goodchild** (Richard George). Excavations at Frilford, Berks., 1937–8. 13 figures (maps + plans). Oxoniensia, 4, pp. 1–70 + 5 plates. 1939.

4604 —— An Early Iron Age settlement at Standlake, Oxon. [2 figures (pottery) + 2 plans.] Antiq. J., 22, pp. 202–14 + 2 plates. 1942.

4605 —— An Early Iron Age site at Allen's Pit, Dorchester. [6 figures.]

Oxoniensia, 7, pp. 36–60 + plate. 1942; 11/12, 175–81. 1947.

4606 Brailsford (John William). A new microlithic site on West Heath. [3 figures.] Sussex Arch. Collns., 78, pp. 224–29. 1937.

4607 Briscoe (Grace), *Lady*. Combined Beaker and Iron Age sites at Lakenbeath, Suffolk. [14 figures + 2 plans.] Proc. Camb. Antiq. Soc., 42, pp. 92–111 + 4 plates. 1949.

4608 —— A Windmill Hill site at Hurst fen, Mildenhall, [Suffolk]. [6 figures (pottery and flint implements) + map + plan.] Proc. Camb. Antiq. Soc., 47 (1953), pp. 13–24. 1954.

4609 —— Combined Early Iron Age and Romano-British site at Wangford, West Suffolk. [3 figures + 2 plans.] Proc. Camb. Antiq. Soc., 51 (1957), pp. 19–29. 1958.

4610 Bull (J. M.). A prehistoric site at Twitty Fee, Danbury. [Figure.] Essex Nat., 25, pp. 87–93 + plan. 1935.

4611 Burchell (James Percy Tufnell). The Shell Mound industry of Denmark as represented at Lower Halstow, Kent. Proc. PSEA, 5 i, 1925, 73–78 + 8 figures.

4612 —— Further report on the Epi-Palaeolithic factory site at Lower Halstow, Kent. Proc. PSEA, 5 ii, 1926, 217–223 + 4 plates.

4613 —— A settlement of the dolmen period [in Knowle park, Sevenoaks]. (A further note on the Knowle park settlement). [Figure.] Man, 26, p. 114; 27, pp. 112–13. 1926–27.

4614 —— A Final account of the investigations carried out at Lower Halstow, Kent. Proc. PSEA, 5 iii, 1927, 288–96 + 12 figures.

4615 —— Two Mesolithic "floors" in the Ebbsfleet [west of Northfleet] valley of the lower Thames. [12 figures (flints).] Antiq. J., 18, pp. 397–401. 1938.

4617 Burstow (George Philip). Late Bronze Age farmstead on Itford hill, [near Newhaven]. The second season's work. [5 figures.] Sussex County Mag., 25, pp. 130–34. 1951.

4618 —— *and* **Holleyman** (George Albert). A Late Bronze Age settlement on Itford hill. A short account of excavations there in 1949 and 50. Sussex N. & Q., 13, pp. 175–77. 1951.

4619 —— The Late Bronze Age settlement on Itford hill. The excavations of 1951, 2, and 3. Sussex N. & Q., 14, pp. 101–02. 1955.

4620 —— *and* **Holleyman** (George Albert). Excavations at Muntham Court, Findon. Interim report, 1954–5. Sussex N. & Q., 14, pp. 196–98, 232–33. 1956.

4621 —— *and* —— Late Bronze Age settlement on Itford Hill, Sussex (with a note on carbonized cereals, by Hans Helbaek). Proc. Prehist. Soc., 23, 1957, 167–212 + 31 figures + 10 plates.

4622 —— *and* —— Excavations at Plumpton Plain site B, August 1958. [Late Bronze Age site.] Sussex N. & Q., 15, p. 129. 1959.

4623 —— *and others* [**Holleyman** (G. A.), *and* **Norris** (N. E. S.)]. Excavations at Balcombe Quarry, Glynde [IA settlement]. Sussex Notes & Queries, 16 i, pp. 22–24. 1963.

4624 Caiger (J. E. L.). A Belgicte si at Bexley. [Figure (pottery).] Archaeol. Cant., 72 (1958), pp. 186–89. 1959.

4625 Case (Humphrey). Archaeological Notes. Cumnor, Berks. [mesolithic blades]. Oxoniensia, 23, 1958, 130.

4626 —— Archaeological notes: Enstone, Oxon. [Neolithic flint implement and ditch possibly of small Long Barrow.] Oxoniensia, 23, 1958, 131–32 + 1 figure.

4627 Caux (Henry de). A prehistoric site in the Yare valley. Norfolk Arch., 28, pp. 71–75 + plate. 1942.

4628 Chandler (R. H.). On the Clactonian industry at Swanscombe. Proc. PSEA, 6 ii, 1929, 79–130 + 24 figures + 7 tables.

4629 —— Types of Clactonian implements at Swanscombe. Preliminary notice. Proc. PSEA, 6 iv, 1931, 377–78.

4630 Chapman (D. I.) *and* **Hammond** (P. M.). A Preliminary report on investigations in the Deneholes at Hangman's Wood, Grays, Essex [no dating evidence]. Essex Naturalist 31 i, 1962, 1–15 + 1 plate + 2 figures.

4631 Cheney (H. J.). The prehistoric site at Playden. Sussex County Mag., 5, pp. 206–11. 1931.

4632 —— An Aeneolithic occupation site at Playden, near Rye, [Sussex]. [4 figures + map + plan. Pp. 161–63, Report on the pottery, by Stuart Piggott].

Antiq. J., 15, pp. 152–64 + 2 plates. 1935.

4633 Christy (Miller). On the remains of a supposed pile-dwelling at Woodham Walter, Essex. Essex Nat., 13, pp. 280–82. 1904.

4634 Churchill (D. M.). The Stratigraphy of the Mesolithic sites III and V at Thatcham, Berkshire, England. Proc. Prehist. Soc., 28, 1962, 362–70 + 3 figures.

4635 Clark (John Grahame Douglas). A Stone Age site on Swaffham Prior farm. Proc. Camb. Antiq. Soc., 32, pp. 17–23 + plate (implements). 1930.

4636 —— A microlithic flaking site at West Heath, W. Harting. [5 figures.] Sussex Arch. Collns., 73, pp. 145–55. 1932.

4637 —— Early settlement at Runcton Holme, Norfolk, Part I. The first occupation: Neolithic and Beaker remains. Proc. PSEA, 7 ii, 1932–34, 199–202 + 5 figures.

4639 —— Report on an Early Bronze Age site [at Plantation Farm, Shippen hill], in the south-eastern Fens. [8 figures + map. Pottery, etc.] Antiq. J., 13, pp. 266–96 + 6 plates. 1933.

4640 —— A Late Mesolithic settlement site at Selmeston, Sussex. [10 figures + map.] Antiq. J., 14, pp. 134–158. 1934.

4641 —— *etc.* Report on recent excavations at Peacock's farm, Shippen Hill, Cambridgeshire. [16 figures + map + 2 plans. Early Bronze Age, Neolithic "A" and Late Tardenoisïan.] Antiq. J., 15, pp. 284–319 + 6 plates + plan. 1935.

4642 —— Report on a Late Bronze Age site in Mildenhall fen, west Suffolk. [11 figures + map.] Antiq. J., 16, pp. 29–50 + 2 plates. 1936.

4643 —— Mesolithic pit-dwellings. [At Farnham, Surrey.] Antiquity, 11, pp. 476–78 + 2 plates. 1937.

4644 —— A report on trial excavations at Limlow hill, Litlington, Cambridgeshire. [2 figures. Early Iron Age.] Proc. Camb. Antiq. Soc., 38, pp. 170–76 + 2 plates. 1938.

4645 —— *and* **Rankine** (William Francis). Excavations at Farnham, Surrey (1937–38): the Horsham Culture and question of mesolithic dwellings. Proc.

prehist. Soc., 5, 1939, 61–118 + 24 figures.

4646 —— *and* **Fell** (Clare Isabel). The Early Iron Age site at Micklemoor Hill, West Harling, Norfolk, and its pottery [also so Levallois and Clacton flints]. Proc. prehist. Soc., 19, 1953, 1–40 + 21 figures + 6 plates.

4647 —— Excavations at the Neolithic site at Hurst Fen, Mildenhall, Suffolk. Proc. prehist. Soc., 26, 1960, 202–45 + 30 figures + 7 plates.

4648 Clark (J. P. H.). A new prehistoric site at Bost hill, Findon valley, Worthing. Sussex N. & Q., 14, pp. 98–99. 1955.

4648(b) Clarke (William George). A Prehistoric flint-pot at Ringland [Neolithic], Norfolk. Proc. PSEA, 2 i, 1914/1915, 148–51 + 1 plate.

4649 —— *and* **Halls** (H. H.). A "Cissbury type" station at Great Melton [Norfolk]. Proc. PSEA, 2 iii, 1916/17, 374–80 + 3 figures.

4650 —— An Early Neolithic site at Hockham, Norfolk [tranchet arrowheads, scrapers]. Proc. PSEA, 4 i, pp. 92–95 + 1 figure. 1922/24.

4651 Clay (Richard Challoner Cobbe). A Flint factory site at Little Somborne, Hants. Proc. PSEA, 5 i, 1925, 67–72 + 14 figures.

4652 Clinch (George). Prehistoric chambers discovered at Waddon, near Croydon. [2 plans.] Surrey Archaeol. Collns., 17, pp. 181–83. 1902.

4653 —— Ancient subterranean chambers at Waddon, near Croydon. Reliquary, 3rd S. 9, pp. 71–72. 1903.

4654 —— On some ancient subterranean chambers recently discovered at Waddon, near Croydon, Surrey. Man, 3, pp. 20–23. 1903.

4655 —— Recent discoveries [of ancient prehistoric chambers] at Waddon, Surrey. [Figure + plan.] Proc. Croydon N.H. & Sci. Soc., 5 (1902–03), pp. 40–58 + plate. 1903.

4656(a) —— Recent discoveries at Wallington. [Successive habitation Neolithic—Iron Age.] Surrey Archaeol. Collns., 20, pp. 233–35 + plate; 22, pp. 195–96. 1907–09.

4656(b) Cocks (Alfred Hentage). Prehistoric pit-dwellings at Ellesborough. Records of Bucks., 9, pp. 349–61 + plate (Early Iron Age pottery). 1909.

4657 Collins (A. E. P.). An Early Iron Age site on Hills road, Cambridge. Proc. Camb. Antiq. Soc., 41, pp. 76–77 + plate. 1948.

4658 Cook (Norman). A pit dwelling of the Early Iron Age at Rainham, Kent. [Figure. Pottery.) Arch. Cant., 49, pp. 280–83 + plate. 1938.

4659 Cook (W. H.) *and* **Killick** (J. R.). On the discovery of a flint-working site of Palaeolithic date in the Medway valley at Rochester, Kent, with notes on the drift-stages of the Medway. [Halling Man skull.] PPSEA, 4 ii, 1923/24, 133–154 + 4 plates + 7 figures.

4661 Cooper (G. Miles). An account of some British antiquities found at Wilmington. [Bronze Age.] Sussex Arch. Collns., 14, pp. 171–75 + plate. 1862.

4662(a) Coote (C. M. J.). Preliminary report on excavation at Houghton, Huntingdonshire. Trans. Cambs. & Hunts. Arch. Soc., 5, pp. 248–50 + 2 plates (pottery). 1937.

4662(b) Cotton (Percy Horace Gordon Powell) *and* **Pinfold** (G. F.). The Beck find. Prehistoric and Roman site on the foreshore at Minnis bay [Birchington]. Report and catalogue [of a Late Bronze Age hoard of celts and other implements]. [James Beck = finder (a boy of 14).] Arch. Cant., 51 (1939), pp. 191–203 + 5 plates. 1940.

4663 Cottrill (Frank). A Late Bronze Age hearth near Watford. Antiq. J., 19, pp. 81–82. 1939.

4664 Cra'ster (Mary D.). The Aldwick Iron Age settlement, Barley, Hertfordshire [8 figures + 6 plates]. Proc. Camb. Ant. Soc., vol. LIX (1961), pp. 22–46.

4665 —— Aldwick, Barley: recent work at the Iron Age site [5 figures + 1 plate]. Proc. Camb. Ant. Soc., LVIII (1965), 1–11.

4666 Crawford (O. G. S.). A Flint factory at Thatcham, Berks. II. The flint implements and flakes. Proc. PSEA, 3 iv, 500–14 + 4 figures + 1 plate. 1921/22.

4667 Curwen (Eliot). Prehistoric remains from Kingston Buci. [10 figures. Pp. 188–208, commentary on the pottery, by Christopher Hawkes.] Sussex Arch. Collns., 72, pp. 185–217. 1931.

4668 —— Flint implement site at Cowfold. Sussex County Mag., 11, pp. 246–47. 1937.

4669 Curwen (Eliot Cecil). The Lavant caves, Chichester. [Flint-mines.] Sussex N. & Q., 2, p. 81. 1928.

4670 —— A prehistoric site in Kingley Vale, near Chichester. Sussex Arch. Collns., 75, pp. 209–15. 1934.

4671 —— A flint-miner's dwelling and a Bronze Age farm in Sussex. Antiquity, 8, pp. 215–16 + 3 plates. 1934.

4672 —— A Late Bronze Age farm and a Neolithic pit-dwelling on New Barn down, Clapham, nr. Worthing. [13 figures + 5 plans.] Sussex Arch. Collns., 75, pp. 136–70 + plan. 1934.

4673 Dakin (G. F.). A Romano-British site at Orton Longueville, Huntingdonshire [10 figures + 2 plates]. Proc. Camb. Ant. Soc., LIV, 1961, 50–67.

4674 Davey (Norman). Neolithic site at Oxtrey, near Watford. St. Albans Archit. & Archaeol. Soc. Trans., 1930, pp. 65–68 + 5 plates (implements) + plan. 1931.

4675(a) Dawson (G. J.). Excavations at Purwell Farm, Cassington. Oxoniensia, 26/27 1961/62, 1–6 + 3 figures.

4675(b) Densham (H. B. A. Ratcliffe). Middle Brow [near Storrington]. [Site inhabited in Late Bronze Age.] Sussex N. & Q., 11, pp. 155–56. 1947.

4675(c) —— *and* **Densham** (M. M. Ratcliffe). A Celtic farm in Blackpatch [hill, Patching]. [6 figures + 2 plans. Late Bronze Age site.] Sussex Arch. Collns. 91, pp., 69–83. 1953.

4676 Detsicas (A. P.). Greenhithe: excavations at Stone Castle Quarry. Arch. Cantiana, 77, 1962, 200–01.

4677 Dutt (William Alfred). New Palaeolithic site in the Waveney valley. [2 figures.] Man, 8, pp. 41–42, 168–69. 1908.

4678(a) Dyer (James F.). Recent excavations near Hexton. Herts. Countryside, 9, pp. 142–43. 1955.

4678(b) Edgar (William). Borough Hill [Northants] and its history. pp. vi, 118. 8°. London, 1923. [34 figures and plates. Pp. 19–38, camp and tumuli.]

4679 Edmonds (Michael). Orpington, Well Hill: mesolithic sites. Arch. Cantiana, 77, 1962, 199–200.

4680 Edwardson (A. R.). Excavations at Gainsborough Road, Bury St.

Edmunds. Proc. Suffolk Inst. Archaeol., 27, pp. 89–95 + plate (urns). 1957.

4681 Evans (*Sir* Arthur) *and* **Smith** (Reginald Allender). Find of Late-Celtic antiquities at Welwyn, Herts. Proc. Soc. Antiq., 2 S. 24, pp. 3–6. 1911.

4682 Featherstonhaugh (G. W.). Account of an excavation in the Chalk near Norwich. Proc. Geol. Soc., London, 1, 1827, 35.

4683 Fell (Clare Isobel). The Early Iron Age settlement at Fengate, Peterborough. [11 figures.] Archaeol. J., 100 (1943), pp. 188–223 + 2 plates. 1945.

4684 —— An Early Iron Age settlement, at Linton, Cambridgeshire. [4 figures + plan. Tools and pottery.] Proc. Camb. Antiq. Soc., 46 (1952), pp. 31–42. 1953.

4685 Field (Laurence F.). Castle hill, Newhaven. Sussex Arch. Collns., 80, pp. 263–68. 1939.

4686 Fox (*Sir* Cyril). Excavations at Foxton, Cambridgeshire, in 1922. Proc. Camb. Antiq. Soc., 25, pp. 37–46. 1922.

4687 —— A Settlement of the early Iron Age at Abingdon Pigotts, Cambs., and its subsequent history; as evidenced by objects preserved in the Pigott collection. Proc. PSEA, 4 ii, pp. 211–33 + 6 plates + 4 figures. 1923/24.

4688 —— *and* **Wolseley** (Garner R.). The Early Iron Age site at Findon Park, Findon, Sussex. [5 figures + map + 2 plans.] Antiq. J., 8, pp. 449–60. 1928.

4689 Francis (Alfred George). A shell-mound on a prehistoric creek at Southchurch, Essex, probably belonging to the Beaker period of the Bronze Age. [2 figures + map + plan.] Trans. Southend Ant. Soc., 1, pp. 208–29. 1925.

4690 —— A west Alpine and Hallstatt site at Southchurch, Essex. [4 figures + map.] Antiq. J., 11, pp. 410–418 + map. 1931.

4691 Francis (D. L.). Iron Age finds at Stoke clump, [Hammerstone and spindle whorl]. Sussex N. & Q., 14, p. 280. 1957.

4692 Frere (Sheppard Sunderland). An Iron Age site near Epsom. [Figure + 2 maps + plan.] Antiq. J., 22, pp. 123–138. 1942.

4693 —— An Iron Age site at West Clandon, Surrey, and some aspects of Iron Age and Romano-British culture in the Wealden area. [8 figures + 2 maps.] Archaeol. J., 101 (1944), pp. 50–67. 1946.

4694 —— *and* **Hogg** (Alexander Hubert Arthur). An Iron Age and Roman site on Mickleham downs. [2 figures.] Surrey Archaeol. Collns., 49, pp. 104–06. 1946.

4695 Garrood (Jesse Robert). Iron Age and Romano-British site at Salome Lodge, Leighton, [Hunts.]. Trans. Cambs. & Hunts. Arch. Soc., 6, pp. 66–72 + 3 plates. 1947.

4696 —— An Iron Age and Roman site at Houghton, [Hunts.]. [Figure (pottery).] Trans. Cambs. & Hunts. Arch. Soc., 6, pp. 155–58. 1947.

4697 Gell (A. S. R.). An Early Iron Age site at Lakenheath, Suffolk. [3 figures + plan. Pottery.] Proc. Camb. Antiq. Soc., 42, pp. 112–16. 1949.

4698 Greenfield (Ernest). A Neolithic pit and other finds from Wingham, East Kent [pottery, antler comb & flints]. Arch. Cant., 74, 1960, pp. 58–72 + 3 figures.

4699 Halahan (B. C.). Flint sites in Chiddingfold. [Figure.] Surrey Archaeol. Collns., 37, p. 239. 1927.

4700 Harding (Joan M.). Interim report on the excavation of a Late Bronze Age homestead in Weston Wood, Albury, Surrey. Surrey Arch. Collections, 61, 1964, 10–17 + 2 figures + 2 plates.

4701 Harrison (E. E.). A Pre-Roman and Romano-British site at Charterhouse, Godalming [Iron Age A and Second B]. Surrey Arch. Collections, 58, 1961, 21–34 + 7 figures.

4702 Harrison (James Park). Additional discoveries at Cissbury. J. Anthrop. hist., 7, pp. 412–33 + plate + plan. 1878.

4703 Harrison (Kenneth). A Note on High Lodge, Mildenhall. Proc. prehist. Soc., 4, 1938, 326–28 + 1 figure.

4704 Hastings (F. A.). Excavation of an Iron Age site at Hawk's Hill, Fetcham. Surrey Arch. Collections, 59, 1962, 86–88 + 1 figure.

4705 —— Hawk's Hill, Fetcham [IA farmstead]. Surrey Arch. Collections, 60, 1963, 82.

4706 —— Excavations of an Iron Age farmstead at Hawk's Hill, Leatherhead. Surrey Arch. Collections, 62, 1965, 1–43 + 14 figures + 1 plate.

4707 Haward (F. N.). A workshop site of primitive culture at Two-Mile-Bottom, Thetford [Mesolithic]. Proc. prehist. Soc. E.A., 1 iv, 1913/14, 461–67 + 4 figures.

4708 Hawkes (Charles Francis Christopher). Runcton Holme, Part II. The second occupation: a peasant settlement of the Iceni. Proc. prehist. Soc. E.A., 7 ii, pp. 231–62 + 52 figures. 1932–34.

4709 —— A Middle-Late Bronze Age date for the occupation-site at Playden, near Rye. Antiq. J., 15, pp. 467–71. 1935.

4710 —— A site of the Late Bronze–Early Iron Age transition at Totternhoe, Beds. [4 figures + map.] Antiq. J., 20, pp. 487–91. 1940.

4711 Head (John Frederick). Early Iron Age pits at Bledlow. Records of Bucks., 14, pp. 149–50. 1944.

4712 —— *and* **Piggott** (Cecily Margaret). An Iron Age site at Bledlow, Bucks. [6 figures + 2 maps.] Records of Bucks., 14, pp. 189–209 + plate. 1942.

4713 Hewitt (H. Dixon). Notes on some flint-chipping sites at Risby, Suffolk. Proc. prehist. Soc. E.A., 3 i, 1918/19, 67–72 + 2 plates + 1 figure.

4714 Hind (F.). The Clifton (Nottm.) Bronze Age pile settlement and the Broxtowe (Nottm.) Early Iron Age settlement. pp. 8. 8°. Nottingham, 1940. [4 figures + plan. *Reprint from* Nottinghamshire Guardian.]

4715 Holleyman (George Albert) *and* **Curwen** (Eliot Cecil). Late Bronze Age lynchet settlements on Plumpton Plain, Sussex. Proc. prehist. Soc., 1, 1935, 16–38 + 43 figures.

4716 —— Excavations on Itford hill, Sussex. [Late Bronze Age hut enclosures.] Arch. News Letter, 2, p. 180. 1950.

4717 —— Bronze-Age farmstead on Itford hill. [3 figures.] Sussex County Mag., 24, pp. 171–74. 1950.

4718 —— Itford hill excavations. [3 figures.] Sussex County Mag., 29, pp. 15–18. 1955.

4719 —— *and* **Burstow** (George Philip). Excavations at Muntham Court, Findon, Sussex. [3 figures. (2 figures). Iron Age site.] Arch. News Letter, 5, pp. 204–05; 6, pp. 101–02. 1955–57.

4720 Holmes (Thomas Vincent). On Deneholes. Trans. Essex Field Club, 3, 1883, 48–58.

4721 —— Miscellaneous notes on deneholes, 1883. Trans. Essex Fld. Club, 4, 1885, 87–110 + 5 figures.

4722 —— The deneholes of Kent. [10 figures.] V.C.H., Kent, 1, pp. 446–54. 1908.

4723 Hubbard (Arthur John) *and* **Hubbard** (George). Neolithic dew-ponds and cattle-ways. pp. x, 69 + 25 plates. 8°. London, 1905.

4724 Hurd (Howard). On a Late-Celtic village near Dumpton Gap, Broadstairs, [Kent]. [8 figures.] Archaeologia, 61, pp. 427–38 + plate + 3 plans. 1909.

4725 —— The discovery of a Late-Celtic settlement near Dumpton Gap, Broadstairs, Kent. Proc. Soc. Antiq., 2 S. 22, pp. 508–11. 1909.

4726 Hutchinson (Jonathan). Prehistoric remains lately found at Haslemere, Surrey, and some pottery from Late-Keltic graves. [4 figures + plan of urnfield.] Proc. Soc. Antiq., 2 S. 21, pp. 217–28. 1906.

4727 James (H. A.). The Folly in Cobham Park. Antiquity, 35 (1961), pp. 151–52.

4728 Johnston (David E.). Two Iron Age sites at Sandy. Beds. Archaeologist, 2, pp. 33–34 + 3 plates. 1959.

4729 Jones (E. C. H.). Orpington Mesolithic site. [2 figures (flints).] Arch. Cant., 65 (1952), pp. 174–78. 1953.

4730 Jones (Harry). On the discovery of some supposed vestiges of a pile dwelling in Barton mere, near Bury St. Edmunds. Q. J. Suffolk Inst. Arch., 1, pp. 31–36. 1869.

4731 Jones (M. U.). Excavations at Stanton Low, in the Upper Ouse Valley, during March, 1957 [5 figures + 4 plates]. Records of Bucks., 16 (3), 1957/8, 198–215.

4732 Keef (P. A. M.). Flint-chipping sites and hearths on Bedham hill near Pulborough. [7 figures + map + plan.] Sussex Arch. Collns., 81, pp. 215–35. 1940.

4734 —— *and others*. A Mesolithic site on Iping Common, Sussex, England (with J. J. Wymer and G. W. Dimbleby). Proc. prehist. Soc., 31, 1965, 85–92 + 3 figures.

4735 Kempson (G. H.). An early

wealden settlement at Kirdford. [Early Bronze Age—Mediaeval.] Sussex N. & Q., 5, pp. 21–22. 1934.

4736 Kenworthy (Joseph W.). A supposed Neolithic settlement at Skitts hill, Braintree, Essex. [17 figures + map + plan.] Essex Nat., 11, pp. 94–126 + 2 plates. 1899.

4737 —— A supposed Neolithic settlement at Skitts hill, Braintree, Essex. Reliquary, 3rd S. 7, pp. 121–23. 1901.

4738 Kenyon (Kathleen Mary). Excavations in Southwark [some EBA flints]. Surrey archaeol. Soc. Res. Papers, 5, 1959, 1–112 + 8 plates + 37 figures.

4739 —— Excavations in Southwark. (Research Papers of the Surrey Archaeological Society, No. 5.) Guildford, 1959, pp. 111, 8 plates + 37 figures.

4740 Kew, Royal Botanic Gardens. Aldwick, Barley: recent work at Iron Age site. Appendix III: Charcoal samples. Proc. Camb. Ant. Soc., LVIII, 1965, 9.

4741 Lacaille (Armand Donald) *and* **Oakley** (Kenneth Page). The palaeolithic sequence at Iver, Bucks. With an appendix on the geology, by K. P. Oakley. [Map.] Antiq. J., 16, pp. 420–43 + 5 plates. 1936.

4742 Lambert (C. A.). Aldwick, Barley: recent work on the Iron Age site. Appendix II: Weed seeds. Proc. Camb. Ant. Soc., LVIII (1965), 7–8.

4743 Layard (Nina Frances). A winter's work on the Ipswich Palaeolithic site. [Figure.] J. Anthrop. Inst., 36, pp. 233–36 + 2 plates. 1906.

4744 —— Account of a palaeolithic site in Ipswich. Proc. Camb. Antiq. Soc., 11, pp. 493–502. 1906.

4745 —— "Coast finds" by Major Moore at Felixstowe Ferry. Proc. PSEA, 2 i, 1914/15, 132–34 + 1 plate.

4746 —— The Mundford pebble industry [Aurignacian/Mousterian?]. Proc. prehist. Soc. E.A., 3 i, 1918/19, 150–57 + 4 figures + 1 plate.

4747 —— The Stoke Bone-bed, Ipswich [tortoise-core, Mousterian]. Proc. prehist. Soc. E.A., 3 ii, 1919/20, 210–19 + 5 figures.

4748 —— A Late Palaeolithic settlement in the Colne valley, Essex. [8 figures.] Antiq. J., 7, pp. 500–14 + 2 plates. 1927.

4749 Leach (Arthur). Dew-ponds. Woolwich Ant. Soc., Ann. Rpt., 14 (1908), pp. 83–89. 1909.

4750 Leaf (C. S.). Report on the excavation of two sites in Mildenhall fen [Suffolk]. [8 figures + 2 plans. Hayland house (Neolithic) and Fifty farm (Beaker habitation site).] Proc. Camb. Antiq. Soc., 35, pp. 106–27 + 3 plates (Neolithic bowl; beaker). 1935.

4751 Leakey (L. S. B.). Preliminary excavations of a Mesolithic site at Abinger common, Surrey. *Research Papers of the Surrey Archaeological Society*, 3. pp. 44 + 5 plates + 2 plans. 4°. [Guildford], 1951. [13 figures.]

4752 Leeds (Edward Thurlow). Further discoveries of the Neolithic and Bronze Ages at Peterborough. [15 figures (pottery).] Antiq. J., 2, pp. 220–237. 1922.

4753 —— A Neolithic site at Abingdon, Berks. [6 figures + 2 maps + plan.] Antiq. J., 7, pp. 438–64 + 2 plates. 1927.

4754 —— A Neolithic site at Abingdon, Berks. (Second report.) [4 figures + plan. *See also* 9, p. 37.] Antiq. J., 8, pp. 461–77 + 3 plates. 1928.

4755 —— An Iron Age site near Radley, Berks. [3 figures (pottery).] Antiq. J., 11, pp. 399–404. 1931.

4756 —— Recent Iron Age discoveries [at Chadlington, Cassington and Dorchester in Oxfordshire] and [at Radley], north Berkshire. [2 figures.] Antiq. J., 15, pp. 30–41 + 4 plates + plan. 1935.

4757 Lewis (Geoffrey D.). A possible mesolithic site at Angmering. Sussex Arch. Collections, 98, 1960, 12–13 + 1 figure.

4758 —— An Iron Age and Roman site at West Torring, Worthing. Sussex Arch. Collection, 98, 1960, 21–22.

4759 Little (R. I.). The Atwood School Iron Age and Romano-British site, Sanderstead. Surrey Arch. Collections, 58, 1961, 112–13.

4760 —— The Atwood Iron Age and Romano-British site, Sandershead, 1960. Surrey Arch. Collections, 61, 1964, 29–38 + 3 figures.

4761 Lowerison (Bellerby). An Aurignacian floor at Heacham, Norfolk. Proc. prehist. Soc. E.A., 1 iv, 1913/14, 475 + 1 plate.

4762 Lowther (Anthony William George). An Early Iron Age oven at St. Mary's hill, near Guildford. [2 figures (pottery).] Surrey Archaeol. Collns., 43, pp. 113–15 + plate (loom-weight). 1935.

4763 —— Excavations at Purberry Shot, Ewell, Surrey. A pre-Roman and Roman occupation site. [30 figures (pottery, etc.) + 2 plans.] Surrey Archaeol. Collns., 50, pp. 9–46 + 4 plates. 1949.

4764 Manning (W. H.). Excavation of an Iron Age and Roman site at Chadwell St. Mary, Essex [settlement from IA–4th c. A.D.]. Trans. Essex Arch. Soc., 3 Ser. 1 (1962), pt. 2, 127–40 + 7 figures.

4765 Margary (Ivan Donald). An Early Iron Age site near Merle common, Limpsfield. Surrey Archaeol. Collns., 42, pp. 110–11 + plate. 1934.

4766 —— Early Iron Age site at Danehill. Sussex N. & Q., 6, p. 29. 1936.

4767 Marr (J. E.). A Late Palaeolithic site on Wretham Heath, near Thetford. Proc. prehist. Soc. E.A., 1 iii, 1912/1913, 374–77 + 1 plate.

4768 ——, **King** (W. B. R.) and **Lethbridge** (Thomas Charles). An Upper Palaeolithic site near Fen Ditton. [Figure (implements.)] Proc. Camb. Antiq. Soc., 25, pp. 16–20. 1922.

4769 —— and **Burkitt** (Miles Crawford). A Neolithic site north-west of Cambridge. Proc. Soc. Antiq. Soc., 25, pp. 11–15. 1922.

4770(a) Marshall (Kenneth). Excavations at a Mesolithic site near High Beach, Epping Forest. Essex Naturalist, 30 iii, 1959, 163.

4770(b) —— A Denehole at Purfleet, Essex [no dating evidence]. Essex Naturalist, 31 iv, 1965, 271–73 + 2 plates + 1 figure.

4771 Martin (E. A.). Dew ponds. Trans. Eastbourne N.H. Soc., 8, pp. 151–152. 1921.

4772 Migeod (Frederick William Hugh). Cissbury. pp. 34. 8⁰. Worthing, 1950.

4773 Moir (James Reid). The discovery of a flint "workshop-floor" in Ivry Street, Ipswich. Proc. prehist. Soc. E.A., 1 iv, 1913/14, 475–79 + 2 plates.

4774 —— An Early Mousterian floor discovered at Ipswich. [4 figures.] Man, 18, pp. 98–100. 1918.

4775 —— An Early Neolithic floor discovered at Ipswich. [5 figures.] Man, 20, pp. 84–89. 1920.

4776 —— A Natural "Eolith" factory beneath the Thanet sand. Geol. Mag., 58, pp. 187–89, 1921.

4777 —— On an early Chellian–Palaeolithic workshop-site in the Pliocene forest bed of Cromer, Norfolk. (Further discoveries, etc.) [20 figures. (18 figures).] J. R. Anthrop. Inst., 51, pp. 385–418 + plate; 55, pp. 311–39 + 2 plates. 1921–25.

4778 —— An early Palaeolith from the glacial till at Sidestrand, Norfolk. [Figure.] Antiq. J., 3, pp. 135–37. 1923.

4779 —— Further researches in the Forest Bed of Cromer, Norfolk [Chellean flints]. Proc. Prehist. Soc. E.A., 5 iii, pp. 273–81, 8 figures. 1927.

4780 —— and **Hopwood** (A. Tindell). Excavations at Brundon, Suffolk (1935–1937) [Palaeolithic]. Proc. prehist. Soc., 5, 1939, 1–32 + 18 figures.

4781 Money (James H.). Excavations at High Rocks, Tunbridge Wells, 1954–56. Sussex Arch. Collections, 98, 1960, 173–221 + 2 plates + 25 figures.

4782 —— Excavations at High Rocks, Tunbridge Wells, 1954–56. Supplementary Note. Sussex Arch. Collections, 100, 1962, 149–51 + 1 figure.

4783 Money (Walter). Notes on a pile-structure in Grimsbury forest. [Berks.] Trans. Newbury F.C., 2 (1872–1875), pp. 150–53. 1878.

4784 Moore (John W.). Neolithic finds at Fairlight, Hastings. Sussex N. & Q., 14, p. 173. 1956.

4785 Myres (John Nowell Linton). A prehistoric settlement on Hinksey hill, near Oxford. [4 figures + 2 plans. Early Iron Age and Romano-British. pp. 377–85, Report on the pottery, by Christopher Hawkes; pp. 386–88, Report on the flints, by Christopher Hawkes.] J. Brit. Archaeol. Ass., N.S. 36, pp. 360–390. 1930.

4786 —— A prehistoric and Roman site on Mount farm, Dorchester. [8 figures (pottery, etc.). Bronze Age to Roman period.] Oxoniensia, 2, pp. 12–40 + 2 plates. 1937.

4787 Nasmyth (G. C. H.). Prehistoric pits in Kent. [Polished flint axe, etc.] Antiquity, 7, pp. 90–91 + plate. 1933.

4788 Newnham (W.). A Mesolithic site at Bishop's wood, Warninglid. Sussex N. & Q., 15, pp. 63–64. 1958.

4789 Newton (W. N.). On deneholes or drainage pits and their relation to Grime's Graves, or first Antler-pick period. [2 figures.] Man, 28, pp. 78–83. 1928.

4790 Norris (Norman Edward Stanley). An early habitation site at Eastwick. [Plan.] Sussex County Mag., 10, pp. 843–44. 1936.

4791 —— etc. An Iron Age and Romano-British site on Slonk hill, Shoreham. [Plan.] Sussex N. & Q., 12, pp. 150–54. 1949.

4792 —— and **Burstow** (George Philip). A prehistoric and Romano-British site at West Blatchington, Hove. [12 figures + map + 8 plans. pp. 8–12, Prehistoric (Late Bronze Age to Iron Age); pp. 45–48, Pre-Roman pottery, by G. P. Barstow.] Sussex Arch. Collns., 89, pp. 1–56 + plan; 90, pp. 421–40. 1950–1952.

4793 Oakley (Kenneth Page) and **Leakey** (Mary). Report on excavations at Jaywick Sands, Essex (1934), with some observations on the Clactonian Industry, and on the fauna and geological significance of the Clacton Channel. Proc. prehist. Soc., 3, 1937, 217–58 + 11 figures + 1 plate.

4794 Ogilvie (D. J. R.). Denehole at Bramling. Arch. Cant., 74, 1960, pp. 190–92 + 1 figure.

4795 Parsons (John). Broomwood Bronze Age settlement, St. Paul's Cray, Kent. Arch. Cant., 76, 1961, pp. 134–42 + 3 figures.

4796 Parsons (W. J.) and **Curwen** (Eliot Cecil). An agricultural settlement on Charleston Brow, near Firle beacon. [5 figures + plan. Normal settlement of c. 500 B.C. to A.D. 500). Sussex Arch. Collns., 74, pp. 164–80 + plan. 1933.

4797 Payne (George), jun. Celtic remains discovered at Grovehurst, in Milton-next-Sittingbourne. Arch. Cant., 13, pp. 122–26 + 2 plates (flint implements). 1880.

4798 Peake (A. E.). An account of a flint factory, with some new types of flints, excavated at Peppard common, Oxon. [27 figures + map.] Archaeol. J., 70, pp. 33–68. 1913.

4799 —— A Cave site at Nettlebed, S. Oxon. [late Aurignacian–early Magdalaine]. Proc. PSEA, 2 i, 1914/15, 71–80 + 3 plates.

4800 —— A prehistoric site at Kimble, S. Bucks. Proc. PSEA, 2 iii, 1916/17, 437–58 + 3 figures.

4801 —— Further excavations at Grime's Graves. Presidential Address. Proc. PSEA, 2 iii, 1916/17, 409–36 + 9 figures + 1 plate.

4802 Peake (Harold John Edward). A flint factory at Thatcham, Berks. 1. Report of site and excavations. Proc. PSEA, 3 iv, 1921/22, 499–500 + 1 figure.

4803 —— and **Coghlan** (Herbert Henry), etc. Recent discoveries (Early Iron Age remains) on Boxford common. [pp. 142–49, 2 plans. The pottery and other objects, by Christopher Hawkes.] Trans. Newbury F.C., [6] 1930–33, pp. 103–04, 136–50, 211–17. 1933.

4804 Peake (William Brian). Mount's Wood dene-hole. Trans. Dartford Antiq. Soc., 5, pp. 25–30. 1935.

4805 Pengelly (William). Kent's cavern and glacial or pre-glacial man. Rpt. & Trans. Devon. Assoc., 16, pp. 480–88. 1884.

4806 Penn (W. S.). The Romano-British settlement at Springhead; excavation of Temple I, Site C1 [Celtic-Roman type temple]. Arch. Cant., 73, 1969, pp. 1–61, + 15 figures + 6 plates.

4807 Perkins (John Bryan Ward). Iron Age site in Essex. [Figure.] Antiq. J., 17, pp. 194–95. 1937.

4808 —— An Early Iron Age site at Crayford, Kent. Proc. prehist. Soc., 4, 1938, 151–68 + 11 figures + 1 plate.

4809 Petch (D. F.). An Iron Age site, Sleaford. Rpts. & Papers Lincs. A. & A.S., 9, 1961, 12.

4810 Philip (Alexander John). A prehistoric civilization on the banks of the Thames. [Figure. Around Gravesend.] Home Counties Mag., 13, pp. 46–56 + 3 plates. 1911.

4811 Philp (Brian J.). A Romano-British villa site at Swarling, Kent [Late Celtic cemetery and Belgic pottery]. Arch. Cant., 74, 1960, pp. 186–90 + 2 figures.

4812 —— Reports from local secretaries and groups: West Kent Border [Hayes Common LBA farmstead, Neolithic–BA site]. Arch. Cantiana, 79, 1964, lxi–lxii.

4813 Piggott (Cicily Margaret) *and* **Seaby** (Wilfred Arthur). Early Iron Age site at Southcote, Reading. Proc. prehist. Soc., 3, 1937, 43–57 + 8 figures.

4814 Piggott (Stuart). Early Iron Age rubbish pits at Knighton hill, Berks. Antiq. J., 7, p. 517. 1927.

4815 —— A prehistoric village site at Knighton hill, Compton Beauchamp, [Berks.]. Berks, Bucks & Oxon. Archaeol. J., 31, pp. 25–27. 1927.

4816 —— Excavation of an Early Iron Age site at Knighton hill, near the White Horse hill, Berks. [3 figures.] Man, 28, pp. 97–101. 1928.

4817 —— An early settlement at Theale, near Reading, Berks. [Early Bronze Age, Iron Age A and C. Pottery.] Trans. Newbury F.C., 7 (1934–37), pp. 146–49. 1937.

4818 Posnansky (Merrick). Neolithic finds from Attenborough, near Nottingham. [Figure.] Antiq. J., 38, pp. 87–89. 1958.

4820 Pull (J. H.). Some discoveries at Findon. [12 figures + plan.] Sussex County Mag., 7, pp. 470–72, 506–08, 597–600, 653–55, 727–30, 810–14. 1933.

4821 Rahtz, P. A. Row Down, Lambourn. Berks. Scientific Addendum, by L. Bick. Berks. Arch. J., 60, 1962, 25–29.

4822 Rankine (William Francis). A Mesolithic site at Farnham. [9 figures + 2 plans.] Surrey Archaeol. Collns., 44, pp. 24–46. 1936.

4825 Reader (Francis W.). Further notes on the pile-dwelling site at Skitt's hill, Braintree, Essex. A report on the excavation of a portion of the relic-bed, October, 1900. [2 figures + plan.] Essex Nat., 14, pp. 137–47. 1905.

4826 —— A Neolithic floor in the bed of the Crouch river, and other discoveries near Rayleigh, Essex. [8 figures + 2 maps.] Essex Nat., 16, pp. 249–64 + 5 plates. 1911.

4827 Reid (Clement). The Palaeolithic deposits at Hitchin and their relation to the Glacial Epoch. Trans. Herts. N.H.S. & F.C., 10, 1898–1901, 14–22.

4828 —— Further note on the Palaeolithic deposits at Hitchin. Trans. Herts. N.H.S. & F.C., 11, 1902/03, 63–64.

4829 Renfrew, Jane. Aldwick, Barley: recent work at the Iron Age site. Appendix IV: Grain impressions from the Iron Age sites of Wandlebury and Barley. Proc. Camb. Ant. Soc., LVIII, 1965, 10–11.

4830 Richardson (*Mrs.* C. J.). Prehistoric site at Waddon, Croydon. Antiq. J., 3, pp. 147–48. 1923.

4831 Richardson (Katharine Margaret). An Iron Age A site [at Chinnor common, Bucks.,] on the Chilterns. [8 figures + map + plan.] Antiq. J., 31, pp. 132–48 + 3 plates. 1951.

4832 Riley (D. N.). A Late Bronze Age and Iron Age site on Standlake downs, Oxon. [3 figures + plan. Appendices: i. The pottery (1943); ii. Six urns in the Ashmolean museum (1857), by R. J. C. Atkinson; iii. The human remains (1943), by Beatrice M. Blackwood.] Oxoniensia, 11/12, pp. 27–43 + plate. 1947.

4833 Robarts (N. F.). Notes on a section of clay with flints near Woldingham. Proc. Croydon N.H. & Sci. Soc., 6, pp. 11–14. 1903.

4384 Row (Prescott). A Late Celtic burial and a series of Early Iron Age occupation sites at Waddon, Croydon, Surrey [with some earlier flint flakes]. Proc. PSEA, 5 i, 1925, 80–82 + 1 plate.

4835 —— A burial of the Iron Age and a series of Early Iron Age occupation sites at Waddon, Croydon, Surrey. [Page of figures of flints.] Surrey Archaeol. Collns., 37, pp. 59–63. 1926.

4836 Rudsdale (E. J.). Early Iron Age site at Hatfield Peverel. [Figure (pottery).] Trans. Essex Archaeol. Soc., N.S. 19, pp. 315–16. 1930.

4837 Sainty (J. E.). A flaking site on Kelling Heath, Norfolk. PPSEA, 4 ii, 1923/24, 165–76 + 7 figures.

4838 —— Further notes on the flaking site on Kelling Heath, Norfolk. PPSEA, 5 i, 1925, 56–61 + 5 plates.

4839 —— An Acheulean Palaeolithic workshop site at Whitlingham, near Norwich. Proc. PSEA, 5 ii, 1926, 176–213 + 21 figures.

4840 —— The Kelling flaking site. Proc. PSEA, 5 iii, 1927, 283–87 + 9 figures.

4841 Salvage (S.). A note on the Mesolithic site at Salmeston. J. & Trans.

Eastbourne N.H. & Arch. Soc., 13 iii, p. 17. 1953.

4842 Savory (Hubert Newman). An early Iron Age site at Long Wittenham, Berks. [2 figures.] Oxoniensia, 2, pp. 1–11 + 2 plates. 1937.

4843 Seaby (Wilfred Arthur). Some pre-Roman remains from south Reading. [Ring earthwork on Marshall's hill: pottery and implements.] Berks. Archaeol. J., 36, pp. 121–25 + 2 plates. 1932.

4844 —— Early Iron Age settlement at Southcote, Reading. Berks. Archaeol. J., 37, pp. 83–84. 1933.

4845 Sheridan (R.). Rescue excavation of a Mesolithic site at Greenham Dairy Farm, Newbury, 1963. Trans. Newbury Dist. Fld. Club, xi iv, 1967, 66–73 + 3 figures.

4846 Sherlock (J. W.). The Early Iron Age site at Asheldham. Essex Rev., 55, pp. 215–16. 1946.

4847 Shrubsole (George). The ponds on the downs. (The dew pond question.) Trans. Eastbourne N.H. Soc., 12 ii, pp. 24–29; 12 iv, pp. 24–25. 1939, 1946.

4848 Sieveking (Gaude G.). Ebbsfleet: Neolithic sites. Arch. Cant., 74, 1960, pp. 192–94.

4849 Slade, C. F. A Late Neolithic site at Sonning, Berkshire [6 figures + 4 plates]. Berks. Arch. J., 61, 1963/4, 4–19.

4850 Smith (Charles Roach). The caves or pits in Kent, and in the parish of Tilbury in Essex. [Anterior to Pliny.] Collectanea Antiqua, 6, pp. 243–47. 1868.

4851 Smith (Reginald Allender). A Palaeolithic industry at Northfleet, Kent. Archaeologia, 62, pp. 515–32 + 3 plates. 1911.

4852 —— *and* **Dewey** (Henry). Researches at Rickmansworth, [Herts.]; report on excavations made in 1914 on behalf of the British Museum. Archaeologia, 66, pp. 195–224. 1915.

4853 —— On prehistoric and Anglo-Saxon remains discovered by Capt. L. Moysey at Howletts, near Bridge, Kent. Proc. Soc. Antiq., 2 S. 30, pp. 102–13 + 3 plates. 1918.

4854 Smith (V. Gerard). Kitchen midden at Seaford. Sussex N. & Q., 5, pp. 251–52. 1935.

4855 —— Iron Age and Romano-British site at Seaford. Sussex Arch. Collns., 80, pp. 293–305. 1939.

4856 Smith (Workington George). On a Palaeolithic floor at [Stoke Newington common,] north-east London. J. Anthrop. Inst., 13, pp. 357–84 + 15 plates (flints, etc.) + map. 1884.

4857 —— Primaeval man: a Palaeolithic floor near Dunstable. [7 figures.] Natural Science, 1, pp. 664–70. 1892.

4858 —— Notes on the Palaeolithic floor near Caddington. [40 figures + plan. Gaddesden Row, Herts., Round Green, Luton, South Beds.] Archaeologia, 67, pp. 49–74. 1916.

4859 Snelling (A. J. R.). Excavations at the Globe Pit, Little Thurrock, Grays, Essex, 1961. Essex Naturalist, 31 iii, 1964, 199–208.

4860 Solomon (J. D.). Palaeolithic and Mesolithic sites at Motston, Norfolk. [14 figures.] Man, 31, pp. 275–78. 1931.

4861 Stebbing (William Pinckard Delane). Iron Age hearth at Finglesham near Eastry, Kent. Arch. Cant., 41, pp. 69–70. 1929.

4862 —— An Early Iron Age site at Deal. [Hut. Pottery.] Arch. Cant., 46, pp. 207–09. 1934.

4863 —— An early Belgic rubbish pit, Mill Hill, Deal. Arch. Cant., 60 (1947), pp. 125–26. 1948.

4864 Swaffer (Spencer F.). A Late Iron Age site, east of Cuckmere Haven. Sussex Notes & Queries, 16, 3, 1964, 102.

4865 Tebbutt (Charles Frederick). Palaeolithic industries from the Great Ouse gravels at and near St. Neots [with appendices by J. E. Marr and M. C. Burkitt]. Proc. PSEA, 5 ii, 1926, 166–73 + 3 plates.

4866 —— Early Iron Age settlement on Jack's Hill, Great Wymondley, Herts. Proc. PSEA, 6 iv, 1931, 371–74 + 2 plates + 1 figure.

4867 Tester (P. J.). An Acheulian site at Orpington. [Figure (hand-axes).] Archaeol. Cant., 72 (1958), pp. 194–97. 1959.

4868 —— Interim report on the discovery of a Palaeolithic site at Cuxton, Kent. Arch. Cantiana, 78, 1963, xlviii.

4869 Thomas (Nicholas W. de l'Eglise). Excavations at Vicarage field, Stanton Harcourt, 1951. With an appendix [pp. 23–28] on secondary Neolithic wares in the Oxford region. [6 figures +

2 plans. Pp. 4–7, 12–23, Neolithic pits, and finds.] Oxoniensia, 20 (1955), pp. 1–28 + plate + plan. 1957.

4870 Toms (Herbert S.). The Park Brow [Sompting] platforms. [Figure. Bronze Age.] Sussex Arch. Collns., 65, pp. 251–53. 1924.

4871 —— Ancient ponds near Cissbury. [3 plans.] Sussex County Mag., 1, pp. 404–07. 1927.

4872 —— Ancient ponds near Patcham. [Figure + 3 plans.] Sussex County Mag., 8, pp. 486–90. 1934.

4873 —— Ancient ponds near Falmer: Broad Shackles and Buckland Bank. [2 figures + 3 plans.] Sussex County Mag., 8, pp. 546–50. 1934.

4874 Trollope (Edward), *bp. of Nottingham*. British hut-circles at Tetney [Lincs.]. Assoc. Archit. Socs.' Rpts., 14, pp. 220–23. 1878.

4875 Turner (J.). On an Early Palaeolithic workshop site at Stonecross, Luton, Chatham. Proc. PSEA, 5 iii, 1927, 299–305 + 15 figures.

4876 Tylecote (R. F.). *and* **Owles** (Elizabeth). A Second Century iron smelting site at Ashwicken, Norfolk [a pre-Roman pit on site]. Norfolk Archaeology, xxxii (iii), 1960, 142–62 + 16 figures.

4877 Walker (Frederick George). A recently discovered Neolithic site at Gamlingay, Cambridgeshire. [Map.] Proc. Camb. Antiq. Soc., 15, pp. 64–67 + 2 plates. 1910.

4878 Walker (John William). Prehistoric and Roman finds at Aston Tirrold [Berks.], *etc.* Antiq. J., 10, pp. 49–51. 1930. *Reprinted in* Berks. Archaeol. J., 34, pp. 15–18. 1930.

4879 Warren (Samuel Hazzledine). On the correlation of the prehistoric floor at Hullbridge, with similar beds elsewhere. Essex Nat., 16, pp. 265–82. 1911.

4880 —— The Mosvinian industry of Clacton-on-Sea, Essex. Proc. PSEA, 3 iv, pp. 597–602 + 2 figures. 1921/22.

4881 Watson (M. B.). Iron Age site on Bridge Hill. Arch. Cantiana, 78, 1963, 185–88 + 1 figure.

4882 Wenlock (Christopher). Dewponds of the Sussex downs. [9 figures.] Sussex County Mag., 13, pp. 231–37. 1939.

4883 Whitwell (J. B.). Iron Age site, Ancaster. Rpts. & papers Lincs. A. & A.S. 10, 1964, 60–61.

4884 Williams (*Mrs.* Audrey). Excavations at Beard Mill, Stanton Harcourt, Oxon., 1944. [6 figures + 2 plans. Iron Age A2.] Oxoniensia, 16 (1951), pp. 5–22 + 2 plates. 1953.

4885 Wolseley (Garnet R.) *and* **Smith** (Reginald Allender). Discoveries [on Park Brow] near Cissbury. [5 figures + plan. Early Iron Age. Pottery, *etc.*] Antiq. J., 4, pp. 347–59. 1924.

4886 Wood (E. S.). Prehistoric settlement at Farnborough, Kent. [Figure (flint implements). Late Neolithic or Early Bronze Age.] Arch. Cant., 60 (1947), pp. 122–25. 1948.

4887 Worsfold (F. H.). A Report on the Late Bronze Age site excavated at Minnis Bay, Birchington, Kent, 1938–40. Proc. prehist. Soc., 9, 1943, 28–47, 10 figures + 4 plates.

4888 —— An Early Iron Age site at Borden [near Sittingbourne]. [3 figures + plan. Coarse pottery.] Arch. Cant., 61 (1948), pp. 148–55 + plate. 1949.

4889 Wymer (John). Excavations at Thatcham, Berks., 1958 [Mesolithic]. Trans. Newbury Dist. Fld. Club, 10 iv, 1958, 31–48 + 9 figures.

4890 —— Excavations on the Mesolithic site at Thatcham, Berks.—1958. Interim Report [8 figures]. Berks. Arch. J., 57, 1959, 1–24.

4891 —— Excavations at Thatcham, Berks. (Second Interim Report) [Mesolithic]. Trans. Newbury Dist. Fld. Club, xi i, 1960, 12–19 + 3 figures.

4892 —— Excavations at the Maglemosian sites at Thatcham, Berkshire, England (with a report on the animal bones, by Judith E. King). Proc. prehist. Soc., 28, 1962, 329–61 + 13 figures + 4 plates.

4893 —— Excavations at Thatcham. Final Report [Mesolithic]. Trans. Newbury Dist. Fld. Club, xi ii, 1963, 41–52 + 2 plates + 4 figures.

(b) Zone 2 [CBA Group 12]

4894 Adorian (Paul) *and* **Keil** (Fred). Excavations near Eldon Seat, Encombe, Corfe Castle. Report on the excavations of 1960–61. Proc. Dorset N.H. & A.S., 83, 1962, 84.

4895 Annable (F. Kenneth). Mesolithic working floor [Salisbury and Downtown]. [3rd session of excavations. Mesolithic and Neolithic B–Beaker.] Wilts. Arch. Mag., 57, p. 13. 1958.

4896 —— Grange Penning, Little Avebury: Iron Age [A] and later occupation. Wilts. Arch. Mag., 57, pp. 232–33. 1959.

4897 [Anon.] Early Iron Age village at All Cannings, Wilts. J. Brit. Archaeol. Ass., N.S. 27, pp. 110–12. 1921.

4898 [Anon.] Discovery of a [Late Neolithic] hearth-site at Shaftesbury. N. & Q., Som. & Dorset, 25, pp. 276–77. 1950.

4899 [Anon.] Discovery of Celtic remains at Basingstoke. Reliquary, 24, p. 128. 1883.

4900 Applebaum (Shimon). The Agriculture of the British Early Iron Age as exemplified at Figheldean Down, Wiltshire. Proc. prehist. Soc., 20, 1954, 103–114 + 1 figure.

4901 Arkell (*Sir* T. Noel) *and* **Arkell** (William Joscelyn). A new Bronze Age site at Highworth. Wilts. Archaeol. Mag., 50, p. 373. 1944.

4902 Ashbee, Paul. The Wilsford shaft. Antiquity, 37 (1963), 116–20.

4903 Bailey (C. J.). An Early Iron Age/Romano-British site at Pin's Knoll, Litton Cheney. Interim Report. Proc. Dorset N.H. & A.S., 81, 1960, 124–26.

4904 —— Second interim report on excavations at Pin's Knoll, Litton Cheney. Proc. Dorset N.H. & A.S., 85, 1963, 95–6.

4905 Barnes (William). Pilsdon. Proc. Dorset Antiq. F.C., 7, pp. 102–05. 1886.

4906 Benson (G. C.). Iron Age settlement at Ventnor. Proc. I. of W. N.H. & Arch. Soc., 4, p. 97 + plate. 1948.

4907 —— A Belgic occupation site at Gill's Cliff, Ventnor. [4 figures + 2 plans. Iron Age.] Proc. I. of W., N.H. & Arch. Soc., 4, pp. 303–11. 1953.

4908 Bersu (Gerhard). Excavations at Woodbury, near Salisbury, Wiltshire (1938). Proc. prehist. Soc., 4, 1938, 308–13 + 1 plate.

4909 —— Excavations at Little Wood-bury, Wiltshire. Part 1: The settlement as revealed by excavation. Proc. prehist. Soc., 6, 1940, 30–111 + 32 figures + 7 plates.

4910 Boon (George C.). Roman Silchester [with some discussion of pre-Roman settlement]. London (Parrish), 1957, pp. 245.

4911 Brailsford (John) *and* **Jackson** (J. Wilfrid). Excavations at Little Woodbury, Wiltshire (1938–39). Part II: The pottery; Part III: the animal remains. Proc. prehist. Soc., 14, 1948, 1–23 + 7 figures + 1 plate.

4912 —— Excavations at Little Woodbury. Part IV: Supplementary excavation, 1947; Part V: The small finds. Proc. prehist. Soc., 15, 1949, 156–68 + 8 figures.

4913 Brooke (J. W.). British midden on the banks of the Kennet, Marlborough. [Early Neolithic.] Wilts. Archaeol. Mag., 26, p. 410. 1892.

4914 Burkitt (M. C.) *and others* [T. T. Paterson *and* C. J. Mugridge]. The Lower Palaeolithic industries near Warsash, Hampshire. Proc. prehist. Soc., 5, 1939, 39–50 + 8 figures.

4916 Calkin (John Bernard) *and* **Piggott** (Cecily Margaret). Iron Age A habitation site at Langton Matravers. [4 figures + plan.]. Proc. Dorset Archaeol. Soc., 60 (1938), pp. 66–72. 1939.

4917 —— *and* **Piggott** (Stuart). A Neolithic A habitation site at Corfe Mullen. [Figure + plan.] Proc. Dorset Archaeol. Soc., 60 (1938), p. 73. 1939.

4918 —— Neolithic pit at Southbourne, [Hants.]. [2 figures.] Proc. Dorset Archaeol. Soc., 69 (1947), pp. 29–32 + 2 plates (pottery). 1948.

4919 —— A Roman site at Wilkswood, Langton Matravers. Proc. Dorset N.H. & A.S., 81, 1960, 120–22.

4920 Cambridge (Octavius Pickard). Woodbury hill. Proc. Dorset Antiq. F.C., 7, pp. 93–98 + plate. 1886.

4921 Clay (Richard Challoner Cobbe). An Early Iron Age site on Fifield Bavant down. Wilts. Archaeol. Mag., 42, pp. 457–96 + 25 plates + plan. 1924.

4922 —— An inhabited site of La Tène I date on Swallowcliffe down. (Supplementary report on the Early Iron Age village.) [2 figures (3 figures).] J. Wilts. Archaeol. Mag., 43, pp. 59–93 +

12 plates + plan; pp. 540–47. 1925–26.

4923 Clay (Richard Challoner Cobb). Pit-dwelling of the Beaker period at Lymore, Hants. [Figure (beaker) + plan.] Antiq. J., 8, pp. 95–96. 1928.

4924 Collins (W. G.). A prehistoric site at Conkwell, near Bradford-on-Avon. [2 figures (flints).] [Surface finds of various dates Neol.–Roman]. Antiquary, 48, pp. 380–87. 1912.

4925 Cooke (J. H.). On the discovery of an undisturbed midden and firehearth at Chark near Gosport, [Hants.]. Man, 23, pp. 85–90. 1923.

4926 Cunliffe (Barry). Report on a Belgic and Roman site at the Causeway, Horndean (1959) [Belgic potsherds, loom weights *etc.*]. Papers & Proc., Hants. F.C., 22, pt. 1, pp. 25–29 + 2 figures. 1961.

4927 —— Report on the excavations on the Roman pottery kiln at Hallcourt Wood, Shedfield, Hampshire (1960). [Some Romanised Belgic forms.] Papers & Proc. Hants. F.C., 22, pt. 1, 1961, pp. 8–24 + 7 figures.

4928 —— Summary report on excavations near Eldon Seat, Encombe, 1963 [Iron Age A settlement, farming]. Proc. Dorset N.H. & A.S., 85, 1963, 98–9.

4929 —— Winchester excavations 1949–1960. Vol. I. Winchester, 1964, 190 pp. + 9 plates + 66 figures.

4930 —— Excavations near Eldon Seat, Encombe, Corfe Castle, 1964 [Iron Age bucket urns]. Proc. Dorset N.H. & A.S., 86, 1964, 109.

4931 Cunnington (Henry). Description of the opening of a British dwelling-pit at Beckhampton. Wilts. Archaeol. Mag., 23, pp. 65–68. 1887.

4932 Cunnington (*Mrs.* Maud Edith). Notes on a Late Celtic rubbish heap near Oare, Wiltshire. [6 figures.] Man, 9, pp. 18–21. 1909.

4933 —— A Late Celtic inhabited site at All Cannings Cross farm. [Figure + plan.] Wilts. Archaeol. Mag., 37, pp. 526–38 + 6 plates. 1912.

4934 —— Hut circles (?) at Old Shepherd's Shore. [Mounds in Bishop's Cannings parish.] Wilts. Archaeol. Mag., 38, pp. 632–33. 1914.

4935 ——A village site of the Hallstatt period [on All Cannings Cross farm] in Wiltshire. [2 figures.] Antiq. J., 2, pp. 13–19 + 2 plates. 1922.

4936 —— The Early Iron Age inhabited site at All Cannings Cross farm, Wiltshire. pp. 204 + 51 plates + map + plan. 4⁰. Devizes, 1923.

4937 Cunnington (William). Relics of ancient population on Oldbury hill, Wilts. [Implements, etc.]. Wilts. Archaeol. Mag., 23, pp. 213–22 + plan. 1887.

4938 Dewar (H. S. L.). Excavations at Walls Field, Charminster (Interim Report) [RB Building + IA sherds]. Proc. Dorset, N.H. & A.S., 82, 1961, 86–7.

4939 —— *and* **Aitken** (G. N.). Excavations at Somerleigh Court [RB masonry]. Proc. Dorset N.H. & A.S., 86, 1964, 155–57 + 1 figure.

4940 Dimbleby, G. W. The ancient forest of Blackamore. Antiquity, 35, 1961, pp. 123–28; 36, 1962, pp. 136–37.

4941 Draper (J. C.). A Mesolithic site on Old Winchester hill. [3 figures (flints).] Papers & Proc. Hants. F.C., 17, pp. 293–97. 1952.

4942 —— A secondary Neolithic site on Oxenbourne down, Butser. [2 figures.] Papers & Proc. Hants. F.C., 19, pp. 180–83. 1956.

4943 Drew (Charles Douglas). Early Iron Age site at West Parley. [Corrigenda & addenda, 52, p. 19.] Proc. Dorset Archaeol. Soc., 51, pp. 232–36 + 2 plates. 1830.

4944 Farrar (Raymond Anthony Holt.) An Early Iron Age beach-head at Bindon hill, West Lulworth. Proc. Dorset Archaeol. Soc., 72 (1950), pp. 80–82. 1951.

4945 —— Iron Age remains at Grimstone reservoir. Proc. Dorset Archaeol. Soc., 72 (1950), pp. 88–89. 1951.

4946 —— An Iron Age and Romano-British site at Poundbury farm, Bradford Peverel. Proc. Dorset Archaeol. Soc., 72 (1950), pp. 89–90. 1951.

4947 —— A Celtic settlement, possibly manufacturing shale armlets, near Bradle Barn, Church Knowle. Proc. Dorset Arch. Soc., 78 (1956), p. 76. 1957.

4948 —— A Neolithic pit at Sutton Poyntz, Weymouth. [2 figures.] Proc. Dorset Arch. Soc., 79 (1957), pp. 112–13. 1958.

4949 Farrar (Raymond Anthony Holt). Excavations near Eldon Seat, Encombe, Corfe Castle [IA "A" and RB]. Proc. Dorset N.H. & A.S., 83, 1962, 83–84.

4950 —— Iron Age and Romano-British occupation at Southwell, Portland [Iron Age A and Romano-British pottery]. Proc. Dorset N.H. & A.S., 85, 1963, 101.

4951 —— Roman-British finds near Sandy Barrow, Osmington [RB and possibly IA "A" sherds]. Proc. Dorset N.H. & A.S., 85, 1963, 101–02.

4952 —— Iron-age, Romano-British, and mediaeval finds near Rope Lake, Kimmeridge [Iron Age A armlet + sherds + RB sherds]. Proc. Dorset N.H. & A.S., 85, 1963, 102.

4953 —— Roman and possibly pre-Roman remains at Rempstone, Corfe Castle [Quern]. Proc. Dorset N.H. & A.S., 85, 1963, 103–04.

4954 —— Iron Age or Roman occupation on Furgey Island, Poole Harbour [Iron A "B" tin]. Proc. Dorset N.H. & A.S., 85, 1963, 104.

4955 —— Iron Age and Roman occupation on Green Island, Poole Harbour [IA & RB sherds]. Proc. Dorset N.H. & A.S., 85, 1963, 104–05.

4956 —— A Romano-British site at Bailie Gate, Sturminster Marshall [Pit]. Proc. Dorset N.H. & A.S., 85, 1963, 105.

4957 —— *and* **Longworth** (Ian H.). Neolithic and early Bronze Age occupation at Poundbury, Dorchester [Rinyo-Clacton and Wessex II of EBA sherds]. Proc. Dorset N.H. & A.S., 86, 1964, 106–107 + 1 figure.

4958 —— Romano-British pits in the commonfield of Sturminster Marshall. Proc. Dorset N.H. & A.S., 86, 1964, 115.

4959 —— Romano-British site on Turlin Moor, Poole. Proc. Dorset N.H. & A.S., 86, 1964, 115–16.

4960 —— Romano-British occupation at Creech Grange, Steeple [RB sherds]. Proc. Dorset N.H. & A.S., 86, 1964, 116.

4961 —— The Romano-British site at Norden, Corfe Castle [shale table leg & RB sherds]. Proc. Dorset N.H. & A.S., 86, 1964, 116–17.

4962 —— The Iron Age and Romano-British site at Compact Farm, Worth Matravers [Iron Age A, B & C and RB sherds]. Proc. Dorset N.H. & A.S., 86, 1964, 118.

4963 —— Iron Age, Romano-British and mediaeval remains from Weston Farm, Worth Matravers [Iron Age A and RB sherds]. Proc. Dorset N.H. & A.S., 86, 1964, 118.

4964 —— Iron Age and Romano-British occupation at Godlingston Farm, Swanage [sherds and slingstones]. Proc. Dorset N.H. & A.S., 86, 1964, 118–19.

4966(a) Fox (Charles Frederick). A Bronze Age refuse pit at Swanwick, Hants. (Further finds.) [Figure + map. (Figure).] Antiq. J., 8, pp. 331–36 + plate; pp. 30–33, 1928–30.

4966(b) Fox (Joseph Plunket Bushe). Excavations at Hengistbury head [Hants.] in 1912–13. [Early Iron Age.] Proc. Soc. Antiq., 2 S. 26, pp. 212–15. 1914.

4967 Frend (William Hugh Clifford). Some further Iron Age and Roman sites in the Isle of Purbeck. Proc. Dorset Archaeol. Soc., 71 (1949), pp. 51–53. 1950.

4968 Harding (D. W.) *and* **Blake** (I. M.). An Early Iron Age settlement in Dorset. Antiquity, 37 (1963), 63–64.

4969 Hawkes (Charles Francis Christopher). The Twyford down village, the abandonment of St. Catharine's hill, and the first settlement of Winchester. Papers & Proc. Hants. F.C., 13, pp. 208–212. 1936.

4970(a) Hewer (T. F.). Guy's rift, Slaughterford, Wilts.: an Early Iron Age habitation. [2 figures.] Proc. Spelaeolog. Soc., 1925, pp. 229–37. *Reprinted in* Wilts. Archaeol. Mag., 43, pp. 483–87 + plate. 1926.

4970(b) Higgs (Eric). Excavations at a Mesolithic site at Downtown, near Salisbury, Wiltshire. Proc. prehist. Soc., 25, 1959, 209–32 + 14 figures + 2 plates.

4971 Hooley (Reginald W.). The finds at Worthy down, Winchester, Early Iron Age site. J. Brit. Archaeol. Ass., N.S. 30, pp. 137–38. 1924.

4972 —— Excavation of an Early Iron Age village on Worthy down, Winchester. [Figure.] Papers & Proc. Hants. F.C., 10, pp. 178–92. + 4 plates + plan 1929.

4974 Johnston (J. L. Forde). Preliminary report on excavations on Knowle hill, Dorset. [Early Iron Age.] Proc. Dorset Arch. Soc., 79 (1957), pp. 106–07. 1958.

4975 Kell (Edmund). Investigation into the rude pit habitations of the ancient Britons in Gallibury and Rowborough, Isle of Wight. J. Brit. Archaeol. Ass., 11, pp. 305–13 + plan. 1855.

4976 Kendall (Henry George Ommanney). Investigations at Knowle farm pit [Savernake, Wilts.] [3 figures.] Man, 6, pp. 38–41. 1905.

4977 —— Investigations at Knowle farm pit. [Palaeolithic and Mesolithic implements.] Wilts. Archaeol. Mag., 34, pp. 299–307. 1906.

4978 —— Palaeolithic periods at Knowle farm pit. [Savernake forest.] Proc. Soc. Antiq., 2 S. 23, pp. 453–64 + 2 plates (implements). 1911.

4979 —— Dwelling pits on Winterbourne Monkton down. Wilts. Archaeol. Mag., 38, pp. 108–10 + plate. 1913.

4980 —— Excavations on Hackpen hill, Wilts. [25 figures (palaeolithic implements) + map + plan.] Proc. Soc. Antiq., 2 S. 28, pp. 26–48. 1916.

4981 Laidler (Barbara) *and* **Young** (W. E. V.). A surface flint industry from a site near Stonehenge. [6 figures + plan.] Wilts. Archaeol. Mag., 48, pp. 150–60. 1938.

4982 Liddell (Dorothy Mary). Excavations at Meon hill. [10 figures. La Tène II to Romano-British times. Pp. 137–39, Report on human remains, by M. L. Tildesley (probably Anglo-Saxon).] Papers & Proc. Hants. F.C., 12, pp. 127–62 + 8 plates + plan. 1933.

4983 —— Report of the Hampshire Field Club's excavations at Meon hill. Second season, 1933. [12 figures. Iron Age A I to La Tène II. Pp. 23–33, 47–54 + 7 figures, pottery; pp. 39–42, Report on animal remains, by J. Wilfrid Jackson.] Papers & Proc. Hants. F.C., 13, pp. 7–54 + 13 plates + 3 plans. 1935.

4984 Mace (Angela). An Upper Palaeolithic open-site at Hengistbury Head, Christchurch, Hants. Proc. prehist. Soc., 25, 1959, 233–59 + 14 figures + 2 plates.

4985 Meyrick (Owen). Notes on some Early Iron Age sites in the Marlborough district. [2 figures + 2 plans.]

Wilts. Archaeol. Mag., 51, pp. 256–63. 1946.

4986 Musty (J. W. G.). A pipe-line near Old Sarum: prehistoric, Roman and Medieval finds including two twelfth century lime kilns. [5 figures + plan.] Wilts. Arch. Mag., 57, pp. 179–91. 1959.

4987 Nicholas (R. E.). Record of a prehistoric industry in tabular flint at Brambridge and Highfield, near Southampton. Pp. 92 + 2 plates. 8°. Southampton, 1916. [44 figures + 2 plans.]

4988 Ozanne (Paul C.). Further discoveries at Net Down, Shrewton, Wiltshire. Archaeol. News Letter, 7 ii, 1961, 44 + 1 figure.

4989 Palmer (Susann). Mesolithic sites on the shore of the fleet near Weymouth. Proc. Dorset N.H. & A.S., 84, 1963, 101.

4990 —— Prehistoric stone industries of the Fleet-area, Weymouth [4 figures]. Proc. Dorset N.H. & A.S., 85, 1963, 107–15.

4991 Parkes (A.). Recent discoveries at Warsash. [Late Bronze and Early Iron Ages.] Papers & Proc. Hants. F.C., 16, pp. 190–91. 1945.

4992 Percival (Sidney Theodore) *and* **Piggott** (Stuart). Neolithic and Early Bronze Age settlement at Broom Hill, Michelmersh, Hants. [3 figures.] Antiq. J., 14, pp. 246–53 + 2 plates. 1934.

4993 Piggott (Stuart). The Bronze Age pit at Swanwick, Hants.: a postscript. Ant. J., 43, 1963, 286–87.

4995 Poole (Hubert Frederick). An undisturbed early Neolithic site near Sandown, Isle of Wight. [2 figures (flints).] Papers & Proc. Hants. F.C., 10, pp. 25–34 + plate. 1927.

4996 Pope (Alfred). Some dew-ponds in Dorset. pp. 14 + 4 plates. 8°. Dorchester, 1912.

4997 —— Some dew-ponds in Dorset. Proc. Dorset Antiq. F.C., 32, pp. 22–33 + 4 plates. 1912.

4998 Rahtz (Philip A.). Excavations at Shearplace Hill, Sydling St. Nicholas, Dorset, England (with a report on the pottery, by A. M. ApSimon). [BA.] Proc. prehist. Soc., 28, 1962, 289–328 + 23 figures + plates.

4999(a) —— *and* **ApSimon** (A. M.). Neolithic and Beaker sites at Downton, near Salisbury, Wiltshire. WAM, 58, 1962, No. 210, 116–41 + 17 figures + plate.

4999(b) Railston (*Mrs.* V. Pleydell) *and* **Drew** (Charles Douglas). Iron Age and Romano-British settlement at Milborne St. Andrew. Proc. Dorset Archaeol. Soc., 52, pp. 10–18 + 6 plates (pottery, etc.) + 2 plans. 1931.

5000 Rankine (William Francis). A Mesolithic site on the foreshore at Cams, Fareham, Hants. [Figure + map.] Papers & Proc. Hants. F.C., 17, pp. 141–42. 1952.

5001 —— A Mesolithic chipping floor at the Warren, Oakhanger, Selborne, Hants. Proc. prehist. Soc., 18, 1952, 21–35 + 9 figures.

5002 —— Hampshire, Mesolithic excavation, interim report. [Flaking floor on the Warren at Oakhanger.] Arch. News Letter, 6, p. 122. 1958.

5003 —— *and* **Rankine** (W. H.). Further excavations at a Mesolithic site at Oakhanger, Selborne, Hants. Part I: Archaeology. (Part II: Fossil pollen and charcoal, by G. W. Dimbleby.) Proc. prehist. Soc., 26, 1960, 246–62 + 8 figures + 1 table.

5004 —— Mesolithic folk movements in Southern England. Further evidence from Oakhanger, Hants., Phase II. Archaeol. News Letter, 7 iii, 1961, 63–65 + 1 figure.

5005 Reid (Clement). An early Neolithic kitchen-midden and tufaceous deposit at Blashenwell, near Corfe Castle. Proc. Dorset Antiq. F.C., 17, pp. 66–75. 1896.

5006 Richardson (Katharine Margaret). The excavation of Iron Age villages on Boscombe down west. [15 figures + 3 plans. Pp. 166–68, Report on human remains, by A. J. E. Cave.] Wilts. Archaeol. Mag., 54, pp. 123–68 + 6 plates + plan. 1951.

5008 Stevens (Frank). "The Highfield pit dwellings", Fisherton, Salisbury, excavated May, 1866, to September, 1869. [9 figures. Early Iron Age. Pp. 618–19, Report on the human bones, by M. L. Tildesley.] Wilts. Archaeol. Mag., 46, pp. 579–624 + plan. 1934.

5009 Stone (John F. S.). A settlement site of the Beaker period, on Easton down, Winterslow, S. Wilts. Wilts.

Archaeol. Mag., 45, pp. 366–72 + 3 plates. 1931.

5010 —— Three "Peterborough" dwelling pits and a doubly-stockaded Early Iron Age ditch at Winterbourne Dauntsey. Wilts. Archaeol. Mag., 46, pp. 445–53 + 3 plates + 2 plans. 1934.

5011 —— A Late Bronze Age habitation site on Thorny down, Winterbourne Gunner, S. Wilts. [5 figures + plan.] Wilts. Archaeol. Mag., 47, pp. 640–59 + plan. 1937.

5012 —— A Middle Bronze Age site at Stockbridge, Hampshire. Proc. prehist. Soc., 4, 1938, 249–57 + 5 figures.

5013 —— The Deverel-Rimbury settlement on Thorny Down, Winterbourne Gunner, S. Wilts. Proc. prehist. Soc., 7, 1941, 114–33 + 8 figures + 3 plates.

5014 —— *and* **Young** (W. E. V.). Two pits of grooved ware date near Woodhenge. [5 figures + plan.] Wilts. Archaeol. Mag., 52, pp. 287–306. 1948.

5015 Stone (Percy). The Down pits in the Isle of Wight. [2 figures + 2 maps. No evidence for British villages, but due to pipes in the chalk.] Proc. Soc. Antiq., 2 S. 24, pp. 65–78. 1912.

5016 Stuart (James D.) *and* **Birkbeck** (James M.). Note on an excavation [of a prehistoric village] on Twyford down [Winchester]. Papers & Proc. Hants. F.C., 12, p. 271. 1934.

5017 —— *and* —— A Celtic village on Twyford down [Winchester], excavated 1933–1934. [6 figures. Iron Age. Pottery types till end of 1st c. A.D.—when site probably deserted for Winchester.] Papers & Proc. Hants. F.C., 13, pp. 188–207 + 5 plates + 2 plans. 1936.

5018 Summers (P. G.). A Mesolithic site, near Iwerne Minster, Dorset. Proc. prehist. Soc., 7, 1941, 145–46 + 1 figure.

5019 Thomas (Nicholas). A Neolithic pit on Waden hill, Avebury. [Figure (pottery).] Wilts. Archaeol. Mag., 56, pp. 167–71. 1955.

5020 Toms (G. S. C.). Interim Report of excavations at Bagwood Coppice, Bere Regis [RB settlement]. Proc. Dorset N.H. & A.S., 84, 1963, 103–06.

5021 Toms (G. S. C.). Second interim report of excavations at Bagwood, Bere Regis. [Roman-British possibly habitation site.] Proc. Dorset N.H. & A.S., 85, 1963, 99–100.

5022 —— Third interim report of excavations at Bagwood, Bere Regis. [RB working hollow.] Proc. Dorset N.H. & A.S., 86, 1964, 111–12.

5023 Troubridge (*Sir* Thomas), *bart.* A Mesolithic village [at Beaulieu] in Hampshire. [3 figures + plan.] Papers & Proc. Hants. F.C., 13, pp. 184–87. 1936.

5024 —— A Mesolithic village [at Beaulieu] in Hampshire. [3 figures + plan.] Antiq. J., 16, pp. 200–02. 1936.

5025 Tucker (J. H.). Mesolithic sites in Wiltshire. [Figure.] Wilts. Archaeol. Mag., 55, pp. 330–32. 1954.

5026 Underwood (Guy). Early British settlement at Farleigh Wick and Conkwell, Wilts. [Figure + 3 plans.] Wilts. Archaeol. Mag., 51, pp. 440–52 + plate + plan. 1946.

5027 Wacher (John Stewart). Interim report on excavations at Litton Cheney. [Bronze Age, etc.] Proc. Dorset Arch. Soc., 78 (1956), p. 84. 1957.

5028 Warren (Frank). Possible Early Iron Age site at Lainston. Papers & Proc. Hants. F.C., 12, p. 187. 1933.

5029 Warren (Samuel Hazzledine) *and others*. An Early Mesolithic site at Broxbourne sealed under boreal peat. [Herts.] [9 figures + map + plan.] J. R. Anthrop. Inst., 64, pp. 101–28. 1934.

5030 Weaver (*Sir* Lawrence). Discoveries at Amesbury [Wilts.]. [4 figures. Bronze Age. Stone and copper axe-hammers.] Antiq. J., 1, pp. 125–30. 1921.

5031 Wheeler (*Sir* Robert Eric Mortimer). An Early Iron Age "beach-head" at Lulworth, Dorset [and earthwork on Bindon hill]. [2 figures + plan.] Antiq. J., 33, pp. 1–13 + 5 plates + 2 maps. 1953.

5032 Williams (Audrey). Excavations at Allard's quarry, Marnhull, Dorset. [21 figures + 3 plans. Iron Age A, B and C: pottery, etc.] Proc. Dorset Archaeol. Soc., 72 (1950), pp. 20–75 + 2 plates. 1951.

(c) Zone 3 [CBA Groups 8, 13]

5033 [Anon.] Report on the excavations at Milber down, 1937–8. [6 figures + 3 maps + 2 plans.] Proc. Devon Archaeol. Expl. Soc., 4, pp. 27–66 + 14 plates + plan. 1949.

5034 [Anon.] Excavations at Kestor. Arch. News Letter, 4, pp. 62, 178. 1951–1952.

5035 Ashbee (Paul). Halangy Down, St. Mary's, Isles of Scilly. Cornish Arch., 3, 1964, 86.

5036 —— Excavations at Halangy Down, St. Mary's, Isles of Scilly, 1964: Interim Report. Cornish Arch., 4, 1965, 36–40 + 1 figure + 2 plates.

5037 —— Excavations at Halangy Down, St. Mary's, Isles of Scilly, 1965 and 1966. Cornish Arch., 5, 1966, 20–27.

5038 Balch (Herbert Ernest). On the exploration of a Late Celtic and Romano-British cave-dwelling at Wookey hole. (Further excavations, etc.) Proc. Soc. Antiq., 2 S. 23, pp. 403–06; 25, pp. 201–03. 1911–13.

5039 —— *and* **Troup** (R. D. R.). A Late Celtic and Romano-British cave-dwelling at Wookey-hole, near Wells, Somerset. (Further excavations at *ditto*.) [12 figures + plan. (2 figures (pottery)).] Archaeologia, 62, pp. 565–92 + 2 plates; 64, pp. 337–46 + plate. 1911–13.

5040 —— Wookey hole: its caves and cave-dwellers. pp. xiii, 268 + 36 plates. 4°. London, 1914. [55 figures.]

5041 —— Excavations at Wookey Hole and other Mendip caves, 1926–7. [25 figures.] Antiq. J., 8, pp. 193–210. 1928.

5042 —— Mendip—the great cave of Wookey hole. Third edition. pp. vii, 108 + 24 plates. 8°. Bristol, 1947.

5043 —— Mendip—Cheddar, its gorge and caves. Second edition. pp. vii, 102 + 33 plates. 8°. Bristol, 1947.

5044 —— Mendip—its swallet caves and rock shelters. Second edition. Pp. vi, 156 + 35 plates + table (man and wild beasts). 8°. Bristol, 1948.

5045 Barnwell (Edward Lowry). Beehive hut, Bosphrennis, in the parish of Zennor, Cornwall. [7 figures + plan.] Arch. Camb., 3rd S. 9, pp. 120–29. 1863.

5046 Beynon (F.). The Deposits in

the Torbryan Caves. Trans. & Proc. Torquay nat. Hist. Soc., 5, 1928, 153–159 + 1 figure.

5047 Benyon (F), **Dowie** (H. G.) *and* **Ogilvie** (Arthur H.). Report on the excavations in Kent's Cavern, 1926–9. Trans. & Proc. Torquay nat. Hist. Soc., 5, 1929, 237–42.

5048 —— The Cow Cave, Chudleigh [Agilian implements]. Trans. & Proc. Torquay nat. Hist. Soc., 6, 1930–34, 127–132.

5049 Blake (J. E. H.). Some remains of the Bronze Age at Mathon [Hereford-shire]. [2 figures.] B'ham. Arch. Soc., Trans., 39 (1913), pp. 90–93. 1914.

5050 Blake (T. W. Lex). Prehistoric man at [Gough's cave,] Cheddar. N. & Q. Som. & Dorset, 9, pp. 1–2 + plate. 1905.

5051 Blight (John Thomas). Account of an ancient British village in Cornwall. [2 figures + 2 plans. Chysanster.] Archaeol. J., 18, pp. 39–46 + plan. 1861.

5052 —— Notice of underground chambers at Boscaswell, in the parish of S. Just in Penwith. [Plan.] J. Roy. Instn. Cornwall, 1 ii, pp. 6–7. 1864.

5053 —— An account of remarkable subterranean chambers at Trelowarren, the seat of Sir R. R. Vyvyan, bart., in the county of Cornwall. [2 figures + 2 plans.] Archaeologia, 40, pp. 113–18 + plate. 1866.

5054 —— Discovery and exploration of caves or subterranean chambers at Castallack and Treveneague near Penzance. [Figure + plan. Pottery, etc.] Proc. Soc. Antiq., 2 S. 3, pp. 498–502. 1867.

5055 British Association. First (second, third, fourth, fifth) report of the Committee for exploring Kent's cavern, Devonshire. 5 pts. Rpt. Brit. Ass., 1865–69.

5056 Bulleid (Arthur). Discovery of a British village near Glastonbury. N. & Q. Som. & Dorset, 3, pp. 42–43, 122–25. 1893.

5057 —— The prehistoric British village at Glastonbury. [Report on paper to Brit. Assocn.] N. & Q., 8 S. 4, p. 306. 1893.

5058 —— A British village of lake or marsh dwellings [near Glastonbury] in

Somerset. Cardiff Nats'. Soc., Rpt. & Trans., 2S. 7, ii (1892–98), pp. 50–51. 1894.

5059 —— The lake village near Glastonbury. Proc. Somerset Arch. Soc., 40 (1894), pp. 141–51 + 4 plates + 2 plans. 1894.

5060 —— *and* **Gray** (Harold St. George). The Glastonbury lake village. An account of the excavations undertaken during 1904 (—1905). [Plan. (6 figures).] 50 (1904), pp. 68–93 + 6 plates; 51 (1905), pp. 77–104 + 4 plates + plan. 1905–06.

5061 —— *and* —— The Glastonbury ... (1905 and 1906). [9 figures. pp. 130–31, Report on the seeds and grain found ... 1905, by Clement Reid (7 figures + plan).] 52 (1906), pp. 94–131 + 5 plates + plan; 53 (1907), pp. 101–47 + 6 plates. 1907–08.

5062 —— *and* —— The Glastonbury lake village. A full description of the excavations and relics discovered, 1892–1907. 2 vol. 4°. Glastonbury, 1911–17. [101 plates.]

5063 —— *and* —— Meare lake-village. Proc. Somerset Arch. Soc., 56 (1910), pp. 38–43; 57 (1911), pp. 42–47; 58 (1912), pp. 38–41. 1911–13.

5064 —— *and* —— The lake villages in the neighbourhood of Glastonbury. Report of the Committee, *etc.* Rept. Brit. Ass., 1911, 1914, 1915, 1922.

5065 —— *and* —— The Meare Lake excavations, 1928 (—1929), *and subsequent years.* Proc. Somerset Arch. Soc., 74 (1928), pp. 152–53, *etc.* 1929 *etc.*

5066 —— *and* —— The Meare lake village. A full description of the excavations and the relics from the eastern half of the next village, 1910–1933. pp. xv, xl, 280 + 53 plates and plans. 2 vol. 4°. Taunton, 1948–53. [82 figures and plans.]

5067 Bullows (Wilfred L.). Notes on prehistoric cooking site and camping ground in Sutton park, Warwickshire, excavated October 1926. B'ham. Arch. Soc., Trans., 52 (1927), pp. 291–300 + plate + 2 plans. 1930.

5068 Burnard (Robert). Prehistoric Dartmoor. 1. The hut-circles. [5 figures + plan.] Reliquary, 3rd S. 8, pp. 87–95. 1902.

5069 —— Exploration of the hut circles in Broadun ring and Broadun.

Rpt. & Trans. Devon. Assoc., 26, pp. 185–96. + 3 plans. 1894.

5070 Burnard (Robert). Exploration of Carn Brê, [Illogan, West Cornwall]. [7 figures (flints): (3 figures + plan).] Reliquary, N. [3rd] S. 2, pp. 45–49, 108–11. 1896.

5071 Burrow (Edward J.) *etc.* Excavations on Leckhampton hill, Cheltenham, during the summer of 1925. [4 figures + 3 plans. Early Iron Age. pp. 91–101, The tumulus, by W. H. Knowles; pp. 101–07, Notes on the finds, by A. E. W. Paine.] Trans. Bristol & Glos. Arch. Soc., 47, pp. 81–112 + 7 plates + plan. 1925.

5073 Cantrill (Thomas Crossbee). A prehistoric flint factory at Great Packington, Warwickshire. [Figure + map.] B'ham. Arch. Soc., Trans., 35 (1909), pp. 99–103. 1910.

5074 —— A flint-factory [on the eastern borders of Cannock chase] in south Staffordshire. [Neolithic.] Antiquary, 47, pp. 229–30. 1911.

5076 Christie (Patricia M.). Carn Enny excavations: Interim Report on the 1964 season. Cornish Arch., 4, 1965, 24–30 + 1 figure + 1 plate.

5077 —— Carn Enny: a brief note on the 1965 excavations. Cornish Arch., 5, 1966, 17–19.

5078 Churchill (D. M.). The Kitchen Midden site at Westward Ho!, Devon, England: ecology, age, and relation to changes in land an sea level (with an appendix, by J. J. Wymer). [Mesolithic]. Proc. prehist. Soc., 31, 1965, 74.

5079 Clark (Evelyn V.) *and others.* The Fogou of Lower Boscaswell, Cornwall (with E. B. Ford and Charles Thomas). Proc. prehist. Soc., 23, 1957, 213–19 + 2 figures.

5080 —— Cornish Fogous. pp. xix, 152 + 16 plates + 10 line illustrations. London, 1961.

5082 Clark (John Grahame Douglas). A Neolithic house at Haldon, Devon. Proc. prehist. Soc., 4, 1938, 222–23 + 1 figure.

5083 Clay (Richard Challoner Cobbe). Excavations at Chelm's Combe, Cheddar. Report on the bone and flint implements. Proc. Somerset Arch. Soc., 72 (1926), pp. 113–15 + plate. 1927.

5084 —— Excavations at Chelm's Combe, Cheddar. Report on the pottery. [5 figures. Neolithic–Early Iron Age.] Proc. Somerset Arch. Soc., 72 (1926), pp. 106–13 + 3 plates. 1927.

5085 Clifford (Elsie Margaret). A prehistoric and Roman site at Barnwood near Gloucester. [19 figures + plan. Pp. 202–07 + 2 plates, The Barnwood people, by Sir Arthur Keith.] Trans. Bristol & Glos. Arch. Soc., 52, pp. 201–54 + 13 plates. 1930.

5086 —— An Early Iron Age site at Barnwood, Gloucestershire. [8 figures + plan.] Trans. Bristol & Glos. Arch. Soc., 56, pp. 227–35 + 5 plates. 1934.

5087 —— An Enclosure on Crickley Hill, Gloucestershire [post-Roman earthwork but finds neolithic flints and IA brooch]. Trans. Bristol & Glos. Arch. Soc., 83, pp. 40–48 + 3 figures + 1 plate. 1964.

5088 Cooper (N. C.). Excavations at Chelm's Combe, Cheddar. Human remains. Proc. Somerset Arch. Soc., 72 (1926), pp. 101–06. 1927.

5089 Crawford (Osbert Guy Stanhope). The work of giants. 4 maps. Antiquity, 10, pp. 162–74 + 9 plates. 1936.

5090 —— Celtic fields on the Long Mynd. [Map.] Antiquity, 28, pp. 168–70 + plate. 1954.

5091 Crofts (C. B.) *and* **Parchett** (Florence M.). Bodrifty, Mulfra. Interim Report 1950–1952. Proc. West Cornwall F.C., N.S. 1, pp. 15–20. 1953.

5092 Davies (J. A.). Aveline's hole, Burrington combe: an upper Palaeolithic station. Proc. Somerset Arch. Soc., 68 (1922), pp. 21–26 + plates (implements, etc.). 1923.

5093 —— *and* **Tratman** (E. K.). Recent discoveries in the Mendip caves. Somerset Arch. Soc., Proc. Bath branch, [5] 1924–28, pp. 25–30 + 4 plates (fibulae, etc.). 1924.

5094 Dawkins (W. Boyd). On a hyaena-den at Wookey Hole, near Wells [? Middle Acheulian implement.] J. Geol. Soc. London, 18, 1862, 115–26 + 5 figures.

5095 —— On a hyaena-den at Wookey Hole, near Wells. No. II. J. Geol. Soc., London, 19, 1863, 260–74 + 8 figures.

5096 Dewar (H. S. L.). An Iron Age farmstead at Podimore. Proc. Somerset

Arch. Soc., 97 (1952), p. 189 + plate. 1953.

5097 Dodd (J. Phillip). A possible Bronze Age site near Quatford. [Figure.] Trans. Shropshire Archaeol. Soc., 54, pp. 149–52. 1952.

5098 Douch (H. L.). Tredarvah, Penzance [EBA–MBA domestic site]. Cornish Arch., 3, 1964, 85.

5099 Dowie (H. G.). The Excavation of a cave at Torbryan. J. Torquay nat. Hist. Soc., 4, 1924, 261–68 + 3 figures.

5100 —— Note on recent excavations in Kent's Cavern, Torquay [Upper Aurignacian]. Proc. PSEA, 5 iii, 1927, 306–07.

5101 Dudley (Dorothy). A Late Bronze Age settlement on Trewey downs, Zennor, Cornwall. [7 figures + map + 2 plans. pp. 127–28, The pottery, by C. A. Ralegh Radford; pp. 128–30, The stone artifacts, by A. D. Lacaille.] Archaeol. J., 98 (1941), pp. 105–30 + 4 plates. 1942.

5102 —— Excavations at Bodrifty, Mulfra hill, Cornwall. [Plan. Iron Age "A" hut circle.] Antiquity, 26, pp. 90–92. 1952.

5103 —— An excavation at Bodrifty [farm], Mulfra hill, near Penzance, Cornwall. [4 figures + 7 plans. Early Iron Age hut circles.] Archaeol. J., 113 (1956), pp. 1–32 + 6 plates. 1957.

5104 —— Smallacombe and Trewortha Downs [LBA-type huts & pounds]. Cornish Archaeol., No. 2, 1963, 56.

5105 —— Nor-nour, Isles of Scilly. Cornish Arch., 3, 1964, 87.

5106 —— Nor'nour, Isles of Scilly. Cornish Arch., 4, 1965, 65–66.

5107 Dunning (Gerald Clough). Bronze Age settlements and a Saxon hut near Bourton-on-the-Water, Gloucestershire. [5 figures + map.] Antiq. J., 12, pp. 279–93 + 3 plates + plan. 1932.

5109 Edmonds (Richard). The beehive British dwellings at Bosphrennis, and Chapel Euny, near Penzance. Ann. Rpt. Roy. Instn. Cornwall, 45, pp. 71–74. 1863.

5110 Elwes (E. V.). On some drawings connected with Kents Cavern. J. Torquay nat. Hist. Soc., 2, 1919, 292–96.

5111 Fowler (P. J.). A Native homestead of the Roman period at Porth

Godrevy, Gwithian. Cornish Archaeology, No. 1, 1962, 17–60 + 14 figures.

5112 Fox (Aileen Mary), *Lady Fox*. Excavations at Kestor, an Early Iron Age settlement near Chagford, Devon. [4 figures + map + 4 plans.] Rpt. & Trans. Devon. Assoc., 86, pp. 21–62 + 14 plates + 3 plans. 1954.

5113 —— Huts and enclosures on Gripper's hill, in the Avon valley, Dartmoor. [Plan.] Rpt. & Trans. Devon. Assoc., 87, pp. 55–62 + plate + plan. 1955.

5114 —— Excavations on Dean moor, in the Avon valley, 1954–1956. The Bronze Age settlement. [8 figures + 2 maps + 4 plans.] Rpt. & Trans. Devon. Assoc., 89, pp. 18–77 + 11 plates + map + 5 plans. 1957.

5115 Gould (Sabin Baring). An ancient settlement on Trewortha marsh. [2 figures. Hut-circles.] J. Roy. Instn. Cornwall, 11, pp. 57–70 + plate + plan, pp. 289–90 + plate + plan. 1891–93.

5116 —— Hut circles at Tavy Cleave. Rpt. & Trans. Devon. Assoc., 26, pp. 197–98. 1894.

5117 —— Report on the exploration of hut circles, etc., near Wedlake farm, Petertavy. Rpt. & Trans. Devon. Assoc., 37, pp. 141–45 + plan. 1905.

5118 Gray (Harold St. George). The Glastonbury lake village. p. 15. 8°. London, 1906. [5 figures + plan.] [*Reprinted from* Memorials of Old Somerset.]

5119 —— Excavations at Combe beacon, Combe St. Nicholas, 1935. [3 figures. Neolithic pottery, implements, *etc.*] Proc. Somerset Arch. Soc., 81 (1935), pp. 83–107 + 4 plates + plan. 1936.

5120 —— Excavations at the Meare lake village, 1948 (—1949). Arch. News Letter, 1 ix, p. 3:2, p. 107. 1949.

5121 —— The Meare Lake village, 1949–50. (—1951). (—1952). (—1953). Proc. Somerset Arch. Soc., 95 (1950), pp. 170–71; 96 (1951), p. 231; 97 (1952), pp. 187–88; 98 (1953), pp. 157–59. 1951–55.

5122 —— Meare Lake village (east village) mound xiv, northern half, 1950. Proc. Somerset Arch. Soc., 101/102, pp. 154–56. 1958.

5123 —— Excavations at the Glastonbury lake village, in July, 1902. [Figure.] Proc. Somerset Arch. Soc., 48 (1902), pp. 102–21 + plate + 2 plans. 1963.

5124 Gray (J. W.) *and* **Brewer** (G. W. S.). Evidences of ancient occupation on Cleeve hill. [Figure + map.] Proc. Cotteswold Nat. Club., 15, pp. 49–57 + plate. 1904.

5125 Greenaway (R. D.). The British village at Carwen, near Blisland, Cornwall. [2 figures.] [JA.] J. Roy. Instn. Cornwall, 22, pp. 50–61 + plan. 1926.

5127 Guthrie (A.). Goldherring, Sancreed. Cornish Archaeol., No. 2, 1963, 56.

5128 Hawkes (Charles Francis Christopher). The lake-villages of Glastonbury and Meare. Archaeol. J., 107 (1950), pp. 87–90. 1952.

5129 —— Wookey hole. (Note on recent exploration in Wookey hole, from a report by E. J. Mason.) [Used in Iron Age and in Romano-British times.] Archaeol. J., 107 (1950), pp. 92–94. 1952.

5130 Hantin, F. Excavation at Broomfield Hill, near Broomfield, Somerset [Iron Age "A" sherds]. N. & Q. Somerset & Dorset, 28, 1964, pt. 280, pp. 187–89.

5131 Hencken (Hugh O'Neill). An excavation at Chysauster, 1928. [3 figures + map + 2 plans.] J. Brit. Archaeol. Ass., N.S. 34, pp. 145–64. 1928.

5132 —— An excavation by H.M. Office of Works at Chysauster, Cornwall, 1931. [4 figures + 9 plans.] Archaeologia, 83, pp. 237–84 + 4 plates + plan. 1933.

5133 Hichens (J. H.). The Story of Brixham and Kents Cavern. Trans. & Proc. Torquay nat. Hist. Soc., 7, 1936, 1–10.

5134 Hickling (M. J. L.) *and* **Seaby** (Wilfred Arthur). Finds from Cockles Wood cave, Nettlebridge, Somerset. [2 figures. Grooved and Beaker ware, flints and human remains.] Proc. Somerset Arch. Soc., 96 (1951), pp. 193–202. 1952.

5136 Horne (Ethelbert). Excavations in the Seven Acre field, Camerton. [Early Iron Age.] Somerset Arch. Soc.,

Proc. Bath branch, [7] 1934–38, pp. 86–89 + plate + plan; pp. 136–39 + plate + plan. 1935–36.

5137 —— An Early Iron Age site at Camerton, Somerset. [2 figures. Pottery, *etc.*] Proc. Somerset. Arch. Soc., 83 (1937), pp. 155–65 + plate + plan. 1938.

5138 Houlder (Christopher H.). Excavation of a Neolithic Settlement on Hazard hill, Totnes. Arch. News Letter, 3, pp. 65–66. 1951.

5139 Hunt (Arthur R.). Kent's Cavern: some doubts and difficulties. Jl. Torquay nat. Hist. Soc., 1, 1914, 267–71.

5141 Iago (William). The fogou, or cave, at Halligey, Trelowarren. J. Roy. Instn. Cornwall, 8, pp. 243–63 + 3 plates + 3 plans. 1884.

5142 Jones (William Arthur). Langport, the Llongborth of Llywarch Hên's elegy, and the site of an ancient British town of the same name. Proc. Somerset Arch. Soc., 4 (1853), pp. 44–59, 128. 1854.

5143 Julian, *née* **Pengelly** (Hester Forbes). The Palaentological and archaeological finds in Kent's cavern. Rpt. & Trans. Devon. Assoc., 50, pp. 258–67. 1918.

5144 —— Notes on some Kent's Cavern specimens. Trans. & Proc. Torquay nat. Hist. Soc., 5, 1927, 12–17.

5145 Lake (P. M. B.). A new plan of Kent's Cavern. Trans. & Proc. Torquay nat. Hist. Soc., 6, 1930–34, 331–332 + 1 figure.

5146 Lowe (Harford J.). Plan of Kent's Cavern. J. Torquay nat. Hist. Soc., 2, 1915, 23–24 + 1 figure.

5147 —— The Caves of Tor Bryan, their excavators, excavation, products, and significance. J. Torquay nat. Hist. Soc., 2, 1918, 199–213 + 1 figure + 2 plates.

5148 —— The Needles of Kent's Cavern, with reference to needle origin [?Magdalenian]. J. Torquay nat. Hist. Soc., 2, 1920, 325–36 + 1 figure.

5149 —— Kent's Cavern anthropology and the Ice Ages. J. Torquay nat. Hist. Soc., 3, 1922, 71–83 + 1 figure.

5150 —— The Excavation products of Kent's Cavern and their distribution. J. Torquay nat. Hist. Soc., 4, 1923, 6–9 + 1 plate.

5151 —— Ice Age theories and Kent's

Cavern. J. Torquay nat. Hist. Soc., 4, 1926, 295–302 + 2 figures.

5152 McMurtrie (James). Notes on ancient British remains found in a lias quarry at Tyning, Radstock. [Quern, spindle whorl, black pottery, *etc.*] Proc. Bath N.H. & Ant. F.C., 9, pp. 39–49. 1901.

5154 Marsden (John G.). A workshop floor near Porthcurno, Cornwall. Proc. prehist. Soc. E.A., 2 i, 1914/15, 41–42 + 1 plate.

5155 —— A further note on workshop floor near Porthcurno. Proc. prehist. Soc. E.A., 2 ii, pp. 173–75 + 2 plates. 1915/16.

5156 Morland (John). Ancient British village at Glastonbury. Proc. Somerset Arch. Soc., 38 (1892), pp. 26–30. 1892.

5157 Moysey (C. F.). A flint implement factory site near Milverton, Somerset [?date]. Proc. prehist. Soc. E.A., 2 iv, pp. 521–23 + 1 figure. 1917/18.

5158 Munro (Robert). The discovery of an ancient lake-village [at Glastonbury] in Somersetshire. Antiquary, 26, pp. 247–52. 1892.

5159 —— The British lake-village near Glastonbury. Letters and papers . . . published by the Glastonbury Antiquarian Society. Fourth edition, revised. pp. 27 + 4 plates + 2 plans. 8°. Taunton, 1904.

5160 New (Herbert). Stone-boiling mound at Pelsall, near Walsall, visited September 16th, 1913. B'ham Arch. Soc., Trans., 40 (1914), pp. 14–15. 1915.

5161 Ogilvie (Arthur Hebden). Some Kents Cavern questions. Trans. & Proc. Torquay nat. Hist. Soc., 6, 1930–34, 193–200.

5162 Ormerod (George Wareing). On the hut-circles on the eastern side of Dartmoor. J. Brit. Archaeol. Ass., 20, pp. 299–308 + plan. 1864.

5163 Palmer (L. S.). Some early British remains from a Mendip cave. [2 figures + map. The "Kelticcavern".] J.R. Anthrop. Inst., 51, pp. 200–15 + 7 plates. 1921.

5164 Parry (R. F.). Excavation at the caves, Cheddar. [Plan. pp. 106–13 + 4 plates, flint implements found in Gough's cave, 1927–28; pp. 118–21 + 2 plates, Report on human remains from

Gough's cave, by Sir Arthur Keith and N. C. Cooper.] Proc. Somerset Arch. Soc., 74 (1928), pp. 102–21 + 7 plates. 1929.

5165 —— Excavations at Cheddar. [3 figures + plan. i. The caves; ii. Soldier's hole pp. 57–58, Report on a mandible from the caves, by N. C. Cooper.] Proc. Somerset Arch. Soc., 76 (1930), pp. 46–63 + plate. 1931.

5167 Pengelly (William). Recent researches in Bench Cavern, Brixham, Devon. [Flint implement—not described.] Trans. Edinburgh Geol. Soc., 5, 1885/88, 507–12.

5168 —— Recent researches in Bench Cavern, Brixham, Devon. [1 flint flake artifact.] Advm. of Sci., 1887, 710–11.

5169 Phillips (E. N. Masson). Excavation at possible Romano-British site at Stoke Gabriel [enclosure and field system—may be earlier]. Devon Notes & Queries, 27, 1958, 312.

5170 —— Stoke Gabriel excavations. Interim Report 1959. [Some BA sherds, but site RB.] Rep. & Trans. Devonshire Association, XCII, 1960, 449–53.

5171 —— Excavation of a Romano-British site at Lower Well Farm, Stoke Gabriel, Devon [IA—RB]. Proc. Devon arch. Expl. Soc., N.S. No. 23, 1966, 3–34 + 62 figures + 4 plates.

5172 Pickard (Ransom). A Celtic site on Coombe down. [Plan.] Rpt. & Trans. Devon. Assoc., 84, pp. 159–62. 1952.

5173(a) Pleydell (John Clavell Mansell). Lake dwellings at Glastonbury. Proc. Dorset Antiq. F.C., 19, pp. 172–175. 1898.

5173(b) Pollard (Sheila H. M.). Neolithic and Dark Age settlements on High Peak, Sidmouth, Devon. Proc. Devon arch. Expl. Soc., N.S., No. 23, 1966, 35–59 + 13 figures.

5174 Pool (Peter Aubrey Seymour). The Courtyard-house site at Higher Bodinnar, Sancreed, Cornwall: an early plan. [Iron Age.] Antiquity, 35, 1961, pp. 314–16.

5175 Prestwich (*Sir* Joseph). On the bone-cave at Brixham in Devonshire. J. Geol. Soc., London, 16, 1860, 189–90.

5176 —— Report on the exploration of Brixham cave. [pp. 549–52 + 3 figures, Remarks on the worked flints, by

Sir John Evans.] Phil. Trans. Roy. Soc., 163, pp. 471–572 + 7 plates. 1873.

5177 Purnell (F.) *and* **Webb** (E. W.). An Iron Age "A" site [in Sandy lane, Leckhampton] near Cheltenham. [Figure (pottery).] Trans. Bristol & Glos. Arch. Soc. 69 (1950), pp. 197–99. 1952.

5178 Rahtz (Philip). Barrow Mead, Bath, Somerset. [Iron Age "B" ditches and pits underlying med. earthwork.] Proc. Somerset A. & N.H.S. 105, 1960/61, 61–76 + 2 relevant figures.

5179 Reid (Clement) *and* **Reid** (Eleanor). On a probable Palaeolithic floor at Praa Sands (Cornwall) [doubtful]. Q.J. Geol. Soc., London, 60, 1904, 106–12 + 2 figures.

5180 Rivers (Augustus Henry Lane Fox Pitt). Report on excavations made in the Pen pits, near Penselwood, Somerset. pp. 13 + 3 plates. 4°. London, 1884.

5181 Robinson (R. S. Gavin). Flint workers and flint users in the Golden Valley. [Neolithic to Iron Age.] Trans. Woolhope N.F.C., 1933–35, pp. 54–63 + 6 plates. [Herefords.] 1938.

5182 —— The pre-historic occupation of Cefn hill, near Craswell. [Neol.—BA.] Trans. Woolhope N.F.C., 32 (1946–48), pp. 32–37 + 4 plates + map. 1949.

5183 —— Notes on Bronze Age settlements on Abbey farm, Crasswall. [Map.] Trans. Woolhope N.F.C., 33 (1949–51), pp. 112–17 + 2 plates. 1952.

5184 Rogers (Ernest Henry). Stratification of the cave earth in Kents cavern. [4 figures (flints). pp. 75–77, classification of existing flint implements.] Proc. Devon Archaeol. Expl. Soc., 5, pp. 68–91 + plan. 1955.

5185 Russell (Vivien) *and* **Pool** (P. A. S.). Excavation of a Romano-British hut at Boscreege in Gulval. Cornish Archaeol., No. 2, 1963, 19–22 + 2 figures.

5186 Seaby (Wilfrid Arthur). Mesolithic chipping floor at Fideoak farm, Bishop's Hull. Proc. Somerset Arch. Soc., 95 (1950), pp. 169–70. 1951.

5187 Shorter (Alfred H.). Hut circle sites in the parishes of Ashburton, Hennock and Christow, Devon. [1901–]. Devon N. & Q., 24, pp. 14–16. 1950.

5188 Simpson (Brian) *and* **Rogers** (Inkermann). A chipping-floor at Or-

leigh Court, [Buckland Brewor] north Devon. [7 figures + 2 maps. Mesolithic and neolithic.] Antiq. J., 17, pp. 299–309. 1937.

5189 Smart (T. William Wake). Account of some ancient British antiquities discovered . . . in Kent's cavern, near Torquay. J. Brit. Archaeol. Ass., 2, pp. 171–74. 1846.

5190 Smith (C. Nancy S.). A prehistoric and Roman site at Broadway. [Figure (bone implement).] Trans. Worcs. Archaeol. Soc., N.S., 23 (1946), pp. 57–74 + 2 plates. 1947.

5191 Smith (Elsie E.). An attempt to date a surface-site on Mutter's moor, Sidmouth. [Figure (rubber flint). Neolithic.] Proc. Devon. Archaeol. Expl. Soc., 4, pp. 133–39. 1952.

5192 Smith (Reginald A.). Some recent finds in Kent's Cavern. Trans. & Proc. Torquay nat. Hist. Soc., 8, 1940, 59–60 + 1 plate.

5193 Somerset Archaeological Society. Excavations at Chelm's combe, Cheddar, 1925–26. pp. 32 + 7 plates + plan. 8°. 1926.

5194 Stone (J. Harris). Crows-anwra, the beehive huts, and St. Euny's well, Cornwall. [6 figures.] Antiquary, 45, pp. 49–54. 1909.

5195 Sutcliffe (A. J.) *and* **Zeuner** (F. E.). Excavations in the Torbryan Caves, Devonshire. I: Tornewton Cave. Proc. Devon arch. expl. Soc., V, v + vi, 1957/58, 127–45 + 3 plates.

5196 Sykes (C. M.) *and* **Whittle** (S. L.). The Birdcombe Mesolithic site, Wraxall. Proc. Somerset A. & N.H.S., 104, 1959/60, 106–23 + 6 figures + 2 plates.

5197 —— *and* —— A flint-chipping site on Tog-Hill, near Marshfield. [Mesolithic, some use Neolithic in BA.] Trans. BGAS, 84, 1965, 5–14 + 4 figures.

5198 Tebbs (B. N.). Villages of the Late Iron Age in Cornwall. Trans. & Proc. Torquay nat. Hist. Soc., 8, 1939, 17–26 + 1 plate.

5199 Thomas (Charles). An Early Iron Age site at Carwynnen, Camborne. [Figure.] Proc. West Cornwall F.C., N.S. 1, pp. 48–53. 1954

5200 —— Antiquities at Trink farm, Lelant, Cornwall. Proc. West Cornwall F.C., N.S. 1, pp. 109–70. 1956.

5201 **Thomas** (Charles). Excavations at Gwithian, Cornwall, 1953–58. [3 figures + map + plan.] Archaeol. News Letter, 6,pp. 131–38. 1958.

5202 —— Gwithian: ten years' work (1949–1958). West Cornwall Field Club. pp. 35. 4⁰. Gwithian, 1958. [Map + 7 plans. pp. 7–16, Prehistory.]

5203 —— Trial excavations at Mulfra Vean, 1954. [EIA—Roman period court-yard house.] Cornish Archaeol., No. 2, 1963, 23–28 + 3 figures.

5204 —— Gwithian [BA]. Cornish Arch., 3, 1964, 84.

5205 **Thomas** (Ivor). Kynance excavations. [MBA—EIA; cairn and huts.] Cornish Archaeol., No. 2, 1963, 57.

5206 **Threipland** (Leslie Murray). An excavation at St. Mawgan-in-Pyder, North Cornwall. [28 figures + 2 maps + 9 plans. Early Iron Age camp and hut circles. Site influenced by availability of stream tin.] Archaeol. J., 113 (1956), pp. 33–81 + 6 plates + plan. 1957.

5207 **Vachell** (E. T.). Kent's Cavern: its origin and history. J. Torquay nat. Hist. Soc. XI, 1953, 51–73 + 3 figures.

5208 —— "Tor Rocks" site, Broad-sands [no evidence found] [thought to be Neol.—BA from earlier surface finds]. Proc. Devon arch. expl. Soc., v, vi, 1958, 168.

5209 **Vulliamy** (Colwyn Edward). An uncharted village [on the western slope of Mulfrahill] in Cornwall. Man, 20, pp. 121–22 + plan. 1920.

5212 **Whittington** (G.). Strip lynchets in the Glocestershire Cotswold [explanation by analogy of lynchets at Blewburton Hill]. Trans. Bristol & Glos. A.S., 79, 1960, pt. ii, 212–20 + 4 figures.

5213 **Wicks** (A. T.). Prehistoric remains at Grapnell, Dinder, Somerset. Wells Nat. Hist. & Arch. Soc. Rpt., 1933, pp. 1–4. 1934.

5215 **Willock** (Edward Hulse). A Neolithic site at Haldon. (A further note, *etc*.) [Map. (8 figures).] Proc. Devon Archaeol. Expl. Soc., 2, pp. 244–63 + 10 plates + plan; 3, pp. 33–43 + plate. 1936–37.

5216 **Woods** (Gertrude MacAlpine). A surface site in S.E. Devon. Proc. PSEA, 5 i, 1925, 83–85 + 5 figures.

5217 —— A stone-age site in south-east Devon. [Flint implement factory at Beer.] Proc. Devon Archaeol. Expl. Soc., 1, pp. 10–14 + 3 plates. 1929.

5218 —— *and* **Woods** (Roland MacAlpine). Excavations (further excavations) in a dry valley in Beer, S.E. Devon. [5 figures (flints) + plan. Figure. ?Upper Palaeolithic.] Proc. Devon Archaeol. Expl. Soc., 2, pp. 28–39; 3, pp. 44–50 + plate. 1933–37.

5219 —— *and* —— Excavations in a dry valley in Beer, S.E. Devon [Mousterian]. Proc. PSEA, 7 iii, 1934, 354–65 + 5 figures + 1 plate.

5220 **Worth** (Richard Nicholls). A hut cluster ["below Shell Top towards Lee Moor"] on Dartmoor. [Plan.] Rpt. & Trans. Devon. Assoc., 22, pp. 237–39. 1890.

5221 **Wright** (Reginald W. M.). The Avon settlement [Bath]. [Various Neol. —IA.] Somerset Arch. Soc., Proc. Bath branch, [8] 1939–47, pp. 129–31. 1941.

5222 **Zeuner** (F. E.). Excavations at the site called "The Old Grotto", Torbryan [only passing reference to prehistoric finds, but containing description of cave]. Rep. & Trans. Devonshire Association XCII, 1960, 311–330.

(d) Zone 4
[CBA Groups 3, 4, 5, 6]

5223 **Alexander** (G. M. M.). Finds from the Mesolithic habitation—site at Star Carr, Seamer, near Scarborough, Yorks. B.M.Q., 19, pp. 52–54. 1954.

5224 **Armstrong** (Albert Leslie). Exploration of Harborough cave, Brassington [Derbs.]. [9 figures + plan. Mostly Early Iron Age finds.] J. R. Anthrop. Inst., 53, pp. 402–16 + plate. 1923.

5225 —— Further evidences of Maglemose culture [from Skipsea, near Hornsea] in East Yorkshire. [3 figures. Flints.] Man, 23, pp. 135–38. 1923.

5226 —— Excavations at Mother Grundy's parlour, Creswell Crags, Derbyshire, 1924. [18 figures + plan.] J. R. Anthrop. Inst., 55, pp. 146–78 + plate. 1928.

5227 —— Pin Hole cave excavations,

Creswell Crags, Derbyshire. Discovery of an engraved drawing of a masked human figure [Upper Aurignacian (Fort-Robert)]. Proc. PSEA, 6 i, 1928–29, 27–29 + 3 figures.

5228 Armstrong (Albert Leslie). Excavations at Creswell Crags, Derbyshire, 1924–26. (1926–28.) (1928–32.) The Pin Hole cave. Trans. Hunter Arch. Soc., 3, pp. 116–22 + 4 plates; pp. 332–34 + 1 plate; 4, pp. 178–84 + 1 plate. 1929–37.

5229 —— Excavations in the Pin Hole Cave, Creswell Crags, Derbyshire [Aurignacian-Magdalenian]. Proc. PSEA, 6 iv, 1931, 330–34 + 1 figure.

5230 —— Report on the excavation of Ash Tree cave, near Whitwell, Derbyshire, 1949 to 1957. J. Derbs. Archaeol. Soc., 76, pp. 57–64. 1956.

5231 Atkinson (W. G.). Report on the exploration of Bonfire Scar cave and Dobson cave, near Scales in Furness. [Human remains of Early Iron Age.] Trans. Cumb. & Westm. Ant. Soc., N.S. 27, pp. 110–16 + plate. 1927.

5232 Bankier (A. M.). Native site, The Heugh, Birtley. Arch. Æliana 38, 1960, 247 + 1 figure.

5233 Bemrose (William). Exploration of the Harborough Rocks cave [near Brassington, Derbs.] [Pottery, etc.] Proc. Soc. Antiq., 2 S. 22, pp. 9–12. 1907.

5234 Beynon (Vernon Bryan Crowther). Notes on some Rutland antiquities. [Figure (Neolithic skull and celt). Pp. 50–52, prehistoric.] Antiquary, 43, pp. 50–56. 1907.

5235 Booth (John). Traces of prehistoric man in the vicinity of Settle. [Victoria cave: cave at Kirkdale.] Yorks. N. & Q. (ed. Forshaw), 4, pp. 232–34. 1908.

5236 Bramwell (D.). The excavation of Dowel Cave, Earl Sterndale, 1958–9 [Neolithic burials; other finds Pleistocene to EIA]. D.A.J., 79, 1959, 97–109 + 13 figures.

5237 Brewster (T. C. M.). The excavation of Staple Howe [IA "A"]. East Riding Arch. Research Committee, Malton, 1963.

5238 Buckley (Francis). A Microlithic industry, Marsden, Yorkshire. pp. 15. 8⁰. London [1921].

5239 Bu'lock (John D.). Possible remains of Celtic fields at Kellsall in Cheshire. Trans. Lancs. & Ches. Ant. Soc., 64 (1954), pp. 24–26 + plan.

5240 Carrington (Samuel). An account of the excavations and discoveries in Thor's cave, Wetton dale, near Dovedale, Derbyshire. [7 figures.] Reliquary, 6, pp. 201–12 + 3 plates. 1866.

5241 Cherry (J.). Esmeals sand-dunes occupation sites—Phase 1, flint working [7 figures + 1 plate + 1 map]. Trans. C. & W.A. & A.S., N.S. 63, 1963, 31–52.

5242 Clark (Edwin Kitson). Excavation at Pulehill, near Marsden [Yorks.], on the Huddersfield and Manchester road. Proc. Soc. Antiq., 2 S. 18, pp. 125–29 + plate (urn with perforated lugs). 1900.

5243 Clark (John Grahame Douglas). A Mesolithic habitation-site in Yorkshire. [At Star Carr, Seamur, Scarborough.] Antiquity, 23, pp. 207–08. 1949.

5244 —— A preliminary report on excavations at Starr Carr, Seamer, Scarborough, Yorkshire, 1949. Proc. prehist. Soc., 15, 1949, 52–69 + 2 figures + 10 plates.

5245 —— Preliminary report on excavations at Starr Carr, Seamer, Scarborough, Yorkshire (second season 1950). Proc. prehist. Soc., 16, 1950, 109–129 + 8 figures + 8 plates.

5246 —— Excavations at the Mesolithic site of Star Carr, Yorkshire, 1949–1950. [7 figures.] Archaeology, 4, pp. 66–70. 1951.

5247 —— The Mesolithic hunters of Star Carr. Trans. Lancs. & Ches. Ant. Soc., 63 (1952–53), pp. 183–90 + 2 plates. 1954.

5248 —— Excavations at Star Carr. An Early Mesolithic site at Seamer, near Scarborough, Yorkshire. pp. 200 + 24 plates. [80 figures.] 4⁰. Cambridge, 1954.

5249 —— Excavations at Star Carr: an Early Mesolithic site at Seamer, near Scarborough, Yorkshire, 24 plates, 80 text figures, 21 tables, Cambridge 1954. [repr. 1971.]

5250 —— Star Carr, a Mesolithic site in Yorkshire. [5 figures + map + plan.] Recent archaeol. excavations in Britain, pp. 1–20 + 3 plates. 1956.

5251 Clark (John Grahame Douglas) *and* **Godwin** (H.). A Maglemosian site at Brandesburton, Holderness, Yorkshire. Proc. prehist. Soc., 22, 1956, 6–22 + 8 figures + 3 plates.

5252 Collingwood (Robin George). Prehistoric settlements near Crosby, Ravensworth [Westm.]. [Map & 9 plans.] Trans. Cumb. & Westm. Ant. Soc., N.S. 33, pp. 201–26. 1933.

5253(a) Collingwood (William Gershorn). Hut-circles at Greendale. [Plan.] Trans. Cumb. & Westm. Ant. Soc., N.S. 28, pp. 371–76 + plate. 1928.

5253(b) Collins (E. R.). Upper Palaeolithic sites in Nidderdale [Aurignacian] [Gouthwaite Reservoir, Yorkshire]. Proc. PSEA, 7 ii, 1932–34, 185–87 + 1 figure.

5254 Cornwall (Ian W.). Excavations at Star Carr, Seamer, Yorks. (1951). 1950 season. [Mesolithic site.] Arch. News Letter, 3, pp. 141–42; 4, 78–79. 1951–52.

5255 Coupland (George). A Microlithic industry, Durham [Tardenoisean]. Proc. PSEA, 5 i, 1925, 62–64, 1 plate.

5256 —— A Microlithic flint industry on the Durham coast. pp. 6. [Figure.] 8°. *n.p.* [1932].

5257 —— A Mesolithic industry at the Beacon, S.E. Durham. pp. 7 + plate. 8°. *n.p.* 1948.

5258 Cowen (John David). Excavations on Heddon Law, 1925. [Plan.] Proc. Soc. Antiq. Newc., 4th S. 6, pp. 76–78. 1933.

5259 Cowling (E. T.) *and* **Strickland** (H. J.). Two Mesolithic riverside sites. [Leathley bridge, Topcliffe. Plan and 2 figures.] Yorks. Archaeol. J., 36, pp. 455–62. 1947.

5260 Cox (John Charles). On a newly discovered bone cave [on Longcliffe ridge, above Brassington] in Derbyshire. [Rains cave.] Reliquary, N.S. 2, pp. 237–39. 1888.

5261 Cross (*Hon.* Marjorie). A prehistoric settlement on Walney island [Lancs.]. [42 figures. Neolithic and Bronze Age implements, *etc.*] Trans. Cumb. & Westm. Ant. Soc., Part 1, N.S. 38, pp. 160–63 + 5 plates; Part 2, 39, pp. 262–83 + 3 plates; Part 3, 42, pp. 112–21; Part 4, 46, pp. 67–76 + plate; Part 5, 47, pp. 68–77; Part 6, 49,

pp. 1–9; Part 7, 50, pp. 15–19. 1938–50.

5262 Davies (J.). A Mesolithic site on Blubberhouses Moor, Wharfedale, West Riding of Yorkshire. Yorks. Arch. Journ., 41 (i) 1963, 61–70, 2 figures.

5263 Davis (James W.). On a pile dwelling recently discovered at Ulrome, in Holderness, Yorkshire [?date]. Advm. Sci., 1883, 567–68.

5264 Dawkins (*Sir* William Boyd). Report on the results obtained by the Settle Cave Exploration Committee out of Victoria Cave in 1870. [2 figures. Neolithic: also Roman Jewellery, *etc.*] J. Anth. Inst., 1, pp. 60–70 + 2 plates. 1871.

5265 —— *and* **Mello** (J. M.). Further discoveries in the Cresswell Caves, with notes on the Mammalia by the former. [Solutrian.] J. Geol. Soc., London, 35, 1879, 724–35 + 7 figures.

5266 Dobson (John). Report on an ancient settlement at Stone Close, near Stainton-in-Furness. Trans. Cumb. & Westm. Ant. Soc., N.S. 12, pp. 277–84 + plan. 1912.

5267 Duncombe (*Hon.* Cecil). Evidence of lake dwellings on the banks of the Costa, near Pickering, North Riding of Yorkshire. J. Anthrop. Inst., 28, pp. 150–54 + plate. 1899.

5268 Dymond (Charles William), **Ferguson** (Richard Saul) *etc.* An ancient village in Hugill [Westm.]. [Figure.] Trans. Cumb. & Westm. Ant. Soc., 12–14 + plan; 14, pp. 460–69. 1893–97.

5269 Dymond (Charles William) *and* **Hodgson** (T. H.). An ancient village near Turelkeld. [Figure.] Trans. Cumb. & Westm. Ant. Soc., N.S. 2, pp. 38–52 + plate + 2 plans. 1902.

5270 Fair (Mary Cicely). Additional remains at Greendale, near Wastwater. [Hut-circles.] Trans. Cumb. & Westm. Ant. Soc., N.S. 31, p. 209 + 2 plates. 1931.

5271 —— A re-consideration of the lakeside site at Ehenside tarn, west Cumberland. [Plan. Neolithic hearth, *etc.*] Trans. Cumb. & Westm. Ant. Soc., N.S. 32, pp. 57–62. 1932.

5272 Fox (W. Storrs). Notes on the excavation of Harborough cave, near Brassington, Derbyshire. [Figure + plan.] Proc. Soc. Antiq., 2 S. 22, pp. 129–35. 1908.

5273 Fox (W. Storrs). Harborough cave, near Brassington. i. Description of the excavations. [Figure + plan.] J. Derbs. Archaeol. Soc., 31, pp. 89–96 + 2 plates. 1909.

5274 —— and **Read** (*Sir* Charles Hercules). Ravencliffe cave. [Figure + 2 plans. Neolithic–Roman occupation.] J. Derbs. Archaeol. Soc., 32, pp. 141–51 + 3 plates. 1910.

5275 —— Ravencliffe cave. [Figure.] J. Derbs. Archaeol. Soc., N.S. 3, pp. 71–78 + plate + plan. 1930.

5276 Gillam (J. P.). Excavations at Tullie House, Carlisle, 1954–56. Report on the Romano-British coarse pottery [3 figures]. Trans. C. & W.A. & A.S., N.S., lxiv, 1964, 29–41.

5277 Greenwell (William) *and* **Gatty** (Reginald A.). The pit dwellings at Holderness. [2 figures. Neolithic.] Man, 10, pp. 86–90. 1910.

5278 Hall (George Rome). An enquiry into the origin of certain terraced slopes in North Tynedale. Nat. Hist. Trans. Northumberland & Durham 3, 1868/70, 32–53 + 1 figure.

5279 —— An account of researches in ancient circular dwellings, near Birtley, Northumberland. Archaeologia, 45, pp. 355–74 + 2 plans. 1877.

5280 —— An account of the Gunnar peak camp, North Tynedale, and of excavations in the ancient circular and other dwellings. [Ancient British or Romano–British.] Arch. Æl., N. [2nd] S. 10, pp. 12–37 + 3 plans. 1885.

5281 Hodgson (*Mrs.* Alice). Excavations above Milkingstead, Eskdale. Trans. Cumb. & Westm. Ant. Soc., N.S. 28, pp. 149–51 + plans (6 cairns). 1928.

5282 Jobey (George). A note on Farhill crags [native site]. [Figure (food vessel). Site destroyed by quarrying.] Proc. Soc. Antiq. Newc., 5th S. 1, pp. 350–51. 1955.

5283 —— Excavations at the native settlement, Grubeon cottage, Northumberland. [3 figures + 4 plans. Site occupied in second century AD or later. Native pottery mostly degenerated Iron Age.] Arch. Æl., 4 S. 35, pp. 163–79. 1957.

5284 —— An Iron Age homestead at West Brandon, Durham. Arch. Æliana,

40 (1962), 1–34 + 10 figures + 3 plates.

5285 —— Excavations of a native settlement at Marden, Tynemouth. Arch. Æliana, 41, 1963, 19–35 + 7 figures + 2 plates.

5286 Jackson (John Wilfrid). Preliminary (Further, Third) report on the exploration of "Dog holes" cave, Warton crag, near Carnforth, Lancashire. [Implements, pottery, *etc.* Pp. 14–19, (73–74), (108–15), human remains.] Trans. Lancs. & Ches. Ant. Soc., 27 (1909), pp. 1–32 + 2 plates + plan; 28 (1910), pp. 59–81 + 2 plates; 30 (1912), pp. 99–130 + plate. 1910–13

5287 —— Report on the recent explorations at the Dog Holes, Warton Crag. [Interments: ?Bronze Age.] Trans. Cumb. & Westm. Ant. Soc., N.S. 13, pp. 55–58. 1913.

5288 —— Creswell caves [Derbs.]. Trans. Lancs. & Ches. Ant. Soc., 44 (1927), pp. 1–7. 1929.

5289 Jones (G. D. B.) *and* **Thompson** (F. H.). Excavations at Main Tor and Brough-on-Noe, 1965 [IA + Roman]. D.A.J., 85, 1965, 123–26 + plates.

5290 Kelly (J. H.). Excavations at Reynard's Cave, Dovedale. D.A.J., 80, 1960, 117–23 + 1 plate + 1 figure.

5291 Lomas (John). A Mesolithic site in South Derbyshire. D.A.J., 79, 1959, 119–22 + 1 figure.

5292 Lowndes (R. A. C.). Excavation of a Romano-British farmstead at Eller Beck [2 figures]. Trans. C. & W.A. & A.S., N.S. 64, 6–13, 1964.

5293 Manby (T. G.). A Neolithic site at Driffield, East Riding of Yorkshire. [4 figures + plan.] Yorks. Archaeol. J., 39, pp. 169–78. 1957.

5294 —— A Neolithic site at Craike hill, Garton Slack, East Riding of Yorkshire. [7 figures + 2 plans.] Antiq. J., 38, pp. 223–36. 1958.

5295 March (Henry Colley). The early neolithic floor of East Lancashire. Advm. of Sci., 1887, 912.

5296 Martindale (J. A.). An ancient British village in Kentmere. Trans. Cumb. & Westm. Ant. Soc., N.S. 1, pp. 175–85 + plan. 1901.

5297 Mello (J. Magens). Palaeolithic man at Creswell [caves]. J. Derbs. Archaeol. Soc., 1, pp. 15–24. 1879.

5298 Moore (John W.). Excavations

at Beacon Hill, Flamborough Head, East Yorkshire [Neolithic—Beaker settlement "hollow"]. Yorks. Arch. Journ., 41 (ii), 1964, 191–202 + 4 figures.

5299 Morris (J. P.). Report of explorations conducted in the Kirkhead cave at Ulverstone [Lancs.]. Mems. Anthrop. Soc. London, 2, pp. 358–63. 1866.

5300 Mullins (E. H.). The ossiferous cave at Langwith. [2 figures. Pp. 145–50 + 2 plates. Notes on flints: pp. 155–57, Report on a cranium, by Sir Arthur Keith (Late Palaeolithic or Early Neolithic).] J. Derbs. Archaeol. Soc., 35, pp. 137–58 + 5 plates + plan. 1913.

5301 Musson (Reginald Coulson). A Bronze Age cave site in the Little Bolland area of Lancashire. Report of excavation. [4 figures + 2 plans.] Trans. Lancs. & Ches. Ant. Soc., 59 (1947), pp. 161–70 + 2 plates. 1948.

5302 Nickson (D.) *and* **Macdonald** (J. H.). A preliminary report on a Microlithic site at Drigg, Cumberland. [4 figures + plan.] Trans. Cumb. & Westm. Ant. Soc., N.S. 55, pp. 17–29 + 2 plates. 1956.

5303 Norbury (William). Lindow common as a peat bog: its age and its people. Trans. Lancs. & Ches. Ant. Soc., 2 (1884), pp. 61–75 + plate. 1885.

5304 Philips (Judith T.). An Iron Age site at Driffield, East Riding, Yorks. Yorks. Arch. Journ., 40 (ii), 1960, 183–91 + 8 figures.

5305 Powell (T. G. E.). *and others*. Excavations at Skelmore Heads near Ulverston 1957 and 1959 (with Clare I. Fell, John X. W. P. Corcoran and F. Barnes). [6 plates + 11 figures.] Trans. C. & W.A. & A.S., N.S., 63, 1963, 1–30.

5306 Radley (Jeffrey) *and* **Mellars** (P.). A Mesolithic structure at Deepcar, Yorkshire, England, and the affinities of its associated flint industries. Proc. prehist. Soc., 30, 1964, 1–24 + 10 figures.

5307 —— *and* **Cooper** (L.). An occupied cave of the Bronze Age, Bunter's Hill Wood, Beeley. D.A.J., 86, 1966, 93–98 + 4 figures.

5308 Raistrick (Arthur). Excavation of a [bone] cave at Bishop Middleham, [Co.] Durham. [Figure + map + plan.

Pp. 119–21, report on human remains, by Sir Arthur Keith.] Arch. Æl., 4th S. 10, pp. 111–22 + plate (skull). 1933.

5309 —— A Mesolithic site on the South-East Durham coast. Trans. Northern Naturalists Union, 1 iv, 1936, 207–16 + 3 figures.

5310 —— Prehistoric cultivations at Grassington, West Yorkshire. [The "Borrans". 3 figures. Hut-circles, *etc*.] Yorks. Archaeol. J., 33, pp. 166–74 + plate + map. 1938.

5311 Roeder (Charles). On a newly discovered Neolithic settlement at the Red Noses, New Brighton, near Liverpool. Trans. Hist. Soc. Lancs. & Ches., 50, pp. 123–30 + 2 plates. 1900.

5312 Rooke (Hayman). Description of certain pits [in Linda Spring wood near Crich] in Derbyshire. [Plan. Queries—"British town".] Archaeologia, 10, pp. 114–17. 1792.

5313 Sandeman (Edward). Excavation discoveries in the Derwent Valley. [Bronze Age or Early Iron Age mould for casting rings: from Derwent dam.] J. Derbs. Archaeol. Soc., 92, pp. 73–75 + plate. 1910.

5314 Sheppard (Thomas). Excavations at Eastburn, East Yorkshire. [Pp. 35–42, Iron Age remains.] Yorks. Archaeol. J., 34, pp. 35–47 + 5 plates. 1938.

5315 Smith (Henry Ecroyd). The limestone caves of Craven and their ancient inhabitants. Trans. Hist. Soc. Lancs. & Ches., [17] N.S. 5, pp. 199–230 + 2 plates. 1865.

5316 Smith (Reginald Allender). Notes on the finds in the Harborrow cave. [2 figures.] Proc. Soc. Antiq., 2 S. 22, pp. 135–45. 1908.

5317 —— Harborough cave, nr. Brassington. ii. Description of the finds. [17 figures.] J. Derbs. Archaeol. Soc., 31, pp. 97–114 + plate. 1909.

5318 —— Lake-dwellings in Holderness, Yorks., discovered by Thos. Boynton, 1880–1. [11 figures + plan. Ulrome, *etc*.] Archaeologia, 62, pp. 593–610 + plate + plan. 1911.

5319 —— On the ancient lake-dwellings discovered by Thomas Boynton at Ulrome and elsewhere in Holderness. Proc. Soc. Antiq., 2 S. 23, pp. 490–92. 1911.

5320 Spence (Joseph E.). An early settlement on Moor Divock. [Plan.] Trans. Cumb. & Westm. Ant. Soc., N.S. 34, pp. 45–49 + plate. 1934.

5321 —— An early settlement near Askham [Cumberland]. [On Skirsgill hill.] Trans. Cumb. & Westm. Ant. Soc., N.S. 35, pp. 61–65 + 6 plates + plan. 1935.

5322 Stead (Iain M.). An excavation at Yearsley, North Riding, 1961 [Bronze Age]. Yorks. Arch. Journ., 41 (i), 1963, 19–20 + 1 figure.

5323 Tate (George). An account of the British settlement called Greaves Ash in Northumberland. Arch. Camb., 3rd S. 7, pp. 201–08 + plan. 1861.

5324 —— On the old Celtic town at Greaves Ash, near Linhope, Northumberland, with an account of diggings recently made into this and other ancient remains in the valley of the Breamish. Hist. Berwick. Nat. Club, 4, pp. 293–316 + 5 plates + plan. 1861.

5325 Thompson (F. H.). Infirmary Field Excavation, 1957. Chester Arch. Jl., 49, 1962, 1–3.

5326 Tyson (John C.). Preliminary report of excavations at the Iron Age settlement in Canklow wood, Rotherham. Trans. Hunter Arch. Soc., 6, pp. 271–77 + 3 plates. 1950.

5327 Wacher (John Stewart). Excavations at Martinsthorpe, Rutland, 1960 [surface find BA flint scraper]. Trans. Leic. Arch. Soc., 39, 1963–64, 11 + 1 figure.

5328 Walker (D.). A site at Stump Cross, near Grassington, Yorkshire, and the age of the Pennine microlithic industry. Proc. prehist. Soc., 22, 1956, 23–28 + 2 figures + 1 plate.

5329 Walker (M. J.). A flint working site from Ilkley Crags [mesolithic]. Yorks. Arch. Journ., 41 (ii), 1964, 183–84 + 1 figure.

5330 Ward (John). On Rains cave, Longcliffe, Derbyshire. [Plan.] Reliquary, N.S. 3, pp. 14–24 + 2 plates. 1889.

5331 —— On Rains cave, Longcliffe, Derbyshire. (Second report.—The excavation and general results). (Third report.—The pottery, the human and animal remains). [Plan. (4 figures + plan).] J. Derbs. Archaeol. Soc., 11,

pp. 31–45 + 3 plates; 14, pp. 228–50; 15, pp. 161–76 + 2 plates. 1889–92, 1893.

5332 —— Recent cave-hunting in Derbyshire. [i. Rains cave, near Brassington (6 figures + plan): ii. Thirst house, Deepdale (15 figures + plan).] Reliquary, N. [3rd] S. 2, pp. 209–20; 3, pp. 87–98. 1896–97.

5333 Waterman (Dudley M.), **Kent** (B. W. J.) *and* **Strickland** (H. J.). Two Iron Age sites with "Iron Age A" pottery in the West Riding of Yorkshire. [Occupation site at Grafton, 6 figures: tumulus on Roomer common, near Masham, plate, figure, plan.] Yorks. Archaeol. J., 38, pp. 383–97 + plate. 1954.

5334 Willett (Frank) *and* **Seddon** (Thomas). Excavations [of pillow-mounds] in Everage Clough, Burnley, 1951. Trans. Lancs. & Ches. Ant. Soc., 63 (1952–53), pp. 194–200 + 2 plates + plan.

5335 —— Excavations at Castle Croft, Blackrod, Lancashire, 1952. [?Neolithic and mediaeval.] Trans. Lancs. & Ches. Ant. Soc., 63 (1952–53), pp. 201–06 + plate (flints).

5336 Wood (Eric S.). Settlement site at Hutton-le-Hole, North Riding. Yorks. Archaeol. J., 36, p. 265; 37, pp. 1–3. 1946–48.

(e) ZONE 5
[CBA Group 2]

5337 Allen (E. E.). A Stone Age flint chipping site in vale of Towy; Llanegwad parish. [?Neolithic.] Trans. Carmarthenshire Ant. Soc., 28, pp. 92–94 + plate. 1938.

5338 —— Flint chipping floor in the Towy valley. Proc. Swansea Sc. Soc., 2, pp. 107–18. 1939.

5339 —— *and* **Rutter** (J. G.). A survey of the Gower caves with an account of recent excavations. Part 1. Proc. Swansea Sc. Soc., 2, pp. 221–46, 263–90. 1944–47.

5340 —— *and* —— Gower caves, with an account of recent excavations. 8°. Swansea, 1946. pp. 28 + 14 plates + 49 figures.

5341 [**Anon.**] Neolithic caves at Perthi Chwarea, near Llandegla. Proc. Llandudno F.C., 13 (1926–27), pp. 25–27. 1927.

5342 Banks (Richard William). On the crannog in Llangors lake [near Brecon]. Arch. Camb., 4th S. 3, pp. 146–48. 1872.

5343 Baynes (Edward Neil). The shell-mounds of Newborough warren. [Figure (bone needles).] Anglesey Ant. Soc. Trans., 1927, pp. 34–37. 1927.

5344 Breese (Charles E.). Cytian Gwyddelod [hut circles] in the ville of Gest [Carnarvonshire]. Arch. Camb., 77, p. 396. 1922.

5345 Burgess (C. B.) *and* **Boon** (George C.). Current work in Welsh archaeology: excavations and discoveries. Bull. Board Celtic Studies, 19 iv, 1962, 335–54 + 6 figures + 4 plates.

5346 Cantrill (Thomas Crosbee). The shell-mounds on Laugharne burrows, Carmarthenshire. [16 figures + map + 2 plans. Early Iron Age occupation.] Arch. Camb., 6th S. 9, pp. 433–72. 1909.

5347 Chambers (G. C.). A note upon Muriau'r Dre (Tre'r Gwyddelod) [hut circles], Carnarvonshire. [Plan.] Arch. Camb., 6th S. 3, pp. 282–84. 1903.

5348 Crawford (Osbert Guy Stanhope). Account of excavations at Hengwm, Merionethshire, August and September, 1919. [3 figures + 6 plans.] Arch. Camb., 6th S. 20, pp. 99–128 + 9 plates + 5 plans: 76, pp. 305–06. 1920–21.

5349 Cunnington (Maud Edith). Notes on objects from an inhabited site on the Worms head, Glamorgan. [4 figures.] Arch. Camb., 6th S. 20, pp. 251–56. 1920.

5350 Davies (Ellis). Hut circles and ossiferous cave on Gop farm, Gwannysgor, Flintshire. [Plan.] Arch. Camb., 80, pp. 436–38. 1925.

5351 Drinkwater (C. H.). Ancient British hut-dwellings near Bula, Merionethshire. [Plan.] Arch. Camb., 5th S. 5, pp. 26–28. 1888.

5352 Dumbleton (E. N.). On a crannoge, or stockaded island, in Llangorse lake, near Brecon. Arch. Camb., 4th S. 1, pp. 192–98. 1870.

5353 Evans (George Eyre). Kidwelly shell-mounds on the burrows. Trans. Carmarthenshire Ant. Soc., 7, pp. 3–4. 1911.

5354 Falconer (H.). On the ossiferous caves of the Peninsula of Gower, in Glamorganshire, S. Wales. J. Geol. Soc., London, 16, 1860, 487–91.

5356 Fox (Aileen Mary) *Lady Fox*. An account of John Storrie's excavations on Barry Island in 1894–5. [Bronze Age occupation.] Cardiff Nat. Soc. Rpt. & Trans., 69 (1936), pp. 12–38 + 4 plates + map. 1938.

5357 Fox (Cyril). A settlement of the Early Iron Age (La Tène I subperiod) on Merthyr Mawr Warren, Glamorgan. Arch. Cambrensis, 82 i, 1927, 44–66, 8 figures.

5358 Gardner (Lloyd). A prehistoric mound [at Llanfoist] near Abergavenny [Mon.]. Arch. Camb., 6th S. 13, pp. 349–50. 1913.

5359 George (T. Neville). A Mesolithic site in Gower. Proc. Swansea Sc. Soc., 1935, pp. 289–94. 1935.

5360 Glenn (Thomas Allen). Exploration of Neolithic station near Gwaenysgor, Flintshire. [14 figures + plan.] Arch. Camb., 6th S. 14, pp. 247–70. 1914.

5361 —— Prehistoric and historic remains at Dyserth castle [Flintshire]. [10 figures + plan (3 figures). Occupation in Neolithic and Bronze Ages.] Arch. Camb., 6th S. 15, pp. 47–56, 249–52. 1915.

5363 Gresham (Colin A.). Megalithic site, Roe-Wen East, Caernarvonshire. Arch. Camb., 114, 1965, 180–81 + 1 figure.

5364 Griffith (J. E.). British antiquities found [in hut-circles] at Plas-Bach, near Cerring Ceinwen, Anglesey. Arch. Camb., 5th S. 9, pp. 242–43 + plate. 1892.

5365 Griffiths (William Eric). The development of native homesteads in North Wales. [5 plans. Hut groups, *etc.*] Antiquity, 25, pp. 174–86. 1951.

5366 —— Excavations on Pemmaen-Mawr (Caern.) 1950. [Mounds just stone clearance dumps.] Arch. Camb., 101 ii, 1951, 163.

5367 —— The excavation of an enclosed hut-group at Cae'r-mynydd in Caernarvonshire. [3 figures + map +

plan. Iron Age "B".] Antiq. J., 39, pp. 33–60 + plate + plan. 1959.

5368 Grimes (William Francis). A new Upper Palaeolithic site in S.W. Wales. [Cave at Monkton, near Pembroke.] Bull. Bd. Celtic Stud., 6, pp. 286–87. 1932.

5369 —— Priory Farm cave, Monkton, Pembrokeshire with a report on the human and animal remains, by Lionel F. Cowley. Arch. Camb., 88 i, 1933, 88–100 + 5 figures.

5370 —— Note on excavations in Wales in 1935. Proc. prehist. Soc., N.S. 1, 1935, 144–46.

5371 —— Coygan Cave, Llansedyrain, Carmarthenshire [Monsherian]. Arch. Camb., 90 i, 1935, 95–111 + 7 figures.

5372 —— *and* **Hyde** (H. A.). A prehistoric hearth at Radyr, Glamorgan, and its bearing on the nativity of beech (fagus sylvatica L.) in Britain. [Plan. Early Iron Age.] Cardiff Nat. Soc. Rpt. & Trans., 68 (1935), pp. 46–54 + plate. 1937.

5373 —— Clegyr Boia [short note]. [Neolithic univall. IA hill fort.] Arch. J., 119, 1962, 336.

5375 Hesketh (G. E.). An account of excavations in the cave in big covert, Maeshafu, Llanferres. Flintshire Hist., Soc. Publns., 15, pp. 141–48 + plate + plan. 1955.

5376 Hughes (H. Harold). Remains of a circular hut at Llanysturdwy [?IA]. Arch. Camb., 83 i, 1928, 216–18 + 1 plate.

5377 Humphreys (George Alfred). Prehistoric remains, Kendrick's cave, Great Orme's Head, Llandudno. Proc. Llandudno F.C., 2 (1907–08), pp. 49–57. 1909.

5378 Jerman (H. Noel). Oak piles from the peat in north Breconshire. [?remains of hut-poles.] Bull. Bd. Celtic Stud., 7, pp. 329–30. 1934.

5379 Jones (Harry Longueville). Maev Beuno [near Barriew, Montgomeryshire]. [Figure. Maenhir, Neolithic.] Arch. Camb., 3rd S. 3, pp. 299–301. 1857.

5380 —— Ty Illtyd, [at Mannest farm in the parish of Llanhamlach] Brecknockshire. [2 figures + plan.] [Neolithic] Arch. Camb., 3rd S. 13, pp. 347–55 + plate. 1867.

5381 Leach (Arthur L.). Note on the discovery of prehistoric hearths at Swanlake [Pembrokeshire]. [General.] [Plan.] Arch. Camb., 6th S. 9, pp. 243–45, 367. 1909.

5382 —— Nanna's cave, Isle of Caldey [Pemb.]. [9 figures + map. (3 figures). Late Palaeolithic occupation.] Arch. Camb., 6th S. 16, pp. 155–80; 17, pp. 71–89. 1916–17.

5383 —— Kitchen-middens on Giltar Point, near Tenby. Arch. Camb., 87 ii, 1932, 359–63 + 2 figures.

5384 Lethbridge (Thomas Charles) *and* **David** (H. E.). Excavation of a house-site on Gateholm, Pembrokeshire [Iron Age]. Arch. Camb., 85 ii, 1930, 366–74 + 6 figures.

5385 Lines (H. H.). Celtic remains at Llanfairfechan. Antiquary, 27, pp. 58–61. 1893.

5386 —— Remains at Muriam Gwyddelod, near Harlech. The walls of the Irishmen. Antiquary, 29, pp. 76–81, 111–14. 1894.

5387 Livens (Roger G.). An enclosed hut-group at Thearddur Bay. Trans. Anglesey Antiq. Soc. Fld. Club, 1962, 86 + 1 figure.

5388 Lowe (Walter Bezant). Gwern Engan, near the Sychnant pass [Carnarv.] [2 figures + plan. Hut-circle village.] Proc. Llandudno F.C., 8 (1913–15), pp. 32–35. 1917.

5389 Morris (John H.). Exploration of Newmarket (Gop) caves. [Plan. Human bones found.] Northern Flintshire, 1, pp. 32–38 + plate (flint-axe). 1913.

5390 O'Neil (Bryan Hugh St. John). Excavations at Caeran ancient village, Clynnog, Caernarvonshire, 1933 and 1934. [7 figures + plan.] Antiq. J., 16, pp. 295–320 + 6 plates + plan. 1936.

5391 Owen (Elias). Arvona antiqua—ancient dwellings, or cyttiau, near Llanllechid [Carnarvonshire]. Arch. Camb., 3rd S. 12, pp. 215–28 + 3 plans (early enclosures). 1866.

5392 —— A group of ancient circular and oblong buildings at Coed Uchaf, Llanllechid [Carnarvonshire]. Arch. Camb., 4th S. 3, pp. 239–48 + 2 plates + map + 3 plans. 1872.

5393 Pape (Thomas). Prehistoric

settlement [from Newborough], Angle-sey. [5 figures.] Antiq. J., 7, pp. 196–97. 1927.

5394 Pape (Thomas). A prehistoric settlement [at Newborough warren] in Anglesey. [3 (2) figures.] Anglesey Ant. Soc. Trans., 1927, pp. 23–33; 1928, pp. 21–27. 1927–28.

5395 Peate (Iorwerth Cyfeiliog). A reputed lake dwelling site near Tregaron [Cards.]. Antiquity, 2, p. 473. 1928.

5396 Penniman (T. K.). Culver hole cave, Llangennith, Gower. Bull. Bd. Celtic Stud., 6, pp. 90–92, 196–97. 1931–32.

5397 —— Culver hole cave, Llangen-nith, and vicinity. Bull. Bd. Celtic Stud., 7, pp. 417–18. 1935.

5398 Phillips (Charles William). The excavation of a hut site at Parc Dinmor, Penmon, Anglesey. [Iron Age.] Arch. Camb., 87 ii, 1932, 247–59 + 4 figures.

5399 —— The excavation of a hut group at Pant-y-saer in the parish of Llanfair-Mathafarn-Eithaf, Anglesey [said to be RB but cf. BA sites today]. Arch. Camb., 89 i, 1934, 1–36 + 12 figures.

5400 Prichard (Hugh). Huts of Ardudwy [Merioneth.]. Arch. Camb., 4th S. 12, pp. 17–30 + 2 plates. 1881.

5401 Ridgway (Maurice H.) *and* **Leach** (Geo. B.). Prehistoric flint workshop site near Abersoch, Caernar-vonshire. Arch. Camb., 99 i, 1946, 78-84 + 3 figures.

5402 Savory (Hubert Newman). The excavation of a Neolithic dwelling and a Bronze Age cairn at Mount Pleasant farm, Nottage (Glam.). Cardiff Nat. Soc. Rpt. & Trans., 81 (1950/52), pp. 75–92 + 4 plates + plan. 1953.

5403 Smith (F. Gilbert). Sidelights on the pigmy workshop discovered at Prestatyn. Proc. Llandudno F.C., 16, pp. 42–49. 1931.

5404 Sollas (William Johnson). Pavi-land cave: an Aurignacian station in Wales. [23 figures.] J. R. Anthrop. Inst., 43, pp. 325–74 + 4 plates. 1913.

5405 Stanley (*Hon.* William Owen). On the remains of the ancient circular habitations in Holyhead Island, called Cyttiau'r Gwyddelod, at Ty Mawr, on the S.W. slope of Holyhead mountain. (Notices of relics found by Albert Way).

[7 figures + 2 plans.] Archaeol. J., 24, pp. 229–44 + 3 plates. 1867.

5406 —— On the remains of ancient circular habitations in Holyhead Island, called Cyttiau'r Gwyddelod, at Ty Mawr, on the S.W. side of of Holyhead moun-tain. [8 figures + plan.] Arch. Camb., 3rd S. 14, pp. 385–433 + 3 plates + map + plan. 1868.

5407 —— Ancient circular habitations, called Cyttiau'r Gwyddelod, at Ty Mawr in Holyhead island; with notices of other early remains there. [6 figures + 2 plans.] Archaeol. J., 26, pp. 301–22 + 6 plates + 4 plans. 1869.

5408 —— Recent excavations at Ty Mawr, Pen y Bonc, Twr and Mynydd Gof Du in Holyhead island, with notices of ancient relics found at Cerrig Ddewi, and at Old Geir, in Anglesey. [8 figures + plan.] Archaeol. J., 27, pp. 147–64 + 12 plates. 1870.

5409 —— Ynys Lyrad [hut clusters], Anglesey. Arch. Camb., 4th S. 9, pp. 134–35 + 2 plans. 1878.

5410 Style (A. Hurrell). Notes on a Pembroke cave. pp. 10 + plate. 8°. Pembroke [1907?].

5411 Thomas (Roger). A prehis-toric flint factory discovered at Aberyst-wyth. [2 plans.] Arch. Camb., 6th S. 12, pp. 211–16. 1912.

5412 —— *and* **Dudlyke** (E. R.). A flint chipping floor at Aberystwyth. [10 figures.] J. R. Anthrop. Inst., 55, pp. 73–89 + 2 plates. 1925.

5413 Wainwright (G. J.). The ex-cavation of a Mesolithic site at Freshwater West, Pembrokeshire. [4 figures + plan.] Bull. Bd. Celtic Stud., 18, pp. 196–205. 1959.

5414 —— The re-examination of a chipping floor at Frainslake, Pembroke-shire, and its affiliated sites. Bull. Board Celtic Studies, 19 i, 1960, 49–56 + 3 figures.

5415 Williams (Audrey). Clegyr Boia, St. David's (Pemb.): Excavation in 1943. [Neolithic—IA "A".] Arch. Camb., 102 i, 1952, 20–47 + 13 figures + 6 plates.

5416 Williams (Jacob Picton Gor-don). The Nab head flint factory [Pem-broke]. [Azilian.] Trans. Carmarthen-shire Ant. Soc., pt. 16, 1925, p. 33.

5417(a) —— Druidston haven chip-ping floors [Pembroke]. Trans. Carmarthenshire Ant. Soc., pt. 16, 1925, pp. 43–44.

5417(b) Williams (Jacob Picton Gordon). The Nab head [Pemb.] chipping floor. [6 figures.] Arch. Camb., 81, pp. 86–110. 1926.

5418 Williams (John). On Carn Goch, in Caermarthenshire. Arch. Camb., 3rd S. 2, pp. 40–48. 1856.

5420 Wood (James George). Y Garn Llwyd, erroneously called the Gaer Llwyd. [Newchurch, Mon.] Arch. Camb., 6th S. 10, pp. 305–12. 1910.

(f) Zone 6
[CBA Group 1 plus Ireland and Isle of Man]

5421 Astley (Hugh John Dukinfield). Some further notes on the Langbank crannog. J. Brit. Archaeol. Ass., N.S. 9, pp. 59–64 + plate. 1903.

5422 Bersu (Gerhard). Excavation of Celtic round houses at Ballakeigan and Ballanorris, Isle of Man. Antiq. J., 24, p. 152. 1944.

5423 Bigger (Francis Joseph) *and* **Fennell** (William J.). Souterrain at Stranocum, Co. Antrim. Ulster J. Arch., 3, 1897, 202–03 + 2 figures.

5424 —— *and* —— Souterrain in the parish of Ardboe, Co. Tyrone. Ulster J. Arch., 4, 1897, 65–67 + 3 figures.

5425 Bruce (John). Report and investigations upon the Langbank pile dwelling. [La Tène.] Trans. Glasgow Arch. Soc., 2nd S. 5, pp. 43–53 + 6 plates + plan. 1905.

5426 Bruce (J. R.) *and others* [**Megan** (E. M.) *and* **Megan** (B. R. S.)]. A Neolithic site at Ronaldsway, Isle of Man. Proc. prehist. Soc., 13, 1947, 139–60 + 11 figures + 8 plates.

5427 Calder (Charles T.). A summary of the report on the excavation of a Neolithic temple at Stanydale in the parish of Sandsting, Shetland, given to the Society of Antiquaries of Scotland. [Figure + plan.] Arch. News Letter, 3, pp. 111–14. 1951.

5428 —— Excavations in Whalsay, Shetland, 1954–5. [Dwelling and temple pre-EIA; 2 cairns EBA.] Proc. Soc. Ant. Scotland, 94, 1960/61, 28–45 + 8 figures + 3 plates.

5429 Case (Humphrey). A Neolithic site at Goodland, Co. Antrim. Arch. News Letter, 5, p. 19. 1954.

5430 Childe (Vere Gordon). Skara Brae: a "Stone Age" village in Orkney. [Figure (bone tools). Probably Bronze Age.] Antiquity, 5, pp. 47–59 + 4 plates + plan. 1931.

5431 —— Skara Brae, a Pictish village in Orkney. pp. xiii, 208 + 62 plates + plan. 8°. London, 1931. [24 figures. pp. 185–97, an account of the skeletons and their probable affinities, by Thomas H. Bryce.]

5432 —— Age of Skara Brae. ["Prebroch".] Man, 32, p. 191. 1932.

5433 —— Notes on excavations in Scotland in 1935. Proc. prehist. Soc., N.S. 1, 1935, 142–44 + 1 plate.

5434 —— A new Skara Brae [at the Braes of Rinyo, Ronsay, Orkney]. [Figure. Beaker period.] Antiq. J., 18, pp. 402–03. 1938.

5435 —— Ancient dwellings at Skara Brae, Orkney. *Ministry of Works.* pp. 20 + 8 plates + plan. 8°. Edinburgh, 1950.

5436 Chinnock (Edward J.). Recent antiquarian discoveries at [High Banks farm, parish of] Kirkcudbright. Trans. Dumfries. Ant. Soc., 6 (1887–90), pp. 263–67 + plate (urns). 1890.

5437 Coles (Frederick R.). A prehistoric colony at Anwoth. Trans. Dumfries. Ant. Soc., 7 (1890–91), pp. 17–24. 1891.

5438 Davidson (James Milne). A stone flaking site at Burghead, Morayshire. Trans. Glasgow Archaeol. Soc., N.S. 11, pp. 28–30. 1947.

5439 Dimbleby (Geoffrey William). Iron Age land use on Bonchester Hill. Proc. Soc. Ant. Scotland, 93, 1959–60, pp. 237–38.

5440 Donnelly (W. A.). Discovery of a crannog [at Dumbarton] on the shore of the Clyde. J. Brit. Archaeol. Ass., N.S. 4, pp. 282–89, 364–74. 1898.

5441 —— The mound dwellings of Auchingaich [Dunbartonshire]. J. Brit. Archaeol. Ass., N.S. 6, pp. 363–57 + plate. 1900.

5442 Dunbar (J. G.) *and* **Hay** (G. D.). Excavations at Lous, Stobo, 1959–60. Proc. Soc. Ant. Scotland, 94, 1960–61, 196–210 + 6 figures + 2 plates.

5443 Edgar (William). A Tardenoisian site at Ballantrae, Ayrshire. [Figure (artifacts).] Trans. Glasgow Archaeol. Soc., N.S. 9, pp. 184–88. 1939.

5444 Evans (Emyr Estyn). Notes on excavations in Northern Ireland in 1935. Proc. prehist. Soc., N.S. 1, 1935, 140–42.

5445 —— A late Neolithic site in county Antrim. H.M.S.O. pp. viii, 71 + 8 plates. 8°. Belfast, 1953. [26 figures.]

5446 Farrer (James). Note of excavations in Sanday, one of the north isles of Orkney. [2 figures.] Proc. Soc. Antiq. Scot., 7, pp. 398–401. 1870.

5447 Feachem (Richard William). Glenachan Rig homestead, Cardon, Peebleshire [suggested LBA]. Proc. Soc. Antiq. Scotland, 92, 1958–59, 15–24 + 7 figures + 1 plate.

5448 —— The palisaded settlements at Harehope, Peeblesshire. Excavations, 1960. [LBA/EIA settlement.] Proc. Soc. Ant. Scotland, 93, 1959–60, 174–91 + 10 figures.

5449 Grieve (Symington). Griddle or Greidel Ine or Een, otherwise known as Griadae Fhinn, Kilchoan, Ardnamurchan. Trans. Edinb. F.N. & Micr. Soc., 1900–11, pp. 1–16 + 4 plates + plan. 1911.

5450 Grigor (John). Notice of the remains of two ancient lake dwellings or crannoges, in the loch of the Clans . . . Nairnshire. (Further explorations, etc.) Proc. Soc. Antiq. Scot., 5, pp. 116–19 +plan, pp. 332–35 +plate. 1865.

5451 Hamilton (John R. C.). Iron Age settlement in the Shetlands. Recent excavations at Jarlshof. Arch. News Letter, 4, pp. 159–60. 1952.

5452 —— An Iron Age settlement in the Shetlands. [6 figures.] Archaeology, 6, pp. 104–07. 1953.

5453 —— Jarlshof, Shetland. Ministry of Works. pp. 37 + 8 plates + plan. 8°. Edinburgh, 1953.

5454 Harkness (Robert). On a crannoge found in Drunkeery lough, near Bailieborough, Co. Cavan, Ireland. [2 plans.] Archaeologia, 39, pp. 483–90. 1863.

5455 Hunt (Arthur R.). The Borness Cave, Kirkcudbrightshire. Advm. Sci., 1883, 561.

5456 Jackson (John Wilfrid). Excavations at Ballintory caves, Co. Antrim. [Further excavations.] (Third report.) Irish Naturalists J., 5, pp. 104–41 + 4 plates; 6, pp. 31–42, 1934, 1936.

5457 Jervise (Andrew). An account of the excavation of the round or beehive shaped house, and other underground chambers, at West Grange of Conan, Forfarshire. Proc. Soc. Antiq. Scot., 4, pp. 492–99 + plate. 1863.

5458 Leask (H. G.). Notes on excavations in the Irish Free State in 1935. Proc. prehist. Soc., N.S. 1, 1935, 138–39.

5459 Lethbridge (Thomas Charles). A settlement site of the Beaker period at Sana Bay, Ardnamurcham, Argyll. [2 figures.] Man, 27, pp. 173–74. 1927.

5460 —— Excavations at Kilpheder, South Uist, and the problem of Brochs and wheelhouses. Proc. prehist. Soc., 18, 1952, 176–93 + 9 figures + 1 plate.

5461 Livens (Robin G.). Excavations at Terally (Wigtownshire), 1956. [Early Iron Age. Cists, etc.] [General—sites of various periods.] Trans. Dumfries. Ant. Soc., 3rd S. 35 (1956–57), pp. 85–102 + plate + 8 maps + 2 plans. 1958.

5462 Mackie (Evan W.). A dwelling site of the earlier Iron Age at Balevullin, Tiree, excavated in 1912 by A. Henderson Bishop. Proc. Soc. Ant. Scotland 96, 1962–63, 155–83 + 5 figures + 3 plates.

5463 Maclaren (A.). Excavations at Keir Hill, Gargunnock. Proc. Soc. Antiq. Scotland, 91, 1960, 78–83 + 3 figures.

5464 MacRitchie (David). An Aberdeenshire mound-dwelling. [4 figures + plan. Cromar.] Antiquary, 33, pp. 135–39. 1897.

5465 ——Two Midlothian souterrains. [3 figures + 2 plans. Middleton and Crichton.] [Not prehist. as Roman Stones incorporated.] Reliquary, N. [3rd] S. 5, pp. 174–78. 1899.

5466 —— Notice of a Hebridean earth-house. [2 figures + plan. Arinabost, Coll.] Antiquary, 43, pp. 414–16. 1907.

5467 Mann (Ludovic Maclellan). Prehistoric pile structures [at Stoneykirk, Wigtownshire] in south-west Scotland.

Antiquary, 41, pp. 287–93, 333–40. 1905.

5468 Mann (Ludovic Maclellan). A Galloway stone-age village [in Stoneykirk parish, Wigtownshire]. Trans. Dumfries. Ant. Soc., 20 (1907–08), pp. 74–95. 1909.

5469 Mapleton (R. J.). Notice of an artificial island in Loch Kielziebar [Argyleshire]. Proc. Soc. Antiq. Scot., 7, pp. 322–24. 1870.

5470 Monteith (James). The crannog at Lochend, Coatbridge, Lanarkshire, with a report on the osseous remains by John R. Robb. [12 figures + plan.] Trans. Glasgow Archaeol. Soc., N.S. 9, pp. 26–43. 1937.

5471 Munro (Robert). A crannog in Lochan Dughaill, near Tarbert, Argyllshire, showing indications of a circular wooden house. [4 figures.] Proc. Soc. Antiq., 2 S. 16, pp. 179–82. 1896.

5472 —— A cave at Oban, containing human remains and a prehistoric refuse heap. [9 figures.] [Mesolithic.] Proc. Soc. Antiq., 2 S. 16, pp. 182–93. 1896.

5473 —— The Dumbuck "crannog" [Dunbartonshire]. [?Early Iron Age.] Proc. Soc. Antiq., 2 S. 18, pp. 379–86. 1901.

5474 Neely (G. J. H.). Excavations at Ronaldsway, Isle of Man. [4 figures + map.] Antiq. J., 20, pp. 72–86 + 6 plates + map. 1940.

5475 Newall (Frank). Early open settlement in Renfrewshire [BA to post Roman]. Proc. Soc. Ant. Scotland, 95, 1961–62, 159–70 + 7 figures.

5476 Peach (B. N.) *and* **Horne** (J.). Notes on a shell mound at Tongue Ferry, Sutherland [dolorite "celt" & coarse pot sherd]. Trans. Edinburgh Geol. Soc., 6, 1890/93, 303–08.

5477 Petrie (George). Notice of ruins of ancient dwellings at Skara, bay of Skaill, in the parish of Sandwick, Orkney, recently excavated. Proc. Soc. Antiq. Scot., 7, pp. 201–19 + 3 plates + plan. 1870.

5478 Proudfoot (V. B.). Excavations at the Cathedral Hill, Downpatrick. Arch. News Letter, 5, pp. 87–88. 1954.

5479 Ritchie (P. R.). An earthhouse at South Unigarth, Sandwick, Orkney. [Orcadian earth houses group; excavated into soft rock.] Proc. Soc. Ant. Scotland, 92, 1958–59, 118–19 + 1 figure + 1 plate.

5480 Rivet (A. L. F.). Tor Wood Broch (NS 833849). [Note for Summer Meeting, 1964 with whole page plan.] Arch. J., 121, 1964, 194–95.

5481 Robertson (A. D.). Druidical altar, Craigmaddie, parish of Baldernock, Stirlingshire. [Figure.] Trans. Glasgow Archaeol. Soc., 2, pp. 4–10. 1883.

5482 Smith (Reginald Allender). The Skara Brae village in Orkney. [Tools, beads, etc.] B.M.Q., 7, pp. 127–28 + plate. 1933.

5483 Smith (W. S.). The Souterrain at Tiogracey. Ulster J. Arch., 3, 1896, 58.

5484 —— The souterrain at Holywell, near Antrim. Ulster J. Arch., 3, 1897, 137–39 + 1 figure.

5485 Somerville (Boyle). A newly discovered souterrain near Ballineen, county Cork, Irish Free State. Antiq. J., 10, pp. 244–50 + plan. 1930.

5486 Stuart (John). An account of some subterraneous habitations [in the parishes of Auchindoir and Kildrummy] in Aberdeenshire. Archaeol. Scot., 2, pp. 53–58. 1822.

5487 Thomas (F. W. L.). Notice of a beehive house in the island of St. Kilda. [Plan.] Proc. Soc. Antiq. Scot., 3, pp. 225–32. 1862.

5488 Webb (Robert). Glanworth [Co. Cork] and its "sweat house". [Neol. and IA]. J. Antiq. Ass. Brit. Isles, 3, 1932, pp. 82–88 + 1 figure + 1 plate.

5489 Young (Alison) *and* **Richardson** (K. M.). A Cheardach Mhor, Drimere, South Uist [2nd cent. A.D. wheelhouse and later occupations]. Proc. Soc. Ant. Scotland, 93, 1959–60, 135–73 + 15 figures + 6 plates.

D. MATERIAL FINDS

1. STONE OBJECTS IN GENERAL

5490 Abbott (W. J. Lewis). The eolithic problem. Man, 9, pp. 148–52. 1909.

5491 —— The pygmy implements. Man, 9, pp. 178–81. 1909.

5492 —— On the classification of the British stone age industries, and some new and little known, well-marked horizons and cultures. J. R. Anthrop. Inst., 41, pp. 458–81 + 19 plates (flints). 1911.

5493 Allchin (Bridget). The stone-tipped arrow (with 16 pp., plates, 43 line drawings and 4 maps). Records many aspects of Stone Age cultures of great value in the interpretation of the long period during which man lived solely by hunting and food-gathering. September, 1966.

5494 Barnes (Alfred S.). Note on the paper by Mr. F. N. Haward on "The origin of the rostro-carinate industry". Proc. prehist. Soc. EA, 3 ii, 1919/20, 259–60.

5495 Barnes (S.) *and* **Moir** (James Reid). A criticism of Mr. S. Hazzledine Warren's views on eoliths [in Q.J.G.S., 76, pp. 238–53, 1921]. [*See also* pp. 82–83 (S. H. Warren's reply).] Man, 23, pp. 51–55, 119–21. 1923.

5496 —— Modes of prehension of some forms of Upper Palaeolithic implements. Proc. PSEA, 7 i, 1932–34, 43–56 + 13 figures.

5497 Barnwell (Edward Lowry). Querns. [Especially Welsh.] Arch. Camb., 4th S. 12, pp. 30–43 + 4 plates. 1881.

5498 Bell (A. Montgomerie). Flint sickles. Antiquary, 45, pp. 430–31. 1909.

5500 Brotherton (Bertram). A remarkable quartzite implement [Rostro-carinate!] Proc. PSEA, 6 iv, 1931, 304–55 + 1 figure + 2 plates.

5501 Buckman (James). On worked flints. Proc. Dorset Antiq. F.C., 2, pp. 97–103 + 2 plates. 1878.

5502 Burchell (James Percy Tufnell). The origin and evolution of the Epi-palaeolithic axe: an hypothesis. Man, 26, pp. 50–52. 1926.

5503 Burkitt (Miles C.). Classification of burins and gravers. [Upper Palaeolithic.] Proc. prehist. Soc. EA, 3 ii, 1919/20, 306–10 + 2 figures.

5504 Clark (John Grahame Douglas). Discoidal polished flint knives—their typology and distribution. [Beaker associations.] Proc. PSEA, 6 i, 1928–29, 41–54 + 7 figures.

5505 —— The date of the plano-convex flint-knife in England and Wales. [Early Bronze Age.] Antiq. J., 12, pp. 158–62 + plate. 1932.

5506 —— Note on some flint daggers of Scandinavian type from the British Isles. [6 figures. Neolithic.] Man, 32, pp. 186–90. 1932.

5507 —— The curved flint sickle blades of Britain. Proc. PSEA, 7 i, 1932–34, 67–81 + 7 figures + 2 plates.

5508 —— Derivative forms of the *Petit tranchet* [transverse arrowhead] in Britain. [12 figures.] Archaeol. J., 91 (1934), pp. 32–58. 1935.

5509 Clift (J. G. Neilson). A study in eoliths. J. Brit. Archaeol. Ass., N.S. 15, pp. 129–48 + 2 plates. 1909.

5510 Curwen (Eliot). Blunted axe-like implements. [Neolithic axes with blunted edges.] Proc. prehist. Soc., 5, 1939, 196–201 + 14 figures.

5511 Curwen (Eliot Cecil). Querns. [42 figures. Neolithic, etc. i. Non-rotating hand-mills; ii. Rotating hand-mills. Figures 4–13, Pre-Roman rotary querns from Wessex.] Antiquity, 11, pp. 133–51 + 4 plates. 1937.

5512 —— More about querns. [29 figures.] Antiquity, 15, pp. 15–32 + 4 plates. 1941.

5513 Dewey (Henry). Some flat-based celts from Kent and Dorset. [?Neolithic.] Proc. prehist. Soc. EA, 3 ii, 1919/20, 267–76 + 1 figure.

5514(a) Evans (*Sir* John). Account of some further discoveries of flint implements in the Drift on the continent and in England. Archaeologia, 39, pp. 57–84 + 4 plates. 1863.

5514(b) Evans (*Sir* John) *KCB.* Ancient stone implements, weapons, and ornaments of Great Britain. 8º. London, 1872.

5515 Evans (*Sir* John) *KCB*. The ancient stone implements, weapons and ornaments of Great Britain. Second edition, revised. pp. xviii, 747 + 2 plates. 8º. London, 1897. [477 figures.]

5516 —— Some recent discoveries of Palaeolithic implements. [Acheulian.] Q. J. Geol. Soc. London, 64, 1908, 1–7 + 2 plates.

5517 Fell (Clare Isobel). The Cumbrian type of polished stone axe and its distribution in Britain. Proc. prehist. Soc., 30, 1964, 39–55 + 3 figures. [Neolithic.]

5518 Flower (J. W.). On the relative ages of the stone implement periods in England. J. Anth. Inst., 1, pp. 274–95 + 4 plates. 1872.

5519 Gardner (G. B.). Letter on "elf-bolts". Folklore, 73, 1962, 282–83.

5520 Garrod (Dorothy Annie Elizabeth). Solutrean implements in England. [4 figures.] Man, 25, pp. 84–85. 1925.

5521 Gatty (Reginald A.). Pigmy flint implements. [4 figures.] Reliquary, 3rd S. 6, pp. 15–24. 1900.

5522 Grimes (William Francis). The Early Bronze Age flint dagger in England and Wales. Proc. PSEA, 6 iv, 1931, 340–55 + 3 figures.

5523 Halls (H. H.). Flint harpoon barbs. Proc. PSEA, 1 iii, p. 306 + 1 plate. 1912/13. [*See* Relph, A. E., Antiquary, Sept. 1907.]

5524 —— An animistic implement of "cissbury type". [?Microlith core.] Proc. PSEA, 3 iii, pp. 461–62 + 1 figure. 1920/21.

5525 Haward (F. N.). The problem of the eoliths. Proc. PSEA, 1 iii, pp. 347–59 + 11 plates + 8 figures. 1912/13.

5526 Hill (J. D.). Surface implements of a late Palaeolithic site. Proc. PSEA, 2 iv, 1917/18, 519–21 + 2 figures.

5527 Hughes (Thomas McKenny). On the [British] evidence bearing upon the early history of man which is derived from the form, condition of surface, and mode of occurrence of dressed flints. Archaeol. J., 54, pp. 363–76 + 4 plates. 1897.

5528 —— On sources of error in assigning objects found in sands and gravels to the age of those deposits, with special reference to the so-called eoliths. [Figure.] Archaeol. J., 69, pp. 205–14 + 3 plates. 1912.

5530(a) Jerman (H. Noel). Some further unrecorded finds from East Central Wales. Arch. Camb., 91 i, 1936, 118–28 + 7 figures.

5530(b) Jones (S. J.). Typology and distribution of perforated stone axes—studies in regional consciousness and environment. Not in BM cat. No reference, but quoted in Arch. Camb., 85 ii, 1930, 407.

5532 Kelley (Pat Harper). Acheulian flake tools. Proc. prehist. Soc., 3, 1937, 15–28 + 8 figures.

5533 Kendall (Henry George Ommanney). The case for eoliths restated. Man, 7, pp. 84–86. 1907.

5534 —— Pygmy flints. [Figure.] Man, 7, p. 133. 1907.

5535 —— Palaeolithic microliths. [7 figures.] Man, 8, pp. 103–04. 1908.

5536 —— Eoliths—their origin and age. Presidential address. PPSEA, 3 iii, 1920/21, 333–52 + 3 plates + 6 figures.

5537 Kendrick (*Sir* Thomas Downing). A note on English arrowheads. Man, 32, pp. 43–44. 1932.

5538 Knight (R. P.). Conjectures concerning the instruments called celts. Archaeologia, 17, pp. 220–23 + 2 plates. 1814.

5539 Knowles (*Sir* Francis H. S.). *bart.* Stoneworker's progress: a study of stone implements in the Pitt Rivers Museum. *Pitt Rivers Museum, Occasional Papers on Technology*, 6. pp. 120. 8º. Oxford, 1953. [24 figures.]

5540 Lacaille (Armand Donald). Lower Palaeolithic tools with retouched edges. [2 figures.] Antiq. J., 22, pp. 56–59. 1942.

5541 —— Palaeolithic implements manufactured in naturally holed flints, from Rossington, Yorks, and Dartford, Kent. [2 figures.] Antiq. J., 24, pp. 144–46. 1944.

5542 —— Some flint implements of special interest from Lincolnshire, Hampshire, and Middlesex. [7 figures.] [General—Palaeolithic—BA.] Antiq. J., 26, pp. 180–85. 1946.

5543 —— Massive Acheulian implements from Thames and Solent gravels. Man, 60, 1960, 103–04 + 3 figures.

5544 Lacaille (Armand Donald). Three grinding-stones, I: Overton Down, Wiltshire; II: Fort-Harrouard, Eure-et-Loire; III: Luss, Dunbartonshire. Ant. J., 43, 1963, 190–96 + 2 plates. [Wessex BA.]

5545 Lebour (Nona). White quartz pebbles and their archaeological significance. [?passport after purification by death.] Trans. Dumfries. Ant. Soc., 3 S. 2 (1923–14), pp. 121–34. 1914.

5546 Lomas (Joseph). On some flint implements found in the glacial deposits of Cheshire and North Wales. Trans. Hist. Soc. Lancs. & Ches., 50, pp. 111–22 + plate. 1900.

5547 Lort (Michael). Observations on celts. Archaeologia, 5, pp. 106–18 + 4 plates. 1779.

5548 Lukis (Frederick C.). The elf-shot and the elfin-dart of the north. Reliquary, 8, pp. 207–08 + plate. 1868.

5549 March (Henry Colley). Pigmy flint implements in barrows. [3 figures.] [Beaker burial.] Reliquary, 3rd S. 7, pp. 123–26. 1901.

5550 Moir (James Reid). The flint implements of sub-crag man. Proc. PSEA, 1 i, pp. 17–43 + 8 plates. 1908/10.

5551 —— On the evolution of the earliest palaeoliths from the Rostro-carinate implements. [21 figures. Suffolk material.] J. R. Anthrop. Inst., 46, pp. 197–20. 1916.

5552 —— The ancestry of the Mousterian palaeolithic flint implements. Proc. PSEA, 2 iv, 1917/18, 508–19 + 6 figures.

5553 —— The flaking and flake characteristics of a pre-Red Crag rostro-carinate flint implement. Proc. PSEA, 2 iv, 1917/18, 524–39 + 14 figures.

5554 —— A few notes on the sub-crag flint implements [?man-made]. Proc. PSEA, 3 i, pp. 158–61. 1918/19.

5555 —— The transition from Rostro-carinate flint implements to the tongue-shaped implements of river-terrace gravels. [16 figures.] Phil. Trans. Roy. Soc., B, 209, pp. 329–50 + 7 plates. 1920.

5556 —— A series of Rostro-carinate implements not hitherto described. [5 figures.] Man, 21, pp. 116–20. 1921.

5557 —— Solutrean flint implements in England. Man, 25, pp. 21–23. 1925.

5558 —— A double-ended Rostro-carinate flint implement. Proc. PSEA, 6 ii, 1929, 76–78 + 2 plates + 1 figure.

5559 —— Rostro-carinates and hand-axes. [2 figures.] Antiq. J., 10, pp. 46–48. 1930.

5560 —— and **Burchell** (James Percy Tufnell). Flint implements of Upper Palaeolithic facies from beneath the uppermost boulder clay of Norfolk and Yorkshire. [5 figures.] Antiq. J., 10, pp. 359–83 + 4 plates. 1930.

5561 —— A primitive transitional hand-axe from beneath the Red Crag. [3 figures.] Man, 32, pp. 61–63. 1932.

5562 —— Two St. Acheul blades. [2 figures. From Swanscombe, Kent and from Corfe Mullen, Dorset.] Antiq. J., 15, pp. 74–76. 1935.

5563 —— and **Burchell** (James Percy Tufnell). Diminutive flint implements of Pliocene and Pleistocene Age. [27 figures.] Antiq. J., 15, pp. 119–33. 1935.

5564 —— Rostro-carinates and rostrate hand-axes. [2 figures.] Antiq. J., 19, pp. 282–84. 1939.

5565 Munro (Robert). Notes on flint saws and sickles. [14 figures.] Ill. Arch., 1, pp. 176–93. 1893.

5566 Passmore (A. D.). Hammer-stones. Proc. PSEA, 3 iii, pp. 444–47. 1920/21.

5567 Paterson (T. T.). Core, culture and complex in the Old Stone Age. Proc. prehist. Soc., XI, 1945, 1–19 + 6 figures.

5568 Petch (D. F.). Polished stone and flint axes. Rpts. & Papers, Lincs. A. & A.S., 8, 1959, 4–5.

5569 —— Polished stone and flint axes. Rpts. & Papers, Lincs. A. & A.S., 9, 1961, 4.

5570 —— Querns of the prehistoric and Roman periods [saddle & bee-hive IA]. Rpts. & Papers, Lincs. A. & A.S., 9, 1962, 94.

5571 Phillips (C. W.). Pebbles from early ploughs in England. [EIA or Viking?] Proc. prehist. Soc., 4, 1938, 338–39 + 1 figure.

5572 Powell (D. F. W. Baden). Experimental Clactonian technique. Proc. prehist. Soc., 15, 1949, 38–41 + 4 figures.

5573 Prestwich (Joseph). Notes on some further discoveries of flint implements in bed of post-Pliocene gravel and clay; with a few suggestions for search elsewhere. J. Geol. Soc. London, 17, 1861, 362–68.

5574 Radley (Jeffrey). One ultimate form of the "petit tranchet" derivative arrowhead [mesolithic—Beaker]. Yorks. Arch. Journ. 41 (ii), 1964, 203–08 + 13 figures.

5575 Rankine (W. F.). Pebbles of non-local rock from Mesolithic chipping floors. Proc. prehist. Soc., 15, 1949, 193–94 + 1 figure.

5576 —— Artifacts of Portland chert in Southern England. Proc. prehist. Soc., 17, 1951, 93–94 + 1 figure.

5577 —— Quartzite pebble mace-heads with hour-glass perforation: their distribution in England. [Map.] Arch. News Letter, 4, pp. 53–55. 1951.

5578 —— Implements of coloured flint in Britain: their distribution and the derivation of raw materials. [Map.] Arch. News Letter, 4, pp. 145–49. 1952.

5579 —— A study of quartzite mace-heads. Functional interpretation and perforation technique. [2 figures + 3 tables.] Arch. News Letter, 4, pp. 186–88. 1953.

5580 —— Blade-segment implements from Mesolithic sites. [Figure.] Arch. News Letter, 5, pp. 86–87. 1954.

5581 —— Some Mesolithic gravers. [Figure.] Arch. News Letter, 5, pp. 201–04. 1955.

5582 —— Microliths. [Figure.] Arch. News Letter, 6, pp. 63–67. 1956.

5583 Roe (F. E. S.). The battle-axe series in Britain. Proc. prehist. Soc., 32, 1966, 199–245 + 8 figures + 2 maps.

5584 Sainty (J. E.). The problems of the Crag [Eoliths]. Proc. PSEA, 6 ii, 1929, 57–75 + 11 figures + 2 plates.

5585 Schwarz (Alfred). Some suggestions for organised research on flint implements. Proc. PSEA, 1 iv, pp. 449–54. 1913/14.

5586 Smith (Reginald A.). Surface implements of Palaeolithic type. Proc. PSEA, 1 iv, pp. 468–72 + 4 figures. 1913/14.

5587 —— Origin of the Neolithic celt. [27 figures.] Archaeologia, 67, pp. 27–48. 1916.

5588 —— On three rare flint implements from Northfleet (Kent), Le Moustier (Dordogne), and Ipswich (Suffolk).

[3 figures.] Proc. Soc. Antiq., 2 S. 30, pp. 160–66. 1918.

5589 —— The chronology of flint daggers. [11 figures.] Proc. Soc. Antiq., 2 S. 32, pp. 6–22. 1919.

5590 —— Hoards of Neolithic celts. [4 figures.] Archaeologia, 71, pp. 113–24 + 2 plates. 1921.

5591 —— Flint implements of special interest. [18 figures.] [Chellean—Neolithic.] Archaeologia, 72, pp. 25–40. 1922.

5592 —— The perforated axe-hammers of Britain. [48 figures. Bronze Age.] Archaeologia, 75, pp. 77–108. 1926.

5593 —— Flint arrow-heads in Britain. [38 figures.] Archaeologia, 76, pp. 81–106. 1927.

5594 Smith (W. Campbell). Jade axes from sites in the British Isles. Proc. prehist. Soc., 29, 1963, 133–72 + 3 figures + 2 tables + 5 plates.

5595 —— The distribution of jade axes in Europe with a supplement to the catalogue of those from the British Isles. Proc. prehist. Soc., 31, 1965, 25–33 + 1 figure. [Neol.—BA.]

5596 Smith (Worthington George). Nature-made eolithic implements. [3 figures.] Man, 7, pp. 99–100. 1907.

5597 —— Eoliths. [4 figures.] Man, 8, pp. 49–53 + plate. 1908.

5598 Sollas (William Johnson). A flaked flint from the Red Crag [?Aurignacian]. Proc. prehist. Soc. EA, 3 ii, 1919/20, 261–67 + 1 plate + 1 figure.

5599 Solly (E.). Palaeolithic man and his implements. Rep. Rugby School N.H. Soc., 29–36.

5600 Sturge (William Allen). The bearing of the Drayson theory on the problems presented by striated Neolithic flints. Proc. prehist. Soc. EA, 1 iii, 1912/13, 254–96 + 10 plates + 1 figure.

5601 Underwood (W.). Animistic forms in certain flints, showing human work. Proc. prehist. Soc. EA, 1 i, pp. 106–08. 1908–10.

5602(a) Vulliamy (Colwyn Edward). A note on proto-Neolithic flint implements from the Chiltern hills. [Figure.] Man, 27, pp. 131–34. 1927.

5602(b) —— The problem of the Pre-chellean industries. Man, 29, pp. 3–5. 1929.

5603 Wade (A. G.). The graver or

burin in England. [Figure. From Farnham, Surrey.] [Palaeolithic—Aurignacian.] Antiq. J., 5, pp. 283–84. 1925.

5604 Warhurst (Alan). Flint implements found near Maidstone [and now in its museum]. [Figure. From East Malling and Higham. Early to Middle Bronze Age.] Arch. Cant., 64 (1951), pp. 161–63. 1952.

5605 Warren (Samuel Hazzledine). On the original of eolithic flints by natural causes, especially by the foundering of drifts. J. Anthrop. Inst., 35, pp. 337–64 + plate. 1905.

5606 Whincupp (William). On the deposit of flint implements in France and England. J. Brit. Archaeol. Ass., 22, pp. 155–59. 1866.

5607 Whitwell (J. B.). Polished stone and flint axes. Rpts. & Papers, Lincs. A. & A.S., 10, 1963, 1–2.

5608 —— Polished stone and flint axes. Rpts. & Papers, Lincs. A. & A.S., 10, 1964, 57–58.

2. STONE OBJECTS BY ZONES

(a) Zone 1
[CBA Groups 7, 9, 10, 11A, 11B, 14]

5609 Abbott (W. J. Lewis). Implements from Cromer Forest Bed and the Admiralty section [?]. Proc. prehist. Soc. EA, 3 i, 1918/19, 110–14 + 1 figure.

5610(a) Alexander (E. M. M.). Stone celt from Pimlico. [Figure.] Antiq. J., 16, pp. 95–96. 1936.

5610(b) Allen (Edward Heron). Neolithic celt found at Selsey. Sussex Arch. Collns., 66, p. 232. 1925.

5611 [Anon.] Palaeolith from raised beach [in Slindon park] in Sussex. [Figure.] Antiq. J., 5, pp. 72–73. 1925.

5612 [Anon.] Palaeoliths from Beaconsfield [Bucks.]. [Figure.] Antiq. J., 7, pp. 314–15. 1927.

5613 [Anon.] A partly polished chert adze from Thakeham, Sussex. [Figure. Neolithic.] Antiq. J., 14, pp. 426–28. 1934.

5614 [Anon.] An implement from Warren hill [between Icklingham and Mildenhall, Suffolk]. [St. Acheul.] Antiq. J., 12, pp. 68–69 + plate. 1932.

3615 [Anon.] Flint dagger from Upchurch. [Kent.] Antiq. J., 14, pp. 298–99. 1934.

5616 [Anon.] A palaeolithic problem. [St. Acheul hand-axe from High Wycombe, Bucks.] Antiq. J., 18, p. 75 + plate. 1938.

5617 [Anon.] A remarkable [Palaeolithic] flint core [from the bank of the Stour near Canterbury]. [Figure.] Antiq. J., 19, p. 317. 1939.

5618 [Anon.] A flint dagger from Hornsey. [Beaker period.] Antiq. J., 19, p. 440 + plate. 1939.

5619 Arkell (William Joscelyn). Palaeoliths (More Palaeoliths) from the Wallingford fan-gravels. [6 figures + map.] Oxoniensia, 8/9, pp. 1–18; 11/12, pp. 173–75. 1944, 1947.

5620 —— Three Oxfordshire palaeoliths and their significance for pleistocene correlation. Proc. prehist. Soc., XI, 1945, 20–31 + 3 figures.

5621 —— A palaeolith from the Hanborough terrace [Oxon.]. [Figure.] Oxoniensia, 11/12, pp. 1–4. 1947.

5622 Armstrong (Albert Leslie). Notched dagger of flint [from Flixboro, near Scunthorpe, Lincs.]. [Figure. Early Bronze Age.] Antiq. J., 9, pp. 36–37. 1929.

5623 Asten (H. H. Godwin). On the discovery of some worked flints, cores, and flakes from Blackheath, near Chilworth and Bramley, Surrey. J. Anthrop. Inst., 13, pp. 137–43 + map. 1883.

5624 Babington (Charles Cardale). On a flint hammer, found near Burwell [Cambs.]. Antiq. Comm. (Camb. Antiq. Soc.), 2, pp. 201–02. 1862.

5625 Barley (M. W.). A flint dagger from Staythorpe, Notts., and other finds from the Newark area. Proc. prehist. Soc., 16, 1950, 184–86 + 3 figures.

5626 Barnes (Alfred S.). The dimensions of flint implements. [On the Clactonian Industry at Swanscombe.] Proc. PSEA, 6 ii, 1929, 117–30 + 7 tables.

5627 Batstone (R. F. S.). Mesolithic flints from Epsom downs and Ewell. [Figure.] Surrey Archaeol. Collns., 48, pp. 150–51. 1943.

5628 Bell (Alexander Montgomerie). Remarks on the flint implements from the chalk plateau of Kent. [Palaeolithic.] J. Anthrop. Inst., 23, pp. 266–84 + 3 plates (flints). 1894.

5629 Bell (Alexander Montgomerie). Implementiferous sections at Wolvercote (Oxfordshire) [dating dicey: Chellean—Magdalenian]. Q. J. Geol. Soc. London, 60, 1904, 120–32.

5630 Benton (Gerald Montagu). Stone axe-hammer from Tendring [Essex]. Trans. Essex Archaeol. Soc., N.S. 21, pp. 125–27. 1937.

5631 —— Peforated stone adze-like axe from Cressing. Trans. Essex Archaeol. Soc., N.S. 22, pp. 132–33. 1940.

5632 Bevan (J. T.). A Berkshire palaeolith (from Englefield). [Figure.] Antiq. J., 5, pp. 428–29. 1925.

5633 Biddle (Martin). Prehistoric and Roman finds from the Colne Valley, near Hemper Mills, Watford. [Hollow-base arrow-head; plano-convex point, *etc.*] Trans. St. Albans & Herts. archit. & archaeol. Soc., 1961, 77–89 + 4 figures.

5634 Birks (S. Graham Brade). A [Another] palaeolith from Sturry [Kent]. [2 figures.] Antiq. J., 9, pp. 244–46. 1929.

5635 Blackmore (H. P.). The Piltdown flints. Man, 23, pp. 98–99. 1923.

5636 Boswell (P. G. H.) *and* **Moir** (James Reid). The Pleistocene deposits and their contained Palaeolithic flint implements at Foxhall road, Ipswich. [24 figures.] J. R. Anthrop. Inst., 53, pp. 229–62. 1923.

5637 Bowes (Armstrong). Palaeoliths found in England. [From St. Stephen's, Canterbury: from Hoarth, Kent: from East Runton, Norfolk.] Antiq. J., 8, pp. 517–18 + 3 plates. 1928.

5638 Boyson (Ambrose P.) Flint arrow-head found at Seaford. Sussex Arch. Collns., 46, p. 236. 1903.

5639 Brachi (R. M.). Flint adze from Hambledon. [Mesolithic. Figure.] Surrey Archaeol. Collns., 49, p. 90. 1946.

5640 Brooks (I.). Pudding stones. Herefordshire Countryside, No. 72, 1964, 169.

5641 Burchell (James Percy Tufnell). A rare [Palaeolithic] flint from [Sturry] Kent. [Figure.] Antiq. J., 3, pp. 261–62. 1923.

5642 —— Palaeolithic implements from Kirmington, Lincolnshire, and

their relation to the 100-foot raised beach of Late Pleistocene times. [8 figures + map.] Antiq. J., 11, pp. 262–72. 1931.

5643 —— Two rostrate hand-axes from Swanscombe, Kent. [2 figures. Acheulian.] Antiq. J., 15, pp. 545–46. 1935.

5644 —— Hand-axes later than the Main Coambe-Rock of the lower Thames valley. [5 figures.] [Palaeolithic.] [Acheul and Levallois.] Antiq. J., 16, pp. 260–64. 1936.

5645 —— *and* **Moir** (James Reid). Eoliths of a late prehistoric date. [6 figures. Stone Court valley and Ebbsfleet valley, Kent.] Antiq. J., 19, pp. 185–92. 1939.

5646 Burkitt (Miles Crawford). Notes on the implements (from Cambridgeshire gravels). J. Geol. Soc. London, 75, 1919, 241–44 + 1 plate.

5647 —— Six interesting flint implements now in Cambridge. [Figures. i–iii, from Cambridge; iv–v, from Heacham, Norfolk; iv, from Altarnum, Cornwall. J. Antiq. J., 11, pp. 55–57. 1931.

5648 —— Eoliths: a test specimen [from Bolton's pit, Ipswich]. [2 figures.] Man, 32, pp. 190–91. 1932.

5649 —— A Levallois flake in Babraham park, Cambs. [Figure.] Antiq. J., 25, p. 147. 1945.

5650 Burstow (George Philip). Palaeolithic implements from Newhaven. Sussex N. & Q., 13, p. 41. 1950.

5651 Burton (C. E. C. H.). Mesolithic and Bronze Age flints at Westham, Pevensey. Sussex N. & Q., 8, pp. 43–44. 1940.

5652 Bury (Henry). Some "flat-faced" palaeoliths from Farnham. Proc. PSEA, 2 iii, 1916/17, 365–74 + 4 figures.

5653 Butler (L. A. S.). Church Close, Langton-by-Spilsby, a deserted medieval village. Rpts. & Papers, Lincs. A. & A.S., 9, 1962, 125–33 + 3 figures.

5654 Calkin (John Bernard). Pygmy and other flint implements found at Peacehaven. [5 figures + plan.] Sussex Arch. Collns., 65, pp. 224–41. 1924.

5655 —— Implements from the higher raised beaches of Sussex. Proc. PSEA, 7 iii, 1934, 333–47 + 26 figures.

5656 Carpenter (L. W.). A palaeolithic hand-axe from Banstead heath, Walton-on-the-Hill. [Figure.] Surrey Archaeol. Collns., 54, pp. 136–37. 1955.

5657 —— Tranchet axes from Walton Heath and Walton-on-the-Hill. [Mesolithic.] Surrey Arch. Collections, 58, 1961, 108 + 1 figure.

5658 —— Tranchet axe from Lower Kingswood. [Mesolithic.] Surrey Arch. Collections, 58, 1961, 109 + 1 figure.

5659 —— Flint arrowheads from Surrey—some recent finds. Surrey Arch. Collections, 58, 1961, 109–11 + 1 figure.

5660 Case (Humphrey). Mesolithic finds in the Oxford area. [5 figures + 2 maps.] Oxoniensia, 17/18 (1952/53), pp. 1–13. 1954.

5661 —— The flint implements from the Summerstown—Radley Terrace. [Acheulian.] Q. J. Geol. Soc. London, 111, 1955/56, 236–37 + 1 figure.

5662 Chandler (R. H.). Implements of Les Eyzies-type and a working floor in the river Cray valley. [Upper Aurignacian—La Madelaine.] Proc. PSEA, 2 i, 1914/15, 80–98 + 7 figures.

5663 —— The implements and cores of Crayford. [Mousterian]. Proc. PSEA, 2 ii, 1915/16, 240–48 + 8 figures.

5664(a) Cheal (Henry). A Shoreham Palaeolith. [Figure.] Sussex Arch. Collns., 64, pp. 187, 189. 1923.

5664(b) Chitty (Lily Frances). Axe-hammer from [Haslington,] Cheshire. [Figure. Bronze Age.] Antiq. J., 7, pp. 522–23. 1927.

5665 Chown (Eileen). Flint arrowhead at Sedlescombe. [Mesolithic.] Sussex N. & Q., 13, p. 321. 1953.

5666 Clark (John Grahame Douglas). Some hollow-scrapers from Seaford. [Figure.] Sussex Arch. Collns., 68, pp. 273–76. 1927.

5667 —— Rubbing-stones of flint. [Figure. Neolithic. From Bishopstone, Peacehaven and Westdean.] Sussex Arch. Collns., 70, pp. 200–02. 1929.

5668 —— A new pigmy site [at Seaford] in Sussex. [Figure.] Man, 30, pp. 2–3. 1930.

5669 —— and **Binnall** (R.). Note on two flints from Hastings. [Figure. Upper Palaeolithic.] Man, 31, p. 250. 1931.

5670 —— Two flint daggers from the Fens. [Figure. From Bottisham Lock and near Windy hall, Isleham fen. Usually associated with class A of Beaker pottery.] Antiq. J., 13, pp. 52–53. 1933.

5671 —— Some unrecorded finds of microliths from England (?Horsham). Proc. PSEA, 7 iii, 1934, 421–23 + 1 figure.

5672 Clark (J. P. H.). Flint-work at Wiston. Sussex N. & Q., 14, pp. 226–27. 1957.

5673 —— Uncommon types of flint implements [from Sussex sites]. Sussex N. & Q., 15, pp. 22–23. 1958.

5674 Clarke (W. G.). Implements of sub-crag man in Norfolk. Proc. PSEA, 1 ii, pp. 160–68 + 3 plates. 1910/12.

5675 —— Some Barnham palaeoliths. Proc. PSEA, 1 iii, pp. 300–03 + 2 plates. 1912/13.

5676 ——Norfolk implements of Palaeolithic "cave" types. Proc. PSEA, 1 iii, pp. 338–45 + 6 plates. 1912/13.

5677 —— The Norfolk sub-crag implements. Proc. PSEA, 2 ii, 1915/16, 213–22 + 5 figures.

5678 Clinch (George). On some wrought flints found at West Wickham in Kent. [5 figures.] Arch. Cant., 14, pp. 85–90. 1882.

5679 —— Neolithic implements found at Rowes farm, West Wickham, Kent. [8 figures.] Antiquary, 15, pp. 233–38. 1887.

5680 —— Palaeolithic implements [from Minster in] the Isle of Thanet. [Figure.] Reliquary, 3rd S. 7, pp. 57–58. 1901.

5681 Cockrill (H. W.). Implements in a sand-stratum at Lyng. Proc. PSEA, 1 ii, pp. 169–70 + 1 plate. 1910/12.

5682 Coghlan (Hubert Henry). Stone hammers in the Newbury Museum. [7 figures.] Trans. Newbury F.C., 8, pp. 280–89. 1946.

5683 Coleridge (A. H. B.). Bronze Age arrowhead at Leatherhead. [Figure.] Surrey Archaeol. Collns., 42, pp. 109–10. 1934.

5684 Collar (Hubert). Neolithic axe from Elsenham. [Figure.] Trans. Essex Archaeol. Soc., N.S. 24, p. 149. 1951.

5685 Collins (A. E. P.). A flint flake from Aston Tirrold [Berks.]. [Early

Bronze Age. Now in Reading Museum.] Berks. Archaeol. J., 50, p. 101 + plate. 1947.

5686 Compton (C. H.). Palaeolithic implements from Hanwell. J. Brit. Archaeol. Ass., N.S. 13, pp. 123–24 + plate. 1907.

5687 Cook (Norman) *and* **Owen** (W. E.). A flint implement of rostro-carinate type from Brasted. [Figure. Post-glacial, but undatable.] Arch. Cant., 45, pp. 278–80. 1933.

5688 Copsey (H. W.). Surface flint from Sonning. [Appendix to paper by Slade, C. F.] Berks. Arch. J., 61, 1963/4, 19.

5689 Corder (Henry). Stone implements from the neighbourhood of Chelmsford, Essex. [Neolithic spear-head/dagger.] Trans. Epping Forest & County of Essex F.C., 2, pp. 29–30 + 1 figure. 1882.

5690 Cornwall (Ian W.). Humanly-struck flakes from gravels in Hertford-shire. [Figure.] Univ. London, Inst. Archaeol., Ann. Rpt., 4 (1946–7), pp. 39–45. 1948.

5691 —— The Clacton flint industry; a new interpretation. Arch. News Letter, 3, pp. 31–32. 1950.

5692 Cowther (Anthony William George). Three stone axes from Ash-tead. [Figure. ?Neolithic.] Surrey Archaeol. Collns., 51, pp. 141–42. 1950.

5693 Cox (J.). Implements from the glacial deposits of North Norfolk. [Mousterian, rostro-carinate.] Proc. PSEA, 3 ii, pp. 200–05 + 4 figures. 1919/20.

5694 Cragg (William A.). Stone axe or hammer [from Threckingham]. [Early Bronze Age.] Lincs. N. & Q., 23, pp. 57–58 + plate. 1934.

5695 —— Axe-head from [Threcking-ham,] Lincolnshire. [Figure.] Antiq. J., 15, p. 59. 1935.

5696 Cra'ster (Mary D.). Archaeo-logical notes: Neolithic axes. Proc. Camb. Ant. Soc., LVII, 1965, 141 & 143.

5697 Crawshay (de Barri). Eoliths found "in situ" at South Ash, Kent. Proc. PSEA, 4 ii, pp. 155–62 + 3 plates + 3 figures. 1923/24.

5698 Curwen (Eliot). Notes on some uncommon types of stone implements found in Sussex. [2 figures. Neolithic—

Bronze Age.] Sussex Arch. Collns., 69, pp. 76–91. 1928.

5699 —— A Sussex [holed] stone im-plement [from Wolstonbury]. [Figure. Late Bronze or Early Iron Age. Of foreign stone. ?use.] Sussex N. & Q., 2, pp. 165–67. 1929.

5700 —— Hoard of [flint] celts from [Clayton hill near Hurstpierpoint,] Sussex. Antiq. J., 9, pp. 42–43 + plate, 152. 1929.

5701 —— Two stone implements from Deans, Piddinghoe. [Figure. Early Bronze Age.] Sussex Arch. Collns., 71, pp. 252–54. 1930.

5702 —— Some noteworthy flints from Sussex. [Figure.] Sussex Arch. Collns., 73, pp. 197–200. 1932.

5703 —— *and* **Curwen** (Eliot Cecil). A flint sickle-flake from Selmeston, Sussex. [2 figures.] Antiq. J., 14, pp. 389–92. 1934.

5704 —— Non-crescentic sickle-flints from Sussex. [3 figures from Salvington, Lancing and Plumpton Plain.] Antiq. J., 16, pp. 85–90 + plate. 1936.

5705 —— On Sussex flint arrow-heads. [2 figures. General distribution, types and their distribution, chronology.] Sussex Arch. Collns., 77, pp. 15–25. 1936.

5706 —— Flint daggers of the Early Bronze Age from [Stoke down, north of Chichester,] Sussex. [Figure.] Sussex N. & Q., 8, pp. 69–70. 1940.

5707 —— A mace-head from Washing-ton. [Figure. Bronze Age.] Sussex N. & Q., 9, pp. 133–34. 1943.

5708 —— A perforated stone hoe from Ringmer. [Figure. Early Bronze Age.] Sussex N. & Q., 10, pp. 76–78. 1944.

5709 —— A flint dagger factory near Pulborough, Sussex. [Figure. Early Bronze Age.] Antiq. J., 29, pp. 192–93. 1949.

5710 Curwen (Eliot Cecil). A sickle-flint from [Beckley] near Rye, Sussex. [2 figures.] Antiq. J., 18, pp. 278–79. 1938.

5711 —— Axes of igneous rock found [at Dallington] in Sussex. [Fig-ure. Earliest Neolithic.] Sussex N. & Q., 8, pp. 67–69. 1940.

5712 —— Burnishing stones for pottery. [2 polished triangular pebbles found with Iron Age pottery near Horsted Keynes, Sussex.] Antiquity, 15, pp. 200–01 + 2 plates. 1941.

5713 Curwen (Eliot Cecil). A flint sickle from Beddingham hill. [Figure. Neolithic B.] Sussex N. & Q., 8, p. 189. 1941.

5714 —— Plano-convex knife with corn-gloss. [Figure. From Tonge Hill, near Sittingbourne, Kent.] Antiq. J., 24, pp. 64–65. 1944.

5715 —— A hand-axe from the Chichester gravels. Proc. prehist. Soc., 12, 1946, 172–73 + 1 figure.

5716 —— A palaeolithic from the Chichester gravels. [Figure.] Sussex N. & Q., 11, pp. 99–101. 1947.

5717 —— A sickle-flint from Seaford, Sussex. [2 figures.] Antiq. J., 29, pp. 193–95. 1949.

5718 —— Two sickle-flints from Seaford. [Figure.] Sussex N. & Q., 13, pp. 196–97. 1952.

5719 —— Iver. [1st cent. quern in Lewis Museum.] (1 plate.) Record of Bucks., 17(3), 1963, 209.

5720 Darbishire (R. D.). On the implements from the chalk plateau in Kent, their character and importance. Mems. Manch. Lit. & Phil. Soc., 46, pp. 1–18 + 6 plates. 1901.

5721(a) Davey (F. W. G.). Palaeoliths (from Beeston) near Nottingham. [5 figures.] Antiq. J., 8, pp. 91–93. 1928.

5721(b) Davies (John Langdon). Pygmy gravers [burins, from between Leith hill and Coldharbour] in Surrey. [Figure.] Antiq. J., 6, pp. 82–83. 1926.

5722 Densham (H. B. A. Ratcliffe). Flint implements from Broadwater. [Neolithic or Early Bronze Age.] Sussex N. & Q., 11, pp. 113–14. 1947.

5723 —— Stone implements from Durrington [Worthing]. [Figure. Early Bronze Age mace head.] Sussex N. & Q., 12, pp. 87–89. 1948.

5724 Dewey (Harry). Implements from the clay-with-flints of North Kent. [2 figures.] Antiq. J., 4, pp. 147–49. 1924.

5725 —— On Chellean implements from the gravel of Hyde Park, London. S. Geol. Soc. London, 81, 1925, cxxvi–cxxvii.

5726 —— *and* **Smith** (Reginald Allender). Flints from the Sturry gravels,

Kent. [25 figures + map + 2 plans.] Archaeologia, 74, pp. 117–36. 1925.

5727 —— Palaeoliths in Hyde Park. [2 figures.] Antiq. J., 6, pp. 73–75. 1926.

5728 Dillon (Harold). On flint implements, &c., found in the neighbourhood of Ditchley, Oxon. J. Anth. Inst., 5, pp. 30–33. 1875.

5729 Dines (H. G.). The Flint industries of Bapchild [Mousterian Early Levallois] [one looks like a Thames pick to me!]. Proc. PSEA, 6 i, 1928–29, 12–26 + 8 figures + 2 plates.

5730 Dormer (Ernest W.). A palaeolithic implement from Woodley [Berks.]. Berks. Archaeol. J., 34, p. 66. 1930.

5731 Dudding (Reginald C.). Neolithic stone axe (found at Welton-le-Marsh]. Lincs. N. & Q., 18, p. 97 + plate. 1925.

5732 Dutt (William Alfred). Palaeolithic implements in east Suffolk. [2 figures.] Antiquary, 44, pp. 60–64. 1908.

5733 Edwardson (A. B.). Flint dagger of Beaker period [from Burnt Fen, Cambs.]. Proc. Camb. Antiq. Soc., 51 (1957), p. 82 + plate. 1958.

5734 —— Two neolithic axes from Suffolk. Proc. Suffolk Inst. Arch., 29 ii, 1962, 216 + 1 plate.

5735 Evans (*Sir* John). A neolithic celt found near Berkhamsted Common. Trans. Herts. N.H.S. & F.C., 12, 1904, pp. 157–58 + 1 figure.

5736 —— On a recent Palaeolithic discovery near Rickmansworth. Trans. Herts. N.H.S. & F.C., 13, 1906, 65–66 + 2 plates.

5737 —— Recent discoveries of palaeolithic implements in Hertfordshire and Bedfordshire. Trans. Herts. N.H. & F.C., 14, 1909/12, 1–4 + 1 plate + 1 figure.

5738 Evens (E. D.) *and* **Wallis** (F. S.). Polished axe from cop round barrow Bledlow. [Of greenstone: original provenance possibly St. Ives, Cornwall.] Records of Bucks., 13, pp. 440–41. 1939.

5739 Fancourt (St. John F. M.). The discovery of prehistoric implements at Danecroft, Stowmarket. [7 figures. Neolithic.] Proc. Suffolk Inst. Arch., 13, pp. 113–32. 1909.

5740 Fardell, *Canon*. Flint sickle from [Wreningham,] Norfolk. [Figure. Neolithic.] Antiq. J., 9, pp. 249–50. 1929.

5741 Flower (J. W.). On some flint implements lately found in the valley of the Little Ouse river, near Thetford. [Acheulean.] J. Geol. Soc. London, 23, 1867, 45–46 + 6 figures.

5742 —— On the distribution of flint implements in the drift, with reference to some recent discoveries in Norfolk and Suffolk. [Abstract.] J. Geol. Soc. London, 25, 1869, 272–73.

5743 —— On some recent discoveries of flint implements of the drift in Norfolk and Suffolk, with observations on the theories accounting for their distribution. [Acheulean.] J. Geol. Soc. London, 25, 1895, 449–60 + 1 plate.

5744 Fowler (J.). Palaeoliths found at Slindon. [Figure.] Sussex Arch. Collns., 70, pp. 197–200. 1929.

5745 —— Palaeolith from [Chithurst, near Midhurst,] West Sussex. [Figure.] Sussex N. & Q., 3, pp. 158–59. 1931.

5746 Fox (Cyril). Flint axe and "chisel" found at Newmarket Heath. [Neolithic.] Proc. PSEA, 5 i, 1925, 79 + 1 plate.

5747 Frere (John). Account of flint implements discovered at Hoxne in Suffolk. Archaeologia, 13, pp. 204–05 + 2 plates. 1797.

5748 Frere (Sheppard Sunderland). Three flint implements from Shimpling [near Diss]. [Figure. Neolithic.] Norfolk Archaeol., 27, pp. 29–30. 1939.

5749 —— Axe hammer from Loddon, Norfolk. [Figure. Early Bronze Age.] Antiq. J., 23, pp. 154–55. 1943.

5750 —— Polished [flint] axes from Guildford and Leith hill, and South Norwood. [2 figures.] Surrey Archaeol. Collns., 49, pp. 90–92. 1946.

5751 —— Polished axe from Bury hill, Dorking. [Figures.] Surrey Archaeol. Collns., 49, pp. 92–93. 1946.

5752 Froom (F. R.). An axe of Dorset chert from a mesolithic site at Kintbury. [1 figure.] Berks. Arch. J., 61, 1963/4, 1–3.

5753 Gardner (J. W.). A flint dagger from Canterbury. [Beaker "A" complex.] Arch. Cant., 62 (1949), pp. 142–43 + plate. 1950.

5754 Garrood (Jesse Robert). Neolithic mace-heads from [Kimbolton, Wood Walton and Holywell], Hunts. [Figure.] Antiq. J., 6, p. 188. 1926.

5756 —— Palaeoliths from the lower Ouse. [Figure. Hand-axe from Hartford, Hunts., etc.] Antiq. J., 13, pp. 313–15. 1933.

5757 —— Hand-axe from Holywell, St. Ives, Hunts. [Figure. Late St. Acheul or Le Moustier.] Antiq. J., 19, pp. 329–30. 1939.

5758 —— Stone chisels from Wood Walton, Huntingdonshire. Antiq. J., 21, pp. 346–47 + plate. 1941.

5759 —— A perforated hammer stone and axe hammer from [Eynesbury cemetery, Howitts Lane and from Sawtry Roughs,] Huntingdonshire. [Bronze Age.] Trans. Cambs. & Hunts. Arch. Soc., 6, pp. 191–92 + plate. 1947.

5760 Gatty (Reginald A.). Pigmy flint implements from the sand-beds at Scunthorpe in Lincolnshire. [3 figures.] Man, 2, pp. 18–22. 1902.

5761 Gower (Harry D.). Flints found at Waddon marsh. [Figure.] Proc. Croydon N.H. & Sci. Soc., 6, pp. 20–23 + plate. 1903.

5762 Griffith (A. F.). On a flint implement found at Barnwell, Cambs. Camb. Antiq. Comm., 4, pp. 177–80 + 2 plates. 1878.

5763 Grimes (William Francis). A stone axe from Iver, Buckinghamshire. [Figure.] Records of Bucks., 14, pp. 361–64. 1946.

5764 Grinsell (Leslie Valentine). A stone axe of Scandinavian type from Enfield. [Figure. Early Bronze Age.] Trans. London & Middx. Arch. Soc., N.S. 10, pp. 308–09. 1951.

5765 Grove (Leonard Robert Allen) *and* **Warhurst** (Alan). Southborough: polished flint axe. [Figure.] Arch. Cant., 68 (1954), pp. 211–13. 1955.

5766 Halls (H. H.). Implements from a station at Cranwich, Norfolk. Proc. prehist. Soc. EA, 1 iv, 1913/14, 454–457 + 7 plates.

5767 Hancox (R. H.). Some Suffolk arrow-heads. [3 figures. Neolithic.] Antiquary, 43, pp. 88–91. 1907.

5768 Harrison (*Sir* Edward). Palaeolith from the North Downs. [Figure. Ightham, Kent.] Antiq. J., 12, pp. 294–96. 1932.

5769 Harrison (E. E.). Polished flint axe from Godalming. Surrey Arch. Collections, 59, 1962, 86 + 1 figure.

5770 Harrison (E.E.) Three flint implements from Surrey. [Late Neolithic/EBA.] Surrey Arch. Collections, 61, 1964, 99–100 + 1 figure.

5771 —— Polished flint axe from Horne. Surrey Arch. Collections, 62, 1965, 122 + 1 figure.

5772 Haward (F. N.). The origin of the "Rostro-carinate implements" and other chipped flints from the Basement Beds of East Anglia. Proc. prehist. Soc. EA, 3 i, 1918/19, 118–46 + 8 figures + 5 plates.

5773 Hayden (W.). On some prehistoric flint implements found on the South Downs near Chichester. [At Bourhill.] J. Brit. Archaeol. Ass., 50, pp. 131–38. 1894.

5774 Hearne (E. J. Frazer). Flint implements of probable metal-age date from Barnham. [4 figures.] Sussex N. & Q., 5, pp. 57–60. 1934.

5776 Herring (I. J.). Two prehistoric finds from Chingford. ["Thames pick" and Neolithic flint axe.] Essex Nat., 30, p. 112 + plate. 1958.

5777 Hewett (W. P.). A palaeolith from Dorking. [Figure.] Antiq. J., 15, p. 343. 1935.

5778 Hockings (E. F.). Arrowheads. [2 figures. i. Bronze Age from West Blatchington; ii. Beaker period from Balsdean, Rottingdean.] Sussex N. & Q., 13, pp. 112–13. 1951.

5779 Hodges (H. W. M.). A perforated stone axe-hammer from Cockhaise farm, Lindfield. [?Early Bronze Age.] Sussex N. & Q., 15, pp. 32–39 + plate. 1958.

5780 Hogg (Alexander). The flint implements of Addington. Proc. Croydon N.H. & Sci. Soc., 4, pp. 257–62. 1897.

5781 Hogg (Alexander Hubert Arthur). Flint implements from Shooters Hill. [Figure.] Woolwich Ant. Soc., Ann. Rpt., 23, pp. 43–44. 1926.

5782 Holden (E. W.). Flint artifacts from Arlington and Hailsham. Sussex Notes & Queries, 16, 7, 1966, 221–25 + 1 figure.

5783 —— Polished flint axe from Hellingly. Sussex Notes & Queries, 16 (9), 1967, 321.

5784 Holling (F.) *and* **Harrison** (E. E.). Three polished flint axes from West Surrey. Surrey Arch. Collections, 62, 1965, 122 + 1 figure.

5785 Hollis (Edwin). Stone adze from Wendover. [Early Bronze Age.] Records of Bucks., 13, pp. 227–28 + plate. 1936.

5786 Honywood (Thomas.) Discovery of flint implements near Horsham, in St. Leonard's forest. Sussex Arch. Collns., 27, pp. 177–83 + 2 plates. 1877.

5787 Hooper (Wilfrid). Neolithic implements from Redhill and Reigate. Surrey Archaeol. Collns., 37, p. 90 + plate. 1926.

5788 —— Pygmy flints from Reigate. [Figure.] Surrey Archaeol. Collns., 37, pp. 238–39. 1927.

5789 —— Pigmy burins in Surrey and Sussex. Proc. PSEA, 6 ii, 1929, 136–39 + 14 figures.

5790 —— The micro-burin [or beaked pigmy graver] on Sussex pigmy sites. [Figure.] Sussex Archaeol. Collns., 70, pp. 203–04. 1929.

5791 —— A palaeolith from [Woodhatch, Reigate,] Surrey. [Figure.] Antiq. J., 17, p. 318. 1937.

5792 —— Palaeolithic flint from Reigate. [Figure.] Surrey Archaeol. Collns., 45, pp. 140–41. 1937.

5793 Irwin (John). Edenbridge: Palaeolithic flint implements. Arch. Camb., 76, 1961, 204–05.

5794 Jamieson (A. W.). Some Sussex implements. [?Solutrean.] Proc. PSEA, 3 i, pp. 108–10 + 1 figure. 1918/19.

5795 Jeffery (R. W.). Slindon hand axe. [Late Acheulian.] Sussex N. & Q., 14, p. 242. 1957.

5796 Johnson (J. P.). Palaeolithic implements from the low-level drift of the Thames valley: chiefly from Ilford and Grays, Essex. [5 figures.] Essex Nat., 12, pp. 52–57. 1901.

5797 —— Neolithic implements from the North Downs near Sutton, Surrey. [Figure.] Essex Nat., 12, pp. 117–19. 1901.

5798 —— Eolithic implements from the plateau gravel around Walderslade, Kent. [7 figures.] Essex Nat., 12, pp. 207–17. 1902.

5799 Keef (P. A. M.). Flint arrowheads at Trotton. [Figure. Neolithic.]

Sussex N. & Q., 13, pp. 202–03. 1952.

5800 Kelly (David B.). Researches and discoveries in Kent: Ashford. Arch. Cant., 76, 1961, p. 191 + 1 figure.

5801 —— Researches and discoveries in Kent: Marden [Neolithic flint axe] Nettlestead [ditto partly polished]. Arch. Cant., 76, 1961, p. 200.

5802 —— Researches and discoveries in Kent: Ilcombe [Thames pick]. Arch. Cant., 76, 1961, p. 202.

5803 Kendall (H. G. O.). Middle Glacial and pre-crag implements in South Norfolk. Proc. PSEA, 2 i, pp. 31–35 + 2 plates. 1914/15.

5804 —— Chipped flints from below the Boulder Clay at Hertford. Proc. PSEA, 2 iii, 1916/17, 352–59.

5805 —— Arrowheads at Grimes Graves. Proc. PSEA, 5 i, 1925, 64–66 + 1 plate.

5806 Kennard (A. S.). Notes on a palaeolith from Grays, Essex. [Figure.] Essex Nat., 13, pp. 112–13 + plate. 1903.

5807 —— Note on a Neolithic arrowhead from Upton Park, Essex. [Figure.] Essex Nat., 13, p. 114. 1903.

5808 Kennedy (Robert A.). Recent finds of stone implements [acquired by Brighton Museum]. Sussex N. & Q., 15, pp. 130–31. 1959.

5809 Kensington (*Mrs.* L. M.). A flint from West Chiltington. [Figure.] Sussex Arch. Collns., 74, p. 242. 1933.

5810 King (C. Cooper). Discovery of a flint implement station in Wishmoor Bottom, near Sandhurst [Surrey]. J. Anth. Inst., 2, pp. 365–72 + plate + map. 1873.

5811 Lacaille (Armand Donald). Quartzites taillés de la région Londonienne. [5 figures + 2 maps.] Comptes rendu, 12. Congrés préhist. de France, pp. 609–29. 1936.

5812 —— A Levallois side-scraper from brickearth at Yiewsley, Middlesex. Antiq. J., 18, pp. 55–57 + plate. 1938.

5813 —— The Palaeolithic contents of the gravels at East Burnham, Bucks. (A summary of discoveries in the higher part of the Boyn Hill terrace.) [Map.] Antiq. J., 19, pp. 166–81 + 5 plates. 1939.

5814 —— The palaeoliths from the gravels of the lower Boyn Hill terrace around Maidenhead. [Map.] Antiq. J., 20, pp. 245–71 + 7 plates. 1940.

5815 —— Palaeoliths from brickearth in South-East Buckinghamshire. [5 figures + 2 plates.] Records of Bucks., 16 (4), 1959, 274–88.

5816 —— The Muswell Hill axe [early Neolithic]. Trans. London & Mddsx. A.S., 20 ii (1960), p. 81 + 1 plate.

5817 —— On Palaeolithic choppers and cleavers. [6 pull-out figures.] Records of Bucks., 16(5), 1960, 330–41.

5818 —— Remarkable stone implements from Piccadilly and Swanscombe, Kent. Ant. J., 40, 1960, 65–66.

5819 —— The Palaeoliths of Boyn Hill, Maidenhead. Ant. J., 41, 1961, pp. 154–85.

5821 Lankester (*Sir* Edwin Ray). On the discovery of a novel type of flint implements below the base of the Red Crag of Suffolk, proving the existence of skilled workers of flint in the Pliocene age. Phil. Trans. Roy. Soc., B202, pp. 283–336 + 4 plates. c. 1912

5822 —— Description of the first specimen of the Rostro-Carinate industry found beneath the Norwich Crag. *Royal Anthropological Institute, Occasional Papers*, 4. pp. 18 + 3 plates. 8°. London, 1914.

5823 —— A remarkable flint implement from Piltdown. [2 figures.] Man, 21, pp. 59–62. 1921.

5824 —— A remarkable flint implement from Selsey bill. Proc. Roy. Soc., B, 92, pp. 162–68 + 4 plates. 1921.

5825 Laver (Henry). Flint-implements at Walton-on-Naze and Lexden, Essex. Essex Nat., 2, pp. 187–88. 1888.

5826 Layard (Nina Frances). A recent discovery of Palaeolithic implements in Ipswich. (Further excavations on a Palaeolithic site in Ipswich.) [Figure.] J. Anthrop. Inst., 33, pp. 41–43 + 2 plates; pp. 306–10 + 2 plates. 1903.

5827 —— Finger grips: an interpretation of worked hollows found on many surface flints [found in Norfolk and Suffolk]. [2 figures.] Man, 17, pp. 89–90 + plate. 1917.

5828 —— Flint tools showing well-defined finger-grips. Proc. Suffolk Inst. Arch., 17, pp. 1–12 + 18 plates. 1921.

5829 Layard (Nina Frances). Solutrian blades from South-Eastern England. Proc. PSEA, 6 i, 1928–29, 55 + 1 plate.

5830 —— Neolithic hoard [of flint celts] from [Canewdon,] Essex. [Figure.] Antiq. J., 11, pp. 57–58. 1931.

5831 Leeds (Edward Thurlow). Four polished stone axes [from Kencot, Oxon.]. Oxoniensia, 3, pp. 168–69 + plate. 1938.

5832 (Lewis (Geoffrey D.). Polished axehead from Worthing. [Early Bronze Age. In Worthing Museum.] Sussex N. & Q., 13, p. 186. 1951.

5833 —— Mesolithic implements from Billingshurst. Sussex Arch. Collections, 98, 1960, 12.

5834 —— Hand-axe from High Salvington, Worthing. [Late Acheulian ovate.] Sussex Archaeological Collections, 98 (1960), 12.

5835 —— Flint axehead from Nutbourne Common. Sussex Arch. Collections, 98, 1960, 13.

5836 Lingwood (Edward). Neolithic flint implements found at Baylham, Suffolk. Proc. Suffolk Inst. Arch., 7, pp. 209–11 + plate. 1890.

5837 Lovett (Edward). The gunflint manufactury at Brandon, with reference to its connection with the Stone Age. Proc. Croydon Micr. & N.H. Club, 3, pp. 113–21. 1886.

5838 Lowther (Anthony William George). Two Neolithic stone maceheads. [In Guildford Museum.] Surrey Archaeol. Collns., 45, pp. 141–42 + plate. 1937.

5839 —— Flint trancher-axe from Ashtead. (Flint axes from Ewhurst, etc.). [Figure.] Surrey Arch. Collns., 55, p. 118. 1958.

5840 MacLeod (D.). Flint axes from Horley. [Figure.] Surrey Arch. Collns., 55, pp. 119–20. 1958.

5841 Malden (Henry Elliot). Prehistoric implements from Dorking and Limpsfield. [Neolithic polished flint axe & ?BA grooved ?hammer stone.] Surrey Archaeol. Collns., 37, pp. 89–90 + plate. 1926.

5842 —— A Surrey stone implement. [No date.] [Figure. From Limpsfield. Mining tool.] Antiq. J., 6, p. 181. 1926.

5843 Marr (J. E.). An implement

from Higham, Suffolk. PPSEA, 4 ii, 1923/24, 163–64 + 1 figure.

5844 Marsden (John G.). Note on Le Moustier flints from Acton, West Drayton and Iver. Proc. PSEA, 5 iii, 1927, 297–98 + 2 figures.

5845 —— St. Acheul implements from high-level gravel at Denham, Bucks. Proc. PSEA, 6 ii, 1929, 131–35 + 7 figures.

5846 Migeod (Frederick William Hugh). Recent finds of palaeoliths in the Worthing area. [2 figures. *See also* pp. 146, 176.] Sussex County Mag., 16, pp. 96–99. 1942.

5847 Mitford (Rupert Leo Scott Bruce). A hoard of Neolithic axes from Penslake, Surrey. [Figure.] Antiq. J., 18, pp. 279–84. 1938.

5848 Moir (James Reid). Flint implements of man from the middle glacial gravel and the chalky boulder clay of Suffolk. Proc. PSEA, 1 iii, pp. 307–19 + 3 plates. 1912/13.

5849 —— A defence of the "humanity' of the pre-river valley implements of the Ipswich district. Proc. PSEA, 1 iii, pp. 368–74 + 1 figure + 1 plate. 1912/13.

5850 —— Flint implements of man from the Middle Glacial gravel and chalky boulder clay of Suffolk. Man, 13, pp. 36–37. 1913.

5851 —— The fractured flints of the Eocene "Bull-head" bed at Coe's Pit, Bramford near Ipswich. Proc. PSEA, 1 iv, pp. 397–404 + 2 plates. 1913/14.

5852 —— On the further discoveries of flint implements of man beneath the base of the red crag of Suffolk. Proc. PSEA, 2 i, pp. 12–31 + 8 plates. 1914/15.

5853 —— A series of pre-Palaeolithic implements from Darmsden, Suffolk. Proc. PSEA, 2 ii, 1915/16, 210–13 + 4 plates.

5854 —— The evolution of the rostro-carinate implement from the primitive Kentian plateau implements. [4 figures.] Man, 17, pp. 42–43. 1917.

5855 —— The ancient flint implements of Suffolk. [7 figures.] Proc. Suffolk Inst. Arch., 16, pp. 98–134. 1918.

5856 —— On the occurrence of humanly-fashioned flints, etc., in the middle glacial gravel at Ipswich, Suffolk.

[45 figures.] J. R. Anthrop. Inst., 49, pp. 74–93 + 2 plates. 1919.

5857 Moir (James Reid). A series of humanly-fashioned flints found in the cliffs and on the shore at Mundesley, Norfolk. [Pre-Chellean—Neolithic.] Proc. PSEA, 3 ii, pp. 219–43 + 5 figures. 1919/20.

5858 —— On the occurrence of flint implements in the glacial chalky boulder clay of Suffolk. [13 figures.] J. R. Anthrop. Inst., 50, pp. 135–52 + 2 plates. 1920.

5859 —— A description of the humanly-fashioned flints found during the excavations at High Lodge, Mildenhall. Proc. PSEA, 3 iii, pp. 367–79 + 6 figures. 1920/21.

5860 —— Further discoveries of humanly-fashioned flints in and beneath the Red Crag, Suffolk. Proc. PSEA, 3 iii, pp. 389–430 + 30 figures + 4 plates. 1920/21.

5861 —— Four Suffolk flint implements. [4 figures. From Southwold, Charsfield, Hoxne, and Nacton.] Antiq. J., 2, pp. 114–17. 1922.

5862 —— An Early Palaeolithic flint implement from West Runton, Norfolk. [2 figures.] Man, 22, pp. 34–36. 1922.

5863(a) —— The Red Crag flints of Foxhall [Ipswich]. Man, 22, pp. 104–05. 1922.

5863(b) —— The great flint implements of Cromer, Norfolk. pp. 39 (including 6 plates). 4°. Ipswich, 1923.

5864 —— On some further flint implements of Pliocene age discovered in Suffolk. Proc PSEA, 4 i, pp. 46–56 + 10 figures. 1922/24.

5865 —— A series of Solutré blades from Suffolk and Cambridgeshire. Proc. PSEA, 4 i, pp. 71–81 + 7 figures. 1922/24.

5866 —— An unusual implement of Neolithic form found at Bawdsey, Suffolk [Thames pick]. Proc. PSEA, 5 i, p. 86 + 1 colour plate. 1925.

5867 —— The silted-up lake of Hoxne, and its contained flint implements [various Upper Palaeolithic]. Proc. PSEA, 5 ii, 1926, 137–65 + 13 figures.

5868 —— Upper Palaeolithic man in East Anglia. Proc. PSEA, 5 ii, 1926, 232–52 + 13 figures.

5869 —— A palaeolith from Sidestrand, Norfolk. [Figure.] Antiq. J., 7, pp. 515–16. 1927.

5870 —— Palaeolithic implements from the cannon-shot gravel, Norfolk. [Late Acheulean.] Proc. PSEA, 6 i, 1928–29, 1–11 + 8 figures + 2 plates.

5871 —— A remarkable object from beneath the Red Crag [at Bramford, Suffolk]. [4 figures. Sling-stone.] Man, 29, pp. 62–65. 1929.

5872 —— Some hitherto (further) unpublished implements. [5 figures. Acheulean hand-axe from Sidestrand, Norfolk, etc. (5 figures, Cromer and Ipswich).] Antiq. J., 9, pp. 239–43. 1929.

5873 —— A Chellean hand-axe from the Cromer forest bed. [4 figures. From foreshore, West Runton, Norfolk.] Antiq. J., 9, pp. 101–04. 1929.

5874 —— A polished hand-axe from West Runton, Norfolk. [Figure. St. Acheul.] Antiq. J., 10, pp. 143–45. 1930.

5875 —— A hand-axe from beneath the Norwich Crag. [Early Chellean.] Proc. PSEA, 6 iii, 1930, 222–25 + 2 figures.

5876 —— A hand-axe from the Upper chalky boulder clay. [Figure. Early Mousterian. From Ipswich.] Man, 31, pp. 7–9. 1931.

5877 —— Further hand-axes from the Cromer forest bed. [2 figures. Now in Ipswich museum.] Man, 31, pp. 191–94. 1931.

5878 —— Further discoveries of flint implements in the brown Boulder Clay of Northwest Norfolk. [Upper Aurignacian.] Proc. PSEA, 6 iv, 1931, 306–315 + 13 figures.

5879 —— Further Solutré implements from [Felixstowe and Ipswich] Suffolk. [4 figures.] Antiq. J., 12, pp. 257–61. 1932.

5880 —— Hand-axes from glacial beds at Ipswich. [Rostro-carinate, Mousterian, Acheulian.] Proc. PSEA, 7 ii, 1932–34, 178–84 + 7 figures.

5881 —— A giant hand-axe from Sheringham, Norfolk. [Chellean.] Proc. PSEA, 7 iii, 1934, 327–32 + 9 plates.

5882 —— The Darmsden flint implements. [Pre-Acheulean.] [Essex.] Proc. prehist. Soc., 1, 1935, 93–97, 11 figures.

5883 —— A St. Acheul hand-axe from

[Overstrand on] the Cromer coast. [Figure.] Antiq. J., 15, pp. 73–74. 1935.

5884 Moir (James Reid). The age of the pre-Crag flint implements. [20 figures.] J. R. Anthrop. Inst., 65, pp. 343–74 + 2 plates. 1935.

5885 —— Hand-axes from the Cromer forest-bed. [Figure. From East Runton and Beeston, Norfolk.] Antiq. J., 16, pp. 91–93. 1936.

5886 —— Four flint implements. [4 figures. 2 Early Solutré blades from Bramford Road, Ipswich. Hand-axe from Warren Hill pit, Suffolk. St. Acheul hand-axe from Swanscombe (Kent).] Antiq. J., 18, pp. 258–61. 1938.

5887 —— A pre-Crag side-scraper [from Ipswich]. Antiq. J., 22, pp. 54–56. 1942.

5888 Morris (C.) *and* **Anthony** (J. E.). Pudding stones. Hertfordshire Countryside, 18, No. 70, 1963, 81–82.

5889 Morris (Harry). A suggestion as to the border-land between palaeoliths and pre-paleoliths. Trans. Eastbourne N.H. Soc., 9, pp. 21–27. 1925.

5890 Musson (Reginald Coulson). Two stone axes from Hampden park, Eastbourne. [Figure.] Sussex N. & Q., 13, pp. 84–86. 1950.

5891 Newton (William M.). Kent: flint implements. The occurrence in a very limited area of the rudest with the finer forms of worked stones. [Greenhithe.] Man, 1, pp. 81–82 + plate. 1901.

5892 Nichols (John F.). Flint arrowhead from Godalming. Surrey Arch. Collections, 57, 1960, 100.

5893 Nightingale (R. C.). The Stone Age in Beechamwell. Proc. PSEA, 1 iii, pp. 320–21. 1912/13.

5894 Norman (Philip). Notes on some flint implements found at Keston, Kent. [Figure.] Proc. Soc. Antiq., 2 S. 17, pp. 216–21. 1898.

5895 O'Neil (Helen E.). A greenstone axe from Dean, near Charlbury, Oxfordshire. Oxoniensia, 24, 1959, 102–103 [1 figure].

5896 Paterson (T. T.) *and* **Fagg** (B. E. B.). Studies on the palaeolithic succession in England No. 11. The Upper Brecklandian Acheul (Elveden . Proc. prehist. Soc., 6, 1940, 1–29 + 19 figures.

5897 —— *and* **Tebbutt** (Charles Frederick). Studies in the palaeolithic suc-

cession in England, No. 111: Palaeoliths from St. Neots, Huntingdonshire. Proc. prehist. Soc., 13, 1947, 37–46 + 6 figures.

5898 Peake (Harold John Edward). Mesolithic implements at Newbury. [Figure.] Trans. Newbury F.C., 7 (1934–37), pp. 50–51. 1937.

5899 Petch (D. F.). A Palaeolithic hand-axe from Harlaxton. Rpts. & Papers, Lincs. A. & A.S., 9, 1961, 3–4 + 1 figure.

5900 —— Flint knives from Nocton and Salmonby, and a flint sickle from Thorney. [Secondary Neolithic.] Rpts. & Papers, Lincs. A. & A.S., 9, 1961, 6 + 3 figures.

5901 —— Three stone implements, Middle Rasen. [Wessex type battle-axe, hour-glass perf. hammer & unfinished axe.] Rpts. & Papers, Lincs. A. & A.S., 9, 1961, 6–7 + 2 figures + 1 plate.

5902 —— Stone battleaxes from Ropsley and Grainsby. [Late Neolithic boat-shaped + 2 broken EBA types.] Rpts. & Papers, Lincs. A. & A.S., 9, 1961, 7 + 2 figures.

5903 —— A Bronze Age hammerstone, Faldingworth. Rpts. & Papers, Lincs. A. & A.S., 9, 1961, 7 + 1 figure.

5904 —— Palaeolithic implements from Faldingworth and Sleaford. [Acheulian hand-axes.] Rpts. & Papers, Lincs. A. & A.S., 9, 1962, 90–91 + 3 figures.

5905 —— A barbed and tanged arrowhead, Edenham. Rpts. & Papers, Lincs. A. & A.S., 9, 1962, 91.

5906 —— Polished stone and flint axes found in Lincolnshire. Rpts. & Papers, Lincs. A. & A.S., 9, 1962, 91.

5907 —— A stone axe-hammer, Welby. [MBA.] Rpts. & Papers, Lincs. A. & A.S., 9, 1962, 91–92.

5908 —— Bronze Age mace-heads, Glentham and Legsby. [EBA hour-glass perf. and MBA straight perf.] Rpts. & Papers, Lincs. A. & A.S., 9, 1962, 92 + 2 figures.

5909 Portans (R. D.). Flint implements recently found in the neighbourhood. Trans. Eastbourne N.H. Soc., N.S. 2, pp. 94–96. 1889.

5910 Posnansky (Merrick). A levalloisian implement from Lake Welbeck,

Nottinghamshire. [Figure + plan.] Antiq. J., 38, pp. 85–86. 1958.

5911 Posnansky (Merrick). The Lower and Middle Palaeolithic industries of the English East Midlands. Proc. prehist. Soc., 29, 1963, 357–94 + 13 figures.

5912 Powell (D. F. W. Baden). Palaeoliths from the Fen District. [Levallois & Acheulian.] Proc. prehist. Soc., 16, 1950, 29–41 + 16 figures.

5913 Prestwich (Joseph). On the occurrence of palaeolithic flint implements in the neighbourhood of Ightham, Kent, their distribution and probable age. J. Geol. Soc., London, 45, 1889, 270–97 + 3 plates.

5914 —— On the primitive characters of the flint implements of the chalk plateau of Kent, with reference to the question of their glacial or preglacial age. [Pp. 263–67, On certain rude implements from the North Downs; pp. 267–70, Notes by De Barri Crawshay.]. J. Anthrop. Inst., 21, pp. 246–76 + plate + map. 1892.

5915 Prigg (Henry). On a ground stone implement, from Flempton, near Bury St. Edmonds, Suffolk. J. Anthrop. Soc. London, 6, pp. cvii–viii. 1868.

5916 —— On a ground stone implement, from Flempton, near Bury St. Edmunds. Q. J. Suffolk Inst. Arch., 1, p. 21. 1869.

5917 Pyddoke (Edward). An Acheulian implement from Slindon [Sussex]. [Figure.] Univ. London, Inst. Archaeol., Ann. Rpt., 6 (1948–49), pp. 30–33. 1950.

5918 Quick (Richard). The Eolithic stone age, or notes on eoliths from Kent. [Figure.] J. Brit. Archaeol. Ass., N.S. 6, pp. 332–42. 1900.

5919 Radley (Jeffrey) *and* **Mellars** (P.). Hail Mary Hill: a mesolithic surface site in the Rother valley. [Sauvelerrian affinities.] Trans. Hunter archaeol. Soc., 8 v, 1963, 307–11 + 2 figures.

5920 Rankine (William Francis). Discoveries in the gravels of the fifty-foot terrace at Farnham, Surrey. Proc. prehist. Soc., N.S. 1, 1935, 148–49 + 1 figure.

5921 —— Tranchet axes of South-western Surrey. [Neolithic. 2 figures + map.] Surrey Archaeol. Collns., 46, pp. 98–113. 1938.

5922 —— Slate artefacts [from Frensham]. [Page of figures.] Surrey Archaeol. Collns., 47, pp. 88–90. 1941.

5923 —— Some remarkable flints from west Surrey Mesolithic sites. [5 figures.] Surrey Archaeol. Collns., 49, pp. 6–19. 1946.

5924 —— Late Levallois point from C terrace, Farnham. [Palaeolithic flake implement. Figure.] Surrey Archaeol. Collns., 50, p. 132. 1949.

5925 —— Flint implement from the brickearth overlying D terrace, Farnham. [Figure. Mesolithic.] Surrey Archaeol. Collns., 50, pp. 133–34. 1949.

5926 —— A Neolithic axe of sandstone from Runfold, Farnham. [Figure.] Surrey Archaeol. Collns., 50, pp. 134–35. 1949.

5927 —— A Neolithic axe of volcanic rock from Frensham. [Figure.] Surrey Archaeol. Collns., 50, pp. 135–36. 1949.

5928 —— A perforated implement [quartzite hammer] from Ash. [Bronze Age. Figure.] Surrey Archaeol. Collns., 50, p. 137. 1949.

5929 —— A perforated implement o diorite from Wisley. [Figure. Bronze Age.] Surrey Archaeol. Collns., 50, p. 138. 1949.

5930 —— Stone "maceheads" with Mesolithic associations from south-eastern England. Proc. prehist. Soc., 15, 1949, 70–76 + 3 figures.

5931 —— Some palaeoliths from the Farnham terrace gravels. [4 figures.] Surrey Archaeol. Collns., 54, pp. 1–9. 1955.

5932 Reader (Francis W.). On a polished stone axe from Doddinghurst, Essex. Essex Nat., 13, p. 193 + plate. 1904.

5933 —— Flint axe found at Pleshey, Essex. Essex Nat., 15, p. 18 + plate. 1907.

5934 Rice (Robert Garroway). On some Palaeolithic implements from the terrace gravels of the river Arun and the Western Rother. [3 figures.] Proc. Soc. Antiq., 2 S. 20, pp. 197–207. 1905.

5935 —— Report on an unusual palaeolithic implement and an unfinished neolith found at West Chiltington [Sussex]. [2 figures.] Proc. Soc. Antiq., 2 S. 32, pp. 79–82. 1920.

5936 Robarts (N. F.). The plateau gravel, Upper Norwood, and assorted Eolithic implements. Proc. Croydon N.H. & Sci. Soc., 6, pp. 14–18. 1903.

5937 —— Eolithic implements in Surrey. Proc. Croydon N.H. & Sci. Soc., 6, pp. 195–204. 1908.

5938 Rouse (Edward Clive). Discovery of [Palaeolithic] flint implements at Normer hill, Denham. Records of Bucks., 12, pp. 147–48. 1929.

5939 —— A polished celt from [Rush Green] Denham. [Late Neolithic.] Records of Bucks., 12, pp. 420–21. 1933.

5940 Rowe (A. W.). Palaeolithic implements from the Boulder Clay near Felstead. J. & P. Essex Fld. Club, 4, 1884/87, xcvi–xcvii.

5941 —— Neolithic celts at Felstead. Essex Nat., 1, p. 62. 1887.

5942 Sainty (J. E.) *and* **Solomon** (J. D.). Some Norfolk Palaeolithic discoveries. Implement, ferous gravels in East Anglia. Proc. PSEA, 7 ii, 1932–34, 171–77 + 7 figures.

5943 —— Flint implements from the "stone bed" of the north Norfolk coast. Proc. PSEA, 7 iii, 1934, 323–26 + 10 figures.

5944 —— Three Combe-Capelle hand-axes from Norfolk. Proc. prehist. Soc., N.S. 1, 1935, 98–100 + 3 figures.

5945 —— *and* **Watson** (A. Q.). Palaeolithic implements from Southacre. Norfolk Arch., 28, pp. 183–86 + 2 plates. 1948.

5946 Shelley (John). Communication on rude flint flakes found at Reigate. [2 figures.] [Meso. + Palaeo.] Proc. Soc. Antiq., 2 S. 1, pp. 70–77. 1860.

5947 Sheridan (R. A.). A Palaeolith [*sic*] from Thatcham. Trans. Newbury Dist. Fld. Club, xi, i, 1960, 18–19 + 1 figure.

5948 Shrubsole (O. A.). On certain less familiar forms of Palaeolithic flint implements from the gravel at Reading. J. Anthrop. Inst., 14, pp. 192–200 + plate. 1884.

5949 —— On the valley-gravels about Reading, with special reference to the Palaeolithic implements found in them. J. Geol. Soc. London, 46, 1890, 582–94.

5950(a) —— On flint implements of a primitive type from old (pre-glacial)

hill-gravels in Berkshire. J. Anthrop. Inst., 24, pp. 44–49 + plate. 1894.

5950(b) Smart (T. William Wake). Notes on worked flints found in the neighbourhood of Hastings. Sussex Arch. Collns., 19, pp. 53–60 + plate. 1867.

5951 Smith (Reginald Allender). Striated flints of Neolithic appearance found on the surface at Icklingham, Suffolk. Proc. Soc. Antiq., 2 S. 23, pp. 238–49 + 2 plates. 1910.

5952 —— Flint-finds in connection with sand. [9 figures (flints from Ipswich) + plan (Ipswich).] J. R. Anthrop. Inst., 44, pp. 376–84. 1914.

5953 —— On flint implements from the palaeolithic "floor" at Whipsnade, Bedfordshire. [10 figures + map.] Proc. Soc. Antiq., 2 S. 31, pp. 39–50. 1918.

5954 —— On a polished flint implement of palaeolithic type [from Clapton park, London], and a celt of Cissbury type with palaeolithic patina [from Heacham, Norfolk. [2 figures.] Proc. Soc. Antiq., 2 S. 31, pp. 50–56. 1918.

5955 —— A ground axe of igneous rock [found at Hewfield]. [Figure. Dolmen period (3000–2000 B.C.).] Sussex Arch. Collns., 67, pp. 217–18. 1926.

5956 —— A flint celt from Middleton [near Bognor]. Sussex Arch. Collns., 68, pp. 276–77. 1927.

5957 —— Palaeolith found at West Bognor. [Figure.] Sussex Arch. Collns., 70, pp. 196–97. 1929.

5958 —— Implements from high-level gravel near Canterbury. [Acheulean.] Proc. PSEA, 7 ii, 1932–34, 165–70 + 5 figures.

5959 —— Flints from Farnham, Surrey. B.M.Q., 9, pp. 52–53 + plate. 1934.

5961 Smith (V. Gerard). St. Acheul hand-axe found at Piddinghoe. Sussex N. & Q., 10, p. 161. 1945.

5962 Smith (W. Campbell). Source of the stone used in a mace-head from Dorchester, Oxfordshire. Proc. prehist. Soc., 33, 1967, 455–56 + 1 plate.

5963 Smith (Worthington George). On Palaeolithic implements from [Shacklewell, Middlesex] in the valley of the Lea. J. Anthrop. Inst., 8, pp. 275–79. 1879.

5964 —— Palaeolithic implements from [Hanwell, Middlesex, in] the valley of the Brent. J. Anthrop. Inst., 9, pp. 316–20. 1880.

5965 Smith (Worthington George). Pre-historic stone pestle from Epping forest. [Figure.] Essex Nat., 2, pp. 4–5. 1888.

5966 —— Neolithic and palaeolithic scrapers, replaced and reworked. [4 figures.] Essex Nat., 2, pp. 67–68. 1888.

5967 —— Palaeolithic implements— large and heavy examples. [2 figures.] Essex Nat., 2, pp. 97–101. 1888.

5968 —— Stone saucer from Kempston [Beds.]. [Figure.] Arch. Camb., 5th S. 8, p. 158. 1891.

5969 —— Palaeolithic implement found [in Woburn Place] near the British Museum. [Figure.] Man, 9, p. 88. 1909.

5970 —— Flint flakes of tertiary and secondary age. [4 figures. From Dunstable Downs, etc.]. Man, 12, pp. 196–98. 1912.

5971 Solomon (J. D.). The implementiferous gravels of Warren hill [near Mildenhall, Suffolk]. [7 figures.] J. R. Anthrop. Inst., 63, pp. 101–10. 1933.

5972 Spurrell (Flaxman Charles John) On implements and chips from the floor of a palaeolithic workshop [c. half a mile N.N.E. of Crayford church, Kent]. [3 figures.] Archaeol. J., 137, pp. 294–99 + 2 plates. 1880.

5973 —— On the discovery of the place where palaeolithic implements were made at Crayford [?date]. J. Geol. Soc. London, 36, 1880, 544–48 + 3 figures + 1 plate.

5974 —— Palaeolithic implements found in west Kent. [3 figures. Ightham, Erith and Hayes.] Arch. Cant., 15, pp. 89–103 + plate. 1883.

5975 —— Notes on rude implements from the North Downs. Archaeol. J., 48, pp. 315–19. 1891.

5976 Stevens (Joseph). Stone implements found in the Thames river [at Reading]. J. Brit. Archaeol. Ass., 39, pp. 344–46 + plate. 1883.

5977 Stopes (H.). Unclassified worked flints [especially from the Thames valley]. J. Anthrop. Inst., 30, pp. 299–304 + 6 plates. 1900.

5978 Sturdy (David) *and* **Case** (Humphrey). Recent excavations in Christ Church and nearby [some Neolithic and EBA flints]. Oxoniensia, 26/27, 1961, 19–37 + 11 figures.

5979 Sturge (W. Allen). The polished axe found by Canon Greenwell in a flint pit at Grime's graves. Man, 8, pp. 166–68. 1908.

5980 —— Implements of the later palaeolithic "cave" periods in East Anglia. Proc. PSEA, 1 ii, pp. 210–32 + 14 plates. 1910/12.

5981 Talbot (Keith). Palaeolith from plateau gravel [at Tokers Green, Oxon.]. [Figure. Hand-axe.] Antiq. J., 5, p. 73. 1925.

5982 Taylor (Brian Hope). Two flint-axes from Farthing down, Coulsdon. [2 pages of figures. Late Neolithic or Early Bronze Age.] Surrey Archaeol. Collns., 49, pp. 94–98. 1946.

5983 Tebbutt (Charles Frederick) *and* **Burkitt** (Miles Crawford). A recent find of a flint implement [near St. Neots] in Huntingdonshire showing certain peculiar features. [2 figures.] Man, 32, pp. 140–41. 1932.

5984 Tester (P. J.). A Palaeolithic implement found on the high plateau between Folkestone and Dover. [Figure.] Arch. Cant., 62 (1949), pp. 140–42. 1950.

5985 —— Palaeolithic flint implements from the Bowman's Lodge gravel pit, Dartford heath. [4 figures + plan.] Arch. Cant., 63 (1950), pp. 122–34. 1951.

5986 —— Three associated Neolithic axes from Pembury. [3 figures.] Arch. Cant., 64 (1951), pp. 57–62. 1952.

5987 —— Early use of the levallois technique in the Palaeolithic succession of the lower Thames. [Figure (Swanscombe).] Arch. News Letter, 4, pp. 118–19. 1952.

5988 —— Surface Palaeoliths from Standardhill farm, near Elham. [2 figures.] Arch. Cant., 65 (1952), pp. 85–89. 1953.

5989 —— A discovery of Acheulian implements in the deposits of the Dartford Heath terrace. [2 figures.] Arch. Cant., 66 (1953), pp. 72–76. 1954.

5990 —— A flint dagger from Bexley. Beaker folk A.] Arch. Cant., 69 (1955), pp. 204–05 + plate. 1956.

5991 —— Neolithic axes from Darenth, Bexley and East Wickham. Arch. Cantiana, 73, 1959, pp. 209–11 + 1 figure.

5992 Tester (P. J.). A Prehistoric saddle-quern from Bexley. Arch. Cantiana, 78, 1963, 183–84.

5993 Thomas (Nicholas). A flint Knife of Beaker type from Bestwood, Notts. Trans. Thoroton Soc., 62 (1958), 23.

5994 Todd (A. E.). Early flake implements from "clay-with-flints" on the Eastbourne Downs. [Clactonian?] Proc. PSEA, 7 iii, 1934, 419–20 + 1 figure.

5995 —— Early palaeoliths from the summit of the South Downs. [Rostrocarinate and 3 ovates]. Proc. prehist. Soc. N.S. 2, 1936, 140–43 + 4 figures.

5996 Toke (N. E.). Flint implements. Folkestone and the country around, ed. John W. Walton (South-Eastern Union of Scientific Societies). pp. 85–87. 1925.

5997 Toms (Herbert S.). Notes on pigmy flint implements found in Sussex. [Figure.] Antiquary, 51, pp. 246–50. 1915.

5998 Treacher (Llewellyn). On the occurrence of stone implements in the Thames valley between Reading and Maidenhead. [2 figures + map.] Man, 4, pp. 17–19 + plate. 1904.

5999 Turner (D. J.). Mesolithic implement from Sanderstead. Surrey Arch. Collections, 60, 1963, 82 + 1 figure.

6000 —— Barbed and tanged arrowhead, Barnes Common. Surrey Arch. Collections, 62, 1965, 122 + 1 figure.

6001 Turner (J.). An Association of thin-butted celts with leaf shaped arrowheads at Drow Hill, Capstone North, Kent. [Neolithic.] Proc. PSEA, 5 ii, 1926, 214–16 + 1 figure + 1 plate.

6002 Waddington (Quintin). Neolithic mace-head from [Bank of England site] London. [Figure.] Antiq. J., 8, pp. 518–19. 1928.

6003 Wade (A. G.). Palaeolith from Farnham [Surrey]. [Figure.] Antiq. J., 7, pp. 313–14. 1927.

6004 ——Palaeoliths from Farnham. [Figure.] Antiq. J., 15, pp. 57–59. 1935.

6005 Walker (F. M.). Axe hammer from the Fens. [Figure.] [Bronze Age—boat shaped.] Antiq. J., 10, pp. 385–86. 1930.

6006 Warburton (J. S.). Some implements of "Cissbury type" found in Norfolk. Proc. PSEA, 1 iv, pp. 420–27 + 3 plates. 1913/14.

6007 Warhurst (Alan). Flint implement from Cranbrook. [Figure. Mesolithic. Now in Maidstone Museum.] Arch. Cant., 65, (1952), p. 192. 1953.

6008 Warren (S. Hazzledine). Note on some Palaeolithic and Neolithic implements from east Lincolnshire. [3 figures.] Man, 7, pp. 146–48. 1907.

6009 —— Notes on the Palaeolithic and Neolithic implements of east Essex. Essex Nat., 16, pp. 46–51 + 6 plates. 1909.

6010 —— The Red Crag flints of Foxhall. [Foxhall road, Ipswich.] Man, 22, pp. 87–89. 1922.

6011 —— Palaeolithic and Neolithic implements from the Thames valley and elsewhere. Essex Nat., 21, pp. 67–77 + 2 plates. 1923.

6012 Webb (Wilfred Mark). A Neolithic stone-hammer from Braintree, Essex. [Figure.] Essex Nat., 13, pp. 95–96. 1903.

6013 Wheatley (Sydney Williams). Find of flint instruments and workshop at Frindsbury. Arch. Cant., 38, pp. 183–84. 1926.

6014 White (G. M.). An Acheulean hand-axe from Chichester. Proc. PSEA 7 iii, 1934, 420–21 + 1 figure.

6015 Whitwell (J. B.). Barbep and tanged arrowheads and scrapers, Glentham and Legsby. Rpts. & Papers, Lincs. A. & A.S., 10, 1963, 2.

6016 —— Barbed and tanged arrowheads, Castle Bytham and Revesby. Rpts. & Papers, Lincs. A. & A.S., 10, 1963, 2.

6017 —— Stone adze, Bassingham. Rpts. & Papers, Lincs. A. & A.S., 10, 1964, 58.

6018 —— Perforated axe hammer, Harrington. Rpts. & Papers, Lincs. A. & A.S., 10, 1964, 58.

6019 —— Stone axe hammer, East Torrington. Rpts. & Papers, Lincs. A. & A.S., 10, 1964, 58.

6020 —— Flint dagger, Alford. [Beaker.] Rpts. & Papers, Lincs. A. & A.S., 10, 1964, 58 + 1 figure.

6021 Wight (Edward). A palaeolith from Stopham. [Figure.] Sussex N. & Q., 9, p. 17. 1942.

6022 Willett (Edgar). On a recent find of worked flints in Tilgate forest.

[Neol. & BA.] Sussex Arch. Collns., 55, pp. 123–25 +2 plates. 1912.

6023 Williams (Audrey). Axe-head from Shephall, Hertfordshire. [Figure.] Antiq. J., 27, pp. 80–81. 1947.

6024 Williams (Francis R. B.). Flint implements from Grayford [Kent]. [2 figures.] Reliquary, 3rd S. 7, pp. 271–72. 1901.

6025 Williamson (F.). "Bury" Collection of flint implements from Farnham, Surrey. [Palaeoliths & mesolithic.] Surrey Archaeological Collections, 57, 1960, 100.

6026 Winbolt (Samuel Edward). A Neolithic celt found at Selsey. [Figure.] Sussex County Mag., 3, p. 869. 1929.

6027 —— A Late Pleistocene flint point [from Paper Harrow park, Godalming, Surrey]. [Figure.] Antiq. J., 9, pp. 152–53. 1929.

6028 —— A Neolithic celt from [Colgate] St. Leonard's forest. [Figure.] Sussex Arch. Collns., 73, p. 201. 1932.

6029 —— Bronze Age flints at Frant. Sussex N. & Q., 7, p. 93, 126–27. 1938.

6030 Wittering (W. O.). Puddingstones. Hertfordshire Countryside, No. 71, 1963, 131–32 + 1 plate.

6031 Worsfold (F. H.). Observations on the provenance of the Thames Valley pict, Swalecliffe, Kent. [Early Neolithic.] Proc. PSEA, 5 ii, 224–31 + 4 plates. 1926.

6032 Wortham (B. Hale). Neolithic implements discoverd at Stifford, south Essex. [3 figures.] Antiquary, 45, pp. 287–88. 1909.

6033 —— Palaeolithic implements in south-east Herts. and south Essex. [5 figures.] Antiquary, 48, pp. 57–60. 1912.

6034 Wright (Arthur G.). On the discovery of palaeolithic implements in the neighbourhood of Kennet, Cambs. pp. 2 + 8 plates. Sm. 4°. n.p. 1886.

6035 Wyatt (James). Flint implements in the drift in Bedfordshire. [2 figures.] Notes Beds. Archit. & Archaeol. Soc., 1, pp. 145–56 + 3 plates. 1861.

6036 —— Flint implements in the Drift [Beds.]. Assoc. Archit. Socs.' Rpts., 6, pp. 71–93 + 5 plates (flints from Biddenham, Beds.). 1861.

6037 —— On the flint implements in the Drift, discovered near Bedford. pp.

17 + 3 plates. 8°. Bedford, 1861. [2 figures.]

6038 —— On some further discoveries of flint implements in the gravel near Bedford. J. Geol. Soc. London, 18, 1862, 113–14.

6039 Wyley (J. F.). An Abbevillian hand-axe from the Vale of St. Albans. Proc. prehist. Soc., 20, 1954, 237 + 1 figure.

6040 Wymer (J.). Palaeoliths from gravel of the ancient channel between Caversham and Henley at Highlands near Henley. Proc. prehist. Soc., 22, 1956, 29–36 + 22 figures.

6041 Young (John T.). On some Palaeolithic fishing implements from the Stoke Newington and Clapton gravels. J. Anthrop. Inst., 14, pp. 83–84. 1884.

6042 Zeuner (F. E.). A group VI Neolithic axe from Minster Lovell, Oxfordshire. Proc. prehist. Soc., 18, 1952, 240–41 + 1 plate.

(b) Zone 2 [CBA Group 12]

6043 [Anon.] Palaeoliths from the New Forest. [Figure.] Antiq. J., 7, pp. 188–89. 1927.

6044 Arkell (William Joscelyn). Glazed flints [from Knowle, Collingbourne, etc.]. Wilts. Archaeol. Mag., 45, pp. 233–34. 1930.

6045 —— A palaeolith from Sherborne. [Figure.] Proc. Dorset Archaeol. Soc., 68 (1946), pp. 31–32. 1947.

6046 —— Palaeolith from gravels at Sutton Benger. Wilts. Archaeol. Mag., 50, p. 290 + plate. 1943.

6047 Ashbee (Paul). A "single-piece" flint sickle from Titchfield haven. [Figure. Neolithic.] Papers & Proc. Hants. F.C., 19 (1956), pp. 280–82. 1957.

6048 Blackmore (H. P.). Discovery of flint implements in the higher level gravel at Milford hill, Salisbury. [Figure.] Archaeol. J., 21, pp. 243–45. 1864.

6049 —— On the discovery of flint implements in the drift at Milford Hill, Salisbury. J. Geol. Soc. London, 21, 1865, 250–52.

6050 —— On the recent discovery of flint implements in the drift of the valley of the Avon. [?Palaeolithic.] Wilts. Archaeol. Mag., 10, pp. 221–33. 1867.

6051 Bond (William Ralph Garneys). A specialised Mesolithic flint implement from Blashenwell. [Scoop for extracting limpets.] Proc. Dorset Archaeol. Soc., 62 (1940), pp. 37–38 + plate. 1941.

6052 Bowen (H. Collin). A flint arrowhead from Wareham. Proc. Dorset Arch. Soc., 79 (1957), pp. 107–08. 1958.

6053 Brooks (Howard). Palaeolith from Plateau gravel [St. George's hill, Weymouth]. Antiq. J., 16, p. 199. 1936

6054 Buckman (James). The flint implements and weapons of Dorset. J. Brit. Archaeol. Ass., 28, pp. 220–21. 1872.

6055 Calkin (J. Bernard) *and* **Green** (J. F. N.). Palaeoliths and terraces near Bournemouth. [Acheulian.] Proc. prehist. Soc., 15, 1949, 21–37 + 22 figures.

6056 Clay (Richard Challoner Cobb). A flint implement from Pucknall, Hants. [Figure.] Man, 24, p. 133. 1924.

6057 —— Flint implements from the Nadder valley, south Wilts. Wilts. Archaeol. Mag., 43, pp. 156–62 + 2 plates. 1925.

6058 —— Polished flint knives, with particular reference to one recently found at Durrington. [Figure. Bronze Age.] Wilts. Archaeol. Mag., 44, pp. 97–100. 1928.

6059 —— A remarkable flint implement [from Sutton Mandeville, Wilts.]. [Figure. Bronze Age.] Man, 28, pp. 5–6. 1928.

6060 Clayton (G. L.). A flint flake from Grayshott. Paper & Proc. Hants. F.C., 17, p. 54. 1952.

6061 Clift (J. G. Neilson). Neolithic implements from Dorset. J. Brit. Archaeol. Ass., N.S. 13, pp. 172–75 + folding plate. 1907.

6062 Collins (W. G.). Worked flints from the river-drift at Holt, Wilts. [Figure. Palaeolithic.] Antiquary, 47, pp. 179–83. 1911.

6063 Collum (V. C. C.). Basalt weapon-head from Rotherley down, Rushmore. Wilts. Archaeol. Mag., 46, pp. 94–96. 1932.

6064 Cook (Norman C.). Stone axe from Southampton. [Figure.] Papers & Proc. Hants. F.C., 17, p. 55. 1952.

6065 Corcoran (J. X. W. P.). A Scandinavian axehead from the Isle of Wight. [Neolithic.] Proc. I.O.W. nat. Hist. & archaeol. Soc., 5 viii, 1963, 357–58 + 1 figure.

6066 Cunnington (Edward). Flint implements found at Portesham during 1894 and 1895. [Neolithic.] Proc. Dorset Antiq. F.C., 17, pp. 192–93. 1896.

6067 Cunnington (Maud Edith). A "Thames pick" of Iron Age date [from Casterley camp, Wilts.]. Man, 25, pp. 134–35. 1925.

6068 Cunnington (William). On some Palaeolithic implements from the plateau-gravels, and their evidence concerning "Eolithic" man. J. Geol. Soc. London, 54, 1898, 291–300 + 4 figures.

6069 Cunnington (William) *and* **Cunnington** (William A.). The Palaeolithic implements and gravels of Knowle, Wilts. Wilts. Archaeol. Mag., 33, pp. 131–38. 1903.

6070 Dale (William). The Palaeolithic implements of the Southampton gravels. Papers & Proc. Hants. F.C., 3, pp. 261–64 + plate. 1896.

6071 —— Neolithic implements from the neighbourhood of Southampton. Papers & Proc. Hants. F.C., 4, pp. 183–85 + 2 plates. 1901.

6072 —— Notes on the character and forms of implements of the Palaeolithic age from the neighbourhood of Southampton. Proc. Soc. Antiq., 2 S. 21, pp. 37–42. 1905.

6073 —— Neolithic implements from Hampshire. Proc. Soc. Antiq., 2 S. 21, pp. 263–66. 1906.

6074 —— The implement-bearing gravel beds of the valley of the lower Test. [Hants.] Arch. Camb., 6th S. 12, p. 245. 1912.

6075 —— The implement-bearing gravel-beds of the lower valley of the Test [Hants.]. [5 figures.] Proc. Soc. Antiq., 2 S. 24, pp. 108–16 + 5 plates: 25, pp. 46–51. 1912–13.

6076 —— Hampshire flints. Demarcation of the Stone Ages. Papers & Proc. Hants. F.C., 7 i, pp. 20–24 + 3 plates. 1914.

6077 —— [Palaeoliths from Dunbridge, Hants.]. [10 figures.] Proc. Soc. Antiq., 2 S. 30, pp. 20–32 + plate. 1918.

6078 Davies (Henrietta F.). The shale industries at Kimmsridge, Dorset.

[7 figures + map. Two industries, one from beginning of Early Iron Age, the other from the early part of the Roman occupation.] Archaeol. J., 93 (1936), pp. 200–19 + 3 plates. 1937.

6079 Dewar (H. S. L.). Mesolithic and other worked flints at Bryants puddle, Dorset. Proc. Dorset N.H. & A.S., 83, 1962, 82.

6080 Dixon (S. B.). On some uses of flint implements. Wilts. Archaeol. Mag., 19, pp. 96–102. 1881.

6081 —— On the Palaeolithic flint implements from Knowle, Savernake forest. [pp. 144–45, The Knowle polish, by E. H. Goddard.] Wilts. Archaeol. Mag., 33, pp. 139–45. 1903.

6082 Draper (J. C.). Stone industries from Rainbow bar, [Titchfield haven] Hants. [Figure. *See also* 4, p. 3 (letter from S. Hazzledine Warren).] Arch. News Letter, 3, pp. 147–49. 1951.

6083 —— Upper Palaeolithic type flints from Long Island, Langstone Harbour, Portsmouth. Papers & Proc. Hants. F.C., 22, pt. ii, 1962, pp. 105–06 + 1 figure.

6084 Engleheart (George Herbert). On Neolithic flints lying below the present surface at Dinton. Wilts. Archaeol. Mag., 36, pp. 86–89. 1909.

6085 —— Surface implements from [Fovant] Wiltshire. [2 Figures. Neolithic.] Antiq. J., 3, pp. 144–45. 1923.

6086 —— A probable source of the material of some Wiltshire prehistoric axe-hammers. [Chesil beach.] Wilts. Archaeol. Mag., 45, pp. 73–74. 1930.

6087 Evans (John) (*FGS*) (*FSA*). On some recent discoveries of flint implements in Drift-deposits in Hants. and Wilts. [?Acheulian from description.] J. Geol. Soc. London, 20, 1864, 188–94 + 1 figure.

6088 Farrar (Raymond Anthony Holt). A [Neolithic] polished axe from Portisham. [Figure.] Proc. Dorset Arch. Soc., 78 (1956), pp. 83–84. 1957.

6089 —— An Early Bronze Age arrow-head from East Stoke, near Wool [short note]. Proc. Dorset N.H. & A.S., 85, 1963, 102.

6090 —— A flint pick from New Mills Heath, Corpe Castle [short note]. Proc. Dorset N.H. & A.S., 86, 1964, 117.

6091 —— Flints from Harman's Cross, Corfe Castle. Proc. Dorset N.H. & A.S., 86, 1964, 117–18.

6092 —— A possible quernstone from Manor Farm, Studland. Proc. Dorset N.H. & A.S., 86, 1964, 118.

6093 Goddard (Edward Hungerford). The gloss on flints from Knowle and Collingbourne. Wilts. Archaeol. Mag., 41, pp. 183–84. 1920.

6094 —— Stone implements of uncommon type found in Wiltshire. Wilts. Archaeol. Mag., 41, pp. 365–77 + 2 plates. 1921.

6095 Gray (Harold St. George). A remarkably thin flint arrowhead from Maiden Castle. Man, 4, pp. 161–62. 1935.

6096 Grinsell (Leslie Valentine). A palaeolith from Heytesbury. [Figure.] Wilts. Archaeol. Mag., 54, pp. 436–37. 1952.

6097 —— A flint dagger from Avebury. [Figure.] Wilts. Archaeol. Mag., 55, pp. 176–77. 1953.

6098 Grist (C. J.). Some eoliths from Dewlish [Dorset] and the question of origin. J. R. Anthrop. Inst., 40, pp. 192–208 + 2 plates. 1910.

6099 Hawkes (Charles Francis Christopher). Two palaeoliths from Broom, Dorset. Proc. prehist. Soc., 9, 1943, 48–52 + 3 figures.

6100 Hookey (T. P.). A Thames pick from Shorwell. [Figure. Mesolithic implement.] Proc. I. of W. N.H. & Arch. Soc., 4, p. 268. 1952.

6101 Ingram (A. H. Winnington). On a piece of perforated slate found at Aldington, Worcestershire, as illustrative of the ancient use of slate tablets discovered in barrows in Wiltshire. [Concave. ?used as shooting brace.] [Wrist guard. Beaker.] Wilts. Archaeol. Mag., 10, pp. 109–13 + 2 plates. 1867.

6102 Jones (J. B.). A north Wilts. celt. [From downs between Aldbourne Warren and Wanborough plain. Ground stone axe of Neolithic type.] Wilts. Archaeol. Mag., 53, pp. 133–34. 1949.

6103 Kendall (Henry George Ommanney) *and* **Whitaker** (W.). Palaeolithic implements, etc., from Hackpen Hill, Winterbourne Bassett, and Knowle Farm pit (Wiltshire). J. Geol. Soc. London, 65, 1909, 166–68.

6104 —— Flint implements from the surface near Avebury: their classification and dates. [13 figures.] Proc. Soc. Antiq., 2 S. 26, pp. 73–88. 1914.

6105 Kendall (Henry George Ommanney). Scraper-core industries in North Wilts. [?]. PPSEA, 3 iv, 1921/22, 515–41 + 18 figures.

6106 —— Two flint celts from [Tollard Royal], Dorset. [2 figures.] Antiq. J., 3, pp. 139–42. 1933.

6107 —— Some flint tools of the Iron Age: a singular series. [11 figures. From Laverstock down, Wilts.] Antiq. J., 5, pp. 158–63. 1925.

6108 King (D. Grant). Ground and polished Stone axe from Euridge. [Late Neolithic.] WAM, 58, 1962, No. 210, 219–20 + 1 figure.

6109 Kitchin (E. Hugh). Nodule implements in the Bournemouth district— pp. 22 + 19 plates. 4°. Cambridge, 1936.

6111 Linton (E. C.). A large palaeolith from [Edmondsham], Dorset. [Figure.] Antiq. J., 13, pp. 159–61. 1933.

6112 —— Palaeoliths from [Luzborough,] Hants. [3 figures.] Antiq. J., 15, pp. 193–94. 1955.

6113 Mellor (A. Shaw). Stone axe found near Biddestone, Wilts. [Neolithic.] Wilts. Archaeol. Mag., 53, p. 254. 1949.

6114 Newall (Robert Stirling). Polished stone celt with grooves on the edges [from Liddington, Wilts.]. [Figure.] Wilts. Archaeol. Mag., 37, pp. 613–14 + plate. 1912.

6115 —— Circular stone perforated mace head from near Bilbury camp, Wylye. Wilts. Archaeol. Mag., 43, pp. 348–49 + plate. 1926.

6116 —— Two shale cups of the Early Bronze Age [in Salisbury Museum] and other similar cups. [2 figures.] Wilts. Archaeol. Mag., 44, pp. 111–17. 1928.

6117 Piggott (Cecily Margaret). A flint axe of Scandinavian type from [the bank of the Stour near Canford,] Dorset. [Figure. Early Bronze Age.] Proc. Dorset Archaeol. Soc., 67 (1945), p. 28. 1946.

6118 Piggott (Stuart). Two foreign stone axes from Hampshire. [Neolithic, polished, volcanic.] Proc. prehist. Soc., N.S., 1, 1935, 154.

6119 Poole (Hubert F.). Palaeoliths

from Great Pan farm, Isle of Wight. [4 figures.] Papers & Proc. Hants. F.C., 9, pp. 305–19. 1925.

6120 —— Flint arrow-head types of the Isle of Wight. Proc. I. of W. N.H. & Arch. Soc., 1, pp. 436–14 + 2 plates. 1926.

6121 —— Upper Palaeolithic implement from Grange chine: Le Moustier implement of rare type. [2 figures.] Proc. I. of W. N.H. & Arch. Soc., 1, pp. 609–10. 1928.

6122 —— A laurel-leaf point from Brighstone. [Figure. Solutrean flint implement.] Proc. I. of W. N.H. & Arch. Soc., 1, pp. 690–92. 1928.

6123 —— Stone axes found in the Isle of Wight. Proc. I. of W. N.H. & Arch. Soc., 1, pp. 652–58 + plate: 2, pp. 27–38 + 4 plates. 1929–30.

6124 —— The gravel and flint implements of Bleak down, Isle of Wight. [7 figures.] Papers & Proc. Hants. F.C., 12, pp. 20–47. 1932.

6125 —— Flint knives found in the Isle of Wight. Proc. I. of W. N.H. & Arch. Soc., 2, pp. 190–95 + 3 plates. 1932.

6126 —— Le Moustier implements from gravel new Rew Street, Isle of Wight. [3 figures.] Papers & Proc. Hants. F.C., 13, pp. 173–78. 1936.

6127 —— Additional records of stone implements found in the Isle of Wight. 1. Microliths and arrowheads. 2. Stone axes. 3. Flint knives and other stone implements. Proc. I. of W. N.H. & Arch. Soc., 3, pp. 122–27 + plate; pp. 263–69 + plate; pp. 270–78 + 4 plates. 1939–41.

6128 —— On a tribrachial implement of flint in the Carisbrooke castle museum. [N/D but cf. modern ceremony with bull's horns, Roy. Antediluvian Ord. Buffaloes.] Proc. I. of W. N.H. & Arch. Soc., 3, pp. 279–82 + plate. 1941.

6129 —— Flint implements of Upper Palaeolithic types found at Havenstreet, Isle of Wight. [3 figures.] Proc. I. of W. N.H. & Arch. Soc., 3, pp. 370–77. 1943.

6130 Rankine (W. F.). A ground flake from Dinton. [Figure. Neolithic.] Wilts. Archaeol. Mag., 56, pp. 188–89. 1955.

6131 —— A blade graver from Dinton. [Figure.] [Palaeolithic.] Wilts. Archaeol. Mag., 56, p. 189. 1955.

6132 Read (C. J.). The flint implements of Bemarton and Milford hill, near Salisbury. [Palaeolithic.] Wilts. Archaeol. Mag., 22, pp. 117–23 + 5 plates + 2 plans. 1885.

6133 Renn (D. F.). A flint axe from Fareham. [Neolithic A—EBA.] Papers & Proc. Hants. F.C., 21, pt ii, 1959, p. 113 + 1 figure.

6134 Short (W. F.). Stone axes, etc., from Donhead St. Mary. Trans. Salisbury F.C., 1, pp. 34–35. 1890.

6135 Simpson (D. D. A.). Plano-convex flint knife. WAM, 58, 1962, No. 210, 226 + 1 figure.

6136 —— Discoidal flint knife. [Late Neolithic.] WAM, 58, 1962, No. 210, 226 + 1 figure.

6137 Smallcombe (W. A.). A flint sickle with associated objects from East Knoyle, Wiltshire. Proc. prehist. Soc., 3, 1937, 158–59 + 3 figures.

6138 Smith (Reginald Allender). A palaeolith from [Edmondsham], Dorset. B.M.Q., 7, pp. 126–27 + plate. 1933.

6139 Stevens (Edward Thomas). Flint chips. A guide to prehistoric archaeology as illustrated by the collection in the Blackmore Museum, Salisbury. pp. xxvi, 593, xxxviii + plate. 8⁰. London, 1870. [125 figures.]

6140 Stevens (Joseph). Notes on some worked flints found at St. Mary Bourne [Hants.]. [Neolithic.] Wilts. Archaeol. Mag., 11, pp. 106–12. 1869.

6141 Stone (J. F. S.). An axe-hammer from Fifield Bavant, Wilts., and the exploitation of Presilite. [Figure + map. Late Neolithic.] Antiq. J., 30, pp. 145–51 + plate. 1950.

6142 Stron (Frederick). Acheulian ovate from Bembridge. Proc. I. of W. N.H. & Arch. Soc., 4, p. 95 + plate. 1948.

6143 Thomas (Herbert H.). Stone celt from [Box, east of Bath,] Wiltshire. [Figure. Neolithic.] Antiq. J., 6, pp. 442–44. 1926.

6144 —— Dolerite celt from [Bursledon,] Hampshire. [Figure. Neolithic.] Antiq. J., 9, pp. 377–78. 1929.

6145 Thurnam (John). On four leaf and lozenge-shaped flint javelin-heads from an oval barrow near Stonehenge; and the leaf-shaped type of flint arrowhead, and its connection with long barrows. [2 figures.] Wilts. Archaeol. Mag., 11, pp. 40–49. 1869.

6146(a) Way (Albert). Notes on an unique [tribrachial] implement of flint, found, as stated, in the Isle of Wight. [Figure.] Archaeol. J., 30, pp. 28–34 + plate. 1873.

6146(b) Weekes (Ethel Lega). Conbett's stone axe-hammer. [Figure. Early Bronze Age. From Botley(?), Hants.] Antiq. J., 16, pp. 96–97. 1936.

6147 Westropp (Hodder Michael). On Ventuor flints. J. Anth. Inst., 3, pp. 69–70. 1873.

6148 Willett (Edgar). On a collection of Palaeolithic implements from Savernake. J. Anthrop. Inst., 31, pp. 310–15 + 2 plates. 1901.

6149 Willis (G. W.). Hampshire palaeoliths and the clay-with-flints. Papers & Proc. Hants. F.C., 16, pp. 253–56 + 4 plates + map. 1947.

6150 Young (W. E. V.). Dual-period stone implement from West Kennett. [Figure. Early Bronze Age.] Wilts. Archaeol. Mag., 53, pp. 184–90. 1949.

(c) Zone 3 [CBA Groups 8, 13]

6151 [Anon.] An early British fragment [from Barnwood, Glos.]. [Iron Age.] [4 figures. Decorated stone cone.] Antiq. J., 14, pp. 59–61. 1934.

6152 [Anon.] A palaeolith found near Gloucester. Antiq. J., 16, p. 91. 1936.

6153 [Anon.] Neolithic axe-head [from Trent]. N. & Q. Som. & Dorset, 23, pp. 28–29. 1939.

6154 Arnold (Edwin L.). Pygmy implements from Cornwall. Proc. prehist. Soc. EA, 1 iii, 1912/13, 334–36.

6155 Bowen (A. R.). Considerations on certain flint implements and other antiquities from the Worcester and Malvern district. [Figure. Neolithic and Bronze Age.] Trans. Worcs. Archaeol. Soc., N.S. 26 (1949), pp. 32–37. 1950.

6156 Brent (Francis). On the occurrence of flint flakes, and small stone implements, in Cornwall. J. Roy. Instn.

Cornwall, 8, pp. 58–61; 14, pp. 417–19. 1886, 1900.

6157 Britton (Mark). Palaeoliths from [Halberton], Devonshire. [2 figures.] Antiq. J., 15, pp. 343–45. 1935.

6158 Brushfield (Thomas Nadauld). Description of a perforated stone implement found in the parish of Withycombe Raleigh. [Stone hammer, Neolithic.] Rpt. & Trans. Devon Assoc., 22, pp. 208–11 + plate. 1890.

6159 Bullen (R. Ashington). Polished stone implements from Harlyn Bay. [2 figures. Early Iron Age.] [Cornwall.] Man, 8, pp. 74–75. 1908.

6160 Burnard (Robert). Dartmoor stone implements and weapons. Rpt. & Trans. Devon Assoc., 29, pp. 378–85 + 8 plates. 1897.

6161 Cantrill (Thomas Crossbee) *and* **Cockin** (G. M.). Neolithic flints from a chipping-floor at Carnock wood, near Rugeley, south Staffordshire. North Staffs. F.C., Trans., 51, pp. 85–98 + plate + map. 1917.

6162 —— A flint arrow-head from Stone, Kidderminster. [Barbed and tanged. Bronze Age, c. 1800 B.C.] Trans. Worcs. Archaeol. Soc., N.S. 4, pp. 127–28. 1928.

6163 —— Flint flakes from the Shrewsbury and Wellington district. [Figure.] Trans. Shropshire Archaeol. Soc., 46, pp. 19–30. 1931.

6164 Cardew (Cornelius E.). Flint axe-head from St. Enoder parish. J. Roy. Instn. Cornwall, 19, pp. 140–42 + plate. 1912.

6165 Cardew (John Haydon). The surface flint implements of the Cotteswold hills. Trans. Bristol & Glos. Arch. Soc., 15, pp. 246–53 + 10 plates. 1891.

6166 Carpenter (Miss) *and* **Burkitt** (Miles Crawford). Flint implements from the Severn basin. [2 figures. From Kidderminster and Wroxeter.] Antiq. J. 14, pp. 63–65. 1934.

6167 Childe (V. Gordon). An exotic stone adze from Tuckingmill, Camborne, Cornwall. Proc. prehist. Soc., 17, 1951, 96 + 1 plate.

6168 Chitty (Lily Frances). Stone celt from the Longmynd. [Pre-Dolmen date, c. 4000 B.C.] Trans. Shropshire Archaeol. Soc., 43 (4th S. 10), p. xi. 1926.

6169 —— Perforated stone axe-hammers found in Shropshire. [Figure. List of 28.]. Bull. Bd. Celtic Stud., 4, pp. 74–91. 1927.

6170 —— Stone celt found in Clunton, Shropshire. Trans. Shropshire Archaeol. Soc., 45 (4th S. 12), pp. i–ii. 1929.

6171 —— Small perforated stone adze from High Hatton, Stanton-upon-Hine heath, Shropshire. [Figure.] Trans. Shropshire Archaeol. Soc., 45 (4th S. 12), pp. ii–v. 1929.

6172 —— Flint implements recently found in Shropshire, south of the Severn, with a supplementary note on two newly-recorded stone axe-hammers. [2 figures.] Trans. Shropshire Archaeol. Soc., 53, pp. 24–36 + 4 plates. 1949.

6173 —— Lozenge-shaped flint arrowhead from Poston, Peterchurch. Trans. Woolhope N.F.C., 34 (1952–54), pp. 36–37. 1955.

6174 —— Notes on a stone pestle found in the river Severn below Ford, West Shropshire. Trans. Shropshire A.S., 57 iii, 1964, 180–84 + 1 figure + 1 plate.

6175 Clarke (W. E. H.). An ancient British mortar discovered at Hereford. Trans. Woolhope N.F.C., 1914–17, pp. 278–79.

6176 Clifford (Elsie Margaret). A Palaeolith from Gloucestershire. [Acheulian axe.] Proc. prehist. Soc., 3, 1937, 465–66 + 1 figure.

6177 —— Palaeolith from the upper Thames valley [near Lechlade, Glos.]. [Figure.] Antiq. J., 19, p. 193. 1939.

6178 —— Palaeolithic implement from Little Alne, Alcester, Warwickshire. Proc. prehist. Soc., 9, 1943, 52–54 + 2 figures.

6179 ——, **Garrod** (D. A. E.) *and* **Gracie** (H. S.). Flint implements from Gloucestershire. [4 figures. Palaeolithic and later.] Antiq. J., 34, pp. 178–87. 1954.

6180 —— Palaeolithic implements from Little Alne, Alcester, Warwickshire. Proc. prehist. Soc., 29, 1963, 429.

6181 Cra'ster (Mary D.). Two stone axes in Gloucester Museum. [Figure. Neolithic. i. From Robinswood Hill, Gloucester; ii. From Clement's End, near Coleford.] Trans. Bristol & Glos.

Arch. Soc., 73 (1954), pp. 228–29. 1955.

6182 Dallas (James). A stone celt from Budleigh Salterton. [Figure. Now in Albert Memorial Museum, Exeter.] Notes & Gleanings . . . Devon & Cornwall, 3, pp. 129–30. 1890.

6183 Dewar (H. S. L.). Neolithic axe from Shapwick Heath. Notes & Queries for Somerset & Dorset, 27, pt. 270, 1959, 233.

6184 Dewey (Henry). Flint implements from the Torquay area. [2 figures.] Proc. Devon Archaeol. Expl. Soc., 4, pp. 129–32. 1953.

6185 Dodd (J. Phillip). Stone axe found near Alveley, S.E. Shropshire. [Group VI Langdale, EBA.] Trans. Shropshire A.S., 56 (1959) II, 125–28 + 2 figures.

6186 Dudley (Dorothy). Stone pendants from Cornwall. [Figure. From Paul and Lelissick, Padstow (Late Bronze Age).] Proc. West Cornwall F.C., N.S. I, pp. 171–72. 1956.

6187 Dunning (Gerald Clough). Stone axe from Foxcote, Andoversford, Gloucestershire. [Figure. Late Neolithic.] Trans. Bristol & Glos. Arch. Soc., 58, pp. 284–85. 1936.

6188 Dyer (W. T. Thistleton). On some flint-flakes from the valley of the Chur at Cirencester. Proc. Cotteswold Nat. Club, 5, pp. 271–72. 1871.

6189 Edmonds (U. M.). Two chert implements from a garden in the Blackdowns (now in Taunton Castle Museum). [i. Mallet, adze-hammer, or hoe; ii. Scraper. Both Neolithic—Bronze Age.] N. & Q. Som. & Dorset, 27, pp. 147–48. 1957.

6190 Edwards (W. H.). Notes on some Worcestershire flint implements. [Mostly Neolithic.] B'ham. Arch. Soc., Trans., 41 (1915), pp. 1–4 + 2 plates. 1916.

6191 Evans (*Sir* John). On a discovery of Palaeolithic implements in the valley of the Axe. J. Anthrop. Inst., 7, pp. 499–501. 1878.

6192 Falconer (J. P. E.). The flints of the Bath downs (South Cotswolds). Somerset Arch. Soc., Proc. Bath branch, [8] 1939–47, pp. 289–91 + plate. 1944.

6193 Fielden (Marjory Eckett). A celt and mortar-stone [from Corringdon, Devon]. [Early Bronze Age.] Devon

& Cornwall N. & Q., 17, pp. 43–44 + plate. 1932.

6194 Finney (Frank). Flint implements found at Stone, Kidderminster. [Bronze Age.] B'ham Arch. Soc., Trans., 54 (1929–30), pp. 75–76. 1932.

6195 Gardner (J. W.). A flint "point" from Callow hill. [Figure. Neolithic.] Proc. Somerset Arch. Soc., 96 (1951), pp. 231–33. 1952.

6196 —— Mesolithic finds from the Bath downs. [Micro-burin. *See also* p. 146, The micro-burin in north Somerset, by C. M. Sykes.] Arch. News Letter, 5, p. 74. 1954.

6197 Gould (J. T.) *and* **Gathercole** (P. W.). Flint implements from near Bourne Poole, Aldridge [Staffs.]. [Figure.] B'ham Arch. Soc., Trans., 74 (1956), pp. 53–55. 1958.

6198 Gracie (H. S.). Surface flints from Leonard Stanley, Gloucestershire. [4 figures. Mesolithic.] Trans. Bristol & Glos. Arch. Soc., 60, pp. 180–89. 1938.

6199 —— Surface flints from Long Newnton, Gloucestershire. [10 figures.] Trans. Bristol & Glos. Arch. Soc., 63, pp. 172–89. 1942.

6200 Gray (Harold St. George). A remarkably thin arrowhead from Cannington Park camp, near Bridgwater, Somerset. [Figure.] Man, 6, pp. 149–50. 1906.

6201 —— An [thin] arrowhead of rare type from Banwell camp, Somerset. [Figure.] Man, 7, p. 56. 1907.

6202 —— A remarkably thin arrowhead from Cannington Park camp, near Bridgwater. [2 figures.] Proc. Somerset Arch. Soc., 52 (1906), pp. 157–59. 1907.

6203 —— Palaeolith from the Axe gravels [Broom, Somerset]. [Figure.] Antiq. J., 7, pp. 71–72. 1927.

6204 —— Stone axe found at North Patherton, Somerset. [Figure. Neolithic.] Antiq. J., 23, p. 52. 1943.

6205 Grinsell (Leslie Valentine). A Palaeolithic implement from Beckford, Worcestershire. Ant. J., 40, 1960, 67–68.

6206 Guthrie (A.). Sickle flint from Knill's monument [St. Ives]. [Figure.] Proc. West Cornwall F.C., N.S. I, p. 85. 1954.

6207 Hodgson (Thomas Vere). Memorandum on flint implements found on

Dartmoor. Rpt. & Trans. Devon Assoc., 51, pp. 175–76 + plate. 1919.

6208 Horne (Ethelbert). An ornamental spindle-whorl [from Camerton Somerset]. [Figure. Early Iron Age.] [Stone.] Antiq. J., 15, p. 199. 1935.

6209 Jones (Herbert C.). Flints of the Clun valley. [2 figures.] Trans. Caradoc & Severn Valley F.C., 9, pp. 263–67. 1934.

6210 Jones (John). On some flint implements, and the geological age of the deposit in which they were found upon Stroud hill. Proc. Cotteswold Nat. Club. 3, pp. 97–111 + plate. 1865.

6211 Kendall (Henry George Ommanney). Flint implements in Cornwall [various dates]. Proc. PSEA, 2 i, 1914/15, 58–59.

6212 —— Eoliths from Braydon [Glos.] and elsewhere. Proc. Cotteswold N.F.C., 22, pp. 123–35 + 4 plates. 1925.

6213 Lacaille (Armand Donald). Flaked quartz tools from [Camborne,] Cornwall. [Figure.] Antiq. J., 22, pp. 215–16. 1942.

6214 —— Palaeoliths from the lower reaches of the Bristol Avon. [4 figures + map.] Antiq. J., 34, pp. 1–27 + 2 plates + map. 1954.

6215 —— Artifacts of Graig Lwyd rock from Nailsworth, Glos. [Figure + 2 maps. Late Neolithic.] Trans. Bristol & Glos. Arch. Soc., 74 (1955), pp. 5–14 + plate. 1956.

6216 Lowe (Harford J.). The stone implements from the Breccia of Kents Cavern [?Chellean]. J. Torquay nat. Hist. Soc., 2, 1916, 80–87 + 1 plate.

6217 Lucy (W. C.). A slight history of flint implements, with especial reference to our own and adjacent areas. Proc. Cotteswold Nat. Club, 10, pp. 22–38 + 4 plates. 1892.

6218 Marriot (R. A.). The astronomical clue to the age of the stone implements in Kent's Cavern. J. Torquay nat. Hist. Soc., 2, 1919, 257–70 + 2 figures.

6219 Marsden (J. G.). Core cultures at the Land's End. [?Aurignacian/ Magdalenian/Azilian.] Proc. prehist. Soc. EA, 3 i, 1918/19, 59–66 + 3 figures + 2 plates.

6220 —— Note on flint and other stone implements from south-west Pen-

with. J. Roy. Instn. Cornwall, 20, pp. 483–96 + 10 plates + map. 1920.

6221 —— Flint implements of Le Moustier type from Camborne. J. Roy. Instn. Cornwall, 21, pp. 48–55 + 3 plates. 1922.

6222 Moir (James Reid). Chert implments of Clacton type from the "clay and flints" of south-east Devon. Proc. Devon Archaeol. Expl. Soc., 2, p. 40. 1933.

6223 Montague (Leopold A. D.). Flint implements on Lundy. [Figure. See also pp. 302, 341.] Devon & Cornwall N. & Q., 16, pp. 257–59. 1931.

6224 Moore (Henry Cecil). Remarks on flint flakes found near Ledbury. [Neolithic.] Trans. Woolhope N.F.C., 1893–94, pp. 191–93. 1896.

6225 Moysey (C. F.). Neolithic flint implements from West Somerset. Trans. & Proc. Torquay nat. Hist. Soc., 5, 1928, 81–89 + 1 plate.

6226 New (Herbert). Neolithic scraper [found in Selly Oak, 1915]. B'ham Arch. Soc., Trans., 42 (1916), p. 78. 1917.

6227 Nicol (Mary D.). Three Levalloisian flakes from Broom, Chard. [3 figures.] Proc. Devon Archaeol. Expl. Soc., 2, pp. 120–23. 1934.

6228 Oakley (Kenneth Page). Cowry shell and flint cores from Ashen Plains, Dursley, Gloucestershire. [2 figures. Neolithic—Bronze Age.] Trans. Bristol & Glos. Arch. Soc., 64, pp. 89–95. 1943.

6229 O'Neil (Helen E.). A Palaeolithic flint implement from Bourton-on-the-Water. [Middle Acheulian?] Proc. Cotteswold Naturalists F.C., 34 iv, 1965, 225–27 + 1 figure.

6230 Oswald (Adrian). Macehead from Bloxwich [Staffs.]. [?date.] B'ham Arch. Soc., Trans., 71 (1953), p. 135 + plate. 1955.

6231 Parfitt (Edward). On Palaeolithic implements . . . found at Broom, in the valley of the Axe. Rpt. & Trans. Devon Assoc., 16, pp. 501–04. 1884.

6232 Passmore (A. D.). Rarity of large flint implements in Gloucestershire. [No indigenous flint, etc.] Man, 14, pp. 134–35. 1914.

6233 Peake (A. E.). Surface Palaeolithic implements from the Chilterns. Proc. PSEA, 2 iv, 1917/18, 578–87 + 10 figures.

6234 Pengelly (William). Notes on vessels made of Bovey lignite and of Kimmeridge coal. Rpt. & Trans. Devon Assoc., 4, pp. 105–08. 1871.

6235 —— On a flint implement found on Torre-Abbey Sands, Torbay [in Submerged Forest]. Advm. Sci., 1883, 564–65.

6236 Phillips (E. N. Masson). Bunter quartzite artifacts from coastal sites in South Devon. [5 figures + map.] Rpt. & Trans. Devon Assoc., 90, pp. 129–45 + 3 plates. 1958.

6237 Pickard (Ransom). A Palaeolithic implement from Exeter and a note on the Exeter gravels. [Figure.] Proc. Devon Archaeol. Expl. Soc., 2, pp. 207–12 + plate + map. 1935.

6238 —— Another hand-axe from [Exeter,] Devon. [Figure.] Antiq. J., 16, pp. 93–95. 1936.

6239 —— A Neolithic celt from near Moretonhampstead. [Pp. 172–73 + map. List of Devon celts and hammers. *See also* 80 (1948), pp. 235–36, notes on list by R. H. Worth.] Rpt. & Trans. Devon Assoc., 78, pp. 171–75 + plate + map. 1946.

6240 Pierce (Kate). Neolithic arrowheads [from Nether Swell, Glos.]. [Figure.] Antiq. J., 9, p. 35. 1929.

6241 Pitchford (Wilfred Watkins). A perforated stone implement from Dudmaston, nr. Bridgnorth. (Supplementary note, by Lily F. Chilty.) [Figure.] Trans. Shropshire Archaeol. Soc., 52, pp. 129–38 + plate + map. 1947.

6242 —— A quern-stone of uncommon type [from Smestow, Staffs.]. [Neolithic.] Trans. Shropshire Archaeol. Soc., 52, pp. 119–21 + plate + map. 1948.

6243 Pritchard (John Emanuel). Celt at Ozleworth. Trans. Bristol & Glos. Arch. Soc., 44, p. 312 + plate. 1922.

6245 Rogers (Ernest Henry). Drift Palaeoliths from the Teign valley. Proc. Devon Archaeol. Expl. Soc., 5, pp. 27–28. 1953.

6246 Royle (Ernest). A stone hammer found at Aller Vale, Newton Abbot [Wessex type]. Proc. Devon Arch. Expl. Soc., v iv, 1956, 122–23.

6247 Seaby (Wilfred Arthur). Palaeolithic hand-axe from Cheddon Fitzpaine. [Figure.] Proc. Somerset Arch. Soc., 95 (1950), pp. 168–69. 1951.

6248 Shaw (C. T.). A stone implement from Thorverton [Devon]. Proc. Devon Archaeol. Expl. Soc., 2, p. 124. 1934.

6249 Shotton (Frederick William). Palaeolithic implements found near Coventry. [Acheulian.] Proc. PSEA, 6 iii, 1930, 174–81 + 3 figures + 1 plate.

6250 —— Early Palaeolithic implements from [Baginton,] near Coventry. B'ham Arch. Soc., Trans., 54 (1929–30), pp. 72–73. 1932.

6251 —— Flint implements from fields around Coventry. [Figure.] Proc. Coventry N.H. Soc., 1, pp. 65–71. 1933.

6252 —— Stone implements of Warwickshire. B'ham Arch. Soc., Trans., 58 (1934), pp. 37–52 + 8 plates. 1937.

6253 —— A stone battle-axe found at Coventry. [Early Bronze Age.] B'ham Arch. Soc., Trans., 60 (1936), p. 151 + plate. 1940.

6254 —— Graig Lwyd axes from the Coventry neighbourhood. [2 figures.] Proc. Coventry N.H. Soc., 2, pp. 76–81. 1949.

6255 —— Two unrecorded stone implements from the Coventry district. [Figure. i. Polished stone axe from Corley moor (Neolithic); ii. Small hand-axe from the river Sowe (Lower Palaeolithic).] Proc. Coventry N.H. Soc., 2, pp. 177–79. 1952.

6256 —— Notes on two stone axes from [King's Norton and Lapworth] near Birmingham. B'ham Arch. Soc., Trans., 68 (1949–50), pp. 125–26 + plate. 1952.

6257 —— Neolithic axes from Shenstone, Orgreave (near Alrewas) and Brereton (near Rugeley), south Staffordshire and Birmingham [Handsworth]. B'ham Arch. Soc., Trans., 73 (1955), pp. 117–18 + plate. 1957.

6258 —— Notes on two flint arrowheads from Warwickshire. [Neolithic.] Proc. Coventry Dist. nat. Hist. & Scient. Soc., iii 2 (1958), 53–54 + 1 figure.

6259 —— Two Acheulian implements from the Warwickshire–Worcestershire Avon. Proc. Coventry Dist. N.H. & S. Soc., iii 4, 1960, 110–12 + 1 figure.

6260 —— Two hand-axes from the Warwickshire Avon. [Middle Acheulian and Late Acheulian.] Trans. Birmingham Arch. Soc., 79, 1960/61, 120–22 + 2 figures.

6261 Smallwood (G. W.). Flint and other stone implements found at Mary Tavy, Devon. [BA.] Proc. PSEA, 2 iii, 1916/17, 349–51 + 1 figure.

6262 Smith (Elsie E.). Flint implements from Sidmouth. [2 figures. Eoliths and discoidal flint knives of the Bronze Age. (3 figures. Early Bronze Age tranchets, etc.).] Proc. Devon Archaeol. Expl. Soc., 3, pp. 42–44, 167–71. 1946/47.

6263 —— Notes on a series of flints from Woodbury Common. [Mesolithic and Neolithic "petit-tranchet".] Proc. Devon Archaeol. Exploration Soc., v iv, 1956, 117–21 + 3 figures.

6264 Smith (Isobel F.). Transversely sharpened axe from Cornwall. Proc. prehist. Soc., 29, 1963, 429 + 1 figure.

6265 Smith (Reginald Allender) *and* **Rogers** (Ernest Henry). Five Palaeolithic implements from the Kingswear district. [5 figures.] Proc. Devon Archaeol. Expl. Soc., 3, pp. 51–52. 1937.

6266 —— Notes on a Neolithic celt from Torquay. Trans. & Proc. Torquay nat. Hist. Soc., 7, 1938, 239 + 1 plate.

6267 Somervail (Alexander). Notes on a collection of worked flints from the neighbourhood of North Bovey, recently acquired by the Torquay Natural History Society. Jl. Torquay nat. Hist. Soc., 1, 1909, 8–11.

6268 Terry (W. Neville). A Neolithic tanged arrow-head from Withington, Glos. [Figure.] Trans. Bristol & Glos. Arch. Soc., 70 (1951), p. 142. 1952.

6269 Thomas (Charles). A polished stone adze from St. Just-in-Penwith. [Figure.] Proc. West Cornwall F.C., N.S. 1, pp. 90–92. 1954.

6271 Ward (Joseph Heald). Neolithic axe-head at Silverton. Devon N. & Q., 2, p. 125. 1902.

6272 Wedlake (A. L.) *and* **Wedlake** (D. J.). Some Palaeoliths from the Doniford gravels on the coast of West Somerset. Proc. Somerset. A. & N.H.S., 107, 1963, 93–100 + 12 figures.

6273 Whitehouse (D. B.). A flint dagger of the EBA from Diglis, Worcester. Trans. Worcs. A.S., Vol. 37, N.S. 1960, 24–26 + 1 figure.

6274 Whitley (Nicholas). On some flint arrowheads (?) from near Baggy Point, North Devon. J. Geol. Soc. London, 18, 1862, 114–15.

6275 —— The flint implements from Drift, not authentic. [15 figures.] J. Roy. Instn. Cornwall, 1 ii, pp. 19–49. 1864.

6276 —— On recent flint finds in the South-West of England. [Various.] [*See also* note (anon.) in Arch. Camb., 3rd S. 12, pp. 77–81, 1866.] Trans. R. Inst. Cornwall, 2, 1866–67, 121–24.

6277 —— A critical examination of the flints from Brixham cavern, said to be knives and human implements. pp. 28 + plate. 8°. London, 1877. [*Reprinted from* J. Victoria Institute, 11.]

6278 Witchell (Edwin). On a deposit at Stroud containing flint implements, land and freshwater shells etc. [flakes, cores, arrowheads — not described]. J. Geol. Soc. London, 20, 1864, 378 + figures.

6279 Worth (Richard Hansford). A flint implement of Palaeolithic type from [Brent moor,] Dartmoor. Rpt. & Trans. Devon Assoc., 63, pp. 359–60 + plate. 1931.

6280 —— On a stone implement found near Wheal Jewell, Marytavy. Rpt. & Trans. Devon Assoc., 66, pp. 315–16 + plate. 1934.

6281 Wright (J. A.) *and* **Shotton** (F. W.). A Graig Llwyd celt from Gibbet hill. [Figure. Neolithic—from axe factory of Graig Llwyd, Penmaenmawr.] Proc. Coventry N.H. Soc., 1, p. 116. 1935.

6282 Young (Thomas). Pigmy flint implements in north Devon. Rpt. & Trans. Devon Assoc., 38, pp. 261–69. 1906.

(d) Zone 4 [CBA Groups 3, 4, 5, 6]

6283 Alcock (Leslie). Polished stone axes of Lake District origin from Leeds. [Figure. Neolithic.] Yorks. Archaeol. J., 39, pp. 391–94. 1958.

6284 Anderson (T. W.). Axe-hammer found near Silloth. [Late Bronze Age.] Trans. Cumb. & Westm. Ant. Soc., N.S. 17, p. 254. 1917.

6285 Andrew (Walter Jonathan).

Discovery of a Neolithic celt on Rowarth moor. [Plate opposite p. 241 in vol. 25.] J. Derbs. Archaeol. Soc., 24, p. 172. 1902.

6286 [Anon.] A Neolithic hammer [from Foolow]. [Figure. Now in Sheffield Museum.] Yorks. N. & Q. (ed. Forshaw), 1, p. 276. 1904.

6287 [Anon.] Prehistoric axe: Yorkshire find at West Melton. [*c.* 4000 B.C.] J. Brit. Archaeol. Ass., N.S. 28, p. 132. 1922.

6288 [Anon.] A palaeolith from Leicester. [Figure.] Antiq. J., 12, pp. 306–07. 1932.

6289(a) [Anon.] Polished stone axe from Acton Brook. [Figure.] J. Chester & N. Wales Arch. Soc., N.S. 39, p. 109. 1952.

6289(b) [Anon.] Granite axe from Hollowmoor heath. [Figure.] J. Chester & N. Wales Arch. Soc., N.S. 39, p. 109. 1952.

6290 [Anon.] A perforated stone axe from Edge. [Figure.] J. Chester & N. Wales Arch. Soc., N.S., 41, p. 85. 1954.

6291 [Anon.] A perforated stone axe from Bexton. [Figure.] J. Chester & N. Wales Arch. Soc., N.S. 41, p. 85. 1954.

6292 [Anon.] An expanding flint axe from Lyme park [Chester]. [Bronze Age.] J. Chester & N. Wales Arch. Soc., N.S. 42, p. 48. 1955.

6293 [Anon.] Worked flints from Hoole [near Chester]. [Figure. Early Bronze Age. Now in Grosvenor Museum, Chester.] J. Chester Arch. Soc., 43, p. 47. 1956.

6294 [Anon.] [Polished] stone axe from Kingsley [Cheshire]. [Figure. Now in Grosvenor Museum, Chester.] J. Chester & N. Wales Arch. Soc., 44, p. 51. 1957.

6295 [Anon.] [Polished] stone axe from Oxton, Birkenhead. [Figure.] J. Chester & N. Wales Arch. Soc., 44, p. 52. 1957.

6296 [Anon.] Circular hammer-stone from Frodsham. [Figure. Bronze Age.] J. Chester & N. Wales Arch. Soc., 44, pp. 52–53. 1957.

6297 [Anon.] Flint arrowhead from Marton. [Figure. Now in Grosvenor Museum, Chester.] J. Chester & N. Wales Arch. Soc., 44, p. 53. 1957.

6298 Armstrong (Albert Leslie). The evidence of S. York's surface implements relative to classification and dating. Proc. prehist. Soc. EA, 3 ii, 1919/20, 277–89 + 4 figures.

6299 —— Neolithic axe found at Peak Forest [quarry] (Derbs.). J. Brit. Archaeol. Ass., N.S. 31, pp. 262–64. 1925.

6300 —— Notched dagger of flint [from Demon's Dale, Derbyshire]. Antiq. J., 13, pp. 161–62. 1933.

6301 Auden (George Augustus). Two Neolithic implements found near York. [From Aldwark moor, and from Skipwith.] Yorks. Archaeol. J., 20, pp. 256–57 + plate. 1909.

6302 Bailey (Francis Arthur). Neolithic axe found at Whiston [Lancs.]. Trans. Hist. Soc. Lancs. & Ches., 93 (1941), p. 124 + plate. 1942.

6303 —— Stone axe-hammer found at Altcar, 1949. [Figure. Bronze Age.] Trans. Hist. Soc. Lancs. & Ches., 101 (1949). 1950.

6304 Barnes (F.) *and* **Hobbs** (J. L.). Four perforated stone implements from Low Furness. Trans. Cumb. & Westm. Ant. Soc., N.S. 47, pp. 243–45 + plate. 1947.

6305 —— Flint implements from Plain Furness. [Figure.] Trans. Cumb. & Westm. Ant. Soc., N.S. 51, pp. 1–3. 1951.

6306 —— *and* **Hobbs** (J. L.). Implements from Plain Furness. [Figure.] Trans. Cumb. & Westm. Ant. Soc., N.S. 52, p. 178. 1952.

6307(a) Beynon (Vernon Bryan Crowther). The Neolithic find at Great Casterton, Rutland, August 1905, with a note on a Neolithic celt found at Oakham. Rutland Mag., 3, pp. 13–21 + plate. 1907.

6307(b) Bird (W. C. Soden). A stone axe-hammer [from Gunnerton quarry, Northumberland]. Proc. Soc. Antiq. Newc., 4th S. 10, p. 63. 1942.

6308 Birley (Eric). Stone objects from Ambleside. [1 figure]. Trans. Cumb. & Westm. Ant. Soc., N.S. LXI, 1961, 297–98.

6309 Blake (Brian). An axe-hammer from Solway Moss. [Figure. Now at Tullie House.] Trans. Cumb. & Westm. Ant. Soc., N.S. 55, pp. 317–18 + plate. 1956.

6310 Bowles (Charles Eyre Bradshaw). Neolithic celt. [Polished stone axe from Taddington, Derbs.] J. Derbs. Archaeol. Soc., 30, p. 142 + plate. 1908.

6311 Briscoe (John Potter). Ancient stone implements [in Derbyshire]. [List of places where found.] Notts. & Derbs. N. & Q., 2, pp. 122–23. 1894.

6312 Brooke (Susan). A stone axe and other finds from the Yearsley district. [Neolithic and Bronze Age. Plan.] Yorks. Archaeol. J., 38, pp. 359–66 + 3 plates. 1954.

6313 Brunner (Roscoe). Stone celt from [Acton brook, Acton Bridge,] Cheshire. [Figure.] Antiq. J., 7, pp. 60–61. 1927.

6314 Buckley (Francis). Yorkshire gravers [microremains]. PPSEA, 3 iv, 1921–22, 542–47 + 3 figures.

6315 —— Early Tardenois remains at Bamborough, etc. [2 figures (pigmy flints; now in Blackgate Museum).] Proc. Soc. Antiq. Newc., 3rd S. 10, pp. 319–23. 1922.

6316 Chew (John R.). Flint adze from Bacup [Lancs.] [Figure.] Antiq. J., 8, p. 90. 1928.

6317 Chitty (Lily Frances). Perforated stone hammer from Crimpsall, Doncaster. [Bronze Age. Figure.] Yorks. Archaeol. J., 37, pp. 128–30. 1949.

6318 Clark (E. Kitson). Polished stone axehead found [at Norristhorpe,] near Heckmondwike. Yorks. Archaeol. J., 20, p. 104. 1909.

6319 —— Find of a [thin butted] celt [on Booth moor] near Halifax. Yorks Archaeol. J., 26, pp. 304–05. 1922.

6320 Cockerton (R. W. P.). A palaeolith from Hopton. [Figure (hand axe).] J. Derbs. Archaeol. Soc., 74, pp. 153–55 + plate. 1954.

6321 Collins (E. R.). The discovery of an early Palaeolithic implement in Yorkshire. PPSEA, 3 iv, 1921/22, 603–06 + 2 plates + 1 figure.

6322 —— The Palaeolithic implements of Nidderdale, Yorkshire. Proc. PSEA, 6 iii, 1930, 156–73 + 14 figures.

6323 Cooper (John). A Neolithic celt from Bason Bank, south Cumberland. Trans. Cumb. & Westm. Ant. Soc., N.S. 18, p. 105 + plate. 1918.

6324 Coupland (Florence) *and* **Coupland** (George). Further Tardenoisian discoveries on the north-east coast. Proc. prehist. Soc., N.S. 1, 1935, 154.

6325 Cowen (John David). Stone axe found near Longhoughton. Proc. Soc. Antiq. Newc., 4th S. 6, pp. 202–03 + plate. 1934.

6326 —— A Bronze Age axe-head from Broomwood camp, Edlingham. Proc. Soc. Antiq. Newc., 4th S. 10, p. 204. 1944.

6327 Cowling (E. T.). Flint implement sites in mid-Wharfedale. [2 figures + plan.] Yorks. Archaeol. J., 33, pp. 34–48. 1938.

6328 —— Two discoidal flint knives from Yorkshire. Yorks. Arch. Journ., 41 (i), 1963, 17–18 + 1 figure.

6329 Cowper (Henry Swainson). Unrecorded and unusual types of stone implements. [2 figures. Local stone implements (Troutbeck, Westm.; Hawkeshead and Coniston, Lancs.).] Trans. Cumb. & Westm. Ant. Soc., N.S. 34, pp. 91–100. 1934.

6330 Cox (E. W.). Flints found in Wirral. J. Arch. Soc. Chester, N.S. 5, pp. 108–11 + plate. 1895.

6331 Croft (W. R.). Discovery of stone and flint weapons and other implements near [Cupwith hill, Marsden,] Huddersfield. Yorks. Archaeol. J., 9, pp. 255–56. 1886.

6332 Cross (*Hon.* Marjorie). Two stone axe-hammers from Silecroft [Cumberland]. [Figure.] Trans. Cumb. & Westm. Ant. Soc., N.S. 49, pp. 213–14. 1949.

6333 —— A rough stone axe from the Millom area. [Figure.] Trans. Cumb. & Westm. Ant. Soc., N.S. 50, p. 199. 1950.

6334 Cudworth (W.). Implement from the Calf hole, Skyrethorns, Upper Wharfedale, Yorkshire. [Figure. Palaeolithic.] Reliquary, N.[3rd]S. 1, pp. 160–61. 1895.

6335 Davies (J.) *and* **Rankine** (W. F.). Mesolithic flint axes from the West Riding of Yorkshire. Yorks. Arch. Journ., 40 (ii), pp. 209–14 + 3 figures. 1960.

6336 —— A polished discoidal flint knife from Slatepit Moor, Lancashire: a communication. Trans. Lancs. &

Cheshire Antiq. Soc., 71, 1961, 160–62 + 1 figure.

6337 Davis (James W.). On the discovery of chipped flints beneath the peat on the Yorkshire moors, near Halifax. Yorks. Archaeol. J., 6, pp. 125–28. 1881.

6338 Dawkins (*Sir* William Boyd). On the stone mining tools from Alderley Edge, Cheshire. J. Anth. Inst., 5, pp. 2–5 + plate. 1875.

6339 —— Neolithic axe found at Great Budworth, Cheshire. Trans. Lancs. & Ches. Ant. Soc., 39 (1921), p. 195 + plate. 1923.

6340 Dickinson (J. C.). A stone axe of the Pointed Butt type from Lindale-in-Cartmel. [Figure. Early Neolithic.] Trans. Cumb. & Westm. Ant. Soc., N.S. 35, pp. 70–71. 1935.

6341 Dixon (D. D.). Ancient British flint implements found at Low Farnham, Coquetdale. Hist. Berwick. Nat. Club, 10, pp. 347–49 + 2 plates. 1883.

6342 Dobson (John). Neolithic implements found in Furness. [i. Stone hammer found at Backbarrow; ii. Polished celt from Baycliff. (Stone hammer from Walney.).] Trans. Cumb. & Westm. Ant. Soc., N.S. 14, pp. 272–73 + plate, pp. 492–93 + plate. 1914.

6343 Dolby (M. J.). A discoidal polished flint knive from Whitwell [pre-Beaker Secondary Neolithic]. D.A.J., 84, 1964, 120–23 + 1 figure.

6344 Dymond (D. P.). Four prehistoric implements from the Vale of York [3 polished stone axes and 1 flint dagger]. Yorks. Arch. Journ., 41 (ii), 1964, 178–82 + 4 figures.

6345 Egglestone (William Morley). Neolithic flint implements in Weardale. [2 figures. (3 figures.)] Proc. Soc. Antiq. Newc., 3rd S. 4, pp. 205–08; 5, pp. 106–07, 115–17. 1910–11.

6346 —— [Three Neolithic celts found at Stanhope in upper Weardale.] Proc. Soc. Antiq. Newc., 3rd S. 7, pp. 178–79 + plate. 1916.

6347 —— Prehistoric stone axes from upper Weardale. [Figure.] Proc. Soc. Antiq. Newc., 3rd S. 7, pp. 194–96. 1916.

6348 Fair (Mary Cicely). A note on some west Cumberland stone axes. Trans. Cumb. & Westm. Ant. Soc., N.S. 35, pp. 259–61. 1935.

6349 —— A petit tranchet derivative from Eskmeals sandhills [west Cumberland]. Trans. Cumb. & Westm. Ant. Soc., N.S. 38, pp. 311–12 + plate. 1938.

6350 —— Flint knife [from Seascale]. [Figure. Bronze Age.] Trans. Cumb. & Westm. Ant. Soc., N.S. 38, pp. 312–13. 1938.

6351 Fell (Clare Isobel). Three polished stone axes. [2 figures. From Kirkby Thore and Ulverston.] Trans. Cumb. & Westm. Ant. Soc., N.S. 54, pp. 1–4. 1955.

6352 Ford (T. D.) *and* **Hughes** (R. G.). Two perforated quartzite maceheads from Derbyshire. [Mesolithic.] D.A.J., 83, 1963, 102–03.

6353 Fox (W. Storrs). Bronze Age Whetstone [from Hungry Bentley]. [Figure.] J. Derbs. Archaeol. Soc., N.S. 2, pp. 373–74. 1927.

6354 Frankland (Edward Percy). Flint implement found at Ash fell, Ravenstonedale. Trans. Cumb. & Westm. Ant. Soc., N.S. 30, p. 222. 1930.

6355 Garlic (S. L.). A quern stone found at Stretton. J. Derbs. Archaeol. Soc., 75, pp. 155–56. 1955.

6356 Gatty (Reginald A.). Pigmy flint implements. [2 figures.] Trans. Lancs. & Ches. Ant. Soc., 20 (1902), pp. 219–33. 1903.

6357 Gray (T.). A stone axe from Little Salkeld [Cumberland]. Trans. Cumb. & Westm. Ant. Soc., N.S. 46, p. 292. 1946.

6358 Grove (Leonard Robert Allen). Flat-sided axe from Wykeham, near Scarborough. [Figure.] Yorks. Archaeol. J., 34, pp. 2–3. 1938.

6359 Gunstone (A. J. H.). Some prehistoric implements found in West Derbyshire. D.A.J., 82, 1962, 105–06.

6360 Handley (William). Stone axe found at Weston Point [near Runcorn]. [Figure. Neolithic.] Trans. Hist. Soc. Lancs. & Ches., 55/56 (1903/04, N.S. 19/20), pp. 326–27. 1905.

6361 Harrison (Joseph). Some Brotherelkeld finds. [Stone axes and sling balls.] Trans. Cumb. & Westm. Ant. Soc., N.S., 37 p. 216 + 2 plates. 1937.

6362 Heathcote (John Percy). Flint adze found at Oldham's farm, Newhaven [Derbs.]. [Figure.] [Beaker.] J. Derbs.

Archaeol. Soc., 59 (N.S. 12, 1938), pp. 96–97. 1939.

6363 Henley (Doreth) *Baroness*. Stone implements found in the parish of Lanercost, Cumberland. [Bronze Age.] Trans. Cumb. & Westm. Ant. Soc., N.S. 31, pp. 135–36 + plate. 1931.

6364 Himsworth (J. B.). Some flint artifacts from local sites. Trans. Hunter. Arch. Soc., 5, pp. 239–40 + 2 plates. 1943.

6365 Hogg (Robert). A perforated stone axe-hammer from Annfield, Cockermouth [Cumberland]. Trans. Cumb. & Westm. Ant. Soc., N.S. 50, p. 202. 1950.

6366 —— Millstone, Birdoswald. [1 figure.] (Native.) Trans. Cumb. & Westm. Ant. & Arch. Soc., N.S. 62, pp. 322–23. 1962.

6367 —— Perforated stone axe-hammer, Temple Sowerby. [1 figure.] Trans. Cumb. & Westm. Ant. & Arch. Soc., N.S. 62, pp. 324–25. 1962.

6368 —— Polished stone axe. [1 figure.] Trans. Cumb. & Westm. Ant. & Arch. Soc., N.S. 64, pp. 373–74. 1964.

6369 Howchin (W.). Notes on a find of pre-historic implements in Allendale, with notice of similar finds in the surrounding district. [Neolithic—BA?] Nat. Hist. Trans. N'umberland & Durham, 7, 1878–80, 210–22.

6370 Hughes (R. G.). Note on a quartzite macehead with hour-glass perforation. [Mesolithic.] J. Derbs. Archaeol. Soc., 76, p. 64. 1956.

6371 Hume (Abraham). On certain implements of the stone period. Hist. Soc. Lancs. & Ches., Proc., 3, pp. 32–50 + 3 plates. 1851.

6372 Jackson (Edwin). On a stone celt found near Cockermouth. [Late Neolithic.] Trans. Cumb. & Westm. Ant. Soc., N.S. 6, pp. 149–50. 1906.

6373 Jackson (John Wilfrid). A lance-point of Upper Palaeolithic type from Victoria cave, Settle, Yorkshire. Antiq. J., 25, pp. 147–48 + plate. 1945.

6374 —— Note on a perforated stone hammer found at Chelmorton. J. Derbs. Archaeol. Soc., 72 (N.S. 25), p. 124. 1952.

6375 Jobey (George). A polished stone axe from Haydon Bridge, Northumberland. [Figure.] Arch. Æliana, 4 S. 32, pp. 347–48. 1959.

6376 —— Three polished stone axeheads from Northumberland. [Neolithic.] Arch. Æliana, 39, 1961, 378–80 + 1 figure.

6377 Kaye (Walter Jenkinson). A polished celt found at Harrogate. Yorks. Archaeol. J., 26, p. 188. 1922.

6378 Kelly (Paul Vincent). An unfinished stone axe from Barrow [-in-Furness]. Trans. Cumb. & Westm. Ant. Soc., N.S. 36, pp. 227–28. 1936.

6379 Kent (B. W. J.). A Bronze Age whetstone from Carpley Green, Wensleydale. [Figure.] Yorks. Archaeol. J., 33, pp. 115–16. 1938.

6380 —— A polished flint axe from Harrogate. [Figure. Late Neolithic.] Yorks. Archaeol. J., 33, pp. 116–17. 1938.

6381 Law (R.) *and* **Horsefall** (James). An account of small flint implements found beneath peat on the Pennine Chain [microliths]. Advm. Sci., 1884, 924.

6382 Leach (George Bertram). Flint implements from Worsthorne moors, Lancashire. [5 figures + plan. Mesolithic—Bronze Age.] Trans. Hist. Soc. Lancs. & Ches., 103 (1951), pp. 1–22. 1952.

6383 Leadman (Alexander Dionysius Hobson). Discovery of flint arrowheads near Boroughbridge. Yorks. Archaeol. J., 7, p. 495. 1882.

6384 Legh (*Hon.* Richard). Jadeite celt from [Lyme Park, N.E.] Cheshire. [Late Neolithic.] Antiq. J., 12, p. 167 + plate. 1932.

6385 McIntyre (James). Four polished stone axes [3 from Belmont and one from Keswick]. Trans. Cumb. & Westm. Ant. Soc., N.S. 37, pp. 152–54 + 2 plates. 1937.

6386 Manby (T. G.). A Creswellian flint point from Minning Low. DAJ, 82, 1962, 104–05 + 1 figure.

6387 Monkman (Charles). Prehistoric remains in the gravel beds at Malton [Yorks.]. [Polished stone axe.] Reliquary, 8, pp. 184–85 + plate. 1868.

6388 —— On ancient flint and stone implements from the surface soil of Yorkshire. Yorks. Arch. J., 1, pp. 24–40 + 3 plates. 1870.

6389 —— On the finding of flint implements in the valley-gravels and in the Hessle clay of Yorkshire. (Supplementary remarks.) Yorks. Arch. J., I, pp. 41–57 + 2 plates; 334–36. 1870.

6390 Moorhouse (Anthony). Stone implements from the Kirkby Londsdale district. Trans. Cumb. & Westm. Ant. Soc., N.S. 7, pp. 64–66 + 2 plates. 1907.

6391 North (Oliver Henry). Some recent local finds of stone implements. [Stone hammers, Bronze Age (Figure).] Trans. Cumb. & Westm. Ant. Soc., N.S. 34, pp. 113–15 + 2 plates; 36, pp. 129–131 + 4 plates; 37, pp. 155–56 + 2 plates. 1934–37.

6392 —— A stone axe hammer from Threlkeld. Trans. Cumb. & Westm. Ant. Soc., N.S. 43, p. 200 + plate. 1943.

6393 —— A polished celt [from Culgaith] and an axe-hammer [from Swarthmoor, Ulverston]. Trans. Cumb. & Westm. Ant. Soc., N.S. 45, pp. 191–192 + plate. 1945.

6394 —— A polished stone axe from Holme, Westmorland. Trans. Cumb. & Westm. Ant. Soc., N.S. 48, p. 217 + plate. 1948.

6395 —— Another polished stone axe-head from Yealand [Conyers]. Trans. Cumb. & Westm. Ant. Soc., N.S. 57, p. 170. 1951.

6396 Nuttall (T. E.). The occurrence of palaeoliths in north-east Lancashire. Proc. PSEA, 2 i, 1914/15, 61–71 + 6 plates.

6398 Palmer (L. S.). Another palaeolith from Yorkshire. [Figure + map. Irton, near Scarborough.] Man, 34, pp. 86–88. 1934.

6399 Pearson (T. Gibson). Two stone implements found in Furness. [Late Neolithic.] Trans. Cumb. & Westm. Ant. Soc., N.S. 11, p. 483 + plate (annular stone from Barrow-in-Furness). 1911.

6400 Phelps (Joseph James). Stone implement found at Winton, Eccles [Lancs.]. [Neolithic.] Trans. Lancs. & Ches. Ant. Soc., 40 (1922–23), pp. 43–44 + plate. 1925.

6401 Pickering (A. J.). Flint implements from the ploughlands of south-west Leicestershire. [Neolithic.] Proc. PSEA, 2 iv, 1917/18, 549–63 + 4 figures + 4 plates.

6402 Plint (R. G.). Notes: Stone axe-hammer from Skelsmergh. Trans. Cumb. & Westm. Ant. & Arch. Soc., N.S. 60, p. 200. 1960.

6403 —— Notes: Stone axe roughout from Scout Scar. Underbarrow Scar nr. Kendal. Trans. Cumb. & Westm. Ant. & Arch. Soc., N.S. 60, pp. 200–01, 1960.

6404 —— Flint axe from Whitbarrow [note] S. Westm. Trans. Cumb. & Westm. Ant. & Arch. Soc., N.S., 64, p. 376. 1964.

6405 —— Flint scraper from Great Langdale [note]. Trans. Cumb. & Westm. Ant. & Arch. Soc., N.S. 64, pp. 376–77.

6406 Posnansky (M.). A Palaeolithic implement from near Shipley hill, Ratcliffe-on-the-Wreak. With a note on Shipley hill [tumulus]. [Figure + map.] Trans. Leic. Arch. Soc., 31, pp. 30–34 + plate. 1955. 1964.

6407 Preston (H.). Re-chipped greenstone axes [in Yorkshire]. [2 figures.] Vascorlum, 18, pp. 20–22. 1932.

6408 —— Flints from a microlithic industry at Finchale Nab, Co. Durham. Proc. Soc. Antiq. Newc., 4th S. 8, pp. 162–63. 1938.

6409 Priestley (J. H.). Local flints [Yorks.] and their prehistoric sequence. Trans. Halifax Antiq. Soc., 1936, pp. 93–133; 3 plates (interpaginated). 1936.

6410 Radley (Jeffrey). Late Upper Palaeolithic and mesolithic surface sites in South Yorkshire. Trans. Hunter archaeol. Soc., 9 i, 1964, 38–50 + 4 figures.

6411 Riley (D. N.). A group of flint arrowheads from Ughill Moor, near Sheffield. [Clark's type H: hollow base, and G: convex base.] Trans. Hunter archaeol. Soc., 8 iv, 1962, 236–37 + 1 figure.

6412 Ryde (G. Harry). Two [Neolithic] celts from Barlow and Somersall. J. Derbs. Archaeol. Soc., N.S. 1, pp. 116–17. 1924.

6413 Sheppard (Thomas). Yorkshire Neolithic implements. North Western Naturalist, 1940, pp. 50–135 + 6 plates. 1940.

6414 Shorter (Alfred H.). Discoveries of flints near Stanhope, in Weardale, Durham. [Figure.] Proc. Soc. Antiq. Newc., 4th S. 7, pp. 27–31. 1935.

6415 Simpson (Grace.) A flint arrow-head from Lazonby fell [Cumberland]. [Figure.] Trans. Cumb. & Westm. Ant. Soc., N.S. 51, pp. 170–71. 1951.

6416 Smedley (Norman). A notched flint dagger from Doncaster. [Figure. Early Bronze Age?] Yorks. Archaeol. J., 37, pp. 254–56. 1950.

6417 Smith (D. J.). A grooved stone maul from Greenleighton, near Rothbury. Arch. Æliana, 41, 1963, 230–33 + 1 figure.

6418 —— A grooved stone axe from Co. Durham. Arch. Æliana, 41, 1963, 233–35 + 1 figure.

6419 —— A Quernstone from Nafferton, Northumberland. [Roman Iron Age.] Arch. Æliana, 42, 1964, 290 + 1 figure.

6420 —— Thefts from the Museum (of Antiquities of the University of Newcastle-upon-Tyne). Arch. Æliana, 43, 1965, 318 + 1 plate.

6421 —— A stone battle-axe (from the Hexham district). [EBA.] Arch. Æliana, 43, 1965, 318 + 1 plate.

6422 Smythe (J. A.). Note on a flint implement found [on Braid hill] near Newcastle. Proc. Univ. Durham Phil. Soc., 3, pp. 13–14. 1906.

6423 Southward (John). A stone axe from Silver Tarn, Braystones. [Neolithic.] Trans. Cumb. & Westm. Ant. Soc., N.S. 37, pp. 215–16 + plate. 1937.

6424 Sturge (W. Allen). Thin arrowheads. [From Ringham [nr. Derbs.]. Man, 7, p. 37. 1907.

6425 Sutcliffe (William Henry). Flint implements. Trans. Lancs. & Ches. Ant. Soc., 21 (1903), pp. 111–19 + 5 plates. 1904.

6426 —— *etc.* Pigmy flint implements: their provenance and use. Trans. Lancs. & Ches. Ant. Soc., 30 (1912), pp. 1–27 + plate. 1913.

6427 Taylor (Michael W.). On the discovery of stone moulds for spear-heads at Croglin, Cumberland, and on the process of casting in bronze. [Late Bronze Age. P. 288, list of 15 moulds, with references.] Trans. Cumb. & Westm. Ant. Soc., 7, pp. 279–88 + plate. 1884.

6428 Thomas (Nicholas W. de l'E.) A polished flint axe from Thornborough Circles. (N.R.) [Neolithic.] York.

Arch. Journ., 41 (i), 1963, 14–15 + 1 figure.

6429 Thompson (B. L.). Prehistoric axes from Windermere. [Note.] Trans. Cumb. & Westm. Ant. & Arch. Soc., N.S., 62, p. 330. 1962.

6430 —— A polished stone axe from Grasmere. [Note.] Trans. Cumb. & Westm. Ant. & Arch. Soc., N.S., 63, p. 281. 1963.

6431 Thompson (Frederick Hugh). Miscellanea: Hammer-stone from Agden, Nr. Altrincham. [1 figure.] Journ. Chester Arch. Soc., 45, 1958, 71.

6432 —— Miscellanea: Perforated stone hoe from Stockport. [1 plate.] Chester Arch. Soc. Jl., 46 (1959), 79.

6433 —— Miscellanea: Stone axe-hammer from Old Withington, Nr. Macclesfield. Chester Arch. Soc. Jl., 47 (1960), 33.

6434 —— Miscellanea: Flint knife from Ruabon Mountain. [1 figure.] Chester Arch. Soc. Jl., 48 (1961), 43.

6435 —— Miscellanea: Flint arrow-head from Bickerton Hill. Chester Arch. Soc. Jl., 48 (1961), 43.

6436 —— Miscellanea: Stone axe-hammer from Pinsley Green. [1 figure.] Chester Arch. Soc. Jl., 49, 1962, 57.

6437 —— Miscellanea: Stone axe-hammer from Norbury. [1 figure.] Chester Arch. Soc. Jl., 49, 1962, 57.

6438 Thomson (W. H.). [Perforated stone hammer of Early Bronze Age from Alexandra park, Manchester.] [Figure.] Trans. Lancs. & Ches. Ant. Soc., 59 (1947), pp. 219–20. 1948.

6439 Trechmann (C. T.). Mesolithic flints from the submerged forest at West Hartlepool. [Maglemose.] Proc. prehist. Soc., N.S. 2, 1936, 161–68 + 1 figure + 1 plate.

6440 Vassall (Harry Greame). Neolithic celt [found at Milton, Repton]. J. Derbs. Archaeol. Soc., 32, p. 76 + plate. 1910.

6441 "G. G. W.") *and* **Beer** (Roy Giliad). A stone axe head from Skelton-on-Ure. Yorks. Archaeol. J., 36, p. 130 + plate. 1945.

6442 Walker (John William). Flint implements found near Wakefield. [6 figures.] Antiq. J., 12, pp. 449–51. 1932.

6443 —— Mesolithic flints from the

Wakefield district. [Figure.] Yorks. Archaeol. J., 32, pp. 170–71. 1933.

6444 Warren (S. Hazzledine). Palaeoliths from Nidderdale, Yorkshire. [*See also* p. 62 (note by E. R. Collins); p. 93 (reply).] Arch. News Letter, 3, p. 3. 1950.

6445 Watson (William Henry). Stone implements found at Braystones, Cumberland, with remarks on probable Neolithic settlements in the neighbourhood. [Figure (celt and quern).] Trans. Cumb. & Westm. Ant. Soc., N.S. 3, pp. 91–93. 1903.

6446 Watts (Arthur). Pre-historic axe found near Witton Gilbert, Co. Durham. [Figure + plan.] Proc. Soc. Antiq. Newc., 3rd S. 7, pp. 252–57 + plate. 1915.

6447 —— Notes on flint weapons and tools from Northumbria. Proc. Cotteswold N.F.C., 23, pp. 115–19 + 4 plates. 1928.

6448 Webster (Graham). Stone implements in Cheshire. [2 figures. i. flint flakes from Peckforton mere; ii. Perforated stone hoe from Coole Pilate.] J. Chester & N. Wales Arch. Soc., N.S. 38, p. 173. 1951.

6449 Willett (Frank). A Scandinavian flint axe from Manchester. [Early Bronze Age.] Trans. Lancs. & Ches. Ant. Soc., 63 (1952–53), pp. 191–93 + plate + distribution map. 1954.

6450 Williamson (Frederick). Stone axe-hammer found at Derby. [Now in Derby Museum.] J. Derbs. Archaeol. Soc., 52 (N.S. 5, 1931), p. 114. 1932.

6451 Wooler (Edward). Perforated stone hammer found [at Wolsingham] in Weardale. [Bronze Age.] Proc. Soc. Antiq. Newc., 3 vol. S. 6, p. 92 + plate. 1913.

(e) Zone 5 [CBA Group 2]

6452 Allen (E. E.). Stone celt found at Mumbles. Proc. Swansea Sc. Soc., 2, pp. 17–18. 1939.

6453 Allen (John Romilly). Note on a perforated stone axe-hammer found [at Llanrhian] in Pembrokeshire. [9 figures. Pp. 231–34, list of perforated stone axe-hammers found in barrows in Great Britain.] Arch. Camb., 6th S. 3, pp. 224–38 + 2 plates. 1903.

6454 [Anon.] Circular flint knife found in Trefeglwys. [Figure.] Collns. rel. to Montgom., 6, pp. 215–16. 1873.

6455 [Anon.] Crescent-shaped object found at Llandrindod. [Stone.] [Figure.] Arch. Camb., 11, 6th ser., pp. 147–49. 1911.

6456 [Anon.] Neolithic axes in the Society's museum. [From Llandeilo Fawr and Llanfair ar y bryn.] Trans. Carmarthenshire Ant. Soc., 27, p. 64 + plate. 1937.

6457 [Anon.] Carmarthenshire stone implements. [Early Bronze Age. i. Flint axe from Llanegwad: ii. Spearhead, Llanelly.] Trans. Carmarthenshire Ant. Soc., 28, p. 89 + plate. 1938.

6458 Anwyl (*Sir* Edward). The querns of Anglesey. [Mostly Bronze Age.] Antiquary, 44, pp. 7–10. 1908.

6459 Baynes (Edward Neil). A stone axe-hammer of North American type [found at Beaumaris]. Anglesey Ant. Soc. Trans., 1933, pp. 29–33 + 3 plates. 1933.

6460 —— Two stone objects of early type. [Stone hammers from Pencraig, Llangefni, Anglesey and a query.] Anglesey Ant. Soc. Trans., 1934, pp. 25–26 + plate. 1934.

6461 —— A stone axe-hammer from Llanddona. Anglesey Ant. Soc. Trans., 1934, p. 192 + plate. 1934.

6462 Breese (Charles E.). Palaeolithic stone axe-head and other stone implements found near Beddgelert. [Figure.] Arch. Camb., 6th S. 8, pp. 403–04. 1908.

6463 Cantrill (Thomas Crosbee). Note on a collection of flints from Dale, Pembrokeshire. [Figure. Neolithic.] Arch. Camb., 6th S. 19, pp. 193–97. 1919.

6464 Carter (Charles). Perforated stone object found at Rossett. Arch. Camb., 86 i, 1931, 179 + 1 figure.

6465 Chitty (Lily F.). Perforated stone axe-hammers found in Carnarvonshire. Arch. Camb., 83 i, 1928, 223–26 + 4 figures.

6466 —— Ethnographical specimens reported as Cambrian. Arch. Camb., 86 i, 1931, 184–85.

6467 Cunnington (Maud Edith).

Note on a stone mould from [Worms' head, Glamorganshire], South Wales. [2 figures.] Man, 20, pp. 67–68. 1920.

6468 Daniel (Glyn Edmund). Two polished stone axe-heads from Carmarthenshire. Arch. Camb., 91 ii, 1936, 306–09 + 2 figures.

6469 Davies (A. Stanley). Bronze Age finds on Plynlymon Moorland. [Flint barbed and tanged arrow-heads and spalls.] Arch. Camb., 90 i, 1935, 153–56 + 2 figures.

6470 Davies (Ellis). A Bronze Age stone pestle from Caergai, near Llanuwchllyn. Arch. Camb., 88 i, 1933, 106 + 1 figure.

6471 —— Stone-axe hammer from Rhayader. Arch. Camb., 88 i, 1933, 107 + 1 figure.

6472 —— Stone axe and mace-head, Tafern Faig. Arch. Camb., 90 ii, 1935, 306 + 1 figure.

6473 —— Stone axe-hammer, Penarth, Clynnog. Arch. Camb., 90 ii, 1935, 311 + 1 figure.

6474 —— A hoard of large flint flakes from Penmachno, Caernarvonshire. Arch. Camb., 94 i, 1939, 106–07 + 1 figure.

6475 —— Stone axe, Rhuddlan. [Graig Llwyd.] Arch. Camb., 102 ii, 1953, 169.

6476 Davies (J.). Stone axes from near Dinas, Llanfairfechan. [Neolithic.] Trans. Caernarvons. hist. Soc., 22, 1961, 1–5 + 1 plate.

6477 —— Prehistoric stone blades from Parwyd, near Aberdaron. Trans. Caernarvons. hist. Soc., 23, 1962, 23–24.

6478 Dawkins (*Sir* William Boyd). On a find of Neolithic celts near Crickhowell, Breconshire. [Figure.] Arch. Camb., 6th S. 18, pp. 1–5. 1918.

6479 Dudlyke (E. R.). Two arrow-heads from Kerry, Montgomeryshire. [Figure.] Arch. Camb., 80, pp. 206–09. 1925.

6480 Dunn (C. J.). Flints from the Radnor Basin. Trans. Radnors. Soc., 34, 1964, 42–50 + 5 figures.

6481 —— Some additions to flints from the Radnor Basin (Radnorshire Society Transactions, xxxiv, 1964). Trans. Radnors. Soc., 35, 1965, 21.

6482 Evans (Evan). [9] stone implements, [recently found in] Anglesey. [9

figures.] Arch. Camb., 6th S. 8, pp. 292–94. 1908.

6483 Evans (George Eyre). Perforated stone hammer [from Marchgwyn Cilmaenllwyd, Carmarthenshire] in the Society's museum. [Early Bronze Age.] Trans. Carmarthenshire Ant. Soc., 27, p. 48 + plate. 1937.

6484 Forde (Cyril Daryll). A plano-convex knife from [near Dolgelly], Merionethshire. [Figure. Early—Middle Bronze Age.] Antiq. J., 15, pp. 346–47. 1935.

6485 Fox (*Sir* Cyril). Llanelly. Stone javelin. [Bronze Age.] Trans. Carmarthenshire Ant. Soc., 16, pp. 54–55 + plate. 1925.

6486 —— Axe of Graig Lwyd rock from Brecknockshire. Arch. Camb., 98 i, 1944, 142–43 + 1 figure.

6487 Glenn (Thomas Allen). Distribution of Neolithic implements in northern Flintshire. [2 figures + map.] Arch. Camb., 6th S. 13, pp. 181–90. 1913.

6488 —— Finds on the Rhyl foreshore. [3 polished Graig Lwyd axes, 6 flint implements.] Arch. Camb., 85 ii, 1930, 424–25 + 1 figure.

6489 Grimes (William Francis). Stone axe from Trefer Quarry, Caernarvonshire. Arch. Cambresnsis, 83 i, 1928, 195–97 + plate.

6490 —— A fragmentary stone axe from Sker, Glamorgan. [Graig Lwyd.] Arch. Camb., 84 i, 1929, 147–49 + 1 figure.

6491 —— A stone axe from Kenfig Burrows, Glamorgan. Arch. Camb., 84 i, 1929, 149–50 + 1 figure.

6492 —— A holed axe-hammer from Dolgelley, Merioneth. Arch. Camb., 84 i, 1929, 150–51 + 1 figure.

6493 —— Polished stone axes from Cowbridge and Welsh St. Donats, Glamorgan. Arch. Camb., 85 i, 1930, 210–12 + 2 figures.

6494 —— Polished stone axe from Meline, Pembrokeshire. Arch. Camb., 86 ii, 1931, 361 + 1 figure.

6495 —— Surface flint industries around Solva, Pembrokeshire. [EBA.] Arch. Camb., 87 i, 1932, 179–92 + 5 figures.

6496 —— Recent finds of stone implements. Arch. Camb., 87 ii, 1932, 406–08 + 3 figures.

6497 Grimes (William Francis). Notes on recent finds of perforated axe-hammers in Wales. [BA.] Arch. Camb., 90 ii, 1935, 267–78 + 6 figures.

6498 —— A grooved hammer from Plandiomwyn, Carmarthenshire [?date]. Arch. Camb., 97 ii, 1943, 235–36 + 1 figure.

6499 Hayes (Peter). Moel y Gaer, Llanbedr. Flint scraper. [Figure. Bronze Age.] Flintshire Hist. Soc. Pubns., 17, pp. 88–89. 1957.

6500 —— Caerwys, Babell: polished stone axe, spindle whorl, stone bead. Flints. hist. Soc. publns., 18, 1960, 169 + 3 figures.

6501 Hemp (Wilfrid James). Flint barbed arrow-head from The Rivals [Carnarvonshire]. [Figure.] Arch. Camb., 78, pp. 147–48. 1923.

6502 Higgins (H.). A small axe-hammer from Trefriw. Arch. Camb., 83 ii, 1928, 348–49 + 1 figure.

6503 Hughes (Harold). Grooved stone found in Bangor. Arch. Camb., 85 i, 1930, 201–03 + 2 figures.

6504 —— Mullers or grinding stones from Braich y Dinas [Penmaenmawr]. Arch. Camb., 85 i, 1930, 203–04 + 2 figures.

6505 —— Flint arrow-head found at the chambered tomb of Pant-y-saer, Anglesey [leaf-shaped]. Arch. Camb., 89 ii, 1934, 335 and 336 + 1 figure.

6506 —— Stone axe from Castellior, Menai Bridge. Arch. Camb., 90 i, 1935, 151 and 152 + 1 figure.

6507 —— Hammer stone from Llanerchymedd. Arch. Camb., 91 i, 1936, 142–44 + 1 figure.

6508 —— Hammer stone found near Caernarvon. Arch. Camb., 91 i, 1936, 144 + 1 figure.

6509 —— Arrowhead from the Great Ormes Head. Arch. Camb., 92 ii, 1937, 330–31 + 1 figure.

6510 —— Grooved hammer-stone at Llanfaer yn Neubwll, Anglesey. Arch. Camb., 93 i, 1938, 134 + 1 figure.

6511 —— Stone axe from Llanddaniel Fab, Anglesey [polished, Neolithic]. Arch. Camb., 93 i, 1938, 139 + 141 + 1 figure.

6512 Hughes (Meredith J.). Celt found in the Gop cave, Newmarket, Flintshire. Arch. Camb., 6th S. 12, p. 243 + plate. 1912.

6513 Hughes (Thomas McKenny). On the occurrence of Felstone implements of the Le Moustier type in Portnewydd cave, near Cefn, St. Asaph. J. Anth. Inst., 3, pp. 387–92 + plate. 1874.

6514 Hyde (H. A.). On the date of an axe-hammer from Llangeitho, Cardiganshire. Proc. prehist. Soc., 5, 1939, 166–72 + 3 figures.

6515 Jerman (H. Noel). Some recent discoveries on the Kerry Hills, Montgomeryshire. Arch. Camb., 88 i, 1933, 107 + 1 figure.

6516 —— Unrecorded finds from east central Wales. Bull. Bd. Celtic Stud., 7, pp. 331–32. 1934.

6517 —— Perforated stone axe-hammer from Anglesey. Arch. Camb., 91 i, 1936, 147 + 1 figure.

6518 —— Perforated stone hammer in the National Library of Wales. Arch. Camb., 91 i, 1936, 148–49 + 1 figure.

6519 Jones (J. F.). A grooved hammer from Rhandirmwyn, Carmarthenshire, [and] new earthwork. Carmarthen. Antiquary, 2, pp. 40–41. 1946.

6520 Jones (S. J.). Perforated stone axe-hammers found in Wales. [Figure. List of 43.] Bull. Bd. Celtic Stud., 3, pp. 343–56. 1927.

6521 Lacaille (Armand Donald). A hand axe from Pen-y-lan, Cardiff. [2 figures. Acheulian.] Antiq. J., 34, pp. 64–67. 1954.

6522 Laws (Edward). Notice of two stone implements from Pembrokeshire. [2 figures. In Tenby museum.] Arch. Camb., 5th S. 6, pp. 314–16. 1889.

6523 Leach (Arthur L.). An implement of crystalline quartz, from Freshwater West, Pembrokeshire. [Figure. ?Neolithic.] Arch. Camb., 6 S. 11, pp. 78–80. 1911.

6524 —— Stone implements from soil-drifts and chipping-floors, etc., in south Pembroke. [12 figures + 3 maps.] Arch. Camb., 6th S. 13, pp. 391–432 + 3 plates. 1913.

6525 —— A perforated stone-hammer from [Manorbier], south Pembrokeshire. [Figure.] Arch. Camb., 6th S. 18, pp. 349–50. 1918.

6526 —— Stone implements from the Nals Head, St. Bride's, Pembrokeshire. Arch. Camb., 88 ii, 1933, 229–36 + 3 figures.

6527 Lewis (Herbert P.). A polished stone celt from the neighbourhood of the Llandegla sepulchral caves. [3 figures.] Arch. Camb., 79, pp. 404–08 + map. 1924.

6528 Lukis (John Walter). The flint implements of the drift period. Cardiff Nat. Soc., Rpt. & Trans., 5 (1873), pp. 28–33. 1874.

6529 Manby (T. G.). The Bodwrdin Mould, Anglesey [stone]. Proc. prehist. Soc., 32, 1966, 349.

6530 Mathias (A. G. O.). Celts found in Pembroke. [2 Neolithic felsite polished axes.] Arch. Camb., 83 i, 1928, 208–09 + 1 plate.

6531 —— A barbed and tanged flint arrowhead from Freshwater West, Castle Martin, Pembs. Arch. Camb., 84 ii, 1929, 333 + 1 figure.

6532 —— Stone-axe found near Pembroke [polished, fine-grain stone]. Arch. Camb., 85 i, 1930, 203–05 + 1 figure.

6533 —— Hammer-stones from the Castlemartin floors, south Pembrokeshire. Arch. Camb., 85 i, 1930, 205–06 + 2 figures.

6534 O'Neil (Bryan Hugh St. John). A polished celt from Trefeglwys, Montgomeryshire. Arch. Camb., 86 ii, 1931, 356–58 + 3 figures.

6535 Owen (D. Edmondes). A stone [axe-] hammer, found near Rhayader [Radnor]. [2 figures.] Arch. Camb., 6 S. 11, pp. 151–54. 1911.

6536 Pape (Thomas). Newborough warren flints in 1928. Anglesey Ant. Soc. Trans., 1929, pp. 95–96. 1929.

6537 Peate (Iorwerth Cyfeiliog). Arrow-heads from Bugeilyn [Montgomeryshire]. [Figure.] Arch. Camb., 80, pp. 196–202, 415–16. 1925.

6538 —— Stone axe and holed hammer-stone from [Bwlchyddwyallt], north Cardiganshire. [Figure. Now in museum of Univ. Coll., Aberystwyth. Neolithic.] Arch. Camb., 80, pp. 202–03. 1925.

6539 —— Some Teifiside [south Cards.] holed stones. [Figure.] Arch. Camb., 80, pp. 205–06. 1925.

6540 —— Flints from [Solfach], Pembrokeshire. [2 figures.] Arch. Camb., 80, pp. 416–19. 1925.

6540 —— Flints from [Solfach], Pembrokeshire. [2 figures.] Arch. Camb., 80, pp. 416–19. 1935.

6541 —— More arrowheads from Bugeilyn [barbed and tanged and leaf]. Arch. Camb., 83 ii, 1928, 344–45 + 1 figure.

6542 —— Arrowheads and flints from Bugeilyn. Arch. Camb., 85 i, 1930, 200–01 + 1 figure.

6543 —— An axe-hammer from Arthog, Merioneth. Arch. Camb., 85 ii, 1930, 407 + 1 figure.

6544 Price (William Fred). Neolithic celt found at Colwyn Bay. [Figure.] Arch. Camb., 5th S. 15, pp. 92–93. 1898.

6545 Prichard (Hugh). A perforated stone found [at Bodrwyn] in Anglesey. Arch. Camb., 4th S. 5, pp. 10–17 + 2 plates. 1874.

6546 Prothero (R. M.). Polished axe, Merthyr Tydfil, Glamorgan. [Neolithic felsite.] Arch. Camb., 99 ii, 1947, 292–94 + 3 figures.

6547 Pye (W. R.). Notes on the collection of flints, Lower Lloyney, Clyro. [Mesolithic—BA.] Trans. Radnors. Soc., 30, 1960, 57–61 + 3 figures.

6548 Savory (Hubert Newman). Semi-perforated stone from Cardiganshire. [MBA but use unknown.] Arch. Camb., 95 ii, 1940, 243–44 + 1 figure.

6549 —— Boat-shaped stone axe-hammer from Llanfachreth, Merionethshire. Arch. Camb., 99 i, 1946, 113–14 + 1 plate.

6550 —— Boat-shaped stone axe-hammer from Llanfachreth, Merioneth. Bull. Bd. Celtic Stud., 12, pp. 58–59. 1946.

6551 —— Two polished flint axes of unusual type from the Usk valley [one passage grave type]. Arch. Camb., 99 ii, 1947, 286–90 + 2 figures.

6552 —— Nordic flint axe from Crickhowell, Brecknockshire. Bull. Bd. Celtic Stud., 12, p. 125. 1948.

6553 —— Polished stone axe from Rhos-on-Sea, Denbighshire. Bull. Bd. Celtic Stud., 12, p. 125. 1948.

6554 —— Polished stone axe from Llangunllo, Radnorshire. Bull. Bd. Celtic Stud., 12, p. 126. 1948.

6555 —— Perforated axe-hammer from Clarbeston, Pembrokeshire. Bull. Bd. Celtic Stud., 13, p. 110. 1949.

6556 Savory (Hubert Newman). Flint [second *ditto*] arrow-head from Mynydd Wysg, Brecknockshire. Bull. Bd. Celtic Stud., 13, p. 110, 162. 1949.

6557 —— Axe of Pembrokeshire stone from [Dinas Powis], Glamorganshire. Bull. Bd. Celtic Stud., 13, pp. 245–46. 1950.

6558 —— Stone mace-head from Cilrhedyn East (Carm.). Bull. Bd. Celtic Stud., 14, p. 85. 1950.

6559 —— Hoard of stone axes from Newport (Mon.). Arch. Camb., 101 ii, 1951, 166–67 + 2 figures.

6560 —— [Lower Palaeolithic] drift implement from Penylan, Cardiff. Bull. Bd. Celtic Stud., 15, p. 67. 1952.

6561 —— Perforated stone axe-hammer from [somewhere in] Anglesey. [Bronze Age.] Bull. Bd. Celtic Stud., 15, pp. 68–69 + plate. 1952.

6562 —— Perforated axe-hammer from Lampeter (Card.). Bull. Bd. Celtic Stud., 15, p. 158 + plate. 1953.

6563 —— Stone axe-heads from [Llandudno,] Caernarvonshire. Bull. Bd. Celtic Stud., 15, p. 225. 1953.

6564 —— Stone mace-heads from [Dolwen,] Denbighshire and [Abercwmboi,] Glamorgan. Bull. Bd. Celtic Stud., 15, pp. 303–04. 1954.

6565 —— [Mesolithic] microlith from [Clyro area,] Radnorshire. Bull. Bd. Celtic Stud., 16, p. 49. 1954.

6566 —— Neolithic axe-heads from [Caerleon and Newport,] Monmouthshire. [Now in Newport museum.] Bull. Bd. Celtic Stud., 16, p. 49. 1954.

6567 —— Neolithic axe-head from the Lleyn [peninsula, Caernarvonshire]. Bull. Bd. Celtic Stud., 16, p. 50. 1954.

6568 —— Barbed and tanged arrowheads from [Cardiff,] Glamorgan and [Portskewett,] Monmouthshire. [Middle Bronze Age. Now in National Museum of Wales.] Bull. Bd. Celtic Stud., 16, p. 50. 1954.

6569 —— Perforated axe-hammer from the Lleyn [Caernarvonshire]. [Now in National Museum of Wales.] Bull. Bd. Celtic Stud., 16, p. 208. 1955.

6570 —— Stone axe-heads from [Penarth], Glamorgan. Bull. Bd. Celtic Stud., 16, p. 208. 1955.

6571 —— Polished stone axe-head from Dol-Berthog, Llandrindod. Radnorshire Soc. Trans., 26, p. 4. 1956.

6572 —— Stone axe-head from [Heronston,] Glamorgan. Bull. Bd. Celtic Stud., 17, p. 53. 1956.

6573 —— Stone axe-head from [Plas Penmynydd,] Anglesey. Bull. Bd. Celtic Stud., 17, p. 53. 1956.

6574 —— Chert javelin-head from [Banwen,] Glamorgan. Bull. Bd. Celtic Stud., 17, pp. 53–54. 1956.

6575 —— Stone axe-head hoard from [Penarth], Glamorgan. Bull. Bd. Celtic Stud., 17, pp. 194–95 + plate. 1957.

6576 —— Axe-head from Llaneilian. [Neolithic.] Trans. Anglesey Antiq. Soc. Fld. Club, 1959, 58–59 + 1 figure.

6577 —— Neolithic implements from east Glamorgan. Trans. Cardiff Nat. Soc., 86 (1956–57), pp. 24–25. 1959.

6578 —— Flint arrow-head found at Marianglas. Trans. Anglesey Antiq. Soc. Fld. Club, 1960, 53.

6579 —— Current work in Welsh archaeology: excavations and discoveries. Bull. Board Celtic Studies, 20 ii, 1963, 165–67 + 1 figure.

6580 Smith (Worthington George). Stone hammer from Moel Fenlli [Denbighshire]. [Figure.] Arch. Camb., 5th S. 1, pp. 305–08. 1884.

6581 —— Flint scraper from Gogerddan [Cards.]. [Figure.] Arch. Camb., 5th S. 15, p. 287. 1898.

6582 Storrie (John). Interesting discovery [of Bronze Age implements] at Llantwit Major. [Figure.] Arch. Camb., 5th S. 4, pp. 151–55. 1887.

6583 Thomas (Roger). Pigmy flints found at Newport (Pem.). Arch. Camb., 78, pp. 324–26. 1923.

6584 Wainwright (G. J.). A reinterpretation of the Microlithic industries of Wales. Proc. prehist. Soc., 29, 1963, 99–132 + 15 figures + 1 plate.

6585 Ward (Frank). Flint implement found near Trawsfynydd [scraper]. Arch. Camb., 94 ii, 1939, 226 + 1 figure.

6586 Way (Albert). Supplementary notices of relics recently obtained by the Hon. William Owen Stanley, in his researches in Holyhead island. Archaeol. J., 28, pp. 144–54 + 3 plates. 1871.

6587 Webley (D.). Neolithic sandstone disk from Crom Cadlan, Breckn. Bull. Bd. Celtic Stud., 15, p. 303. 1954.

6588 Webley (D.). Flint surface finds [in 1954] in Glamorgan, Monmouthshire, and Brecknockshire (–1955). (–1956). [39 worked flints from 26 sites. (27 flints from 16 sites).] Bull. Bd. Celtic Stud., 16, pp. 210–11, 298; 17, pp. 116–17. 1955.

6589 Williams (Audrey). Hammer or mace from Oxwich, Glamorgan. Arch. Camb., 91 ii, 1936, 309 + 1 figure.

6590 Williams (Geoffrey) and **Williams** (Lorna). A note on the collection of flint implements from Old Forest Farm, Clyro, Radnorshire. Trans. Radnors. Soc., 31, 1961, 47–52 + 2 figures.

6591 Williams (V. E. Nash). Stone axe-hammer from Pentregalar, Llanfyrnach. Arch. Cambrensis, 82 ii, 1927, 387–90 + 2 figures.

6592 —— A polished celt from Blaina, Monmouthshire. Arch. Camb., 86 i, 1931, 176 + 1 plate.

6593 —— Spindle whorls found at Corwen, Merioneth [EIA type] [stone]. Arch. Camb., 94 i, 1939, 107 + 1 figure.

(f) Zone 6
[CBA Group 1 plus Ireland and Isle of Man]

6594 [Anon.] Find at East Mains, west Berwickshire. [Neolithic hammer.] J. Brit. Archaeol. Ass., N.S. 29, p. 257. 1923.

6595 Breuil (Henri) *abbé*. Les calcaires taillés de Sligo, Irelande. Man, 28, p. 119. 1928.

6596 —— Objects of palaeolithic type found near Comrie, Perthshire, Scotland. [Clactonian flakes.] Proc. prehist. Soc., 3, 1937, 463–64 + 1 plate.

6597 Burchell (James Percy Tufnell) *and* **Moir** (James Reid). The evolution and distribution of the hand-axe in North-East Ireland. Proc. PSEA, 7 i, 1932–34, 18–34 + 1 plate + 19 figures.

6598 Childe (Vere Gordon). Rare flint [microburin] in Hawick museum. Trans. Hawick Archaeol. Soc., 1942, p. 31. 1942.

6599 Coles (John M.). A "Bann point" from Dumfriesshire. Trans. Dumfries . . . 43, 1966, 147 + 1 figure.

6600 Corrie (John M.). Pigmy flint implements found in Roxburghshire

and Berwickshire. Trans. Hawick Archaeol. Soc., 1920, pp. 13–16 + plate. 1920.

6601 —— A small perforated hammer recently discovered in the parish of Dunscore. Trans. Dumfries. Ant. Soc., 3 S. 14 (1926–28), pp. 54–56. 1930.

6602 Cowley (Charles H.) Manx pigmy flints. [2 figures.] J. Brit. Archaeol. Ass., N.S. 27, pp. 159–67. 1921.

6603 Craw (James Hewat). On the occurrence of a flint axe in the parish of Foulden. [Figure.] Hist. Berwick Nat. Club, 23, p. 456. 1918.

6604 Davidson (James Milne). Note on the evolution of stone hammers in Scotland. [Figure.] Trans. Glasgow Archaeol. Soc., N.S. 8, Suppl., pp. 11–14. 1934.

6605 Dow (John). Remarks on the ancient weapon denominated the celt. Archaeol. Scot., 2, pp. 199–207. 1822.

6606 Dunover (George Victor). On worked flint flakes from Carrickfergus and Larne. J. Geol. Soc. London, 25, 1869, 48–50.

6607 Evans (*Sir* John). On some discoveries of stone implements in Lough Neagh, Ireland. Archaeologia, 41, pp. 397–408 + coloured plate. 1867.

6608 Falkiner (W.). Notes on some stone finds at Killucan, Co. Westmeath. [Figure.] Antiquary, 36, pp. 298–301. 1960.

6609 Gogan (Liam S.). A perforated double-axe of stone from [Curraboy Knox, near Ballinrobe], county Mayo. [Figure.] Man, 33, pp. 128–30. 1933.

6611 Gray (A. F.). A collection of stone artifacts from Redpoint, Loch Torridon, Ross-shire. Proc. Soc. Ant. Scotland, 93, 1959–60, 236–37.

6612 Hardy (James). On some flint implements and rude ornaments of prehistoric people in Berwickshire. Hist. Berwick. Nat. Club, 6, pp. 410–15; 7, pp. 264–68 + 4 plates; 8, pp. 160–68 + 4 plates; pp. 543–47 + 3 plates. 1872–1878.

6613 —— On a flint scraper found on Gullane links [East Lothian]. [Figure. In museum of Society of Antiquaries of Scotland.] Hist. Berwick. Nat. Club, 10, p. 372. 1883.

6614 Hawkes (Charles Francis Christopher). A stone battle-axe from [the river Bann at Kilrea, Co. Londonderry], northern Ireland. [Figure. Mesolithic.] Antiq. J., 17, pp. 72–73 + plate. 1937.

6615 Holden (J. Sinclair). A peculiar Neolithic implement from [the Glens of] Antrim. [Flint saws.] J. Anth. Inst., 4, pp. 19–20 + plate. 1874.

6616 Keiller (Alexander). Two axes of Presely stone from [co. Antrim], Ireland. [+ 4 from Wales.] Antiquity, 10, pp. 220–21 + 2 plates. 1936.

6617 Knowles (William James). Flint implements from [Portglenore in] the valley of the Bann. J. Anthrop. Inst., 10, pp. 150–53. 1880.

6618 —— A flint implement from Ballycastle. Ulster J. Arch., 4, 1897, 8–11 + 2 figures.

6619 —— Irish flint arrow- and spearheads. J. Anthrop. Inst., 33, pp. 44–56 + 8 plates. 1903.

6620 —— The antiquity of man in Ireland, being an account of the older series of Irish flint implements. [89 figures (flints).] J. R. Anthrop. Inst., 44, pp. 83–121. 1914.

6621 Lacaille (Armand Donald). Silex Tardenoisieus de Shewalton (Comté d'Ayr), Ecosse. [4 figures + map.] Bull. Soc. préhistorique franc., 1931, pp. 307–12. 1931.

6622 —— The microlithic industries of Scotland. [8 figures + map.] Trans. Glasgow Archaeol. Soc., N.S. 9, pp. 56–74. 1937.

6623 —— The scraper in prehistoric culture. (Its evolution; its penetration into Scotland; its survivals). [5 figures.] Trans. Glasgow Archaeol. Soc., N.S. 11, pp. 38–83. 1947.

6624 —— A stone industry from Morar, Inverness-shire; its Obanian (Mesolithic) and later affinities. [13 figures + 2 maps.] Archaeologia, 94, pp. 103–39 + 3 plates. 1951.

6625 —— Stone basins. (Some examples from the west of Scotland as guides to typology.) [15 figures. Prehistoric and later.] Trans. Glasgow Archaeol. Soc., N.S. 12, pp. 41–93. 1953.

6626 —— Stone Age tools. [5 figures.] Trans. Glasgow Archaeol. Soc., N.S. 13, pp. 17–32. 1954.

6627 —— A perforated stone implement from Glen Fruin, Dunbartonshire.

Proc. Soc. Ant. Scotland, 96, 1962/63, 348–50 + 1 plate.

6628 Layard (Nina Frances). The older series of Irish flint implements. [2 figures.] Man, 9, pp. 81–85 + plate. 1909.

6629 Lowson, *Dr.* Flint implement found in a Park Place garden [Stirling]. Trans. Stirling N.H. & Arch. Soc., 1914–19, pp. 88–89. 1919.

6630 Mann (Ludovic Maclellan). Perforated stones of unknown use. Trans. Glasgow Archaeol. Soc., N.S. 6, pp. 289–97 + 5 plates. 1916.

6631 Maxwell (J. Harrison). Flint saw found at Roughrigg reservoir, near Airdrie. [Figure. ?Early Bronze Age.] Trans. Glasgow Archaeol. Soc., N.S. 10, pp. 76–77. 1941.

6632 Mitchell (Arthur). Notice of flint flakes found in the parish of Abernethy, Strathspey. Proc. Soc. Antiq. Scot., 6, pp. 251–52. 1868.

6633 —— On some remarkable discoveries of rude stone implements in Shetland. [9 figures.] Proc. Soc. Antiq. Scot., 7, pp. 118–34. 1870.

6634 Moir (James Reid) and **Burchell** (James Percy Tufnell). The Sligo artefacts. Man, 28, pp. 118–19. 1928.

6635 Murray (David). Note on a stone axe found at Mollandhu, Dunbartonshire. Trans. Glasgow Archaeol. Soc., N.S. 1, p. 515. 1890.

6636 Paterson (H. M. Leslie). Pygmy flints in the Dee valley. [3 figures.] Man, 13, pp. 103–05. 1913.

6637 Petrie (George). Notice of some rude stone implements found in Orkney. [Figure.] Proc. Soc. Antiq. Scot., 7, pp. 135–36. 1870.

6638 Richards (E. E.) *and* **Stoyle** (A. E. Blin). A study of the homogeneity in composition of an Irish thick-butted axe. Archaeometry, 4, 1961, 353–55 + 1 figure.

6639 Roberts (George E.). On some arrow-heads and other implements of quartz and flint from the Bin of Cullen (Elginshire). J. Anthrop. Soc. London, 2, p. lxiv. 1864.

6640 Scott (J. G.). Two flint daggers found in Scotland. Proc. Soc. Ant. Scotland, 95, 1961–62, 304–05 + 1 figure.

6641(a) Scott (T.). Collection of flint

arrow-heads, spear-heads, knives, scrapers, borers, flakes—about 600 in all—from Craigsfordmains mostly. Hist. Berwick. Nat. Club, 14, pp. 166–69 + 5 plates. 1894.

6641(b) Smith (G. S. Graham). Anvil stones: with special reference to those from Skelmuir, Aberdeenshire [?working floor]. Proc. prehist. Soc. EA, 3 i, 1918/19, 33–58 + 4 figures + 2 plates.

6642 Stevenson (Robert Barron Kerr). Note on a stone-axehammer from Locharbriggs. [Figure. Bronze Age.] Trans. Dumfriess. Ant. Soc., 3rd S. 25 (1946–1947), pp. 173–75. 1948.

6643 —— Stone axe from Dhuloch. [Figure.] Trans. Dumfriess. Ant. Soc., 3rd S. 28 (1949–54), pp. 186–87. 1951.

6644 —— Some unfinished flint artefacts [showing projection for gripping, later to be trimmed off]. [Figure.] Proc. Soc. Antiq. Scot., 90 (1956–57), p. 221. 1959.

6645 —— Notes on flints, etc., from Ruberslaw. Trans. Hawick Archaeol. Soc., 1957, p. 56 + plate. 1958.

6646 Truckell (Alfred Edgar). A Neolithic axe roughout. Trans. Dumfries. . . . 42, 1965, 149 + 1 figure.

6647 Whelan (C. Blake). The implementiferous raised beach gravels of south-east Antrim. [4 figures.] Man, 28, pp. 186–89. 1928.

6648 —— The tanged flake industry of the river Bann, county Antrim. Antiq. J., 10, pp. 134–38 + plate. 1930.

6649 —— Peculiar celt from [Derryaghy, co. Antrim], Ireland. [Figure. Late Neolithic polished axe-head.] Antiq. J., 12, pp. 298–99. 1932.

6650 —— Cordate hand-axe of Chalcolithic Age [from Rathlin Island]. [Figure.] Antiq. J., 15, pp. 194–95. 1935.

6651 —— [Flint] implement from Larne [co. Antrim] raised beach. [Figure.] Antiq. J., 15, pp. 465–66. 1935.

6652 —— The palaeolithic question in Ireland. Report of XVI Internat. Geol. Congress, Washington, 1933, pp. 1209–1218. 1936.

6653 Wilson (Daniel). On the class of stone vessels known in Scotland as druidical paterae. [2 figures. i.e. found in connection with "druidical" circles.] Proc. Soc. Antiq. Scot., 1, pp. 115–18. 1855.

3. CERAMIC OBJECTS IN GENERAL

6654 Abercromby (*Hon.* John). The oldest Bronze Age ceramic type in Britain; its close analogies on the Rhine; its probable origin in central Europe. J. Anthrop. Inst., 32, pp. 373–97 + 13 plates + map. 1902.

6655 —— A method of arranging British Bronze Age ceramic in chronological order. Trans. Glasgow Archaeol. Soc., N.S. 5, pp. 54–60. 1908.

6656 —— A study of Bronze Age pottery of Great Britain & Ireland, and its associated grave-goods. 2 vol. 4°. Oxford, 1912. [110 plates (1611 illustrations of pottery and 155 examples of grave-goods).]

6657 [Anon.] Finger-nail decoration. [Late Bronze Age.] Antiq. J., 8, p. 98 + plate. 1928.

6658 ApSimon (A. M.). Food vessels. Bull. Inst. of Arch. London, 1, 1958, 24–36 + 3 figures.

6659 Case (Humphrey). Abingdon ware. [Neolithic pottery. Test for being porous.] Antiquity, 29, pp. 236–37. 1955.

6660 Childe (Vere Gordon). Neolithic pottery. Antiquity, 6, pp. 89–90. 1932.

6661 —— The continental affinities of British Neolithic pottery. [Figure + map. Pp. 58–66, Peterborough ware.] Archaeol. J., 88 (1931), pp. 37–66 + 11 plates. 1932.

6662 Clarke (David Leonard). Beaker Pottery of Great Britain and Ireland (Gulbenkian Archaeological ser.). Vols. 1 and 2, numerous tables, 14 diagrams, 9 plates, 1110 drawings 12 in. by 9 in. Cambridge, 1970.

6664 Corcoran (John X. W. P.). Tankards and tankard handles of the British Early Iron Age. Metal. Proc. prehist. Soc., 18, 1952, 85–102 + 3 figures + 5 plates.

6665 Cunnington (Maud Edith). Was there a second Belgic invasion (represented by bead-rim pottery)? Antiq. J., 12, pp. 27–34. 1932.

6666 Devizes Museum. Cross on "incense cup". [Figure. Bronze Age.] Antiq. J., 6, pp. 182–84. 1926.

6667 Fitzjohn (G. J. Monson). Drinking vessels of bygone days, from the Neolithic age to the Georgian period. pp. 144. 8⁰. London, 1927.

6668 Gray (Harold St. George). The Beaker class of fictilia found in association with remains of the Roman period. [Pottery.] Antiquary, 42, pp. 18–20. 1906.

6669 Grimes (William Francis). The La Tène art style in British Early Iron Age pottery. Proc. prehist. Soc., 18, 1952, 160–75 + 12 figures.

6670 Hawkes (Charles Francis Christopher). Patterns on early pottery. Antiq. J., 10, pp. 166–67 + plate. 1930.

6671 Hawkes (Jacquetta). The significance of channelled ware in Neolithic western Europe. [9 figures. Pp. 147–53, Britain.] Archaeol. J., 95 (1938), pp. 126–73 + 5 plates. 1939.

6672 Hayes (J. W.). Prehistoric and aboriginal pottery manufacture. [A little material on British pottery and kilns.] J. R. Anthrop. Inst., 41, pp. 260–77. 1911.

6673 Hobden (G.). Early British pottery. Trans. Hawick Archaeol. Soc., 1903, pp. 65–66. 1903.

6674 Hodges (Henry W. M.). Thin sections of prehistoric pottery: an empirical study. Bull. Inst. of Arch. London, 3, 1962, 58–68 + 1 figure + 2 plates.

6675 Hughes (Thomas M'Kenny). The early potters' art in Britain. [Pp. 223–29, British.] Archaeol. J., 59, pp. 219–37 + plate (mediaeval). 1902.

6676 Jewitt (Llewellyn). The ceramic art of Great Britain, *etc.* 2 vol. 8⁰. London, 1878. [Vol. 1, pp. 1–23 (with 77 figures), prehistoric.]

6677 —— Ceramics of the ancient Britons. [5 figures.] Antiquary, 1, pp. 106–10. 1880.

6678 Longworth (Ian H.). The origins and development of the primary series in the collared urn tradition in England and Wales. Proc. prehist. Soc., 27, 1961, 263–306 + 12 figures.

6679 Mackay (R. Robertson). Beaker coarse wares. An analysis of beaker domestic pottery. Archaeol. News Letter, 7 v, 1961, 99–104 + 7 figures.

6680 Matson (Frederick R.), *editor.*

Ceramics and man. Methuen, London, 1966, 301 pp.

681 Phené (John Samuel). On a British terra-cotta vase from Berigonium, and British sepulchral urns from other localities. J. Brit. Archaeol. Ass., 27, pp. 355–64. 1871.

6682 Piggott (Stuart). The Neolithic pottery of the British Isles. [20 figures + 3 maps. Pp. 67–110, Windmill hill ware; pp. 110–34, Peterborough ware; pp. 134–58, Annotated list of sites of both wares.] Archaeol. J., 88 (1931), pp. 67–158 + 4 plates. 1932.

6683 —— The mutual relations of the British Neolithic ceramics. Proc. PSEA, 7 iii, 1934, 373–81 + 6 figures.

6684 Repton (John Adey). Remarks on [the difference between] British and Roman urns. J. Brit. Archaeol. Ass., 9, pp. 59–62 + plate. 1853.

6685 Savory (Hubert Newman). A corpus of Welsh Bronze Age pottery. Part 3, Pygmy cups, Middle Bronze Age (*c.* 1400—1000 B.C.). [3 figures + 2 maps.] Bull. Bd. Celtic Stud., 18, pp. 89–118. 1958.

6686 Sheppard (Thomas). The evolution of the potter's art. pp. xx. 4⁰. London [19—?]. [62 figures.]

6687 Smith (Reginald Allender). The development of Neolithic pottery [in England]. [8 figures. Peterborough, etc.] Archaeologia, 62, pp. 340–52 + 3 plates. 1910.

6688 Stevens (Frank). Twisted cord decoration on Bronze Age pottery. [3 figures.] Man, 36, pp. 79–81. 1936.

6689 Wakefield (Hugh). English prehistoric pottery. *Victoria & Albert Museum, Small picture book,* 26. pp. 2 + 32 plates. 8⁰. London, 1952. [32 pots, Neolithic—Belgic period.]

6690 Walters (Henry Beauchamp). History of ancient pottery, *etc.* 2 vol. 8⁰. London, 1905.

6691 Wheeler (Robert Eric Mortimer) *Kt.* The Saint-Pol-de-Léon pot. [Notes and News, cf. pots from Maiden Castle.] Antiq., 34 (1960), p. 58.

6692 Winstone (B.). On some primitive ornamentation found on primitive pottery. [Figure.] J. Brit. Archaeol. Ass., N.S. 3, pp. 213–18. 1897.

4. CERAMIC OBJECTS BY ZONES

(a) Zone 1
[CBA Groups 7, 9, 10, 11A, 11B, 14]

6693 Ade (Charles). On some urns lately found in a tumulus at Alfriston. [Figure.] Sussex Arch. Collns., 2, pp. 270–71. 1849.

6694 Ade (John Stephen) *discoverer*. Discovery of [Celtic] cinerary urns at Alfriston. Sussex Arch. Collns., 37, pp. 193–94. 1890.

6695 Allchin (J. H.). Discoveries of prehistoric pottery in the Maidstone district. [Figure.] Arch. Cant., 27, pp. lxxvi–lxxviii + plate. 1905.

6696 [Anon.] Ancient British drinking cup [in Northampton Museum]. [Bronze Age. Found near Brixworth.] Northants. N. & Q., 5, p. 81 + plate. 1894.

6697 [Anon.] [Cinerary urn of the Late Bronze Age from Mistley, near Manningtree.] [Figure.] Antiquary, 49, p. 4. 1913.

6698 [Anon.] A new handled-beaker [from Newton-in-the-Willows, Northants.]. [Figure. Early Bronze Age.] Antiq. J., 5, pp. 430–31. 1925.

6699 Barnard (G. V.). A handled beaker from Norfolk. Proc. prehist. Soc., 7, 1941, 144 + 1 figure.

6700 Baynes (Edward Neil). A Neolithic bowl and other objects from the Thames at Hedsor, near Cookham. [2 figures.] Antiq. J., 1, pp. 316–20. 1921.

6701 Benton (Gerald Montagu). Cinerary urns of the Late Bronze Age discovered at Shalford, Essex. [Figure.] Antiq. J., 4, pp. 265–67. 1924.

6702 —— Late Bronze Age and Early Iron Age pottery discovered at Shalford [near Braintree]. [2 figures.] Trans. Essex Archaeol. Soc., N.S. 17, pp. 125–28. 1926.

6703 Bradford (John Spencer Purvis). Neolithic "B" pottery from near Eynsham [Oxon.]. Antiq. J., 23, pp. 51–52 + plate. 1943.

6704 Brent (Cecil). British urn [from Summer-hill, three miles from Canterbury]. J. Brit. Archaeol. Ass., 22, pp. 241–42 + plate. 1866.

6705 Briscoe, Grace. Giant Beaker and rustical ware from Lakenheath, Suffolk, and reproduction of ornament. [3 figures.] Cambridge Antiq. Soc. Proc., 53, 1959, 1–7.

6706 Budgen (William). Halstatt pottery from Eastbourne. [5 figures.] Antiq. J., 2, pp. 354–60. 1922.

6707 Bull (Frederick William). Bronze Age pottery from [Tyringham, near Newport Pagnell], Bucks. [Figure.] Antiq. J., 8, p. 354. 1928.

6708 Burchell (James Percy Tufnell) *and* **Moir** (James Reid). Upper Palaeolithic pottery from Ipswich and Swanscombe [Kent]. [2 figures. Pp. 177–78, note by Stuart Piggott.] Man, 34, pp. 175–77. 1934.

6709 —— Some recent discoveries in the Ebbsfleet Valley. [Neolithic pottery.] Proc. prehist. Soc., 4, 1938, 336 + 1 plate.

6710 —— *and* **Piggott** (Stuart). Decorated prehistoric pottery from the bed of the Ebbsfleet, Northfleet, Kent. [9 figures. Neolithic to Early Bronze Age.] Antiq. J., 19, pp. 405–20. 1939.

6711 Case (Humphrey). Beaker pottery from the Oxford region: 1939–1955. [5 figures.] Oxoniensia, 21 (1956), pp. 1–21 + distribution map. 1957.

6712 —— Archaeological Notes, Dorchester, Oxon. [early and late RB pots]. Oxoniensia, 23, 1958, 131.

6713 Chandler (Raymond H.). Note on some prehistoric pottery from Dartmouth heath. [Figures.] Woolwich Ant. Soc., Ann. Rpt., 16 (1910), pp. 25–27. 1911.

6714 Chown (*Mrs.* Eileen). Painted Iron Age pottery at Sedlescombe. [2 figures.] Sussex N. & Q., 11, pp. 148–51. 1947.

6715 Clark (J. G. D.). Notes on the Beaker pottery of the Ipswich Museum. Proc. PSEA, 6 iv, 1931, 356–61 + 4 plates + 2 figures.

6716 Clarke (Roy Rainbird). Bronze Age beaker from Cromer. [Figure.] Antiq. J., 16, pp. 203–04. 1936.

6717 Clegg (John). Bronze Age urn at Lynchmere. Sussex N. & Q., 14, pp. 133–34. 1955.

6718 Cole (William). Ancient ["Late Celtic"] urns at Braintree. [Figure.] Essex Nat., 13, pp. 110–12. 1903.

6719 Cook (Norman). Early Iron Age pottery from Chiddingstone. [Figure.] Arch. Cant., 45, pp. 280–83. 1933.

6720 Cooper (Joseph). On some recently discovered ancient British urns [at Itford, parish of Beddingham]. Sussex Arch. Collns., 29, pp. 238–39. 1879.

6723 Couchman (John Edwin). Neolithic spoons found [on the boundary of Hurstpierpoint and Clayton] in Sussex. [6 figures.] Proc. Soc. Antiq., 2 S. 31, pp. 108–19 + 2 plates. 1919.

6724 —— The Hassocks neolithic spoons. [Figure.] Antiq. J., 14, pp. 422–23. 1934.

6725 Curle (Alexander Ormiston). Neolithic vessels from the Thames [at Mortlake and at Putney]. [? figures.] Antiq. J., 4, pp. 149–50 + plate. 1924.

6726 Curwen (Eliot) *and* **Curwen** (Eliot Cecil). Two [Bronze Age] beakers and an Early Iron Age urn. [Figure. In Society's museum. Beakers found at Brighton in 1830: urn from somewhere on Downs.] Sussex Arch. Collns., 76, pp. 1–5 + plate. 1935.

6727 —— Perforated rim-lugs from Friston, Sussex. [Figure. Early Iron Age.] Antiq. J., 21, pp. 62–64. 1941.

6728 Curwen (Eliot Cecil). A type "A" beaker from Park Brow, Sompting. [Figure.] Sussex N. & Q., 7, pp. 58–59. 1938.

6729 Denington (R. F.) *and* **Gallant** (Louie). The Iron Age pottery from Thorney Farm, Iver. [4 figures.] Record of Bucks., 17 (4), 1964, 240–56.

6730 Dunning (Gerald Clough). Iron Age pot from Caesar's camp, Wimbledon. [Figure.] Antiq. J., 12, p. 437. 1932.

6731 —— Neolithic and Iron Age pottery from Danbury, Essex. [2 figures.] Antiq. J., 13, pp. 59–62. 1933.

6732 —— Iron Age pottery from Danbury, Essex. [4 figures.] Antiq. J., 14, pp. 186–90. 1934.

6733 —— Bronze Age beakers found [at Kempston, Turvey, Shefford and Clifton], in Bedfordshire. Antiq. J., 18, pp. 284–86 + 2 plates. 1938.

6734 Elsley (Frederick H.). Reconstruction of a Bronze Age beaker or drinking cup from Titsey. [*c*. 2000 B.C. Only known specimen from Surrey.] Surrey Archaeol. Collns., 26, pp. 150–51. 1913.

6735 Evans (*Sir* Arthur John). Late Celtic pottery from an ancient British urnfield at Aylesford, Kent. (A Late Celtic cemetery at Aylesford.) Proc. Soc. Antiq., 2 S. 13, pp. 18–20, 125–26. 1889–90.

6736 Fox (*Sir* Cyril). An unusual beaker from [Somersham?] Huntingdonshire. [Figure.] Antiq. J., 4, pp. 131–33. 1924.

6737 —— A food-vessel [of the Early Bronze Age] from the David Pennaut collection [in the University Museum, Cambridge]. [3 figures.] Arch. Camb., 80, pp. 184–90. 1925.

6738 Franks (*Sir* Augustus Wollaston) Two British urns . . . recently found near Brandon, in Suffolk. [2 figures.] Proc Soc. Antiq., 2 S. 5, pp. 270–75. 1872.

6739 Frere (D. H. S.). Late Neolithic grooved ware near Cambridge. [2 figures + plan.] Antiq. J., 23, pp. 34–41. 1943.

6740 Frere (Sheppard Sunderland). A food-vessel from Needham, Norfolk. [Figure + map. Bronze Age.] Antiq. J., 20, pp. 272–74. 1940.

6741 —— Beaker sherd from Chanctonbury. [Figure.] Sussex N. & Q., 9, p. 156. 1943.

6742 —— [Early] Iron Age vessel from Esher. [Figure.] Surrey Arch. Collns., 56, p. 159. 1959.

6743 —— Late Bronze Age pot from Farnham. Surrey Arch. Collections, 58, 1961, 112 + 1 plate.

6744 Gowing (C. N.). A Beaker bowl from Chesham. [1 plate + 1 figure.] Record of Bucks., 17 (2), 1962, 127–28.

6745 Gardner (Eric). Bronze Age urns of Surrey. [Figure + 2 plans.] Surrey Archaeol. Collns., 35, pp. 1–29 + 11 plates. 1924.

6746 —— Prehistoric pottery [2 urns] from Weybridge [Surrey]. [2 figures. Early Iron Age.] Antiq. J., 5, pp. 74–76. 1925.

6747 —— Neolithic pottery [from Weybridge and Croydon, Surrey]. [2 figures.] Antiq. J., 5, pp. 431–32. 1925.

6749 Gell (A. S. R.). Grooved ware from West Runton, Norfolk. Antiq. J., 29, p. 81. 1949.

6750 Glendenning (S. E.). A "Handled Beaker" from Bodney, Norfolk. Proc. PSEA, 7 i, 1932–34, 107–110 + 2 plates + 1 figure.

6751 Green (H. J. M.). Neolithic pottery from the Great Ouse Valley. [1 plate + 1 figure.] Proc. Camb. Ant. Soc., vol. LIV (1961), pp. 17–18.

6752 Grimes (W. F.). Beaker from East Tuddenham. Proc. PSEA, 7 iii, 1934, 424 + 1 plate.

6753 Hardy (H. R.), **Curwen** (Eliot Cecil) *and* **Hawkes** (Charles Francis Christopher). An Iron Age pottery site near Horsted Keynes. [6 figures + plan.] Sussex Arch. Collns., 78, pp. 252–65. 1937.

6754 Hardy (William Kyle). Neolithic and other pottery from Enborne gate gravel-pit. (Middle Palaeolithic implements from Enborne gate.) Trans. Newbury F.C., 7 (1934–37), p. 127, 185, 1937.

6755 —— A Bronze Age cinerary urn, found on the hill to the south of Newbury, 1935. [Figure.] Trans. Newbury F.C., 7 (1934–37), pp. 180–81. 1937.

6756 Harrison (E. E.). Iron Age and Romano-British pottery from Compton. Surrey Arch. Collections, 61, 1964, 101–02 + 1 figure.

6757 Hartley (Brian Rodgerson). Notes on pottery from some Romano-British Kilns in the Cambridge area. [2 figures.] Cambridge Antiq. Soc. Proc., LIII, 1959, 23–28.

6758 Hawkes (Charles Francis Christopher). The pottery from the sites on Plumpton Plain. Proc. prehist. Soc., 1, 1935, 39–59 + 13 figures.

6759 —— The Caburn pottery and its implications. Sussex Arch. Collns., 80, pp. 217–62. 1939.

6760 —— The pottery from Castle hill Newhaven. [9 figures. Late Bronze Age—Romano-British.] Sussex Arch. Collns., 80, pp. 269–92. 1939.

6761 —— Early Iron Age pottery from Linford, Essex. Trans. Essex Arch. Soc., 3 Ser. 1 (1962), pt. 2, 83–87.

6762 Hodson (F. R.). Some pottery from Eastbourne, the "Marnians" and the pre-Roman Iron Age in southern England. Proc. prehist. Soc., 28, 1962, 140–55 + 3 figures + 2 plates.

6763 Holland (Peter Crossley). Iron Age pottery from Chinnor, Oxon. [Figure.] Oxoniensia, 7, pp. 108–09. 1942.

6764 Hore (K. D.). Iron Age sherds from Keston. Arch. Cantiana, 78, 1963, 184.

6765 Hull (Mark Reginald). New Bronze Age beakers. [3 figures. From Little Holland and Sible Hedingham, Essex. In Colchester museum.] Antiq. J., 9, pp. 250–53. 1929.

6766 —— The ancient pottery found at Twitty Fee, Danbury. [2 figures.] Essex Nat., 25, pp. 109–20 + 4 plates. 1936.

6767 Jessup (Ronald Frederick). Cinerary urn from Stodmarsh. [Figure. Bronze Age.] Arch. Cant., 43, pp. 296–97. 1931.

6768 —— Two Early Bronze Age beakers. [From Ightham, Kent and from Kew Gardens.] Antiq. J., 12, pp. 169–70 + plate. 1932.

6769 —— Early Bronze Age beakers. [Figure (Sturry beaker). Also from Ightham, Barham, Bromley, Dover.] Arch. Cant., 45, pp. 174–78 + plate. 1933.

6770 —— A cooking-pot from Chilham, Kent. [Figure. Early Iron Age.] Antiq. J., 16, p. 467. 1936.

6771 —— "Incense-cup" from Canterbury. [Figure. Middle Bronze Age.] Arch. Cant., 48, pp. 243–44. 1936.

6772 Kendrick (*Sir* Thomas Downing). A beaker from Ware. [Beaker period "A".] Antiq. J., 20, p. 103 + plate. 1940.

6773 Lacaille (Armand Donald). Prehistoric pottery found at Iver, Bucks. [2 figures + 2 plans. Neolithic sites.] Records of Bucks., 13, pp. 287–99 + 2 plates. 1937.

6774 —— [Early] Iron Age pottery from Lent Rise, Burnham, Bucks. [Figure.] Antiq. J., 19, pp. 82–83. 1939.

6775 —— *and* **Corder** (Philip). A Belgic clay pot-stand [from Burnham, Bucks.]. [Figure.] Antiq. J., 23, pp. 58–59. 1943.

6776 Latter (Robert Booth). Discovery of fragments of ancient British, Romano-British and Roman pottery in a chalk cavern in Camden park, Chislehurst, near Bromley, Kent. Arch. Cant., 1, pp. 137–42. 1858.

6777 Laver (Henry). Early British urn [from] Wix, Essex. Essex Nat., 1, p. 35. 1887.

6778 —— Early British urns near Wayland, Suffolk. Essex Nat., 1, p. 35. 1887.

6779 —— Discovery of Celtic [cinerary] urns at Colchester. Essex Nat., 3, p. 116. 1889.

6780 —— On a recent discovery of Celtic urns at [Water Lane,] Colchester. Trans. Essex Archaeol. Soc., N.S. 4, pp. 18–20 + plate. 1893.

6781 —— Discovery of a Late Celtic pottery at Shoebury. Trans. Essex Archaeol. Soc., N.S. 6, pp. 222–24 + plate. 1898.

6782 —— Find of Late Celtic pottery at Little Hallingbury, Essex. Trans. Essex Archaeol. Soc., N.S. 9, pp. 348–50 + plate. 1906.

6783 Lee (Austin). The Lincolnshire beakers of the Early Bronze Age. Assoc. Archit. Socs'. Rpts., 38, pp. 209–12 + 5 plates. 1927.

6784 Leeds (Edward Thurlow). On Neolithic pottery from Buston farm, Astrop [near King's Sutton, Northants.]. Oxfordshire Archaeol. Soc., Rpts., 1912, pp. 114–18 + 2 plates. 1913.

6785 —— Notes on early British pottery. [Figure (beaker in Colchester museum).] Antiq. J., 2, pp. 330–38. 1922.

6786 —— Bronze Age urns from Long Wittenham [Berks.]. [Figure.] Antiq. J., 9, pp. 153–54. 1929.

6787 —— Three beakers from [the Devil's Quoits,] Oxfordshire. [Figure.] Antiq. J., 11, pp. 59–60. 1931.

6788 —— A handled beaker from Eynsham, Oxfordshire. Antiq. J., 11, pp. 280–81 + plate. 1931.

6789 —— Beakers of the upper Thames district. [3 figures, map + 2 plans.] Oxoniensia, 3, pp. 7–30 + 4 plates. 1938.

6790(a) —— New discoveries of Neolithic pottery in Oxfordshire. [2 figures + map. Cassington and Stanton Harcourt.] Oxoniensia, 5, pp. 1–12 + 3 plates. 1940.

6790(b) Le Neve (Peter). An extract of a letter, giving an account of a large number of urns dug up at North Elmham in Norfolk. Phil. Trans. Roy. Soc., XXVIII, 1713, 257–60.

6791 Leney (F.). Handled beaker in the Norwich Museum. Proc. PSEA, 6 iii, 1930, 248 + 1 plate.

6792 Lethbridge (Thomas Charles) *and* **O'Reilly** (Maureen Margaret). Three beakers recently acquired by the Museum of Archaeology and Ethnology, Cambridge. [From Whittlesford, Hilgay and Barton Bendish.] Proc. Camb. Antiq. Soc., 37, pp. 74–75 + 2 plates. 1937.

6793 Lewis (Geoffrey D.). Late Bronze Age pot from Yapton. Sussex Arch. Collection, 98, 1960, 17–18 + 1 figure.

6794 —— Late Bronze Age pot from Findon Valley, Worthing. Sussex Arch. Collection, 98, 1960, 18 + 1 figure.

6795 —— Iron Age pot from Highdown Hill. Sussex Arch. Collection, 98, 1960, 18.

6796 Lowther (Anthony William George). Object of gritted hand-made ware from Ashstead, Surrey. [Figure. Iron Age "A".] Antiq. J., 21, p. 347. 1941.

6797 —— Iron Age pottery from Wisley, Surrey. Proc. prehist. Soc., XI, 1945, 32–38 + 4 figures.

6798 —— Iron Age pottery from sites at Ewell and Ashstead. [2 figures.] Surrey Archaeol. Collns., 50, pp. 139–41. 1949.

6799 —— Iron Age pottery from Hawk's hill, Fetcham. [2 figures.] Surrey Archaeol. Collns., 50, pp. 142–43. 1949.

6800 —— Iron Age pottery from St. George's hill camp, Weybridge. [2 figures.] Surrey Archaeol. Collns., 51, pp. 144–47. 1950.

6801 —— Iron Age "A" pot from Milford. [Figure.] Surrey Arch. Collns., 55, p. 124. 1958.

6802 Mallowan (Max Edgar Lucien). Food-vessel from near Henley-on-Thames. [Early Bronze Age.] Antiq. J., 18, p. 412 + plate. 1938.

6803 Maynard (Guy). A rare urn from [Brantham, on the Stour estuary,] Suffolk. [Figure.] Antiq. J., 5, pp. 73–74. 1925.

6804 Moir (James Reid). Two Late Bronze Age urns from [Manningtree and Ipswich] East Anglia. [2 figures.] Man, 19, pp. 6–7. 1919.

6805 Murray (Katherine Maud Elizabeth) *and* **Pilmer** (J. G.). A cinerary urn found at Westbourne. [Middle Bronze Age.] Sussex N. & Q., 13, pp. 159–60. 1951.

6806 Musson (Reginald Coulson). An illustrated catalogue of Sussex Beaker and Bronze Age pottery. [9 figures.] Sussex Arch. Collns., 92, pp. 106–24. 1954.

6807 Newton (M. A.). Iron Age pottery from Telscombe Tye. Sussex N. & Q., 12, pp. 18–19. 1948.

6808 O'Neil (Bryan Hugh St. John). Beaker found at Barnham, West Suffolk. [Figure.] Antiq. J., 24, pp. 147–48. 1944.

6809 Ozanne, Paul C. The Pottery [Aldwick Iron Age Settlement, Barley]. Proc. Camb. Ant. Soc., LIV (1961), 36–45.

6810 Parker (John). Discovery of British pottery [near High Wycombe]. Records of Bucks., 6, pp. 259–60 + plate. 1888.

6811 —— British urns recently discovered near Wycombe, Bucks. Proc. Soc. Antiq., 2 S. 12, pp. 338–46. 1889.

6812 Patchett (Florence M.). Bronze Age cinerary urn from Duneton hill. [2 figures.] Sussex N. & Q., 7, pp. 52–54. 1938.

6813 Peake (Harold John Edward). Beaker from Barham, Kent. [Figure.] Antiq. J., 14, pp. 183–84. 1934.

6814 —— A beaker and a four-legged bowl from Inkpen, Berks. Antiq. J., 16, pp. 97–98 + plate. 1936.

6815 —— A beaker and a four-legged bowl from Inkpen, Berks. [2 figures.] Trans. Newbury F.C., 7 (1934–37), pp. 186–87. 1937.

6816 Petch (D. F.). Bronze Age urns, Blankney or Metheringham. [LBA.] Rpts. & Papers, Lincs. A. & A.S., 9, 1961, 9–11 + 2 figures + 1 plate.

6817 Phillips (Charles William). Neolithic "A" bowl from [Great Ponton,] near Grantham [Lincs.]. [Figure.] Antiq. J. 15, pp. 347–48. 1935.

6818 Piggott (Cecily Margaret). The Iron Age pottery from Theale. [3 figures.] Trans. Newbury F.C., 8, pp. 52–60 + plate. 1938.

6819 Piggott (Stuart). Neolithic pottery and other remains from Pangbourne, Berks., and Caversham, Oxon. Proc. PSEA, 6 i, 1928–29, 30–39 + 3 figures + 2 plates.

6820 —— Neolithic pottery spoon from Kent. Proc. prehist. Soc., N.S. 1, 1935, 150–51 + 1 figure.

6821 —— Handled beakers. [2 in Museum of Archaeology, Cambridge. ?copies in clay of wooden mugs turned from a log on a lathe.] Antiquity, 9, p. 348 + plate. 1935.

6822 Ransom (William). Late Celtic pottery recently found near Hitchin. [Figure.] Proc. Soc. Antiq., 2 S. 13, pp. 16–18. 1889.

6823 Riley (D. N.). Neolithic and Bronze Age pottery from Risby Warren and other occupation sites in North Lincolnshire. Proc. prehist. Soc., 23, 1957, 40–56 + 10 figures + 2 plates.

6824 Rowe (Arthur). Early British pottery [from Margate]. [Figure. La Tène I period.] Antiq. J., 5, pp. 164–65. 1925.

6825 Rudolf (William de M.). Sherds of a Belgic vessel from Westhall. Proc. Suffolk Inst. Arch., 29 ii, 1962, 223–24 + 1 figure.

6826 Smallcombe (W. A.). A Neolithic bowl from Pangbourne. Berks. Archaeol. J., 50, p. 101 + plate. 1947.

6827 Smedley (Norman) *and* **Owles** (Elizabeth). Pottery of the Early Middle Bronze Age in Suffolk. Proc. Suffolk Inst. Arch., 29 ii, 1962, 175–97 + 4 figures + 6 plates.

6828 —— *and* —— Bronze Age pottery from Suffolk—an additional note. Proc. Suffolk Inst. Arch., 29 iii, 1963, 355–56 + 1 figure.

6829 Smith (Isobel F.). Late Beaker pottery from the Lyonesse surface and the date of the transgression. [2 figures. Excavations at Lion Point, Clacton, Essex.] Univ. London, Inst. Archaeol., Ann. Rpt., 11, pp. 29–42 + plate. 1955.

6830 Smith (Reginald Allender). A two-handled cup of black ware from the Thames. [4 figures. From Surrey foreshore, opposite Barn Elms. Bronze Age.] Proc. Soc. Antiq., 2 S. 25, pp. 84–88 + plate. 1913.

6831 —— Two cinerary urns of the Early Iron Age found at Deal. [6 figures.] Proc. Soc. Antiq., 2 S. 26, pp. 129–33. 1914.

6832 —— A Late Celtic cinerary urn found at Letchworth Garden-city,

Herts. [2 figures.] Proc. Soc. Antiq.,
2 S. 26, pp. 238–40 + plate. 1914.

6833 Smith (Reginald Allender).
Pottery finds at Wisley [Surrey]. [8
figures. Neolithic.] Antiq. J., 4, pp.
40–45 + 2 plates. 1924.

6834 —— Two prehistoric vessels.
[Neolithic bowl from the Thames near
Wallingford, and urn from Southern
hill, Reading (Hallstatt period).] Antiq.
J., 4, pp. 127–30 + plate. 1924.

6835 Spokes (Peter Sydney). Roman
and pre-Roman pottery found in Little
Horsted. Sussex N. & Q., 4, pp. 150–54.
1933.

6836 Stebbing (William Pinckard Delane). Bucket-urns found near Deal.
Antiq. J., 17, pp. 73–76. 1937.

6837 —— Pre-Roman, Roman and
post-Roman pottery from burials at
Worth, East Kent. Antiq. J., 17, pp.
310–12. 1937.

6838 Swan (A. C.). Neolithic pottery
from Badshot long-barrow. [Figure.]
Surrey Archaeol. Collns., 47, pp. 90–92.
1941.

6839 Tebbutt (Charles Frederick).
Beakers from [St. Neots,] Huntingdon-
shire. [Figure (stone axes). Bronze Age.]
Antiq. J., 10, pp. 384–85 + plate. 1930.

6840 —— A prehistoric pottery vessel
from the Fens. Antiq. J., 13, pp. 54–55.
1933.

6841 —— Archaeological notes: Neolithic pottery from Buckden, Hunts.
[1 figure.] Proc. Camb. Ant. Soc., 58,
1965, 141–42.

6842 Toms (Herbert S.). Notes on a
Late Celtic urn found near Brighton. [2
figures.] Antiquary, 48, pp. 223–26. 1912.

6843 Warren (Samuel Hazzledine) *and*
Smith (Isobel F.). Neolithic pottery
from the submerged land-surface of the
Essex coast. [2 figures.] Univ. London,
Inst. Archaeol., Ann. Rpt., 10, pp. 26–
33 + plate. 1934.

6844 Watts (H.). Bronze Age beaker
[at Slade End, Berks.]. Berks. Archaeol.
J., 39, p. 99. 1935.

6845 Westell (William Percival).
Cinerary urns found [at Willian] near
Letchworth [Herts.]. [Figure.] Antiq.
J., 4, pp. 268–69. 1924.

6846 White (G. M.). Neolithic pottery from Selsey Bill. [Figure.] Sussex
N. & Q., 4, p. 217. 1933.

6847 Whitwell (J. B.). An unusual
rim probably from an Iron Age vessel,
North Willingham. Rpts. & Papers,
Lincs. A. & A.S., 10, 1963, 4 + 1 figure.

6848 —— Iron Age pottery, Crow-
land Wash. Rpts. & Papers, Lincs.
A. & A.S., 10, 1963, 4.

6849 —— Beaker sherds, Tattershall
Thorpe. Rpts. & Papers, Lincs. A. &
A.S., 10, 1964, 60.

6850 Wickham (D. A.). Recent discoveries in Thurrock area. [LBA food-
vessel; BA funerary urn.] Proc. Essex
Arch. Soc., xxv, iii, 1960, 385–86 + 1
plate.

6851 Williams (John Foster). Iron
Age pottery from Boxford, Suffolk.
Antiq. J., 6, p. 309. 1926.

6852 Wilson (Arthur Ernest). The
evolution of Sussex Iron Age pottery.
[9 figures + 9 maps.] Sussex Arch.
Collns., 87, pp. 77–111. 1948.

6853 Winbolt (Samuel Edward). The
Greek vases from Selsey. [5th—3rd c.
B.C. ?prehistoric trade; ?brought by
early Roman colonists as decorations.]
Sussex N. & Q., 4, pp. 61–62. 1932.

6854 —— Loom-weights from a kiln
[at Badwell Ash, Suffolk]. [Figure.
Latest Bronze or Earliest Iron Age.]
Antiq. J., 15, pp. 474–75 + plate. 1935.

6855 Wright (Arthur G.). Rare find
of Late Celtic pottery at Colchester.
[Figure.] Reliquary, 3rd S. 11, pp. 131–
32. 1905.

6856 —— Late Celtic pottery at
Colchester. [2 figures.] Reliquary, 3rd
S. 12, pp. 203–05. 1906.

6857 —— Early pottery in Colchester
Museum. [6 figures (Bronze Age and
Late Celtic).] Reliquary, 3rd S. 15, pp.
51–56. 1909.

(b) Zones 2 and 3
[CBA Groups 8, 12, 13]

6858 [Anon.] Cinerary urns from
Gunwalloe. J. Roy. Instn. Cornwall, 13,
p. 438 + plate. 1898.

6859 ApSimon (Arthur M.). Cornish
Bronze Age pottery. [Figure.] Proc.
West Cornwall F.C., 2, pp. 36–46. 1958.

6860 Ashbee (Paul). An urn from
Par beach, St. Martin's, Isles of Scilly.

[Figure. Bronze Age.] Proc. West Cornwall F.C., N.S. 1, pp. 123–24. 1955.

6861 Auden (Thomas). Discovery of cinerary urns at Little Ryton. [Probably Late Iron Age.] Trans. Shropshire Archaeol. Soc., 3rd S. 6, p. xx. 1906.

6862 Brailsford (John William). The pottery found during the excavation of a pond-barrow on Sheep down, Winterborne Steepleton, Dorset. [Bronze Age.] Arch. News Letter, 1 xii, pp. 12–14. 1949.

6863 Brooke (J. W.). British urns at Temple, near Marlborough. Wilts. Archaeol. Mag., 26, p. 411. 1892.

6864 Burnard (Robert). Discovery of a prehistoric cooking pot *in situ* [on Raddick hill, near Princetown] on Dartmoor. [Figure.] Reliquary, N. [3rd] S. 2, pp. 225–26. 1896.

3865 Calkin (John Bernard). Buckets, barrels and globulars. [Deverel-Rimbury pottery; Middle and Late Bronze Age; Dorset and Hants. coast.] Proc. Dorset Arch. Soc., 79 (1957), pp. 104–05. 1958.

6866 —— Barrels, buckets and globulars. [Deverel-Rimbury pottery in coastal regions of Dorset and Hampshire. Middle Bronze Age.] Arch. News Letter, 6, p. 111. 1958.

6867 —— Middle Bronze Age urn from South Afflington. [1 plate.] Proc. Dorset N.H. & A.S., 81, 1960, 118–19.

6868 —— Middle Bronze Age urn from Furgebrook, Church Knowle. [1 figure.] Proc. Dorset N.H. & A.S., 81, 1960, 121.

6869 Chatwin (Philip Boughton). Beaker from Baginton, Warwickshire. [Figure.] Antiq. J., 12, pp. 171–72. 1932.

6870 Chitty (Lily Frances). Twin food-vessels preserved at Aqualate hall, [Forton], Staffordshire. [Early Bronze Age.] Antiq. J., 9, pp. 137–40 + plate. 1929.

6871 Clay (Richard Challoner Cobbe). Two cinerary urns of the Bronze Age from Little Ryton, near Condover. [Figure.] Trans. Shropshire Archaeol. Soc., 43 (4th S. 10), pp. xxxiii–xxxv. 1926.

6872 Clifford (Elsie Margaret). Two finds of Beaker pottery from Gloucester-shire [also flint and hammer stone]. Trans. Bristol & Glos. Arch. Soc., 83, pp. 34–39 + 3 figures. 1964.

6873 —— Early Iron Age pottery from Rodborough Common and Duntisbourne Abbots. Trans. Bris. & Glos. Arch. Soc., 83, pp. 145–46 + 1 figure. 1964.

6874 Cook (Norman C.). A late Bronze Age urn from Coombe. Papers & Proc. Hants. F.C., 17, p. 56 + plate. 1952.

6875 Cornwall (Ian W.) *and* **Hodges** (Henry W. M.). Thin sections of British Neolithic pottery: Windmill Hill —a test site. Bull. Inst. of Arch. London, 4, 1964, 29–33.

6876 Cox (James Stevens). A note on ribbed 'Durotrigian' bowls at Ilchester, Somerset. [1 figure.] Proc. Dorset N.H. & A.S., 85, 1963, 94–95.

6877 Crawford (Osbert Guy Stanhope). Description of a vase found on Nunwell down, Isle of Wight. [Figure. Bronze Age.] Man, 13, pp. 19–22. 1913.

6878 —— Note on the discovery of two Bronze Age urns at Storry Cross, in the parish of Minstead, New Forest, December 28th, 1912. [Figure.] Papers & Proc. Hants. F.C., 6, Suppl., pp. 33–36. 1913.

6879 Crofts (C. B.). Bronze Age find at St. Buryan. [Small pot.] Devon & Cornwall N. & Q., 23, p. 315. 1949.

6880 Cunnington (Maud Edith). On some fragments of Arretine ware and other pottery from a Late Celtic rubbish heap at Oare, Wilts. [3 figures.] Reliquary, 3rd S. 15, pp. 57–61. 1909.

6881 —— Bronze Age cinerary urn found at Knowle, Little Bedwyn. [Figure.] Wilts. Archaeol. Mag., 42, pp. 245–46. 1923.

6882 —— List of [81] Bronze Age "drinking cups" found in Wiltshire. Wilts. Archaeol. Mag., 43, pp. 267–84. 1926.

6883 —— Cinerary urn from Figheldean. Wilts. Archaeological Mag., 43, p. 398 + plate. 1926.

6884 —— Cinerary urns from Knowle, Little Bedwyn. Wilts. Archaeol. Mag., 43, p. 399. 1926.

6885 —— Bronze Age beaker from Beckhampton. Wilts. Archaeol. Mag., 43, pp. 399–400 + plate. 1926.

6886 Cunnington (Maud Edith). The pottery from the long barrow at West Kennet, Wilts. pp. 19 + 13 plates. 4⁰. Devizes, 1927.

6887 —— A [Bronze Age cinerary] urn from Wexcombe down. Wilts. Archaeol. Mag., 49, pp. 164–65 + plate. 1940.

6889 Cunnington (William). A comparison of two remarkable urns in the Stourhead collection at Devizes. [From Kingston Deverill, Wilts. and from Crendon, Bucks.] Wilts. Archaeol. Mag., 26, pp. 317–19 + plate. 1892.

6890 Dobson (Dina Portway). A beaker from [Brean Down beach,] Somerset. Antiq. J., 18, p. 172 + plate. 1938.

6891 Donovan (Helen Evangeline) *and* **Dunning** (Gerald Clough). Iron Age pottery and Saxon burials at Foxcote manor, Andoversford, Gloucestershire. [3 figures + map + plan.] Trans. Bristol & Glos. Arch. Soc., 58, pp. 157–70 + plate. 1936.

6892 Dowie (H. G.). A note on the urn discovered near Marldon. J. Torquay nat. Hist. Soc., 4, 1923, 15–17 + 1 plate.

6893 Dunning (Gerald Clough). Bronze Age beakers found in the Isle of Wight. [2 figures + map. List.] Proc. I. of W. N.H. & Arch. Soc., 2, pp. 292–98 + 2 plates. 1933.

6894 —— Late Bronze Age urn from Lower Swell, Gloucestershire. [Figure.] Antiq. J., 15, pp. 471–73. 1935.

6895 —— A beaker from Bourton-on-the-Water, Gloucestershire. Proc. prehist. Soc., 3, 1937, 163–64.

6896 Edwards (J. H.). Bucket-urn from Baginton, Warwickshire. [Figure. Late Bronze Age.] Antiq. J., 18, pp. 412–14. 1938.

6897 Farrar (Raymond Anthony Holt). Recent finds from West Orchard Farm and Bradle Barn, Church Knowle. [Iron Age "A" and "C" and RB sherds.] Proc. Dorset N.H. & A.S., 85, 1963, 102–03.

6898 —— Romano-British sherds from Langton Maltravers. Proc. Dorset N.H. & A.S., 85, 1963, 105.

6899 —— Late Bronze Age and Roman finds at Bokerly Dyke, Pentridge. [LBA sherd.] Proc. Dorset N.H. & A.S., 85, 1963, 106.

6900 —— Surface finds at Bulbury camp, Lytchett Minster. [RB sherds.] Proc. Dorset N.H. & A.S., 86, 1964, 115.

6901 —— A Bronze Age collared urn from Bere Down, Bere Regis. Proc. Dorset N.H. & A.S., 86, 1964, 115.

6902 —— Romano-British and Mediaeval pottery from Town's End, Corfe Castle. [IA "C" and RB sherds.] Proc. Dorset N.H. & A.S., 86, 1964, 117.

6903 Fowler (Peter J.). A note on archaeological finds from the A.E.A. effluent pipe-line, Winfaith Heath, to Arish Mell, 1959. [Some RB pottery]. [6 figures.] Proc. Dorset N.H. & A.S., 84, 1963, 125–31.

6904 Fox (*Lady* Aileen Mary). An Iron Age bowl from Rose Ash, North Devon. Ant. J., 41, 1961, 186–98.

6905 Gardiner (Charles Irving). The discovery of a beaker [from Ivy Lodge farm] near Woodchester. Proc. Cotteswold N.F.C., 24, pp. 103–06 + plate. 1930.

6906 Gray (Harold St. George). Discovery of Neolithic pottery on Meare heath, Somerset. Proc. Somerset Arch. Soc., 82 (1936), pp. 160–62 + plate. 1937.

6907 Guthrie (A.). Miscellaenous sherds from Sennen. [BA—Medieval.] Cornish archaeol. No. 1, 1962, 118–19 + 1 figure.

6908 Hawkes (Charles Francis Christopher). A new handled beaker, with spiral ornament, from Kempsey, Worcestershire. [Figure + map.] Antiq. J., 15, pp. 276–83 + plate. 1935.

6909 Herdman (D. W.). Prehistoric vessel from Hawling. [Transition Late Bronze—Early Iron Age.] Trans. Bristol & Glos. Arch. Soc., 55, pp. 381–82 + plate. 1933.

6910 Hooley (Reginald W.). Hallstatt pottery from Winchester. [Figure.] Papers & Proc. Hants. F.C., 10, pp. 63–68 + plate. 1927.

6911 Hull (Mark Reginald). Five Bronze Age beakers from north-east Essex. [Halstead, St. Osyth, Alresford, Ardleigh and Colchester.] Antiq. J., 26, pp. 67–69 + plate. 1946.

6912 Iago (William). Notice of a cinerary urn found in a barrow at Hustyn in St. Breock, Cornwall. J. Roy. Instn. Cornwall, 7, pp. 141–47 + 2 plates. 1882.

6913 Ingram (A. H. Winnington). On the ancient use of a small clay cup, found near Coughton in Warwickshire, *etc*. Wilts. Archaeol. Mag., 12, pp. 122–26 + plate. 1870.

6914 Jewitt (Llewellynn). Note on a [Celtic] cinerary urn from Stone, Staffordshire. [Figure.] Reliquary, 6, p. 64. 1866.

6915 Leeds (Edward Thurlow). Neolithic spoons from Northern Swell, Gloucestershire. Antiq. J., 7, pp. 61–62 + plate. 1927.

6916 Maxwell (I. S.). A sherd from the submerged forest at Porthcurnick Beach. [IA.] Cornish Arch., 4, 1965, 90–91 + 1 figure.

6917 Musty (John). Beaker finds from South Wiltshire. Wilts. Archaeol. Mag., 58, 1963, No. 211, 414–16 + 1 figure.

6918 Newall (Robert Stirling). Beaker and food-vessel from barrow no. 25, Figheldean. Wilts. Archaeol. Mag., 44, p. 118 + plate. 1928.

6919 Passmore (A. D.). On some Bronze Age pottery of "food vessel" type. [2 figures (pottery from Overton and Ogbourne St. Andrews, Wilts.)] 38, pp. 586–88. 1914.

6920 —— A pottery button from Upham. [Bronze Age.] Wilts. Archaeol. Mag., 46, p. 102 + plate. 1932.

6021 Patchett (Florence M.). Cornish Bronze Age pottery. [17 figures + 9 maps.] Archaeol. J., 101 (1944), pp. 17–49 + 7 tables; 107 (1950), pp. 44–65. 1946, 1952.

6922 —— The Bronze Age beaker from Tregiffian farm, St. Buryan. [Figure.] Proc. West Cornwall F.C., N.S. 1, pp. 23–24. 1953.

6923 —— A Middle Bronze Age urn from Lelissick, Padstow. [Figure.] Proc. West Cornwall F.C., N.S. 1, p. 43. 1954.

6924 Piggott (Cecily Margaret). Late Bronze Age urns from Swindon. [2 figures.] Wilts. Archaeol. Mag., 48, pp. 353–56. 1938.

6925 —— Report on the pottery from Winklebury camp, Hants. [Figure. Iron Age "AI."] Papers & Proc. Hants. F.C., 15, pp. 56–57. 1941.

6926 Piggott (Stuart). A remarkable bowl from the Avebury megalithic avenue. Proc. prehist. Soc. N.S. 1, 1935, 147–48 + 1 plate.

6927 —— A pottery spoon from the Mendips. [Neolithic.] Proc. prehist. Soc., N.S. 2, 1936, 143 + 1 figure.

6928 —— Handley Hill, Dorset—a neolithic bowl and the date of the entrenchment. Proc. prehist. Soc., N.S. 2, 1936, 229–30 + 1 figure.

6929 —— Neolithic pottery from Hackpen, Avebury. [Figure.] Wilts. Archaeol. Mag., 48, pp. 90–91. 1937.

6930 —— An Early Bronze Age vessel from Ashley hill, near Salisbury. [Figure.] Wilts. Archaeol. Mag., 51, pp. 384–85. 1946.

6931 Ratcliffe (Joseph Riley). A cinerary urn (from Christchurch, Hants.]. [Bronze Age.] B'ham Arch. Soc., Trans., 52 (1927), p. 300 + plate. 1930.

6932 Rustell (V.) *and* **Patchett** (Florence M.). A beaker from Trevedra common, St. Just-in-Penwith. [Figure. Bronze Age.] Proc. West Cornwall F.C., N.S. 1, pp. 41–42. 1954.

6933 Shaw (C. T.). Bronze Age urns from Honiton. [3 figures + map.] Proc. Devon Archaeol. Expl. Soc., 2, pp. 191–97 + plate. 1935.

6934 Shortt (Hugh de Sansmarez). Pygmy cups from Boscombe down west. [Figure. Bronze Age. In Salisbury museum.] Wilts. Archaeol. Mag., 48, pp. 462–65. 1939.

6935 —— Bronze Age beakers from Larkhill and Bulford. [3 figures.] Wilts. Archaeol. Mag., 51, pp. 381–83. 1946.

6936 Smart (T. William Wake). Our ancient British urns [i.e. in Dorset County Museum]. Proc. Dorset Antiq. F.C., 12, pp. 180–86 + plate. 1891.

6937 Somerscales (M. I.). Further sherds from Phillack Towans. Cornish Arch., 4, 1965, 86–87 + 1 figure.

6938 Stone (John F. S.). Pygmy cup from Winterbourne Dauntsey. [Late Bronze Age. In Salisbury Museum.] Wilts. Archaeol. Mag., 49, p. 234 + plate. 1940.

6939 —— Some grooved ware pottery from the Woodhenge area. Proc. prehist. Soc., 15, 1949, 122–27 + 2 figures.

6941 Treffry (J. T.). An account of a British sepulchral urn, discovered in the neighbourhood of Place. Ann. Rpt. Roy. Instn. Cornwall, 22 (1840), pp. 63–67. 1841.

6942 Waterman (Dudley M.). A

beaker from [Lower Farringdon,] Hampshire. [Figure.] Antiq. J., 27, p. 80. 1947.

6943 Wight (M.). Broadway: a prehistoric loom weight. [Reprinted from *Country Life* for March 29, 1941: figure there also.] Trans. Worcs. Archaeol. Soc., N.S. 20 (1943), p. 49. 1944.

(c) Zones 4, 5, 6
[CBA Groups 1, 2, 3, 4, 5, 6]

6944 Addyman (P. V.), **Coles** (J. M.) *and* **Hartley** (C. E.). A Late Bronze Age vessel from Flaxby. Yorks. Arch. Journ., 41 (ii), 1964, 184–90 + 2 figures.

6945 [Anon.] Cinerary urn from Kelsall. [Figure. Middle Bronze Age.] J. Chester & N. Wales Arch. Soc., N.S. 39, p. 110. 1951.

6946 Armstrong (Albert Leslie). A cinerary urn of the Bronze Age from Dronfield Woodhouse [Derbyshire.] Trans. Hunter. Arch. Soc., 2, pp. 109–15 + 1 plate. 1924.

6947 Barnes (F.). Pottery from prehistoric sites, North End, Walney Island. [6 figures + plan.] Trans. Cumb. & Westm. Ant. Soc., N.S. 55, pp. 1–16 + plate. 1956.

6948 Barnwell (Edward Lowry). The Caergwrle [Flintshire] cup. Arch. Camb., 4th S. 6, pp. 268–74 + coloured plate. 1875.

6949 —— The Abermeurig cup. ["Incense-cup" found at Talsarn, Cards.] Arch. Camb., 4th S. 10, pp. 222–25 + plate. 1879.

6950 Baynes (Edward Neil). Cinerary urns found at Plâs Penrhyn, Anglesey. Arch. Camb., 84 ii, 1929, 229–36 + 3 figures.

6951 —— Cinerary urns found at Plâs Penrhyn, Anglesey. [3 figures. Late Bronze Age.] Anglesey Ant. Soc. Trans., 1930, pp. 26–32. 1930.

6952 Brewis (Parker) *and* **Cowen** (John David). An encrusted cinerary urn of the Bronze Age. [From Ryton on Tyne.] Arch. Æl., 4th S. 6, pp. 197–98 + plate. 1929.

6953 Brewis (William Parker). Bronze Age food vessel from Amble,

Northumberland. Proc. Soc. Antiq. Newc., 4th S. 4, p. 251 + plate. 1930.

6954 Brewster (T. C. M.). A Bronze Age beaker from Staxton, Scarborough, Yorks., and a new local Beaker complex. [Figure.] Ann. Rpt. Yorks. Phil. Soc., 1951, pp. 13–15. 1952.

6955 Carter (Charles). Cinerary urn from Menai Bridge. Arch. Camb., 85 ii, 1930, 405–07 + 2 figures.

6956 Case (Humphrey). Irish Neolithic pottery: distribution and sequence. Proc. prehist. Soc., 27, 1961, 174–233 + 30 figures.

6957 Childe (Vere Gordon). The Danish Neolithic pottery from the coast of Durham. Arch. Æl., 4th S. 9, pp. 84–88 + 3 plates. 1932.

6958 —— *and* **Warwick** (G. T.) etc. Cinerary urns from Kirk Ireton. [Figure + map. Middle Bronze Age.] J. Derbs. Archaeol. Soc., 68 (N.S. 21), pp. 31–36 + plate. 1948.

6959 Chitty (Lily Frances). A beaker-like vessel from Bushmills, Co. Antrim. [Degenerate example of a beaker of the Early Bronze Age.] Antiq. J., 13, pp. 259–65 + 2 plates. 1933.

6960 —— Notes on the Irish affinities of three Bronze Age food-vessels of type Ia found in Wales. Bull. Bd. Celtic Stud., 9, pp. 275–83 + plate. 1938.

6961 —— Pottery spindle-whorl from Pentrefelin, Caernarvonshire. [Iron Age.] Arch. Camb., 97 ii, 1943, 232–34 + 1 figure.

6962 Clark (Mary Kitson). The Yorkshire food-vessel. [3 figures + map.] Archaeol. J., 94 (1937), pp. 43–63 + plate. 1938.

6963 Cockroft (A.). On the recent discovery of seven prehistoric urns at Blackheath, in Stansfield, Yorkshire. Yorks. N. & Q. (ed. Forshaw), 1, pp. 261–62. 1904.

6964 Corrie (John M.). An incense-cup from Cairngill, Kirkcudbrightshire. [Bronze Age.] Trans. Dumfries. Ant. Soc., 3 S. 15 (1928–29), pp. 50–54 + 3 plates. 1929.

6965 Cottrill (Frank). Another [Early] Bronze Age beaker from [Noseley,] Leicestershire. [Figure.] Antiq. J., 21, pp. 232–34. 1941.

6966 Cowen (John David). A beaker

from [Norham castle estate,] Northumberland. [Figure.] Antiq. J., 29, p. 195 + plate. 1949.

6967 Davies (Ellis). A sepulchral urn from Caergwrle, Flintshire. Arch. Camb., 84 ii, 1929, 333–36 + 2 figures.

6968 —— Beaker from Tremadoc, Caernarvonshire. Arch. Camb., 86 ii, 1931, 363–64 + 1 figure.

6969 Davies (John). The find of British urns near Capel Cynon, in Cardiganshire. [Figure.] Arch. Camb., 6th S. 5, pp. 62–69 + 5 plates. 1905.

6970 Dunning (Gerald Clough). Beaker from Flixton, E.R. Yorks. [Figure.] Antiq. J., 13, pp. 53–54. 1933.

6971 —— A beaker from [Melton Mowbray,] Leicestershire. [Figure. Now in Leicester Museum.] Antiq. J., 17, p. 71. 1937.

6972 Earwaker (John Parsons). The recent discovery of urns at Penmaenmawr. [Figure (bronze pins).] Arch. Camb., 5th S. 8, pp. 33–37 + 2 plates. 1891.

6973 Edwards (Arthur J. H.). Cinerary urns at Monklaw, Jedburgh. [Report by J. C. Brash in incinerated bones from Bronze Age urn.] Trans. Hawick Archaeol. Soc., 1935, p. 35. 1935.

6974 Evans (George Eyre). Bronze Age urns: prehistoric finds at Llandyssul [Carmarthenshire]. J. Brit. Archaeol. Ass., N.S. 29, pp. 262–63. 1923.

6975 —— Bronze Age urns found at Bwlchygroes. [Figure.] Trans. Carmarthenshire Ant. Soc., 17, pp. 58–59. 1923.

6976 —— [Two Bronze Age] urns found on Blaendyffryn farm [Cards.]. Trans. Carmarthenshire Ant. Soc., 18, pp. 76–77. 1925.

6977 Fair (Mary Cicely). A Mid Bronze Age cinerary urn found near Holmrook, Cumberland. Trans. Cumb. & Westm. Ant. Soc., N.S. 44, p. 161 + plate. 1944.

6978 Fell (Clare Isobel). Middle Bronze Age urns from Furness. Trans. Cumb. & Westm. Ant. Soc., N.S. 57, pp. 9–12 + plate. 1958.

6979 —— and **Hogg** (Robert). A food-vessel from Springfield, near Ainstable. [1 figure + 1 plate.] Trans. Cumb. & Westm. Ant. Soc., N.S. 62, pp. 27–30. 1962.

6980 Fowler (Margaret J.). Beaker sherds from Stenson, Derbyshire. [2 figures.] J. Derbs. Archaeol. Soc., 73, pp. 121–26. 1953.

6981 Fox (*Sir* Cyril). On two beakers of the Early Bronze Age recently discovered [at Cyffic, Carmarthenshire, and at Cwm-du, Brecknockshire] in South Wales; with a record of the distribution of beaker pottery in England and Wales. [8 figures.] Arch. Camb., 80, pp. 1–31 + map. 1925.

6982 —— Note on four sepulchral vessels of the Bronze Age from [Hillbury barrow, Wrexham (2), from Holt (Denbighshire) and from Whitford, Flint,] North Wales. [5 figures.] Arch. Camb., 80, pp. 177–84. 1925.

6983 —— The beaker from Hen-Dre'r Gelli, Rhondda, Glamorgan. [Figure.] Arch. Camb., 81, pp. 180–81. 1926.

6984 —— A Bronze Age cinerary urn from Llanbedr, Merioneth. Arch. Cambrensis, 81 ii, 1926, 400–01 + 1 figure.

6985 —— Gorsedd Bran urn. [Tumulus on Mod Heraethog (Denbigh—Cerrig-y-Drud).] Arch. Cambrensie, 81 ii, 1926, 413–14 + 1 figure.

6986 —— An encrusted urn of the Bronze Age from Penllwyn, near Aberystwyth. Trans. Carmarthenshire Ant. Soc., 20, pp. 9–10 + plate. 1926.

6987 —— An "encrusted" urn of the Bronze Age from [Penllwyn, Cardiganshire,] Wales: with notes on the origin and distribution of the type. [Figure. Pp. 128–33, List with references.] Antiq. J., 7, pp. 115–33 + 8 plates + map. 1927.

6988 —— The Penllwyn urn. [Bronze Age.] Cards. Antiq. Soc. Trans., 5, pp. 34–36. 1927.

6989 —— Encrusted urns. [Figure. Bronze Age.] Antiq. J., 8, pp. 355–56 + plate (fragments from Jamestown, Stepaside, Co. Dublin). 1928.

6990 Fox (W. Storrs). Cinerary urns found [on Stanton moor] in Derbyshire. [Figure. Bronze Age.] Antiq. J., 6, p. 189. 1926.

6991 —— Bronze Age pottery from Stanton moor. J. Derbs. Archaeol. Soc., N.S. 2, pp. 199–209 + 3 plates. 1927.

6992 —— Bronze Age beaker [from

Stoney Middleton dale]. [Figure.] J. Derbs. Archaeol. Soc., N.S. 2, pp. 372–73. 1927.

6993 Fox (W. Storrs). Bronze Age urns [from near Bakewell] in Derbyshire. [2 figures.] Antiq. J., 7, pp. 67–69. 1927.

6994 Gaffikin (M.). Food-vessel from [Rubane farm, Kircubbin], Co. Down. [Plan. Bronze Age.] Antiq. J., 12, pp. 299–301 + plate. 1932.

6995 Gógan (Liam J.). Encrusted urns. [2 figures. From Mullaghreelan, Kilkea, Co. Carlow.] Antiq. J., 9, pp. 154–56. 1929.

6996 —— An Irish food-vessel of the megalithic period. [Figure.] Man, 32, pp. 257–59. 1932.

6997 Griffiths (William Eric). Notes on some of the prehistoric pottery of Anglesey. Anglesey Ant. Soc. Trans., 1956, pp. 1–10 + 4 plates. 1956.

6998 —— The typology and origins of beakers in Wales. Proc. prehist. Soc., 23, 1957, 57–90 + 8 figures.

6999 —— A Pre-Roman vessel from Pen Llystyn, Caernarvonshire. Arch. Camb., 108, 1959, 114–25 + 2 figures.

7000 Grimes (William Francis). Bronze Age pottery from near Dolgelley, Merioneth. Bull. Bd. Celtic Stud., 6, p. 195. 1932.

7001 —— Incense cups from Cardiganshire. Arch. Camb., 87 ii, 1932, 409–11 + 2 figures.

7002 —— Bronze Age urn from Pen-y-Lan, Llandyssul, Carmarthenshire. Trans. Carmarthenshire Ant. Soc., 29, pp. 114–16 + 2 plates. 1939.

7003 Hallam (A. M.). A collared urn of the Middle Bronze Age from Chorley, Lancs. Trans. Lancs. & Cheshire antiq. Soc., 73/74, 1963/64, 189–91 + 1 figure.

7004 Hanbury (W. H.). Bronze Age urns found near Willington. J. Derbs. Archaeol. Soc., 59 (N.S. 12, 1938), p. 95. 1939.

7005 Hardy (James). On an urn found on the Galla-law near Luffness, East Lothian. Hist. Berwick. Nat. Club, 10, pp. 306–07 + plate. 1883.

7006 —— On a cinerary urn at Otterburn, Morebattle, Roxburghshire. [Figure.] Hist. Berwick. Nat. Club, 11, pp. 177–79. 1885.

7007 —— On a British urn found at Mackswill, near Gordon, Berwickshire. [Figure.] Hist. Berwick. Nat. Club, 11, pp. 193–94. 1885.

7008 —— On urns and other antiquities found round the southern skirts of the Cheviot hills. [31 figures.] Hist. Berwick. Nat. Club, 11, pp. 269–314 + 2 plates. 1885.

7009 —— On British urns found at Hoprig, near Cockburnspath, Berwickshire. Hist. Berwick. Nat. Club, 12, pp. 13–37 + 6 plates. 1887.

7010 Hayes (R. H.) *and* **Rutter** (J. G.). The discovery of a handled beaker in a fissure near Helmsley, Yorkshire. [Figure. Late Neolithic.] Antiq. J., 35, pp. 223–24. 1955.

7011 Henderson (John). On sections exposed in making a drain through the Queen's Park at Holyrood [pot sherds on lake edge—not dated]. Trans. Edinburgh Geol. Soc., 5, 1885/88, 406–09 + 1 figure.

7012 Henslow (J. S.). On supposed British cinerary urns, found at the village of Kingston, near Derby, in 1844. [12 figures.] J. Brit. Archaeol. Ass., 2, pp. 60–63. 1846.

7013 Hodgson (Katherine S.). A Bronze-Age beaker from Ainstable. [Figure.] Trans. Cumb. & Westm. Ant. Soc., N.S. 48, pp. 215–16. 1948.

7014 Hodgson (Katherine Sophia). Three unpublished collections of Bronze Age pottery: Netherhall, Garlands and Aglionby. [8 figures.] Trans. Cumb. & Westm. Ant. Soc., N.S. 56, pp. 1–17 + plate. 1957.

7015 Hogg, Robert. Romano-British triple vase, Botchergate, Carlisle. [1 plate.] Trans. Cumb. & Westm. Ant. Soc., N.S. 62, pp. 27–30. 1962.

7016 Hughes (Henry Harold). Spindle-whorls from Braich y Dinas, Penmaenmawr. Arch. Camb., 86 i, 1931, 183–84 + 3 figures.

7017 Jackson (John Wilfrid). Peterborough (Neolithic "B") pottery from High Wheeldon cave, Earl Sterndale, near Buxton. [2 figures.] J. Derbs. Archaeol. Soc., 71 (N.S. 24), pp. 72–76. 1951.

7018 James (*Mrs.* R.). Sepulchral urn found at Rhinderston, Pembrokeshire. Arch. Camb., 5th S. 15, p. 195 + plate. 1898.

7019 Jewitt (Llewellynn). Observations on Celtic pottery, derived from the examination of grave mounds in Derbyshire and the neighbouring counties. [15 figures.] Reliquary, 2, pp. 61–70. 1862.

7020 Jobey (George). Bronze Age pottery from High Buston, Northumberland. [3 figures.] Arch. Æl., 4 S. 35, pp. 269–72. 1957.

7021 —— Food-vessels from Callahy and Ashington, Northumberland. Arch. Æliana, 38, 1960, 241–42 + 2 figures.

7022 Jones (E. K.) *and* **Vaughan** (E. R.). Discovery of cinerary urn at Staylittle, near Llanbrynmair, Montgomeryshire. [3 figures + plan (of tumulus).] Arch. Camb., 6th S. 4, pp. 285–90. 1904.

7023 Kendall (Hugh Percy). A Bronze Age urn [from Aislaby moors, near Whitby]. [Figure.] York. Archaeol. J., 32, pp. 243–44. 1935.

7024 Law (Robert). Discovery of burial urns at Todmorden, Yorkshire. [Bronze Age.] J. Brit. Archaeol. Ass., N.S. 4, pp. 277–82. 1898.

7025 Leyland (Francis A.). British sepulchral urns found [at Tower Hill, near Warley] in the parish of Halifax. Bowman (William): Reliquiae Antiquae Eboracenses: (Leeds), pp. 26–28 + coloured plate. 1855.

7026 Livens (Roger). A Beaker find from Denbighshire and its significance. Arch. Camb., 114, 1965, 112–19 + 3 figures.

7027 Longworth (Ian). Sherd from Scremerston Hill, Northumberland. [Food-vessel.] Arch. Æliana, 40, 1962, 280–81 + 1 figure.

7028 —— An Early Iron Age vessel from Muckle Skerry. Proc. Soc. Ant. Scotland, 96, 1962–63, 354–55.

7029 Manby (T. G.). Neolithic "B" pottery from East Yorkshire. [3 figures + map showing distribution.] Yorks. Archaeol. J., 39, pp. 1–8. 1956.

7030 —— A cinerary urn from Welburn, N.R. [Figure. Late Bronze Age.] Yorks. Archaeol. J., 39, pp. 395–96. 1958.

7031 —— Beakers from the Howardian hills, N.R. [Figure.] Yorks. Archaeol. J., 39, pp. 397–99. 1958.

7032 —— Early Iron Age pottery from Melbourne, South Derbyshire.

J. Derbs. Archaeol. Soc., 83, pp. 100–02 + 1 figure. 1963.

7033 —— Food-vessels from Derbyshire. J. Derbs. Archaeol. Soc., 84, pp. 117–20 + 1 figure. 1964.

7034 Martin (J. W.). Cinerary urn found at Newtonrigg, Holywood, in Cairn valley railway cutting, May, 1901. Trans. Dumfries. Ant. Soc., 17 (1902–03), p. 238. 1906.

7035 Mayer (Joseph). On the British urns found at West Kirby. [Figure.] Hist. Soc. Lancs. & Ches., Proc., 1, pp. 153–55. 1849.

7036 Moore (John W.) *and* **Manby** (T. G.). A Rinyo-clacton vase from Wykeham, North Riding, Yorks. York. Arch. Journ., 40 (iv) 1962, 619–21 + 1 figure.

7037 Newbigin (A. J. W.). Neolithic "A" pottery from Broom Ridge, Ford, Northumberland. Proc. prehist. Soc., N.S. 1, 1935, 155–56 + 1 plate.

7038 —— A food vessel from Linkey law, near Chatton, Northumberland. [Figure. ?Neolithic.] Proc. Soc. Antiq. Newc., 5th S. 1, pp. 148–50. 1952.

7039 Newbigin (Nancy). Some Bronze Age pottery from Rothbury. [Figure.] Proc. Soc. Antiq. Newc., 4th S. 7, pp. 32–33. 1935.

7040 —— Neolithic "A" pottery from Ford, Northumberland. [Figure.] Arch. Æl., 4th S. 12, pp. 148–57 + plate. 1935.

7041 —— The Neolithic pottery of Yorkshire. Proc. prehist. Soc., 3, 1937, 189–216, 7 figures + 5 plates.

7042 —— The Neolithic pottery of Yorkshire. Prehistory, 1937, pp. 189–216. 1937.

7043 —— A Bronze Age beaker from Whitwell hill, N.E. Yorks. [Figure.] Yorks. Archaeol. J., 33, pp. 119–20. 1938.

7044 O'Ferrall (R. S. M.). Cinerary urn found near Eyam. [3 figures. Early Bronze Age.] J. Derbs. Archaeol. Soc., 34, pp. 51–54 + plate. 1912.

7045 Pearson (Andrew). British urns found at Wilmslow. [2 figures.] Cheshire N. & Q., 3 S. 5, pp. 55–56. 1900.

7046 Peate (Iorwerth Cypeifiog). Incense cup and cinerary urn [from Penyberth farm, Cards.]. [Figure. Now in museum of Univ. Coll., Aberystwyth.] Arch. Camb., 80, pp. 203–05. 1925.

7047 Peate (Iorwerth Cypeifiog). New light on a Cardigan cinerary urn. Arch. Camb., 87 i, 1932, 201.

7048 Piggott (Stuart) *and* **Childe** (Vere Gordon). Neolithic pottery from Larne. Proc. PSEA, 7 i, 1932–34, 62–66 + 2 plates + 2 figures.

7049 —— The pottery from the Lligwy burial chamber, Anglesey. Arch. Camb., 88 i, 1933, 68–72 + 2 figures.

7050 —— The pottery from the Lligwy burial chamber?, Anglesey. Anglesey Ant. Soc. Trans., 1934, pp. 23–24 + 2 plates. 1934.

7051 —— *and* **Newbigin** (Nancy). A beaker from the Skipsea peat, Yorkshire. Proc. prehist. Soc., N.S. 2, 1936, 230–31 + 1 figure.

7052 Prichard (Hugh). Cinerary urns found at Cae Mickney, Anglesey. Arch. Camb., 4th S. 13, pp. 210–18 + plate. 1882.

7053 Radley (Jeffrey). The base of an urn from Totley Moor. J. Derbs. Archaeol. Soc., 84, p. 128 + 1 figure. 1964.

7054 Reid (R. C.). Note on a cinerary urn from Garrochar. [Bronze Age.] Dumfriess. Ant. Soc. Trans., 3rd S. 23 (1940–44), pp. 136–42 + plate: 24, p. 18. 1946–47.

7055 Reid (R. W.). Cinerary urns from Aberdeenshire. [6 in Anthropological Museum of University of Aberdeen.] Antiq. J., 7, pp. 517–18 + 2 plates. 1927.

7056 Ridgway (Maurice H.). Bronze Age urn from Astbury, Cheshire. [Figure + plan.] Trans. Lancs. & Ches. Ant. Soc., 59 (1947), pp. 155–60 + plate. 1948.

7057 Roberts (Edward). [Urn found at Bryncastell, Penarth, Caernarvonshire.] [2 figures.] Arch. Camb., 6th S. 10, pp. 399–400. 1910.

7058 Robertson (Anne S.). A Bronze Age cinerary urn from Kinsteary, Nairn. [Figure. Late Bronze Age.] Trans. Glasgow Archaeol. Soc., N.S. 12, pp. 37–38. 1953.

7059 Savory (Hubert Newman). Collared rim urn of early type from Llanbrynmair, Montgomeryshire. Arch. Camb., 95 ii, 1940, 244 + 1 figure.

7060 —— Some unpublished Late Middle Bronze Age pottery from West Wales. With notes on the origin of the "pygmy cup". Arch. Camb., 96 i, 1941, 31–48 + 11 figures + 1 plate.

7061 —— Cinerary urns from Llanychaer, Pembrokeshire. [MBA.] Arch. Camb., 99 i, 1946, 115–16 + 1 figure.

7062 —— A Bronze Age cinerary urn from Maes-y-Barker. Caernarvonshire Hist. Soc. Trans., 8, pp. 96–97. 1947.

7063 —— A Bronze Age cinerary urn from Maes-y-Barker, Caernarvonshire. [MBA.] Arch. Camb., 100 i, 1948, 100–01 + 1 figure.

7064 —— Beaker from Caerphilly (Glam.). Bull. Bd. Celtic Stud., 14, pp. 168–69. 1951.

7065 —— Anomalous beaker urn from Merthyr Mawr warren (Glam.). Bull. Bd. Celtic Stud., 15, p. 157. 1953.

7066 —— Some new Beaker sherds from Merthyr Mawr warren. Cardiff Nat. Soc. Rpt. & Trans., 82 (1952/53), pp. 39–43 + plate + plan. 1955.

7067 —— A corpus of Welsh Bronze Age pottery. [3 figures + map. (10 figures + map).] Bull. Bd. Celtic Stud., 16, pp. 215–41 + 3 plates; 17, pp. 196–233. 1955–57.

7068 Scott (Lindsey). A vessel from the Outer Hebrides. Proc. prehist. Soc., 4, 1938, 336–37 + 1 plate.

7069 Sheppard (Thomas). Early pottery (Bronze Age beaker) on the Yorkshire wolds. [7 figures.] Trans. E. Riding Antiq. Soc., 27, pp. 167–73. 1934.

7070 —— Miniature Bronze-Age cinerary urns. [2 figures.] Trans. E. Riding Antiq. Soc., 29, pp. 1–5. 1949.

7071 Shirley (G. W.). A group of burial urns found at Palmerston, Dumfries, 1930. [3 figures + plan.] Trans. Dumfries. Ant. Soc., 3 S. 17 (1930–31), pp. 79–94. 1932.

7072 Simpson (D. D. A.). Food-vessels in south-west Scotland. Trans. Dumfries Ant. Soc., 42, pp. 25–50 + 9 figures. 1965.

7073 Simpson (Grace). A "pygmy cup" from Old Penrith. [Figure. Bronze Age. *See also* 52, pp. 182–83.] Trans. Cumb. & Westm. Ant. Soc., N.S. 51, pp. 171–72. 1951.

7074 Stanley (*Hon.* William Owen). Presaddfed [Caernarvonshire] urns. Arch. Camb., 4th S. 6, pp. 126–28 + plate. 1875.

7075 Steer (Kenneth Anthony). Note on Iron Age pottery from Bunkle Edge [Berwick]. Hist. Berwick. Nat. Club, 32, p. 49. 1950.

7076 Tait (John). Two beakers from Scremerston, Northumberland. ["B" beaker.] Arch. Æliana, 43, 1965, 315–17 + 1 figure.

7077 —— and **Hurrell** (Mary M.). Beakers from Northumberland. pp. 73 + 3 figures + 4 plates + 105 illustrations. Newcastle-upon-Tyne, 1965.

7078 Taylor (George). Cinerary urn found at Blackburn mill, Cockburnspath parish; 30th January 1934. [Bronze Age.] Hist. Berwick. Nat. Club, 28, p. 173 + plate. 1933.

7079 Turnbull (John). Notice of an urn found at Manderston, Berwickshire. Hist. Berwick. Nat. Club, 10, pp. 304–05 + plate. 1883.

7080 Tyneside Naturalists' Field Club. Note on cinerary urns found at Humbledon Hill, near Sunderland. Nat. Hist. Trans. Northumb. & Durham 5, 1873/76, 97–98.

7081 Vulliamy (Colwyn Edward). A Bronze Age cup from [Ffostill, Breconshire,] Wales. [Figure.] Man, 27, pp. 219–20. 1927.

7082 —— A Bronze Age cup from Breconshire. Arch. Cambrensis, 83 i, 1928, 192–94 + 1 plate.

7083 Walker (Iain C.). An unpublished beaker from Nairnshire. Proc. Soc. Ant. Scotland, 95, 1961–62, 305–06 + 1 figure.

7084 Ward (John). Cinerary urn and incense cup, Stanton moor, Derbyshire. [2 figures. Bronze Age.] Antiquary, 22, pp. 112–14. 1890.

7085 —— Cinerary urns and incense cups, Stanton Moor, Derbyshire. [2 figures.] J. Derbs. Archaeol. Soc., 13, pp. 45–51. 1891.

7086 —— Cinerary urns recently discovered in Stanton moor, Derbyshire. [5 figures.] Reliquary, 3rd S. 6, pp. 25–31. 1900.

7087 —— Bronze Age cinerary urn from near Llangynidr, Breconshire. [Figure.] Arch. Camb., 6th S. 19, pp. 95–100. 1919.

7088 Webley (D.). A Neolithic potsherd from Vaynor (Breckn.). Bull. Bd. Celtic Stud., 16, pp. 298–99. 1956.

7089 Wenham (Peter). Iron Age "A" pottery at Kilnsea, near Hornsea, Yorks. Yorks. Arch. Journ. 40 (ii), 1960, 310–13 + 2 figures.

7090 Wheeler (*Sir* Robert Eric Mortimer). Prehistoric beakers found in Wales. [Figure.] Bull. Bd. Celtic Studies, 1, pp. 182–87. 1922.

7091 —— A new beaker from [Llancaiach Isaf farm, Gellygaer, Glamorgan,] Wales. [Figure. Skull also, showing oldest trace of rickets in this country—Sir A. Keith.] Antiq. J., 3, pp. 21–23. 1928.

7092 Williams (Audrey). Prehistoric and Roman pottery in the museum of the Royal Institution of South Wales, Swansea. [Beaker, BA, IA.] Arch. Camb., 94 i, 1939, 21–29 + 5 figures.

7093 Willmot (G. F.). Neolithic "B" pottery from Yorkshire. Proc. prehist. Soc., 4, 1938, 338 + 1 figure.

7094 Wilson (J.). The small urn recently found at Greystone, Dumfries. [Bronze Age.] Trans. Dumfries. Ant. Soc., 5 (1886–87), pp. 38–41 + plate. 1888.

7095 Young (Hugh W.). Cinerary urn found near Buckie, in Banffshire. [Figure. Bronze Age.] Reliquary, N. [3rd] S. 1, pp. 229–30. 1895.

7096 —— Two sepulchral urns from the north-east of Scotland. [2 figures. Afforsk, Banffshire, and Tarland, Aberdeenshire. Bronze Age.] Reliquary, N. [3rd] S. 2, pp. 178–79. 1896.

7097 —— Sepulchral urn from Leslie, Aberdeenshire. [Figure.] Reliquary, N. [3rd] S. 3, p. 49. 1897.

5. METAL OBJECTS IN GENERAL

7098 Alexander (John). The origin of penannular brooches. Proc. prehist. Soc., 30, 1964, 429–30 + 1 figure.

7099 Allen (Derek). Iron currency bars in Britain. Proc. prehist. Soc., 33, 1967, 307–35 + 2 figures + 5 plates.

7100 [Anon.] A Bronze Age problem. [2 figures. Socketed standard.] Antiq. J., 15, pp. 466–67. 1935.

7101 Barber (James) and **Megan** (J. V. S.). A decorated Iron Age bridle-bit in the London Museum: its place in art and archaeology. Proc. prehist. Soc., 29, 1963, 206–13 + 1 figure + 2 plates.

7102 Broholm (Hans Christian), **Larsen** (William P.) *and* **Skjerne** (Godtfred). The lures of the Bronze Age. An archaeological, technical and musicological investigation. pp. 129 + 30 plates. 4⁰. Copenhagen, 1949.

7103 Brewis (W. Parker). The bronze sword in Great Britain. Archaeologia, 73, pp. 253–65 + 15 plates. 1923.

7104 Burke (J.) *and* **Megan** (J. V. S.). British decorated axes: a footnote on fakes. Proc. prehist. Soc., 32, 1966, 343–46 + 4 plates.

7105 Butcher (Charles H.). Essex Bronze [Age] implements and weapons in the Colchester Museum. Trans. Essex Archaeol. Soc., N.S. 16, pp. 258–67 + 2 plates. 1923.

7106 Carpenter (*Sir* H. C. H.). Early Iron Age craftsmanship. [2 figures (bronze spear-head from Roscrea, Co. Tipperary) and (iron spear-head, Golden Lane, London).] Antiq. J., 9, pp. 376–77. 1929.

7107 Childe (Vere Gordon). Double-looped palstaves in Britain. [Figure + map.] Antiq. J., 19, pp. 320–23. 1939.

7108 Clark (John Grahame Douglas). Fresh evidence for the dating of gold lunulae. [2 maps. ?Early Bronze Age.] Man, 32, pp. 40–41. 1932.

7109 —— The halberd in Bronze Age Europe. Proc. prehist. Soc., 4, 1938, 223–25 + 1 figure.

7110 Coles (John M.). Irish Bronze Age horns and their relation with northern Europe. Proc. prehist. Soc., 29, 1963, 326–56 + 6 figures + 2 plates.

7111 Cowen (John David). The earliest bronze swords in Britain and their origins on the Continent of Europe. Proc. prehist. Soc., 17, 1951, 195–213 + 4 figures + 2 maps + 6 plates.

7112 —— Bronze swords in northern Europe: a reconsideration of Sprockhoff's *Griff zungenschwerter*. [British origin postulated.] Proc. prehist. Soc., 18, 1952, 129–47 + 4 plates.

7113 —— The Hallstatt sword of Bronze: on the Continent and in Britain. Proc. prehist. Soc., 33, 1967, 377–454 + 15 figures + 6 maps + 20 plates.

7114 Dunning (Gerald Clough). The swan's-neck and ring-headed pins of the Early Iron Age in Britain. [7 figures + map. Lists.] Archaeol. J., 91 (1934), pp. 269–95 + plate. 1935.

7115 Evans (Emyr Estyn). The Bronze [Age] spear-head in Great Britain and Ireland. [2 distribution maps.] Archaeologia, 83, pp. 187–202 + 2 plates. 1933.

7116 Evans (*Sir* John). The ancient bronze implements, weapons, and ornaments of Great Britain and Ireland. pp. xix, 509. 8⁰. London, 1881. [540 figures.]

7117 Fowler (Elizabeth). The origins and development of the penannular brooch in Europe. Proc. prehist. Soc., 26, 1960, 149–77 + 14 figures.

7118 —— Celtic metalwork of the fifth and sixth centuries A.D. [giving ancestry in Iron Age]. Appendices 8 + figures 9. Arch. J., 120, 1963, 98.

7119 Fox (*Sir* Cyril). The socketed bronze sickles of the British Isles; with special reference to an unpublished specimen from Norwich. Proc. prehist. Soc., 5, 1939, 222–48 + 12 figures + 3 plates.

7120 —— The distribution of currency bars. [Figure and distribution map of finds. Early Iron Age "B". Majority from Forest of Dean iron.] Antiquity, 14, pp. 427–33. 1940.

7121 —— The non-socketed bronze sickles of Britain. Arch. Camb., 96 ii, 1941, 136–62 + 6 figures + 4 plates.

7122 —— Celtic mirror handles in Britain with special reference to the Colchester handle. [Western IA "B".] Arch. Camb., 100 i, 1948, 24–44 + 13 figures + 3 plates.

7123 —— The study of early Celtic metalwork in Great Britain. [Map.] Arch. News Letter, 4, pp. 81–84. 1952.

7124 —— The study of early Celtic metalwork in G.B. pt. 2. [2 figures.] Arch. News Letter, 4, pp. 97–102. 1952.

7125 —— Triskeles, palmettes and horse-brooches. Proc. prehist. Soc., 18, 1952, 47–54 + 4 figures + 2 plates.

7126 Friend (J. Newton). Iron in antiquity, with special reference to local currency bars, and their relation to early British water clocks. Trans. Worcs. Nat. Club, 7, pp. 99–112. 1919.

7127 Greenwell (William) *and* **Brewis** (William Parker). The origin, evolution, and classification of the Bronze [Age] spear-head in Great Britain and Ireland. Archaeologia, 61, pp. 439–72 + 23 plates. 1 909.

7128 Greenwell (William) *and* **Brewis** (William Parker). The development of the bronze spearhead in the United Kingdom. Proc. Soc. Antiq., 2 S. 22, pp. 492–96. 1909.

7129 Hawkes (Charles Francis Christopher). The Needwood forest torc. [Iron Age]. Brit. Mus. Q., 11, pp. 3–4 + plate. 1936.

7130 —— La Tène I brooches from Deal, Preston Candover [Hants.], and East Dean [Sussex]. [3 figures.] Antiq. J., 20, pp. 276–79. 1940.

7131 —— Bronze-workers, cauldrons, and bucket-animals in Iron Age and Roman Britain. [6 plates + 2 maps.] Aspects of archaeology. . . . Essays presented to O. G. S. Crawford, pp. 172–99 + 3 plates. 1951.

7132 —— Gold ear-rings of the Bronze Age, East and West. Folklore 71, 1961, 438–74 + 4 figures + 4 plates.

7133 Hemp (Wilfrid James). The trunnion celt in Britain. [Figure.] Antiq. J., 5, pp. 51–54. 1925.

7134 Henshall (Audrey Shore). Four Early Bronze Age armlets. Proc. prehist. Soc., 30, 1964, 426–29 + 1 figure.

7135 Jope (E. M.). Dagger of the Early Iron Age in Britain. Proc. prehist. Soc., 27, 1961, 307–43 + 14 figures + 8 plates.

7136 Kimmig (Wolfgang). Bronze-situlen ans dem Rheinischen Gebirge, Hunsrück—Eifel—Westerwald [reference to ringhandled types, cf. London Cauldron]. Ber. Romano-german. Komm. 43/44, 1962/63, 31–106, 50 plates + 13 figures.

7137 Maryon (Herbert). Some prehistoric metalworkers' tools. [18 figures (1–13 tracers.).] Antiq. J., 18, pp. 243–250. 1938.

7138 Megan (B. R. S.) *and* **Hardy** (E. M.). British decorated axes and their diffusion during the earlier part of the Bronze Age. Proc. prehist. Soc., 4, 1938, 272–307 + 17 figures + 6 plates.

7139 Megan, J. V. S. A British bronze bowl of the Belgic Iron Age from Poland. Ant. J., 43, 1963, 27–37 + 4 plates.

7140 Navarro (José Maria de). Zu einigen Schwertscheiden aus La Tène [some British, e.g. Llyn Cerrig Bach]. Ber. Rom—german—Komm. 40, 1959, 79–119 + 21 plates + 6 figures.

7141 —— The Finds from the Site of La Tène, Vol. 1: Scabbards and the Swords Found in Them, 2 vol., demy 4°. Pt. 1: Text, 392 pp., 37 text figures, 3 maps. Pt. 2: Catalogue and Plates, 108 pp., 159 plates. Cambridge, 1972.

7142 Nevill (Francis). An account of some ancient trumpets, and other pieces of antiquity found in the County of Tyrone in Ireland. Phil. Trans. Roy. Soc., xxviii, 1713, 250–72 + 3 figures.

7143 O Ríordáin (Seán Pádraig). The halberd in Bronze Age Europe. A study in prehistoric origins, evolution, distribution, and chronology. [65 figures + 4 maps + plan. Pp. 196–99, Ireland; pp. 199–204, Great Britain.] Archaeologia, 86, pp. 195–321. 1937.

7144 Perkins (John Bryan Ward). Iron Age metal horses' bits of the British Isles. Proc. prehist. Soc., 5, 1939, 173–192 + 11 figures + 4 plates.

7145 —— The Iron Age horseshoe. [Figure.] Antiq. J., 21, 1941, pp. 144–149, 238.

7146 Piggott (Cicely Margaret). The Late Bronze Age razors of the British Isles. Proc. prehist. Soc., 12, 1946, 121–141 + 10 figures.

7147 Piggott (Stuart). Metal-work of the north British Iron Age. Arch. News Letter, 1 vi, pp. 10–12. 1948.

7148 —— Swords and scabbards of the British Early Iron Age. Proc. prehist. Soc., 16, 1950, 1–28 + 13 figures + 3 plates.

7149 —— Bronze double-axes in the British Isles. Proc. prehist. Soc., 19, 1953, 224–26 + 1 figure.

7150 —— The carnyx [animal-headed war-trumpet] in Early Iron Age Britain. [2 figures. Tattershall ferry find; Deskford boar's head.] Antiq. J., 39, pp. 19–32 + 6 plates. 1959.

7151 Praetorius (C. J.). Bronze [Age] trumpets [found in Ireland]. [3 figures. P. 119, List.] Reliquary, N. [3rd] S. 5, pp. 116–19. 1899.

7152 Rainbow (Herbert N.). Socketed and looped iron axes from the British Isles. [Figure. List of 11. Between Bronze and Early Iron Ages (700–400B.C.).] Archaeol. J., 85 (1928), pp. 170–75 + plate. 1930.

7153 Read (*Sir* Charles Hercules). On a bronze object of the Late-Celtic period recently added to the British Museum. [Stirrup-like object. No history.] Archaeologia, 66, pp. 349–52 + plate. 1915.

7154 Ridgeway (*Sir* William) *and* **Smith** (Reginald Allender). Early Italian brooches. [27 figures. Bronze Age onwards. Including various examples from English sites, e.g. Ixworth (Suffolk), Alton (Hants.), *etc.*] Proc. Soc. Antiq., 2 S. 21, pp. 97–118 + plate. 1906.

7155 Royal Anthropological Institute, *Ancient Mining and Metallurgy Committee*. Studies of British and Irish celts. (—of Irish and British early copper artifacts). [9 figures.] Man, 53, pp. 97–101 + plate; 54, pp. 18–27. 1953–54.

7156 Smith (Margaret A.). Some Somerset hoards and their place in the Bronze Age of southern Britain. Proc. prehist. Soc., 25, 1959, 144–87 + 7 figures + 4 maps.

7157 Smith (Reginald Allender). Ancient British iron currency. [4 figures.] Proc. Soc. Antiq., 2 S. 20, pp. 179–95. 1905.

7158 —— On Irish [and English] serpentine latchets. [15 figures + distribution map.] Proc. Soc. Antiq., 2 S. 30, pp. 120–31. 1918.

7159 —— Two early British bronze bowls. [7 figures. Early Iron Age. From Cerrig-y-Drudion, Denbighshire, and from Youlton farm, E. Cornwall.] Antiq. J., 6, pp. 276–83. 1926.

7160 Trump (Bridget A. V.). The origin and development of British Middle Bronze Age rapiers. Proc. prehist. Soc., 28, 1962, 80–102 + 19 figures.

7161 Walker (W. Foot). The Bronze [Age] axe: the seven stages of its development in Britain (2000–500 B.C.). Pp. 39 + plate (Bronze axe trade routes). 8°. Hull, 1939. [5 figures.]

7162 Ward (Gordon). The Iron Age horseshoe and its derivatives. [6 figures + distribution map.] Antiq. J., 21, pp. 9–27 + plate. 1941.

7163 Wilson, D. M. On the dating of two spurs. Ant. J., 45, 1965, 111–12.

6. METAL OBJECTS BY ZONE

(a) Zone 1
[CBA Groups 7, 9, 10, 11A, 11B, 14]

7164 Allen (Edward Heron). An early British armlet [from West Street, Chichester]. [Figure. Bronze Age.] Sussex Arch. Collns., 67, pp. 218–19. 1926.

7165 —— Treasure trove at Selsey. [Bronze Age gold circlet from shore.] Sussex N. & Q., 6, pp. 180–81. 1937.

7166 Allan (John). The Snettisham find. [Figure. 13 gold coins.] Num. Chron., 6 S. 8, pp. 233–35. 1948.

7167 Allen (John Romilly). An S-shaped fibula of Late Celtic design from Lakenheath, Suffolk. [2 figures.] Reliquary, 3rd S. 13, pp. 62–63. 1907.

7168 [Anon.] [Bronze mirror from Desborough, Northants.] [Figure. La Tène.] Antiq. J., 4, pp. 151–53. 1924.

7169 [Anon.] Hallstatt brooches from Sussex. [2 figures.] Sussex Arch. Collns., 65, pp. 253–54. 1924.

7170 [Anon.] Bronze Age hoard from [Park Brow], Sussex. [2 figures.] Antiq. J., 6, pp. 444–46. 1926.

7171 [Anon.] An Early Iron Age brooch [from the Thames in Syon reach]. [Figure.] Antiq. J., 11, p. 60. 1931.

7172 [Anon.] Hoard of Bronze [Age] implements [from Bexley Heath, Kent]. Antiq. J., 11, pp. 170–71 + plate. 1931.

7173 [Anon.] [Ancient British earrings of bronze, found at Colchester]. [Figure.] Essex Rev., 43, p. 237. 1934.

7174 [Anon.] Bronze [Age] hoard from East Dean [Sussex]. [Brighton laps and ring-headed pins.] Antiq. J., 16, pp. 461–62 + plate. 1936.

7175 [Anon.] Treasure trove from [Selsey], Sussex. [Figure. Late Bronze Age bracelet.] Antiq. J., 17, pp. 321–22. 1937.

7176 [Anon.] [Two] gold bracelets from Waddesdon, Bucks. [Late Bronze Age.] Antiq. J., 21, p. 162 + plate. 1941.

7177 ApSimon (Arthur M.). A decorated Bronze [Age] dagger of Arreton down type from the Thames near Bourne End [Berks.]. Berks. Archaeol. J., 54, pp. 119–23 + 2 plates. 1955.

7178 Armstrong (Albert Leslie). Flat

bronze celt from Risby Warren, Scunthorpe, N. Lincs. [Figure.] Antiq. J., 11, pp. 279–80. 1931.

7179 Ashbee (Paul). Two Early Bronze Age axes [in Maidstone Museum]. [Figure.] Arch. Cant., 65 (1952), pp. 180–83. 1953.

7180 Baggaley (J. W.). Bronze shield from the river Trent [near Carlton-on-Trent], Nottinghamshire. [Figure.] Antiq. J., 30, p. 195 + plate. 1950.

7181 Bagshawe (Thomas Wyatt). Early Iron Age objects from Harpenden. [2 figures.] Antiq. J., 8, pp. 520–22 + 2 plates (bucket-handle). 1928.

7182 Bally (E. F.). Bronze celts found near Cumberlow, Baldock, Herts. [2 figures.] J. Anth. Inst., 6, pp. 195–96. 1876.

7183 Banks (*Sir* Joseph) *bart.* Observations on an ancient celt found near Boston in Lincolnshire. Archaeologia, 19, pp. 102–04 + plate. 1821.

7184 Benson (G. Vere). Find in a Lewes garden. [Bronze Age ring.] Sussex County Mag., 11, p. 67. 1937.

7185 Boyson (Ambrose P.). Bronze [Age] bracelets found at Hand Cross, Crawley. Sussex Arch. Collns., 49, p. 172. 1906.

7186 Brailsford (John William). A founders hoard from Dartford, Kent, with a note on socketed bronze swords. Proc. prehist. Soc., 13, 1947, 175–77 + 4 figures.

7187 —— The Snettisham [Norfolk] treasure. [Three electrum torcs and gold bracelet. Early Iron Age.] Brit. Mus. Q., 16. pp. 29–80 + plate. 1952.

7188 Briscoe (Grace) *Lady.* A [Middle] Bronze [Age] spearhead from Mildenhall [Suffolk]. Antiq. J., 32, p. 199 + plate. 1952.

7189 —— *and* **Furness** (Audrey). A hoard of Bronze Age weapons from Eriswell, near Mildenhall [Suffolk]. [Figure.] Antiq. J., 35, pp. 218–19 + 2 plates. 1955.

7190 Briscoe (John Potter). Ancient Bronze [Age] implements in Notts. Notts. & Derbs. N. & Q., 2, pp. 109–10. 1894.

7191 British Museum. The Selsey [gold] bracelet. [Figure. Late Bronze Age.] Antiq. J., 6, pp. 308–09. 1926.

7192 British Museum. Flesh-hook from [Little Thetford], Cambs. [2 figures.] Antiq. J., 9, pp. 255–56. 1929.

7193 Britton (Dennis). The Isleham hoard, Cambridge. Antiq., 34, 1960, pp. 279–82.

7194 Budgen (William). Bronze celts found at Eastbourne. [Figure.] Sussex Arch. Collns., 61, p. 144. 1920.

7195 Butcher (Charles H.). A hoard of bronze discovered at Grays Thurrock [Essex]. [3 figures. Bronze Age.] Antiq. J., 2, pp. 105–08. 1922.

7196 Butterfield (W. Ruskin). Bronze palstave found at Flimwell. Sussex N. & Q., 5, pp. 51–52 + plate. 1934.

7197 Cane (L. B.). Socketed celts [in Suffolk]. [Distribution map of Bronze Age socketed celts in Suffolk.] Proc. Suffolk Inst. Arch., 23, pp. 79–82 + plate. 1939.

7198 Carpenter (*Sir* H. C. H.). An ancient spearhead. [Figure. From Golden Lane, London: now in British Museum. Bronze Age. Microscopic examination.] *Nature*, 1929, June 15.

7199 Carpenter (L. W.). An Early Bronze Age flat axe. Surrey Arch. Collections, 58, 1961, 111–12 + 1 figure.

7200 Case (Humphrey J.). The Standlake Iron Age sword. Oxfordshire Archaeol. Soc., Rpts., 87 (1949), pp. 7–8 + plate. 1951.

7201 —— [Late Bronze Age sword from] Witney, Oxon. Oxoniensia, 22 (1957), p. 106 + plate. 1958.

7202 Clarke (Edward Daniel). An account of some antiquities found at Fulbourn in Cambridgeshire. [5 bronze weapons.] Archaeologia, 19, pp. 56–60 + plate. 1821.

7203 Clarke (Roy Rainbird). Norfolk Iron Age find. Arch. News Letter, 3, p. 4. 1950.

7204 —— Gold ornaments of the Bronze Age from Norfolk. Archaeol. J., 106 (1949), pp. 57–58 + plate. 1951.

7205 —— A Celtic torc-terminal from North Creake, Norfolk. [Iron Age.] Archaeol. J., 106 (1949), pp. 59–61 + plate. 1951.

7206 —— A hoard of metalwork of the Early Iron Age from Ringstead, Norfolk. Proc. prehist. Soc., 17, 1951, 214–25 + 8 figures + 4 plates.

7207 —— *and* **Dolley** (R. H. M.).

The Early Iron Age treasure from Snettisham, Norfolk. Proc. prehist. Soc., 20, 1954, 27–86 + 16 figures + 16 plates.

7208 Clarke (Roy Rainbird) *and* **Hawkes** (Charles Francis Christopher). An Iron anthropoid sword from Shouldham, Norfolk, with related continental and British weapons. Proc. prehist. Soc., 21, 1955, 198–227 + 6 figures + 4 plates + 2 maps.

7209 —— The Snettisham treasure. [2 figures + 4 maps + plan. Early Iron Age.] Recent archaeol. excavations in Britain, pp. 21–42 + 4 plates. 1956.

7210 Cocks (Alfred Hencage). On a hoard of Bronze [Age] implements from near Bradwell. [2 figures.] Records of Bucks., 9, pp. 431–40 + plate. 1909.

7211 Coles (John M.). A flat axe from Chatteris Fen, Cambs. [2 figures.] Proc. Camb. Ant. Soc., 56/57, 1962/63, 5–8.

7212 Collins (A. E. P.). An unusual bronze from Wantage. Berks. Archaeol. J., 51, pp. 66–67 + plate. 1949.

7213 Collyer (H. C.). Bronze implements found at Carshalton and Croydon. Surrey Archaeol. Collns., 21, pp. 208–09 + plate. 1908.

7214 Corcoran (John X. W. P.). Tankards and tankard handles of the British Early Iron Age: a handle from Burwell Fen, Cambridgeshire. Proc. prehist. Soc., 18, 1952, 239 + 2 plates.

7215 —— Tankard handle from Puddlehill, near Dunstable, Bedfordshire. Proc. prehist. Soc., 23, 1957, 233 + 1 plate.

7216 Corder (Henry). Note on some ancient bronze implements ("socketed celts") from the neighbourhood of Little Baddow, Essex. Trans. Epping Forest & Cty. Essex F.C., 2, 1882, 31.

7217 Cowen (John David). A bronze sword from Folkestone. [Figure. Late Bronze Age.] Arch. Cant., 65 (1952), pp. 90–91. 1953.

7218 Cra'ster (Mary D.). Archaeological notes: a Bronze Age spear from Mildenhall. [1 figure.] Proc. Camb. Ant. Soc., 54, 1961, 127.

7219 —— Archaeological notes: an Iron Age bridle cheek-piece from Ashwell, Herts. [1 plate.] [Bronze.] Proc. Camb. Ant. Soc., 55, 1961, 65.

7220 Curwen (Eliot). [Socketed] Bronze [Age] celt [from Burgess Hill]. Sussex N. & Q., 5, p. 91. 1934.

7221 —— A [Middle] Bronze Age rapier from [Hope-in-the-Valley, near Lewes], Sussex. [Figure.] Sussex N. & Q., 7, pp. 129–30. 1939.

7222 —— The Coombe hill [Jevington] hoard of Bronze [Age] axes. Sussex N. & Q., 8, pp. 108–10 + plate. 1940.

7223 Curwen (Eliot Cecil). A bronze cauldron from Sompting, Sussex. [6 figures. Late Bronze Age.] Antiq. J., 28, pp. 157–63 + 4 plates. 1948.

7224 —— A bronze cauldron from Sompting. [Figure.] Sussex N. & Q., 12, pp. 9–11. 1948.

7225 —— Fragment of a bronze cauldron from Ditchling. [Figure.] Sussex N. & Q., 12, pp. 11–12. 1948.

7226 Dale (William). Discovery of a bronze bucket of the Early Iron Age at Weybridge in Surrey. [Figure.] Proc. Soc. Antiq., 2 S. 21, pp. 464–69 + plate. 1907.

7227 Devenish (D. C.). Local bronze implements in Kingston-upon-Thames Museum. Surrey Arch. Collections, 61, 1964, 1–9 + 2 figures + 4 plates.

7228 Dixon (Frederick). On bronze or brass relics, celts, &c., found in Sussex. Sussex Arch. Collns., 2, pp. 260–69 + plate. 1849.

7229 Evans (*Sir* John). A hoard of bronze antiquities found [at Yattendon] in Berkshire. Proc. Soc. Antiq., 2 S. 7, pp. 480–85. 1878.

7230 —— On a hoard of Bronze [Age] objects found in Wilburton fen, near Ely. [6 figures.] Archaeologia, 48, pp. 106–14 + plate. 1884.

7231 —— A bronze hoard from Felixstowe, Suffolk. [5 figures.] Proc. Soc. Antiq. 2 S. 11, pp. 8–12. 1885.

7232 —— On a hoard of Bronze [Age] instruments found [near Branston hall] in Lincolnshire. [Socketed celts.] Proc. Soc. Antiq., 2 S. 22, pp. 3–5 + plate. 1907.

7233 Finch (Alan G.). Bronze palstave from Reigate Heath. Surrey Arch. Collections, 57, 1960, 101 + 1 figure.

7234 Flower (John Wickham). Notice of a hoard of bronze implements found at Beddington, Surrey. Surrey

Archaeol. Collns., 6, pp. 125–26 + plate. 1874.

7235 Fox (*Sir* Cyril). A Late Celtic fire-dog [from Lord's Bridge, Burton, Cambs.]. [3 figures.] Antiq. J., 6, pp. 316–18. 1926.

7236 —— A Celtic mirror from Great Chesterford [Essex[. Antiq., 34 (1960), pp. 207–10.

7237 Frere (Sheppard Sunderland). A Late Bronze Age hoard from Banstead. [Figure + map.] Surrey Archaeol. Collns., 47, pp. 95–98 + plate (lumps of metal for casting). 1941.

7238 —— Two Bronze Age implements from Weybridge. [2 figures.] Surrey Archaeol. Collns., 49, pp. 100–102. 1946.

7239 —— *and* **Hooper** (Wilfrid). Late Bronze Age celt from Betchworth. Surrey Archaeol. Collns., 49, p. 102 + plate. 1946.

7240 —— Bronze objects from Farnham. [Figure.] Surrey Archaeol. Collns., 49, pp. 103–04. 1946.

7241 Gowing (C. N.). Two socketed axes from Princes Risborough. A socketed axe from Great Hampden. [2 figures.] Record of Bucks., 17 (2), 1962, 128.

7242 J. A. G. Two bronze spearheads from Conington [Hunts.]. [Middle Bronze Age.] Trans. Cambs. & Hunts. Arch. Soc., 7, p. 18 + plate. 1952.

7243 Gage (John). Account of a British buckler, found in the bed of the river Isis, between Long Wittenham and Dorchester, in Oxfordshire. [Map.] Archaeologia, 27, pp. 298–300 + plate. 1838.

7244 Gardner (Eric). A Late Keltic knife found at Weybridge. [Early Iron Age.] Surrey Archaeol. Collns., 28, pp. 183–84 + plate. 1915.

7245 Garrood (Jesse Robert). Bronze spearhead found at Conington, Hunts. Trans. Cambs. & Hunts. Arch. Soc., 4, p. 252. 1930.

7247 Godwin (H.) *and others*. A Bronze Age spear-head found in Methwold Fen, Norfolk. [M. E. Godwin, J. G. D. Clark, and M. H. Clifford.] [Basal loop e.g. Late Middle BA.] Proc. PSEA, 7 iii, 1934, 395–98 + 3 figures + 1 table.

7248 Goodman (C. H.). Note on a bronze palstave found at Warlingham. Proc. Croydon N.H. & Sci. Soc., 6, p. 58 + plate. 1904.

7249 Goodwin (C. W.). On two British shields recently found in the Isle of Ely, and now in the collection of the Cambridge Antiquarian Society. Quarto Publications of the Cambridge Antiquarian Society, 2, xiv, pp. 7–13 + 4 plates. 1862.

7250 Grace (R.). Additions to the Bronze Age hoard from Broadoak, Sturry, Kent. [Figure. Implements.] Antiq. J., 24, pp. 148–49. 1944.

7251 Green (Barbara). An Iron Age pony-bit from Swanton Morley, Norfolk. Proc. prehist. Soc., 28, 1962, 385–86 + 1 plate.

7252 Greenwell (William). On some rare forms of bronze weapons and implements. [Figure. Pp. 3–4, blade from Kimberley, Norfolk.] Archaeologia, 58, pp. 1–16. 1902.

7253 Grove (Leonard Robert Allen). Bronze spearhead from Windsor, Berkshire. [Figure.] Berks. Archaeol. J., 49, pp. 67–68. 1946.

7254 —— *and* **Terry** (W. Neville). Four bronze implements. [Figures. i. Flat axe from Fishponds, Ightham; ii. Flanged axe from Ashford; iii. Palstave from Sheerness; iv. Socketed axe from Burham.] Arch. Cant., 62 (1949), pp. 143–45. 1950.

7255 —— A bronze spearhead from Caversham. [Figure. Now in Royal Museum, Canterbury.] Berks. Archaeol. J., 53, pp. 118–19. 1952.

7256 —— Two bronze socketed axes from West Peckham. Arch. Cant., 68 (1954), p. 210. 1955.

7257 Guermonprez (H. L. F.). Find of celts at Bognor. [3 figures. "A packet of bronze palstaves of the flanged type".] Sussex Arch. Collns., 66, pp. 225–31. 1925.

7258 Gurney (Robert). A bronze shield from Sutton, Norfolk. Proc. prehist. Soc. EA, 3 ii, 1919/20, 209–10 + 1 plate.

7259 Hall (E. T.) *and* **Roberts** (G.). Analysis of the Moulsford torc. Archaeometry, 5, 1962, 28–32 + 1 plate.

7260 Halsey (Gerald). [Late] Bronze [Age] hoard from [Somerleyton], Suffolk.

[In British Museum. Celts, etc.] Antiq. J., 8, pp. 236–37 + plate. 1928.

7261 Harvey (W.). Discovery of five bronze celts at Waldron. [Figure.] Sussex Arch. Collns., 9, p. 366. 1857.

7262 Hawkes (Charles Francis Christopher). A La Tène bronze handle from Welwyn [Herts.] [Figure. Red enamel bosses.] Antiq. J., 15, pp. 351–54. 1935.

7263 —— A Hallstatt bronze sword from the Thames at Taplow [Bucks.]. Antiq. J., 18, pp. 185–87 + plate. 1938.

7264 —— *and* **Jacobsthal** (Paul). A Celtic bird-brooch from Red Hill, near Long Eaton, Notts. [Figure. Pre-Roman Iron Age.] Antiq. J., 25, pp. 117–24 + plate. 1945.

7265 —— *and* **Smith** (M. A.). On some buckets and cauldrons of the Bronze and Early Iron Ages: the Nannau, Whigsborough, and Heathery burn bronze buckets and the Colchester and London cauldrons. [8 figures + 4 maps.] Antiq. J., 37, pp. 131–98 + 4 plates. 1957.

7266 —— The newly-found gold torc from Moulsford, Berkshire. Antiquity, 35 (1961), pp. 240–42.

7267 —— Archaeological significance at the Moulsford torc analysis. Archaeometry, 5, 1962, 33–37.

7268 Hearne (E. J. Frazer). A Bronze [Age] hoard from Flansham, near Middleton [-on-Sea]. [2 figures. Palstaves, etc.] Sussex Arch. Collns., 81, pp. 204–09. 1940.

7269 Hodges (H. W. M.). A palstave adze from Pusey, Berkshire. [Distribution map.] Oxoniensia, 20 (1955), pp. 93–95 + plate. 1957.

7270 Hollis (Edwin). Four Bronze [Age] implements [in Bucks. County Museum]. Records of Bucks., 11, pp. 349–50 + 3 plates. 1924.

7271 —— Bronze [Age] chisel from [Princes Risborough], Bucks. [Figure.] Antiq. J., 14, p. 56. 1934.

7272 Jessup (Ronald Frederick). Bronzes from the Medway [at Rainham, Kent]. [Figure. Rapier of Middle Bronze Age.] Antiq. J., 13, pp. 465–66. 1933.

7273 —— A Bronze Age hoard from Sturry, Kent. Antiq. J., 23, pp. 55–56 + plate. 1943.

7274 Keef (P. A. M.). Two gold penannular ornaments from Harting beacon, Sussex. [Iron Age A2.] Antiq. J., 33, pp. 204–06 + plate. 1953.

7275 Kelly (D. B.). Researches and discoveries in Kent: Strood. [Leaf-shaped Bronze Age sword.] Arch. Cantiana, 77, 1962, 207–08.

7276 Kendrick (*Sir* Thomas Downing). An ornamented spearhead of the late La Tène period from the Thames at London. [Figure.] Man, 31, pp. 173–74 + plate. 1931.

7277 —— Celtic sword from the river Witham [Lincs.]. [La Tène.] Antiq. J., 19, pp. 194–95 + plate. 1939.

7278 Leeds (Edward Thurlow). Two Bronze Age hoards from Oxford. [Implements, *etc.*, from Burgesses' meadow and from Leopold Street.] Proc. Soc. Antiq., 2 S. 28, pp. 147–53 + plate. 1916.

7279 —— Looped palstave from [near Ollerton], Nottinghamshire. [Figure.] Antiq. J., 5, pp. 165–66. 1925.

7280(a) —— A bronze cauldron from the river Cherwell [at Shipton-on-Cherwell], Oxfordshire, with notes on cauldrons and other bronze vessels of allied types. [11 figures. Close of Bronze Age or Early Iron Age.] Archaeologia, 80, pp. 1–36 + 10 plates. 1930.

7280(b) —— Torcs of the Early Iron Age in Britain. [From Ulceby, Lincs., *etc.*] Antiq. J., 13, pp. 466–68 + 2 plates. 1933.

7281 Lewis (Geoffrey D.). Late Bronze Age hoard from East Preston. Sussex Arch. Collections, 98, 1960, 17.

7282 —— Late Bronze Age palstave from Worthing. Sussex Arch. Collections, 98, 1960, 17.

7283 —— Late Bronze Age palstave from Ferring. Sussex Arch. Collections, 98, 1960, 17.

7284 Liversidge, Joan. A bronze bowl and other vessels from Icklingham, Suffolk. [1 plate.] Proc. Camb. Ant. Soc., LV, 1961, 6–7.

7285 Lowther (Anthony William George). Looped palstave from Frensham. [Middle Bronze Age.] Surrey Archaeol. Collns., 50, p. 137 + plate. 1949.

7286 —— Cast bronze ornament, of Late Bronze Age date, from St. Catharine's hill, Guildford. [Figure.] Surrey Archaeol. Collns., 51, pp. 143–44. 1950.

7287 Lowther (Anthony William George). A Late Bronze Age sword from Charlwood. [Figure + map.] Surrey Arch. Collns., 55, pp. 122–23. 1958.

7288 Maryon (Herbert). The Bawsey torc. Antiq. J., 24, pp. 149–51. 1944.

7289 May (Jeffrey). Some bronze implements from Nottinghamshire [flat axe, spearhead, palstave, swords]. Trans. Thoroton Soc., 66 (1962), 9–19 + 2 figures.

7290 Monckton (?). A Bronze [Age] hoard from the City. [Figure. Founder's hoard (scrap metal) from Great St. Thomas Apostle, near Mansion House station.] Antiq. J., 13, pp. 297–99. 1933.

7291 Moore (Ivan E.). Bronze Age axes from Halesworth and district. [4 figures.] Proc. Suffolk Inst. Arch., 24, pp. 121–23. 1949.

7292 Neve (George). Gold finger ring of Celtic type. [Found at Bettenham farm, Cranbrook. Figure.] Arch. Cant., 9, p. 12. 1874.

7293 Norwich Castle Museum. Bronze Age metalwork in Norwich Castle Museum. Norwich, 1966, pp. 55 + 95 figures + 5 plates.

7294 O'Reilly (Maureen Margaret). A hoard of tools and weapons belonging to the Late Bronze Age found . . . in Green End road, Cambridge. Proc. Camb. Antiq. Soc., 32, pp. 59–61 + 2 plates. 1932.

7295 —— Three Bronze [Age] weapons from East Anglia. [Feltwell, Norfolk and Little Downham, Cambs.] Proc. Camb. Antiq. Soc., 36, pp. 162–63 + 2 plates. 1936.

7296 Osbourne (A. O'Neill). The Hayne Wood [bronze-founder's] hoard [Saltwood, Kent]. [Figure. Late Bronze Age.] Antiq. J., 19, pp. 202–06 + plate. 1939.

7297 Oswald (Adrian). An Iron Age brooch from [Gringley-on-the-Hill,] Notts. [Figure.] Antiq. J., 18, pp. 410–11. 1938.

7298 Payne (George). A hoard of [181] bronze weapons and implements discovered . . . at Ebbs Fleet, near Minster, in Thanet. [3 figures.] Proc. Soc. Antiq., 2 S. 14, pp. 309–11. 1893.

7299 Peake (Harold John Edward).

Description of a bronze flat celt in the Newbury Museum. With a report on an analysis of the alloy by John J. Manley. Man, 14, pp. 112–13. 1914.

7300 —— A bronze socketed axe-head from Lambourne Woodlands. [Figure.] Trans. Newbury F.C., 8, pp. 77–78. 1938.

7301 Penniman (T. K.) *and* **Allen** (L. M.). A metallurgical study of four Irish Early Bronze Age ribbed halberds in the Pitt Rivers Museum, Oxford. Man, 60, 1960, 85–89 + 6 figures.

7302 Petch (D. F.). Bronze axes from Yaddlethorpe, Skinnand and Holton-le-Moor. Rpts. & Papers, Lincs. A. & A.S., 8, 1959, 6–8 + 4 figures.

7303 —— A bronze sword, Appleby. R. & P., Lincs. A. & A.S., 8, 1959, 8 + 1 figure.

7304 —— A bronze spearhead, Coningsby. Rpts. & Papers, Lincs. A. & A.S., 8, 1959, 8 + 1 figure.

7305 —— A Bronze Age spearhead, Temple Bruer [basal-loop]. Rpts. & Papers, Lincs. A. & A.S., 9, 1961, 7–9 + 1 figure.

7306 —— A Late Bronze Age sword, Tattershall Thorpe. Rpts. & Papers, Lincs. A. & A.S., 9, 1961, 9 + 1 plate.

7307 —— A bronze axe from Tatershall. Rpts. & Papers, Lincs. A. & A.S., 9, 1961, 9, 1 figure.

7308 —— A flat bronze axe, Walcot. Rpts. & Papers, Lincs. A. & A.S., 9, 1962, 92–3 + 1 figure.

7309 —— A Bronze palstave, Temple Bruer. Rpts. & Papers, Lincs. A. & A.S., 9, 1962, 93 + 1 figure.

7310 —— A socketed bronze axe Billinghay. Rpts. & Papers, Lincs. A. & A.S., 9, 1962, 93 + 1 figure.

7311 —— A Bronze Age rapier, Glentham. Rpts. & Papers, Lincs. A. & A.S., 9, 1962, 93 + 1 figure.

7312 —— A bronze dagger from Witham at Lincoln. Rpts. & Papers, Lincs. A. & A.S., 9, 1962, 93–4 + 1 figure.

7313 Phillips (Charles William). [Late] Bronze Age sword from [Worlaby], Lincolnshire. [Figure.] Antiq. J., 14, pp. 300–01. 1934.

7314 —— Bronze Age sword from [Billinghay Dales,] Lincolnshire. [Figure.] Antiq. J., 15, p. 349. 1935.

7315 Piggott (Cicily Margaret). A Late Bronze Age hoard from Blackrock in Sussex and its significance. Proc. prehist. Soc., 15, 1949, 107–21 + 6 figures.

7316 Pirie (E. J. E.). Boughton Aluph. [Bronze handle-mount. ?80–75 B.C.] Archaeol. Cant., 72 (1958), pp. 212, 214 + plate. 1959.

7317 —— Researches and discoveries in Kent: Orpington. [Bronze Age socketed axe.] Arch. Cant., 73, 1959, p. 230.

7318 Pollitt (William). Bronze-founder's hoard from Southend-on-Sea. [Late Bronze Age.] Antiq. J., 6, p. 309. 1926.

7319 —— Bronze [Age] objects from [Shoebury], south-east Essex. Antiq. J., 12, p. 74 + plate. 1932.

7320 Pretty (Edward). On the golden armillae in the [Kent Archaeological] Society's museum. [From the Medway, near Aylesford (Celtic) and from Canterbury (Roman).] Arch. Cant., 5, pp. 41–44 + 2 coloured plates. 1863.

7321 Prigg (Henry). On a hoard of Bronze [Age] antiquities from Reach, Cambridgeshire. J. Brit. Archaeol. Ass., 36, pp. 56–62 + plate. 1880.

7322 —— Discovery of an ancient British sword at Chippenham, Cambridgeshire. Northants. N. & Q., N.S. I, p. 22. 1885.

7323 —— On the recent discovery of a bronze sword, at Chippenham, Cambridgeshire, with notices of similar discoveries in the western district of Suffolk. Proc. Suffolk Inst. Arch., 6, pp. 184–94 + plate. 1888.

7324 Read (*Sir* Charles Hercules). Bronze scabbard of Late-Celtic work found at Hunsbury camp, near Northampton. [Figure.] Archaeologia, 52, p. 761–62 + plate. 1890.

7325 —— On a find of bronze implements from Shoebury, Essex. [Figures (palstave, adze and penannular armlet).] Proc. Soc. Antiq., 2 S. 14, pp. 174–79. 1892.

7326 —— Two hoards of Bronze [Age] implements from Grays Thurrock, Essex, and Southall, Middlesex. [Figure. Pp. 330–34, Notes on (i) the composition of the bronze, copper, etc. and (ii) on experiments on the manufac-

ture of ancient bronze, by William Rowland.] Proc. Soc. Antiq., 2 S. 16, pp. 327–34. 1897.

7327 —— [Bronze Age dagger and chisel found in High Down camp, Sussex]. [Figures.] Proc. Soc. Antiq., 2 S. 18, pp. 386–88. 1901.

7328 —— A Bronze [Age] spear-head found in the Thames at Taplow, Berks. [Figure.] Proc. Soc. Antiq., 2 S. 19, pp. 287–89. 1903.

7329 —— Dagger-blade of the Bronze Age from Sproughton, Suffolk. [Figure.] Proc. Soc. Antiq., 2 S. 22, pp. 86–88. 1908.

7330 Rice (R. Garraway). Late Bronze Age founder's hoard, found at Wandsworth, Surrey. [Figure. 9 implements + 8 lumps of founder's metal.] Antiq. J., 3, pp. 343–44. 1923.

7331 Robertson (William Archibald Scott). Gold torques from Dover. Arch. Cant., 12, pp. 317–20 + plate. 1878.

7332 Roskill (V.). The Bronze [Age] implements of the Newbury region. [11 figures.] Trans. Newbury F.C., 8, pp. 10–41. 1938.

7333 Row (Prescott). A founder's hoard of prehistoric bronze implements discovered in Shunaway plantation, Coulsdon, Surrey. [9 figures.] Surrey Archaeol. Collns., 38, pp. 75–78. 1930.

7334 Serocold (Pearce) *Col.* Bronze hoard from Burnham [Bucks.]. [19 palstaves.] Antiq. J., 13, p. 55 + plate. 1933.

7335 Sheppard (Thomas). Rare Bronze Age implement at Messingham [Lincs.]. Lincs. N. & Q., 19, p. 65 + plate. 1927.

7336 Shortt (Hugh de Sansmarez). A looped bronze palstave from St. George's hill, Surrey (ditto from Sheerwater, near Woking). [3 figures.] Surrey Archaeol. Collns., 55, pp. 121–22. 1958.

7337 —— Another spur of the first century A.D. from Suffolk. [2 figures, I plate.] Ant. J., 44, 1964, 60–61.

7338 Skinner (Edward). British bronze weapons found near Norwich. Northants. N. & Q., N.S. I, pp. 57–58. 1885.

7339 Smith (Charles Roach). Gold torques and armillae discovered in Kent. [Celtic.] Arch. Cant., 9, pp. 1–11 + 2 plates. 1874.

7340 Smith (Reginald Allender). On a Late Celtic mirror found at Desborough Northants, and other mirrors of the period. [13 figures.] Archaeologia, 61, pp. 329–46 + 2 plates. 1909.

7341 —— A hoard of metal [objects] found at Santon Downham, Suffolk. [11 figures. Pegs, bridle-bits, ferrules, etc.] Proc. Camb. Antiq. Soc., 13, pp. 146–63 + 3 plates. 1909.

7342 —— A Bronze Age hoard dredged from the Thames off Broadness [Essex]. [5 Figures (implements).] Proc. Soc. Antiq., 2 S. 23, pp. 160–71 + plate. 1910.

7343 —— Thin bronze vessels including water-clocks of the Early Iron Age, discovered at Wotton, Surrey. [15 figures.] Proc. Soc. Antiq., 2 S. 27, pp. 76–95. 1915.

7344 —— Bronze vessels of the Early Iron Age found at Wooton in 1914. [15 figures.] Surrey Archaeol. Collns., 29, pp. 1–24. 1916.

7345 —— On circular bronze shields with especial reference to a specimen from the Lea valley. [2 figures. Early Iron Age.] Proc. Soc. Antiq., 2 S. 31, pp. 145–51. 1919.

7346 —— Gold armlet from the British Bronze Age [from Selsey Bill]. Brit. Mus. Q., 1, pp. 14–15 + plate. 1926.

7347 —— Selsey treasure trove. [Bronze Age. Two gold bracelets.] Brit. Mus. Q., 11, pp. 122–23 + plate. 1937.

7348 —— A Celtic bronze from [Icklingham,] Suffolk. Brit. Mus. Q., 10, pp. 27–28 + plate. 1935.

7349 Stevens (Joseph). Notes on a Bronze [Age] sword and an iron spearhead found in the Thames [at Henley]. Trans. Berks. Arch. Soc., 1880/81, pp. 63–64 + plate. 1881.

7350 —— On a Bronze [Age] sword . . . found at Henley-on-Thames. J. Brit. Archaeol. Ass., 38, pp. 275–77 + plate. 1882.

7351 Stodart (Edward). [A gold] torques found at Boyton, in Suffolk. [Figure.] Archaeologia, 26, p. 471. 1836.

7352 Taylor (Henry). Palstave from Cuckfield. Sussex N. & Q., 10, p. 90. 1944.

7353 Tebbutt (C. F.). Celtic linch-pin heads from Colne Fen, Huntingdonshire. Ant. J., 41, 1961, 235–38.

7354 Terry (W. Neville). A further note [to mention on p. 148 of vol. 63] on the bronze spear-head from Chartham. [Figure. Late Bronze Age.] Arch. Cant., 65 (1952), pp. 198–200. 1953.

7355 Tester (P. J.). The Bexley Heath Bronze Age hoard. Archaeol. Cant., 71 (1957), pp. 232–33. 1958.

7356 Thompson (Frederick Hugh). A Bronze [Age] spear-head from Donington-on-Bain, Lincolnshire. [Figure.] Antiq. J., 34, p. 238. 1954.

7357 Trechmann (C. T.). Two hoards of Bronze [Age] implements. [3 figures. i. From Brighton; ii. From Newport, co. Mayo.] Proc. Soc. Antiq., 2 S. 28, pp. 153–64. 1916.

7358 Ward (Gordon). Horse shoes at Lewes Museum. [Figure. Pp. 38–40, The Celtic group.] Sussex N. & Q., 7, pp. 38–43. 1938.

7359 Ware (Samuel). Battle-axeheads, found near Clare, in Suffolk. [Figure.] Archaeologia, 31, pp. 496–97. 1846.

7360 Way (Albert). Account of the discovery of an armilla of pure gold, in clearing a coppice near Wendover in Buckinghamshire in 1847. Archaeologia, 33, pp. 347–49 + plate. 1849.

7361 Westell (William Percival). Bronze knife found at Letchworth. [Figure.] Antiq. J., 20, p. 275. 1940.

7362 Wheeler (*Sir* Robert Eric Mortimer). Bronze [Age] implements from the city of London. [Figure. 12, various sites.] Antiq. J., 7, pp. 294–98 + plate. 1927.

7363 White (R. Holt). The discovery of gold bracelets near Crayford. [Figure. Bronze Age.] Antiquary, 43, pp. 126–28. 1907.

7364 Whitwell (J. B.). A bronze palstave, Bramsby. [MBA.] Rpts. & Papers, Lincs. A. & A.S., 10, 1963, 2 + 1 figure.

7365 —— A flat bronze axe, South Kyme. Rpts. & Papers, Lincs. A. & A.S., 1963, 2 + 1 figure.

7366 —— A socketed axe, Branston Fen. Rpts. & Papers, Lincs. A. & A.S., 10, 1963, 2 + 1 figure.

7367 Winbolt (Samuel Edward). Two Slinfold finds.—A British gold ring. Sussex N. & Q., 4, pp. 63–64. 1932.

7368 Winbolt (Samuel Edward). A Late Bronze Age hoard from Flansham. [Figure.] Sussex N. & Q., 7, pp. 78–80. 1938.

7369 Wymer (J. J.). The discovery of a gold torc at Moulsford. [3 plates.] Berks. Arch. J., 59, 1961, 36–37.

(b) Zone 2
[CBA Group 12]

7370 [Anon.] Late Celtic bronze enamelled cheek-piece of bit [found at Middle Chase farm, Bowerchalke, Wilts.]. [Figure.] Wilts. Archaeol. Mag., 43, p. 352. 1926.

7371 [Anon.] An early British bronze "spoon". [Figure. From Andover, Hants.] Antiq. J., 13, pp. 464–65. 1933.

7372 [Anon.] Bronze Age spear-head from Muckleford. Proc. Dorset Archaeol. Soc., 54, p. lxxvii + plate. 1933.

7373 Britton (D.). A study of the composition of Wessex culture bronzes. Archaeometry, 4 (1961), 39–52.

7374 Case (Humphrey). The Mere, Roundway, and Winterslow Beaker culture knives. [Figure.] Wilts. Archaeol. Mag., 55, pp. 135–38. 1953.

7375 Coles (John M.). The Hilton (Dorset) gold ornaments. Antiquity, 37, 1963, 132–34.

7376 Crawford (Osbert Guy Stanhope.) A gold torc and a double-looped palstave [from a barrow at Blackwater 2½ miles north-west of Christchurch, Hants.] [Figure + 2 distribution maps. Late Bronze Age: c. 1000 B.C. with bibliographies for both objects.] Proc. Soc. Antiq., 2 S. 24, pp. 39–49. 1912.

7377 Cunnington (Maud Edith). A note on some brooches from [Brixton Deverill,] Wiltshire. [Figure. Early Iron Age to late Romano-British.] Man, 21, pp. 132–33. 1921.

7378 —— Brooches from Cold Kitchen hill [Brixton Deverell, Wilts.]. Wilts. Archaeol. Mag., 42, pp. 67–69. 1922.

7379 —— Late Bronze Age gold bracelet from Clench common [near Marlborough]. [Figure.] Wilts. Archaeol. Mag., 42, pp. 69–70. 1922.

7380 —— Prehistoric gold in Wilts. [2 figures. Wilts. barrows on direct route of traffic in Irish gold.] Antiq. J., 5, pp. 68–70. 1925.

7381 —— Bronze arrow-head from [Water Dean Bottom, Salisbury plain,] Wilts. [Figure.] Antiq. J., 6, p. 182. 1826.

7382 Dale (William). Ancient bronze weapons from the neighbourhood of Southampton. [Early Bronze Age.] Papers & Proc. Hants. F.C., 3, pp. 265–66 + plate. 1896.

7383 —— A hoard of Bronze [Age] implements discovered at Pear Tree, near Southampton. Proc. Soc. Antiq., 2 S. 17, pp. 129–32. 1898.

7384 Darwin (W. E.). A hoard of bronze implements found at Bitterne. Papers & Proc. Hants. F.C., 3, pp. 53–66 + 2 plates. 1894.

7385 Drew (Charles Douglas). Palstaves from Dewlish, Dorset. Antiquity, 7, p. 221 + plate. 1933.

7386 —— Bronze Age hoard from Haselbury Bryan. Proc. Dorset Archaeol. Soc., 56 (1934), pp. 131–32 + plate (2 bracelets and bronze torc). 1935.

7387 —— A Late Bronze Age hoard from Lulworth, Dorset. [Figure (flesh-hook).] Antiq. J., 15, pp. 449–51 + plate. 1935.

7388 Dunning (Gerald Clough). Hoard of palstaves found at Werrar, near Northwood. Proc. I. of W. N.H. & Arch. Soc., 2, p. 616 + plate. 1936.

7389 Farrar (Raymond Anthony Holt). A Late Bronze Age hoard from Grimstone, Stratton. Proc. Dorset N.H. & A.S., 86, 1964, 115.

7390 Fowler (Margaret J.). The typology of brooches of the Iron Age in Wessex. [Figure. La Tène I-III.] Archaeol. J., 110 (1953), pp. 88–105. 1954.

7391 Fox (*Sir* Cyril). A La Tène weight from Winchester. [2 figures.] Antiq. J., 10, pp. 250–53. 1930.

7392 Franks (*Sir* Augustus Wollaston). Note on bronze weapons found on Arreton down, Isle of Wight. [2 figures.] Archaeologia, 36, pp. 326–31 + plate. 1855.

7393 Goddard (Edward Hungerford). Notes on objects of the Bronze Age found in Wiltshire. [15 figures.] Reliquary, 3rd S. 14, pp. 242–49. 1908.

7394 —— Notes on implements of the

Bronze Age found in Wiltshire, with a list of all known examples found in the county. [29 figures.] Wilts. Archaeol. Mag., 37, pp. 92–158, 455 + 7 plates: 38, p. 115: 39, pp. 477–84: 40, pp. 359–60 (supplementary list). 1911–17, 1919.

7395(a) Gray (Harold St. George). Notes on the Allington [down, N. Wilts.] gold torc. [Figure. Found 1844. Late Bronze Age.] Wilts. Archaeol. Mag., 36, pp. 435–38. 1910.

7395(b) Grove (Leonard Robert Allen). Two bridle spurs from Basingstoke. [Figure. Early Iron Age. In Reading Museum.] Papers & Proc. Hants. F.C., 13, pp. 179–80. 1936.

7396 Hawkes (Charles Francis Christopher). Sicilian bronze [shaft-hole] axe from [beach near] Hengistbury head. Antiquity, 12, pp. 225–28 + plate; *see also* pp. 350–51. 1938.

7397 —— A Celtic bronze from Bury Hill camp, near Andover, Hants. [Figure.] Antiq. J., 20, p. 121. 1940.

7398 —— An iron torc from Spettisbury rings, Dorset. [Figure. Early Iron Age.] Archaeol. J., 97 (1940), pp. 112–14. 1941.

7399 Hooley (Reginald W.). Note on a hoard of iron currency-bars found on Worthy down, Winchester. [Figure. Early Iron Age.] Antiq. J., 1, pp. 321–27. 1921.

7400 —— Note on a hoard of iron currency bars found on Worthy down, Winchester. [Early Iron Age.] Papers & Proc. Hants. F.C., 12, pp. 236–40 + plate. 1934.

7401 Meyrick (Owen). Bronze [Age] implement from Manningford, Bohune down. Wilts. Archaeol. Mag., 54, pp. 228. 1951.

7402 Moule (Henry Joseph). Notes on bronze. [Pp. 49–104, Dorset-found Celtic and Roman bronze objects in the Dorset County Museum (celts, weapons, jewellery, etc.).] Proc. Dorset Antiq. F.C., 21, pp. 40–104. 1900.

7403 —— Catalogue of local bronze antiquities in the Dorset County Museum pp. 104. 8º. Dorchester, [1900].

7404 Oliver (Vere Langford). [11] Bronze Age rapiers and swords from Dorset. Proc. Dorset Archaeol. Soc., 58 (1936), pp. 26–29 +3 plates. 1937.

7405 Temple (Amelia Mary) *Viscountess Palmerston.* Gold torques found near Romsey, Hants. Archaeologia, 39, pp. 505–08 + plate. 1863.

7406 Passmore (A. D.). Early Iron Age bronze horse bit roller. Wilts. Archaeol. Mag., 45, p. 94 + plate. 1930.

7407 Piggott (Cecily Margaret). A Late Bronze Age razor from Chilmark. [Figure.] Wilts. Archaeol. Mag., 53, pp. 254–55. 1949.

7408 Piggott (Stuart). The Arreton Down Bronze Age hoard. Antiq. J., 27, pp. 177–78 + plate (implements). 1947.

7409 Roberts (R.). A description of some ancient gold ornaments found [at Hilton,] in Dorsetshire. [*See also* 5, pp. 47–48.] Proc. Dorset Antiq. F.C., 4, pp. 158–59. 1880.

7410 Sherwin (Gerald Ambrose). A second Bronze [Age] hoard of Arreton down types found [at Moon's hill, Totland], in the Isle of Wight. [13 figures.] Antiq. J., 22, pp. 198–201. 1942.

7411 —— A second bronze hoard of Arreton down type found in the Isle of Wight. Ant. J., 22. *Reprinted in* Proc. I. of W.N.H. & Arch. Soc., 3, pp. 378–82. 1943.

7412 Shortt (Hugh de Sansmarez). Bronze palstave from Mere. Wilts. Archaeol. Mag., 48, p. 470. 1939.

7413 —— A hoard of bangles from Ebbesbourne Wake, Wilts. [Plan (Elcombe down). Bronze Age.] Wilts. Archaeol. Mag., 53, pp. 104–12 + plate. 1949.

7414 —— A bronze founder's hoard near Ansty hollow. [Late Bronze Age.] Wilts. Archaeol. Mag., 53, p. 134. 1949.

7415 —— A La Tène I fibula from Cold Kitchen hill. [Figure.] Wilts. Archaeol. Mag., 53, pp. 134–35. 1949.

7416 —— A La Tène I fibula from Micheldever, Hants. [Figure.] Papers & Proc. Hants. F.C., 17, pp. 56–57. 1952.

7417 —— A La Tène I fibula from Fisherton Delamere. [Figure.] Wilts. Archaeol. Mag., 56, p. 195. 1955.

7418 Simpson (D. D. A.). Bronze looped palstave. Wilts. Archaeol. Mag., 58, No. 210, p. 227 + 1 figure. 1962.

7419 Smith (Charles Roach). A hoard of Bronze [Age] bracelets at Brading, I.W. J. Brit. Archaeol. Ass., 38, pp. 423–24. 1882.

7420 Smith (Reginald Allender). An early British [bronze] spoon [from Andover, Hants.]. Brit. Mus. Q., 8, pp. 74–75 + plate. 1933.

7421 Stevens (Frank). La Tène I fibula from Salisbury. [Figure.] Wilts. Archaeol. Mag., 47, p. 285. 1935.

7422 Stone (John F. S.). A decorated Bronze [Age] axe from Stonehenge down. [Figure.] Wilts. Archaeol. Mag., 55, pp. 30–33. 1953.

7423 Sumner (Heywood). Bronze [Age] hoard in the New Forest. Antiq. J., 7, pp. 192–93 + plate. 1927.

(c) Zone 3
[CBA Groups 8, 13]

7424 Allies (Jabez). Ancient bronze ornament found at Perdeswell, near Worcester. [Figure. 20 small pieces twisted and tooled.] Archaeologia, 30, pp. 554–55. 1844.

7425 [Anon.] A gold torc found at Yeovil. [Late Bronze Age.] J. Brit. Archaeol. Ass., N.S. 15, p. 117. 1909.

7426 [Anon.] A Somerset find [of a solid hand-wrought gold wire torque of c. 500 B.C.]. [Inquiry at Yeovil.] Num. Circular, 17, col. 11672. 1909.

7427 Barker (W. R.). An ancient bronze collar from Wraxall, Somerset. [Late Celtic period. Now in Bristol Museum.] Proc. Clifton Antiq. Club, 3, pp. 89–94 + plate. 1897.

7428 Benton (Sylvia). The Pelynt sword-hilt. Proc. prehist. Soc., 18, 1952, 237–38 + 2 plates.

7249 Bulleid (Arthur). Bronze palstave, Peasedown St. John. Proc. Somerset Arch. Soc., 75 (1929), p. 98 + plate. 1930.

7430 Burnard (Robert). Bronze [Age objects] on Dartmoor. [2 figures.] Reliquary, N. [3rd] S. 1, pp. 103–05. 1895.

7431 Childe (Vere Gordon). Bronze dagger of Mycenaean type, Pelynt, Cornwall. Proc. prehist. Soc., 17, 1951, 95 + 1 plate.

7432 Chitty (Lily Frances). Three Bronze [Age] implements from the Edgebold brickyard, Meole Brace, Shropshire. [3 figures. Palstaves, and trunnion celt.] Antiq. J., 5, pp. 409–14. 1925.

7433 —— Bronze spear-head found near the Day House, Charrington. [Late Bronze Age.] Trans. Shropshire Archaeol. Soc., 43 (4th S. 10), pp. vii–viii. 1926.

7434 —— Bronze implements from the Edgebold brickfield, nr. Shrewsbury. [Late Bronze Age.] Trans. Shropshire Archaeol. Soc., 43 [4th S. 10], pp. viii–ix. 1926.

7435 —— Bronze dirk found near the Whetstones circle, Montgomeryshire–Shropshire border. [Middle Bronze Age.] Trans. Shropshire Archaeol. Soc., 43 (4th S. 10), pp. xxvii–xxx. 1926.

7436 —— Bronze dirk found near the Whetstones Circle, Montgomeryshire–Shropshire border, with notes on its neighbouring antiquities. Arch. Cambrensis, 81 ii, 1926, 409–13 + 1 figure.

7437 —— Bronze spear-head from Petton. [Middle Bronze Age. In Shrewsbury Museum.] Trans. Shropshire Archaeol. Soc., 44 (4th S. 11), pp. iv–v + plate. 1927.

7438 —— Bronze implements found near Castle Bryn Amlurg, Bettws-y-Crwyn [Salop.]. [Bronze Age.] Trans. Shropshire Archaeol. Soc., 44 (4th S. 11), pp. v–vii. 1927.

7439 —— Bronze halberd said to have been found in Shropshire. Arch. Camb., 83 i, 1928, 209–11.

7440 —— The Willow Moor bronze hoard, Little Wenlock, Shropshire. [2 figures + map. Late Bronze Age.] Antiq. J., 8, pp. 30–47 + 2 plates. 1928.

7441 —— Bronze palstave from [Preeswood], Shropshire. [Figure.] Antiq. J., 9, pp. 253–55. 1929.

7442 —— Bronze palstave from Preeswood. (*Ditto* from Knockin.) [Middle Bronze Age.] Trans. Shropshire Archaeol. Soc., 45 (4th S. 12), pp. v–vi. 1929.

7443 —— Archaeological notes. 1. Bronze looped palstave from Whixall moss, north Shropshire. (2. Stone implement reported from Builwas). [Figure of palstave.] Trans. Shropshire Archaeol. Soc., 47, pp. 73–77. 1933.

7444 —— Bronze dagger found on Caradoc, All Stretton. [Figure. Bronze Age.] Trans. Shropshire Archaeol. Soc., 49, pp. i–ii. 1938.

7445 Chitty (Lilly Frances). Bronze implements from the Oswestry region of Shropshire. Arch. Camb., 95 i, 1940, 27–35 + 4 figures.

7446 —— Bronze palstave found at Pontesbury, Shropshire. [Figure.] Trans. Shropshire Archaeol. Soc., 54, pp. 145–48. 1952.

7447 —— Bronze axe hoard from Preston-on-the-Weald moors, Shropshire. [2 figures.] Trans. of the Shropshire Archaeol. Soc., 54, pp. 240–54. 1953.

7448 —— Late Bronze Age spearhead from the Great Doward [hill], south Herefordshire. Trans. Woolhope N.F.C., 34 (1952–4), pp. 21–23. 1955.

7449 Dodd (J. Phillip). The Eardington bronze hoard [LBA chisel, gouge, 2 palstaves.] Trans. Shropshire A.S., 56 iii, 1960, 213–17 + 2 figures.

7450 Edwards (J. H.). Recent discoveries of Bronze Age relics near Coventry. [2 figures.] Proc. Coventry N.H. Soc., 1, pp. 45–47. 1932.

7451 Ellacombe (Harry Thomas). A torques, found at Wraxall, in the county of Somerset. Archaeologia, 30, p. 521. 1844.

7452 Ellis (*Sir* Henry). Account of a gold torquis found in Needwood forest in Staffordshire. Archaeologia, 33, pp. 175–76 + plate. 1849.

7453 Fisher (C. H.). Two Bronze [Age] spear-heads from Rodborough, near Stroud. [Figure.] Proc. Cotteswold Nat. Club, 13, pp. 85–87. 1899.

7454 Fowler (Elizabeth). A note on a penannular brooch from Godrevy Headland, Gwithian. [1st–3rd cent. A.D.] Cornish archaeol. No. 2, 1963, 76 + 1 figure.

7455 Fox (*Sir* Cyril). A group of bronzes of the Early Iron Age in Yeovil Museum. [Figure. Rings, etc.] Proc. Somerset Arch. Soc., 96 (1951), pp. 108–11 + plate. 1952.

7456 Franks (*Sir* Augustus Wollaston). On a Late Celtic bronze collar from Wraxall, Somerset. Archaeologia, 54, pp. 495–96 + plate. 1895.

7457 Garrett (C. Scott). Two socketed bronze axes from Gloucestershire, (a) From Sling Common near Coleford. Trans. Bristol & Glos. A.S., 76, 1957, 146–48 + 1 figure.

7458 Gaythorpe (Harper). Notes on a socketed Bronze [Age] celt [from Bristol]. Proc. Bath N.H. & Ant. F.C., 9, pp. 294–300 + 2 plates + plan. 1901.

7459 Gray (Harold St. George). [Late Bronze [Age] sword found on Pitney moor, Somerset. Proc. Somerset Arch. Soc., 47 (1901), pp. 230–33 + plate. 1902.

7460 —— A copper celt from Staple Fitzpaine, Somerset. [Figure. Bronze Age.] Man, 4, pp. 13–14. 1904.

7461 —— A copper celt from Staple Fitzpaine. [Figure. Bronze Age.] Proc. Somerset Arch. Soc., 50 (1904), pp. 110–12. 1905.

7462 —— The gold Torc found at Yeovil, 1909. [Pp. 144–47, Distribution of ancient British gold torcs, with list of localities and references.] Coroners' Society Annual Report, 1909–10, pp. 135–47 + plate. 1910.

7463 —— The gold torc found at Yeovil, 1909. [Figure. Bronze Age. Pp. 78–84, Distribution, with a list of localities and references.] Proc. Somerset Arch. Soc., 55 (1909), pp. 66–84 + plate. 1910.

7464 —— A gold ornament found at Castle Cary, Somerset. [Figure. Late Bronze Age.] Antiq. J., 5, pp. 141–44. 1925.

7465 —— Bronze celt from Staple Fitzpaine, in Taunton Castle Museum. [Analysis: 92·46 per cent copper, 6·94 per cent tin. *See also* **7460**.] Man, 27, p. 207. 1927.

7466 —— [Late] Bronze [Age] chisel from Ham Hill, south Somerset. [Figure.] Antiq. J., 8, pp. 241–42. 1928.

7467 —— Bronze scabbard found at Meare, Somerset. [Figure. La Tène II.] Antiq. J., 10, pp. 154–55. 1930.

7468 —— Bronze [Age] implements, found in the parish of Old Cleeve, Somerset. [Palstaves, etc.] Proc. Somerset Arch. Soc., 77 (1931), pp. 136–37. 1932.

7469 —— Bronze implements found [Ham Hill and Camerton, Somerset], in south-west Britain. [Figure.] Antiq. J., 14, pp. 424–25. 1934.

7470 —— Double-looped palstave found at Curland, near Taunton. [2 figures + distribution map.] Antiq. J., 17, pp. 63–69. 1937.

7471 —— Bronze [Age] spearhead

found at Shapwick, Someerseet. [Figure.] Antiq. J., 26, p. 70. 1946.

7472 Gray (Harold St. George). Bronze finger-ring from Meare lake village. [Figure.] Antiq. J., 31, p. 75. 1951.

7473 Green (Charles). Some Bronze [Age] implements from [Bourton-on-the-Water, etc.], Gloucestershire. [Figures.] Antiq. J., 15, pp. 196–98. 1935.

7474 Grinsell (Leslie Valentine). A socketed bronze adze from [Barrow Gurney], Somerset. [Figure. List with references.] Antiq. J., 33, pp. 203–04. 1953.

7475 —— Two socketed bronze axes from Gloucestershire, (b) From Oldland near Bristol. Trans. Bristol & Glos. A.S., 76, 1957, 148–49 + 1 figure.

7476 —— A bronze torc from Winscombe, Somerset. N. & Q. Somerset & Dorset, 28, 1966, pt. 283, pp. 259–60 + 1 figure.

7477 Hallam (A. D.). A pair of cauldron-handles in the Somerset County museum. [Bronze Age.] Proc. Somerset Arch. Soc., 95 (1950), pp. 171–72 + plate. 1951.

7478 Harford (Charles Joseph). An account of some antiquities discovered on the Quantock hills in Somersetshire, in the year 1794. Archaeologia, 14, pp. 94–98 + plate (torque). 1803.

7479 Hawkes (Charles Francis Christopher). The Towednack [Cornwall] gold hoard. [Figure + plan. Bronze Age.] Man, 32, pp. 177–86 + plate. 1932.

7480 Hitchins (Malachy) *Rev.* Account of antiquities discovered in Cornwall. Archaeologia, 15, pp. 118–21 + plate. 1806.

7481 Hudd (Alfred Edmund). Discovery of Bronze [Age] implements at Coombe dingle, Westbury-upon-Trym. [2 figures (flanged celt and chisel).] Proc. Soc. Antiq., 2 S. 18, pp. 237–40. 1901.

7482 —— Four Bronze [Age] implements from Coombe Dingle, Gloucestershire. Proc. Clifton Antiq. Club, 5, pp. 118–21 + plate. 1904.

7483 Humphreys (Humphrey Francis). A bronze palstave from [Burton Green] near Kenilworth. B'ham Arch. Soc., Trans., 65 (1943–44), pp. 141–42 + plate. 1949.

7484 Hutchinson (Peter Orlando). Bronze [Age] celt found near Sidmouth.

Rpt. & Trans. Devon Assoc., 5, pp. 82–83. 1872.

7485 Meyrick (Samuel Rush). Description of two ancient British shields, preserved . . . at Goodrich Court, Herefordshire. Archaeologia, 23, pp. 92–97 + plate. 1831.

7486 Nankivell (Florence). A Bronze razor or tranchet from Riviere Towans, Hayle. [Figure.] Proc. West Cornwall F.C., 2, pp. 29–31. 1957.

7487 O'Neil (Bryan Hugh St. John). Hoard of [bronze socketed] axes from Bourton-on-the-Water, Gloucestershire. Antiq. J., 21, pp. 151–52. 1941.

7488 Oswald (Adrian). Bronze axehead from Henley-in-Arden. [Early Bronze Age.] B'ham Arch. Soc., Trans., 71 (1953), p. 135 + plate. 1955.

7489 Perkins (John Bryan Ward). An Iron-Age linch-pin of Yorkshire type from [Trevelgue], Cornwall. [Figure.] Antiq. J., 21, pp. 64–67 + 3 plates. 1941.

7490 Pettigrew (Thomas Joseph). [3 torques from Wedmore, Somerset.] J. Brit. Archaeol. Ass., 21, pp. 232–33 + plate. 1865.

7491 Read (*Sir* Charles Hercules). A Late Celtic dagger-sheath from [West Buckland], Somerset. Proc. Soc. Antiq., 2 S. 25, pp. 57–59 + plate. 1913.

7492 Rickard (T. A.). The Falmouth ingot of tin. Man, 32, pp. 195–96. 1932.

7493 Rocke (Thomas Owen). The Bronze [Age] relics of Broadward, Shropshire. Arch. Camb., 4th S. 3, pp. 338–44. 1872.

7494 Sanders (S. S.). Bronze palstave found at Whitley, near Coventry. B'ham Arch. Soc. Trans., 54 (1929–30), pp. 71–72 + plate. 1932.

7495 Smirke (Edward). Observations on the gold gorgets or lunettes found near Padstone, and now in the museum at Truro. [Figure (celt).] J. Roy. Inst. Cornwall, 2, pp. 134–42 + 2 plates, p. 172. 1866.

7496 —— Some account of the discovery of a gold cup in a barrow [near the Cheese-wring] in Cornwall, A.D. 1837. (Supplementary notices . . . by Albert Way.) [Figure.] Archaeol. J., 24, pp. 189–202 + 2 plates. 1867.

7497 —— Some account of the discovery of a gold cup in a barrow [in

Rillaton manor] in Cornwall, A.D. 1837. J. Roy. Instn. Cornwall, 3, pp. 34–48 + 3 plates. 1868.

7498 Smith (Reginald Allender). An iron currency-bar of the early British period found within the earthwork in Meon hill, Gloucestershire, 1824. Proc. Soc. Antiq., 2 S. 22, pp. 337–43. 1908.

7499 —— An iron currency-bar of a new denomination from Salmonsbury camp, Bourton-on-the-Water, Gloucestershire. [Figure.] Proc. Soc. Antiq., 2 S. 27, pp. 69–76. 1915.

7500 —— Side-lights on Italian "bow-pullers". [19 figures. Including Late Celtic example found on the Polden hills, Somerset and on Firle beacon, Sussex, etc.] Proc. Soc. Antiq., 2 S. 29, pp. 24–41. 1916.

7501 —— Note on two bronze bracelets belonging to the Royal Institution of Cornwall. [Figure. Early Iron Age.] Proc. Soc. Antiq., 2 S. 32, pp. 97–101. 1920.

7502 —— On some recent exhibits. [3 figures. 2 gold crescents and celt from Harlyn Bay, Cornwall.] Antiq. J., 2, pp. 93–97. 1922.

7503 —— Treasure-trove from Towednack (Cornwall). [Gold torc. Bronze Age.] Brit. Mus. Q., 7, pp. 48–49 + plate. 1932.

7504 —— The Rillaton [moor] gold cup. [From barrow between Hurlers and Cheesewring.] Brit. Mus. Q., 11, pp. 1–3 + plate. 1936.

7505 Terry (W. Neville). A [Late] Bronze [Age] spear-head from Moreton-in-Marsh, [Glos.] [Figure.] Trans. Bristol & Glos. Arch. Soc., 72 (1953), pp. 150–51. 1954.

7506 Thomas (Charles). Two decorated Bronze [Age] axes from St. Erth. [Figure.] Proc. West Cornwall F.C., N.S. 1, pp. 87–89. 1954.

7507 —— A flat axe from Prea Sands. Cornish archaeol., No. 2, 1963, 77 + 1 figure.

7508 Thomas, Nicholas. A small Celtic bronze from Cleeve Prior, Worcs. Ant. J., 44, 1964, 245–47.

7509 Tucker (Charles). Notices of antiquities of bronze found in Devon. [Figure. From various localities.] Archaeol. J., 24, pp. 110–22 + 3 plates. 1867.

7510 Way (Albert). Antiquities of bronze found in Devonshire. Archaeol. J., 26, pp. 339–51 + 2 plates. 1869.

7511 Williams (Arthur Moray). Socketed axe and spearhead from Bredon hill. [Late Bronze Age and late Middle Bronze Age.] Trans. Worcs. Archaeol. Soc., N.S. 31 (1954), pp. 49–50 + plate. 1955.

(d) Zone 4
[CBA Groups 3, 4, 5, 6]

7512 A (L. A.). Bronze Age axe. [Wincobank, near Sheffield]. J. Brit. Archaeol. Ass., N.S. 29, pp. 145–48. 1923.

7513 [Anon.] Bronze weapon and implements found at Rainton-cum-Newby [N. Riding]. Yorks. Archaeol. J., 20, pp. 103–04. 1909.

7514 [Anon.] Bronze axe-head found at Kirkby Malzeard. [Figure.] Yorks. Archeol. J., 20, pp. 254–55. 1909.

7515 [Anon.] Two looped palstaves ... found in the Stannylands ... between Wilmslow and Styal [Cheshire]. Trans. Lancs. & Ches. Ant. Soc., 31 (1913), pp. 149–50 + plate. 1914.

7516 [Anon.] A Bronze [Age] spearhead from Caldbeck. [Figure.] Trans. Cumb. & Westm. Ant. Soc., N.S. 15, p. 191. 1915.

7517 [Anon.] Bronze palstave found near Buxton. J. Derbs. Archaeol. Soc., 55 (N.S. 8, 1934), p. 93. 1935.

7518 [Anon.] Palstave from Great Sutton. J. Chester & N. Wales Arch. Soc., N.S. 39, p. 110. 1951.

7519 [Anon.] A bronze palstave of an Italian type [found at Chester]. [Figure.] J. Chester & N. Wales Arch. Soc., N.S. 40, pp. 63–64. 1953.

7520 Archaeological Institute. Bronze Collar, found at Embsay, in Yorkshire. Archaeologia, 31, p. 517 + plate. 1846.

7521 Argles (Thomas Atkinson). [Later] Bronze [Age] spearhead from Whitbarrow. Trans. Cumb. & Westm. Ant. Soc., N.S. 21, p. 273. 1921.

7522 Armstrong (Albert Leslie). "Carib" type of axe found in Yorkshire. Proc. PSEA, 2 i, 1914/15, 59–61.

7523 —— Analyses of Bronze [Age

mplements and foundry metal. [Pal-staves from Windsor, Hull Museum, etc.] Man, 26, pp. 164–67. 1926.

7524 Armstrong (Albert Leslie). Bronze brooch from [Steyforth hill, Stainburn moor], Yorkshire. [Figure. La Tène IV type.] Antiq. J., 8, pp. 526–27. 1928.

7525 Auden (George Augustus). Late Celtic sword found at Thorpe, near Bridlington, Yorkshire. [Figure. Now in York Museum.] Reliquary, 3rd S. 12, pp. 269–70 + plate. 1906.

7526 Baggaley (J. W.). Bronze age instruments found in Sheffield and district. Trans. Hunter Arch. Soc., 5, p. 99 + 1 plate. 1943.

7527 Barnes (F.). Further prehistoric finds from Furness. [2 figures.] Trans. Cumb. & Westm. Ant. Soc., N.S. 54, pp. 5–8. 1955.

7528 Bartlett (J. E.) *and* **Hawkes** (C. F. C.). A barbed bronze spear-head from North Ferriby, Yorkshire, England. Proc. prehist. Soc., 31, 1965, 370–73 + 2 figures.

7529 Bolam (R. G.). On a Bronze [Age] celt found at Linden [Nhbd.]. Hist. Berwick. Nat. Club. 7, p. 276. 1874.

7530 Bowden (William). [Palstave from Liscard, Cheshire]. Trans. Lancs. & Ches. Ant. Soc., 29 (1911), p. 222 + 2 plates. 1912.

7531 Bowman (George). Bronze palstave, found at Openshawe, Manchester, in 1908. Trans. Lancs. & Ches. Ant. Soc., 27 (1909), pp. 146–47 + plate. 1910.

7532 Brailsford (John William). The Stanwick sword. [Early Iron Age. North Riding.] Brit. Mus. Q., 17, pp. 50–51 + plate. 1952.

7533 Brewis (Parker). The evolution of the bronze spear and sword in Britain. [21 figures.] Proc. Univ. Durham Phil. Soc., 5, pp. 1–18 + plate. 1913.

7534 Brewis (William Parker). A "Sussex loop" [in Blackgate museum, Newcastle]. [Middle Bronze Age. Found near Crawley.] Proc. Soc. Antiq. Newc., 3rd S. 8, p. 60 + plate. 1917.

7535 —— British brooches of the Backworth type in the Black Gate museum, Newcastle-upon-Tyne. Arch. Æl., 3rd S. 21, pp. 173–81 + 6 plates. 1924.

7537 Brewster (T. C. M.). Two celts from Cayton Carr, Scarborough. [Middle Bronze Age metallic axes.] Arch. News Letter, 3, p. 150. 1951.

7538 —— A spear from Flixton Carr, Scarborough, Yorkshire. [Figure. Middle—Late Bronze Age.] Ann. Rpt. Yorks. Phil. Soc., 1951, pp. 15–17. 1952.

7539 —— Four Bronze Age finds in East Yorkshire. Yorks. Archaeol. J., 38, pp. 446–52. 1955.

7540 —— Four finds from East Yorkshire. Yorks. Archaeol. J., 39, pp. 53–57 + 2 plates. 1956.

7541 Butterfield (Rosse). Incised bronze palstave. Bradford Antiquary, 7 (N.S. 5), p. 50. 1933.

7542(a) Childe (Vere Gordon). Note on a bronze dagger found at Hungry Bentley. [Middle Bronze Age.] J. Derbs. Archaeol. Soc., 62 (N.S. 15), pp. 29–30 + plate. 1941.

7542(b) —— Note on a Bronze [Age] battle axe found near Cornhill. Hist. Berwick. Nat. Club, 30, p. 229 + plate. 1942.

7543 Coles (John M.). The Salta Moss rapier. [1 figure + 2 plates.] Trans. Cumb. & Westm. Ant. Soc., N.S. LXI, pp. 16–24. 1961.

7544 Collinge (Walter Edward). An early Italian brooch from [Boroughbridge], Yorks. [Figure. Early Iron Age.] Antiq. J., 10, pp. 54–55. 1930.

7545 Collingwood (William Gershom). Two bronze armlets from Thirlmere. [Early Iron Age.] Trans. Cumb. & Westm. Ant. Soc., N.S. 4, pp. 80–84 + plate. 1904.

7546 Cowen (John David). Two bronze swords from Ewart Park, Wooler. [Figure. Bronze Age. In Black Gate Museum.] Arch. Æl., 4th S. 10, pp. 185–98 + plate. 1933.

7547 —— Fragments of a bronze sword in the Black Gate Museum [Newcastle]. [Bronze Age. Danish type.] Arch. Æl., 4th S. 10, pp. 199–205 + plate. 1933.

7548 —— A Celtic sword-pommel at Tullie House. [Figure. Early Iron Age. From Brough, Westm.] Trans. Cumb. & Westm. Ant. Soc., N.S. 37, pp. 67–71 + plate. 1937.

7550 Cowper (Henry Swainson). Bronze Age relics from Furness. Trans.

Cumb. & Westm. Ant. Soc., N.S. 7, pp. 39–41 + plate (bronze dagger and spear-head). 1907.

7551 Davies (Ellis). The provenance of the gold torc preserved at Eaton Hall, Chester. Arch. Camb., 83 i, 1928, 218–19.

7552 Fair (Mary Cicely). Bronze Age swords and daggers of Cumberland, Westmorland, and Lancashire north of the Sands. Trans. Cumb. & Westm. Ant. Soc., N.S. 45, pp. 34–38. 1945.

7553 —— An interim review of types of Bronze [Age] spear-heads and axes of Cumberland, Westmorland and Lancashire North-of-the-Sands. [Figure.] Trans. Cumb. & Westm. Ant. Soc., N.S. 45, pp. 172–78. 1945.

7554 Fell (Clare Isobel). A Bronze [Age] spear-head from Woundale Raise, Troutbeck [Westmorland]. [Figure.] Trans. Cumb. & Westm. Ant. Soc., N.S. 49, pp. 10–14. 1949.

7555 —— A bronze palstave from Wraysholme Tower, Allithwaite, Lancashire North-of-the-Sands. Trans. Cumb. & Westm. Ant. Soc., N.S. LXIII, p. 281. 1963.

7556 —— A socketed bronze axe from Little Langdale, Lancashire North-of-the-Sands. [1 figure.] Trans. Cumb. & Westm. Ant. Soc., N.S. LXIII, pp. 282–83. 1963.

7557 Ferguson (Richard Saul). On a torque of late Celtic type found in Carlisle. Trans. Cumb. & Westm. Ant. Soc., 6, pp. 196–97. 1883.

7558 Fox (*Sir* Cyril). A bronze pole-sheath from the Charioteer's barrow, Arras, Yorkshire. [Figure. Iron Age.] Antiq. J., 29, pp. 81–83. 1949.

7559 Gaythorpe (Harper). The Urswick [socketed] bronze celts. Trans. Cumb. & Westm. Ant. Soc., N.S. 3, p. 410 + plate. 1903.

7560 Greenwell (William). Antiquities of the Bronze Age found in the Heathery Burn cave, county Durham. [31 figures.] Archaeologia, 54, pp. 87–114 + plan. 1894.

7561 Grimshaw (Bannister). The Edgeworth [Lancs.] palstave. Trans. Hist. Soc. Lancs. & Ches., 67 (1915), pp. 208–09 + plate. 1916.

7562 Grove (Leonard Robert Allen). Bronze spearhead from Allerston, near Pickering. [Figure. With distribution list and map.] Yorks. Archaeol. J., 34, pp. 4–8. 1938.

7563 Hall (George Rome). Notes on two bronze spear-heads found near Birtley, North Tyne. Arch. Æl., N. [2nd] S. 7, pp. 209–11. 1876.

7564 Hardy (James). On a Bronze [Age] spear-head found on Bowsden moor, Northumberland. [Figure.] Hist. Berwick. Nat. Club, 10, pp. 192–94. 1882.

7565 Hawkes (Charles Francis Christopher). Bronzes of the Early Iron Age from Yorkshire. [3 figures. Brooch from York: situla from York.] Antiq. J., 12, pp. 453–55. 1932.

7566 —— An unpublished Celtic brooch from Danes' Graves, Kilham, Yorks. [Figure. Early Iron Age.] Antiq. J., 26, pp. 187–91 + plate. 1946.

7567 Hildyard (Edward John Westgarth). A triple-headed bucket [from the Ribble]. [Late Bronze Age.] Antiq. J., 34, pp. 225–29 + plate. 1954.

7568 Hodgson (Katherine Sophia). A [socketed] Bronze [Age] axe from Ainstable. Trans. Cumb. & Westm. Ant. Soc., N.S. 51, pp. 172–73. 1951.

7569 Holmes (John). Recent discovery of bronze celts. [South-west of Hunslet moor and Beeston, N. Riding.] Yorks. Archaeol. J., 7, pp. 143–44. 1882.

7570 Jackson (John Wilfrid). Bronze Age find [from Congleton], in Cheshire. [Figure. Socketed celt, 2 spearheads and 2 ferrules.] Antiq. J., 7, pp. 62–64. 1927.

7571 —— A Bronze [Age] sword found near Garstang, Lancs. [Figure.] Antiq. J., 14, pp. 178–80. 1934.

7572 Jewitt (Llewellynn). Bronze [Age] celts from Highlow [Derbs.]. [2 figures.] Reliquary, 14, pp. 63–64. 1864.

7573 King (A.) *and* **Walker** (H.). Two stray finds from Giggleswick. [RB brooch and BA socketed axe.] Yorks. Arch. Journ., 41 (iii), 1965, 363–65 + 1 figure.

7574 Kitchingman (Joseph). The Liscard palstave. Trans. Hist. Soc. Lancs. & Ches., 64 (1912), p. 287 + plate. 1913.

7576 MacGregor (Morna). The Early Iron Age metalwork hoard from Stanwick, N.R. Yorks. Proc. prehist. Soc., 28, 1962, 17–57 + 15 figures + 3 plates.

7577 Manby (T. G.). Two bronze daggers from the Peak District. [1 Wessex type; 1 unique.] J. Derbs. Ant. Soc., 78, pp. 95–97 + 1 figure. 1958.

7578 —— A looped palstave from Denshaw. Huddersfield Archaeol. Soc., Quart. Bull., 9, p. 8 + plate. 1959.

7579 —— The Clotherholme anthropoid sword. [IA 3a.] Yorks. Arch. Journ., 41 (i), 1963, 15–17 + 1 figure.

7580 —— Early Bronze Age axes from Yorkshire. Yorks. Arch. Journ., 41 (iii), 1965, 344–55 + 2 figures.

7581 —— A socketed Bronze Age axe from Kirk Ireton. J. Derbs. Ant. Soc., 86, p. 102 + 1 figure. 1966.

7582 Maryon (Herbert). The casting-on of a sword hilt in the Bronze Age. [Figure. From the Tyne, Elswick.] Proc. Soc. Antiq. Newc., 4th S. 7, pp. 41–42. 1935.

7583 —— The gold ornaments from Cooper's Hill, Alnwick. [Figure (hair-ring).] Arch. Æl., 4th S. 16, pp. 101–08 + plate. 1939.

7584 Mattinson (W. K.). *and* **Palmer** (L. S.). Note on a bronze cauldron from Craven, Yorkshire. Proc. prehist. Soc., 3, 1937, 164–65 + 1 figure.

7585 Megan (J. V. S.). A bronze spear-head from the Heathery Burn Cave, Co. Durham. [1 plate + 1 figure.] Ant. J., 44, 1964, 112–14.

7586 Milton (W. Allan). Prehistoric find of a perfect Bronze [Age] spear [from Buxton, Derbs.]. [Figure.] J. Brit. Archaeol. Ass., N.S. 36, pp. 400–01. 1930.

7587 North (Oliver Henry). Two recently discovered Bronze [Age] celts [from Holm Park quarries, now in Tullie House]. Trans. Cumb. & Westm. Ant. Soc., N.S. 36, pp. 142–43 + plate. 1936.

7588 —— A Bronze [Age] axe and other local finds. [Palstave found near Crook.] Trans. Cumb. & Westm. Ant. Soc., N.S. 42, p. 233 + plate. 1942.

7589 —— A Bronze Age spear-head Trans. Cumb. & Westm. Ant. Soc., N.S. 43, p. 70 + plate. 1943.

7590 Parsons (L. J.). A bronze axe found at Newby, Scarborough. [Middle Bronze Age, c. 1400 B.C. Figure.] Ann. Rpt. Yorks. Phil. Soc., 1952, pp. 21–22. 1953.

7591 Powell (Thomas George Eyre). A Late Bronze Age hoard from Welby, Leicestershire. [Now in Leicester Museum.] Arch. News Letter, 1 i, pp. 8–9. 1948.

7592 —— A Late Bronze Age hoard from Welby, Leicestershire. [3 figures + map. Implements, bronze cup, etc.] Archaeol. J., 105 (1948), pp. 27–40 + plate. 1950.

7593(a) Phelps (Joseph James). A gold pendant of early Irish design. [Dug up in 1772 at second Irwell lock near Manchester.] Trans. Lancs. & Ches. Ant. Soc., 33 (1915), pp. 192–200 + plate. 1916.

7593(b) Preston (F. L.). A flat axe from Ashopton (Derbs.). Trans. Hunter archaeol. Soc., 8 iii, 1961, 162 + 2 figures.

7594 Purvis (John Stanley). A looped socketed celt from [Bridlington] Yorkshire. Antiq. J., 16, p. 323 + plate. 1936.

7595 Raistrick (Arthur) *and* **Smythe** (J. A.). A flanged Bronze [Age] celt from Birtley, co. Durham. [Figure + distribution map.] Proc. Univ. Durham Phil. Soc., 9, pp. 47–54. 1933.

7596 —— A bronze palstave from Arncliffe in Litton dale, W. Yorkshire. [Figure. Bronze Age III.] Yorks. Archaeol. J., 31, pp. 95–96. 1934.

7597 Read (*Sir* Charles Hercules). A Late Celtic sword and sheath found at Sadberge, co. Durham. [Figure.] Proc. Soc. Antiq., 2 S. 16, pp. 4–7. 1895.

7598 —— An early British sword of anthropoid type found near Ripon. Proc. Soc. Antiq., 2 S. 27, pp. 214–15 + plate. 1915.

7599 Reveley (Thomas). Silver fibula and torque, found at Orton scar, in Westmorland. Archaeologia, 33, p. 446 + plate. 1852.

7600 Richmond (Ian Archibald). A spear-head of the Middle Bronze Age from Willington, co. Durham. Proc. Soc. Antiq. Newc., 4th S. 9, pp. 143–44. 1940.

7601 Robinson (J. F.). Find of bronze weapons near Medomsley. Proc. Soc. Antiq. Newc., S. 5, 27, pp. 213–16. 1892.

7602 Roes (A.). The bucket-mount from the river Ribble. [Figure. Two animal heads sacred to sun-god?] Antiq. J., 35, pp. 222–23. 1955.

7603 Salt (W. H.). Discovery of Bronze [Age] axes, etc., in Buxton. [Figure.] Reliquary, 3rd S. 6, pp. 125–26. 1900.

7604 Sheppard (Thomas). Note on a French type of bronze axe found at Hull. [Figure.] Antiquary, 36, pp. 246–47. 1900.

7605 —— Bronze sword scabbard of La Tène period from the Trent. [Figure. In Hull Museum.] Yorks. Archaeol. J., 31, p. 94. 1934.

7608 Simpson (Grace). Two [socketed] Bronze [Age] axes from [Carlisle and Greystokes], Cumberland. [2 figures.] Trans. Cumb. & Westm. Ant. Soc., N.S. 51, pp. 173–74. 1951.

7609 Spain (George Redesdale Brooker). Bronze Age axe heads [found at Unthank, Northumberland]. Proc. Soc. Antiq. Newc., 4th S. 4, p. 30 + plate. 1929.

7610 Thompson (B. L.). A bronze palstave from Windermere. Trans. Cumb. & Westm. Ant. Soc., N.S. 58, p. 189 + plate. 1959.

7611 Thompson (Frederick Hugh). Miscellanea: Bronze razor from Holywell. [1 figure.] Journ. Chester Arch. Soc., 45, 1958, 71.

7612 —— Miscellanea: socketed bronze axe and Roman altar from Helsby. [1 figure.] Chester Arch. Soc., Jl., 46, 1959, 79.

7613 Thoresby (Ralph). A letter to Dr. Hans Sloane, R.S. Sec. concerning some ancient brass instruments found in Yorkshire. Phil. Trans. Roy. Soc., XXVI, 1708, 393–94 + 1 figure.

7614 Tolson (Legh). [An early British bronze pony-bit found on Place Fell]. Trans. Cumb. & Westm. Ant. Soc., N.S. 29, p. 331 + plate. 1929.

7615 —— An early British bridle-bit [from Place Fell, Westmorland]. [Figure. Bronze.] Antiq. J., 9, pp. 41–42. 1929.

7616 Trevelyan (*Sir* C. E.) *bart*. Discovery of ancient bronze implements [at Prior Hall farm] near Wallington. [?Late Bronze Age.] Arch. Æl., N. [2nd.] S. 9, pp. 52–53 + 2 plates. 1883.

7617 Waterman (Dudley M.). An Early Bronze Age bracelet from Bridlington, Yorkshire. [2 figures.] Antiq. J., 28, pp. 179–80 + plate. 1948.

7618 Watson (W.). Two brooches of the Early Iron Age from Sawdon, North Riding, Yorkshire. [2 figures.] Antiq. J., 27, pp. 178–82 + plate. 1947.

7619 Willett (Frank). Three tanged bronze sickles in the Manchester Museum. [Figure.] Man, 54, 1954, 106–08.

7620 Wilson (Thomas). British dagger, found at Woodnook, near Wakefield. [Figure.] Bowman (William): Reliquiae Antiquae Eboracenses: (Leeds), pp. 39–40. 1855.

7621 Wooler (Edward). Notes on an ancient bronze spear-head found at Northallerton. [Figure.] Yorks. Archaeol. J., 24, pp. 106–08. 1917.

7622 Yates (George Charles). Bronze [Age] implements of Lancashire and Cheshire. [16 figures. Pp. 139–41, topographical list.] Trans. Lancs. & Ches. Ant. Soc., 13 (1895), pp. 124–41. 1896.

(e) Zone 5
[CBA Group 2]

7623 Alcock (Leslie). The winged object in the Llyn Fawr hoard. [Notes & News.] Antiquity, 35, 1961, pp. 149–151.

7624 [Anon.] Bronze palstave [Northop, Flintshire]. [Figure.] Arch. Camb., 79, p. 409. 1924.

7625 [Anon.] Bronze implements in the Society's museum. Trans. Carmarthenshire Ant. Soc., 27, p. 67 + plate. 1937.

7626 [Anon.] [Socketed] celt from Bangor-on-Dee [near Wrexham]. [Figure. Late Bronze Age.] Antiq. J., 19, p. 208. 1939.

7627 Banks (Richard William). On some Radnorshire Bronze [Age] implements [in the museum of the Royal Irish Academy]. Arch. Camb., 4th S. 6, pp. 17–21 + plate. 1875.

7628 —— An account of Bronze [Age] implements found near Brecon. Arch. Camb., 5th S. 1, pp. 225–27 + plate. 1884.

7629 —— On a Bronze [Age] dagger found at Bwlch y Ddau Faen, Breconshire. Arch. Camb., 5th S. 2, p. 156 + plate. 1885.

7630 Barker (W. R.). Part of a Late Celtic bronze collar found at Llandyssil, Cardiganshire. Proc. Clifton Antiq. Club, 3, pp. 210–13. 1897.

7631 Barnwell (Edward Lowry). Remarks on an iron celt, found in the Berwen mountains, Merionethshire. Arch. Camb., 3rd S. 1, pp. 250–52 + plate. 1855.

7632 —— Bronze [Age] implements. Arch. Camb., 3rd S. 10, pp. 212–31 + 3 plates. 1864.

7633 —— Ornamented celt [from Monach-ty-gwyn, Carnarvonshire]. [Figure. Bronze Age.] Arch. Camb., 4th S. 2, pp. 20–23. 1871.

7634 —— The Rhosnesney [Denbighshire] Bronze [Age] implements. [*See also* pp. 191–92 (note by R. W. Banks).] Arch. Camb., 4th S. 6, pp. 70–73 + plate. 1875.

7635 Baynes (Edward Neil). Holyhead celts. Anglesey Ant. Soc. Trans., 1927, p. 72. 1927.

7636 Bruce (J. Ronald). A socketed celt, found on Garth mountain, Llangollen. [Figure. Bronze Age.] Arch. Camb., 76, pp. 146–47. 1921.

7637 Burgess (C. B.). Two grooved ogival daggers of the Early Bronze Age from South Wales. Bull. Board Celtic Studies, 20 i, 1962, 75–94 + 1 figure + 2 plates.

7638 —— A palstave from Buckley, Flintshire, with some notes on "shield" pattern palstaves. Flints. hist. Soc. publuns. 20, 1962, 92–95 + 2 figures.

7639 Chitty (Lily Frances). Bronze implement from Tyddyn Bach, Llanfachreth, Merioneth. [Bronze tanged spear-head(?) dagger.] Arch. Cambrensis, 81 ii, 1926, 406–09 + 2 figures.

7640 —— Irish copper halberd from the Dolgelley region. [Early Bronze Age.] Bull. Bd. Celtic Stud., 4, pp. 172–73. 1928.

7641 —— Bronze palstave from Berwyne. Arch. Cambrensis, 83 i, 1928, 202.

7642 —— Bronze spear-head found near Mellington, Montgomery, 1927. Arch. Camb., 83 i, 1928, 220–22 + 1 figure.

7643 —— Flat bronze axe now associated with the Guilshield Hoard. Arch. Camb., 94 ii, 1939, 225.

7644 —— Two bronze palstaves from Llandrinio, Montgomeryshire. [Figure. Bronze Age.] Trans. Shropshire Archaeol. Soc., 51, pp. 146–56. 1943.

7645 —— Bronze spear-head from Pennant (Upper Tanat valley), Montgomeryshire. Arch. Camb., 100 i, 1948, 106–08 + 1 figure.

7646 —— Bronze palstave identified as from Clochfaen, Llangurig, Montgomeryshire. Arch. Camb., 100 ii, 1949, 275–77 + 1 plate.

7647 —— Irish bronze axes assigned to the Guilsfield Hoard, Montgomeryshire. Arch. Camb., 114, 1965, 120–29 + 1 figure.

7648 Clinch (George). Bronze [Age] celt found at Crickhowell, Brecknockshire. [Figure.] Arch. Camb., 6th S. 5, pp. 259–60. 1905.

7649 Crawford (Osbert Guy Stanhope) *and* **Wheeler** (*Sir* Robert Eric Mortimer). The Llynfawr and other hoards of the Bronze Age. [4 figures.] Archaeologia, 71, pp. 133–40 + 4 plates. 1921.

7650 Davies (A. Stanley) *and* **Grimes** (William Francis). The Tanglannau (Mallwyd) Bronze [Age] hoard. [Montgomeryshire.] Bull. Bd. Celtic Stud., 7, p. 334: 8, pp. 96–97. 1934–35.

7651 Davies (Ellis). A Bronze palstave [from near St. Asaph], Flintshire. [Figure.] Arch. Camb., 6th S. 16, pp 367–68. 1916.

7652 —— An early bronze hanging-bowl found at Cerrig-y-Drudion. Arch. Cambrensis, 81 ii, 1926, 335–39 + 4 figures.

7653 —— *and* **Hughes** (Henry Harold). Bronze axe found at Trefriw. Arch. Cambrensis, 81 ii, 1926, 404–06 + 2 figures.

7654 —— Bronze socketed axe from Llangollen. Arch. Camb., 90 ii, 1935, 296–97 + 1 figure.

7655 —— Bronze palstave, Pant-yr-Einiog, Mynydd Cennin. Arch. Camb., 90 ii, 1935, 309 + 1 figure.

7656 —— Gold lunula, Brynkir. Arch. Camb., 90 ii, 1935, 309–11 + 1 figure.

7657 —— A small hoard of flanged bronze celts from Betws (or Bettws)-yn-Rhos, Denbighshire. Arch. Camb., 92 ii, 1937, 334–35 + 2 figures.

7658 Davies (Ellis). Bronze spear-head from Llaniestyn, Lleyn, Caernarvonshire. Arch. Camb., 96 ii, 1941, 203–04 + 1 figure.

7659 —— Gloddaeth bronze celts (palstaves), Caernarvonshire. Arch. Camb., 96 ii, 1941, 205 + 1 plate.

7660 Evans (Emyr Estyn). Bronze celt found near Carno, Montgomeryshire. Arch. Cambrensis, 82 ii, 1927, 390–91 + 1 figure.

7661 —— A bronze spear-head from Caernarvonshire [early "lunate"]. Arch. Camb., 93 i, 1938, 134–35 + 1 figure.

7662 Evans (George Eyre). Discovery of [18] Bronze [Age] axe-heads [on Tanglanan mountain, Cwmdugold, Merioneth]. Arch. Camb., 6th S. 2, p. 240. 1902.

7663 —— Part of a Late Celtic bronze collar [found in Llandyssul parish]. Trans. Carmarthenshire Ant. Soc., 21, pp. 1–2 + plate. 1927.

7664 —— Axe found [on Garn Wen farm] in Llanfallteg parish. [Bronze Age.] Trans. Carmarthenshire Ant. Soc., 21, p. 2. 1927.

7665 Evans (W. F.). Bronze [Age] celt found near Cowbridge [Glam.]. [Figure.] Arch. Camb., 6th S. 19, p. 470. 1919.

7666 Fox (*Sir* Cyril). A Late Celtic bronze mirror from [Pant Faelog, Merioneth] Wales. [3 figures.] Antiq. J., 5, pp. 254–57. 1925.

7667 —— A La Tène brooch from Wales: with notes on the typology and distribution of these brooches in Britain. Arch. Cambrensis, 82 i, 1927, 67–112 + 29 figures.

7668 —— La Tène I brooch from Merthyr Mawr, Glamorgan. Arch. Camb., 84 i, 1929, 146–47 + 1 figure.

7669 —— *and* **Hyde** (H. A.). A second cauldron and an iron sword from the Llyn Fawr hoard, Rhigos, Glamorganshire. [11 figures + 4 maps. Late Bronze Age.] Antiq. J., 19, pp. 369–404 + 7 plates + 6 maps. 1939.

7670 —— A palstave from Llanbister, Radnorshire. [Figure.] Radnorshire Soc., Trans., 12, pp. 74–75. 1942.

7671 —— A palstave from Llanbister, Radnorshire. Arch. Camb., 97 i, 1942, 113–14 + 1 figure.

7672 —— An Early Iron Age discovery in Anglesey. [90 objects of bronze and iron from margin of Llyn Cerrig Bach, near Valley, Anglesey.] Anglesey Ant. Soc. Trans., 1944, pp. 49–54 + 3 plates + map. 1944.

7673 —— An Early Iron Age discovery in Anglesey [Llyn Cerrig Bach hoard]. Arch. Camb., 98 i, 1944, 134–38 + 3 figures.

7674 —— A shield-boss of the Early Iron Age from Anglesey with ornament applied by chasing tools. [Llyn Cerrig Bach, cf. various other La Tène motifs.] Arch. Camb., 98 ii, 1945, 199–220 + 11 figures.

7675 —— Anniversary address. [Model of a British chariot, based on that found at Llyn Cerrig, Anglesey]. [Figure.] Antiq. J., 27, pp. 113–19 + 2 plates. 1947.

7676 —— An embossed bronze disc of Llyn Cerrig Bach type in Corinium Museum. [?SW "B".] Arch. Camb., 100 ii, p. 277 + 1 plate. 1949.

7677 Gage (John). Gold British corselet [from Mold, Flint] . . . purchased by the . . . British Museum. Archaeologia, 26, pp. 422–31 + 2 plates. 1836.

7678 Gage (M. A.). Relics found on Foel Hiraddug, in the county of Flint. Collns. rel. to Montgom., 17, pp. 331–32 + plate. 1884.

7679 Gardner (Willoughby). A bronze dagger from near Penmachno, Caernarvonshire. Arch. Camb., 92 i, 1937, 174–75 + 1 figure.

7680 Griffiths (William Eric). Recent finds from North Caernarvonshire. Arch. Camb., 99 ii, 1947, 291–92 + 1 figure.

7681 —— Bronze knife from Maes-yr-Rhyd. [Late Bronze Age.] Caernarvonshire Hist. Soc. Trans., 18, pp 1–2 + plate. 1957.

7682 —— The Pant-y-Maen Bronze [Age] hoard [Pembrokeshire]. [3 figures. Now in St. David's College, Lampeter.] Bull. Bd. Celtic Stud., 17, pp. 118–24. 1957.

7683 —— Palstaves found recently near Bala. [Merioneth.] Arch. Camb., 107, 1958, 121–22 + 1 figure.

7684 Grimes (William Francis). A Bronze [Age] casting in the Guilsfield, Montgomeryshire, hoard. Bull. Bd. Celtic Stud., 5, pp. 393–94. 1931.

7685 Grimes (William Francis). A bronze casting in the Guilsfield Montgomery, hoard. Arch. Camb., 86 ii, 1931, 358–61 + 3 figures.

7686 —— Bronze [Age] implements [from Brecknockshire]. Bull. Bd. Celtic Stud., 7, pp. 332–33. 1934.

7687 —— A find of the Early Iron Age from Llyn Cerrig Bach, Anglesey. Antiquity, 20, pp. 13–15. 1946.

7688 Hawkes (Jacquetta). Recent discoveries in Britain.—Slave chains. [Figure. Iron Age. From Llyn Cerrig lake, Anglesey.] Archaeology, 1, p. 51. 1948.

7689 Hemp (Wilfrid James). A La Tène shield from Moel Hiraddug, Flintshire. Arch. Camb., 83 ii, 1928, 253–84 + 17 figures.

7690 —— A Late Celtic shield from [the hill-fort on Moel Hiraddug], Flintshire. [Figure.] Antiq. J., 8, p. 104–05. 1928.

7691 —— The Hiraddug shield. Arch. Camb., 85 i, 1930, 201.

7692 —— Bronze axe found at Conway. Arch. Camb., 94 i, 1939, 91 + 1 figure.

7693 Higgins (H.). A note on a bronze axe-head found at Trefriw, Carnarvonshire. [Figure.] Man, 27, p. 224. 1927.

7694 Hughes (Henry Harold). Sword found at Gelliniog Wen, Anglesey. [Figure. *See also* p. 367. Early Iron Age.] Arch. Camb., 6th S. 9, pp. 256–57. 1909.

7695 —— Bronze [Age] axe found at Trefriw [Carnarvonshire]. [2 figures.] Arch. Camb., 81, pp. 404–06. 1926.

7696 —— Bronze spear-head from Penmaenmawr. Arch. Cambrensis, 82 i, 1927, 183–84 + 1 figure.

7697 —— Two halberds found at Tonfannan Quarry, Merioneth. [Irish type bronze.] Arch. Camb , 87 ii, 1932, 395–97 + 1 figure

7698 —— Socketed-axe found on the Conway Mountain. Arch. Camb., 87 ii, 1932, 397 + 1 figure.

7699 Hughes (H. R.) *and* **Franks** (*Sir* Augustus Wollaston). On antiquities from the neighbourhood of Abergele [Denbighshire], North Wales. [Horsetrappings. Late Stone Age.] Archaeologia, 43, pp. 536–57 + plate. 1871.

7700 Jerman (H. Noel). Unrecorded Bronze Age implements, etc., from Central Wales. Bull. Bd. Celtic Stud., 7, pp. 75–77. 1933.

7701 —— The dual identity of a Radnorshire Bronze Age hoard. [From Caben Coch. Axes, etc.] Bull. Bd. Celtic Stud., 7, pp. 916–17. 1935.

7702 —— Socketed celt found near Llangollen, Denbighshire, in 1825. Arch. Camb., 91 ii, 1936, 313–14.

7703 —— Contributions to the bibliography of the Harlech torc. Arch. Camb., 96 ii, 1941, 92–94.

7704 Johnston (J. L. Forde). A hoard of flat axes from Moel Arthur, Flintshire. Flint. Hist. Soc. pubctns., 21, pp. 99–100 + 1 figure + 1 plate. 1963.

7705 Jones (Emrys). Mould for socketed chisel found at Abermâd. Arch. Camb., 98 i, 1944, 146 + 1 figure.

7706 Jones (G. D. B.). Excavations and discoveries. Bull. Bd. Celtic Studies, 21 ii, 1965, 171–74.

7707 Jones (Jack Davies). Palstaves of Welsh provenance in the Grosvenor Museum, Chester. Bull. Bd. Celtic Stud., 18, p. 194 + plate. 1954.

7708 Jones (Morris Charles). Bronze spear-head found in Llandinam parish. [Figure.] Collns. rel. to Montgom., 14, pp. 209–70. 1881.

7709 Kendrick (*Sir* Thomas Downing). The gold torc from Holywell, Flintshire. [Middle Bronze Age.] Antiq. J., 19, p. 320 + plate. 1939.

7710 Laws (Edward). Bronze [Age] implements from the shores of Milford haven. [Figure.] Arch. Camb., 6th S. 8, pp. 114–15. 1908.

7711 Morgan (W. Lloyd). Bronze [Age] implements found at Penwylt, Brecknockshire. [Figure.] Arch. Camb., 6th S. 1, pp. 162–64. 1901.

7712 Morris (T. E.). Two palstaves found [at Clynnog] in south Carnarvonshire. [Figure.] Arch. Camb., 6th S. 10, pp. 334–36. 1910.

7713 Noble (F.). The Bronze Age gold torcs from Heyope, in connection with a forgotten episode of 1399 and Richard II. Radnorshire Soc., Trans., 25, pp. 34–38 + plate. 1955.

7714 Peake (Harold John Edward). The introduction of metal into Wales. Cards. Antiq. Soc. Trans., 5, pp. 48–56. 1927.

7715 Powell (Thomas George Eyre). The gold ornament from Mold, Flintshire, North Wales. Proc. prehist. Soc., 19, 1953, 161–79 + 3 figures + 6 plates.

7716 Price (W. Frederick). Bronze [Age] spear-head found at Caerwys [Flintshire]. [Figure.] Arch. Camb., 6th S. 9, p. 506. 1909.

7717 —— [2] Bronze [Age] celts found in the vale of Clwyd. [2 figures.] Arch. Camb., 6th S. 10, p. 323. 1910.

7718 Pughe (William Owen). [A torc of gold, found on Llyn Gwernan, Cader Idris.] Archaeologia, 21, pp. 557–59. 1827.

7719 Sansbury (Arthur R.). Some recent finds in Cardiganshire. [2 palstaves + 1 celt.] Arch. Cambrensis, 82 i, 1927, 200–01.

7720 —— Bronze objects of the Bronze Age found in Cardiganshire. [Figure.] Cards. Antiq. Soc. Trans., 7, pp. 78–86. 1930.

7721 Savory (Hubert Newman). Two palstaves from South Wales. Arch. Camb., 95 i, 1940, 83–84 + 1 figure.

7722 —— Bronze [Age] implements of Welsh provenance acquired by the National Museum of Wales during the war (1939–45). Bull. Bd. Celtic Stud., 12, pp. 59–61. 1946.

7723 —— Two Bronze Age implements from the Towy valley. Carmarthen Antiquary, 2, pp. 5–9. 1946.

7724 —— Hoard of Breton socketed axes from Tintern, Monmouthshire. Arch. Camb., 99 i, 1946, 114–15 + 1 figure.

7725 —— Two unpublished flanged axes from North Wales. Arch. Camb., 99 i, 1946, 117–19 + 2 figures.

7726 —— Bronze hoard from Nevern, Pembrokeshire. Arch. Camb., 99 ii, 1947, 285–86.

7727 —— Socketed palstave from [?Abergele], Denbighshire. Bull. Bd. Celtic Stud., 12, pp. 125–26. 1948.

7728 —— [An Early] Bronze [Age] flat axe from St. Nicholas, Glam. Bull. Bd. Celtic Stud., 13, pp. 54–55. 1948.

7729 —— Bronze palstave from Lower Toch farm, Haverfordwest, Pemb. Bull. Bd. Celtic Stud., 13, p. 55. 1948.

7730 —— A bronze socketed axe of South Wales type from Llanfair Cilge-

dyn, Mon. [?Early Iron Age.] Bull. Bd. Celtic Stud., 13, pp. 55–56. 1948.

7731 —— Palstave from Llysworney, Glam. Bull. Bd. Celtic Stud., 13, p. 110. 1949.

7732 —— Two Bronze rapiers from [Drygarn, Brecknockshire], mid-Wales. Bull. Bd. Celtic Stud., 13, pp. 162–63. 1949.

7733 —— Bronze Age surface finds at Whitesands bay, St. Davids (Pemb.). Bull. Bd. Celtic Stud., 14, p. 84–85. 1950.

7734 —— An [Early] Bronze [Age] flat axe from St. Nicholas. Cardiff Nat. Soc. Rpt. & Trans., 79 (1945/48), p. 58 + plate. 1950.

7735 —— A bronze palstave from Llysworney. Cardiff Nat. Soc. Rpt. & Trans., 79 (1945/48), pp. 58–59 + plate. 1950.

7736 —— [Middle] Bronze [Age] flat axe from [Garn-Wen quarry, Llanglydwen], Carmarthenshire. Bull. Bd. Celtic Stud., 14, pp. 250–51. 1951.

7737 —— New Bronze and Early Iron Age surface finds from Merthyr Mawr warren (Glam.). Bull. Bd. Celtic Stud., 15, pp. 304–07. 1954.

7738 —— Hoard of Late Bronze Age gold torcs from [Llanwrthiol], Brecknockshire. Bull. Bd. Celtic Stud., 16, pp. 50–51 + plate. 1954.

7739 —— Bronze flat axe from [Ystradowen], Glamorgan. Bull. Bd. Celtic Stud., 16, p. 209 + plate. 1955.

7740 —— Bronze flat axe from [Downton, New Radnor], Radnorshire. [Wessex culture (c. 1500–1200 B.C.).] Bull. Bd. Celtic Stud., 16, p. 209 + plate. 1955.

7741 —— Bronze palstave from [Llanddaniel Fab], Anglesey. Bull. Bd. Celtic Stud., 16, pp. 209–10. 1955.

7742 —— Bronze [Age] axe-heads from [Sennybridge and Abercrave], Brecknockshire. Bull. Bd. Celtic Stud., 16, p. 210 + plate. 1955.

7743 —— A hoard of Bronze Age gold torcs from [Cwm-jenkin farm, Heyope, Knighton], Radnorshire. Bull. Bd. Celtic Stud., 16, pp. 212–13 + plate. 1955.

7744 —— New Bronze [Age] implements from east Glamorgan and Monmouthshire. Trans. Cardiff Nat. Soc.,

86 (1956–57), pp. 27–29 + plate. 1959.

7745 Savory (Hubert Newman). A new hoard of La Tène metalwork from Merionethshire. [Tal-y-llyn.] Bull. Board Celtic Studies, 20 iv, 1964, 449–75 + 7 figures + 6 plates.

7746 —— Excavations and discoveries. [Palstave and half-flanged axe.] Bull. Board Celtic Studies, 21 i, 1964, 94–96 + 2 figures.

7747 —— A new hoard of Early Iron Age metalwork from Merioneth. Arch. Camb., 113, 1964, 174–75.

7748 —— The Tal-y-llyn hoard. Antiquity, 38, 1964, pp. 18–31.

7749 —— The Guilsfield hoard. [Welsh BA.] Bull. Bd. Celtic Studies, 21 ii, 1965, 179–96 + 10 figures.

7750 Sayce (R. U.). A new palstave from Anglesey. Arch. Camb., 93 i, 1938, 135–36 + 2 figures.

7751 Schofield (W.). Bronze knife from Graig Fawr, Meliden, Flintshire. Arch. Camb., 99 ii, 1947, 295–96 + 1 figure.

7752 Sheppard (T.). The Parc-y-Meirch hoard, St. George parish, Denbighshire. Arch. Camb., 96 i, 1941, 1–10 + 7 plates.

7753 Summers (H. H. C.). Discovery of bronze axe-heads near Dinas Mawddwy. [Figure.] Collns. rel. to Montgom., 32, pp. 327–30. 1902.

7754 Thrane (Henrik). The rattle pendants from the Parc-y-Meirch hoard, Wales. Proc. prehist. Soc., 24, 1958, 221–227 + 4 figures.

7755 Ward (John). The Bronze Age in Montgomeryshire. The Tir y Mynach or Guilsfield hoard. [Map. (3 figures).] Collns. rel. to Montgom., 41, pp. 1–32 + 11 plates; 43, pp. 110–65 + 21 plates + map. 1930–34.

7756 Way (Albert). Notes of Bronze [Age] celts and of celt-moulds found in Wales. [3 figures.] Arch. Camb., 3rd S. 2, pp. 120–31. 1856.

7757 Webley (D. P.). The Bronze [Age] knife-dagger from Cefn Cilsanws (Breckn.). Bull. Bd. Celtic Stud., 17, pp. 195–96. 1957.

7758 Wheeler (*Sir* Robert Eric Mortimer). Leaf-shaped swords found in Wales. [Bronze Age.] Bull. Bd. Celtic Studies, 1, pp. 344–45. 1923.

7759 —— Prehistoric gold in Wales. Bull. Bd. Celtic Studies, 2, pp. 166–72. 1924.

7760 Willans (J. B.). A Montgomeryshire Bronze celt. [Figure. Found at Talyglarnau, Mallroyd. In Aberystwyth museum.] Collns. rel. to Montgom., 38, p. 249. 1918.

7761 Williams (Audrey). Bronze implements from Swansea, Glamorgan. Arch. Camb., 92 ii, 1937, 333–34 + 2 figures.

7762 Williams (Howel). A flat celt mould from the Lledr valley. [Figure. Bronze Age.] Arch. Camb., 79, pp. 212–13. 1924.

7763 Williams (Stephen W.) *and* **Price** (Benjamin). Bronze celt (Another Bronze celt) from St. Harmon, Radnorshire. Collns. rel. to Montgom., 10, pp. 189–92. 1877.

7764 Williams (Victor Erle Nash). Bronze flat celt from Pen-Lan-Fâch, Moel Trigarn, Pembrokeshire. Arch. Camb., 84 i, 1929, 147–48 + 1 figure.

7765 —— Harness-trapping from Chepstow, Monmouthshire. [La Tène.] Arch. Camb., 87 ii, 1932, 393–94 + 1 figure.

7766 —— A Late Bronze [Age] hoard from [Leckwith, near] Cardiff. Antiq. J., 13, pp. 299–300 + plate. 1933.

7767 Williams (W. Wynn). Bronze [Age] implements and copper cake (Menai bridge and elsewhere). Arch. Camb., 4th S. 8, pp. 206–11 + 3 plates. 1877.

7768 Wood (Samuel). Bronze implements, found in 1862, in a field near Guilsfield, Montgomeryshire, known [as] The Camp. [Figure.] Proc. Soc. Antiq., 2 S. 2, pp. 249–51. 1863.

(f) Zone 6
[CBA Group 1 plus Ireland and the Isle of Man]

7769 Allen (John Romilly). Discovery of a Bronze [Age] caldron at Hatton Knowe, Peeblesshire. [Figure.] Reliquary, 3rd S. 11, pp. 63–65. 1905.

7770 [Anon.] Hoard of gold objects discovered [on Cathedral Hill, Downpatrick, co. Down]. [Late Bronze Age. Unfinished bracelets, etc. ?stock of a goldsmith.] Arch. News Letter, 5, p. 47. 1954.

7771 Armstrong (Edmund Clarence Richard). The localities and distribution of the various types of bronze celts in the National Museum, Dublin. [5 maps.] Proc. Soc. Antiq., 2 S. 27, pp. 253–59. 1915.

7772 Atkinson (Richard John Copland) *and* **Piggott** (Stuart). The Torrs Chamfrein. [5 figures + map. Early Iron Age metalwork found (before 1829) in a morass on the farm of Torrs, Kelton, Kirkcudbrightshire. Now in National Museum. Frontal for a Celtic pony (collar, head-piece and horns.] Archaeologia, 96, pp. 197–235 + 16 plates. 1955.

7773 Campbell (Marion) *and* **Coles** (John M.). The Torran hoard [axes, gouges, etc.]. Proc. Soc. Ant. Scotland, 96, 1962–63, 353–54 + 1 plate.

7774 Childe (Vere Gordon). La Tène brooches from Scottish forts. [Figure.] Antiq. J., 11, pp. 281–82. 1931.

7776 Chitty (Lily Frances). Single-faced palstaves in Portugal and in Ireland [British analogies]. Proc. prehist. Soc., N.S. 2, 1936, 236–38 + 1 figure.

7777 Coffey (George). Bronze spear-head found [at Dogs] near Boho, [co. Fermanagh]. [Figure.] Reliquary, N. [3rd] S. 4, p. 120. 1898.

7778 —— Irish copper celts. [4 figures. Gap between Neolithic and Bronze Ages.] J. Anthrop. Inst., 31, pp. 265–79 + 14 plates. 1901.

7779 Coles (John M.). Scottish swan's-neck sunflower pine. Proc. Soc. Antiq. Scotland, 92, 1959/58, 1–9 + 2 figures.

7780 —— Scottish Late Bronze Age metalwork: typology, distributions and chronology. Proc. Soc. Antiq. Scotland, 93, 1959–60, 16–134 + 7 figures + 9 maps + 5 plates.

7781 —— *and* **Livens** (Roger G.). A bronze sword from Douglas, Lanarkshire. [Ewart Park type.] Proc. Soc. Antiq. Scotland, 91 (1960), 182–86 + 2 figures + 1 plate.

7782 —— *and* **Scott** (J. G.). The Late Bronze Age hoard from Peelhill, Strathaven, Lanarkshire. Proc. Soc. Ant. Scotland, 96, 1962–63, 136–44 + 4 figures.

7783(a) —— Bronze Age metalwork in Dumfries and Galloway. Trans. Dumfries & Gal. Nat. H. & Ant. Soc., 42, pp. 61–98 + 11 figures + 4 plates. 1965.

7783(b) Conyngham (*Lord* Albert Denison) *afterwards* **Denison** (Albert Denison) *Baron Londesborough*. Description of some gold ornaments recently found in Ireland. [5 from New Grange, also collar from Ardrah, co. Donegal.] Archaeologia, 30, p. 137 + plate. 1844.

7784 Corcoran (J. X. W. P.). A bronze bucket in the Hunterian Museum, University of Glasgow. [4 plates + 1 figure.] Ant. J., 45, 1965, 12–17.

7785 Corrie (John M.). A Bronze [Age] chisel from Kirkconnel, Dumfries-shire. Trans. Dumfries. Ant. Soc., 3 S. 15 (1928–29), pp. 54–57 + plate. 1929.

7786 —— Notice of a Bronze [Age] rapier-like blade found in the parish of Tynron, Dumfriesshire, with notes on a hoard of Bronze [Age] rapier blades from [Kirkgunzeon], Kirkcudbrightshire. Trans. Dumfries. Ant. Soc., 3 S. 14 (1926–28), pp. 49–54 + 2 plates. 1930.

7787 Cowen, J. D. A bronze sword from Scotland in the Society's museum. Ant. J., 41, 1961, 232–33.

7788 Craw (James Hewat). Gold armlets from St. Abb's head. [Bronze Age.] Hist. Berwick. Nat. Club, 27, p. 346. 1931.

7789 Currie (Andrew). On an ancient Bronze [Age] axe found near Howford on the Ettrick, [Selkirkshire]. [Figure.] Hist. Berwick. Nat. Club, 10, pp. 596–97. 1884.

7790 Davidson (James Milne). A Bronze [Age] axe-head from [Broadford bay], Skye. [Figure.] Trans. Glasgow Archaeol. Soc., N.S. 10, pp. 73–74. 1941.

7791 Day (Robert). On a bronze leaf-shaped sword found in [Lisletrim bog, co. Monaghan], Ireland. Reliquary, 10, pp. 65–66 + 2 plates. 1869.

7792 Dunlop (Archibald Murray). On two Bronze [Age] celts from Easter Essenside, Ashkirk [Selkirksh.]. [2 figures.] Hist. Berwick. Nat. Club, 11, pp. 492–93. 1886.

7793 Eogan (George). Catalogue of Irish bronze swords. (National Museum of Ireland.) Dublin, 1967, pp. xxxix + 190 + 97 figures.

7794 Evans (*Sir* Arthur John). On a votive deposit of gold objects found on the north-west coast of Ireland. [8 figures. ?1st c. A.D.] Archaeologia, 55, pp. 391–408 + 2 plates. 1897.

7795 Faber (G. S.). An account of certain Bronze [Age] instruments, supposed to be druidical remains, found beneath a large rock on the south side of the Top of Roseberry in Cleveland. Archaeol. Scot., 4, pp. 53–56 + plate. 1857.

7796 Feacham (Richard William de Fécamp). The "Cairnmuir" hoard from Netherurd, Peeblesshire [torques, ring terminal, Gaulish coins; 1st cent. B.C.– 1st cent. A.D.] Proc. Soc. Antiq. Scotland, 91, 1960, 112–16 + 1 figure + 1 plate.

7797 Fell (Clare Isobel). Socketed bronze axe and gauge from [Portree], Skye. [Late Bronze Age.] Antiq. J., 31, p. 72. 1951.

7798 Fox (*Sir* Cyril). Two Celtic bronzes from Lough Gur, Limerick, Ireland. [2 figures. Late 1st or early 2nd c. A.D. Mounted as chariot pole-sheath.] Antiq. J., 30, pp. 190–92 + plate. 1950.

7799 Haddow (J. Muir) *and* **Boyd** (J. D.). Late Bronze Age weapons found at the Atton in Glen Clova. Proc. Soc. Antiq. Scot., 90 (1956–57), pp. 223–25 + plate. 1959.

7800 Harbison (Peter). The daggers and the halberds of the Early Bronze Age in Ireland (Prähistorische Bronze-funde Abt. 6 Bd. 1) 32 *Taf.* Munich, 1968.

7801 —— The axes of the Early Bronze Age in Ireland (Prähistorische Bronzefunde Abt. 9 Bd. 1) 96 *Taf.* Munich, 1968.

7802 Hardy (James). List of some Berwickshire and Border Bronze [Age] implements. Hist. Berwick. Nat. Club, 14, pp. 395–98. 1893.

7803 Kermode (Philip Moore Calrow). Bronze [Age] implements in the Isle of Man. [Probably all imported.] Antiq. J., 3, pp. 228–30. 1923.

7804 Lawson (John). Some golden ornaments found in March 1806, near the house of New Cairnmuir, Peeblesshire. Archaeol. Scot., 4, pp. 217–19 + plate. 1857.

7805 Lennox (James). Note on a Bronze [Age]-socketed axehead found by Mr. Baxter at Annan. Trans. Dumfries. Ant. Soc., 8 (1891–92), p. 80. 1893.

7807 McCulloch (William T.). Notes respecting two bronze shields recently purchased for the museums of the Society; and other bronze shields. ["Ancient British."] Proc. Soc. Antiq. Scot., 5, pp. 165–68 + plate. 1865.

7808 Maxwell (Stuart) *and* **Stevenson** (Robert Barron Kerr). Bronze objects from Kirkconnell. [Late Bronze Age. Pots and sword now in Dumfries Museum.] Trans. Dumfriess. Ant. Soc., 3rd S. 29 (1950–51), pp. 165–66 + plate. 1952.

7809 Morris (David B.). Bronze axe head found at Nyadd. Trans. Stirling N.H. & Arch. Soc., 1911–12, pp. 85–86. 1912.

7810 Murray (David). Note on two Bronze [Age] celts, found at Craigdhu, Arran. Trans. Glasgow Archaeol. Soc., 2, p. 516. 1890.

7811 O'Dell (Andrew C.). St. Ninian's Isle Treasure, Aberdeen University Studies No. 141. Edinburgh, 1960, 47 pp. + plates + maps. [ref. to BA Burial.]

7812 Pegge (Samuel). Observations on some brass celts, and other weapons discovered [in a bog in West-Meath] in Ireland, 1780. Archaeologia, 9, pp. 84–95 + plate. 1789.

7813 Raftery (Joseph). A bronze disc from the river Bann, [co. Antrim], Northern Ireland. [Figure. Early Iron Age.] Antiq. J., 20, pp. 280–81. 1940.

7814 —— The Gorteenreagh hoard. Contributions to the study of Irish Late Bronze Age gold. Arch. News Letter, 4, p. 177. 1953.

7815 Redmond (David). Bronze ornament found at Cookstown. Ulster J. Arch., 4, 1898, 126.

7816 Ridgeway (*Sir* William). An Irish decorated, socketed Bronze [Age] axe. [2 figures.] Man, 19, pp. 161–64 + plate. 1919.

7817 Rynne (Etienne). Late Bronze Age rattle-pendants from Ireland. Proc. prehist. Soc., 28, 1962, 383–85 + 1 figure + 1 plate.

7818 Scott (J. G.). A decorated bronze axe-head from Perthshire. [Megaw & Hardy Type I.] Proc. Soc.

Antiq. Scotland, 91, 1960, 178–79 + 1 figure.

7819 Smith (D. J.). A flat copper axe from Dumbartonshire. Arch. Æliana, 41, 1963, 227–30 + 1 figure.

7820 Smith (John Alexander). Notice of three small Bronze [Age] blades, or instruments believed to be razors, and a bronze socketed celt in the museum of the Society; with remarks on other small bronze blades. [7 figures.] Proc. Soc. Antiq. Scot., 6, pp. 357–71. 1868.

7821 —— Notice of a Bronze [Age] battle-axe found near Bannockburn, now in the museum of the Society. [Figure.] Proc. Soc. Antiq. Scot., 6, pp. 372–74. 1868.

7822 —— Notice of a remarkable bronze ornament with horns, found [at Torrs], in Galloway, now at Abbotsford. Also of a bronze ornament, like a swine's head, found [at Deskford], in Banffshire]. [9 figures.] Proc. Soc. Antiq. Scot., 7, pp. 334–57 + 3 plates. 1870.

7823 —— Notes on bronze sickles; with special reference to those found in Scotland. [2 figures.] Proc. Soc. Antiq. Scot., 7, pp. 375–81. 1870.

7825 Smith (Reginald Allender). On the evolution of Late Keltic pins of the hand type, well known in Scotland and Ireland. [11 figures.] Proc. Soc. Antiq., 2 S. 20, pp. 344–54. 1905.

7826 —— Irish gold crescents. [5 figures. Early Bronze Age.] Antiq. J., 1, pp. 131–39. 1921.

7827 Stevenson (Robert Barron Kerr). Note on some Bronze [Age] axes. Trans. Dumfriess. Ant. Soc., 3rd S. 26 (1947–1948), pp. 123–25 + 2 plates. 1949.

7828 Stokes (Margaret). On two bronze fragments of an unknown object, portions of the Petrie collection, in the museum of the Royal Irish Academy, Dublin. [?Portions of a radiated crown, 3rd c. A.D.] Archaeologia, 47, pp. 473–80 + 5 plates. 1883.

7829 Topp (Celia). The gold ornaments found near the entrance to New Grange in 1842. [Figure.] Univ. London Inst. Archaeol., Ann. Rpt., 12, pp. 53–62 + plate. 1956.

7830 Trump (Bridget A. V.). Daggers, dirks and rapiers of the Scottish Middle Bronze Age. Proc. Soc. Ant.

Scotland, 93, 1959–60, 1–15 + 5 figures.

7831 Walker (Iain C.). Two decorated axes from the Laich of Moray. [Megaw & Hardy Types I and IIIc.] Proc. Soc. Ant. Scotland, 95, 1961–62, 306–07 + 1 plate.

7. OBJECTS OF OTHER MATERIALS

7832 Apling (Harry). Milk teeth as amulets. [From Bronze Age grave at Attleborough, Norfolk.] Folk-lore, 44, p. 236. 1933.

7833 Armstrong (Albert Leslie). Two East Yorkshire bone harpoons [from Atwick (Hornsea), Holderness]. [Figure. Maglemose?] Man, 22, pp. 130–31. 1922.

7834 —— A bull-roarer of Le Moustier Age from Pin Hole cave, Creswell Crags, Derbyshire. [Figure. Bone, with hole for suspension.] Antiq. J., 16, pp. 322–23. 1936.

7835 Beck (Horace Courthope). Faience beads of the British Bronze Age. [2 figures + 2 distribution maps.] Archaeologia, 85, pp. 203–52 + 7 plates. 1936.

7837 Chitty (Lily Frances). Note on a bone implement from the Ellesmere region. [?Late Bronze Age. Now in Shrewsbury Museum.] Trans. Shropshire Archaeol. Soc., 50, pp. 155–57 + plate. 1940.

7838 Clay (Richard Challoner Cobbe). An important bone implement from Cheddar. Antiquity, 3, pp. 344–46 + plate. 1924.

7839 Craw (James Hewat). Jet necklaces from the Borders. [3 figures. Bronze Age.] Hist. Berwick. Nat. Club, 27, pp. 96–103 + plate, p. 106. 1929.

7840 —— On part of a jet necklace in Hawick museum. [Early Bronze Age.] Trans. Hawick Archaeol. Soc., 1930, pp. 30–31 + plate. 1930.

7841 Cuming (Henry Syer). On ancient spear-heads of bone. J. Brit. Archaeol. Ass., 22, pp. 89–92 + plate. 1866.

7842 —— On some bone implements found in London. J. Brit. Archaeol. Ass., 22, pp. 94–101. 1866.

7843 Cunnington (Maud Edith). The age of the "cylindrical notched glass beads" found in Wiltshire barrows. [1450–1250 B.C. Egyptian, of later 18th and earlier 19th dynasties. 3 from Stonehenge, now in Devizes Museum.] Wilts. Archaeol. Mag., 38, pp. 643–45. 1914.

7844 Cunnington (William). On a sepulchral vessel found near Marlborough. [Deal, with 3 external and one internal iron hoops.] Wilts. Archaeol. Mag., 23, pp. 222–28 + plate. 1887.

7845 Curwen (Eliot Cecil). On the use of scapulae as shovels. Sussex Arch. Collns., 67, pp. 139–45. 1926.

7846 —— Probable pressure-flakers of antler from Harrow hill. Sussex Arch. Collns., 68, p. 273. 1927.

7847 Dawson (Charles) *and* **Woodward** (Arthur Smith). On a bone implement from Piltdown (Sussex). J. Geol. Soc. London, 71, 1915, 144–49 + 1 figure + 1 plate.

7848 Evans (Muir). Harpoon found in the North Sea [Fifty miles N.E. of Cromer]. [Mesolithic. Now in Norwich Museum.] Antiquity, 6, p. 218 + plate. 1932.

7849 Fox (Aileen Mary) *Lady Fox and* **Stone** (J. F. S.). A necklace from a barrow in North Molton parish, north Devon. Antiq. J., 31, pp. 25–31 + plate. 1951.

7850 Gardner (Willoughby). A deerantler implement from Llanddone, Anglesey. Arch. Camb., 92 i, 1937, 172–74 + 1 figure.

7851 Garrood (Jesse Robert). A bone implement from the gravel at Somersham, Huntingdonshire. Antiq. J., 26, p. 186 + plate. 1946.

7852 —— A palstave in Bog Oak at Wood Walton. Trans. Cambs. & Hunts. Arch. Soc., 7, p. 82 + plate. 1952.

7853 Gray (Harold St. George). Glass beads found in a cist-burial at Clevedon. [Figure. Early Iron Age.] Proc. Somerset Arch. Soc., 88 (1942), pp. 73–74. 1943.

7854 —— Amber beads found in the parish of Meare, Somerset. [Late Bronze Age.] Proc. Somerset Arch. Soc., 97 (1952), pp. 184–85 + plate. 1953.

7855 Green (Charles). Eel-spears. [3 figures (mostly from Gloucestershire).] Antiquity, 22, pp. 13–20. 1948.

7856 Griffiths (William Eric). Wooden [cooking] trough from Ynys-Crian. [Bronze Age?] Caernarvonshire Hist. Soc. Trans., 18, pp. 2–4 + plate. 1957.

7857 Hawkes (Charles Francis Christopher). Blue glass bead [from Harting down]. [Figure. Early Iron Age.] Sussex N. & Q., 6, pp. 243–44. 1937.

7858 —— A pre-Roman Iron Age glass bead [from Harting down]. [Figure.] Sussex County Mag., 11, p. 611. 1937.

7859 Kendrick (*Sir* Thomas Downing). The Hammeldon Down [Dartmoor] pommel. [Bronze Age amber dagger-pommel in the Plymouth Athenaeum.] Antiq. J., 17, pp. 313–14 + plate. 1937.

7860 Leeds (Edward Thurlow). An early British enamel. [Figure. From Sudeley Castle Collection, Glos.] Antiq. J., 18, pp. 75–76. 1938.

7861 Lewis (Geoffrey D.). Iron Age bead from Worthing. Sussex Arch. Collection, 98, 1960, 18.

7862 MacCallum (Robert E.). A fragment of comb from Dun Scalpsie, Bute. Proc. Soc. Antiq. Scotland, 92, 1958–59, 115–16 + 1 plate.

7863 Manning (Charles Robertson). Bone ornaments forming part of a necklace of the British period, found in Feltwell fen, 1876. Norfolk Arch., 8, pp. 319–25 + 2 plates. 1879.

7864 Martin (Charles Wykeham). On the wooden battle-axe and dagger found at Holingbourn, Kent. [3 figures.] Arch. Cant., 5, pp. 45–54. 1863.

7865 Moir (J. Reid). A series of mineralised bone implements of a primitive type from below the base of the Red and Coralline Crags of Suffolk. Proc. PSEA, 2 i, 1914–15, 116–31 + 7 plates.

7866 —— A shaped bone from Warren Hill, Suffolk. Antiq. J., 17, pp. 179–180 + plate. 1937.

7867 Newstead (Robert). On the discovery of two prehistoric horn implements at Lymm, Cheshire. [Figure. Neolithic.] J. Arch. & Hist. Soc. Chester, N.S. 6, pp. 152–55. 1899.

7868 Piggott (Stuart). A wheel of Iron Age type from co. Durham. Proc. prehist. Soc., 15, 1949, 191 + 1 plate.

7869 —— An Iron Age yoke from

Northern Ireland. Proc. prehist. Soc., 15, 1949, 192–93 + 1 figure + 1 plate.

7870 Piggot (Stuart). Segmented bone beads and toggles in the British Early and Middle Bronze Age. Proc. prehist. Soc., 24, 1958, 227–29 + 1 figure.

7871 —— A tripartite disc wheel from Blair Drummond, Perthshire. [2 figures. Celtic Iron Age.] Proc. Soc. Antiq. Scot., 90 (1956–57), pp. 238–41 + plate. 1959.

7872 Reader (Francis W.). A series of bone objects found in London, York, Colchester, and elsewhere. [6 figures.] Proc. Soc. Antiq., 2 S. 23, pp. 51–58. 1910.

7873 Relph (Arthur E.). The harpoon in Neolithic times. [Figure.] Antiquary, 43, pp. 330–31. 1907.

7874 Roes, A. Horn cheek-pieces. Ant. J., 40, 1960, pp. 68–72.

7875 Royal Anthropological Institute. [Report] on [the authenticity of the] two bone harpoons from Hornsea, E. Yorkshire. Man, 23, pp. 49–50 + plate. 1923.

7876 Sandars (Horace W.). On the use of the deer-horn pick in the mining operations of the ancients. [20 figures + plan. Grimes Graves, etc.] Archaeologia, 62, pp. 101–24 + 3 plates. 1910.

7877 Sandars (N. K.). Amber spacer-beads again. [Notes & News.] Antiq., 34 (1960), pp. 292–95.

7878 Savory (Hubert Newman). Bone implement from Coygan Cave. Arch. Camb., 95 i, 1940, 84 + 1 figure.

7879 Smallwood (G. W.). Potters tools of slate [in association with Neolithic flint implements]. Proc. prehist. Soc. E.A., 3 i, 1918/19, 115–18 + 4 plates.

7880 Smedley (Norman). Iron Age weaving combs from Cambridgeshire and Suffolk. [1 figure.] Proc. Cambs. Ant. Soc., LIV, 1961, 47–49.

7881 Smith (Reginald Allender). Mesolithic harpoons from [Hornsey and from Skipsea Withow], Holderness. Brit. Mus. Q., 4, pp. 108–09 + plate. 1930.

7882 Stevenson (Robert Barron Kerr). A wooden sword of the Late Bronze Age. Proc. Soc. Antiq. Scotland, 91, 1960, 191–93 + 1 plate.

7883 Thomas (Nicholas W. de l'E.). A Neolithic chalk cup from Wilsford in the Devizes Museum: and notes on others. [2 figures.] Wilts. Archaeol. Mag., 54, pp. 452–63. 1952.

7884 Thompson (M. W.). Azilian harpoons. Proc. prehist. Soc., 20, 1954, 193–211 + 5 figures.

7885 Tratman (E. K.). Amber from a Late Palaeolithic cave deposit at Gough's cave, Cheddar, Somerset. Arch. News Letter, 4, p. 119. 1952.

7886 Wood (E. S.). A Clactonian bone implement. Proc. prehist. Soc., 19, 1953, 120–21 + 1 figure.

8. BONES—
HUMAN AND ANIMAL

7887 [Anon.] Human remains in Lough Gur, county Limerick. Anthrop. Rev., 2, pp. 59–60. 1864.

7888 [Anon.] A skeleton in a Yorkshire cave. [Brachycephalic. Female Celt. Bronze Age. Littondale.] Yorks. N. & Q. (ed. Forshaw), 3, p. 19. 1906.

7889 [Anon.] A Palaeolithic skull at Piltdown Common: a new human type. Arch. Camb., 6th S. 13, pp. 215–18. 1913.

7890 [Anon.] The Piltdown skull. Arch. Camb., 6th S. 13, pp. 445–47. 1913.

7891 [Anon.] Discovery of human remains near Ipswich. [Le Moustier.] J. Brit. Archaeol. Ass., N.S. 21, pp. 377–78. 1915.

7892 [Anon.] [Neolithic skeleton at Grassington, Wharfedale.] [Crouched burial.] J. Brit. Archaeol. Ass., N.S. 31, pp. 259–61. 1925.

7893 [Anon.] 15,000-year-old skull. Find in Kent's cavern. J. Brit. Archaeol. Ass., N.S. 32, pp. 144–47. 1926.

7894 [Anon.] Animal bones from archaeological sites in Britain. (Dr. J. W. Jackson's gift to the British Museum (Natural History).) Antiquity, 20, pp. 40–41. 1946.

7895 [Anon.] The Piltdown hoax. [Summary.] Arch. News Letter, 5, p. 63. 1954.

7896 [Anon.]. A new Swanscombe bone. [Right parietal. Found July 30, 1955.] Antiquity, 30, pp. 37–38. 1956.

7897 Barron (G. B.). On a human skull found near Stockport. [No evidence of date—find with Irish Elk] Advm. Sci., 1883, 562–63.

7898 Bate (Dorothea M. A.). Note on recent finds of Dama clactoniana (Cervus browni auctt.) in London and Swanscombe. Proc. prehist. Soc., 3, 1937, 460–63 + 1 figure.

7899 Beddoe (John). The human remains from the Stoney Littleton [long] barrow. Proc. Clifton Antiq. Club, 1, pp. 104–08. 1888.

7900 Bernfeld (W. K.). The physique of Neolithic man. Trans. Cardiff Nat. Soc., 91, 1961/63, 17–22.

7901 Bird (Henry). An account of the human bones found in the round and long tumuli, situated on the Cotswold hills, near Cheltenham. J. Anthrop. Soc. London, 3, pp. lxv–vii. 1865.

7902 Blake (C. Carter). On human remains from Kent's Hole, near Torquay. J. Anthrop. Soc. London, 2, pp. cclxiii–cclxv. 1864.

7903 —— Remarks on the human remains from the Muckle Heog; in the Island of Unst, Shetland. Mems. Anthrop. Soc. London, 1 (1863–64), pp. 299–307 + plate. 1865.

7904 —— Note on the skulls found in the round barrows of the south of England. [Near Blandford, Dorset.] Mems. Anthrop. Soc. London, 3 (1867–1869), pp. 114–19. 1870.

7905 —— Note on a skull from the cairn of Get, Caithness, discovered by Joseph Anderson. Mems. Anthrop. Soc. London, 3 (1867–69), p. 243. 1870.

7906 Bramwell (D.). Recent finds of animal remains in the Middle Trent Valley gravels. J. Derbs. Arch. & N.H. Soc., 81, pp. 137–39. 1961.

7907 Brooke (J. W.). Find of British skeleton on Windmill hill, Avebury. [Late Neolithic or Early Bronze Age.] Wilts. Archaeol. Mag., 26, pp. 410–11. 1892.

7908 Brothwell (Don R.). An Upper Palaeolithic skull from Whaley Rock shelter No. 2, Derbyshire. Man, 61, 1961, 113–16 + 1 plate + 2 figures.

7909 —— Digging up bones. xiii + 194 pp. + 17 plates + 64 text-figures + 5 tables. London, 1963.

7910 —— Appendix Report on human limb bone from Mesolithic floor at Thatcham. Proc. prehist. Soc., 29, 1963, 428.

7911 Bryce (Thomas H.). Note on prehistoric human remains found in the island of Arran. [Figure.] J. Anthrop. Inst., 32, pp. 398–406 + 2 plates. 1902.

7912 Burchell (J. P. T.). Early Neanthropic man and his relation to the Ice Age. Proc. PSEA, 6 iv, 1931, 253–303 + 58 figures.

7913 Buxton (Leonard Halford Dudley). Report on a calvarium from Guy's rift, Slaughterford, Wilts. [2 figures. Early Iron Age.] Wilts. Archaeol. Mag., 43, pp. 487–89. 1926.

7914 —— The Helston calvarium. [3 figures.] Man, 31, pp. 150–52. 1931.

7915 —— Report on the human remains from Culver hole [Llangennith, Gower]. Bull. Bd. Celtic Stud., 6, pp. 198–200. 1932.

7916 Cameron (John). The Bournemouth skull. [Neolithic.] Proc. Dorset Archaeol. Soc., 55 (1933), pp. 179–81. 1934.

7917 —— The skeleton of British Neolithic man, including a comparison with that of other prehistoric periods and more modern times. pp. 272 + 51 plates and figures + 96 tables. 8°. London, 1934.

7918 Cave (Alexander James Edward). Report on human femur from the Stroud alluvium. [From Stroud gas works. Neolithic.] Proc. Cotteswold N.F.C., 26, pp. 103–04. 1936.

7919 —— Report on a human skull from the Freedown, Ringwould, Kent. ["Not far east of two Bronze Age tumuli."] Arch. Cant., 58 (1945), pp. 83–85 + plate. 1946.

7920 Clark (J. G. D.). The Swanscombe skull. Proc. prehist. Soc., 4, 1938, 342.

7921 Clark (Wilfrid E. Le Gros) *kt.* New palaeontological evidence bearing on the evolution of the Hominoidea [references to Piltdown & Swanscombe]. Q. J. Geol. Soc. London, 105, 1949, 225–64 + 10 figures + 5 plates.

7922 —— The fossil evidence for human evolution. Toronto, 1964, 223 pp. + 26 figures.

7923 Collyer (Robert H.). The fossil human jaw from [Ipswich], Suffolk.

[Figure.] Anthrop. Rev., 5, pp. 221–29. 1867.

7924 Cook (W. H.). On the discovery of a human skeleton in a brick-earth deposit in the valley of the river Medway, at Halling, Kent. [3 figures + map + plan. Late Pleistocene.] J. R. Anthrop. Inst., 44, pp. 212–27 + 5 plates. 1914.

7925 Cornwall (Ian W.). Bones for the archaeologist. London, 1956, pp. 255 + 50 figures.

7926 Crawford (Osbert Guy Stanhope). The Kingsclere skeleton. Papers & Proc. Hants. F.C., 7 ii, pp. 61–63. 1915.

7927 Cuming (Henry Syer). Report on ancient remains found at Maiden Castle, Dorsetshire. J. Brit. Archaeol. Ass., 28, pp. 39–45 + plate. 1872.

7928 Cunnington (Maud Edith). Horns of urus said to have been found in a barrow at Cherhill. [Figure (horns and part of skull).] Wilts. Archaeol. Mag., 47, pp. 583–86 + plate (pottery found with skull of urus). 1937.

7929 Curwen (Eliot) *and* **Curwen** (Eliot Cecil). A Beaker skeleton from Goodwood. [With synopsis of Sir Arthur Keith's report.] Sussex N. & Q., 4, pp. 195–97. 1933.

7930 Curwen (Eliot Cecil). Human remains recently discovered [on the golf course] near the Dyke. [Early Bronze Age.] Sussex N. & Q., 3, pp. 87–89. 1930.

7931 Dart (Raymond A.) *and* **Craig** (Dennis). Adventures with the missing link [pp. 251 + 20 half-tone plates + 21 line drawings]. London, 1959.

7932 Davies (Henry Nathaniel). The discovery of human remains under the stalagmite-floor of Gough's Cavern, Cheddar. Q. J. Geol. Soc. London, 60, 1904, 335–48 + 7 figures + 1 plate.

7933 Davis (Joseph Barnard). On the crania of the ancient Britons, with remarks on the people themselves. Proc. Acad. Nat. Sci. Philadelphia, 1857, pp. 40–48. 1858.

7934 —— Note on the distortions which present themselves in the crania of the ancient Britons. [3 figures.] Nat. Hist. Rev., 2, pp. 1–7. 1862.

7935 Dawe (F. Sherwill). Fossil man. Trans. & Proc. Torquay nat. Hist. Soc., 9, 1947, 171–78.

7936 —— Notes on recent work on human evolution. J. Torquay nat. Hist. Soc., 10, 1950, 111–18.

7937 Dawkins (*Sir* William Boyd). On the discovery of Platycnemic men in Denbighshire. [7 figures + 2 plans. Neolithic. Pp. 450–68 + plate. Notes on the human remains, by George Busk.] J. Ethnolog. Soc., N.S. 2, pp. 440–68 + plate (skulls). 1870.

7938 —— On the mammalia and traces of man found in the Robin-Hood Cave. Q. J. Geol. Soc., 32, 1876, 245–58 + 11 figures.

7939 Dawson (Charles). The Piltdown skull (Eoanthropus dawsoni). Hastings & E. Sussex Naturalist, 2, pp. 73–82 + plate, pp. 182–84. 1913–15.

7940 —— *and* **Woodward** (Arthur Smith). On the discovery of a palaeolithic human skull and mandible in a flint-bearing gravel overlying the Wealden (Hastings Beds) at Piltdown, Fletching (Sussex). J. Geol. Soc. London, 69, 1913, 117–51 + 6 plates + 13 figures.

7941 —— *and* —— Supplementary note on the discovery of a palaeolithic human skull and mandible at Piltdown (Sussex). J. Geol. Soc., 70, 1914, 82–92 + 3 figures + 2 plates.

7942 Degerbol (Magnus). On a find of a Preboreal domestic dog (*Canis familiaris* L.) from Star Carr, Yorkshire, with remarks on other Mesolithic dogs. Proc. prehist. Soc., 27, 1961, 35–55 + 1 figure + 6 plates.

7943 Denston (C. B.). Iron Age skeletal remains from Barley. Proc. Camb. Ant. Soc., LIV, 1961, 46.

7944 —— Aldwick, Barley: recent work at the Iron Age Site. Appendix I: Human skeletal remains. Proc. Camb. Ant. Soc., LVIII, 1965, 6–7.

7945 Devereux (Norman). On a skeleton found in a gravel pit at Overbury, Worcestershire. [2 figures. "Late British."] Man, 10, pp. 168–70. 1910.

7946 Dingwall (Doris) *and* **Young** (Matthew). The skulls from excavations at Dunstable, Bedfordshire. [Early and Middle Bronze Age.] Biometrika, 25, pp. 147–57 + 6 plates + table. 1933.

7947 Dormer (Ernest W.). Discovery of human remains at Caversham. [Later Neolithic.] Berks. Archaeol. J., 36, pp. 93–95. 1932.

7948 Duckworth (Wynfrid Laurence Henry) *and* **Shore** (L. R.). Report on the human crania from peat deposits in England. [2 figures.] Man, 11, pp. 134–39. 1911.

7949 —— Notes on some points connected with the excavation of Kent's Cavern, Torquay; with a report on the fragmentary human upper jaw from the granular stalagmite. Jl. Torquay nat. Hist. Soc., 1, 1913, 211–20 + 3 figures.

7950 —— Notes on the collection of human crania, etc., from Guilden Morden [cemetery, Cambs.]. [Figure.] Proc. Camb. Antiq. Soc., 27, pp. 64–71. 1926.

7951 Evans (John Henry). Farewell to Piltdown. Arch. Cant., 69 (1955), pp. 179–86. 1956.

7952 Ewbank (Jane M.) *and others*. Sheep in the Iron Age: a method of study (with D. W. Phillipson, R. D. Whitehouse and E. S. Higgs). Proc. prehist. Soc., 30, 1964, 423–26 + 2 figures.

7953 Farrar (Raymond Anthony Holt). Human remains from Sutton Poyntz and Radipole, Weymouth [with RB sherds]. Proc. Dorset N.H. & A.S., 86, 1964, 114–15.

7954 Ffoulkes (W. Wynn). On the discovery of Platycnemic men in Denbighshire, and notes on their remains. Arch. Camb., 4th S. 3, pp. 22–32 + 3 plates. 1872.

7955 Finny (W. E. St. Lawrence). Primitive man at Sunbury [Surrey]. [Figure. Neolithic bones.] J. Brit. Archaeol. Ass., N.S. 32, pp. 307–08. 1926.

7956 —— Primitive man at Sunbury [lock]. Surrey Archaeol. Collns., 37, pp. 237–38 + plate (skulls). 1927.

7957 Fisher (Osmond) *Rev.* On the occurrence of *Elephas Meridionalis* at Dewlish (Dorset). Second Communication: Human agency suggested [in pit with eoliths]. Q. J. Geol. Soc. London, 61, 1905, 35–38 + 2 plates.

7958 Fowler (Gordon) *and* **Lethbridge** (Thomas Charles). A skeleton of the Early Bronze Age found in the Fens. Proc. PSEA, 6 iv, 1931, 362–64 + 3 plates + 1 figure.

7959 Fox (W. Storrs). A human skeleton in Monsal dale. [Report on skull by Sir Arthur Keith.] J. Derbs.

Archaeol. Soc., 35, pp. 99–102 + plan. 1913.

7960 Frassetto (Fabio). New views on the "dawn man" of Piltdown (Sussex). Man, 27, pp. 121–24 + plate. 1927.

7961 Garson (J. G.). On the osteology of the ancient inhabitants of the Orkney Islands. J. Anthrop. Inst., 13, pp. 54–86 + table. 1883.

7962 —— Notes on some ancient British skulls in the Wiltshire Museum, Devizes. Wilts. Archaeol. Mag., 23, pp. 295–98. 1887.

7963 —— Human remains from Wiltshire. Advm. Sci., 1888, 839–40.

7964 —— Remarks on [ancient British] skulls dredged from the Thames in the neighbourhood of Kew. J. Anthrop. Inst., 20, pp. 20–25. 1890.

7965 —— Shock report on the human skeleton found in the stone circle of Arbor Low in 1901. Archaeologia, 58, pp. 490–91. 1903.

7966 Gedge (J. D.). Our prehistoric ancestors; . . . the Casterton skull. Rutland Mag., 3, pp. 40–42. 1907.

7967 Gillham (J.). Bronze Age [trephined] skull found of Ovingdean. [Figure.] Sussex County Mag., 9, pp. 187–88. 1935.

7968 Gladstone (Reginald J.). Description of a human cranium from the bed of the river Trent [opposite Kelfield, Lincs.], and a comparison of this with ancient and modern British skulls. [8 figures + map. ?Bronze Age.] J. R. Anthrop. Inst., 51, pp. 343–69. 1921.

7969 Goodman (C. N.) *and* **Morant** (Geoffrey M.). The human remains of the Iron Age and other periods from Maiden Castle, Dorset. Biometrika, 31, pp. 295–312 + 3 plates + 2 tables. 1939.

7970 Gray (Harold St. George). Notes on the skeleton and flints found in Gough's cave, Cheddar. N. & Q. Som. & Dorset, 9, pp. 2–5. 1905.

7971 —— Archaeological remains found at Shepton Mallet. [Bronze Age skeleton and urn.] Proc. Somerset Arch. Soc., 80 (1934), pp. 67–68. 1935.

7972 Gray (John). British ethnology. Summary of a paper. Man, 2, pp. 50–52. 1902.

7973 Harrison (G. A.) *and others*.

[J. S. Weiner, J. M. Tanner, N. A. Barniot]. Human biology—an introduction to human evolution, variation and growth. Oxford, 1964, pp. 536 + xvi + 15 figures + 2 plates.

7974 Hepburn (David). On the association of human remains with those of the red deer and the ox in Hailes Quarry, Midlothian. Trans. Edinburgh Geol. Soc., 8, 1898–1905, 197–99.

7975 —— On prehistoric human skeletons found at Merthyr Mawr, Glamorganshire. [Early Bronze Age.] Cardiff Nat. Soc. Rpt. & Trans., 37 (1904), pp. 31–32 + 3 plates. 1905.

7976 —— On prehistoric human skeletons found at Merthyr Mawr, Glamorganshire. [Bronze Age.] Arch. Camb., 6th S. 5, pp. 211–36 + 3 plates. 1905.

7977 Hewitt (H. Dixon). Prehistoric human remains at Little Cornard, Suffolk. Proc. prehist. Soc. E.A., 1 iii, 1912/13, 297–300 + 1 plate.

7978 Hinton (Martin A. C.). Note on the mammalian remains. [On the Clactonian Industry at Swanscombe.] Proc. PSEA, 6 ii, 1929, 94.

7979 Hogg (Alexander J.). On human and other bones found at Whyteleafe, Surrey. Proc. Croydon N.H. & Sci. Soc., 6, pp. 125–31 + plate. 1905.

7980 Holmes (Thomas Vincent). Notes on the geological position of the human skeleton lately found at the Tilbury Docks, Essex. Trans. Essex Fld. Club, 4, 1885, 135–48.

7981 Hooke (Beatrix G. E.) *and* **Morant** (Geoffrey M.). The present state of our knowledge of British craniology in late prehistoric and historic times. Biometrika, 18, pp. 99–104. 1926.

7982 Howells (William White). The prehistoric craniology of Britain. Antiquity, 12, pp. 332–39. 1938.

7983 —— Mankind in the making— the story of human evolution. pp. 382, 8 plates, many unnumberd maps + figures. London, 1960.

7984 Humphreys (John). Neolithic skulls found at Alcester. [First example from Midlands.] Antiq. J., 4, p. 269. 1924.

7985 Irving (Alexander). Recent discoveries of prehistoric horse remains in the valley of the Stort. Trans. Herts. N.H.S. & F.C., 15, 1913–15, 177–81 + 1 plate.

7986 Janssens (Paul A.). Palaeopathology: the diseases and injuries of prehistoric man. pp. xiv + 170. London, 1970.

7987 Jones (Thomas Rupert). Occurrence of platycnemic bones in the ancient burial ground at Kintbury. J. Anth. Inst., 6, pp. 196–98. 1876.

7988 Keith (*Sir* Arthur). A description of the Dartford skull, discovered by W. M. Newton. pp. 3 + 3 plates. 8°. 1910. [Now in museum of the Royal College of Surgeons. Cro-magnon.]

7989 —— Description of the Ipswich skeleton. Proc. prehist. Soc. E.A., 1 ii, 1910/12, 203–09 + 3 plates.

7990 —— Prehistoric man.—Story of the Ipswich skeleton. Arch. Camb., 6th S. 12, pp. 245–46. 1912.

7991 —— Report on the skeleton found near Walton-on-Naze. [4 figures.] J. R. Anthrop. Inst., 42, pp. 128–35. 1912.

7992 —— Report on the human remains found by F. J. Bennett in the central chamber of a megalithic monument at Coldrum, Kent. [5 figures.] J. R. Anthrop. Inst., 43, pp. 86–100. 1913.

7993 —— Report on the [Bronze Age] cranium and femur [found on Nunwell down, Isle of Wight]. [3 figures.] Man, 13, pp. 22–23. 1913.

7994 —— Report on the human and animal remains found at Halling, Kent. [12 figures.] J. R. Anthrop. Inst., 44, pp. 228–40. 1914.

7995 —— Notes on the skeleton found in an Early Bronze Age burial at Upavon, 1915. [3 figures.] Wilts. Archaeol. Mag., 40, pp. 8–11. 1917.

7996 —— [Report on bones from] Bronze Age interment at Lockeridge. Wilts. Archaeol. Mag., 41, pp. 187–88. 1920.

7997 —— Report on human remains received from Mr. A. D. Passmore. [i. From barrow, Wanborough, 38, p. 45; ii. From Ogbourne (Bronze Age), 38, p. 588; iii, iv. From Swinton (Beaker), 38, p. 42. 1913.] Wilts. Archaeol. Mag., 43, pp. 311–12. 1926.

7998 —— Report on a skeleton

found buried in an extended supine position at Mundford and assigned by the finders to the Bronze period. [Note on the Finding, by R. V. Favell.] Proc. PSEA, 5 ii, 1926, 174–75 + 1 figure.

7999 Keith (*Sir* Arthur). Report on a human skull found near the north entrance to Kent's Cavern. J. Torquay nat. Hist. Soc., 4, 1926, 289–94 + 2 figures.

8000 —— Report on a fragment of a human jaw found in Kent's Cavern. Trans. & Proc. Torquay nat. Hist. Soc., 5, 1927, 1–2 + 1 plate.

8001 —— Report on the human remains found by Reginald W. Hooley, at Worthy down, 1921. [Early Iron Age.] Papers & Proc. Hants. F.C., 10, pp. 193–95. 1929.

8002 —— On human remains found in Kent Cavern in 1873. Trans. & Proc. Torquay nat. Hist. Soc., 6, 1930–34, 191–92 + 1 plate.

8003 Kirkby (James W.) *and* **Brady** (George S.). On human and other remains found in a cavern near the Ryhope Colliery [no dating evidence]. Nat. Hist. Trans. Northumberland & Durham, 1, 1866, 148–51.

8004 Lambert (*Sir* Henry C. M.). Bronze Age skeletons found at Banstead. Surrey Archaeol. Collns., 27, p. 141. 1914.

8005 Lartet (M. E.). On the co-existence of man with certain extinct quadrupeds proved by fossil bones, from various Pleistocene deposits bearing incisions made by sharp instruments. J. Geol. Soc. London, 16, 1860, 471–79.

8006 Mackie (S. J.). On some human remains from Muskham [near Newark], in the valley of the Trent, and from Heathery Burn cave, near Stanhope, in Weardale, Durham. [4 figures + 2 plans.] Trans. Ethnol. Soc., N.S. 2, pp. 266–78. 1863.

8007 Marston (Alvan T.). The Swanscombe skull. [12 figures.] J. R. Anthrop. Inst., 62, pp. 339–406 + 6 plates. 1937.

8008 Martin (Edward A.). The earliest men in Sussex. Significance of the Piltdown skull. Sussex County Mag., 17, pp. 310–11. 1943.

8009 Maynard (Guy). Notes on a human skull found at Wendon, Essex. [2 figures. Pp. 247–48. Report on the

cranium, by Sir Arthur Keith.] Essex Nat., 17, pp. 244–48 + plate. 1913.

8010 Millar (Ronald). The Piltdown men. 16 pp., h/t. London, 1970.

8011 Miller (G. S.). The Piltdown jaw. Ann. J. Physical Anth., 1 i, 1918.

8012 Montagu (Montague Francis Ashley). Dislocation of the femur upon the acetabular notch in a pre-Roman Briton [now in Hull Museum]. Trans. E. Riding Antiq. Soc., 27, pp. 131–36. 1934. [*Also in* J. Bone and Joint Surgery, 13, pp. 29–32.]

8013 Moir (J. Reid). The occurrence of a human skeleton in a glacial deposit at Ipswich. Proc. prehist. Soc. E.A., 1 ii, 1910/12, 194–202 + 3 plates.

8014 —— *and* **Keith** (*Sir* Arthur). An account of the discovery and characters of a human skeleton found beneath a stratum of chalky boulder clay near Ipswich. [13 figures. Early Pleistocene.] J. R. Anthrop. Inst., 42, pp. 345–79 + plate. 1912.

8015 —— The Piltdown skull. Antiquary, 50, pp. 21–23. 1914.

8016 —— On the discovery of some human bones, etc., of Neolithic and later date, in the Ipswich district. [Figure.] Man, 16, pp. 97–102 + plate. 1916.

8017 —— On some human and animal bones, flint implements, etc., discovered in two ancient occupation-levels in a small valley, near Ipswich. [42 figures.] J. R. Anthrop. Inst., 47, pp. 367–412 + 2 plates + plan. 1917.

8018 Morant (Geoffrey Miles). A first study of the craniology of England and Scotland from Neolithic to early historic times, *etc*. [Pp. 58–74, English and Scottish skulls of Neolithic and Bronze Age date. The population of England and Scotland from late Bronze Age to Anglo-Saxon times.] Biometrika, 18, pp. 56–98. 1926.

8019 —— The craniology of Ireland. [Including prehistoric.] J. R. Anthrop. Inst., 66, pp. 43–55. 1936.

8020 Mortimer (John Robert). On some crania of the round barrows of a section of the Yorkshire wolds. [2 figures.] J. Anth. Inst., 6, pp. 328–34. 1877.

8021 —— The stature and cephalic index of the prehistoric men whose remains are preserved in the Mortimer

Museum, Driffield. [Late Neolithic—Early Iron Age.] Man, 9, pp. 35–36. 1909.

8022 Mortimer (John Robert). The stature of early man in East Yorkshire. [Driffield Museum.] Trans. E. Riding Antiq. Soc., 17, pp. 23–31. 1910.

8023 Myers (Charles S.). An account of some skulls discovered at Brandon, Suffolk. [Figure. Dolichocephalic=Long barrow types.] J. Anthrop. Inst., 26, pp. 113–28. 1896.

8024 Newbold (Philip). Prehistoric skull found in cave at Ryhope, near Sunderland. Proc. Soc. Antiq. Newc., 3rd S. 5, pp. 242–43 + plate. 1912.

8025 Newton (E. T.). On a human skull and limb-bones found in the Palaeolithic terrace-gravel at Galley Hill, Kent. J. Geol. Soc. London, 51, 1895, 505–27 + 2 figures + 1 plate.

8026 Nuttall (T. E.). The Piltdown skull. Man, 17, pp. 80–82. 1917.

8027 Oakley (Kenneth Page) *and* **Montagu** (Montague Francis Ashley). A reconsideration of the Galley Hill skeleton. [2 figures + map + plan.] Bull. Brit. Mus. (N.H.), Geology, 1, pp. 25–48 + plate. 1949.

8028 —— Solving the Piltdown problem. [8 figures.] Arch. News Letter, 5, pp. 100–01, 121–25, 163–69. 1954.

8029 —— Fragmentary skeleton from Lambourn, Berkshire. Trans. Newbury Dist. Fld. Club, 10 iii, 1956, 54.

8030 —— Ancient preserved brains. Man, 60, 1960, 90–91 + 1 figure.

8031 —— Framework for dating fossil man. London, 1964, pp. x + 335 + 83 figures + 2 maps + 4 charts.

8032 Ovey (Cameron D.). The Swanscombe skull: a survey of research on a Pleistocene site. Roy. Anthrop. Inst. Occasional Paper No. 20. pp. xi + 211 + 25 plates + 65 figures. 4°. London, 1964,

8033 Owen (*Sir* Richard). Antiquity of man, as deduced from the discovery of a human skeleton . . . at Tilbury. pp. 32. 8°. London, 1884.

8034 Parry (L. A.). The Ovingdean skull, with some notes on prehistoric trephining. [Figure. Bronze Age.] Sussex Arch Collns., 90, pp. 40–50. 1952.

8035 Parry (T. Wilson). Prehistoric man and his early efforts to combat

disease. pp. 12 + plate. 8°. London, 1914. [*Reprinted from* Lancet, July 13, 1914. Pp. 7–8, Neolithic trephining in Great Britain.]

8036 —— The art of trephining among prehistoric and primitive peoples: their motives for its practice and their methods of procedure. [11 figures. 5 (Neolithic—Early Iron Age) specimens from Great Britain (6 figures).] J. Brit. Archaeol. Ass., N.S. 22, pp. 33–69. 1916.

8037 —— The prehistoric trephined skulls of Great Britain, together with a detailed description of the operation probably performed in each case. [8 figures.] Proc. Roy. Soc. Med. (Hist. Section), 14, pp. 1–16. 1921.

8038 —— Cranial trephination in prehistoric Great Britain. pp. 23. 8°. London, 1921. [8 figures. Reprinted from Medical Press, Nov. 1921.]

8039 —— The collective evidence of trephination of the human skull in Great Britain during prehistoric times. pp. 7 + 3 plates. 8°. Anvers, 1923. [*Reprinted from* Proc. third Internat. Congress Hist. Med., 1922.]

8040 —— Holes in the skulls of prehistoric man and their significance. [Including British evidence. 5 possible causes, medical and religious.] Archaeol. J., 85 (1928), pp. 91–102 + 6 plates. 1930.

8041 —— The Ovingdean prehistoric skull exhibiting double primitive surgical holing. [Figure.] Man, 35, pp. 56–57. 1935.

8042 —— A comparison between two roundels removed by surgical holing from two prehistoric skulls, lately excavated [at Maiden Castle and on Crichel Down] in the county of Dorset, together with a full description of the push-plough method of operation. [5 figures.] Man, 40, pp. 33–35 + plate. 1940.

8043 Parsons (Frederick Gymer). On some Bronze Age and Jutish bones from Broadstairs, with type contours of all the Bronze Age skulls in the Royal College of Surgeons museum. [13 figures + plan.] J. R. Anthrop. Inst., 43, pp. 550–92. 1913.

8044 —— Bronze Age skulls. [16 British examples.] Arch. Camb., 6th S. 13, pp. 450–51. 1913.

8045 Paterson (T. T.). The Swanscombe skull: a defence. Proc. prehist. Soc., 6, 1940, 166–69 + 2 figures.

8046 Patterson (E. L.). Anatomical report on Bronze Age human skeletal remains from Gallowsclough Hill. Trans. Lancs. & Cheshire antiq. Soc., 70, 1960, 82–83.

8047 Piggott (Stuart). A trepanned skull of the Beaker period from Dorset and the practice of trepanning in prehistoric Europe. Proc. prehist. Soc., 6, 1940, 112–32 + 2 figures + 2 plates.

8048 Powell (D. F. W. Baden) *and* **Oakley** (K. P.). Report on the reinvestigation of the Westley (Bury St. Edmunds) skull site. Proc. prehist. Soc., 18, 1952, 1–20 + 7 figures.

8049 Powers (Rosemary). Ancient preserved brains: a further note. Man, 60 (1960), 91.

8050 Prigg (Henry). On a portion of a human skull of supposed Palaeolithic age from [Westley] near Bury St. Edmunds. J. Anthrop. Inst., 14, pp. 51–55 + 3 plates. 1884.

8051 Reid (R. W.). *and* **Morant** (Geoffrey M.). A study of the Scottish short cist crania. Biometrika, 20B, pp. 379–88 + 10 plates + 2 tables. 1928.

8052 Roberts (D. F.). Skeletal material from Radley [Berks.] and Cassington. [Radley barrow 4, Bronze Age cremation.] Oxoniensia, 15 (1950), pp. 109–10. 1952.

8053 Rolleston (George). Notes on [a male] skeleton found at Cissbury, April, 1878. J. Anthrop. Inst., 8, pp. 377–89 + plate. 1879.

8054 Royal Anthropological Institute—*Swanscombe Committee*. Report on the Swanscombe skull. [21 figures + 2 maps.] J. R. Anthrop. Inst., 68, pp. 17–98 + 6 plates. 1928.

8055 Schuster (E. M. J.). The long barrow and round barrow skulls in the collection of the Department of Comparative Anatomy, the Museum, Oxford. [Figure.] Biometrika, 4, pp. 351–62 + 8 plates + 4 tables. 1906.

8056 Seligman (Charles Gabriel) *and* **Parsons** (Frederick Gymer). The Cheddar man: a skeleton of Late Palaeolithic date. [17 figures.] J. R. Anthrop. Inst., 44, pp. 241–63 + 3 plates. 1914.

8057 Shawcross (F. W.) *and* **Higgs** (Eric S.). The excavation of a Bos

Primigenius at Lowe's Farm, Littleport. [5 figures.] Cambridge Antiq. Soc. Proc., LIV. 1960, 3–16.

8058 Shillitoe (J. S.). Tusk of mammoth in the flood plain gravels at Wolvercote. Oxoniensia, 28, 1963, 93.

8059 Simms (B. B.). Ancient (Staffordshire) crania. [Neolithic—Bronze Age.] North Staffs. F.C., Trans., 65, pp. 55–65 + 5 plates. 1931.

8060 Skerlj, B. Human evolution and Neanderthal man. [Reference to Swanscombe.] Antiquity, 34 (1960), pp. 90–99.

8061 Smith (*Sir* Grafton Elliot). On the exact determination of the median plane of the Piltdown skull. J. Geol. Soc. 70, 1914, 93–99 + 3 figures.

8062 —— The cranial cast of the Piltdown skull. Man, 16, pp. 131–32. 1916.

8063 —— The London skull. [5 figures. Site of Lloyds new building, Leadenhall Street: (now in Anatomical Museum of University College, London. Neandertal.] Nature, 116, pp. 678–80. 1925.

8064 —— Report on the human remains in no. 5 barrow at Dunstable. [2 figures. Bronze Age.] Man, 27, pp. 25–27 + plate. 1927.

8065 Smith (Worthington George). Note on the Tilbury skeleton [disputing great age]. J. & P. Essex Fld. Club, 4, 1885, lxxviii–lxxix.

8066 —— Human skeleton of Palaeolithic Age [at Round Green, N. of Luton, Beds.]. Man, 6, pp. 10–11. 1906.

8067 Spence (T. F.). The anatomical study of cremated fragments from archaeological sites. Proc. prehist. Soc., 33, 1967, 70–83 + 2 figures + 2 tables.

8068 Spielmann (Isidore). Exhibition of a skull dredged on the Manchester Ship canal works. [Not later than Early Bronze Age.] J. Anthrop. Inst., 20, pp. 179–80. 1890.

8069 Squance (T. Coke). Notes on, and deductions from, bones found at Hasting hill, near Sunderland, by Mr. C. T. Trechmann. [Bronze Age.] Ant. Sunderland, 14, pp. 6–11 + plate. 1913.

8070 —— Remarks on two prehistoric skulls, one found in a cave at Ryhope and the other dredged from the bed of the river Wear. [Figure.] Ant. Sunderland, 14, pp. 12–16. 1913.

8071 Stone (John F. S.). A case of Bronze Age cephalotaphy on Easton down in Wiltshire. [2 figures.] Man, 34, pp. 38–39. 1934.

8072 —— A case of Bronze Age cephalotaphy on Easton down, Winterslow. [2 figures.] Wilts. Archaeol. Mag., 46, pp. 563–67. 1934.

8073 Thurnam (John). On the two principal forms of ancient British and Gaulish skulls. [23 figures.] Mems. Anthrop. Soc. London, 1 (1863–64), pp. 120–68, 459–519. 1865.

8074 —— Further researches [to ?] and observations on the two principal forms of ancient British skulls. Mems. Anthrop. Soc. London, 3 (1867–69), pp. 41–80 + 2 plates + 3 tables. 1870.

8075 Tildesley (Miriam Louise). Report on three skeletons from Yarnbury camp. [Iron Age.] Wilts. Archaeol. Mag., 46, pp. 214–17. 1933.

8076 —— Report on the human remains [of the Bronze Age on Easton down in Wiltshire]. Man, 34, pp. 40–42. 1934.

8077 —— The Ovingdean skull. Man, 35, pp. 57–59. 1935.

8078 Turner (*Sir* William). A contribution to the craniology of the people of Scotland, Part 2, Prehistoric, descriptive and ethnographical. Trans. Roy. Soc. Edin., 51, pp. 171–255. 1915.

8079 Underwood (W.). A further review of recent advances in palethnology. Proc. prehist. Soc., E.A., 1 iv, 1913/14, 479–84.

8080 Warren (S. Hazzledine). The dating of early human remains. Essex Nat., 18, pp. 40–59. 1915.

8081 Warwick (R.). Anatomical report upon the skeletal remains of a Bronze Age burial at Burnley, Lancashire. Trans. Lancs. & Ches. Ant. Soc., 62 (1950–51), pp. 207–08. 1953.

8082 Weiner (J. S.), *etc.* The solution of the Piltdown problem. (Further contributions). Bull. Brit. Mus. (N.H.), Geology, 12, pp. 139–46 + 2 plates; pp. 225–87 + 5 plates. 1953–55.

8083 —— The Piltdown forgery. pp. xii, 214 + 9 plates. 8°. London, 1955.

8084 Wells (Calvin P. B.). Bones, bodies and disease. 288 pp. (incl. 48 plates, 41 figures.) London, 1964.

8085 Wells (Lawrence H.). Differences in limb proportions between modern American and earlier British skeletal material. Man, 60, 1960, 139–40.

8086 Wilson (Daniel). Inquiry into the physical characteristics of the ancient and modern Celt of Gaul and Britain. Anthrop. Rev., 3, pp. 52–84. 1865.

8087 Woodward (Arthur Smith) *and* **Smith** (Grafton Elliot). Fourth note on the Piltdown gravel, with evidence of a second skull of Eoanthropus Dawsoni. J. Geol. Soc. London, 73, 1917, 1–10 + 1 plate + 2 figures.

8088 Worth (Richard Nicholls). On the occurrence of human remains in a bone cave at Cattledown [near Plymouth]. [2 figures + plan.] Rpt. & Trans. Devon. Assoc., 19, pp. 419–37 + 2 plates. 1887.

8089 Wright (William). The endocranial cast of the Piltdown skull. Man, 6, p. 158. 1916.

8090 Wymer (Bertram O.). The discovery of the right parietal bone at Swanscombe. Man, 55, p. 124. 1955.

8091 Wymer (John). A further fragment of the Swanscombe skull. [2 figures.] Nature, 176, pp. 426–27. 1955.

8092 —— Further work at Swanscombe, Kent. [Lower Palaeolithic site.] Archaeol. News. Letter, 6, pp. 190–91. 1958.

8093 —— Work at Swanscombe, 1960. Archaeol. News Letter, 7 ii, 1961, 32–33 + 1 figure.

8094 Young (Matthew). The London skull. [4 figures. From excavations of Lloyd's new building, 1925.] Biometrika, 29, pp. 277–321 + 3 plates. 1937.

8095 Young (Thomas). On the occurrence of human remains of Neolithic age near Croyde. Rpt. & Trans. Devon. Assoc., 40, pp. 260–63. 1908.

8096 Young (W. E. V.). Report on Early Bronze Age child skeleton from Beckhampton, Wilts. Wilts. Archaeol. Mag., 53, pp. 324–27. 1950.

9. ASSOCIATED FINDS, MUSEUM AND PRIVATE COLLECTIONS

8097 Abercromby (*Hon.* John). The chronology of prehistoric glass beads and associated ceramic types in Britain. J. Anthrop. Inst., 35, pp. 256–65 + 5 plates. 1905.

8098 Adams (Edward Amery) *and* **Dewey** (Henry). Report on some prehistoric objects from Welstor. [Mainly Bronze Age.] Rpt. & Trans. Devon. Assoc., 82, pp. 321–24 + 3 plates. 1950.

8099 Akerman (John Yonge). An archaeological index to remains of antiquity of the Celtic, Romano-British and Anglo-Saxon periods. pp. xii, 204 + 19 plates. 8°. London, 1847.

8100 Annable (F. Kenneth) *and* **Simpson** (D. D. A.). A guide catalogue of the Neolithic and Bronze Age collections in Devizes Museum. pp. 133, 51 pp. line figures + 10 figures + 10 plates. Devizes, 1964.

8101 [Anon.] Prehistoric implements found near Rhyl. [2 figures. Bronze Age.] Northern Flintshire, 1, pp. 67–69. 1913.

8102 [Anon.] The Evans collection. [i.e. of Sir John Evans. Given by Sir Arthur Evans to Ashmolean Museum, Oxford.] Antiquity, 2, pp. 351–53, 464–66. 1928.

8103 [Anon.] Bronze dagger and cinerary urn from Wraysbury, Bucks. [Early Bronze Age.] Berks. Archaeol. J., 39, p. 99. 1935.

8104 Armstrong (Albert Leslie). The Maglemose remains of Holderness and their Baltic counterparts. [Harpoons and tranchet axes.] PPSEA, 4 i, 1922/24, 57–70 + 2 plates + 5 figures.

8105 —— Prehistoric implements of bone and flint from Bradfield, S. Yorks. Trans. Hunter Arch. Soc., 2, pp. 39–40 + 1 plate. 1924.

8106 —— A bronze palstave, four stone celts, and other prehistoric implements from Sheffield and district. Trans. Hunter Arch. Soc., 2, pp. 246–51 + 2 plates. 1924.

8107 Armstrong (Edmund Clarence Richard). On some gold, bronze and amber ornaments found together near Banagher, King's County. [Figure. End of Irish Bronze Age.] Proc. Soc. Antiq., 2 S. 30, pp. 237–39. 1918.

8108 —— Two Irish Bronze Age finds containing rings. [One from a ruined castle in co. Westmeath: the other from Scotstown, Co. Monaghan.

Both in Royal Irish Academy. Rings, *etc.*] Antiq. J., 3, p. 138 + 2 plates. 1923.

8109 Atkins (W. M.). Archaeological finds in the counties of London and Middlesex, 1960. [Acheulian hand axes; Neolithic knife, *ditto* pot; Beaker flint dagger; BA leaf-shaped sword.] Trans. London & Middlesex Arch. Soc., 20 iv, 1961, 224–25.

8110 Aubrey (John). Wiltshire. The topographical collections of J. Aubrey, A.D. 1659–70. Corrected and enlarged by John Edward Jackson. pp. xiii, 492 + 45 plates. 4°. Devizes, 1862. [Pp. 319–30 + 2 plans, Avebury: pp. 331–33, Silbury.]

8111 Baggaley (J. W.). Bronze and stone implements found in Sheffield and district. Trans. Hunter Arch. Soc., 4, pp. 141–43 + 2 plates. 1937.

8112 Baines (Anthony). Bagpipes. [pp. 140, 78 text figures, 16 plates.] Occasional Papers on Technology No. 9. Pitt-Rivers Museum, Oxford. Oxford, 1960.

8113 Banks (Richard William). The Broadward find. Arch. Camb., 4th S. 4, pp. 202–04. 1873.

8114 Barnes (William). Edge tools in early Britain. Edited by J. E. Acland. Proc. Dorset Antiq. F.C., 37, pp. 133–36. 1916.

8115 Barnwell (Edward Lowry). Some details of the Broadward find [Shropshire]. (Supplementary note.) Arch. Camb., 4th S. 3, pp. 345–55 + 6 plates; 4, pp. 80–83. 1872–73.

8116 Barton (Kenneth James). Worthing Museum archaeological note for 1961. Sussex Arch. Collections, 101, 1963, 20–34.

8117 —— Worthing Museum archaeological report for 1962. Sussex Arch. Collections, 102, 1964, 28–32.

8118 —— Worthing Museum archaeological notes for 1963. Sussex Arch. Collections, 103, 1965, 83–93 + 3 figures.

8119 Bateman (Thomas). A descriptive catalogue of the antiquities and miscellaneous objects preserved in the museum of Thomas Bateman at Lomberdale House, Derbyshire. pp. xii, 307 + 9 plates. [Pp. i–221, Prehistoric.] 8°. Bakewell, 1855.

8120 Bellows (John). On some

bronze and other articles found near
Birdlip. Trans. Bristol & Glos. Arch.
Soc., 5, pp. 137–41 + 2 plates. 1881.

8121 Bemrose (G. J. V.). Report
of Section E: Archaeology. Trans. &
Ann. Rep. North Staffs F.C., 93/94,
1960, 84–91.

8122 Black (George Fraser). Notice
of the principal Scottish antiquities in
the Grierson Museum, Thornhill. [Pp.
108–15, prehistoric implements, *etc.*]
Trans. Dumfries. Ant. Soc., 9 (1892–93),
pp. 108–24. 1894.

8123 Bordaz (Jacques). Tools of the
Old and New Stone Age. 42 h/t + 12
line drawings. Newton Abbot, 1971.

8124 Brailsford (John William). Out-
standing prehistoric and Romano-British acquisitions: 1941–50. Brit. Mus. Q.,
15, pp. 71–72 + plate (Bronze armlets from Castle Newe, Aberdeenshire).
1952.

8125 —— British and medieval an-
tiquities, 1753–1953. (a) Prehistoric and
Romano-British acquisitions. Brit. Mus.
Q., 19, pp. 18–19. 1954.

8126 Brewis (Parker). Notes on prehistoric pottery and a bronze pin from
Ross Links, Northumberland. [3 figures.
Bronze Age.] Arch. Æl., 4th S. 5, pp.
13–25 + 10 plates. 1928.

8127 Briscoe (Grace, *Lady*). Bronze
Age pottery and flint from Joist Fen,
Lakenheath. [2 figures + 1 plate.]
Proc. Camb. Ant. Soc., LVI/LVII, 1962/
1963, 1–4.

8128 British Museum. Guide to the
antiquities of the Stone Age. 10 plates +
142 illustrations. 8º. London, 1902.

8129 —— Guide to the antiquities of
the Early Iron Age. 7 plates + 147
illustrations. 8º. London, 1905.

8130 —— A guide to the antiquities
of the Bronze Age in the Department of
British and mediaeval antiquities. Second
edition. pp. xii, 187 + 10 plates. 8º.
London, 1920. [195 figures.]

8131 —— The Sturge collection. An
illustrated selection of flints from Britain
bequeathed in 1919 by William Allen
Sturge. By Reginald A. Smith. pp. 136
+ 11 plates. 4º. London, 1931.

8132 Burton (C. E. C. H.). Iron Age
pottery and graphite schist at Westham.
Sussex N. & Q., 8, pp. 111–12 + plan.
1940.

8133 —— Flints and pot at Westham.
[Bronze Age.] Sussex N. & Q., 9, pp.
173–74. 1943.

8134 Butler (Jay Jordan) *and* **Smith**
(Isobel F.). Razors, urns, and the
British Middle Bronze Age. [7 figures.]
Univ. London, Inst. Archaeol., Ann.
Rpt., 12, pp. 20–52. 1956.

8135 Calkin (John Bernard). Ancient Bronze Age implements and hoards
[around Bournemouth]. [2 figures.]
Proc. Bournemouth N. Sci. Soc., 43,
pp. 57–66 + plate. 1953.

8136(a) Callander (John Graham).
Notice of an [Early Iron Age] bronze
cup and other objects found apparently
in a sepulchral deposit [of the Roman
period] near Tarland, Aberdeenshire.
[2 figures.] Proc. Soc. Antiq. Scot., 49,
pp. 203–06. 1915.

**8136(b) Cardiff, National Museum
of Wales.** Guide to the collection illus-
trating the prehistory of Wales. By W. F.
Grimes. pp. xv, 254 + 9 plates. 8º.
Cardiff, 1939. [78 figures. Pp. 129–202,
Catalogue.]

8137 Calvert (William K.). The
North Lonsdale Field Club's collection
of antiquities. Trans. Cumb. & Westm.
Ant. Soc., N.S. 51, pp. 174–75. 1951.

8138 Case (Humphries). Archaeological notes: Lechlade, Glos.; Little
Rollright, Oxon.; Nettlebed, Oxon.;
North Leigh, Oxon. Oxoniensia, 23,
1958, 133–34.

8139 —— Archaeological notes: Russell's Water, Oxon.; Stanton Harcourt.
Oxoniensia, 23, 1958, 138.

8140 —— A tin-bronze in bell-beaker
association. Antiquity, 39, 1965, pp.
219–22.

8141 Celoria (Francis). Archaeological finds from the counties of London
and Middlesex added to the Collections
of the London Museum during 1962.
Trans. London & Middlesex A.S., 21 (2),
1965, 140.

8142 Charlton (Edward). On an
enamelled bronze cup [Roman], and a celt
and ring mould, in the possession of
Sir W. Calverley Trevelyan; with observations of the use of metals by the ancient
British and the Romans. [2 figures.]
Arch. Æl. [1st S.], 4, pp. 102–08. 1855.

8143 Chitty (Lily Frances). The D. G.
Goodwin collection of [prehistoric] an-

tiquities [in the Shrewsbury Museum]. [Figure.] Trans. Shropshire Archaeol. Soc., 43 (4th S. 10), pp. xxx–xxxiii. 1926.

8144 Chitty (Lily Frances). Notes on prehistoric implements [from Shropshire]. Trans. Shropshire Archaeol. Soc., 43 (4th S. 10), pp. 233–46. 1926.

8145 —— Notes on recent acquisitions to the prehistoric section, Shrewsbury Museum. [Stone and bronze implements.] Trans. Shropshire Archaeol. Soc., 45 (4th S. 12), pp. 62–74 + 2 plates. 1929.

8146 —— Bronze implements and other objects from Shropshire in the National Museum of Wales, Cardiff. Trans. Shropshire Archaeol. Soc., 50, pp. 143–54 + plate. 1940.

8147 —— Prehistoric and other early finds in the borough of Shrewsbury. (Appendix: A whetstone from Shrewsbury, by G. C. Dunning.) Trans. Shropshire Archaeol. Soc., 54, pp. 105–44 + 6 plates + map. 1951.

8148 Clark (Anthony J.). Ancient weapons from Ripley. [Figure. ?Late Bronze Age and Saxon.] Surrey Archaeol. Collns., 52, pp. 80–82. 1952.

8149 Clark (John Grahame Douglas) *and* **Godwin** (H.). A Late Bronze Age find near Stuntney, Isle of Ely. [4 figures + 2 maps. Wooden vessels, bronze implements. Pp. 63–66, Schedule of ribbed palstaves, with distribution map.] Antiq. J., 20, pp. 52–71 + 2 plates; p. 289. 1940.

8150 —— Neolithic bows from Somerset, England, and the prehistory of archery in north-western Europe. Proc. prehist. Soc., 29, 1963, 50–98 + 21 figures + 8 plates.

8151 Clarke (Joseph). Notes on objects in the Mayer collection relating to Essex: with an account of a discovery of celts and war weapons. Trans. Hist. Soc. Lancs. & Ches., 3rd Ser. 1, pp. 271–84 + 10 plates. 1873.

8152 Clarke (Louis Colville Gray). Prehistoric and Romano-British objects from England in the University Museum of Archaeology and of Ethnology, Cambridge. [A few prehistoric.] Antiq. J., 6, pp. 175–80 + 7 plates. 1926.

8153 Clarke (Roy Rainbird). A bronze cauldron [probably of Early Iron Age] and other antiquities from north-

east Suffolk. Proc. Suffolk Inst. Arch., 23, pp. 219–23 + 3 plates + map. 1939.

8154 Clarke (W. G.). The distribution of flint and bronze implements in Norfolk. Proc. prehist. Soc. E.A., 3 i, 1918/19, 147–49.

8155 Colchester *Borough Council*. What to see in the Castle Museum. pp. 25. 8⁰. Colchester, 1947. [14 figures. Pp. 4–12, Prehistory.]

8156 Cole (Edward Maule). Notes on archaeology in provincial museums. 3.—Driffield. Antiquary, 24, pp. 12–16. 1891.

8157 Cole (Sonia). Forgeries and the British Museum. Antiq., 35, 1961, pp. 103–06.

8158 Coles (Frederick R.). Annotated list of antiquities from the Stewartry of Kirkcudbright, now preserved in the National Museum [Edinburgh]. Trans. Dumfries. Ant. Soc., 15 (1898–99), pp. 32–45. 1900.

8159 Coles (John M.). European Bronze Age shields. Proc. prehist. Soc., 28, 1962, 156–90 + 5 figures + 12 plates.

8160 —— *and others*. A Late Bronze Age find from Pyotdykes, Angus, Scotland, with associated gold, cloth, leather and wood remains (with Herbert Coutts and M. L. Ryder). Proc. prehist. Soc., 30, 1964, 186–98 + 3 figures + 4 plates.

8161 Collins (A. E. P.). Iron Age and Romano-British finds at Wallingford. (Bronzes and pottery from Wallingford.) [Figure (pottery).] Berks. Archaeol. J., 51, pp. 64–66. 1949.

8162 Congresses—*International Congress of Prehistoric and Protohistoric sciences*. Inventaria archaeologrea. Great Britain. 1st (2nd, 3rd etc.) set, G.B. 1 (2, 3 etc.). 4⁰. London, 1955, etc. [Illustrations of Bronze Age material in form of card-inventory.)

8163 Corrie (John M.). Notes on a small collection of antiquities at Broughton house, Kirkcudbright. Trans. Dumfries. Ant. Soc., 3 S. 17 (1930–31), pp. 94–100 + 2 plates. 1932.

8164 Cotton (Percy Horace Gordon Powell) *and* **Crawford** (Osbert Guy Stanhope). The Birchington hoard. [14 bronze axe-heads of palstave type in an earthen bowl.] Antiq. J., 4, pp. 220–226 + 2 plates. 1924.

8165 Couchman (John Edwin). Neolithic spoons and bronze loops. [8 figures. 2 spoons from Sussex (Hurstpierpoint and Clayton).] Sussex Arch. Collns., 61, pp. 65–79. 1920.

8166 Cowen (John David). Museum notes. [Prehistoric axe-heads, etc.] Arch. Æl., 4th S. 26, pp. 127–52 + 6 plates. 1948.

8167 —— The Crawhall Collection. Arch. Æliana, 43, 1965, 1–20 + 1 figure + 2 plates.

8168 Cowper (Henry Swainson). Some miscellaneous finds [in Westmorland]. [7 figures. Bronze Age weapons, etc.] Trans. Cumb. & Westm. Ant. Soc., N.S. 5, pp. 182–87. 1905.

8169 Cra'ster (Mary D.). Archaeological notes: Bronze Age implements. [2 figures.] Proc. Camb. Ant. Soc., LVIII, 1965, 143–44.

8170 Cross (Marjorie) *the hon.* Publication of four prehistoric objects from Millom area. [2 stone axe-hammers, urn and polished stone axe. Bronze Age.] Trans. Cumb. & Westm. Ant. Soc., N.S. 39, pp. 283–84 + 3 plates. 1939.

8171 Cuming (Henry Syer). On Celtic antiquities exhumed in Lincolnshire [jewellery] and Dorsetshire [weapons]. [Figure. Sundry localities.] J. Brit.. Archaeol. Ass., 15, pp. 225–30 + 4 plates. 1859.

8172 —— On British antiquities discovered [in various localities] in Lancashire, and deposited in the museum at Warrington. J. Brit. Archaeol. Ass., 15, pp. 231–36 + 2 plates. 1859.

8173 —— On the weapons of the ancient tribes of Yorkshire. [Figure.] J. Brit. Archaeol. Ass., 20, pp. 101–11 + 3 plates. 1864.

8174 —— On an ancient British snow-knife [from Smithfield, London]. J. Brit. Archaeol. Ass., 24, pp. 125–28 + plate. 1868.

8175 Cummins (W. A.). Notes on some stone tools and medieval pottery from Skyborry, near Knighton. [2 figures + plan.] Trans. Shropshire Archaeol. Soc., 54, pp. 227–33. 1952.

8176 Cunnington (Maud Edith). Early Bronze Age beaker and flint dagger from West Overton. Wilts. Archaeol. Mag., 43, pp. 395–96 + plate. 1926.

8177 —— Cinerary urn and bronze dagger from barrow on Roundway down, near Devizes. [Figure (dagger). Urn, transition Late Bronze and Early Iron Ages.] Wilts. Archaeol. Mag., 45, pp. 82–83 + plate (urn). 1930.

8178 Cunnington (William). Some undescribed articles in the Stourhead collection [in the Wiltshire Museum, Devizes]. [5 figures. Urn from barrow at Kingston Deveril (Early Bronze Age), etc. (2 figures, urn and bone pin from Winterbourne Stoke down).] Wilts. Archaeol. Mag., 21, pp. 256–64; 22, pp. 232–33. 1884–85.

8179 —— Antiquities presented by Sir Henry Hoare, bart. [to the Wiltshire Museum, Devizes]. [c. 70, Prehistoric and Roman.] Wilts. Archaeol. Mag., 22, pp. 341–44. 1885.

8180 Curwen (Eliot). On some Bronze Age axes [from Horsted Keynes]. [Figure.] Sussex N. & Q., 3, pp. 229–32. 1931.

8181 —— Recent presentations to the [Sussex Archaeological] Society's museum, Lewes. [P. 117 + plate, two palstaves, from i. Newhaven and ii. Mayfield. *See also* pp. 181–82 (note on i. by O. S. G. Crawford).] Sussex N. & Q., 6, pp. 115–17 + plate. 1936.

8182 —— Two Bronze [palstaves] and a flint from [Mayfield, etc.,] Sussex [in Society's museum]. Trans. Carmarthenshire Ant. Soc., 27, pp. 50–51 + plate. 1937.

8183 Curwen (Eliot Cecil). The prehistoric collections [of the Sussex Archaeological Society]. [2 figures.] Sussex Arch. Collns., 85, pp. 93–98. 1946.

8184 —— Implements and their wooden handles. [Sickles, etc.] Antiquity, 21, pp. 155–58 & plate. 1947.

8185 —— The Diamond Jubilee of the Brighton and Hove Archaeological Society. Sussex Notes & Queries 16(8), 1966, 261–64.

8186 Davies (A. Stanley). Finds from Nantmel, Radnorshire. Arch. Camb., 89 ii, 1934, 339–40 + 2 figures.

8187 Dawkins (*Sir* William Boyd). A hoard of articles of the Bronze Age, found at Eaton, near Norwich. [6 figures. Implements and weapons.] Proc. Soc. Antiq., 2 S. 11, pp. 42–51. 1885.

8188 Dawson (Charles). Neolithic flint weapon in a wooden haft [from East Dean, near Eastbourne]. Sussex Arch. Collns., 59, pp. 97–98 + plate. 1894.

8189 Derville (M. Teichman). Iron Age discovery (200–100 B.C.) in Romney marsh. [Figure. Blue glass bead).] Arch. Cant., 50, pp. 152–54. 1939.

8190 Dixon (David Dippie) *and* **Hardy** (James). British urn found at Sevenwood, near Alnham, Northumberland, with remarks on other antiquities in that neighbourhood. [2 figures.] Hist. Berwick. Nat. Club, 10, pp. 544–549. 1884.

8191 Dixon (Frederick). On a British sepulchral urn and brass pin, found on Storrington downs. [Figure.] Sussex Arch. Collns., 1, pp. 55–57. 1848.

8192 Doncaster, *Municipal Museum.* Catalogue of antiquities, comprising the Stone and Bronze Ages, the Roman, Saxon mediaeval, and later periods section. Compiled by E. Cornish Senior. pp. 16. 8°. Doncaster, 1913.

8193 Dowie (H. G.). Recent archaeological additions to the museum. Trans. & Proc. Torquay nat. Hist. Soc., 5, 1929, 243–44.

8194 Draper (Warwick Herbert). A Bronze Age find [at Shoebury] in Essex. [3 figures.] Essex Rev., 2, pp. 101–05. 1893.

8195 Dudley (Dorothy). Rosecliston, Cranlock. Cornish Arch., 3, 1964, 83–84.

8196 Dudley (Harold Edgar). Early Iron Age objects discovered at Thealby, Lincs. [Figure (bronze bowl).] Antiq. J., 15, pp. 457–60 + plate. 1935.

8197 Dunning (Gerald Clough). Isle of Wight finds in the Hazzledine Warren Collection [Clactonian]. Proc. I. of W. nat. Hist. & archaeol. Soc., 5 vii, 1962, 333–34.

8198 Edinburgh—*National Museum.* A short guide to the National Museum of Antiquities of Scotland. pp. 23 + 4 plates. 8°. Edinburgh, 1926. [Pp. 4–8, Prehistoric.]

8199 Engleheart (F. H. A.). Artefact from Stoke by Nayland. Proc. Suffolk Inst. Arch., 29 ii, 1962, 217–21 + 1 figure.

8200 Evans (*Sir* Arthur John). Late Celtic dagger [from Hertford Warren, Suffolk], fibula [of bronze, from Beckley, Oxon.], and jet cameo [from near Rochester]. [5 figures.] Archaeologia, 66, pp. 569–72. 1915.

8201 Exeter, *Royal Albert Memorial Museum.* Hembury fort. Exhibition of objects discovered during the excavations (1930–5), and of comparative material from other sites. pp. 16. 4°. Exeter, 1935, [Figure + plan.]

8202 Faraday (Laurence). Ancient Sussex culture in the British Museum. [9 figures.] Sussex County Mag., 10, pp. 39–45, 127–32, 173–77, 285. 1936.

8203 Fox (Aileen). Stone and bronze implements and an iron linch-pin from S.E. Wales [hammer, celt + linch-pin]. Arch. Camb., 98 i, 1944, 141–42 + 1 figure.

8204 Fox (Cyril). Presidential Address to the Cambrian Archaeological Society, Cardiff, 1933 [on National Museum of Wales]. Arch. Camb., 88 ii, 1933, 153–84 + 21 figures.

8205 Francis (*Sir* Frank). The British Museum and British antiquities. Antiquity, 37 (1963), 50–53.

8206 Franks (*Sir* Augustus Wollaston). The collection of British antiquities in the British Museum. (Additions to the collection, etc.) [7 figures.] Archaeol. J., 9, pp. 7–15 + 2 plates; 10, pp. 1–13 + plate; 11, pp. 23–32 + plate. 1852–54.

8207 Freeman (C. E.) *and* **Watson** (W.). Early Iron Age objects from Harpenden: a new interpretation. [Figure. Two bronze bucket-escutcheons in the form of ram-heads, two bronze ring-handles, plus pottery.] Antiq. J., 29, pp. 196–97. 1949.

8208 Frost (Marion). Guide to the museum and art gallery, Worthing. Fourth edition. pp. 19. 8°. Worthing, 1929. [7 figures (palstaves, etc.).]

8209 Gardner (Eric). Some prehistoric and Saxon antiquities found in the neighbourhood of Weybridge. [Pp. 129–31 + 2 plates (pottery, weapons), Bronze Age.] Surrey Archaeol. Collns., 25, pp. 129–35 + 4 plates. 1912.

8210 Garrood (Jesse Robert). Recent discoveries in Hunts. [2 figures. St. Acheul hand-axe from Buckden and socketed adze from Wood Walton.] Antiq. J., 9, pp. 247–49. 1929.

8211 Garrod (Jesse Robert). Iron Age pottery and associated objects in the museum of the Huntingdon Institution. [3 figures.] Trans. Cambs. & Hunts. Arch. Soc., 4, pp. 289–92 + plate. 1930.

8212 —— Stone *and* Bronze implement objects from Castle Hill farm, Wood Walton [Hunts.]. [Neolithic to Roman occupation.] Trans. Cambs. & Hunts. Arch. Soc., 5, pp. 274–77 + 2 plates. 1937.

8213 Gaythorpe (Harper). Prehistoric implements in Furness. Trans. Cumb. & Westm. Ant. Soc., 14, pp. 442–47 + 2 plates. 1897.

8214 —— Pre-historic implements in Furness (and Cartmel). [Bronze Age. (Figure, palstave).] Trans. Cumb. & Westm. Ant. Soc., 15, pp. 161–71 + 4 plates; 16, pp. 152–56; N.S. 4, pp. 325–329 + plate. 1899–1900, 1904.

8215 —— Prehistoric implements in Furness. Trans. Cumb. & Westm. Ant. Soc., N.S. 6, pp. 143–48 + plate. 1906.

8216 Glenn (Thomas Allen). Recent finds near Rhyl. Arch. Camb., 81, pp. 199–203. 1926.

8217 Goddard (Edward Hungerford). The Stourhead collection in the Wiltshire Archaeological Society's museum at Devizes. [51 figures.] Reliquary, N. [3rd] S. 3, pp. 20–36. 1897.

8218 —— The museum of the Wiltshire Archaeological and Natural History Society at Devizes. [26 figures.] Antiquary, 39, pp. 330–35, 369–74. 1903.

8219 Gogan (Liam S.). A composite tool from [Dundrum, Newcastle], a Co. Down sandhill site. [2 figures.] Man, 29, p. 188. 1929.

8220 Gowing (C. N.). A hundred years of the museum. Records of Bucks., 17 (1), 1961, 82–87.

8221 Gray (Harold St. George). The Walter collection in Taunton Castle Museum. [Pp. 27–31, Neolithic and Bronze Age implements from Ham hill.] Proc. Somerset Arch. Soc., 48 (1902), pp. 24–78. 1903.

8222 —— The Stradling collection in the Taunton Castle Museum. [Stone and bronze implements, etc.] Proc. Somerset Arch. Soc., 48 i, pp. 81–87. 1903.

8223 —— The Norris collection in Taunton Castle Museum. Proc. Somerset Arch. Soc., 51 (1905), pp. 136–59 + 2 plates. 1906.

8224 —— Archaeological remains found at Middlezoy. [Figure (bone implement of Early Iron Age).] Proc. Somerset Arch. Soc., 72 (1926), pp. 85–88. 1927.

8225 Green (H. J. M.). An analysis of archaeological rubbish deposits, Part I. Archaeol. News Letter, 7 iii, 1961, 51–54 + 1 figure.

8226 —— An analysis of archaeological rubbish deposits, Part II. Archaeol. News Letter, 7 iv, 1961, 91–93 + 95 + 1 figure.

8227 Grimes (William Francis). Recent finds of prehistoric implements from Wales. Arch. Camb., 85 ii, 1930, 415–16 + 4 figures.

8228 —— Guide to the collection illustrating the prehistory of Wales. *National Museum of Wales.* pp. xv, 354 + 9 plates. 8º. Cardiff, 1939.

—— The prehistory of Wales. [Second edition of last item, revised by H. N. Savory.] pp. xvi, 288. 8º. Cardiff, 1951.

8229 Grinsell (L. V.). The Royce Collection at Stowe-on-the-Wold. [Neolithic—IA.] Trans. Bristol & Glos. Ant. Soc., 83, pp. 5–23 + 2 plates + 2 figures. 1964.

8230 Haevernick (T. E.). Die Glasarmringe und Ringperlen der Mittel- und Spätlatènezeit auf dem Europäischen Festland. [pp. 302, 35 plates, figures and maps.] Römisch-Germanischen Kommission Bonn, Rudolf Habelt. 1960.

8231 Hall (George Rome). An account of the discovery of a British perforated axe-hammer and a Roman silver coin [denarins of Hadrian], near Barrasford, North Tynedale; with notices of other stone implements from this locality. [?Bronze Age.] Arch. Æl., N. [2nd.] S. 12, pp. 116–23 + plate. 1887.

8232 Hardy (James). Bronze dagger and flint arrow head [from Ayton, Berwickshire]. Hist. Berwick. Nat. Club, 14, pp. 391–92 + plate. 1893.

8233 Haverfield (Francis John). Sussex antiquities [in Duke of Northumberland's museum at Alnwick Castle]. Sussex N. & Q., 6, pp. 84–86, 125. 1936.

8234 Hawkes (Charles Francis Christopher). The Marnian pottery and La Tène I brooch from Worth, Kent. [14 figures (pottery): figure (brooch).] Antiq. J., 20, pp. 115–21. 1940.

8235 —— The Deverel urn and the Picardy pin: a phase of Bronze Age settlement in Kent. Proc. prehist. Soc., 8, 1942, 26–47 + 11 figures + 2 plates.

8236 —— The British Museum and British archaeology. Antiquity, 36, 1962, pp. 248–51.

8237 Hayes (P.). Halkyn: copper flat axe, spindle whorl. Flints. hist. soc. publicn., 18, 1960, 169–70 + 2 figures.

8238 Hemp (Wilfrid James). On certain objects mostly of prehistoric [Bronze Age] date discovered near Beddgelert and near Brynkir station [Caernarvonshire]. [8 figures.] Proc. Soc. Antiq., 2 S. 30, pp. 166–84 + map. 1918.

8239 Higgins (R. Brice) *and* **Smith** (R. A.). Flint implements of Moustier type and associated mammalian remains from the Crayford brick-earths. [6 figures.] Man, 14, pp. 4–8, 49–50. 1914.

8240 Hodges (Henry). Artifacts: an introduction to early materials and technology, London, 1966.

8241 Hogg (Robert). Further accessions to the Carlisle Museum. [2 figures (stone implements: late Bronze Age spear-head).] Trans. Cumb. & Westm. Ant. Soc., N.S. 53, pp. 202–08 + plate. 1954.

8242 Holleyman (George Albert). Brighton loops and flint implements from Falmer hill. [Middle Bronze Age.] Sussex N. & Q., 12, p. 60–61. 1948.

8243 Howarth (E.). Bronze and stone celts found in Sheffield. Trans. Hunter. Arch. Soc., 2, pp. 186–88 + 1 plate. 1924.

8244 Hughes (Henry Harold). Collection of antiquities belonging to the late W. Wynn Williams. [6 figures.] Arch. Camb., 6th S. 19, pp. 459–69. 1919.

8245 —— A few further finds from Braich y Dinas, Penmaenmawr [spindle-whorls, pestle, etc.]. Arch. Camb., 87 ii, 1932, 399–401 + 2 figures.

8246 Hugo (Thomas). On celts and their classification. J. Brit. Archaeol. Ass., 9, pp. 63–71 + 3 plates. 1853.

8247 Hulme (Edward Wyndham). Currency bars and water-clocks. [3 figures. Pp. 210–15, Reply, by Reginald A. Smith, and Rejoinder, by E. W. Hulme.] Antiquity, 7, pp. 61–72 + 3 plates. 1933.

8248 —— Sword moulds v. currency bars. pp. 7. 8°. London, 1944. [4 figures. Revised from the British Steelmaker, August, 1944. Caesar's evidence as to iron currency in Celtic Britain.]

8249 Hume (Ivor Noël). Treasure in the Thames. pp. 255 + 43 plates. 8°. London, 1956. [30 figures. pp. 17–52. Prehistoric.]

8250 Hutchinson (William). Account of ["British"] antiquities [at Warton] in Lancashire. [Pottery, etc.] Archaeologia, 9, pp. 211–18 + plate. 1789.

8251 James (Frederick). Remains of the Bronze Age found at Aylesford, Kent. [Figure (implements).] Proc. Soc. Antiq., 2 S. 17, pp. 373–77. 1899.

8252 Jerman (H. Noel). Some unrecorded finds from east central Wales, with observations on the distribution of find-sites in the region of the Upper Severn. Arch. Camb., 89 i, 1934, 112–34 + 8 figures.

8253 Jessup (Ronald Frederick). Bronze Age antiquities from the lower Medway. [2 figures. Stone, antler, bronze: from river, Chatham and marshes.] Arch. Cant., 45, pp. 179–87. 1933.

8254 —— A flint axe [from Ash] and two beakers [from Dover] from east Kent. Antiq. J., 16, pp. 468–69 + plate. 1936.

8255 —— A flint dagger and two beakers from [(i) Capel-le-Ferne and (ii) Folkestone,] east Kent. Antiq. J., 20, pp. 486–87 + 2 plates. 1940.

8256 Jewitt (Llewellynn). Notice of the discovery of some Celtic remains at Stancliffe hall, Darley dale. [3 figures.] Reliquary, 4, pp. 201–06 + 3 plates (pottery). 1864.

8257 —— Notice of the discovery of Celtic remains on the estate of W. S. Ashton, Esq., at Darwen, in Lancashire. Reliquary, 6, pp. 137–38 + 2 plates (cinerary urns). 1866.

8258 Jones (Morris Charles). Some stone implements in the Powysland

Museum. [7 figures.] Collns. rel. to Montgom., 14, pp. 271–78. 1881.

8259 Karlovsky (C. C. Lamberg). Amber and faience. Antiquity, 37, 1963, pp. 301–02.

8260 Kelly (David B.). Researches and discoveries in Kent. Larkfield. Leeds. Arch. Camb., 76, 1961, pp. 197–98.

8261 Kitching (James). Bone, tooth and horn tools of palaeolithic man: an account of the Osteodontokeratic discoveries in Pin Hole Cave, Derbyshire. xiv, 55 pp. + 3 figures + 41 plates. Manchester, 1963,

8262 Knowles (William James). Flint implements, and associated remains found near Ballintoy, Co. Antrim. J. Anthrop. Inst., 7, pp. 202–05. 1878.

8263 Lawrence (G. F.). On the discovery of a prehistoric horn weapon, retaining its original wooden handle, in the Thames [at Hammersmith]. J. Brit. Archaeol. Ass., N.S. 3, pp. 79–80. 1897.

8264 —— Prehistoric London: especially concerning the Late Celtic settlement, as represented in the Guildhall Museum. Archaeol. J., 62, pp. 37–47. 1905.

8265 —— Antiquities from the middle Thames. [3 figures. Objects dredged.] Archaeol. J., 86 (1929), pp. 69–98 + 11 plates + map. 1930.

8266 Leach (George B.). Some surface finds of prehistoric and Roman periods from Ashton, near Chester. [Pp. 53–58, Prehistoric.] J. Chester & N. Wales Arch. Soc., N.S. 35, pp. 53–59 + 2 plates + plan. 1942.

8267 Leeds (Edward Thurlow). Antiquities from Essex in the Ashmolean Museum, Oxford. [Palaeolithic—Anglo-Saxon. Pp. 247–50 + 2 plates, Prehistoric.] Trans. Essex Archaeol. Soc., N.S. 19, pp. 247–54 + 4 plates. 1930.

8268 —— Recent Bronze Age discoveries [at Sutton Courtenay] in Berkshire] and [at Cassington,] Oxfordshire. [Figure + plan.] Antiq. J., 14, pp. 264–276 + 7 plates + plan. 1934.

8269 Lethbridge (Thomas Charles) *and* **O'Reilly** (Maureen Margaret). The Westley collection. [Now in Museum of Archaeology and Ethnology, Cambridge. Stone implements of Neolithic and Bronze Ages: bronze socketed axes and palstaves.] Proc. Camb. Antiq. Soc., 34, pp. 88–92 + 14 plates. 1934.

8270 —— *and* —— Archaeological notes—a bone tool found . . . at Cassington, Oxon., and palstave . . . found at Little Shelford. Proc. Camb. Antiq. Soc., 34, pp. 92–93 + plate 15. 1934.

8271 Livens (Roger G.). A bronze palstave and encrusted urn from Lilliesleaf (Rox.). [Figure.] Trans. Glasgow Archaeol. Soc., N.S. 14, pp. 30–34. 1956.

8272 Lloyd (C.). The Wayside Museum, Zennor. Proc. West Cornwall F.C., N.S. 6, pp. 21–22. 1953.

8273 London—*Guildhall Museum*. Catalogue of the collection of London antiquities. Second edition. pp. x, 411 + 10 plates. 8°. London, 1908. [Pp. 1–22 + plates 1–6, Prehistory.]

8274 London Museum. Catalogue of an exhibition of recent archaeological discoveries (prehistoric and Saxon periods) in Great Britain. Fifth temporary exhibition, 1932. pp. 46. 8°. London, 1932.

8275 —— Archaeological finds from the counties of London and Middlesex added to the collections of the London Museum during 1961. Trans. London & Middsx. Arch. Soc., 21 i, 1963, 78 + 1 figure.

8276 London — *University College Museum*. Catalogue of an exhibition of recent archaeological discoveries in the British Isles. pp. 28. 8°. London, 1929.

8277 MacGregor (Morna) *and* **Simpson** (D. D. A.). A group of Iron Age objects from Barbury Castle, Wilts. Wilts. Archaeol. Mag., 58, 1963, No. 211, 394–402 + 2 figures.

8278 Mackie (S. J.). Bone and bronze relics recently discovered in Heathery Burn cave near Stanhope in Weardale, Co. Durham. [Figure + plan.] Proc. Soc. Antiq., 2 S. 2, pp. 127–32. 1862.

8279 McNaughton (Joseph). Note on a collection of stone and bronze axe heads found in the district, and presented by John E. Shearer, to the Smith Institute, Stirling. Trans. Stirling N.H. & Arch. Soc., 1923–24, pp. 141–42. 1924.

8280 McNeil (Jean). Two implements for ornamenting pottery [from Horn head, Co. Donegal and from Whitepark bay, Co. Antrim]. [2 figures. Bronze Age.] Man, 30, pp. 134–35. 1930.

8281 Malden (Henry Elliot). A cinerary urn and other matters found at [Cotwanding, near] Dorking and Betchworth. [First c. B.C. *See also* 33 (1920), p. 115: flint flakes also found.] Surrey Archaeol. Collns., 26, pp. 149–50 + plate (urn). 1913.

8282 Mitford (Rupert Leo Scott Bruce). Prehistoric and Romano-British antiquities in the British Museum. Antiquity, 35, 1961, pp. 313–14.

8283 Morven Institute of Archaeological Research. Guide to the museum at Avebury, Wiltshire. pp. 15 + 3 plates. 8°. Gloucester [1939].

8284 Munro (Robert). Notes: 1. On a human skeleton, with prehistoric objects, found at Great Casterton, Rutland. 2. On a stone cist containing a skeleton and an urn, found at Largs, Ayrshire. With a report on the urn, by Hon. John Abercromby; and on the skulls, by D. J. Cunningham. [8 figures.] Proc. Roy. Soc. Edin., 26, pp. 279–309. 1906.

8285 Nankivell (Florence). List of Cornish museums. Cornish archaeology, No. 1, 1962, 99–101.

8287 Newbigin (Nancy). A collection of prehistoric material from Hebburn moor, Northumberland. [2 figures. Stone axes, jet objects, flints, etc.] Arch. Æl., 4th S. 19, pp. 104–16 + plate (axes and jet objects). 1941.

8288 Noble (F.). Archaeological finds and other acquisitions of Knighton Secondary School museum from local sources in 1953. (October, 1953—October, 1954.) (October, 1954 to July, 1957.) [2 figures.] Radnorshire Soc., Trans., 23, pp. 16–21; 24, pp. 79–82; 27, pp. 62–71. 1953–54, 1957.

8289 Norwood (J. F. L.). Prehistoric accessions to Hereford Museum, 1957. [Figure.] Trans. Woolhope N.F.C., 35 (1957), pp. 316–20. 1958.

8290 Parsons (H.). Early Bronze Age celts. [Figure. From Ipplepen, Devon and from Stockbridge, Hants.] Antiq. J., 12, pp. 70–71. 1932.

8291 Passmore (A. D.). A hoard of Bronze [Age] implements from Donhead St. Mary, and a stone mould from Bulford, in Farnham Museum, Dorset.

Wilts. Archaeol. Mag., 45, pp. 373–76 + 3 plates. 1931.

8292 —— A flint implement in a horn handle from near Liddington Castle, Wilts. [Figure. Neolithic.] Antiq. J., 23, pp. 52–53. 1943.

8293 Patchett (Florence M.). Food-vessel and flint spear-head, Pentire Glaze, Polzeath, north Cornwall. [2 figures. Both Middle Bronze Age.] Antiq. J., 28, pp. 183–85. 1948.

8294 Payne (George). Catalogue of the museum of local antiquities collected by George Payne. pp. 54. [Pp. 1–9, Celtic period.] 8°. Sittingbourne, 1882.

8295 Peate (Iorwerth Cyfeilwy). Early Bronze Age finds in the Dyfi Basin. Arch. Cambrensis, 81 ii, 1926, 350–62 + 2 figures.

8296 Petch (D. F.). Casual finds of flints and prehistoric pottery. Rpts. & Papers, Lincs. A. & A.S., 8, 1959, 5.

8297 —— Casual finds of prehistoric material. Rpts. & Papers, Lincs. A. & A.S., 9, 1961, 4–5.

8298 Phené (John Samuel). On some early settlers near Conway: their beautiful jewellery and gold work. [7 figures.] J. Brit. Archaeol. Ass., N.S. 3, pp. 241–65 + 5 plates. 1897.

8299 Phillips (Charles William). Some recent finds from the Trent near Nottingham. [5 figures + map. 2 boats and Bronze Age spear-heads and daggers.] Antiq. J., 21, pp. 133–43 + plate, 1941.

8300 Pollitt (William). Bronze Age find in Southend-on-Sea. [Figure (sword, palstave, beaker).] Trans. Essex Archaeol. Soc., N.S. 19, pp. 311–13. 1930.

8301 Raftery (Joseph). A brief guide to the collection of Irish antiquities. [Pp. 96, 10 plates, 97 text-figures.] Dublin, The Stationery Office, 1960.

8302 Raistrick (Arthur), **Spaul** (P.) *and* **Todd** (Eric). The Malham Iron-Age pipe. [i. Archaeology and dating; ii. Nature and anatomy of the bone; iii. Musical analysis of the pipe. 3 figures.] Galpin Soc. J., 5, pp. 1–11 + 2 plates. 1952.

8303 Rankine (William Francis). The Farnham prehistoric museum. [Opened 1939.] Surrey Archaeol. Collns., 47, p. 88. 1941.

8304 Rankine (William Francis). Searching for artifacts. Archaeol. News Letter, 6, pp. 144–46 + plate. 1958.

8305 Rausing (Gad). The bow: some notes on its origin (Acta Archaeologica Lundensia, Series in 8º, 6). pp. 189 + 64 figures. Lund, Sweden, 1967.

8306 Reading Museum. Archaeological notes from Reading Museum. [1 plate.] Berks. Arch. J., 59, 1961, 56–61.

8307 —— Archaeological notes from Reading Museum. [2 plates.] Berks. Arch. J., 61, 1963/64, 96–106.

8308 Rivers (Augustus Henry Lane Fox Pitt). A Bronze [Age] spear, with a gold ferule and a shaft of bog oak, obtained from Lough Gur, county Limerick. J. Ethnol. Soc., N.S. 6, pp. 36–38 + plate. 1869.

8309 —— On the discovery of palaeolithic implements in association with *Elephas primigenius* in the gravels of the Thames Valley at Acton. J. Geol. Soc. London, 28, 1872, 449–65 + 7 figures.

8310 —— Presidential address of Section H [on museum collections & excavations in Wessex]. Advm. Sci., 1888, 825–35 + 2 figures.

8311 Robarts (N. F.). Stone and bronze celts recently discovered in Croydon and neighbourhood. Proc. Croydon N.H. & Sci. Soc., 5, pp. 51–56. 1900.

8312 Roots (William). Some relics of remote times, found in the bed of the river Thames, between Kingston and Hampton Court. [Weapons.] Archaeologia, 30, pp. 490–93. 1844.

8313 Savory (Hubert Newman). A polished stone axe of French type, a beaker and a cinerary urn from Pentreath, Angelsey. Arch. Camb., 95 ii, 1940, 245–47 + 3 figures.

8314 —— Late Bronze Age personal hoard from Llandudno (Caern.). Bull. Bd. Celtic Stud., 16, pp. 51–52 + plate. 1954.

8315 —— Excavations and discoveries. Bull. Board Celtic Studies, 20 iii, 1963, 305–08 + 3 figures.

8316 Sheffield, *Public Museum.* Catalogue of the Bateman collection of antiquities. Prepared by E. Howarth. pp. xxiii, 254. 8º. London, 1899.

[Figures. Pp. 1–190, Celtic or ancient British period. (Stone and bronze implements, urns, crania, querns, etc.) Pp. 191–219, Romano-British period (ornaments, urns, etc.).]

8317 Sheppard (Thomas). Recent prehistoric finds in East Yorkshire. [3 figures: flint arrow-heads and two Bronze Age palstaves.] Trans. E. Riding Antiq. Soc., 24, pp. 65–67. 1923.

8318 —— Bronze Age relics at Elloughton, East Yorks. [2 figures: beaker, bronze dagger and bone pin.] Trans. E. Riding Antiq. Soc., 25, pp. 165–69. 1926.

8319 —— Bronze Age implements (in the Mortimer Museum, Hull). North Western Naturalist, 1941, pp. 9–146 + 7 plates. 1941.

8320 Shore (Thomas William). Prehistoric weapons and implements. Notes on Hampshire discoveries. Shore Memorial Vol. (Hants. F.C.), pp. 70–77. 1911.

8321 Shortt (Hugh de Sansmarez). Notes on prehistoric antiquities, previously unpublished, in the Salisbury and South Wilts. Museum. [5 figures.] Archaeol. J., 104 (1947), pp. 20–26. 1948.

8322 —— Two prehistoric axes. [1: Cornish greenstone; 2: flanged Wessex culture.] Wilts. Arch. Mag., 58, No. 210, pp. 217–18 + 2 figures. 1962.

8323 Smith (Arthur). Implements of the Stone Age, in the City and County Museum, Lincoln. Lincs. N. & Q., 13, pp. 97–101 + 4 plates. 1914.

8324 —— Guide to the Roman and pre-Roman antiquities in the museum. *Newark Municipal Museum, Publication 2.* pp. 80 + 6 plates. 8º. Newark, 1927.

8325 Smith (Isobel) *and* **Wymer** (John J.). The Treacher collection of prehistoric artifacts from Marlow. [4 figures.] Records of Bucks., 17 (4), 1964, 286–300.

8326 Smith (John Alexander). Remarks on a bronze implement, and bones of the ox and dog, found in a bed of undisturbed gravel at Kinleith, near Currie, Mid-Lothian. [4 figures.] Proc. Soc. Antiq. Scot., 5, pp. 84–98. 1865.

8327 —— Notice of a small bronze blade found in a cinerary urn at Balblair, Sutherlandshire, *etc.* [Figure.] Proc. Soc. Antiq. Scot., 7, pp. 475–77. 1870.

8328 Smith (Reginald Allender). Specimens from the Layton collection, in Brentford public library. [30 figures.] Archaeologia, 69, pp. 1–30 + 2 plates. 1920.

8329 —— The Garraway Rice bequest of prehistoric objects. Brit. Mus. Q., 8, pp. 44–45 + plate. 1933.

8330 Smith (Workington George). Dewlish [Dorset] eoliths and elephas meridionalis. Man, 9, pp. 113–14 + plate. 1909.

8331 Spurrell (Flaxman Charles John). On some Palaeolithic knapping tools and modes of using them. J. Anthrop. Inst., 13, pp. 109–18 + plate. 1883.

8332 Stevens (Joseph). Palaeolithic flint implements, with mammalian remains, in the quaternary drift at Reading. J. Brit. Archaeol. Ass., 37, pp. 1–11 + 2 plates. 1881.

8333 Stevenson (Anne H.) *and* **Atkinson** (Richard John Copland). Notes on archaeological material from Dumfriesshire, Kirkcudbrightshire, and Wigtownshire, in the Bishop collection [Hunterian Museum, Glasgow University]. Trans. Dumfriess. Ant. Soc., 3rd S. 30 (1951–1952), pp. 171–78. 1953.

8334 Stopes (Marie Carmichael), **Oakley** (Kenneth Page) *and* **Wells** (Lawrence H.). The discovery of human skulls with stone artifacts and animal bones, in a fissure at Portland. [2 figures. Early Bronze Age.] Proc. Dorset Archaeol. Soc., 74 (1952), pp. 39–47 + 2 plates. 1953.

8335 Stradling (W.). A young turf-bearer's find in the turbaries. [Knives, palstaves and jewellery.] Proc. Somerset Arch. Soc., 5 (1854), pp. 91–94 + 2 plates. 1855.

8336 Struthers (J.). On the human crania and other contents found in short stone cists in Aberdeenshire. Advm. of Sci., 1885, 1225.

8337 Sturdy (David) *and* **Case** (Humphrey). Archaeological notes, 1961. Oxoniensia, 26/27, 1961/62, 336–339.

8338 Swift (Henry). Weapons of the British Bronze period. [6 figures.] J. Antiq. Assoc. Brit. Isles, 2, pp. 135–42. 1932.

8339 Thomas (A. Charles). Unpublished material from Cornish museums: 1 Carn Brea finds in Camborne Public Library. Cornish archaeology, No. 1, 1962, 104–06 + 1 figure.

8340 Thomas (Nicholas). Notes on some Early Bronze Age grave groups in Devizes Museum. [4 figures. Pp. 326–30 + figure, the bronze standard from Hoare's Wilsford barrow 18.] Wilts. Archaeol. Mag., 55, pp. 311–30. 1954.

8341 —— Three pre-Roman antiquities from the Midlands. Trans. Birmingham Arch. Soc., 77, 1959, 1–4 (2 figures).

8342 Thompson (George H.). Notes on urn and flint spear head found at Amble [Nhbd.]. Hist. Berwick. Nat. Club, 14, pp. 121–22 + 2 plates. 1892.

8343 Thoresby (Ralph). Museum Thoresbyanum: or, a catalogue of the antiquities . . . preserved in the repository of R. T. at Leedes. fol. London, 1713. [Pp. 337–48, British, runic, Saxon, and Danish medals (=coins).]

8344 Tebbutt (Charles Frederick). Bronze Age, Iron Age and Saxon objects from Bedfordshire. [2 palstaves from Northill and Belgic urn from Old Warden.] Antiq. J., 34, p. 232 + plate. 1954.

8345 Truckell (Alfred Edgar). The Archaeological collection of the Society. Trans. Dumfries & Gal. Nat. H. & Ant. Soc., 41, pp. 55–56. 1962/63.

8346 Turner (Frederic). Objects found in the Thames at Runnymede. [Neolithic and Early Bronze Age, *etc.*] Surrey Archaeol. Collns., 22, pp. 187–98 + plate. 1909.

8347 Underhill (F. M.). Archaeological notes from Reading Museum. [2 plates + 1 figure.] Berks. Arch. J., 58, 1960, 52–65.

8348 Underwood (W.). A discovery of pleistocene bones and flint implements in a gravel pit at Dovercourt, Essex. Proc. prehist. Soc. E.A., 1 iii, 1912/13, 360–68 + 3 plates.

8349 Warren (Samuel Hazzledine). Note on a prehistoric deposit at Loughton, Essex. [Flints, pottery, *etc.*] Essex Nat., 16, pp. 101–03. 1910.

8350 —— On a palaeolithic (?) wooden spear. J. Geol. Soc. London, 67, 1911, xcix.

8351 Waterman (Dudley M.). A Bronze Age urn with associated flints from Troutsdale, N.R. Yorks. [Figures.]

Ann. Rpt. Yorks. Phil. Soc., 1946–47, pp. 38–40. 1947.

8352 Way (Albert). Notes on certain objects of stag's horn used for hafting stone implements or weapons. Archaeol. J., 21, pp. 54–59 + plate. 1864.

8353 —— Notice of ancient relics found at Llangwyllog in Anglesey. [2 figures.] Arch. Camb., 3rd S. 12, pp. 97–111 + 2 plates. 1866.

8354 Wedlake (A. L.). Mammoth remains and Pleistocene implements found on the west Somerset coast. Proc. Somerset Arch. Soc., 95 (1950), pp. 167–68. 1951.

8355 Westell (William Percival). Roman and pre-Roman antiquities in Letchworth Museum. [Also separately. *Letchworth Museum Publication 2.* 1928.] East Herts. Archaeol. Soc., 7 (1926), pp. 258–81 + 3 plates (pottery), pp. 338–39. 1927.

8356 —— Roman and pre-Roman discoveries at Newinn, Herts. [British native ware urns: Iron Age objects, *etc.*] St. Albans Archit. & Archaeol. Soc., Trans., 1931, pp. 141–50 + 5 plates + plan. 1932.

8357 Williams (Stephen William). Notes on some Bronze [Age] and stone weapons discovered in Wales. [15 figures.] Arch. Camb., 5th S. 12, pp. 241–49. 1895.

8358 Williams (Victor Erle Nash).

Early Iron Age and Roman pottery and other objects from Minchin hole, Gower, Glam. Bull. Bd. Celtic Stud., 12, pp. 62–63. 1946.

8359 Windle (*Sir* Bertram Coghill Alan). Some prehistoric implements of Warwickshire and Worcestershire. B'ham & Midland Inst., Arch. Section, Trans., 23 (1897), pp. 6–14 + 2 plates. 1898.

8360 Winstone (B.). Two prehistoric weapons recently found [at Epping (stone) and at North Weald (bronze)] in Essex. [2 figures.] J. Brit. Archaeol. Ass., 50, pp. 158–68. 1894.

8361 Winwood (M. H.). Ornaments, sickles and weapons of the Bronze Age, found in St. Catherine's Valley, St. Monkswood, near Bath. [3 figures.] Proc. Soc. Antiq., 2 S. 15, pp. 357–60. 1895.

8362 Wyatt (James). Further discoveries of flint implements and fossil mammals in the valley of the Ouse. J. Geol. Soc. London, 20, 1864, 183–188.

8363 Wymer (J.). Archaeological notes from Reading Museum. [Loans and presentations.] Berks. Archaeol. J., 56, pp. 54–58. 1958.

8364 Yorkshire Philosophical Society. A handbook to the antiquities in the grounds and museum. Eighth edition, pp. vii, 246. 8º. York, 1891.

E. CULTURE

1. ECONOMY

(a) Hunting, Farming and Industry

8365 Aberg (F. A.) *and* **Bowen** (H. Collin). Ploughing experiments with a reconstructed Donner upland ard. [Notes and News.] Antiq., 34 (1960), pp. 144–47.

8366 Airy (Wilfrid). On the extensive use of the avoirdupois pound in the ancient British period. Minutes of Proc. hist. Civil Engineers, 186, 1911, pp. 422–24.

8367 [Anon.] The Essex Red Hills exploration. J. Brit. Archaeol. Ass., N.S. 13, pp. 71, 119–20. 1907.

8368 [Anon.] Iron ore [in prehistoric Britain]. N. & Q. Som. & Dorset, 23, pp. 115–16. 1940.

8369 Armstrong (Albert Leslie). Flint-crust engravings, and associated implements, from Grime's Graves, Norfolk. [Mousterian type flint!] PPSEA, 3 iii, 1920/21, 434–43 + 1 plate + 4 figures.

8370 —— Further discoveries of engraved flint-crust and associated implements at Grime's Graves. PPSEA, 3 iv, 1921/22, 548–58 + 3 figures + 1 plate.

8371 —— Discovery of a new phase of early flint minings at Grimes Graves, Norfolk. PPSEA, 4 i, 1922/24, 113–25 + 5 figures + 2 plates.

8372 Armstrong (Albert Leslie). Percy Sladen Memorial Fund excavations. Grimes Graves, Norfolk, 1924. Interim Report. 1. Further researches in the primitive flint mining area. 2. Discovery of an early Iron Age site, of Halstatt culture. PPSEA, 4 ii, 1923/24, 182–93 + 3 plates + 1 figure.

8373 —— Further excavations upon the engraving floor (Floor 85), Grimes' Graves. PPSEA, 4 ii, 1923/24, 194–202 + 7 figures.

8374 —— The Grime's Graves problem on the light of recent researches. Presidential Address, London, November, 1926. Proc. PSEA, 5 ii, 1926, 91–136 + 35 figures.

8375 —— The Percy Sladen Trust excavations, Grime's Graves, Norfolk. Interim Report, 1927–32. Proc. PSEA, 7 i, 1932–34, p. 57 + 2 figures + 2 plates.

8376 —— Grime's Graves, Norfolk. Report on the excavation of Pit 12. Proc. PSEA, 7 iii, 1934, 382–94 + 6 figures + 3 plates.

8377 Arthur (J. R. B.). Prehistoric wheats in Sussex. [4 figures. Spelt in the Iron Age and the method in which it has been stored in the ground.] Sussex Arch. Collns., 92, pp. 37–47. 1954.

8378 Astley (Hugh John Dukinfield). The romance of Grime's graves. J. Brit. Archaeol. Ass., N.S. 20, pp. 37–44. 1914.

8379 Atkinson (Richard John Copland). Neolithic engineering. Antiquity, 35, 1961, pp. 292–99.

8380 —— Neolithic engineering [reply to Lt. Col. B. S. Browne]. Antiquity, 37, 1963, 142–44

8381 Bailey (C. J.). An Early Iron-Age "B" hearth site indicating salt working on the north shore of the fleet at Wyke Regis. [2 figures.] Proc. Dorset N.H. & A.S., 84, 1963, 132–36.

8382(a) Baker (Frederick Thomas). The Iron Age salt industry in Lincolnshire. R. & P. Lincs. A. & A.S., 8, 1959, 26–34 + 1 plate + 5 figures.

8382(b) Barnes (Alfred S.). The technique of blade production in Mesolithic and Neolithic times. Proc. prehist. Soc., 13, 1947, 101–13 + 5 figures.

8383 Booth (A. St. J.) *and* **Stone** (John F. S.). A trial flint mine at Dur-

rington, Wiltshire. [2 figures + plan. Neolithic—Early Bronze Age.] Wilts. Archaeol. Mag., 54, pp. 381–88. 1952.

8384 Bowen (H. Collin). Ancient fields—a tentative analysis of vanishing earthworks and landscapes. Brit. Assoc. 6 plates + 5 figures, pp. xii + 80. London, 1961,

8385 Britton (Dennis). Tradition of metal-working in the Later Neolithic and Early Bronze Age of Britain. Part 1. Proc. prehist. Soc., 29, 1963, 258–325 + 20 figures + 4 plates.

8386 Brothwell (Don and Patricia). Food in Antiquity (Ancient Peoples and Places). 66 photos, 43 line drawings, 3 maps. London, 1969.

8387 Brough (Bennett H.). The early use of iron. [Pp. 247–51, Britain.] J. Iron & Steel Inst., 69, pp. 233–53. 1906.

8388 Browne (B. S.). Neolithic engineering. Antiquity, 37, 1963, 140–44.

8389 Bunch (Brian) *and* **Fell** (Clare Isobel). A stone-axe factory at Pike of Sickle, Great Langdale, Westmorland. [Neolithic—EBA.] Proc. prehist. Soc., 15, 1949, 1–20 + 8 figures + 4 plates.

8390 Caley (Earle R.). Analysis of ancient metals. 184 pp. Oxford, 1964.

8391 Chaplin (Raymond E.). Animals in archaeology. Antiquity, 39, 1965, pp. 204–11.

8392 Clark (Grahame) *and* **Piggott** (Stuart). The age of the British flint mines. [9 figures + map. Grimes graves, Cissbury, etc.] Antiquity, 7, pp. 166–83 + plate. 1933.

8393 —— The introduction of metallurgy to Britain. Proc. prehist. Soc., 3, 1937, 175–76.

8394 —— Seal-hunting in the Stone Age of North-Western Europe: a study on economic prehistory. Proc. prehist. Soc., 12, 1946, 12–48 + 11 figures + 2 plates.

8395 —— Sheep and swine in the husbandry of prehistoric Europe. [P. 124, table for prehistoric Britain.] Antiquity, 21, pp. 122–36. 1947.

8396 —— *and* **Thompson** (M. W.). The groove and splinter technique of working antler in Upper Palaeolithic and Mesolithic Europe. Proc. prehist. Soc., 19, 1953, 148–60 + 6 figures + 4 plates.

8397 —— Stone Age Hunters (with

25 colour plates, 113 black and white illustrations). (Library of the Early Civilizations.) London, 1967.

8398 Clarke (Roy Rainbird). The flint-knapping industry at Brandon. [Confutes Greenwell's theory of continuity from Neolithic times.] Antiquity, 9, pp. 38–56 + 8 plates. 1935.

8399 —— Prehistoric archaeology in Norfolk since 1923, with notes on the Grimes graves flint-mines and the modern flint-industry at Brandon, and on the Iron Age date of Warham camp. Archaeol. J., 106 (1949), pp. 55–57. 1951.

8400 —— Grime's Graves. [Visit.] Trans. London & Middx. Arch. Soc., 20, p. 1. 1959.

8401 Clarke (William George). The antiquity of Grime's graves. Antiquary, 44, pp. 137–39. 1908.

8402 —— Report on the excavations at Grime's Graves, Weeting, Norfolk, March–May, 1914. *Prehistoric Society of East Anglia.* pp. 255 + 36 plates + 3 plans. 8⁰. London, 1915. [Pp. 10–134, Excavations, by A. E. Peake; pp. 134–41, Human Remains, by Sir Arthur Keith; etc.]

8403 —— Are Grime's Graves Neolithic? Proc. PSEA, 2 iii, 1916/17, 339–49.

8404 Coghlan (Herbert Henry). Some aspects of the prehistoric metallurgy of copper. [6 figures.] Antiq. J., 22, pp. 22–38. 1942.

8405 —— Some aspects of prehistoric metallurgy in the south of England. S.E. Naturalist and Antiquary, 56, 1951, 6–16.

8406 —— Notes on prehistoric and early iron in the Old World. *Pitt Rivers Museum, Oxford. Occasional Papers on technology,* 8. pp. 220 + 16 plates. 4⁰. Oxford, 1956. [A little British material.]

8407 Coghlan (Herbert Henry) *and* **Case** (Humphrey). Early metallurgy of copper in Ireland and Britain. Proc. prehist. Soc., 23, 1957, 91–123 + 5 figures.

8408 —— Research upon prehistoric copper metallurgy in England. [7 figures.] Archaeologia Austriaca, 1958 Beiheft 3, pp. 57–69. 1958.

8409 —— *and* **Willows** (R.). A Note upon native copper: its occurrence and properties (Metallurgical appendix, by R. Willows). Proc. prehist. Soc., 28, 1962, 58–67 + 3 plates.

8410 Cope (*Mrs.* E. E.). A Neolithic industry. [British ironworks at Finchampstead Ridges, Berks.] N. & Q., 156, p. 189. 1929.

8411 Crawford (I. A.). A source of charcoal in antiquity. Antiquity, 39, 1965, 139–40.

8412 Crawford (Osbert Guy Stanhope). Superimposed cultivation systems. [Diagram. Celtic and later.] Antiquity, 9, pp. 89–90 + plate. 1935.

8413 Crawfurd (John). On the sources of the supply of tin for the bronze tools and weapons of antiquity. [Negative evidence as regards Britain.] Trans. Ethnolog. Soc., N.S. 3, pp. 350–56. 1865.

8414 Cunnington (R. H.). Military engineering in the Early Iron Age. J. Brit. Archaeol. Ass., N.S. 40, pp. 206–20 + 2 plates. 1935.

8415 Curwen (Eliot) *and* **Curwen** (Eliot Cecil). Harrow hill [Sussex] flint-mine excavation, 1924–5. Report [for] Worthing Archaeological Society. [9 figures + 2 plans. Neolithic.] Sussex Arch. Collns., 67, pp. 103–38. 1926.

8416 —— *and* —— Probable flint-mines near Tolmere pond, Findon. [Plan.] Sussex N. & Q., 1, pp. 168–70. 1927.

8417 Curwen (Eliot Cecil). Prehistoric agriculture in Britain. [6 figures.] Antiquity, 1, pp. 261–89 + 5 plates: *see also* pp. 474–75. 1927.

8418 —— The old flint mines of Sussex. Sussex County Mag., 1, pp. 160–64. 1927.

8419 —— Prehistoric agriculture in Britain. Newcomen Soc. Trans., 9 (1928–29), pp. 36–42. 1930.

8420 —— Ancient cultivations. [Figure + map. Supplementary to his in 1, 26–89.] Antiquity, 6, pp. 389–406. 1932.

8421 —— The early development of agriculture in Britain. Proc. prehistoric Soc., 4, 1938, 27–51 + 9 figures + 2 plates.

8422 —— Plough and pasture. *Past and Present: studies in the history of civilization,* 4. pp. 122 + 14 plates. 8⁰. London, 1946. [21 figures.]

8423 Davidson (James Milne). The

place of Scotland in prehistoric engineering. [16 figures.] Trans. Glasgow Archaeol. Soc., N.S. 13, pp. 33–69. 1954.

8424 Day (Robert). The ancient manufacture of gold in Ireland. pp. 3. 4⁰. *n.p.*, [1890?].

8425 Dent (Anthony) *and* **Goodall** (Daphne Machin). The Foals of Epona. A history of British ponies from the Bronze Age to yesterday. pp. 305 + 33 plates + 52 text-figures + 6 maps. London, 1962.

8426 Farrar (Raymond Anthony Holt). A note on the prehistoric and Roman salt industry in relation to the Wyke Regis site, Dorset. [2 figures.] Proc. Dorset N.H. & A.S., 84, 1963, 137–44.

8427 Fell (Clare Isobel). A stone-axe factory site, Pike o' Stickle, Great Langdale, Westmorland. Trans. Cumb. & Westm. Ant. Soc., N.S. 48, pp. 214–15. 1948.

8428 —— The Great Langdale stone-axe factory. Trans. Cumb. & Westm. Ant. Soc., N.S. 50, pp. 1–14 + 7 plates + 2 maps (distribution of axes). 1950.

8429 —— Further notes on the Great Langdale axe factory. Proc. prehist. Soc., 20, 1954, 238–39.

8430 Fenton (Alexander). Early and traditional cultivating instruments in Scotland. Proc. Soc. Ant. Scotland, 96, 1962–63, 264–317 + 21 figures + 7 plates.

8431 Forbes (R. J.). Studies in ancient technology Vol. I 1955–Vol IX. Leiden, 1964.

8432 Forrest (H. E.). Sheep and early man in Britain. Trans. Caradoc & Severn Valley F.C, 7, pp. 111–15. 1923.

8433 Fox (*Lady* Aileen Mary). Neolithic charcoal from Hembury. Antiquity, 37, 1963, pp. 228–29.

8434 Fryer (W. H.). Notes on the iron ore mines of the forest of Dean and on the history of their working. Trans. Bristol & Glos. Arch. Soc., 29, pp. 311–16. 1906.

8435 Giedion (S.). The Eternal present: Vol I: the Beginnings of architecture. London, 1963. xxi + 588 pp., 500 illustrations including 20 in colour + over 100 drawings, diagrams & maps. Washington D.C., 1964.

8436 Glenn (Thomas Allen). Distribution of the Graig Lloyd axe and its associated cultures. Arch. Camb., 90 ii, 1935, 189–218 + 8 figures.

8437 Goodman (W. L.). A history of woodworking tools. London, 1964, 208 pp., 200 in-text plates and figures.

8438 Gough (John Wiedhofft). The mines of Mendip. pp. x, 269 + 2 maps. 8⁰. Oxford, 1930.

8439 Gowland (William). Copper and its alloys in prehistoric times. [12 figures.] J. Anthrop. Inst., 36, pp. 11–38 + 3 plates. 1906.

8440 —— The metals in antiquity. J. R. Anthrop. Inst., 42, pp. 235–87 + 5 plates. 1912.

8441 Graham (Angus). Spruce and pine timber in two Scottish prehistoric buildings. [Stanydale, Shetland and on west coast of Barra.] Arch. News Letter, 4, pp. 133–37. 1952.

8442 Grant (S. Maudson). Ancient pottery kilns [at Ingoldmells, Lincs.]. Lincs. N. & Q., 8, pp. 33–38 + plate. 1904.

8443 Greenwell (William). On the opening of Grime's graves in Norfolk. J. Ethnolog. Soc., N.S. 2, pp. 419–39 + 2 plates + plan. 1870.

8444 Hamilton (B. C.). Suspected flint mines on Bow hill [overlooking Kingley Vale]. [Plan.] Sussex N. & Q., 4, pp. 246–47. 1933.

8445 Hanbury (W. H.). Notes on an ancient kiln at Parwich. [Figure. ?Bronze Age.] J. Derbs. Archaeol. Soc., 67 (N.S. 20), pp. 92–95 + plate. 1947.

8446 Heizer (Robert F.). Domestic fuel in primitive society. [Skara Brae.] Jl. R. Anthrop. Inst., 93, 1963, 186–94.

8447 Helbaek (Hans). Studies on prehistoric and Anglo-Saxon cultivated plants in England. Proc. prehist. Soc., 6, 1940, 176–78.

8448 —— Early crops in southern England. Proc. prehist. Soc., 18, 1952, 194–233 + 13 figures + 5 plates.

8449 Henshall (Audrey Shore). Textiles and weaving appliances in prehistoric Britain. Proc. prehist. Soc., 16, 1950, 130–62 + 5 figures + 2 plates.

8450 Higgs (Eric S.) *and* **White** (J. Peter). Autumn Killing. Antiquity, 37, 1963, pp. 282–89.

8451 Hodges (Henry). Artifacts: an

introduction to early materials and technology. 248 pp. + 51 figures. London, 1964.

8452 Holleyman (George Albert). The Celtic field-system in south Britain: a survey of the Brighton district. [4 maps. 1000 B.C.–c. 400 A.D.] Antiquity, 9, pp. 443–54 + plate + map. 1935.

8454 Houlder (Christopher H.). A new Neolithic axe-factory in Caernarvonshire. Antiq., 34 (1960), pp. 141–42.

8455 —— The Neolithic axe-factory on Mynydd Rhiw in Lleyn. Trans. Caernarvons. hist. Soc., 21, 1960, 1–5 + 1 plate.

8456 —— The excavation of a Neolithic stone implement factory on Mynydd Rhiw in Caernarvonshire. Proc. prehist. Soc., 27, 1961, 108–43 + 18 figures + 2 plates.

8457 Huntingford (George Wynn Brereton). Ancient agriculture. [10 figures.] Antiquity, 6, pp. 327–37. 1932.

8458 —— Defences against cattle-raiding. [2 figures (Lowbury hill, Berks.).] Antiquity, 8, pp. 429–36 + 3 plates. 1934.

8459 Hutchinson (*Sir* Joseph), *Editor*. Essays on crop plant evolution. pp. 204. Cambridge, 1965.

8460 Jenkin (Alfred Kenneth Hamilton). The Cornish miner. An account of his life above and underground from early times. pp. 351 + plates. 8°. London, 1927. [Chapters 1–3, Prehistory.]

8461 Jessen (Knud) *and* **Helbaek** (Hans). Cereals in Great Britain and Ireland in prehistoric and early historic times. pp. 68. [4 figures.] K. Danske Videnskabernes Selskab, Biol. Skrifter, 3 ii. 1944.

8462 Jope (E. M.), *Editor*. Studies in building history. Essays in recognition of the work of B. H. St. J. O'Neil. pp. 287 + 32 plates + 71 text-figures. London. 1961.

8463 Junghans (Siegfried). Metallanalysen Kupferzeitlicher und Frühbronzezeitlicher Bodenfunde aus Europa (Studien zu den Aufängen der Metallurgie. Band 1). pp. 217 + 30 plates of line-drawings + 14 maps + 2 folding tables. Berlin, 1960.

8464 Kendall (Henry George Ommanney). The flint supplies of the ancient Cornish. Man, 6, pp. 150–51. 1906.

8465 —— The oldest human industry. pp. 19 + plate. 8°. London, 1910. [7 figures.]

8466 —— Grime's Graves: Floors 47 to 59. Proc. prehist. Soc. EA, 3 ii, 1919/20, 290–305 + 5 figures.

8467 —— Further excavations at the Graig Lwyd neolithic stone axe factory, Penmaenmawr. Arch. Cambrensis, 82 i, 1927, p. 141 + 1 map.

8468 Kendall (J. D.). The iron ores of Great Britain and Ireland, *etc.* pp. xvi, 430. 8°. London, 1893.

8469 Knowles (William James). Portstewart [co. Derry] and other flint factories in the north of Ireland. J. Anthrop. Inst., 9, pp. 320–28. 1880.

8470 —— Stone-axe factories near Cushendall, county Antrim. J. Anthrop. Inst., 33, pp. 360–66 + 8 plates. 1903.

8471 Lacaille (Armand Donald). Aspects of intentional fracture. (Being notes on the flaking of some rocks other than flint as exemplified by some Scottish artifacts.) [8 figures.] Trans. Glasgow Archaeol. Soc., N.S. 9, pp. 313–41. 1940.

8472 Laver (Henry). The loom during the Bronze Age in Britain. [2 figures.] Reliquary, 3rd S. 15, pp. 201–06. 1909.

8473 —— The loom in Britain during the Bronze Age. Trans. Essex Archaeol. Soc., N.S. 11, pp. 219–22 + 2 plates. 1911.

8474 Law (William). Flint mines on Church hill, Findon. [Plan.] Sussex N. & Q., 1, pp. 222–24. 1927.

8475 Lethbridge (Thomas Charles). Herdsmen and hermits. Celtic seafarers in the northern seas. pp. xix, 146. 8°. Cambridge, 1950.

8476 Lewis (A. L.). The flint supplies of the ancient Cornish. Man, 7, pp. 21–22. 1907.

8477 Lloyd (John) *F.R.S.* An account of the late discovery of native gold in Ireland. Phil. Trans. Roy. Soc., 86, 1796, 34–37.

8478(a) Lommel (Andreas). The Age of the Early Hunter. (15 colour plates and 60 monochrome illustrations) (Civilisations of the Past).

8478(b) —— German edition of above. Die Welt der frühen Jäger. Munich, 1965.

8479 Lovett (Edward). A very an-

cient industry. [14 figures.] Ill. Arch.
I, pp. 1–10. 1893.

8480 Mann (Ludovoc MacLellan).
Craftsmen's measures in prehistoric times.
pp. 25. 4°. Glasgow [1930]. [6 figures.]

8481 Manning (Charles Robertson).
Grime's graves, Weeting. Norfolk Arch.,
7, pp. 169–77 + plate. 1872.

8482 Mills (Abraham). A mineral-
ogical account of the native gold lately
discovered in Ireland. Phil. Trans. Roy.
Soc., 86, 1796, 38–45 + 1 figure.

8483 Moir (James Reid). The natural
fracture of flint and its bearing upon
rudimentary flint implements. Proc.
prehist. Soc. EA, 1 ii, 1910/12, 171–84
+ 2 plates.

8484 —— Some details of flint fracture. Proc. prehist. Soc. EA, 1 iv,
1913/14, 442–45.

8485 —— Grime's graves, Weeting,
Norfolk. *Ministry of Works*. pp. 24 + 2
plates + plan. 8°. London, 1939.
[Figure.]

8486 Mourant (A. E.) *and* **Zeuner**
(F. E.), *Editors*. Man and cattle. Proceedings of a Symposium on domestica-
tion. 166 pp. + 21 plates + 32 figures.
London, 1963.

8487 Munro (Robert). On prehistoric otter and beaver traps. [Figure.]
Antiquary, 24, pp. 9–11. 1891.

8488 Nenquin (Jacques). Salt: a
study in economic prehistory. [pp. 162
+ 5 maps + 11 plates.] Bruges, 1961.

8489 Nicholls (Henry George). Iron
making in the olden times: as instanced
in the ancient mines, forges, and furnaces
of the Forest of Dean, historically
related, *etc*. 8°. London, 1866.

8490 Oakley (Kenneth P.). Man
the tool-maker. Second edition (revised). *British Museum*. pp. 98 + 3
plates. 8°. London, 1952. [41 figures.]

8491 —— Fire a palaeolithic tool and
weapon. Proc. prehist. Soc., 21, 1955,
36–48 + plate.

8492 O'Callaghan (P.). On the primeval architecture of the British Isles.
Assoc. Archit. Socs.' Rpts., 7, pp. 97–
104. 1863.

8493 Oldham (Charles). The ancient
East Anglian industries: cultivation and
manufacture of woad and manufacture
of gun-flints. Trans. Herts. N.H.S. &
F.C., 16, 1915/17, 37–38.

8494 Payne (F. G.). The plough in
ancient Britain. [3 figures.] Archaeol. J.,
104 (1947), pp. 82–111 + 7 plates. 1948.

8495 Peake (A. E.). Notes on the
implements from the factory sites at
Peppard, Oxon. Proc. prehist. Soc.
EA, 1 iv, 1913/17, 404–20 + 6 plates.

8496 —— Recent excavations at
Grime's Graves. Proc. PSEA, 2 ii, 1915/
1916, 268–319 + 18 figures.

8497 —— Excavations at Grime's
Graves during 1917. Proc. prehist. Soc.
EA, 3 i, 1918/19, 73–93 + 5 figures.

8498 Peake (Harold John Edward).
The excavations at Grime's graves.
Antiquary, 51, pp. 375–79. 1915.

8499 Pegge (Samuel). On the hunting
of the ancient inhabitants of our island,
Britons and Saxons. [E.g. on coins of
Cunobelinus.] Archaeologia, 10, pp.
156–66. 1792.

8500 Penniman (Thomas Kenneth)
and others. Ancient metallurgical furnaces in Great Britain to the end of the
Roman occupation (with Allen, I. M.
and Wootton, A.). Sibrium, 4, 1958/59,
97–127.

8501 Percival (John). Wheat in
Great Britain. 2nd edition. pp. 132 +
80 plates. 8°. London, 1948. [Sum-
marizes discoveries of prehistoric wheat
in Britain.]

8502 Percy (John), *M.D.* Metallurgy,
refractory materials, and fuel. pp. xii,
596. London, 1875.

8503 Petch (D. F.). Iron Age salterns
at Addlethorpe and Wrangle. Rpts. &
Papers, Lincs. A. & A.S., 9, 1961, 13.

8504 Plint (R. G.). Stone axe-factory
sites in the Cumbrian fells. [2 pull-out
maps + 5 plates + 9 figures.] Trans.
Cumb. & Westm. Ant. & Arch. Soc.,
N.S. LXII, pp. 1–26. 1962.

8505 Pull (J. H.). The flint miners of
Blackpatch [Sussex]. pp. 152 + 8 plates
+ map. 8°. London, 1932.

8506 Ramsden (H. F. S.). A Sussex
stone implement; and primitive rope-
making. Sussex N. & Q., 2, pp. 102–05
+ plate, pp. 143–44. 1928–29.

8507 Rann (Ernest H.). A prehistoric factory. Bygone Suffolk, ed.
Cumming Walters, pp. 138–52. [189 ?].

8508 Read (*Sir* Charles Hercules).
On a potter's kiln at Shoebury, Essex.
[Figure. Bronze Age to Roman period.]

Proc. Soc. Antiq., 2 S. 16, pp. 40–42. 1895.

8509 Reader (Francis W.). The Red Hills or salting mounds of Essex. [4 figures + 2 plans.] Woolwich dist. Ant. Soc., Ann. Rpt., 16 (1910), pp. 29–39 + map. 1911.

8510 Red Hills Exploration Committee. Report on the excavations carried out during the years 1906–7. [10 figures. 5 plates + 3 plans of Langenhoe district; 5 plates + plan of Goldhanger. Pp. 190–203, Additional remarks on the pottery and briquetage, by Francis W. Reader.] Proc. Soc. Antiq., 2 S. 22, pp. 164–214 + 10 plates + 4 plans. 1908.

8511 Reid (Clement). Bronze and tin in Cornwall. Man, 18, pp. 9–10. 1918.

8512 Reid (W. F.). Note on a prehistoric Bronze [Age] foundry at St. Columb Porth [near Newquay, Cornwall]. J. Brit. Archaeol. Ass., 47, pp. 333–34. 1891.

8513 Richardson (Derek). A new celt-making floor at Grime's graves. Proc. prehist. Soc., EA, 3 ii, 1919/20, 243–58 + 7 figures.

8514 Rickard (T. A.). Man and metals. A history of mining in relation to the development of civilisation. 2 vol. 8⁰. New York, 1932.

8515 Riehm (Karl). Prehistoric salt boiling. Antiquity, 35, 1961, pp. 181–91.

8516 Ritchie (P. R.). Great Langdale and the Group VIII rock. Proc. prehist. Soc., 19, 1953, 230 + 1 figure.

8517 Roeder (Charles). Prehistoric and subsequent mining at Alderley Edge, with a sketch of the archaeological features of the neighbourhood. Trans. Lancs. & Ches. Ant. Soc., 19 (1901), pp. 77–118 + 2 plates + 3 maps. 1902.

8518 —— and Graves (F. S.). Recent archaeological discoveries at Alderley Edge. [Prehistoric pits and hammers.] Trans. Lancs. & Ches. Ant. Soc., 23 (1905), pp. 17–29 + map. 1906.

8519 Rosenfeld (Andrée). The inorganic raw materials of antiquity. 259 pp. + 26 plates + 30 figures. London, 1965.

8520 Ryder (M. L.). The origin of spinning. Antiquity, 38, 1964, 293–94.

8521 Salisbury (E. F.). Prehistoric flint mines on Long Down, Eartham, 1955–58. Sussex Arch. Collections, 99, 1961, 66–73 + 2 plates.

8522 Sayce (Roderick Urwick). Food through the ages. Montgomerys. Colls., 49, 1946, 266–90.

8523 Schmalz (Robert F.). Flint and the patination of flint artifacts. Proc. prehist. Soc., 26, 1960, 44–49 + 1 figure + 2 plates.

8524 Schubert (H. R.). History of the British iron and steel industry from c. 450 B.C. to A.D. 1775. pp. xxi + 445 + 26 plates + 11 maps. 8⁰. London, 1957.

8525 Seebohm (Mabel Elizabeth). The evolution of the English farm. pp. 376. 8⁰. London, 1927.

8526 Semenov (S. A.). Prehistoric technology. 211 pp. + 105 diagrams + photographs. London, 1964.

8527 Sheppard (Thomas). The origin of materials used in the manufacture of prehistoric stone weapons in East Yorkshire. [12 figures.] Trans. E. Riding Antiq. Soc., 23, pp. 34–54. 1920.

8528 —— Early Bronze measures from Selby. [One for a gallon, and one for a quart.] Yorks. Archaeol. J., 31, pp. 137–40 + plate. 1934.

8529 Simmonds (A. M.). Mesolithic pine cones. Reading Naturalist, No. 12, 1960, 33–34.

8530 Smith (Reginald Allender). On the timekeepers of the ancient Britons. Proc. Soc. Antiq., 2 S. 21, pp. 319–34 + plate + plan. 1907.

8531 —— On the date of Grime's Graves and Cissbury flint-mines. [40 figures.] Archaeologia, 63, pp. 109–58 + 3 plates. 1912.

8532 —— The date of Grime's Graves and Cissbury flint-mines. Proc. Soc. Antiq., 2 S. 24, pp. 278–81. 1912.

8533 —— On the Essex Red hills as saltworks. [2 figures.] Proc. Soc. Antiq., 2 S. 30, pp. 36–54. 1918.

8534 Smith (Robert Trow). English husbandry from the earliest times to the present day. pp. 239 + 16 plates. 8⁰. London, 1951. [Pp. 15–26 + 2 plates, Prehistoric preview.]

8535 —— A history of British livestock husbandry to 1700. pp. x, 286 + 16 plates. 8⁰. London, 1957. [Pp. 1–28, Prehistoric.]

8536 Stevens (Joseph). The flint-works at Cissbury. Sussex Arch. Collns., 24, pp. 145–65 + plate. 1872.

8537 Stone (John F. S.). Easton down, Winterslow, S. Wilts., flint mine excavation, 1930. Wilts. Archaeol. Mag., 45, pp. 350–65 + 7 plates + 2 plans. 1931.

8538 —— A flint mine at Martin's clump, Over Wallop. Papers & Proc. Hants. F.C., 12, pp. 177–80. 1933.

8539 Stones (J. W.). Grasses and man. East Derbyshire Fld. Club Year Book, 1912, 21–26.

8540 Straker (Ernest). Wealden iron: a monograph on the former ironworks in the counties of Sussex, Surrey and Kent, *etc.* pp. xiv, 487 + 3 plates + 8 maps. 8°. London, 1931.

8541 Sturge (W. Allen). The patina of flint implements. Proc. prehist. Soc. EA, 1 ii, 1910/12, 140–57.

8542 Sutherland, C. H. V. Gold. [pp. 196 + 69 plates + 11 drawings and maps.] London, 1959.

8543 Szyrma (Wladyslaw Somerville Lach). The mining tribes of ancient Britain. J. Brit. Archaeol. Ass., N.S. 9, pp. 191–96. 1903.

8544(a) Tansley (*Sir* Arthur George). The British Isles and their vegetation. 2nd edition. pp. 930 + 162 plates. 2 vol. 8°. Cambridge, 1949.

8544(b) Taylor (Brian Hope). Celtic agriculture in Surrey. [4 figures + plan.] Surrey Archaeol. Collns., 50, pp. 47–72 + 3 plates + map. 1949.

8545 Thomson (Donald F.). The seasonal factor in human culture. Illustrated from the life of a contemporary nomadic group. Proc. prehist. Soc., 5, 1939, 209–21 + 2 figures.

8546 Todd (K. R. U.). A Neolithic flint mine at East Horsley. Surrey Archaeol. Collns., 51, pp. 142–43. 1950.

8547 Tylecote (R. F.). Metallurgy in archaeology. pp. 368 + 16 plates + 74 figures. London, 1962.

8548 Wade (A. G.). Ancient flint mines at Stoke Down, Sussex. PPSEA, 4 i, 1922/24, 82–91 + 3 plates + 6 figures.

8549 Wake (Thomas). Early corn milling in Norfolk. Norfolk Arch., 28, pp. 111–16 + 2 plates. 1943.

8550 Ward (John). On Mr. Micah

Salt's diggings around Buxton. J. Brit. Archaeol. Ass., N.S. 6, pp. 209–26. 1900.

8551 Warren (Samuel Hazzledine). The flint supplies of the ancient Cornish. Man, 7, pp. 39–41. 1907.

8552 —— A stone-axe factory at Graig-Lwyd, Penmaenmawr. [76 figures.] J. R. Anthrop. Inst., 49, pp. 342–65. 1919.

8553 —— Excavations at the stone-axe factory of Graig-Lwyd, Penmaenmawr. [21 figures.] J. R. Anthrop. Inst., 51, pp. 165–99 + 3 plates. 1921.

8554 —— The Neolithic stone-axes of Graig Llwyd, Penmaenmawr. [14 figures + plan.] Arch. Camb., 77, pp. 1–32 + 2 plates. 1922.

8555 —— The Neolithic stone axes of Graig Lwyd, Penmaenmawr. [14 figures + map.] Proc. Llandudno F.C., 10 (1923–24), pp. 3–18. 1925.

8556 —— A study of comparative flaking in 1927. [*See also* pp. 22–24 (Mr. Warren's views on flaking, by J. P. T. Burchell); pp. 44–45 (The problem of Rosses flakings, by S. H. Warren); and pp. 101–03 (The necessary qualifications for the study of comparative flint-flaking, by W. J. Lewis Abbott).] Man, 28, pp. 6–8. 1928.

8557 Watson (W.). The lathe in prehistoric Britain. [2 figures.] Arch. News Letter, 1 iii, pp 5–9 1948.

8558 Weeks (William Self). Swine in Britain. [First brought in by Gwydion ab Don Mabinagion legend.] N. & Q., 12 S. 4, pp. 113–14. 1918.

8559 Willett (Ernest Henry). On flint workings at Cissbury, Sussex. [2 figures.] Archaeologia, 45, pp. 337–48 + plate + plan. 1877.

8560 Williams (Lucy). Prehistoric flint knapping at Holyhead. Anglesey Ant. Soc. Trans., 1950, pp. 94–95. 1950.

8561 Winbolt (Samuel Edward). Flint working at Wiston. Sussex N. & Q., 6, p. 57. 1936.

8562 Worth (Richard Nicholls). Ancient mining implements of Cornwall. [2 figures.] Archaeol. J., 31, pp. 53–60 + plate. 1874.

8563 Worthing Archaeological Society. Blackpatch flint-mine excavation, 1922. Report. [11 figures + plan.

Neolithic and Bronze Ages.] Sussex
Arch. Collns., 65, pp. 69–111. 1924.

8564 Wymer (J.). Localised battering
on hand axes. Archaeol. News Letter,
6, p. 139. 1958.

8565 Zeuner (F. E.). A history of
domesticated animals. pp. 560 + 356
illustrations. London, 1963.

(b) Trade and Coinage

8566 Allan (John). The Carn Brea
[Cornwall] hoard of 1749. [Gaulish
coins.] Num. Chron., 6 S. 8, pp. 235–
36. 1948.

8567 Allen (Derek F.). British tin
coinage of the Iron Age. [8 figures +
map. p. 357, 35 find spots.] Trans.
Internat. Num. Congress, London, pp.
351–57. 1936.

8568 —— British tin coinage of the
Iron Age. Trans. Int. Num. Congr.,
1936, 351–57.

8569 —— Belgic coins as illustrations of life in the late pre-Roman Iron
Age of Britain. Proc. prehist. Soc., 24,
1958, 43–63 + 10 plates.

8570 —— Three Celtic coins in
Nottingham Castle Museum. Trans.
Thoroton Society, 65 (1961), 7–9.

8571 [Anon.] Evidences of prehistoric trade between Wiltshire and France.
Wilts. Archaeol. Mag., 43, p. 336. 1926.

8572 [Anon.] Ancient British coins
found in Surrey. [From Farley heath,
etc.] Surrey Archaeol. Collns., 1, pp.
69–70 + 2 plates. 1858.

8573 Arnold (Frederick Henry). Ancient Greek coin [found at Westbourne].
[Hieron II of Syracuse, 275–216 B.C.
? brought by Phoenicians.] Sussex
Arch. Collns., 48, pp. 151–52. 1905.

8574 Baines (J. Manwaring). Ancient British coin from Hastings. [1st
c. B.C. Issued by combined Atrebates
and Regni] Sussex N. & Q., 11, pp.
66–67. 1946.

8575 Berry (M. J.). A British tin
coin from Walton-on-the-Hill. [Map.
Early 1st c. B.C.] Surrey Archaeol.
Collns., 48, pp. 151–52 + plate. 1943

8576 Black (*Sir* Frederick W.). The
Isle of Wight and the ancient tin trade.
[Pp. 505–06, bibliography.] Proc. I. of
W. N.H. & Arch. Soc., 1, pp. 494–
508. 1927.

8577 Borlase (William Copeland).
Historical sketch of the tin trade in
Cornwall from the earliest period to the
present day. pp. 72. [4 figures + 2
plans.] 8°. Plymouth, 1874.

8578 Box (E. G.). British gold coins
found near Westerham, Kent. [2nd c.
B.C. Copied from gold staters of Philip
of Macedon.] Antiquity, 2, pp. 89–90
+ plate (6 coins and "money-box" in
which found). 1928.

8579 Brooke (George Cyril). Coins
in a flint [as money-box]. [14 gold
coins—earliest imitations made in this
country of those of the Atrebates.
Dug up at Squerries, Westerham, Kent.
1st. c. B.C.] Antiq. J., 7, p. 526. 1927.

8580 —— A treasure trove hoard
from [Squerries estate], Westerham. [14
coins. Type derived from Atrebatic
staters.] Brit. Mus. Q., 2, pp. 66–67.
1928.

8581 —— A find of ancient gold
coins at Westerham. [On Squerries
estate. Hollow flint containing 14
coins, 2 Gaulish and 12 probably
British.] Arch. Cant., 40, pp. 25–28 +
plate. 1928.

8582 Buckland ([*Miss*] Anne Walbank). Necklaces in relation to prehistoric commerce. Advm. Sci., 1888,
849–50.

8583 Clark (Hyde). The tin trade of
antiquity. N. & Q., 2 S. 5, pp. 101–03,
218–19, 287. 1858.

8584 Golbert de Beaulieu (J.-B.).
Armorican coin hoards in the Channel
Islands [with implications for Britain].
Proc. prehist. Soc., 24, 1958, 201–10 +
3 plates.

8585 Cotton (Arthur R.). Ancient
British coin [from Epsom common].
[Imitation stater of Philip of Macedon.]
Surrey Archaeol. Collns., 44, pp. 138–39
+ plate. 1936.

8586 Crawford (Osbert Guy Stanhope). Prehistoric trade between England and France. L'Anthropologie. 1913.

8587 Cunnington (Benjamin Howard). A hoard of British coins found at
Chute. Wilts. Archaeol. Mag., 44, pp.
236–39 + 2 plates. 1928.

8588 Cunnington (Edward). The influence of Phoenician colonization, com-

merce and enterprise on England two thousand years ago. Proc. Dorset. Antiq. F.C., 20, pp. 113–21. 1899.

8589 Cunnington (Maud Edith). Coin of Alexander the Great found at Tilshead. [Due to pre-Roman trade with Gaul.] Wilts. Archaeol. Mag., 38, pp. 106–07. 1913.

8590 Dion (R.). Le problème des Cassitérides. Latomus, 11, pp. 306–14. 1952.

8591 Dixon (Ronald). The Cassiterides, Scilly Isles, and Lyonesse. [References.] N. & Q., 11 S. 4, pp. 286–87: 11 S. 6, pp. 88. 1911–12.

8592 Dolley (Reginald Hugh Michael). Grimsby treasure trove (1954). 4 N "Morini"–c. 70 B.C. [Figure.] Num. Chron., 6 S. 15, pp. 242–43. 1955.

8593 —— A surface find of three silver coins of the Dobuni [from Norwood farm near Chippenham]. Brit. Num. J., 28, p. 403. 1957.

8594 Draper (Frederick W. M.). Tin coins found at Sunbury. [317 coins (between 100 and 50 B.C.) and 56 pieces of pottery.] Trans. London & Middx. Arch. Soc., N.S. 10, p. 307. 1951.

8595 Edmonds (Richard). On the Phoenician tin trade with Cornwall. 8⁰. Plymouth, 1868. [*Reprinted from* Rpt. Plymouth Instn., 1867–68.]

8596 Evans (*Sir* John). On a method of casting coins in use among the ancient Britons. [Wooden moulds.] Num. Chron., 17, pp. 18–19. 1854.

8597 —— The coins of the ancient Britons. pp. 424 + 17 plates + 27 figures. London, 1864.

8598 ——The coins of the ancient Britons (with supplement). pp. xvii, 599 + 23 plates + map. 8⁰. London, 1864–1890.

8599 —— Note on a hoard of [109] ancient British coins found at Santon Downham, Suffolk. [Including 2 *dupondii* of Claudius.] Archaeol. J., 27, pp. 92–97. 1870.

8600 Fairholt (Frederic William K.). Early Celtic coins found [between Garlinge and Birdington] in Kent. [Figure.] Num. Chron., 16, pp. 184–86. 1854.

8601 Gill (H. S.). A few remarks on an ancient British coin found on Northernhay, Exeter. Rpt. & Trans. Devon. Assoc., 5, pp. 317–18. 1872.

8602 Green (Emanuel). The early tin trade and the isle of Ictis. pp. 28 + 2 plates. 8⁰. Bath, 1917.

8603 Grierson (Philip). Sylloge of coins of the British Isles, Fitzwilliam Museum, Cambridge. Part 1, Ancient British and Anglo-Saxon coins. *British Academy*. pp. xxii, 70 + 32 plates. 8⁰. London, 1958. [Nos. 1–216 + plates 1–7, British.]

8604 Grinsell (Leslie Valentine). A gold stater [of the Dobuni] from [Southfield farm, Hardwicke], Gloucestershire. Trans. Bristol & Glos. Arch. Soc., 72 (1953), p. 152. 1954.

8605 —— An inscribed gold stater of the Dobunni from King's Weston, Bristol. [Early Iron Age.] Brit. Num. J., 28, p. 175. 1956.

8606 —— A gold stater from Kingswood, Gloucestershire. [British Romic type.] Trans. Bristol & Glos. Arch. Soc., 89, pp. 143–44 + 1 figure. 1964.

8607 Hawkes (Charles Francis Christopher). English channel harbours for pre-historic trade. Proc. I. of W. N.H. & Arch. Soc., 4, pp. 257–59. 1952.

8608 Hawkins (John). On the intercourse which subsisted between Cornwall and the commercial states of antiquity, *etc*. Trans. Roy. Geol. Soc. Cornwall, 3, pp. 113–35. 1827.

8609 Hedges (E. S.) *and* **Robins** (D. A.). Examination of an ancient British bronze coin. The Numismatic Chronicle, 7th Ser. 3, 1963, 233–36 + 2 figures.

8610 —— Tin in social and economic history. pp. xiv + 194 + 32. plates London, 1964,

8611 Hoare (Edward). Ancient British coins found [near Sherborne] in Dorsetshire. [Figure.] Num. Chron., 6, pp. 200–01. 1843.

8612 —— On Celto-Irish ring-money. Num. Chron., 17, pp. 62–83. 1854.

8613 Johnston (Leonard P.). British [gold] coin found at Burpham. [200–150 B.C.] Sussex Arch. Collns., 55, pp. 305–06. 1912.

8614 Jones (Jack Davies). Prehistoric trade in Cheshire. Cheshire Historian, 4, pp. 26–30. 1954.

8615 Kell (Edmund). An account of the discovery of a Roman building in Gurnard Bay, Isle of Wight, and its relation to the ancient British tin-trade of the island. [Presence of Greek coins.] J. Brit. Archaeol. Ass., 22, pp. 351–68 + 2 plates + plan. 1866.

8616 Kent (J. P. C.). The coinage of Great Britain: the pre-Roman series. [5 figures. i. Uninscribed coinages, *c.* 100–30 B.C.; ii. The Belgic struggle for power; iii. The non-Belgic tribes of the north and west.] Arch. News Letter, 6, pp. 73–75, 86–88, 112–14. 1956–58.

8617 Laing (Lloyd R.). Coins and Archaeology. 24 pp. illustrations. London, 1969.

8618 Latchmore (Frank). Exhibition of a collection of British coins. Proc. Camb. Antiq. Soc., 7, pp. 152–56. 1893.

8619 Linecar (Howard). On a find of [317] early British tin coins at Sunbury-on-Thames. [Iron Age.] Brit. Num. J., 26 (1949–51), pp. 339–40. 1952.

8620 Mack (Richard Paston). The coinage of ancient Britain. pp. 152 + 29 plates. 8⁰. London, 1953. [18 maps.]

8621 —— The coinage of ancient Britain, 5. pp. 195 +32 plates. London, 1964.

8622 Malden (Henry Elliot). Ockley: coin of the Roman republic found. [?from early commerce with Gaul.] Surrey Archaeol. Collns., 33, p. 117. 1920.

8623 Manton (J. O.). British stater found near Derby. [150–200 B.C.] J. Derbs. Archaeol. Soc., N.S. 1, pp. 248–49. 1925.

8624 Milne (J. G.). Finds of Greek coins in the British Isles. The evidence reconsidered in the light of the Rackett collection from Dorset. *Ashmolean Museum, Oxford.* pp. 41 + 3 maps. 4⁰. London, 1948.

8625 Onslow (Richard William Alan), *5th Earl of Onslow*. Phoenicians in Britain. N. & Q., 165, pp. 101–02, 193. 1933.

8626 Peake (Harold John Edward) *and* **Fleure** (Herbert John). The way of the sea. *Corridors of time, 6.* pp. viii, 168. 8⁰. Oxford, 1929. [Pp. 106–19 (4 figures + 3 plans, British Isles).]

8627 Phillips (Charles William). British coins from North Lincolnshire. Proc. prehist. Soc., N.S. 2, 1936, 144 + 1 plate.

8628 Poole (Reginald Stuart). The Phoenicians, and their trade with Britain. J. Roy. Instn. Cornwall, 1 iv, pp. 1–10. 1865.

8629 Rickard (T. A.). The Cassiterides, and the ancient trade in tin. J. Roy. Instn. Cornwall, 22, pp. 201–51 + map. 1927.

8630 Rolfe (R. T.). The riddle of the Cassiterides. [Figure. Classical references, etc.] Metal Industry, 31, pp. 361–63, 389–90. 1927.

8631 Russell, *Miss*. Notes on plate of British and other coins, older than the Roman conquest of Britain. 7] figures. In British Museum.] Hist. Berwick. Nat. Club, 10, pp. 375–83 + plate. 1883.

8632 Sammes (Aylett). Britannia antiqua illustrata, or the antiquities of ancient Britain derived from the Phoenicians: Wherein the original trade of this country is discovered, *etc.* Vol. 1 [only]. fol. London, 1676.

8633 Seaby (Wilfed A.). Early British coins found in Berkshire and in the Silchester district. [Pp. 81–91, Inventory of 44.] Berks. Archaeol. J., 42, pp. 75–91 + 2 plates + map; 43, pp. 38–45 + plate. 1938–39.

8634 Smith (Charles Roach). Gold British, or Gaulic coins, found at Bognor and Alfriston in Sussex. Collectanea Antiqua, 1, pp. 9–12 + plate. 1848.

8635 Smith (George). The Cassiterrides: an inquiry into the commercial operations of the Phoenicians in western Europe, with particular reference to the British tin trade. pp. viii, 154. 8⁰. London, 1863.

8636 Smith (Reginald A.). Our neighbours in the Neolithic period. Presidential Address. Proc. PSEA, 2 iv, 1917/18, 479–507 + 14 figures.

8637 —— Foreign relations in the Neolithic period. Proc. prehist. Soc., EA, 3 i, 1918/19, 14–32 + 3 figures + 1 plate.

8638 Smith (Worthington George). Find of [16] British gold coins in a hollow flint near Rochester. [Figure. Evolved from gold stater of Philip II of Macedon.] Proc. Soc. Antiq., 2 S. 24, pp. 318–20. 1912.

8639 Spores (Sidney). Discovery of a Carthaginian coin near the Caburn.

[Figure. *c.* 200 B.C.] Sussex Arch. Collns., 68, pp. 57–59. 1927.

8640 Sutherland (Carol Humphrey Vivian). Ancient British gold coin [from Rochester]. [Figure. Belgic Morini. Second quarter of first century B.C.] Arch. Cant., 46, pp. 206–07. 1934.

8641 Thomas (T. H.). Some devises and ornaments upon ancient British coins. [9 figures.] Arch. Camb., 5th S. 14, pp. 167–71. 1897.

8642 Thompson (F. C.). A note on the composition of British pre-Roman "tin money". Numismatic Chronicle, 7th Ser. 2, 1962, 111–12.

8643 Tylecote (R. F.). The method of use of early iron-age coin moulds. Numismatic Chronicle, 7th Ser. 2, 1962, 101–06 + 4 figures.

8644 Voss (W. A.). British [gold] stater found at Shoebury. [*c.* 90 B.C.] Trans. Essex Archaeol. Soc., N.S. 25, p. 108. 1955.

8645 Whitbourn (Richard). Ancient British coins found in Surrey. [From Farley heath. Vericus, Epaticcus, etc.] Surrey Archaeol. Collns., 2, pp. 14–17 + plate. 1864.

8646 White (John). British coins in gold, electrum, silver and copper in the possession of John White. pp. 2 + plate. 4⁰. *n.p.*, 1773.

8647 Whitwell (J. B.). Iron Age mint, Old Sleaford. Rpts. & Papers, Lincs. A. & A.S., 10, 1964, 61.

(c) Transport

8648 Anderson (Romola) *and* **Anderson** (R. C.). The sailing-ship: six thousand years of history. pp. 212 + 20 plates. 8⁰. London, 1926. [134 figures. Pp. 54–65, Northern ships before the Romans (Brigg, etc.).]

8649 Anderson (Ruth Mary Clementi). Roads of England. Being a review . . . from the days of the ancient trackways to the modern motoring era. pp. xiv, 236. 8⁰. London, 1932.

8650 [Anon.] The ancient boat at Brigg. Walford's Antiquarian, 10, pp. 99–102 + plate. 1886.

8651 [Anon.] Ancient canoe found on the Barton section of the Manchester ship canal. [Figure. Deposited in Owens College museum.] Ill. Arch., 2, pp. 43–45. 1894.

8652 [Anon.] Dug-out canoe [discovered at Marston, near the mouth of Milton creek] in Kent. Antiq. J., 4, pp. 277–78. 1924.

8653 [Anon.] [Three] dug-out canoes in the British Museum. [3 figures.] Antiq. J., 21, pp. 74–75. 1941.

8654 Arnold (James John). Notes on Roman and British roads. Hants. N. & Q., 4, pp. 79–81. 1889.

8655 Atkinson (Alfred). Notes on an ancient boat found at Brigg. [5 figures.] Archaeologia, 50, pp. 361–70. 1887.

8656 Barber (Edward). Ancient boat in Baddiley mere [near Nantwich]. J. Arch. & Hist. Soc. Chester, N.S. 18, pp. 204–12 + plate + plan. 1911.

8658 Barnes (William). Notes on so-called Roman roads. [British origin.] Proc. Dorset Antiq. F.C., 5, pp. 69–80. 1881.

8659 Barnwell (Edward Lowry). Ancient British canoe [from Llyn Llydaw on Snowdon]. Arch. Camb., 4th S. 5, pp. 147–51 + plate. 1874.

8660 Beloe (Edward Milligen). The great fen road and its path to the sea. pp. 8. 8⁰. King's Lynn, 1889.

8661 —— On the great Fen road and its path to the sea. [Argument that it was pre-Roman.] Proc. Camb. Antiq. Soc., 7, pp. 112–30 + 2 plates + 2 maps. 1893.

8662 —— The Padders' Way and its attendant roads. [5 figures. Dates to pre-Roman times.] Proc. Camb. Antiq. Soc., 9, pp. 77–95 + 3 plates. 1895.

8663 Bird (Anthony). Roads and Vehicles (Industrial Archaeology ser., 3) illustrated. London, 1969.

8664 Boehmer (George H.). Prehistoric naval architecture of the north of Europe. [Pp. 537–42 + 2 plates + 13 figures.] Report of W.S. Nat. Museum, 1891, pp. 527–647. 1893.

8665 Boomphrey (Geoffrey). British roads. pp. 184 + 12 plates + 6 maps. 8⁰. London, 1939. [Pp. 7–32, Prehistoric roads.]

8666 Bourke (W. W. L.). Discovery of an ancient British canoe [on the bank of the Hamble, near Botley] in Hampshire. Papers & Proc. Hants. F.C., 1 iii, pp. 90–91 + plate. 1889.

8667 Brock (Edgar Philip Loftus). The discovery of an ancient ship at Brigg, Lincolnshire. J. Brit. Archaeol. Ass., 42, pp. 279–86 + plate. 1886.

8668 Bulleid (Arthur). Ancient canoe found [at British village] near Glastonbury. N. & Q. Som. & Dorset, 3, p. 121 + plate. 1863.

8669 —— Prehistoric boat, found at Shapwick, 1906. Proc. Somerset Arch. Soc., 52 (1906), pp. 51–54 + plate. 1907.

8670 —— Ancient trackway in Meare heath, Somerset. [2 figures + 2 maps.] Proc. Somerset Arch. Soc., 79 (1933), pp. 19–29 + 2 plates. 1934.

8671 Burne (Christopher). Old track from Walbury camp to Tidbury ring. Papers & Proc. Hants. F.C., 8, pp. 104–06. 1917.

8672 Chatterton (Edward Keble). Sailing ships: the story of their development from the earliest times to the present day. pp. xxi, 361. 8°. London, 1909. 130 figures, pp. 95–102 + plate. Brigg boat.

8673 Childe (Vere Gordon). Scottish tracked stones and their significance. [Early Iron Age.] Proc. prehist. Soc., N.S. 2, 1936, 233–36 + 1 figure + 1 plate.

8674 —— The first waggons carts— from the Tigris to the Severn. Proc. prehist. Soc., 17, 1951, 177–94 + 9 figures + 2 plates.

8675 Chitty (Lily Frances). Dug-out canoes from Shropshire (Cheshire, [and] from Oakley Park, Staffordshire). [Ellesmere punt, Bagley boat, Bentley harbour, Knockin canoe, Marton dug out.] Trans. Shropshire Archaeol. Soc., 44 (4th S. 11), pp. 113–33 + 7 plates +map. 1927.

8676 Clark (Edwin Kitson). On a prehistoric route in Yorkshire. [7 figures. Garrowby–Stamford Bridge– Tadcaster–Bramham.] Proc. Soc. Antiq., 2 S. 23, pp. 309–25 + 5 maps. 1911.

8677 —— Lines of communication and their relation in pre-Roman and Roman times to the valleys of tributaries of the Humber. [2 maps of prehistoric tracks and Roman roads.] Archaeol. J., 78, pp. 391–96 + plate. 1921.

8678 Clark (J. G. D.). Early navigation in North Western Europe. [Meso-

lithic.] Proc. prehist. Soc., N.S. 2, 1936, 146.

8679 Clarke (W. G.) *and* **Hewitt** (H. Dixon). An early Norfolk trackway: the "Drove" road. Proc. prehist. Soc. EA, 1 iv, 1913/14, 427–34 + 3 plates + 1 figure.

8680 —— Peddar's Way. Proc. PSEA, 2 i, 1914/15, 51–57 + 2 plates.

8681 —— The Icknield Way in East Anglia. Proc. PSEA, 2 iv, 1917/18, 539–48 + 2 plates.

8682 Clay (Richard Challoner Cobbe). Some prehistoric ways. [2 figures. Double-lynchet ways, cattle ways, etc.] Antiquity, 1, pp. 54–65. 1927.

8683 Clifford (Elsie Margaret) *and* **Simpson** (C. A.). A possible Neolithic trackway [in the Cotswolds]. [Figure + map. Bisley to Notgrove barrow.] Geography, 24, pp. 230–39. 1939.

8684 —— The Severn as a highway in prehistoric times. Trans. Bristol & Glos. Arch. Soc., 68 (1949), pp. 5–13. 1951.

8685 Cochrane (C.). Lost roads of Wessex, illustrated. Newton Abbot, 1969.

8686 Coghlan (Hubert Henry). The Old Way from Basingstoke to Salisbury plain: (—from Basingstoke to Farnham): (—from Salisbury plain to Old Winchester hill). [4 maps.] Trans. Newbury F.C., 7 (1934–37), pp. 151–59 + map; 8, pp. 43–51 + map; pp. 189–203 + map. 1937–40.

8687 —— Ancient roads and the Ridgeway. Trans. Newbury F.C., 101, pp. 6–14. 1953.

8688 Cowling (Eric T.). Rombalds Way: a prehistory of mid-Wharfedale. pp. 185. 4°. Otley, 1946. [70 figures, plates and map.]

8689 Cox (R. Hippisley). The green roads of England. Avebury, pp. xi, 22. 8°. Oxford, 1908.

8691 Cuming (Henry Syer). On the basket boats of the ancient Britons and other primitive tribes. Trans. Brit. Archaeol. Ass., 3, Congress at Gloucester, 1846, pp. 160–69. 1848.

8692 Curwen (Eliot) *and* **Curwen** (Eliot Cecil). Ancient trackways near Saddlescombe. Brighton & Hove Archaeologist, 1, pp. 36–40 + 2 plates + plan. 1914.

8693 —— *and* —— Covered ways on the Sussex downs. Sussex Arch. Collns.,

59, pp. 35–75 + 2 plates + 6 plans. 1918.

8694 Curwen (Eliot Cecil). Neolithic road, Bow Hill. Sussex N. & Q., 2, pp. 80–81. 1928.

8695 Dawkins (*Sir* William Boyd). On the pre-Roman roads of northern and eastern Yorkshire. Archaeol. J., 61, pp. 309–18. 1904.

8696 Dawson (Charles). Ancient boat found at Bexhill. Sussex Arch. Collns., 39, pp. 161–63 + plate. 1894.

8697 Dodds (W.). The Ryton dugout canoe. Arch. Æliana, 42, 1964, 285–88 + 1 figure.

8698 Dudley (Harold Edgar). The one-tree boat at Appleby, Lincolnshire. [3 figures + map.] Antiquity, 17, pp. 156–61 + plate. 1943.

8699 Duignan (W. H.). A British trackway from London to Chester. N. & Q., 5 S. 11, pp. 342–43. 1879.

8700 Dunlop (G. A.). Three dug-out canoes found at Warrington. Trans. Lancs. & Ches. Ant. Soc., 47 (1930–31), pp. 16–26 + 4 plates.

8701 Elwes (Dudley George Cary). A pre-historic boat. A lecture [to the Northampton Library Club]. pp. 36. 8⁰. Northampton, 1903.

8702 Erwood (Frank Charles Elliston). The Pilgrim's Way, its antiquity and its alleged mediaeval use, with special reference to that part of it in the county of Kent. Arch. Cant., 37, pp. 1–20. 1925.

8703 Evans (Emyr Estyn). Ridgeways in north-west Wales. Bull. Bd. Celtic Stud., 8, pp. 84–87. 1935.

8704 Evans (K. Jane). Dugout canoes found in the river Arum. Sussex Notes & Queries, 16, 6, 1965, 185–87.

8705 Feachem (Richard William de Fécamp). A dug-out canoe from Cambuskenneth Abbey. Proc. Soc. Antiq. Scotland, 92, 1958–59, 116–17 + 1 figure.

8706 Forbes (Robert James). Notes on the history of ancient roads and their construction. pp. xi, 182 + 4 tables. 8⁰. Amsterdam, 1934. [35 figures.]

8707 Forbes (Urquhart A.) *and* **Burmester** (Arnold C.). Our Roman highways. pp. xviii, 259 + map. 8⁰. London, 1904. [Figures + maps. Pp. 13–39, Pre-Roman roads.]

8708 Fox (*Sir* Cyril). Canoe discovered in Llangorse lake [Brecknockshire]. [2 figures.] Arch. Camb., 80, pp. 419–22. 1925.

8709 Godwin (Henry). Prehistoric wooden trackways of the Somerset Levels: their construction, age and relation to climatic change. Proc. prehist. Soc., 26, 1960, 1–36 + 15 figures + 4 plates.

8710 Good (Ronald). The old roads of Dorset, *etc.* pp. 101 + 6 plates. 8⁰. Dorchester, 1940.

8711 Graham (James). A pre-Roman trackway to the Sussex iron field. [11 maps in text.] Surrey Archaeol. Collns., 49, pp. 26–55 + map. 1946.

8712 Gregory (John Walter). The story of the road from the beginning down to A.D. 1931. pp. xii, 311 + 4 maps + 16 plates. 8⁰. London, 1931. [Pp. 79–91 + map.]

8713 Gresham (C. A.) *and* **Irvine** (H. C.). Prehistoric routes across North Wales. Antiquity, 37 (1963), 54–58.

8714 Grimes (William Francis). The Jurassic way. [Spread of Iron Age culture across the English lowland. 3 figures + 4 maps.] Aspects of archaeology.... Essays presented to O. G. S. Crawford, pp. 144–71 + plate. 1951.

8715 Grundy (George Beardoe). The ancient highways and tracks of Wiltshire, Berkshire and Hampshire, with the Saxon battlefields of Wiltshire. [Prehistoric ridgeways, Roman roads, etc. 79 in Wilts., 58 in Berks., 56 in Hants.] Archaeol. J., 75, pp. 69–194. 1918.

8716 —— The ancient highways and tracks of Worcestershire and the Middle-Severn basin. [Ridgeways, Romanised roads, saltways, local tracks.] Archaeol. J., 91 (1934), pp. 66–96 + 3 maps; pp. 241–68 + 4 maps; 92 (1935), pp. 98–141 + 2 maps.] 1935–36.

8717 —— The ancient highways of Dorset, Somerset, and south-west England. [Ridgeways, Roman roads (in part 2), etc.] Archaeol. J., 94 (1937), pp. 257–90 + map: 95 (1938), pp. 174–222. 1938–39.

8718 —— The ancient highways of Somerset. [Ridgeways, etc.] Archaeol. J., 96 (1939), pp. 226–97 + map. 1940.

8719 —— Ancient highways of Devon

[Ridgeways, etc.] Archaeol. J., 98 (1941), pp. 131–64 + map. 1942.

8720 —— Ancient highways in Cornwall. Archaeol. J., 98 (1941), pp. 165–180. 1942.

8721 Harley (Laurence S.). Alignments of ancient sites in Essex. New judgment on the old straight track [by Alfred Watkins, 1922]. Essex Nat., 29, pp. 63–76. 1953.

8722 Hawkes (Charles Francis Christopher). Old roads in central Hants. Papers & Proc. Hants. F.C., 9, pp. 324–33 + map. 1925.

8723 Hobkirk (Charles P.). Plagiothecium undulatum in Lincolnshire in pre-historic times. [Moss used in caulking Brigg boat.] Naturalist, 1889, pp. 4–5. 1889.

8724 Homan (W. MacLean). The eastern end of the ridgeway between Rye and Uckfield. Sussex N. & Q., 6, pp. 198–201. 1937.

8725 Hornell (James). British coracles and Irish curraghs, *etc.* 23 plates. 8º. London, 1938. [Reprinted from the Mariner's Mirror.]

8726 Hughes (T. Cann) *and* **Crouch** (Walter). Ancient boats. N. & Q., 9 S. 8, pp. 366, 507–08. 1901.

8727 Joce (Thomas James). An ancient British trackway [across south Devon]. Rpt. & Trans. Devon. Assoc., 43, pp. 262–63 + map. 1911.

8728 —— Quatpath. [Track from Great Haldon to Staverton.] Rpt. & Trans. Devon. Assoc., 63, pp. 307–10 + 2 maps. 1931.

8729 Johnstone, Paul. The Bantry boat. Antiquity, 38, 1964, 277.

8730 Kinahan (George Henry). On a prehistoric road, Duncan's Flow, Ballyalbanagh, co. Antrim. [3 figures.] J. Anth. Inst., 5, pp. 106–10. 1875.

8731 Lethbridge (Thomas Charles). Investigation of the ancient causeway in the fen between Fordy and Little Thetford, Cambridgeshire. [Figure. Late Bronze.] Proc. Camb. Antiq. Soc., 35, pp. 86–89 + plate: 36, pp. 161–62. 1935–36.

8732 —— *and others.* [Fell, C. I. and Bachem, K. E.]. Report on a recently discovered dug-out canoe from Peterborough. Proc. prehist. Soc., 17, 1951, 229–33 + 4 figures.

8733 Lett (H. W.). Canoe found at Portmore, Co. Antrim. Ulster J. Arch., 3, 251–52 + 1 figure. 1897.

8734 Lillie (H. W. R.). The North Downs trackway in Surrey. Surrey Arch. Collections, 61, 1964, 18–28 + 4 figures.

8735 MacDougall (Alexander). The equipment of a dug-out [Figure. Various dimensions.] Antiquary, 45, pp. 145–46. 1909.

8736 Margary (Ivan Donald). An Early [Iron Age] trans-wealden trackway. [From North Downs, west of Titsey park, over Limpsfield common towards Dry Hill camp, Lingfield.] Sussex N. & Q., 11, pp. 62–64. 1946.

8737 —— The early development of tracks and roads in and near East Grinstead. [2 maps.] Sussex N. & Q., 11, pp. 77–81. 1946.

8738 —— The North Downs' main trackways. [Ridgeway in addition to Pilgrims' Way.] Surrey Archaeol. Collns., 52, pp. 29–31. 1952.

8739 —— The North Downs main trackway and the Pilgrims' Way. [9 maps.] Archaeol. J., 109 (1952), pp. 39–53 + 4 plates. 1953.

8740 —— The North Downs trackway in Surrey. Surrey Arch. Collection, 62, 1965, 80–82.

8741 Moore (C. T. J.) *and others.* Probable antiquity of a boat and timber road recently found at Brigg in the county of Lincoln. N. & Q., 7 S. 2, pp. 7, 94. 1886.

8742 Mulholland (T. P. C.). An ancient track in St. Albans. Hertfordshire Countryside, 18, No. 69, 1963, 18–19 + 3 plates.

8743 Newbigin (E. R.). Notes on ancient trackways in the Rothbury district. Proc. Soc. Antiq. Newc., 4th S. 4, pp. 55–59 + plate. 1929.

8744 —— Deep trackways on Simonside hills [Northumberland]. [?Prehistoric.] Hist. Berwick. Nat. Club, 27, pp. 330–33 + plate. 1931.

8745 Noble (William Mackreth). Discovery of an ancient boat in Warboys fen. Trans. Cambs. & Hunts. Arch. Soc., 3, pp. 143–44 + 3 plates. 1914.

8746 O'Neil (Helen E.). Archaeological observations on the Jurassic Way in Northern Oxfordshire and the Cotswolds. Proc. Cotteswold Naturalists F.C., 35 i, 1966, 42–49 + 1 figure.

8747 Pape (Thomas). Ironbridge primitive canoe. North Staffs. F.C., Trans., 65, pp. 157–58 + plate. 1931.

8748 Peake (Harold John Edward). The prehistoric roads of Leicestershire. [Map.] Dryden (A.) Memorials of old Leicestershire, pp. 31–45 + map. 1911.

8749 —— Prehistoric roads. Arch. Camb., 6th S. 17, pp. 346–96. 1917.

8750 Peers (R. N. R.). Dugout canoe from Poole Harbour, Dorset. Proc. Dorset N.H. & A.S., 86, 1964, 131–34 + 3 figures.

8751 Phillips (Charles William). A dug-out boat from the Lea Valley. Proc. prehist. Soc., N.S. 2, 1936, 144–45 + 1 plate.

8752 Pickard (Ransom). Trackways near Cotley Castle. Rpt. & Trans. Devon. Assoc., 62, pp. 347–49 + map. 1930.

8753 —— Tracks to Stoke Hill camp and in St. David's parish, Exeter. Rpt. & Trans. Devon. Assoc., 63, pp. 301–06 + 2 maps. 1931.

8754 —— The central trackway of Dartmoor. [Map.] Rpt. & Trans. Devon. Assoc., 79, pp. 187–91. 1947.

8755 Pike (Gladys). Recent evidence for land transport in Europe outside the Mediterranean area before the Late Bronze Age. Bull. Inst. of Archaeol. London, 5, 1965, 45–60 + 3 figures.

8756 Pope (Alfred). An ancient British trackway [excavated in Dorchester]. Proc. Dorset Antiq. F. C.,21, pp. 105–10 + plate + plan. *See also* 22, pp. 51–52. 1900–01.

8757 Prowse (David Crawford) *and* **Worth** (Richard Hansford). On some guide-stones standing on the course of the old track from Tavistock to Ashburton. [2 maps.] Rpt. & Trans. Devon. Assoc., 66, pp. 317–22 + 2 plates. 1934.

8758 Robinson (R. S. Gavin). Recent discoveries along the Greenway. [Ridge between Golden Valley and Wye valley.] Trans. Woolhope N.F.C., 1936–38, pp. 47–49. 1940.

8759 Rudge (Ernest A.). The Puddingstone track. [The towpath, from Thetford to Nettlebed.] Essex. Nat., 30, pp. 53–55 + 2 plates. 1957.

8760 Russell (Percy). Roads [in Leicestershire.] [Pp. 57–62 + plate + map, Prehistoric tracks.] V.C.H., Leicester, 3, pp. 57–91. 1955.

8761 Sheldon (Gilbert). From trackway to turnpike: an illustration from east Devon. pp. 178 + 3 maps. 8°. London, 1928. [Pp. 3–30, Prehistoric roads.] [Pp. 31–39, The Romano-British period and the rise of Exeter.]

8762 Sheppard (Thomas). Notes on the ancient model of a boat, and warrior crew, found at Roos, in Holderness. (Additional note.) [4 figures.] Trans. E. Riding Antiq. Soc., 9 (1901), pp. 62–74 + 2 plates; 10 (1902), pp. 76–79 + 1 plate. 1902–03.

8763 —— The British boat at Brigg. Naturalist, 1905, p. 165 + plate. 1905.

8764 —— A primitive dreadnought. Naturalist, 1909, pp. 211–12. 1909.

8765 —— The pre-historic boat from Brigg [Lincs.]. [15 figures and plates. Pp. 52–54, bibliography.] Trans. E. Riding Antiq. Soc., 17, pp. 33–54. 1910.

8766 Shore (Thomas William). Old roads and fords of Hampshire. Archaeol. Rev., 3, pp. 89–98. 1889.

8767 Smith (M. Urwick). Ancient boat discovered in R. Nene bed at Peterborough. Arch. News Letter, 3, p. 120. 1951.

8768 Smith (Urban A.). Roman and pre-Roman roads in Hertfordshire. East Herts. Archaeol. Soc., Trans., 5, pp. 117–31 + folding map. 1913.

8769 Spencer (Thomas). Account of an ancient canoe found at Burpham, near the river Arun, on the property of T.S. [2 figures.] Sussex Arch. Collns., 10, pp. 147–50. 1858.

8770 Stirrup (Mark). On the ancient canoe found at Barton-upon-Irwen. Trans. Manchester Geol. Soc., 20, pp. 295–314 + plate. 1890.

8771 Straker (Ernest). A wealden ridgeway. [Rye to Uckfield. *See also* p. 224 (note by I. D. Margary).] Sussex N. & Q., 6, pp. 171–73 + map. 1937.

8772 Sweeting (H. R.). A pre-Roman road in Warwickshire. [Map.] Geography, 23, pp. 258–61. 1938.

8773 Tait (James). On the Black Dyke [Roman road] and some British camps in the West of Berwickshire. Hist. Berwick. Nat. Club, 10, pp. 307–12. 1883.

8774 Tavaré (Frederick Lawrence). Boats. N. & Q., 8 S. 6, p. 275. 1894.

8775 Taylor (Arthur). On the course of the Icknild Way as connected with Norwich castle. Proc. Archaeol. Inst., [3], pp. 17–23. Norwich, 1847

8776 Thropp (James). The pre-historic boat discovered at Brigg. Assoc. Archit. Socs.' Rpts., 18, pp. 129–32 + plate + plan. 1886.

8777 —— A description of an ancient raft recently discovered by Messrs. Judge and Cole, in a field adjoining the brickyard in their occupation . . . situate at Brigg, in the county of Lincoln. Assoc. Archit. Socs.' Rpts., 19, pp. 95–97 + plate. 1887.

8778 Timperly (H. W.) *and* **Brill** (Edith). Ancient trackways of Wessex. 216 pp. + 16 plates + 30 maps. London, 1965.

8779 Traill (William). Discovery of an ancient British dug-out canoe near Walthamstow. [Figure.] Reliquary, 3rd S. 7, pp. 54–55. 1901.

8780 Turner (Edward). British boat found at North Stoke. [Figure.] Sussex Arch. Collns., 12, p. 261. 1860.

8781 Warren (Samuel Hazzeldine). The conglomerate track. Being comments on two papers by Ethel Rudge. Essex Nat. 29, pp. 176–77. 1954.

8782 Watkins (Alfred). Early British trackways, moats, mounds, camps, and sites. pp. 41 + 18 plates + 2 maps. 8°. Hereford, 1922.

8783 —— The proof of ancient track alignment. [Figure.] J. Antiq. Assoc. Brit. Isles, 2, pp. 65–71. 1931.

8784 —— The old straight track: its mounds, beacons, moats, sites and mark stones. 1st ed. pp. xviii, 234. 8°. London, 1925. [129 figures.]

8785(a) —— The Old Straight Track, (97 photos., 33 line drawings). (1925) a reprint. Also Ley Hunter's Manual—a guide to early tracks. pp. 90, plate xv. Hereford, 1927.

8785(b) The ley hunter's manual: a guide to early tracks. pp. 90 + xv plates. 8°. Hereford, 1927. [2 figures + map + 8 plans.]

8786 Watkins (Morgan G.). The Keltic lanes of south Herefordshire. Trans. Woolhope N.F.C., 1895–97, pp. 61–64; 1905–07, pp. 269–72.

8787 Whitaker (H.). Early British trackways [in Yorkshire]. Trans. Halifax Antiq. Soc., 1929, pp. 333–50 + map. 1929.

8788 Whittingham (R. D.). British trackway at Carisbrooke. Proc. I.O.W. nat. Hist. & archaeol. Soc., 5 ii, 1957, 86.

8789 Wildridge (Thomas Tindall). The ancient boat at Brigg. Bygone Lincolnshire, 1, pp. 10–32. 1891.

8790 Wilkinson (T. W.). From track to by-pass. A history of the English road. pp. xvi, 240. 8°. London, 1934.

8791 Williamson (Reginald P. Ross). Notes on Celtic road and lynchets on Traleigh hill. [Plan.] Brighton & Hove Archaeologist, 2, pp. 54–56. 1924.

8792 Wright (C. W.) *and* **Wright** (E. V.). Submerged boat at North Ferriby. [3 figures.] Antiquity, 13, pp. 349–54 + 2 plates. 1939.

8793 Wright (E. V.) *and* **Wright** (C. W.). Prehistoric boats from North Ferriby, East Yorkshire. Proc. prehist. Soc., 13, 1947, 114–38 + 18 figures + 10 plates.

8794 —— The North Ferriby boats—radiocarbon dating [900–600 B.C.]. Proc. prehist. Soc., 26, 1960, 351.

8795 —— *and* **Churchill** (D. M.). The boats from North Ferriby, Yorkshire, England, with a review of the origins of the sewn boats of the Bronze Age. Proc. prehist. Soc., 31, 1965, 1–24 + 11 figures + 9 plates.

8796 Wylie (William Michael). Prehistoric road [of timber] near Brigg in Lincolnshire. [Map.] Proc. Soc. Antiq., 2 S. 10, pp. 110–15. 1884.

8797 Yeo (W. Curzon). Ancient boats. [In bog, near Tuam.] N. & Q., 9 S. 9, p. 194. 1902.

2. LIFE STYLE

(a) Religion

8798 Aitken (Barbara). Letter on ritual breaking of articles. Folklore, 73, 1962, 57–58.

8799 Annett (S. F.). The Long Man of Wilmington [and mythology]. Sussex County Mag., 6, pp. 402–04. 1932.

8800 [Anon.] The Long Man of Wilmington. [Figure.] Sussex County Mag., 2 pp. 497–99. 1928.

8801 [Anon.] The dolmen goddess in Sussex. [Figure. From peat bog near Piltdown.] Sussex County Mag., 2, p. 592. 1928.

8802 Black (George Fraser). Druids and druidism: a list of references. *New York Public Library.* pp. 16. 8⁰. New York, 1920. [Reprinted from Bulletin of New York Public Library.]

8803 Cassar (Paul). Phallic objects from Australia and Wales. Man, 60, 1960, 183.

8804 Christy (Miller). On a strange stone object from a Bronze Age interment [near Saffron Walden] in Essex. [3 figures. ?an idol or sacred object.] Man, 16, pp. 38–42. 1916.

8805 Coles (John M.) The archaeological evidence for a "Bull Cult" in Late Bronze Age Europe. Antiquity, 39, 1965, pp. 217–19.

8806(a) Corcoran (John X. W. P.). Ritual practices in British prehistory. [i. Neolithic; ii. Bronze Age; iii. Iron Age.] Archaeol. News Letter, 6, pp. 179–85, 213–19, 236–41. 1958–59.

8806(b) Couchman (John Edwin). Ancient carving from Piltdown. [Figure. "Dolmen goddess".] Sussex Arch. Collns., 65, pp. 206–09. 1924.

8807 Crawford (Osbert Guy Stanhope). The giant of Cerne and other hill-figures. Antiquity, 3, pp. 277–82 + 2 plates. 1929.

8808(a) —— The eye goddess. pp. 168 + 48 plates. 8⁰. London, 1957. [46 figures. Pp. 88–101 + 7 plates + 4 figures, Ireland; pp. 102–10 + 4 figures, from Ireland to Britain.]

8808(b) Curwen (Eliot Cecil). The antiquities of Windover hill [Wilmington]. [2 figures + plan. Barrows, Long Man, etc.] Sussex Arch. Collns., 69, pp. 92–101. 1928.

8809 Davies (Edward). The mythology and rites of the British druids, ascertained by national documents, etc. pp. xvi, 642 + plate. 8⁰. London, 1809.

8810(a) Dearsly (W. A. St. John). The Wilmington giant. Antiquary, 21, pp. 108–10. 1890.

8810(b) Des Moulins (J.). Antiqua Restorata, a concise historical account of the ancient druids. pp. viii, 58 + plate. 8⁰. London, 1794.

8811 Dowie (H. G.). The earliest European religion [Megalithic]. J. Torquay nat. Hist. Soc., 3, 1921, 34–40.

8812 —— The Kingsteignton idol [no dating evidence but socketed spearhead found nearby]. J. Torquay nat. Hist. Soc., 3, 1922, 137–40.

8813 Edgar (William). Beliefs concerning the soul in prehistoric Scotland. Trans. Glasgow Archaeol. Soc., N.S. 10, pp. 7–25. 1941.

8814 Eliade (Mircea). Pattern in comparative religion. pp. 484. London, 1958.

8815 Elliot (J.). Age of druidical monuments in Britain. Trans. Hawick Archaeol. Soc., 1875.

8816 Grimes (William Francis). A prehistoric temple at London airport (Heathrow). [Figure + 2 plans. Iron Age.] Archaeology, 1, pp. 74–78. 1948.

8817 Grinsell (Leslie Valentine). The breaking of objects as a funerary rite. Folklore, 71, 1961, 475–91.

8818 Hague (D. B.). A phallic object from North Wales. Man, 60, 1960, 92 + 1 figure.

8819 Hare (Henry G.). Druidism. [Derivation of the word. *See also* 8, pp. 299, 550; 9, p. 422.] N. & Q., 3 S. 9, pp. 103–04. 1866.

8820 Hawkes (Charles Francis Christopher). The limestone carving or phallus-idol [from prehistoric site at Broadway, Worcs.]. Trans. Worcs. Archaeol. Soc., N.S. 23 (1946), pp. 66–71 + plate. 1947.

8821 Hawley (William). The old temple on the plain. Hist. Teachers' Miscellany, 1, pp. 13–16. 1922.

8822 Heichelheim (F. M.). The Gogmagog giant of Cambridge. Antiquity, 13, pp. 87–88. 1939.

8823 Hornblower (G. D.). Ancient stone monuments in their religious aspect. Penzance. 1941.

8824 Jackson (John Wilfrid). A figurine from [Ballintry harbour, co. Antrim], Northern Ireland. [Figure. Early Iron Age. Mother-goddess?] Antiq. J., 14, pp. 180–82. 1934.

8825 James (D.). The patriarchal religion of Britain; or a complete manual of ancient British druidism, *etc.* pp. 100. 8⁰. London, 1836.

8826 James (Edwin Oliver). Prehistoric religion: a study in prehistoric archaeology. pp. 300. 8⁰. London, 1957. [14 figures + 3 maps + 5 charts.] Pp. 83–93 + figure + plan, Megalithic burial in the British Isles.]

8827 —— The threshold of religion. The Marett Lecture, 1958 [mention of Paviland]. Folklore, 69, 1958, 160–74.

8828 —— From cave to cathedral: temples and shrines of prehistoric, classical and early Christian times. London, 1965. 404 pp. incl. 152 photographs and 48 text-figures.

8829 Kendrick (*Sir* Thomas Downing). The Druids: a study in Keltic prehistory. pp. xiv, 227 + 9 plates. 8⁰. London, 1927. [3 figures + 2 maps + 9 plans. Pp. 212–21. Passages relating to the Druids in the works of Greek and Latin authors.]

8830 Knight (W. J. F.). Maze symbolism and the Trojan game. Antiquity, 6, 1932, 445–58.

8831 Langton (Robert). An obscure funeral custom. [Fragments of flint, broken pottery and pebbles scattered "through all the mass of the tumulus". *See also* 7, pp. 63–71 *for* Remarks on this paper by M. Colley March, *and* 8, pp. 27–33 + plate *for* Further remarks, by Thomas Kay. Trans. Lancs. & Ches. Ant. Soc., 6 (1888), pp. 58–66. 1889.

8832 Layard (Nina Frances). The Nayland figure-stone. Proc. Suffolk Inst. Arch., 15, pp. 3–8 + plate. 1915.

8833 —— Evidence of human sacrifice in Seacliff Cave, Scotland. Proc. PSEA, 7 iii, 1934, 399–401 + 2 plates.

8834 Leach, John. The smith-god in Roman Britain. Arch. Æliana, 40, 1962, 35–45 + 4 plates.

8835 Leadman (Alexander Dionysius Hobson). A British idol [in the museum] at Aldborough. [Figure.] Reliquary, N.S 8, p. 46. 1894.

8836 Ledwich (Edward). A dissertation on the religion of the Druids. Archaeologia, 7, pp. 303–22. 1785.

8837 Leroi-Gourhan (André). Les Religions de la préhistoire (paléolithique). Paris, 1964, 154 pp. + 16 figures.

8838 Le Rouz (Françoise). Les Druides. pp. 156. Paris, 1961.

8839 Lethbridge (Thomas Charles). Rediscovery of hill figures at Wandlebury. [Figure. "Belgic".] Arch. News Letter, 5, p. 192. 1955.

8840 —— The Wandlebury giants [Cambs.]. [Figure. Hill figures. *See also* pp. 304–05.] Folk-lore, 67, pp. 193–203. 1956.

8841(a) —— Gogmagog: the buried gods. pp. xiii, 181 + 4 plates. 8⁰. London, 1957. [18 figures + map + 2 plans.]

8841(b) Levien (D. V.). Wessex white horses and other turf landmarks on the Great Western Railway. pp. 15 + 12 plates + map. 8⁰. London, 1923.

8842 Lewis (A. L.). The "Nine Stones". [Use of number nine (ceremonies, gods?).] Man, 3, pp. 116–17. 1903.

8843 McKay (J. G.). The deer-cult and the deer-goddess of the ancient Caledonians. Folk-lore, 43, pp. 144–74. 1932.

8844 Mackenzie (Donald A.). Buddhism in pre-Christian Britain. pp. xx, 178 + 12 plates. 8⁰. London, 1928. [9 figures.]

8845 MacMichael (James Holden). Marriage in Celtic Britain. J. Brit. Archaeol. Ass., 48, pp. 154–66, 217–28. 1892.

8846 Mahr (Adolf). A wooden idol from [a bog at Ralaghan, co. Cavan], Ireland. [Now in National Museum, Dublin.] Antiquity, 4, p. 487 + plate. 1930.

8847 Maier (Rudolf Albert). Neolithische Tierknocken—Idole und Tierknocken—Anhängen Europas. Ber. Rom-german. Komm., 42, 1961, 171–306 + 54 plates + 11 figures.

8848 March (Henry Colley). The giant and the maypole of Cerne. Proc. Dorset Antiq. F.C., 22, pp. 101–18 + 2 plates. 1901.

8849 —— The giant and the maypole of Cerne. pp. 19 + 3 plates. 8⁰. Dorchester, 1902.

8850(a) Maringer (Johannes). The gods of prehistoric man. pp. xviii + 219, 63 plates + 57 figures. London, 1960,

8850(b) Marples (Morris). White horses and other hill figures. pp. 223 + 54 plates. 8⁰. London, 1949. [57 figures. Uffington horse, Cerne giant, Long Man of Wilmington, etc.]

8851 Mortimer (John Robert). Evidence of the religious beliefs of the ancient Britons. Yorks. Archaeol. J., 19, pp. 446–52. 1907.

8852 Napper (H. F.). The Cerne giant: a memorial of Corinaeus and Goetmagot. [Memorial of giant and conqueror.] N. & Q. Som. & Dorset, 1, pp. 140–42. 1890.

8853 Newton (William M.). On Palaeolithic figures of flint found in the old river alluvia of England and France and called figure stones, with some of the literature on the subject and an account of its progress. [18 figures.] J. Brit. Archaeol. Ass., N.S. 19, pp. 3–44 + 11 plates. 1913.

8854 Owen (A. L.). The famous Druids. Oxford. pp. 264 + 4 plates. 1962.

8855 Palmer (John). Rock temples of the British Druids. Antiquity, 38, 1964, pp. 285–87.

8856 Passmore (A. D.). The Long Man of Wilmington. [Similarity to coin of Constantius.] Sussex N. & Q., 6, pp. 219, 252 + plate. 1937.

8857 Patte (Etienne). Les Hommes préhistoriques et la religion. pp. 194 + 35 figures. Paris, 1960.

8858 Pegge (Samuel). Observations on the Stanton Moor [Derbs.] urns and druidical temple. Archaeology, 8, pp. 58–62 + plan and plate. 1787.

8859(a) Piggott (Stuart). The Uffington white horse. [Plan. ?1st. c. B.C. With other Early Iron Age representations of horses.] Antiquity, 5, pp. 37–46 + 3 plates. 1931.

8859(b) —— The Druids. 35 photographs + 30 line drawings + 1 map. (Ancient Peoples and Places.) London, 1968.

8860(a) Plenderleath (William Charles). On the White Horses of Wiltshire and its neighbourhood. Wilts. Archaeol. Mag., 14, pp. 12–30 + plate. 1874.

8860(b) —— The White Horses of the Wash of England. With notice of some other ancient turf-monuments. pp. 41. 8º. London, 1885.

8860(c) Pownall (Thomas). Observations on the Dundalk ship temple. Archaeologia, 7, pp. 149–57 + 3 plates. 1785.

8861 —— and **Ledwich** (S.). On the ship-temples in Ireland. Archaeologia, 7, pp. 269–75 + plate. 1785.

8862 Rhys (*Sir* John). Lectures on the origin and growth of religion as illustrated by Celtic heathendom. *Hibbert Lectures, 1886.* pp. xi, 708. 8º. London, 1888. [Pp. 216–34, The god of druidism.]

8863 Róheim (Géza). Cú-chulainn and the origin of totemism. Man, 25, pp. 85–88. 1925.

8864 Ross (Anne). The human head in insular pagan Celtic religion. Proc. Soc. Antiq. Scotland, 91 (1960), 10–43 + 4 plates.

8865 —— The horned god of the Brigantes. Arch. Æliana, 39 (1961), 63–85 + 3 plates + 6 figures.

8866 St. Croix (William de). The Wilmington giant. [5 figures.] Sussex Arch. Collns., 26, pp. 97–112. 1875.

8867 Shore (Thomas William). Traces of ancient sun worship in Hampshire and Wiltshire. Advm. Sci., 1886, 843–44.

8868 Sidgwick (J. B.). The mystery of the Long Man. [4 figures. *See also* pp. 574–75, 647.] Sussex County Mag., 13, pp. 408–20. 1939.

8869 Smart (Thomas William Wake). The Cerne giant. J. Brit. Archaeol. Ass., 28, pp. 65–70. 1872.

8870 —— The Cerne giant. N. & Q. Som. & Dorset, 1, pp. 178–80. 1890.

8871 Smiddy (Richard). An essay on the druids, the ancient churches, and the round towers of Ireland. pp. ix, 242. 8º. Dublin, 1871.

8872 Smith (Reginald Allender). A flint masterpiece [from Grime's Graves]. [Late Neolithic.] Brit. Mus. Q., 6, pp. 103–04 + plate. 1932.

8873 Somerset (F. R.) *4th Lord Raglan.* The temple and the house. 218 pp. + 1 drawing. London, 1964.

8874(a) Spence (James Lewis Thomas Chalmers). The mysteries of Britain, or secret rites and traditions of ancient Britain restored. pp. 256 + plates. 8º. London [1928].

8874(b) Stevens (Joseph). Turf carvings. Winchester, 1875.

8875(a) Thoms (William John). Some observations on the White Horse of Berkshire. [Figure. Uffington.] Archaeologia, 31, pp. 289–98. 1846.

8875(b) Ucko (Peter J.). The interpretation of prehistoric anthropomorphic figures. Jl. R. anthrop. Inst., 92, 1962, 38–54 + 5 figures.

8876 Williams (H. J.). On the druidical remains of the ancient Britons. Assoc. Archit. Socs.' Rpts., 2, pp. 406–422 + plate + 3 plans. 1853.

8877(a) Williams (Meta E.). Concerning druids. N. & Q., 170, pp. 218–219. 1936.

8877(b) Woolner (Diana). The White Horse, Uffington. Trans. Newbury Dist. Fld. Club, xi iii, 1965, 27–44.

(b) Art

8878 Abercromby (*Hon.* John). A Neolithic "Pintadera" (?) from [Biggin], Derbyshire. [6 figures. Portable stamp, with hole for suspension, for imprinting a pattern on the human body.] Man, 6, pp. 69–71. 1906.

8879 Aitchison (*Sir* Walter de Lancey) *bart.* Note on three sculptured rocks in north Northumberland. [Rimside Moor, Lemmington wood, and on South Middleton farm.] Hist. Berwick. Nat. Club, 32, p. 50. 1950.

8880 Allen (John Romilly). The prehistoric rock-sculptures of Ilkley. J. Brit. Archaeol. Ass., 35, pp. 15–25 + 2 plates. 1879.

8881 —— Notice of sculptured rocks near Ilkley, with some remarks on rocking stones. J. Brit. Archaeol. Ass., 38, pp. 156–64 + plate. 1882.

8882 —— The cup-and-ring sculptures of Ilkley. [17 figures.] Reliquary, N. [3rd] S. 2, pp. 65–83, 1896.

8883 —— The chevron and its derivatives. A study in the art of the Bronze Age. [41 figures.] Arch. Camb., 6th S. 2, pp. 182–229 + 12 plates (urns). 1902.

8884 Anderson (R. S. G.). Notes on two cup-and-ring stones [on Blackmyres farm in Kirkmabreck parish] in the Stewartry. Trans. Dumfries. Ant. Soc., 3 S. 14 (1926–28), pp. 140–43. 1930.

8885 [Anon.] Sculptured stone ball found at Glas hill, parish of Towie, Aberdeenshire. [6 figures. Bronze Age.] Reliquary, N.[3rd]S. 3, pp. 102–06. 1897.

8886 [Anon.] Sculptured rock at Traprain Law. Antiquity, 6, pp. 474–75 + 2 plates. 1932.

8887 Armstrong (Albert Leslie). The discovery of engravings upon flint crust at Grime's Graves. [Figure.] Antiq. J., 1, pp. 81–86. 1921.

8888 Astley (Hugh John Dakinfield). On ornaments of jet and cannel coal, on cup-and-ring markings, and on slate weapons, as characteristic of the Neolithic age. J. Brit. Archaeol. Ass., N.S. 6, pp. 164–88 + 12 plates. 1900.

8889 Baildon (William Paley). Cup-and-ring carvings: some remarks on their classification, and a new suggestion as to their origin and meaning. Archaeologia, 61, pp. 361–80. 1909.

8890 Bailey (J. B.). Notes on cup and ring-marked stones found near Maryport. Trans. Cumb. & Westm. Ant. Soc., 9, pp. 435–38 + plate. 1888.

8891 Barnwell (Edward Lowry). Marked stones in Wales. [2 figures.] Arch. Camb., 3rd S. 13, pp. 150–56 + plate. 1867.

8892 Bigger (Francis Joseph). Inscribed stone, Clonduff, co. Down. Ulster J. Arch., 4, 1898, 188 + 1 figure.

8893 Breuil (Henri). Presidential Address for 1934. [Neolithic Art.] Proc. PSEA, 7 iii, 1934, 289–322 + 46 figures.

8894 Brodrick (Alan Houghton). Prehistoric painting. pp. 37 + 44 plates. 8o. London, 1948.

8895 Brown (Gerard Baldwin). The art of the cave dweller; a study of the earliest artistic activities of man. pp. 300 + 98 plates + 4 maps. 8o. London, 1932. [70 figures.]

8896 Browne (H. B.). A "cup-and-ring" marked stone found at Aislaby, near Whitby. [Figure.] Yorks. Archaeol. J., 35, pp. 65–67. 1940.

8897 Bulleid (Arthur). Some decorated woodwork from Glastonbury lake village. [4 figures.] Antiquary, 31, pp. 109–13. 1895.

8898 Campbell of Kilberry (Marion). Two rock carvings discovered in Argyll [cup and ring and other marks]. Proc. Soc. Ant. Scotland, 94, 1960–61, 320–22 + 1 figure.

8899 Childe (Vere Gordon). Rock engravings in [Gleann Domhain, Argyll.

The gorge of the South Esk, Midlothian and Dunadd, Argyll], Scotland. [Hind, fish and stylized animal.] Antiquity, 15, pp. 290–91 + plate. 1941.

8900 Chollot-Legoux (Martha). Arts et techniques de la préhistoire. Paris. 33 pp. of text + 80 pp. of illustrations. 1962. Edition Albert Morance.

8901 Christy (Miller). The Red Crag shell portrait: a comment on the report of the committee. Proc. prehist. Soc., EA, 1 iv, 1913/14, 446–49.

8902 Cocks (William A.). The Ryton [co. Durham] cup and ring marked stone. [Figure.] Proc. Soc. Antiq. Newc., 4th S. 6, pp. 353–54. 1934.

8903 —— A cup-marked stone at Ryton. [Figure.] Proc. Soc. Antiq. Newc., 4th S. 10, pp. 87–88. 1943.

8904 Coles (Frederick R.). The recent cup and ring mark discoveries in Kirkcudbrightshire. Trans. Dumfries. Ant. Soc., 5 (1886–87), pp. 41–52 + 5 plates. 1888.

8905 —— Certain points in connection with cup and ring marks. Trans. Dumfries. Ant. Soc., 9 (1892–93), pp. 8–12 + plate. 1894.

8906 Coles (John M.). A rock carving from south-west Ireland. Proc. prehist. Soc., 31, 1965, 374–75 + 1 figure.

8907 Corrie (John M.). Cup and ring markings in West Kilbride. Trans. Dumfries. Ant. Soc., 20 (1907–08), p. 30. 1909.

8909 Cowan (H. H.). Sculptured rocks [in Northumberland]. Hist. Berwick. Nat. Club, 31, pp. 130–42 + 4 plates. 1948.

8910 Cowling (Eric T.). Cup and ring markings to the north of Otley. [3 figures + map.] Yorks. Archaeol. J., 33, pp. 291–97. 1938.

8911 —— A classification of West [Riding of] Yorkshire cup and ring stones. Archaeol. J., 97 (1940), pp. 115–24 + 2 plates + map. 1941.

8912 —— and **Hartley** (C. E.). A ring-marked rock. The Grey Stone, Harewood Park. Yorks. Arch. Journ., 40 (ii), 1960, 215–16 + 1 plate.

8913 Craw (James Hewat). An inscribed boulder from Grant's House. [?Neolithic.] Hist. Berwick. Nat. Club, 27, p. 30 + plate. 1931.

8914 Crawford (Osbert Guy Stanhope). Rock sculptures. [?natural or intentional engraving.] Antiquity, 8, pp. 463–64 + 2 plates. 1934.

8915 —— The technique of the Boyne carvings. [Neolithic.] Proc. prehist. Soc., 21, 1955, 156–59 + 3 plates.

8917 Davies (J.). A new engraved rock from Wharfedale, West Riding of Yorkshire. Yorks. Arch. Journ., 40 (iv), 1962, 622–26 + 4 plates + 3 figures.

8918 Davison (William B.). Recent discoveries at Rowting Linn (Northumberland monument no. 65). [Rock with seven cup marks, etc.] Proc. Soc. Antiq. Newc., 4th S. 6, p. 178. 1933.

8919 —— and **Davison** (Georgina T.). Report on an excavation of a sculptured rock on North Doddington farm, Doddington, Northumberland. [2 figures.] Proc. Soc. Antiq. Newc., 4th S. 6, pp. 204–05. 1934.

8920 —— A note on two cup and ring-marked rocks at Fowberry park [Chatton, Northumberland]. [2 figures.] Proc. Soc. Antiq. Newc., 4th S. 6, pp. 292–94. 1934.

8921 —— and **Davison** (Georgina T.). Incised rocks at Gled law, near Doddington, Northumberland. Proc. Soc. Antiq. Newc., 4th S. 7, pp. 85–88 + 3 plates. 1935.

8922 —— Sculptured rocks, West Horton [Northumberland]. Hist. Berwick. Nat. Club, 30, p. 37. 1938.

8923 —— Sculptured cist cover from West Horton. (Sculptured rocks at West Horton, Chatton.) Proc. Soc. Antiq. Newc., 4th S. 8, pp. 218–21. 1938.

8924 Deas (George B.). The sculpturings of the caves of Wemyss [Fife]. [4 figures.] Rothmill Quart. Mag., Oct. 1948, pp. 1–7. 1948.

8925 Dymond (Charles William). Cup-markings on Burley moor [Ilkley, Yorkshire]. J. Brit. Archaeol. Ass., 36, pp. 413–17 + plan. 1880.

8926 Edwardson (A. R.). A spirally decoratdd object from Garboldisham. Antiquity, 39, 1965, p. 145.

8927 Evans (Joan). The history of art in Gloucestershire. Trans. Bristol & Glos. Arch. Soc., 81, pp. 5–9. 1962.

8928 Everitt (C. H.). Did Britons paint? J. Antiq. Assoc. Brit. Isles, 2, pp. 85–88. 1931.

8929 Farrar (Raymond Anthony Holt). A Romano-British rider relief from Whitcombe. [1 figure.] Proc. Dorset N.H. & A.S., 86, 1964, 103–04.

8930 Feachem (R. W.). Incised symbols from an Iron Age house. Antiquity, 38, 1964, pp. 56–57.

8931 Ferguson (Spencer C.). A cup-and-ring marked stone from Honey Pots farm, near Edenhall [Cumb.]. [Figure.] Trans. Cumb. & Westm. Ant. Soc., N.S. 10, pp. 507–08 + plate. 1910.

8932 Fox (*Sir* Cyril). Pattern and purpose: a survey of early Celtic art in Britain. Cardiff, 1958, pp. xxix + 160, 83 figures + 80 plates.

8933 Garfitt (G. A.). On a recent discovery of rock sculptures [on Eyam moor and at Great Hucklow] in Derbyshire. [3 figures.] Man, 21, pp. 35–37. 1921.

8934 —— Rock sculptures in Derbyshire. Trans. Hunter Arch. Soc., 2, pp. 182–85 + 1 plate. 1924.

8935 Gow (James Macintosh). Notes on cup-marked stones, old burying-grounds, and curing or charm stone, near St. Fillans, Perthshire. Archaeol. Rev., 2, pp. 102–04. 1889.

8936 Hall (George Rome). On some cup-incised stones, found in an ancient British burial-mound at Pitland hills, near Birtley, North Tynedale. Arch. Æl., N.[2nd.]S. 12, pp. 268–83 + 2 plates. 1887.

8937 —— A possible meaning for pre-historic cup-marked stones. Arch. Æl., N.[2nd.]S. 15, pp. 43–48. 1892.

8938 Hardy (James). On the incised rocks at Morwick. With notices and illustrations by Sarah Dand. Hist. Berwick. Nat. Club, 10, pp. 343–47 + 4 plates. 1883.

8939 Hawkes (Charles Francis Christopher). An engraved La Tène bronze from Arundel Park. [Figure.] Antiq. J., 16, pp. 103–05. 1936.

8940 Hawkes (Jacquetta). A prehistoric carved stone from Arncliffe in Littondale [Yorks.]. [Figure. Bronze Age.] Man, 34, pp. 189–90. 1934.

8941 Hemp (Wilfrid James). Cup markings on rock at Treflys, Caernarvonshire. Arch. Camb., 93 i, 1938, 141 + 3 figures.

8942 —— Cup-marked stone in Caer-narvonshire. Arch. Camb., 99 ii, 1947, 290.

8943 —— A cup-marked stone at Glyndyfrdwy. Arch. Camb., 109, 1960, 181 + plate.

8944 Henry (Françoise). L'Art Irlandais. Pierre qui-Vine, 308 pp., 134 plates (15 in colour) + 34 figures. Yonne, 1963.

8945 Heywood (Nathan). The cup and ring stones on the Panorama rocks, near Rombald's moor, Ilkley, Yorkshire. Trans. Lancs. & Ches. Ant. Soc., 6 (1888), pp. 127–28 + 2 plates. 1889.

8946 Howse (Richard). On the so-called sculptured rocks of north Northumberland. Nat. Hist. Trans. N'umberland & Durham, 7, 1878–80, 365–76.

8947 Hughes (Reginald). The art of pre-Roman Britain. [9 figures.] Traill (H. D.) and Mann (J. S.), Social England, 1, pp. 122–36. 1901.

8948 Isle of Man, *Official Information Department*. A sculptured stone from [near Ramsey], Man. [Early Bronze Age.] Antiquity, 5, pp. 359–60 + plate. 1931.

8949 Johnstone (William). Creative art in Britain from the earliest times to the present. pp. xxvi, 291. 4⁰. London, 1950.

8950 Kendall (Henry George Ommaney). Two chalk carvings from Grime's Graves. [Figure.] Antiq. J., 4, pp. 46–47. 1924.

8951 Kendall (Hugh Percy). Cup and ring stone [on Stoup Brow moor, near Ravenscar]. Yorks. Archaeol. J., 33, pp. 120–21 + plate. 1938.

8952 Kermode (Philip Moore Callow) An engraved stone pillar from [near Ramsey], the Isle of Man. [2 figures. Bronze Age.] Antiq. J., 9, pp. 372–75. 1929.

8953 Kinahan (George Henry). On an inscribed rock surface at Mevagh, Rosguile, county Donegal, Ireland. (Barnes' inscribed dallâns, county Donegal.) [Cups, circles and furrows.] J. Anthrop. Inst., 18, pp. 170–71, 171–74 + plate. 1888.

8954 Kirkwood (James). Note on cup and ring markings at Craigenfeoch, Renfrewshire. [Figure.] Trans. Glasgow Archaeol. Soc., N.S. 9, pp. 81–82. 1938.

8955 Kühn (Herbert). Die Felsbilder

Europas. Vienna, 1952. pp. 322 + 3 plates + 144 figures.

8956 Kühn (Herbert). The rock pictures of Europe. Illustrated, a re-issue. London, 1966.

8957 Lacaille (Armand Donald). A cup-marked sarsen near Marlborough, Wiltshire. Archaeol. News Letter, 7 vi, 1962, 123–29 + 1 plate + 2 figures.

8958 —— Cup-markings in North Drymen, Stirlingshire. [MBA.] Proc. Soc. Ant. Scotland, 96, 1962–63, 351–352 + 1 plate.

8959 Lamb (George). Cup-marked stone found [on the Braid Hills golf course] near Edinburgh. [2 figures.] Reliquary, N.[3rd]S. 3, pp. 231–32. 1897.

8960 Leeds (Edward Thurlow). Celtic art in Britain. [Late Bronze Age onwards.] Man, 32, pp. 205–07. 1932.

8961 —— Celtic ornament in the British Isles down to A.D. 700. pp. xix, 170. 8º. Oxford, 1933. [43 plates and figures. Pp. 63–85, Early British numismatic art.]

8962 Le Page (John). A Baildon moor sculptured stone. [Cup and ring. ?Mid-Bronze Age.] Bradford Antiquary, 9 (N.S. 7), p. 276 + plate. 1952.

8963 Leroi-Gourhan (André). The art of prehistoric man in Western Europe. London, 1968. pp. 543, 739 figures + 56 charts.

8965 Liddell (Dorothy M.). New light on an old problem. [Use of bird bones for decorating Neolithic pottery.] Antiquity, 3, pp. 283–91 + 10 plates. 1929.

8966 Liversidge (Joan). Cirencester: Romano-British wall-paintings from the Dyer Court excavations, 1957. Trans. Bristol & Glos. Arch. Soc., 81, 1962, 41–50 + 8 figures + 2 plates.

8967 Lommel (Andreas). Prehistoric and primitive men. (Landmarks of the World's Art.) London, 1966. pp. 176, 160 colour plates + 105 black and white figures.

8968 Mann (Ludovic MacLellan). The archaic sculpturings of Dumfries and Galloway; being chiefly interpretations of the local cup and ring markings, *etc.* [14 figures.] Trans. Dumfries. Ant. Soc., 3 S. 3 (1914–15), pp. 121–66 + 6 plates. 1915.

8970 Matheson (Colin). Hippocam-pus as a *motif* in Celtic art. Arch. Camb., 86 i, 1931, 179–81 + 2 figures.

8971 Megan (J. V. S.). A bronze bull's head in Glasgow and its affiliations. [Iron Age.] Proc. Soc. Antiq. Scotland, 91, 1960, 179–82 + 1 plate.

8972 —— A bronze mount from Mâcon: a miniature masterpiece of the Celtic Iron Age reappraised. [Reference to Rose Ash Mount and other parallels.] Ant. J., 42, 1962, 24–29 + 1 plate.

8973 Miller (Edward). An unrecorded cup-and-ring marked rock on Jenny's lantern hill. [Figure.] Proc. Soc. Antiq. Newc., 4th S. 11, pp. 281–82. 1949.

8974 Morris (Rupert Hugh). Notes on the spiral ornament in Wales. [6 figures.] Arch. Camb., 6th S. 12, pp. 249–62. 1912.

8975 Munro (W. A.). [Stone with incised figures] at Denholm Hill. [Figure.] Trans. Hawick Archaeol. Soc., 1905, p. 32. 1905.

8976 Navarro (José Maria de). The Celts in Britain and their art. [8 figures.] The Heritage of early Britain, pp. 56–82. 1952.

8977 Newbigin (A. J. W.). A note on cup-marked stones. Arch Æl., 4th S. 10, pp. 206–09. 1933.

8978 Newbigin (Edward Richmond). Cup and ring markings at Tod Crag. Proc. Soc. Antiq. Newc., 4th S. 4, pp. 86–88 + plate. 1929.

8979 —— Incised rocks near Lordenshaws camp. Hist. Berwick. Nat. Club, 27, pp. 327–29. 1931.

8980 —— Notes on a series of unrecorded incised rocks at Lordenshaws [camp, Northumberland]. Arch. Æl., 4th S. 9, pp. 50–67 + 5 plates. 1932.

8981 —— The inscribed rocks of Doddington district. [2 figures.] Proc. Soc. Antiq. Newc., 4th S. 6, pp. 68–71. 1933.

8982 —— A cup-marked stone from Cartington. Proc. Soc. Antiq. Newc., 4th S. 8, pp. 114–16 + plate. 1937.

8983 —— Newly discovered cup-markings in Northumberland. Hist. Berwick. Nat. Club, 30, pp. 33–36. 1938.

8984 —— Note on a newly discovered large group of marked rocks near Millstone burn. Proc. Soc. Antiq. Newc., 4th S. 8, pp. 231–32. 1938.

8985 Newbigin (Nancy). Cup marked rocks on Chirnells moor, Rothbury. [3 figures + plan.] Proc. Soc. Antiq. Newc., 4th S. 6, pp. 345–49. 1934.

8986 Peers (*Sir* Charles Reed). Cantor lectures on ornament in Britain. *Royal Society of Arts.* pp. 39. 8°. London, 1926. [Pp. 3–15 (with 11 figures), Prehistoric.]

8988 Piggott (Stuart) *and* **Daniel** (Edmund Glyn). A picture book of ancient British art. pp. ix, 27 + 73 figures on plates. 4°. Cambridge, 1951.

8989 Pond (W.). Incised stones found [at Great Wyrley], near Cannock. [?Palaeolithic art.] B'ham. Arch. Soc., Trans., 54 (1929–30), pp. 69–70 + 2 plates. 1932.

8990 Powell (Thomas George Eyre). Megalithic and other art: centre and west [refers Boyne culture]. Antiq., 34 (1960), pp. 180–90.

8991 —— Prehistoric art. [World of Art Library.] London, 1966. pp. 286, 263 illustrations (47 in colour), + 1 map.

8992 Quine (John). Early scribed rocks of the Isle of Man, with notes on the early pottery of the island. [5 figures.] Proc. Camb. Antiq. Soc., 24, pp. 77–94. 1922.

8993 Raistrick (Arthur). "Cup and ring" marked stones of West Yorkshire. [Figure and map.] Yorks. Archaeol. J., 32, pp. 33–42. 1934.

8994 Rhodes (J. F.). Romano-British sculptures in the Gloucester City Museum, 1964.

8995 Russell, *Miss.* Some rock-cuttings in Northumberland. [3 figures.] J. Brit. Archaeol. Ass., N.S. 2, pp. 206–214. 1896.

8996 Sieveking (Gale de G.). Exhibition of masterpieces of prehistoric Europe and Roman Britain. Brit. Mus. Q., 26, 3/4, 1963, 118–23.

8997 Simpson (*Sir* James Young) *bart.* On the cup-cuttings and ring-cuttings on the Calder stones near Liverpool. Trans. Hist. Soc. Lancs. & Ches. [7], N.S. 5, pp. 257–62 + 2 plates. 1865.

8998 —— On ancient sculpturings of cups and concentric rings, etc. pp. 148 + 32 plates. Proc. Soc. Antiq. Scot., 6, Appendix. 1867.

8999 Smith (Reginald Allender). A bronze fragment of Late Keltic engraving [from Urswick Stone Walls, Furness]. [4 figures.] Trans. Cumb. & West. Ant. Soc., N.S. 7, pp. 95–99. 1907.

9000 —— Examples of Mesolithic art. [Engraved deer-antler from Romsey and ox-bone implement from the Thames.] Brit. Mus. Q., 8, pp. 144–45 + plate. 1934.

9001 Stevenson (Robert Barron Kerr). Incised symbols from an Iron Age house. Antiquity, 38 (1964), 137–38.

9002 Stopes (Marie Carmichael). The Red Crag shell portrait. Proc. prehist. Soc. EA, 1 iii, 1912/13, 323–32 + 1 plate.

9003 Stuart (John). Note on incised marks on one of a circle of standing stones in the island of Lewis. Proc. Soc. Antiq. Scot., 3, pp. 212–14 + plate. 1862.

9004 Tate (George). The ancient British sculptured rocks of Northumberland and the eastern Borders, with notices of the remains associated with these sculptures. [5 figures.] Hist. Berwick. Nat. Club, 5, pp. 137–79 + 12 plates. 1864.

9005 Taylor (Michael Waistell). On a cup-marked stone found at Redhills, near Penrith. Trans. Cumb. & Westm. Ant. Soc., 6, pp. 110–18 + plate. 1883.

9006 Thomas (Anthony Charles). An inscribed pebble from Porthmeor, west Penwith. [Figure. Now in Wayside Museum, Lennor.] Proc. West Cornwall, F.C., N.S. 1, pp. 166–67. 1956.

9007 —— The animal art of the Scottish Iron Age and its origins. [16 figures + 2 plates.] Arch. J., 118, 1961, 14–64.

9008 —— The interpretation of the Pictish symbols [giving prehistoric ancestry]. 3 appendices + 10 figures + 2 plates. Arch. J., 120, 1963, 31–97.

9009 Thomas (T. H.). [Cup-marked stone near Rhiwderin, Monmouthshire.] [2 figures.] Arch. Camb., 5th S. 12, pp. 233–35. 1895.

9010 Thornley (*Canon*). Ring-marked stones at Glassonby and Maughanby. Kirkoswald. [Figure.] Trans. Cumb. & Westm. Ant. Soc., N.S. 2, pp. 380–83 + 2 plates. 1902.

9011 Toynbee (Jocelyn Mary Catherine). Art in Britain under [and before] the Romans. 8°. Oxford, 1964.

9012 Truckell (Alfred Edgar). A group of separate cup-and-ring marked slabs in the Cairnholy–Auchenlarie District. Trans. Dumfries & Galloway, 40, 1961/62, 192–95 + 8 figures.

9013 Walton (R. H.), *Capt.* A cup-marked stone in the Roman town of Corstopitam. Hist. Berwicks. Naturalists Club, 36 i, 1962, 57 + 1 plate.

9014 —— A group of cup-and-ring marked rocks on Gorwick Sands. Hist. Berwicks. Naturalists Club, 36 i, 1962, 58–59 + 2 plates.

9015 Watkins (Alfred). Cup-marked stone, Llannerch, Radnor Forest. Arch. Camb., 83 ii, 1928, 349–50 + 1 figure.

9016 —— Cup-marked stones, Here-fordshire and Radnorshire. J. Brit. Archaeol. Ass., N.S. 40, pp. 160–61. 1935.

9017 —— Cup-marked stone at Tillington, Hereford. Trans. Woolhope N.F.C., 1933–35, pp. 45–47 + 2 plates. 1938.

9018 Webley (D. P.). Harold's [cup-marked] stones, Trellech (Mon.). Bull. Bd. Celtic Stud., 18, p. 76. 1958.

9019 Wilson (Thomas). Prehistoric art: on the origin of art as manifested in the works of prehistoric man. 8°. Washington, 1898. pp. 664 + 74 plates + 325 figures.

9020 Woodward (Arthur Smith). On an apparently palaeolithic engraving on a bone from Sherborne (Dorset). J. Geol. Soc., 70, 1914, 100–03 + 1 figure.

INDEX

INDEX

A. (L. A.), **7512**
Abbevillian (Chellian), **831, 877, 1037, 4777, 4779, 5591, 5602(b), 5652, 5725, 5873, 5875, 5881, 6039, 6103, 6126, 6233, 6321**
Abbott (G. Wyman), **4581**
Abbott (W. J. Lewis), **804, 1989, 4582, 5490–92, 5609, 8556**
Abdon Burf Camp (Salop), **4198, 4253**
Abell (Henry Francis), **805(a)**
Aber circles (Carn.), **3512**
Abercromby (John) *hon.*, **6654–6, 8097, 8284, 8878**
Aberdeen, University Museum of Anthropology, **7055**
Aberdeenshire (field archaeology), **1802, 1852, 1856, 1884–5, 1904, 1909, 1916**; (specific sites—burials), **3102, 3123, 3128, 3136, 3198, 3210**; (specific sites—circles, henges, etc.), **3524, 3621, 3632, 3641, 3659(a) & (b), 3672, 3711, 3716**; (specific sites—forts, camps, etc.), **4536, 4570**; (all other sites), **5464, 5486**; (material finds—stone), **6641(b)**; (material finds—metal), **7799**; (associated finds, museum and private collections), **8124, 8136, 8336**; (art), **8886**
Aberfeldy stone circle (Perth), **3616**
Aberg (F. A.), **1028, 8365**
Aberystwyth (Cards.), **4384–5, 4387–91, 4507, 4513(b), 5411–12, 6986**
Aberystwyth, University College Museum, **6538, 7046**
Abingdon (Berks.), **2146, 3798, 4753–4**
Abinger (Surrey), **4751**
Acheulean, **83, 879, 940, 941, 942, 1035, 1036, 1057, 1092, 4851, 4867, 4875, 5094–5, 5514, 5516, 5532, 5543, 5562, 5591, 5614, 5616, 5643, 5644, 5661, 5724, 5726, 5741, 5743, 5757, 5762, 5795, 5834, 5845, 5870, 5872, 5874, 5880, 5882–3, 5886, 5896, 5904, 5912–14, 5917, 5942, 5947, 5949, 5958, 5961, 5983, 5989, 5998, 6014, 6055–6, 6075, 6087, 6103, 6142, 6176, 6229, 6233, 6238, 6249, 6259–60, 6442, 6521, 6650, 8045, 8109, 8141, 8210**

Acklam Wood (Yorks.) [round barrows], **2767**
Acland (H. D.), **90**
Acland (John Edward), **1080, 2213, 8114**
Adams (Edward Amery), **8093**
Adams (John), **1990–1**
Addington (Kent), **998, 1995–6, 2000, 2012, 2018, 2046**
Addy (Samuel Oldall), **1394(b)**
Addyman (P. V.), **6944**
Ade (Charles), **6693**
Ade (John Stephen), **6694**
Adlestrop Hill (Glos.), **2487, 2506**
Adorian (Paul), **2214, 4894**
Adzes, **5639, 5785, 6017, 6167, 6171, 6189, 6269, 6316, 6362, 7325, 8210**
Agriculture, **481, 482, 506, 512, 801, 4704–6, 4715–19, 5089–90, 5096, 5439, 8383, 8384, 8386, 8417, 8419–22, 8430, 8447–8, 8457, 8459, 8493, 8501, 8525, 8539, 8544(b), 8549**
Ahier (Philip), **4264**
Ainstable (Cumb.), **2706, 6979, 7568**
Airne (C. W.), **91**
Airy (Wilfrid), **8366**
Aitch (Ian), **3281**
Aitchison (*Sir* Walter de Lancey), *bart.*, **8879**
Aitken (Barbara), **8798**
Aitken (Martin Jim), **438, 439, 440, 442, 443, 444, 445, 446, 447, 544, 3785**
Aitken (W. G.), **3081**
Akerman (John Yonge), **1992–5, 2215, 9099**
Alberbury (Salop), **2467, 2502**
Alcock (Elizabeth), **2598**
Alcock (Leslie), **528, 670, 2598, 3486, 4348–53, 6283, 7623**
Aldbourne (Wilts.) [settlement and round barrow], **2355**
Aldreth Causeway (Camb.), **1070(b)**
Aldwick, Barley (Herts.), **456, 4664–5, 4740, 4742, 4829, 6809, 7943–4**
Alexander (E. M. M.), **5223, 5610**
Alexander (*Sir* J. E.), **3082**
Alexander (John), **448, 1995–6, 2216–18, 4583–4, 7098**
Alfred's Castle, Ashbury (Berks.), **3809**

Entry No.	Corrections
2	Menhios *to read* Menhirs
6(b)	1975 *to read* 1976
82	Thresfall *to read* Threlfall
103(b)	N.F. 2.50 *to be deleted*
125	Closing bracket to be inserted after (Max
138	Beaver *to read* Beaker
233	Halstalt -und *to read* Halstatt- und
277	Umlaut to be deleted from Röm.
	ihne Bedeutung *to read* ihre Bedeutung
292	Cauford cliffs *to read* Canford cliffs
296	winkle pens *to read* winkle pins
313	Megan (J.V.S.) *to read* Megaw (J.V.S.)
360	Hyphen between using and agriculture to be deleted
361	Title British prehistory to come before *Home University Library*, 205
394	The Aisted *to read* The Aisled
418	Indo-Scythiae *to read* Indo-Scythians
465	*Editor to read Editors*
717	Leslie V. Grindsell's *to read* Leslie V. Ginsell's
753	Megan, (J.V.S.) *to read* Megaw, (J.V.S.)
842	Sauveberrian *to read* Sauveterrian
940	Arch. Cantiane *to read* Arch Cantiana
941	staker *to read* stater
1044	A.W.G. Lorother *to read* A.W.G. Lowther
1082	Hyphen to be deleted from middle of word Neolithic
1154	*Editor to read Editors*
1159	Granborne *to read* Cranborne
1330	Kist ovens and *to read* kists, ovens and
1670	Author's name *to read* Evans (T. Lodwig)
1761	Name of journal in reference is Brycheiniog
1823	Lougherew hills *to read* Loughcrew hills
1936	Crannoges *to read* crannogs
2012	Coldvane farm *to read* Coldrum farm
2028	Full point to be deleted after un-urned
2088	Reference *to read* Q.J. Suffolk etc
2238	Grimsell's barrow *to read* Grinsell's barrow
2239	,, ,, ,, ,, ,, ,,
2253	,, ,, ,, ,, ,, ,,
2333	Collingbourne Dacis *to read* Collingbourne Ducis
2389	A heatherworker's *to read* A leatherworker's
2453	Author's first name Jonothan *to read* Jonathan
2459	Avenis *to read* Avening
2488	Remains on. . . *to read* Remains of
2789	Beater *to read* beaker
2828	Bryn Celli Dam *to read* Bryn Celli Ddu
2860	Comma to be deleted after Breos
2935	Caper Garmon *to read* Capel Garmon
3105	Ronsay *to read* Rousay
3115	Cadlingford *to read* Carlingford
3160	Clara *to read* Clava
3219	Clave *to read* Clava
3231	Author's name *to read* Young
3283	Author's name *to read* Annable
3300	The word books to be inserted after published

3614	Calbernish *to read* Callernish
3647	Reference *to read* North Staffs. N.F.C.
3780) 3781)	Arther *to read* Arthur
3872	Hambledown *to read* Harbledown
4035(a)	Bugbury *to read* Buzbury
4067	,, ,, ,, ,,
4219	Oxenton *to read* Oxonton
4241) 4212) 4213)	Castle-au-Dinas *to read* Castle-an-Dinas
4383	Part in square brackets *to read* i. Moel Fenlli (multival.); ii. Moel Gaer (multival.), part of Moel Famma; iii. Moel Arthur (multival.);
4425	Moel Hiraddng *to read* Moel Hiraddug
4429	Braich y Ddinas *to read* Braich y Dinas
4482	,, ,, ,, ,, ,, ,, ,, ,,
4483	,, ,, ,, ,, ,, ,, ,, ,,
4588	Antignacian *to read* Aurignacian
4624	Belgicte si *to read* Belgic site
4639	Shippen hill *to read* Shippea hill
4641	,, ,, ,, ,, ,, ,,
4646	Delete so between also *and* Levallois
4799	Magdalaine *to read* Magdalenian
4848	Author's name *to read* Sieveking (Gale de G.)
4880	Mosvinian *to read* Mousterian
5048	Agilian *to read* Azilian
5182) 5183)	Craswell *to read* Creswell
5197	Note in square brackets *to read after comma*: some use in Neolithic/BA.
5243	Seamur *to read* Seamer
5426	Both authors *to read* Megaw
5434	Ronsay *to read* Rousay
5450) 5454)	Delete e from crannogs in both items
5644	Delete a from Coambe (*to read* Combe Rock)
5716	A palaeolithic *to read* A palaeolith
5729	Close square brackets after Thames pick, and *delete* to me!
5738	Cop round barrow to have capital C
5839	trancher *to read* tranchet
5919	Sauvelerrian *to read* Sauveterrian
5942	Implement, ferous *to read* implementiferous
6031	Pict *to read* pick
6090	Corpe Castle *to read* Corfe Castle
6147	Ventour *to read* Ventnor
6525	Manorbler *to read* Manorbier
6526	Nals Head *to read* Nabs Head
6621	Tardenoisieus *to read* Tardenoisien
6737	Pennaut *to read* Pennant
6878	Storry Cross *to read* Stoney Cross
6903	Winfaith Heath *to read* Winfrith Heath
6934	Author's name *to read* Shortt (Hugh de Sausmarez) also in Items 7336, 7412, 8321
7046	Author's name *to read* Peate (Iorwerth Cyfeiliog) also in Items 8295 and in index

7101) 7104)	Second author *to read* Megaw (J.V.S.)
7136	Second line *to read* situlen aus dem. . . .
7138) 7139)	Authors' names *to read* Megaw (B.R.S.) and Megaw (J.V.S.) respectively
7174	Brighton laps *to read* Brighton loops
7210	Author's name *to read* Cocks (Heneage)
7443	Builwas *to read* Buildwas
7643	Guilshield *to read* Guilsfield
8162	Title *to read* (Inventaria)archaeologica
8211	Author's name *to read* Garrood
8231	denarians *to read* denarius
8330	Author's name *to read* Smith (Worthington George)
8366	Proc. hist. *to read* Proc. inst.
8436	Graig Lloyd *to read* Graig Lwyd
8558	Mabinagion *to read* Mabinogian
8665	Author's name *to read* Boumphrey
8689	Author's name *to read* Hipbisley
8704	river Arum *to read* river Arun
8971	Megan *to read* Megaw
Index	Azilian, second reference to be inserted 5416
"	Bishop's Hull (Somerset) first item 1356
"	Buckets (bronze) handles/mouths *to read* handles/mounts
"	Coquetdale (Nhbd) first item *to read* 1410(b)
"	Cross (Margorie) *the hon.* to be spelt Marjorie
"	Devil's Arrowa *to read* Devil's Arrows
"	Lehnox (James) *to read* Lennox
"	Roads and Tracks to have inserted in order an Item No. 4578
"	Smith (J.J.) *fl.* 1842 2000 (*not* 0000!)
"	Spaul — initial (P) to be inserted